FREE SPEECH AS CIVIC STRUCTURE

Free Speech as Civic Structure

A COMPARATIVE ANALYSIS OF HOW COURTS AND
CULTURE SHAPE THE FREEDOM OF SPEECH

Ronald J. Krotoszynski, Jr.
JOHN S. STONE CHAIR, DIRECTOR OF THE PROGRAM IN
CONSTITUTIONAL STUDIES & INITIATIVE FOR CIVIC ENGAGEMENT,
AND PROFESSOR OF LAW, UNIVERSITY OF ALABAMA, USA

OXFORD
UNIVERSITY PRESS

Oxford University Press is a department of the University of Oxford.
It furthers the University's objective of excellence in research, scholarship,
and education by publishing worldwide. Oxford is a registered trade mark of
Oxford University Press in the UK and in certain other countries.

Published in the United States of America by Oxford University Press
198 Madison Avenue, New York, NY 10016, United States of America.

© Ronald J. Krotoszynski, Jr. 2024

All rights reserved. No part of this publication may be reproduced, stored in a retrieval system,
or transmitted, in any form or by any means, without the prior permission in writing of Oxford
University Press, or as expressly permitted by law, by license or under terms agreed with the
appropriate reprographics rights organization. Inquiries concerning reproduction outside the scope
of the above should be sent to the Rights Department, Oxford University Press, at the address above.

You must not circulate this work in any other form and you must impose this same condition on any
acquirer

Library of Congress Cataloging-in-Publication Data
Names: Krotoszynski, Ronald J., 1967– author.
Title: Free speech as civic structure : a comparative analysis of how courts and culture
shape the freedom of speech / Ronald J. Krotoszynski, Jr.
Description: New York : Oxford University Press, 2024. |
Includes bibliographical references and index. |
Identifiers: LCCN 2023058810 | ISBN 9780197662199 (hardback) |
ISBN 9780197662212 (epub) | ISBN 9780197662205 (updf) | ISBN 9780197662229 (online)
Subjects: LCSH: Freedom of speech. | Courts.
Classification: LCC K3254 .K765 2024 | DDC 342.08/53—dc23/eng/20240117
LC record available at https://lccn.loc.gov/2023058810

DOI: 10.1093/9780197662229.001.0001

Printed by Integrated Books International, United States of America

Note to Readers
This publication is designed to provide accurate and authoritative information in regard to the subject
matter covered. It is based upon sources believed to be accurate and reliable and is intended to be
current as of the time it was written. It is sold with the understanding that the publisher is not engaged
in rendering legal, accounting, or other professional services. If legal advice or other expert assistance is
required, the services of a competent professional person should be sought. Also, to confirm that the
information has not been affected or changed by recent developments, traditional legal research
techniques should be used, including checking primary sources where appropriate.

*(Based on the Declaration of Principles jointly adopted by a Committee of the
American Bar Association and a Committee of Publishers and Associations.)*

You may order this or any other Oxford University Press publication
by visiting the Oxford University Press website at www.oup.com.

I dedicate this book to my friend and partner, Joan. We met incident to this project and, since then, my life has been immeasurably richer—and better—with you in it. I am incredibly grateful that the Fates brought us together. My love, always.

Contents

Preface	xi
Acknowledgments	xvii
List of Abbreviations	xxi

1. *Introduction: The Importance of Text to Securing Rights in a Written Constitution (with Particular Attention to Expressive Freedom)* — 1
   - I. Introduction: The Interrelationship of Text and Fundamental Human Rights Reconsidered — 1
   - II. Common Law Constitutionalism and the (Limited) Role of Constitutional Text — 6
   - III. The Cosmic Turtle Revisited: Judges—Not Text—All the Way Down? — 9
   - IV. Text, Judges, and Expressive Freedoms—Setting the Stage for a Comparative Legal Adventure — 11
   - V. Conclusion: Text Meets Courts — 13

2. *The United States: The Protean First Amendment and the (Very) Limited Relevance of Its Text to the Warp and Weft of Expressive Freedom* — 15
   - I. The First Amendment as a Nontextual Text: The Protean Nature of the First Amendment and the Critical Role of Judges in Protecting Expressive Freedom — 15
   - II. Textualism and Originalism in Constitutional Interpretation and Adjudication: The First Amendment as an Exemplar of Common Law Constitutionalism in Action — 18

Contents

III. Deeply Seated Sociolegal Norms Define the Scope of Freedom of Expression More Reliably Than Constitutional Text—and This Might Apply to Other Substantive Rights Too ... 24

IV. Turtles All the Way Down: The Necessity of Common Law Exegesis in Interpreting and Applying Constitutional Text ... 28

V. Conclusion: Judges, Not the First Amendment's Text, Play the Central Role in Defining and Protecting Speech in the United States ... 31

3. *South Africa: Reconciling the Freedom of Speech with Dignity, Equality, and Human Freedom in the Long Shadow of Apartheid* ... 33

I. Introduction: The Constitutional Court of the Republic of South Africa as the Guardian of Constitutional Rights, Values, and Structures ... 33

II. The South African Constitutional Text: Dignity, Equality, and Human Freedom as the Apex Human Rights and Foundational Constitutional Values ... 39

III. The Underlying Constitutional Reality: Freedom of Expression as a Coequal Constitutional Value in the CCSA's Constitutional Jurisprudence ... 46

   A. *The Hate Speech and Broadcasting Decisions: Speech as a Coequal Constitutional Value* ... 47

   B. *Defamation and the Role of a Free Press in a Democratic Polity* ... 52

   C. *Drawing the Line: The Examples of Julius Sello Malema, Vicki Momberg, and the Edgy Art Student as Potential Propagators of Constitutionally Unprotected Hate Speech* ... 55

   D. *Conclusion: Expressive Freedoms Do Not Hold an Inferior Status as Fundamental Human Rights in Contemporary South Africa* ... 61

IV. The Long Shadow of Apartheid and Freedom of Expression: Lingering Social Skepticism About Even Well-Intentioned Government Efforts to Censor Political Speech ... 62

V. Conclusion: Freedom of Expression as a Coequal Constitutional Value with Dignity, Equality, and Human Freedom ... 67

4. *The United Kingdom: Free Speech as a Sociolegal Norm* ... 69

I. Introduction: The United Kingdom as a Cautionary Tale About the Importance of Text—as Opposed to Judges—in Securing Fundamental Rights ... 69

II. The Pre-HRA 98 Push for a British Bill of Rights and Growing Judicial Solicitude for Expressive Freedom Claims ... 74

III. The Advent of the HRA 98: Bringing Fundamental Human Rights, Including Expressive Freedoms, Home ... 77

Contents

ix

   IV. Expressive Freedom in the United Kingdom After the HRA 98 Comes
Into Force: Plus ça Change, Plus C'est la Même Chose   82

    V. Free Speech as a Common Law Constitutional Right in the
United Kingdom   89

   VI. Conclusion: The Judicial Protection of the Freedom of Expression
in the United Kingdom Constitutes Common Law Constitutionalism
in Action   100

5. *Australia: The Constitutional Protection of Political and Governmental Speech
as an "Implied Freedom" Essential to Facilitating Democratic Deliberation,
the Electoral Process, and Democracy Itself*   103

     I. Introduction: The Absence of an Express Free Speech Provision,
Judicial Implications, and Australia's (Partially) Written Constitution   103

    II. An Introduction to Australia's Implied Freedom of Political and
Governmental Communication   106

   III. Deconstructing the IFPGC: A Collective Interest, a Personal Right,
or A Structural Constraint—Or Perhaps *All Three*?   117

   IV. Does Constitutional Text—or Its Absence—Really Matter to the
Scope of Expressive Freedoms in Australia?   123

    V. Conclusion: The Absence of Text Matters in Australia, But the
Presence of an Express Guarantee of Expressive Freedoms Would
Not Necessarily Work a Constitutional Revolution   132

6. *Israel: Common Law Constitutionalism, Democracy, and Dignity*   135

     I. Introduction: Common Law Constitutionalism and the Judicial Role
in Securing and Safeguarding Fundamental Rights (Including
Freedom of Expression)   135

    II. Israel's Constitutional Architecture: A Founding Without
a Constitution   138

   III. Freedom of Expression as an Unenumerated, Yet Nevertheless
Fundamental, Constitutional Right   140

      A. Kol Ha'am Co. Ltd. v. Minister of the Interior   140

      B. *Freedom of Expression from* Kol Ha'am *to 1992*   142

   IV. The Advent of a Text—Basic Law: Human Dignity and Liberty   149

      A. *The Status of Basic Laws in General*   149

      B. *Basic Law: Human Dignity and Liberty and Basic Law: Freedom of
Occupation—Judicial Review and Freedom of Expression*   153

      C. *Freedom of Expression after* United Mizrahi Bank *and* Golan   156

    V. The (Limited) Relevance of a Text to the Protection of Freedom of
Expression in Israel   158

Contents

VI. Free Speech and Democracy: The Essential Role of a Constitutional
Court as the Guardian of the Democratic Process (Including
Democratic Deliberation)   161

    A. *Dworkin: Unfettered Democracy Is Fundamentally Unjust*   162

    B. *Ely: Judges Have a Duty to Reinforce Democracy and Democratic
Institutions Using the Power of Judicial Review*   164

    C. *Meiklejohn: Freedom of Speech Constitutes an Essential Condition for the
Maintenance of Democratic Self-Government*   165

    D. *Judicial Review Facilitates, Rather than Impedes, the Operation of
Democratic Self-Governance*   166

VII. Conclusion: The Supreme Court of Israel Plays an Essential and
Necessary Role in Facilitating the Operation of Democratic
Self-Government   167

7. *Conclusion: Common Law Constitutionalism in the Service of Expressive
Freedoms Constitutes a Global Rule Rather than an Exception*   169

    I. Text or No Text, Judges Set the Metes and Bounds of Expressive
Freedom   169

    II. Expressive Freedom, Constitutional Text, and the Practice of
Democratic Self-Government   170

    III. Common Law Constitutionalism, in the Context of Judicial
Protection of the Expressive Freedom, Is Inevitable and Universal   172

    IV. Expressive Freedom, Fundamental Rights More Generally, and
Judge-Made Law: The Critical Role of Judges in a Constitutional
Democracy   178

    V. Conclusion: The Protean First Amendment   181

NOTES   183

INDEX   289

Preface

IT IS ENTIRELY natural to think that codifying a human right will have a meaningful impact on both the right's scope of application and the willingness of judges to safeguard it. This might well hold true in general, but, as this book will show, it does not appear to hold true for the protection of expressive freedom (meaning the freedoms of speech, press, assembly, association, and petition). Instead, through a process of common law reasoning and elucidation, judges define and then enforce the metes and bounds of the freedom of expression. This is true in the United States (which has a written Constitution that includes a Bill of Rights). It is also true in other polities—some of which have written constitutions with an express free speech provision (South Africa), some of which have a written constitution that entirely omits a guarantee of freedom of expression (Australia), some of which have a statutory, rather than entrenched, constitutional guarantee of freedom of expression (the United Kingdom), and, finally, some that lack a written constitution as such at all (Israel).

Consider the example of the United States. In the United States, the Bill of Rights begins with the First Amendment—which famously proclaims that "Congress shall make no law" that abridges the constitutional rights of speech, press, assembly, and petition. Yet, since the 1980s, the Supreme Court of the United States has routinely ignored both the precise text of the First Amendment and its original public meaning when hearing and deciding disputes that implicate expressive freedom. In the contemporary United States, the text of the First Amendment does little, if any, meaningful jurisprudential work in the pages of *U.S. Reports*. No less odd, jurists who proclaim their fidelity to textualist originalism as a means of constitutional interpretation abandon this methodology in free speech cases, instead using a dynamic, and purposive, reading

xi

of the First Amendment's Free Speech Clause. The First Amendment thus stands for a general constitutional rule against any and all forms of government censorship that might disrupt the process of democratic deliberation—a process that facilitates an ongoing process of democratic self-government.

My initial thought, as I pondered the potential significance of this state of affairs, began with its implications for textualist originalism as an interpretative methodology. Although many sitting Justices purport to be textualist-originalists, this method of interpretation has relatively few adherents within the U.S. legal academy—and with good reason. It's a well-known fact that judges observe textualist originalism more often in the breach than in the observance when taking this approach permits them to reach congenial results on the merits. A book that simply attacks textualist originalism as a false faith—and a bogus methodological enterprise—would not add much to the ongoing debates about the proper role of judges within a democratic polity.

It is also true that, within some corners of comparative constitutional law, empirical scholars place great emphasis on the text of national constitutions, coding them and then deriving fairly broad, sweeping inferences about the nature of a particular polity based on the text. I have always wondered how well this methodology works when the judges serving on a national constitutional court do not seem to feel much bound to follow the text. In Israel, for example, no text exists that expressly safeguards the freedoms of speech, press, assembly, association, or petition. Yet, since the Supreme Court of Israel's landmark decision in *Kol Ha'am* ("Voice of the People"), the Justices have routinely exercised both strong-form and weak-form judicial review to safeguard expressive freedom. If one were coding Israel's only partially written constitution for speech, it would register as a null set. The reality is considerably more complicated. Israeli judges, from 1953 to the present, have used a process of common law reasoning to afford constitutional protection to the freedom of speech. The Supreme Court of Israel did so first from Israel's status as a democratic state; after the Knesset's enactment, in 1992, of Basic Law: Human Dignity and Liberty, it also did so by declaring the freedom of speech to be an important aspect of human dignity and liberty.

My project evolved as I engaged in the research required to write this book. For that, I should express gratitude to Professor Vicki Jackson, who, incident to a comparative public law workshop organized by Professor Mila Versteeg at the University of Virginia School of Law, and hosted by the Robert H. Smith Center for the Constitution at James Madison's Orange County, Virginia estate, Montpelier, urged me to embark on this project with an open mind and to let my findings dictate my conclusions (rather than vice versa). Vicki's advice, as always, was prescient. I followed her suggestion and the focus of this book evolved over time.

The principal argument that I make and defend in the pages that follow is that free speech law in a democracy is invariably a species of judge-made law. Constitution makers can attempt to circumscribe or limit judicial discretion to recognize, or to refuse to recognize, expressive freedom, but, to paraphrase *Jurassic Park*'s tagline "[judges] find a way." Thus, despite the efforts of the drafters of South Africa's 1996 Constitution to

Preface   ⟶ xiii

signal, repeatedly, the primacy of equality, dignity, and freedom as the apex human-rights values and substantive rights, judges had a different idea—and have instead afforded speech and correlated expressive freedoms a coequal status with dignity, equality, and freedom.

So, too, the framers of Australia's 1901 Commonwealth Constitution borrowed heavily from both the American and Westminster models. When it came to creating judicially enforced fundamental human rights, however, they did not much care for what they saw in the jurisprudence of the *Lochner*-era Supreme Court of the United States. Rather than trusting unelected judges to serve as Platonic Guardians of the basic rights of the citizenry, they instead reposed their faith in the voters under a theory of "democratic constitutionalism."

Legislators, vested by the voters with a warrant to make, amend, and abolish public policies on matters great and small, would be the primary guardians of the rights of the people. Even so, however, in 1992, in a pair of landmark cases, the High Court of Australia (HCA) conjured a limited "freedom" of speech related to governmental and political communications. The absence of text did not prove out to be an impediment to recognition of an implied freedom of governmental and political communication—nor to the HCA's subsequent deployment of judicial review to invalidate federal and state laws that unduly abridged or denied this freedom. In sum, Australian judges, like nature in *Jurassic Park*, found a way.

Another major discovery—and one that probably has salience well beyond the specific context of judicial review to safeguard expressive freedom: judicial culture and the institutional role of courts within a particular system of government matter far more than the precise constitutional text, or absence of relevant constitutional text, to the scope and vibrancy of constitutionally protected expression. Thus, in a system like the United Kingdom, with a strong commitment to parliamentary sovereignty as part of its constitutional DNA, even the addition of a written text, with an express admonition to the domestic courts to have "particular regard" for the freedom of speech, did not much affect the strength of speech rights on the ground.

The Human Rights Act 1998 (HRA 98) was an important, indeed landmark, human rights law in the United Kingdom. But it did not affect very much, if at all, the scope of constitutionally protected speech. As Chapter 4 will show, British judges began recognizing and applying the freedom of speech in the 1970s and 1980s—well before the HRA 98 came onto the legal scene. It turns out that, for the most part, British judges had already done what they were prepared to do regarding judicial protection of speech before the effective date of the HRA 98.

I do not claim—and do not argue—that text (constitutional or statutory) is wholly irrelevant to securing a particular human right or human rights in general. Text can and does often matter. My point is more limited—it matters less than we generally realize. Both its presence and its absence have only a marginal constraining effect on judicial discretion. As between text and independent courts, vested with some kind of power of judicial review, the latter matters much more than the former to safeguarding expressive freedom.

Another somewhat related point: sociolegal culture matters more than text as well. To a greater extent than we perhaps appreciate, a constitution means what We the People think it means (rather than what it actually says). Judges generally do not seek to write opinions that most citizens will find unpersuasive—much less outrageous, offensive, or repulsive. To disregard speech entirely, in favor of unfettered legislative authority to distort the process of democratic deliberation that informs the act of voting, is something that most judges, most of the time, would prefer to avoid. And, as long as elected legislators acquiesce in the assertion of a power of judicial review to protect the process of democratic deliberation, judges will succeed when they assert a checking function in this context.

Indeed, because elected politicians obviously labor under a structural conflict of interest when they regulate speech related to elections and self-government, the necessity of a neutral umpire or referee—an honest broker—is fairly obvious. Judges on constitutional courts routinely undertake this role regardless of what, if anything, the local constitution has to say about freedom of expression. And, at least in the United States, South Africa, the United Kingdom, Australia, and Israel, the judges, not the elected politicians, get to have the last word on the scope and meaning of expressive freedom.

In sum, a project that began as a sustained attack on textualist originalism in the United States as the primary theory of constitutional interpretation evolved and changed as my work on this project progressed. Rather than attacking a straw man (the intellectual bankruptcy of originalism as practiced, now and again, by the contemporary Supreme Court), my project became more of a sustained argument in favor of common law constitutionalism in the specific context of defining and then protecting expressive freedom (particularly in the context of self-government). Even if the framers of a constitution or bill of rights work diligently and comprehensively to define speech rights, these efforts will, at the end of the day, come up short and it will fall to judges to reconcile government efforts to regulate the marketplace of political ideas with the ability of citizens to engage, borrowing Justice William J. Brennan, Jr.'s wonderfully apt turn of phrase, in a process of public debate that is wide open, robust, and uninhibited.

Whether this state of affairs holds true for other fundamental human rights is a question that lies beyond the scope of my immediate project. With respect to speech and other related expressive freedoms, however, borrowing the "Cosmic Turtle" metaphor, it's judges all the way down. This is not to say that judges define speech rights independently of the sociopolitical culture (of which they are a part) or without regard to the institutional limitations associated with the exercise of judicial power (which obviously constrain both what judges may do and how they may do it). It is to say, within the bounds of a particular nation's sociolegal culture, and subject to local constraints on the institutional role and power of the judiciary, that, more often than not, judges will play the leading role in defining and then safeguarding the freedom of expression.

Preface

My argument will proceed across seven substantive chapters. Chapter 1 introduces the question of the relevance of text to the safeguarding of human rights in general and the freedom of speech in particular. Chapter 2 considers how the First Amendment, in the United States, constitutes something of an "atextual-text"—meaning that as much as judges serving on the Supreme Court like to invoke text as a basis for their expressive freedom rulings, the actual text of the First Amendment does little, if any, significant jurisprudential work in contemporary constitutional free speech law. Chapter 3 considers the limited relevance of constitutional text in South Africa—where the jurists serving on the Constitutional Court have elevated speech to a coequal status with the apex human rights values of dignity, equality, and freedom (defined as freedom from unjust imprisonment, torture, and the like), which also constitute expressly protected fundamental rights as well.

Chapter 4 considers the limited effects of the HRA 98 with regard to the scope of expressive freedom in the United Kingdom; there, the addition of a text, with an express admonition to upgrade the status of freedom of expression, had little (if any) practical effect on the scope of these rights. In Chapter 5, Australia's judicially created implied freedom of political and governmental communication receives sustained analysis and critique. Chapter 6 takes up the Supreme Court of Israel's seventy-plus years of work to use a process of common law constitutionalism to secure expressive freedom. Despite the absence of any textual warrant, and the Knesset's failure, in 1993 and again in 1994, to enact a Basic Law that expressly safeguards freedom of expression, the Supreme Court of Israel has successfully (to date, in any event) asserted a power of judicial review to protect speech (and has done so well beyond speech directly related to elections and self-government). Finally, Chapter 7 offers a summary of the preceding chapters—including lessons that this comparative public law exercise teaches—and a brief conclusion.

In sum, text, whether of a constitutional or statutory stripe, certainly matters and it can enable, or inhibit, judicial efforts to safeguard speech. But, as this book will hopefully establish with convincing clarity, judges matter more—a great deal more—to securing successfully the ability of ordinary citizens to speak their version of truth to power.

Ronald J. Krotoszynski, Jr.
Tuscaloosa, Alabama

Acknowledgments

A SCHOLARLY PROJECT of this scope necessarily requires the active support and assistance of many friends and colleagues—in this case, hailing quite literally from around the globe. I had the good fortune of presenting draft chapters at a series of faculty workshops, and conferences, across the jurisdictions canvassed within this book. I should hasten to add that the arguments, ideas, and theories that I present in *Free Speech as Civic Structure* are mine alone—and so too are any errors or omissions. With that important caveat, I wish to thank the institutions and individuals who helped keep me on the right track as I explored the free speech jurisprudence of the highest courts in the United States, South Africa, the United Kingdom, Australia, and Israel—with a particular focus on the central role of judges in developing, shaping, and enforcing the local precedents that govern the freedom of expression.

Starting with Chapter 2 (the United States), the law faculties at Cornell University Law School, Indiana University-McKinney School of Law, and Wayne State University Law School hosted workshops at which I presented an earlier draft of this chapter. In addition, I presented Chapter 2 at conference panels at the University of Paris 1 Panthéon-Sorbonne University School of Law (incident to its annual IMODEV conference), at the National Public Service University, in Budapest, Hungary, and at the 2022 annual meeting of the Southeastern Association of Law Schools. Among those who generously read and commented on earlier drafts of Chapter 2, which reflects the benefit of their thoughtful and constructive input, are Anita Bernstein, Richard Bierschbach, Vince Blasi, Dawn Chutkow, Mike Dorf, Jennifer Drobak, Charlotte Garden, Michael Heise, Vicki Jackson, RonNell Andersen Jones, András Koltay, David

xvii

xviii ᴏ̲ Acknowledgments

Law, Clark Lombardi, Steven Shiffrin (who was an iconic free speech scholar and is much missed), Nelson Tebbe, Bernát Török, Jonathan Weinberg, and George Wright.

I had the good fortune of presenting Chapter 3 (South Africa) at the University of Cape Town Faculty of Law and also at the South African Institute for Advanced Constitutional, Public, Human Rights and International Law (known as "SAIFAC"), an academic center of the University of Johannesburg (and associated with the University of Johannesburg Faculty of Law). I also wish to thank, in particular, David Bilchitz, Joanna Botha, Pierre De Vos, Mark Kende, and Christopher Roederer for their thoughtful and detailed comments on an earlier draft of Chapter 3.

The University of Oxford Faculty of Law, the Edinburgh Law School, at the University of Edinburgh, the University of Leeds School of Law, and the University of Reading School of Law all hosted faculty workshops associated with Chapter 4 (the United Kingdom). I should also offer thanks to Başak Bak, Rachael Craufurd Smith, James Devenney, Liz Fisher, Rebecca Moosavian, and Jake Rowbottom for their extremely helpful comments and reactions to an earlier draft of Chapter 4.

The law faculties at Melbourne University, the University of Sydney, the Australian National University, and Monash University all graciously hosted faculty workshops associated with Chapter 5 (Australia). In addition, I am deeply grateful to Margaret Allars, Ros Dixon, Andrew Kenyon, Justice Michael Kirby, Will Partlett, Heather Roberts, Adrienne Stone, and Normann Witzleb for helping me to better understand the High Court of Australia's implied freedom of political and governmental communication jurisprudence and also for offering highly useful and constructive comments on an earlier draft of Chapter 5.

I was deeply honored to share an early draft of Chapter 6 (Israel) at a lecture hosted by the Supreme Court of Israel. Moreover, I greatly appreciated the very high level of engagement with this project that several of the Justices, and their law clerks, demonstrated at this event. The Hebrew University School of Law, in Jerusalem, hosted a faculty workshop associated with Chapter 6. Professor Rivka Weill, who serves on the law faculty at the Harry Radzyner Law School, at Reichman University, in Herzliya, Israel, organized a session of her Comparative Constitutional Law Seminar focused exclusively on an earlier draft of Chapter 6; it was a genuine pleasure to interact with her law students. I appreciated, very much, the focused attention—and provocative and dynamic reactions—that Professor Weill's students brought to the table (literally). At all three events, I received extremely helpful, and thoughtful, ideas and suggestions for how to further refine and develop my arguments regarding the Supreme Court of Israel's central role in crafting and then operationalizing an implied (constitutional) freedom of expression. Finally, I also wish to acknowledge the assistance of Justice Alex Stein, of the Supreme Court of Israel, who generously engaged my project (with respect to Israel and more broadly as well) and also introduced me to several highly accomplished public law scholars in Israel.

Seattle University School of Law hosted me as a Distinguished Visiting Scholar in Residence during the summers of 2019, 2022, and 2023, while I was working on *Free Speech as Civic Structure*. I want to acknowledge this support; I very much appreciate

Acknowledgments

the hospitality that Seattle University School of Law provided to me during these summer sojourns. In particular, Lori Lamb offered timely and extremely helpful support and assistance—and did so on a consistent basis.

The University of Alabama School of Law provided generous financial support for this multiyear book project—including extensive travel support and magnanimous summer research grants from the University of Alabama Law School Foundation. Deans Mark Brandon and Bill Brewbaker could not have been more supportive of me or my project; I am genuinely grateful to both of them and sincerely appreciate their unflagging support of my scholarly work. The University of Alabama Bounds Law Library provided expert research assistance (not uncommonly on unreasonably short deadlines)—Library Director Casey Duncan, Research Librarian Matthew Neely, and former Research Librarian Seth Brostoff all rendered essential help with locating foreign law materials that were (and are) critical to the success of this book project.

My former student and current research assistant, Trent Gill, UASL '24, provided invaluable assistance on several chapters, notably including Chapter 6 (Israel). Trent also supplied eagle-eyed help with the arduous, but quite essential, task of carefully proofreading and correcting the final page proofs. Finally, Erica Nicholson, my long-term administrative assistant at the University of Alabama School of Law, furnished timely and excellent support for this project (as she does, in candor, for all of my scholarly endeavors).

I should acknowledge that some of the material in Chapter 1 (Introduction), Chapter 2 (the United States), and Chapter 7 (Conclusion) first appeared in print, albeit in a substantially revised form, as:

Ronald J. Krotoszynski, Jr., *Common Law Constitutionalism and the Protean First Amendment*, 25 U. Pa. J. Const. L. 1 (2023).

* * *

Again, I want to thank everyone who facilitated my scholarly journey, over the past six years, as I was researching, then writing and editing, *Free Speech as Civic Structure*. I could not have succeeded in completing a project of this scale and scope without the assistance of so many wonderful friends and colleagues. Help of this sort is both essential and absolutely invaluable. Finally, I should close by once again noting that any and all errors or omissions in the pages that follow are my responsibility alone.

List of Abbreviations

ACTV	Australian Capital Television
Adelaide L. Rev.	Adelaide Law Review
Admin. L. Rev.	Administrative Law Review
Am.	American
Am. J. Int'l L.	American Journal of International Law
Am. J. Leg. Hist.	American Journal of Legal History
Ann. Rev. L. & Soc. Sci.	Annual Review of Law and Social Sciences
Annals of Cong.	Annals of Congress
APSA	Australian Public Service Act
APSC	Australian Public Service Code of Conduct
Ass'n	Association
Auth'y	Authority
BBC	British Broadcasting Corporation
Bd.	Board
Bldg.	Building
BNA	British North America Act of 1867
Broad.	Broadcasting
B.U. L. Rev.	Boston University Law Review
Buff. L. Rev.	Buffalo Law Review
Cambridge L.J.	Cambridge Law Review
Cap.	Capital
Cardozo L. Rev.	Cardozo Law Review
CCSA	Constitutional Court of the Republic of South Africa

xxii ⌒   List of Abbreviations

Chi.-Kent J. Int'l & Comp. L.	Chicago-Kent Journal of International & Comparative Law
CLR	Commonwealth Law Reports
Cnty.	County
Colum. L. Rev.	Columbia Law Review
Comm.	Committee
Comm'n	Commission
Commc'ns	Communications
Comm'r	Commissioner
Const. Comm.	Constitutional Commentary
Const. F.	Constitutional Forum
Constr.	Construction
Contemp. Jewry	Contemporary Jewry
Cornell L. Rev.	Cornell Law Review
Ctr.	Center
Dep't	Department
Dir.	Director
Dist.	District
Div.	Division
Duke J. Comp. & Int'l L.	Duke Journal of Comparative & International Law
Duke L.J.	Duke Law Journal
ECtHR	European Court of Human Rights
Educ.	Education
EFF	Economic Freedom Fighters
Elec.	Electric(al)
Emory Int'l L. Rev.	Emory International Law Review
Emp.	Employment
Eng'rs	Engineers
Ent.	Entertainment
Eur. H.R. Rep.	European Human Rights Report
Eur. Hum. R. L. Rev.	European Human Rights Law Review
FCC	Federal Constitutional Court
Fed.	Federal
Fed. L. Rev.	Federal Law Review
Fed'n	Federation
Fla. St. U. L. Rev.	Florida State University Law Review
Fordham L. Rev.	Fordham Law Review
Gen.	General
Geo. Wash. Int'l L. Rev.	George Washington International Law Review
Geo. Wash. L. Rev	George Washington Law Review
Governance: An Int'l J. of Law, Pol'y, Admin. & Insts.	Governance: An International Journal of Law, Administration, & Institution
Grp.	Group

List of Abbreviations   ⟿ xxiii

Harv. L. Rev.	Harvard Law Review
Hastings Const. L.Q.	Hastings Constitutional Law Quarterly
HCA	High Court of Australia
HCJ	High Court of Justice
HOL	House of Lords
Hosp.	Hospital
HRA 98	Human Rights Act 1998
HRC	Human Rights Commission
Hum.	Human
Hum. Rts. L. Rev.	Human Rights Law Review
IBA	Independent Broadcasting Authority
IFPGC	implied freedom of political and governmental communication
Ind. L.J.	Indiana Law Journal
Ind.	Independent
Indus.	Industrial
Inst.	Institute(ion)
IRA	Irish Republican Army
Isr. L. Rev.	Israeli Law Review
J. Free Speech L.	Journal of Free Speech and Law
J. Rts. & Just.	Journal of Rights and Justice
James Cook U. L. Rev.	James Cook University Law Review
JPL	Jet Propulsion Lab
Just.	Justice
LGBTQ	lesbian, gay, bisexual, transgender, and queer
MAC	Muslims against Crusaders
McGill L.J.	McGill Law Journal
Melb. U. L. Rev.	Melbourne University Law Review
Merchs.	Merchants
Mich. L. Rev.	Michigan Law Review
Minn. L. Rev.	Minnesota Law Review
Monash U. L. Rev.	Monash University Law Review
Nat'l	National
N.C. L. Rev.	North Carolina Law Review
Nev. L.J.	Nevada Law Journal
NFIB	National Federation of Independent Business
NLRB	National Labor Relations Board
Nw. Univ. L. Rev.	Northwestern University Law Review
N.Y. Times	New York Times
N.Y.U. L. Rev.	New York University Law Review
Org.	Organization
PER/PELJ	Potchefstroomse Elektroniese Regstydskrif/ Potchefstroom Electronic Law Journal

xxiv | List of Abbreviations

Plymouth L. & Crim. Justice Rev.	Plymouth Law & Criminal Justice Review
POA	Public Order Act 1986
Prods.	Products
Pub.	Public
Pub. L.	Public Law
Res.	Resources
Rev. Const. Stud.	Review of Constitutional Studies
R.R.	Railroad
Rts.	Rights
Ry.	Railway
SAIFAC	South African Institute for Advanced Constitutional, Public, Human Rights and International Law
SCA	Supreme Court of Appeal
SCC	Supreme Court of Canada
Sch.	School
SCI	Supreme Court of Israel
S.C.R.	Supreme Court Review
SCUK	Supreme Court of the United Kingdom
Se.	Southeastern
Sec'y	Secretary
Serv.	Service
Stan. L. Rev.	Stanford Law Review
Sup. Ct. Rev.	Supreme Court Review
Tel Aviv U. Stud. L.	Tel Aviv University Studies of Law
Tex. L. Rev.	Texas Law Review
U. Chi. L. Rev.	University of Chicago Law Review
U. Cin. L. Rev.	University of Cincinnati Law Review
U. Conn. L. Rev.	University of Connecticut Law Review
U. Miami L. Rev.	University of Miami Law Review
U. Pa. J. Const. L.	University of Pennsylvania Journal of Constitutional Law
U. Pa. L. Rev.	University of Pennsylvania Law Review
U. Tasmania L. Rev.	University of Tasmania Law Review
U. W. Sydney L. Rev.	University of West Sydney Law Review
U.K.H.L.	United Kingdom House of Lords Decision
U.N.S.W. L.J.	University of New South Wales Law Journal
UCLA L. Rev.	UCLA Law Review
UK	United Kingdom
US	United States
Va J. Intl L.	Virginia Journal of International Law
Va. L. Rev.	Virginia Law Review

List of Abbreviations   xxv

Wash. Post	Washington Post
Wis. L. Rev.	Wisconsin Law Review
Wm. & Mary L. Rev.	William & Mary Law Review
Yale L.J.	Yale Law Journal

LIST OF PERIODICAL AND REPORTER ABBREVIATIONS

Adelaide L. Rev.	Adelaide Law Review
Admin. L. Rev.	Administrative Law Review
Am. J. Int'l L.	American Journal of International Law
Am. J. Leg. Hist.	American Journal of Legal History
Ann. Rev. L. & Soc. Sci.	Annual Review of Law and Social Sciences
Annals of Cong.	Annals of Congress
B.U. L. Rev.	Boston University Law Review
CLR	Common Wealth Law Reports
Buff. L. Rev.	Buffalo Law Review
Cambridge L.J.	Cambridge Law Review
Cardozo L. Rev.	Cardozo Law Review
Chi.-Kent J. Int'l & Comp. L.	Chicago-Kent Journal of International & Comparative Law
Colum. L. Rev.	Columbia Law Review
Const. Comm.	Constitutional Commentary
Const. F.	Constitutional Forum
Contemp. Jewr.	Contemporary Jewry
Cornell L. Rev.	Cornell Law Review
Duke J. Comp. & Int'l L.	Duke Journal of Comparative & International Law
Duke L.J.	Duke Law Journal
Emory Int'l L. Rev.	Emory International Law Review
Eur. H.R. Rep.	European Human Rights Report
Eur. Hum. R. L. Rev.	European Human Rights Law Review
Fed. L. Rev.	Federal Law Review
Fla. St. U. L. Rev.	Florida State University Law Review
Fordham L. Rev.	Fordham Law Review
Geo. Wash. Int'l L. Rev.	George Washington International Law Review
Geo. Wash. L. Rev	George Washington Law Review
Governance: An Int'l J. of Law, Pol'y, Admin. & Insts.	Governance: An International Journal of Law, Policy, Administration, & Institution
Harv. L. Rev.	Harvard Law Review
Hastings Const. L.Q.	Hastings Constitutional Law Quarterly
Hum. Rts. L. Rev.	Human Rights Law Review
Ind. L.J.	Indiana Law Journal

List of Abbreviations

Isr. L. Rev.	Israeli Law Review
J. Free Speech L.	Journal of Free Speech and Law
J. Rts. & Just.	Journal of Rights and Justice
James Cook U. L. Rev.	James Cook University Law Review
McGill L.J.	McGill Law Journal
Melb. U. L. Rev.	Melbourne University Law Review
Mich. L. Rev.	Michigan Law Review
Minn. L. Rev.	Minnesota Law Review
Monash U. L. Rev.	Monash University Law Review
N.C. L. Rev.	North Carolina Law Review
Nev. L.J.	Nevada Law Journal
N.Y. Times	New York Times
N.Y.U. L. Rev.	New York University Law Review
N. S. Wales Univ. L. Rev.	New South Wales University Law Review
PER/PELJ	Potchefstroomse Elektroniese Regstydskrif/ Potchefstroom Electronic Law Journal
Plymouth L. & Crim. Justice Rev.	Plymouth Law & Criminal Justice Review
Rev. Const. Stud.	Review of Constitutional Studies
Stan. L. Rev.	Stanford Law Review
Sup. Ct. Rev.	Supreme Court Review
Tel Aviv U. Stud. L.	Tel Aviv University Studies of Law
Tex. L. Rev.	Texas Law Review
U. Chi. L. Rev.	University of Chicago Law Review
U. Cin. L. Rev.	University of Cincinnati Law Review
U. Conn. L. Rev.	University of Connecticut Law Review
U. Miami L. Rev.	University of Miami Law Review
U. Pa. J. Const. L.	University of Pennsylvania Journal of Constitutional Law
U. Pa. L. Rev.	University of Pennsylvania Law Review
U. Tasmania L. Rev.	University of Tasmania Law Review
U. W. Sydney L. Rev.	University of West Sydney Law Review
U.K.H.L.	United Kingdom House of Lords Decision
U.N.S.W. L.J.	University of New South Wales Law Journal
UCLA L. Rev.	UCLA Law Review
Va J. Intl L.	Virginia Journal of International Law
Va. L. Rev.	Virginia Law Review
Wash. Post	Washington Post
Wis. L. Rev.	Wisconsin Law Review
Wm. & Mary L. Rev.	William & Mary Law Review
Yale L.J.	Yale Law Journal

List of Abbreviations   xxvii

LIST OF CASE NAME ABBREVIATIONS

Am.	American
Ass'n	Association
Auth'y	Authority
Bd.	Board
Bldg.	Building
Broad.	Broadcasting
Cap.	Capital
Cnty.	County
Comm.	Committee
Comm'n	Commission
Commc'ns	Communications
Comm'r	Commissioner
Constr.	Construction
Ctr.	Center
Dep't	Department
Dir.	Director
Dist.	District
Div.	Division
Educ.	Education
Elec.	Electric(al)
Emp.	Employment
Eng'rs	Engineers
Ent.	Entertainment
Fed.	Federal
Fed'n	Federation
Gen.	General
Grp.	Group
Hosp.	Hospital
Hum.	Human
Ind.	Independent
Indus.	Industrial
Just.	Justice
Merchs.	Merchants
Nat'l	National
Org.	Organization
Prods.	Products
Pub.	Public
Res.	Resources
R.R.	Railroad

List of Abbreviations

Rts.	Rights
Ry.	Railway
Sch.	School
Se.	Southeastern
Sec'y	Secretary
Serv.	Service

1

Introduction

THE IMPORTANCE OF TEXT TO SECURING RIGHTS IN A WRITTEN CONSTITUTION (WITH PARTICULAR ATTENTION TO EXPRESSIVE FREEDOM)

I. INTRODUCTION: THE INTERRELATIONSHIP OF TEXT AND FUNDAMENTAL HUMAN RIGHTS RECONSIDERED

To what extent does the presence or absence of constitutional text, for example, in a written, entrenched bill of rights, matter to securing those rights within a particular polity? One might assume, reflexively, that it matters a great deal. After all, if a nation's founding arrangements include a written constitution that features a bill of rights enumerating particular fundamental rights, one might reasonably assume that courts would be more solicitous of rights specifically enumerated vis-à-vis rights omitted from the enumeration. As it turns out, at least with respect to the protection of expressive freedom,[1] such an assumption would prove wide of the mark.

The First Amendment sets forth four distinct expressive freedoms[2]—yet only one of these clauses, the Free Speech Clause, does any meaningful work today in the pages of *U.S. Reports*.[3] Good reasons also exist for thinking that at least some of those who wrote and ratified the First Amendment held a narrow view of its scope of application—perhaps meaning nothing more than William Blackstone's definition of the "the freedom of speech" under the common law of England, namely, rules against prior restraints and licensure of the press.[4] Certainly Congress's decision to pass, and President John Adams's decision to sign into law, the Alien Act and Sedition Act, in 1798, lends historical and precedential support to this proposition of a tepid First Amendment that protects a very limited universe of expressive activity.[5] Indeed,

Free Speech as Civic Structure. Ronald J. Krotoszynski, Jr., Oxford University Press. © Ronald J. Krotoszynski, Jr. 2024.
DOI: 10.1093/9780197662229.003.0001

Justice Joseph Story, the author of a very influential early gloss on the meaning of the Constitution and Bill of Rights, concluded that the Alien and Sedition Acts were perfectly constitutional—and did not violate the Free Speech Clause of the First Amendment.[6] At least arguably, the actions of the framing generation, coupled with Story's authoritative early gloss, constitute the best available guides to the original public meaning of the Free Speech Clause.

Even if the First Amendment applied only to Congress ("*Congress* shall make no law. . ."), and meant nothing more than Blackstone's rules against prior restraints and licensing the press, would free speech principles be significantly different today than they presently are? In the pages that follow, using an extended comparative legal analysis and argument, I posit that an irrelevant First Amendment, locked in time and space, like a *Jurassic Park* mosquito frozen in amber, would probably not matter much, if at all, to the scope and vibrancy of expressive freedom in the contemporary United States (and, for that matter, in other constitutional democracies as well, with respect to their local constitutions' inclusion or omission of constitutional guarantees for expressive freedoms). This book's project is to show, hopefully with convincing clarity, that this reality holds true not only in the United States, but also in Australia, Israel, South Africa, and the United Kingdom.

Simply put, in the absence of the First Amendment, the federal courts would have recognized and protected a more generally applicable freedom of speech, as a necessary implication of the Constitution's voting related provisions,[7] because free and fair elections cannot take place without a free and open public debate that is "uninhibited, robust, and wide-open."[8] After all, a polity cannot successfully use elections to legitimate a nation's governing institutions if the voters are not free to discuss and engage each other about the candidates seeking election to public office and their proposed public policies.[9] In the alternative, looking to state constitutions and (more-or-less) consistent practice, the federal courts could find speech to be "deeply rooted in the nation's history and traditions,"[10] and therefore protected under the rubric of substantive due process. Either way, free speech law in the United States would probably not look radically different than it does today were the First Amendment interpreted in a highly restrictive fashion—or entirely missing from the Bill of Rights.

We are deluding ourselves if we attribute the scope and vibrancy of expressive freedom in the contemporary United States to the written-ness of the First Amendment rather than to a sociolegal culture that prizes speech and greatly distrusts government efforts to censor it. And, the principal enforcer of an antigovernment censorship rule in the United States is not the First Amendment (which, after all, cannot enforce itself), but rather the federal and state judiciaries (and especially the U.S. Supreme Court). At the end of the day, then, free speech law, both in the United States and also in the wider world, depends far more on the solicitude of judges than on the accident of constitutional or statutory text.

This is not to say that constitutional text is utterly irrelevant to defining and safeguarding fundamental rights. Plainly, the presence of a relevant text provides a judge, asked to disallow a particular government policy or action as a violation of a particular

Introduction: The Importance of Text

human right, with a basis for providing relief (beyond the judge's own secret inner voice). Text, in other words, can legitimate judicial decisions enforcing the text. But, to stipulate that text sometimes can and does matter is not to say that text invariably matters. It also bears noting that some of the most committed textualist judges, such as Justice Hugo L. Black, who repeatedly announced, in both his opinions from the bench and in his off-the-bench writings, his absolute fealty to the Constitution's text and nothing else,[11] routinely abandon textualism when doing so is essential to reaching results that they find compelling.

In Justice Black's view, "it is language and history that are the crucial factors which influence me in interpreting the Constitution—not reasonableness or desirability as determined by justices of the Supreme Court."[12] Thus, "in order to obtain results thought to be desirable at the time," Black argued that judges could not legitimately "rewrite our basic charter of government under the guise of interpreting it."[13] More recently, Justice Antonin Scalia[14] and failed Supreme Court nominee Judge Robert Bork have espoused a largely identical approach to constitutional interpretation: text *uber alles*.[15]

Yet, interestingly, Justice Black had no problem conjuring an antidiscrimination principle that mirrors the Equal Protection Clause of the Fourteenth Amendment from the Fifth Amendment's Due Process Clause.[16] He did so, without any explanation (or citation to a provision of the Constitution, Bill of Rights, or even existing case law), first in *Korematsu*[17] (an odious decision that the Supreme Court has since expressly disavowed[18]), but voted consistently with majorities in the post-*Brown* era[19] to prohibit the federal government from acting in ways that would violate the Equal Protection Clause if undertaken by a state government.[20] I do not suggest that Justice Black was mistaken in *Korematsu* to apply a principle of equal protection, presumably as an aspect of substantive due process, or in error to join Chief Justice Earl Warren's unanimous decision in *Bolling* to apply this principle to disallow the federal government's policy of operating racially segregated public schools in the District of Columbia.[21] Neither result, however, can be successfully reconciled with a strict "text and only the text" approach to interpreting and applying the Bill of Rights and Fourteenth Amendment.

When faced with federal government policies that discriminated based on race, Justice Black interpreted an open-ended clause located within the Fifth Amendment to ground an anti-discrimination principle no less robust than the express anti-discrimination principle expressly set forth in the Fourteenth Amendment's Equal Protection Clause. Suppose, however, that the U.S. Constitution entirely lacked an explicit Equal Protection Clause, applicable to either the state or federal governments? Would this mean that the Supreme Court would not have decided *Brown v. Board of Education* in the same way (i.e., it would have sustained, rather than invalidated, state segregation of the public schools)? The thesis of this book is that, even in the absence of an express provision of the U.S. Constitution disallowing racial discrimination by the government, the Supreme Court, using a process of common law reasoning, would have discovered such a principle and then invoked it in support of judicial review to disallow government efforts to classify and subordinate citizens based on their racial or ethnic identities.

Moreover, the same would likely also hold true for the freedom of speech. The Supreme Court has not had any need to engage in conjuration, divination, or merely implication from the Constitution's text to ground its aggressive extension of judicial review to protect speech—even odious, hateful, or discriminatory speech.[22] Yet, the text that the Supreme Court has used to ground these outcomes seems somewhat surprising on first glance as a legitimate source of a general constitutional rule against government censorship of speech that rather clearly causes nontrivial social harms.[23] Unlike any other provision of the Bill of Rights, the First Amendment is directed *solely* at one branch of the federal government—namely, Congress.[24] Does this leave the president and the federal courts free to censor speech? For a truly committed textualist interpreter of the Constitution, arguably it should.

Using a comparative legal analysis, the chapters that follow will consider free speech principles in the United States,[25] South Africa,[26] the United Kingdom,[27] Australia,[28] and Israel.[29] Why these particular jurisdictions? The first two jurisdictions, the United States and South Africa, feature written, entrenched constitutions, including extensive bills of rights, that include express guarantees of freedom of expression. Yet, both the U.S. Supreme Court and the Constitutional Court of South Africa largely disregard these texts when defining expressive freedoms and protecting them from undue government abridgement.

The United Kingdom features a text—the Human Rights Act 98 (HRA 98)[30]—that codifies the European Convention for the Protection of Human Rights and Fundamental Freedoms (commonly known as the European Convention on Human Rights)[31] into domestic U.K. law. The HRA 98 instructs judges, whenever possible, to interpret laws and regulations in ways that comply with the European Convention and the European Court of Human Rights judgments interpreting and applying it.[32] Thus, the United Kingdom provides an example of a jurisdiction where, prior to October 2, 2000 (the date the HRA 98 entered into legal force), no express text existed in domestic law safeguarding speech (or any of the other rights enumerated in the European Convention). If constitutional or statutory text is essential to the effective judicial protection of a human right, and the vigor with which judges will go about protecting a right, then one would expect that express codification, coupled with an equally explicit parliamentary mandate to the domestic courts to protect a particular human right, would lead to enhanced judicial solicitude and protection. As Chapter 3 shows, this is not how things turned out. Free speech law in Great Britain changed very little, if at all, before and after the HRA 98. And, this holds true despite Parliament instructing the domestic courts to "have particular regard to the importance of the Convention right to freedom of expression."[33]

Australia and Israel are jurisdictions that lack *any* express constitutional guarantee of expressive freedom. Given this state of affairs, one would probably predict that courts in those countries do not exercise a power of judicial review to protect speech. If one were engaged in an empirical comparative constitutional law analysis of freedom of expression based on directly relevant constitutional text, both jurisdictions would

Introduction: The Importance of Text

appear to constitute null sets.[34] But free speech enjoys meaningful judicial protection in both Australia and Israel. In point of fact, the High Court of Australia (HCA) and Supreme Court of Israel (SCI) both exercise judicial review to protect an implied freedom of speech.

Australia has a written constitution—but it lacks any provision safeguarding speech, press, assembly, or petition (the expressive freedoms expressly set forth in the U.S. First Amendment), or for that matter, a provision on freedom of association (an expressive freedom not expressly mentioned in the First Amendment, but nevertheless protected as an implication from the enumerated provisions, notably including freedom of speech and assembly). Even so, the HCA exercises judicial review to safeguard an implied freedom of political and governmental communication and, since 1992, regularly has invalidated federal and state legislation on free speech grounds.[35]

Israel does not have a formal, entrenched constitution (at all) but instead a series of Basic Laws, enacted between 1960 and 2018, that establish Israel's governing institutions and safeguard certain human rights (including human dignity and liberty).[36] Freedom of speech, however, is not enumerated in any of Israel's Basic Laws. Notwithstanding this fact, however, the SCI has, since the 1950s, claimed and exercised a power of judicial review to protect speech.[37] Indeed, constitutional protection of freedom of expression in Israel is considerably stronger, and more robust, than in Australia (despite both legal systems relying on implications to ground the right) and in the United Kingdom (where the domestic courts have not applied the HRA 98 aggressively in the context of speech rights).

What one will find, if one bothers to look, is a lack of correspondence between constitutional text, or its absence, and the scope and vibrancy of expressive freedoms on the ground. Even so, in the contemporary United States, federal judges, members of Congress, and a good many law professors all espouse a commitment to text as possessing signal importance to legitimating the use of judicial review to protect fundamental human rights.[38] But, in reality, how important is text to safeguarding a particular right? And, in practice, how much does text effectively constrain judges? This book takes as its project assessing the importance of text to securing one set of human rights: expressive freedoms.[39]

It would, of course, go too far to say that text is entirely irrelevant to judicial behavior. As one member of a national constitutional court told me in a private conversation, "If we had a text, whether in an entrenched constitution or a statutory bill of rights, it would give us a hook on which to hang our hat." So, plainly, the presence of a text provides a license, or justification, for judicial solicitude toward a particular right—but this presumes that the judge wants to define and protect the right. In the absence of judicial interest in such an undertaking, the presence of text, by itself, does not mean, and will not mean, that a right will have legal, political, or cultural salience.[40] Thus, text can *facilitate* judicial enforcement of a right but cannot *compel* it. And, at the end of the day, the text means what the courts say it means and, more often than not, judges interpret text in a way that corresponds to widely shared and held moral, philosophical, and cultural values.[41]

Of course, constitutional text might matter more—or less—in some contexts than in others. In the chapters that follow, using a sustained comparative legal analysis, I will show that with respect to safeguarding expressive freedoms, a text is neither a necessary nor a sufficient condition.

II. COMMON LAW CONSTITUTIONALISM AND THE (LIMITED) ROLE OF CONSTITUTIONAL TEXT

The protean nature of the First Amendment raises a larger, and quite important, question about constitutional design: Does text matter? Assuming that text does matter—at least in some instances—should we be concerned when courts purporting to interpret and apply that text choose to ignore it (and, in the case of the First Amendment and expressive freedoms, do so more or less completely)?[42] These questions implicate long-standing arguments about the importance of constitutional text, particularly in the context of safeguarding fundamental human rights, that go all the way back to the Federal Convention, which took place in Philadelphia, Pennsylvania, during the summer of 1787.

For example, one might posit that the specificity of constitutional text will prefigure its ability to bind both the political branches and the judiciary. In the alternative, one might believe that structural provisions might be less susceptible to creative judicial interpretation and application than rights provisions—and therefore potentially do a better job of delimiting how government institutions and actors operate.[43] From this vantage point, the limiting power of constitutional text exists on a continuum or spectrum that depends critically on context. Good reasons exist to question whether either of these postulations actually holds true. The better view might well be that constitutional text means what judges say that it means—nothing more and nothing less.[44] For the moment, however, and for the sake of argument, let us assume that the question is a debatable one and that a legal text might bind the institutions of government (at least in some contexts).

James Madison, generally a strong proponent of the written draft Constitution— which seems to reflect at least some degree of faith in text as a means of constraining the behavior of the institutions of government—nevertheless famously opposed the inclusion of a written bill of rights at the Federal Convention and, for a time, during the ratification debates in the states. When his friend and mentor, Thomas Jefferson, later offered his strenuous objection to the draft constitution's failure to include a written bill of rights, Madison responded that textual guarantees of fundamental human rights were of little—if any—practical utility because they could not, by themselves, constrain a government bent on disregarding them.

In Madison's view, written rights provisions simply do not work: "[E]xperience proves the inefficacy of a bill of rights on those occasions when its countroul [sic] is most needed."[45] He observed that "[r]epeated violations of these parchment barriers have been committed by overbearing majorities in every State" and such violations would likely occur at the federal level as well because "[w]herever the real power in a Government lies, there is the danger of oppression" and "[w]herever there is an interest and power to do wrong, wrong will generally be done."[46]

Thus, Madison had "never thought the omission [of a written bill of rights] a material defect, nor been anxious to supply it even by *subsequent* amendment, for any other reason than that it is anxiously desired by others."[47] Madison posited that federalism would serve as a more reliable safeguard of the people's rights and liberties than an extensive list of human rights.[48]

Of course, Madison fails to explain why *structural* provisions will prove any more efficacious than rights provisions. Delimiting the specific powers of the national government, after all, is no less a "parchment barrier" than rights provisions. What is more, a national government vested with broad powers, including a general power to tax and spend for the general welfare, could, if it wished to do so, consistently move the boundaries of federalism over time in favor of the central government. Indeed, this is arguably precisely what has happened from 1788 to the present. If Madison's argument rests on a theory that state governments could effectively and reliably check ever-broader federal assertions of authority, obvious and immediate problems of collective action and transaction costs arise.

Some structural provisions, such as vesting the state legislatures with the power to select members of the federal Senate, perhaps do provide a self-executing check on the expansion of the federal government's authority.[49] But the actions of the national government in the early years of the Republic, including the creation of a national bank[50] and the Louisiana Purchase,[51] provided almost immediate and convincing evidence of the limited utility and efficacy of structure as an effective check against mission creep by the federal government.[52] In sum, little evidence exists to support Madison's assumption that the text qua text binds the institutions of government any more effectively in the context of structure than it does with respect to substantive rights.

Making a different argument in support of the omission of a bill of rights, Alexander Hamilton, in *Federalist No. 84*, posits that written rights guarantees were at best superfluous and, at worst, dangerous.[53] Defending the failure to include a bill of rights, he argued that such guarantees are not needed when a government has limited, clearly defined powers because "the Constitution ought not to be charged with the absurdity of providing against the abuse of an authority which was not given."[54] Written rights guarantees, moreover, "would even be dangerous" because "[t]hey would contain various exceptions to powers which are not granted" thereby "afford[ing] a colorable pretext to claim more than were granted."[55] As Hamilton puts it, "[f]or why declare that things shall not be done which there is no power to do?"[56] Thus, Hamilton argued that express rights-granting constitutional provisions were unnecessary for a limited constitution, whereas Madison argued that express rights provisions would not, and probably could not, limit a government bent on violating them.

Like Madison's questionable claim that constitutional text related to federalism and structure would effectively constrain the national government, Hamilton's argument lacks persuasive force. A power to tax, for example, implies the power to destroy.[57]

On this count, Chief Justice John Marshall, not Justice Oliver Wendell Holmes, Jr., has the better of this argument: Congress routinely has used usurious taxes as a means of regulating where its direct regulatory authority, at least at the time when Congress enacted the "tax," might have been open to serious constitutional doubts.[58] Indeed, the validity of the Affordable Care Act's mandate for individual citizens to enter the private insurance market ultimately rested on Congress's constitutional taxing authority.[59] Thus, if Congress possesses the power to tax and spend for the general welfare, it could easily and foreseeably use these constitutional powers just like Louisiana's state government under Huey P. Long to impose discriminatory taxes on newspapers critical of the government.

Madison won the battle but lost the war. The ratification conventions in several states, notably including New York and Virginia,[60] made the inclusion of a bill of rights an absolute condition for agreeing to ratify the proposed draft constitution.[61] As Akhil Amar and his coauthor explain, the Antifederalists "were militant advocates for the inclusion of a bill of rights in the new Constitution" and were "suspicious of the extraordinary powers that were to be granted to the federal government by a constitution lacking a bill of rights that would clearly and unequivocally protect certain rights and freedoms."[62] Notwithstanding misgivings about the efficacy of such provisions, the Constitution's proponents (notably including James Madison) found it both politically necessary and expedient to agree to quickly consider and adopt a bill of rights once the reorganized national government came into operation.[63]

Even though Madison ultimately gave up his opposition to including a bill of rights in the Constitution, and in fact introduced the first draft of the amendments that became the Bill of Rights in the House of Representatives on June 8, 1789,[64] his arguments against the efficacy of "parchment barriers" should give a thoughtful person pause. To what extent do the actual words of a constitutional provision matter? Do those words effectively constrain the government? Under Madison's view, written rights guarantees, standing alone, do not and simply cannot prevent the government from abusing its powers.[65] Instead, he believed that the careful use of structural design elements—notably including the separation of powers and federalism—in shaping governing institutions would provide a more durable and efficacious means of securing individual liberty and safeguarding against tyranny.[66]

Madison's point seems, at best, rather dubious. If the efficacy of text depends on whether those who interpret it take it seriously, then the ultimate efficacy of text depends on whether its interpreters prove to be faithful stewards—and not on the inherent power of the text itself to compel respect and compliance. It is certainly true that many judges, lawyers, and legal scholars alike invoke constitutional text as if the words and phrases in the Constitution, Bill of Rights, and subsequent amendments possess talismanic powers. Even so, however, one cannot credibly deny that constitutional text does not perforce have a constraining effect. Consider that China, Cuba, and North Korea all have written constitutions—none of which effectively limits the government's exercise of coercive powers over citizens of those nations.[67] What's more, provisions on structure and institutional design are no more binding on the

Introduction: The Importance of Text ⟿ 9

institutions of government and are not self-evidently less susceptible to being evaded or ignored than are rights-granting provisions.

Simply put, a written constitution, interpreted and enforced by an independent judiciary, may devolve into a mere "parchment barrier" if those holding the reins of government power systematically attack and successfully destroy the institutional independence of the national courts. Thus, although Hungary, Poland, Russia, and Turkey all have written constitutions that once possessed more than a modicum of constraining legal force on the executive and legislative branches of government, these documents largely have fallen into desuetude as effective checks on the scope of these governments' powers today.[68] In all four countries, the political branches have used constitutionally available political controls over the judiciary, including the national constitutional courts, to effectively negate and cancel the judiciary's ability to exercise a meaningful power of judicial review to enforce constitutionally protected human rights. Although this has not (yet) happened in the United States, the fact remains that Congress and the President enjoy constitutional authority to reduce, or even destroy, the ability of the federal courts to interpret and enforce the Constitution and Bill of Rights.

Madison's skepticism about the potential efficacy of written rights provisions, mere "parchment barriers," seems justified. The effective constraining force of constitutional text crucially depends on context, the specificity of the provisions, the willingness of political actors to respect such guarantees voluntarily, and the ability and willingness of the courts to enforce compliance when the political branches disregard constitutional constraints. It is simply not credible to assert that text inevitably will constrain government actions on its own and without regard to any consideration of how the governing institutions within a particular polity interact with each other. One would be going too far to say text never matters and invariably constitutes a mere "parchment barrier"; at the same time, however, one cannot simply assume that constitutional text will, on its own and regardless of context, effectively secure fundamental human rights on the ground—or, for that matter, delimit both the structure and function of a nation's governing institutions.

III. THE COSMIC TURTLE REVISITED: JUDGES—NOT TEXT—ALL THE WAY DOWN?

In one telling of the cosmic turtle myth, the universe sits on a platform, which in turn rests on an elephant, with the elephant standing on the back of a turtle. If one were to ask, "Well, what is the turtle standing on?" a famous reply has it that "it's turtles all the way down."[69] In the case of constitutional interpretation, the meaning of a constitution rests on the judgment of courts (meaning judges). And, despite repeated disclaimers about lacking agency in their interpretations of constitutional text,[70] at the end of the day, it is the judges, not the text, who "say what the law is."[71] Moreover, if constitutional adjudication is, at bottom, a common law endeavor rather than a species of statutory interpretation, this should not really come as a great surprise.

The common law grows interstitially on a case-by-case basis.[72] Contract, tort, and property are, to an important degree, the domain of the judges rather than the legislators in common law jurisdictions.[73] There is a pronounced tendency on the part of judges to disclaim responsibility for potentially controversial results—and a concomitant desire to ground potentially controversial results in constitutional text.[74] This habit of judicial fig-leafing with constitutional text often exists at a level of generality that the text can plausibly support. Even so, however, efforts to ground discretion in text do not change the fact that the judges, not the text, are calling the constitutional shots.[75]

If not the text, then what factor, or factors, matter most to effectively securing a particular human right? In my view, careful comparative legal analysis lends strong support to the hypothesis that the most important factor is the presence of an independent judiciary vested with a power of judicial review—in tandem with executive and legislative institutions that are willing to acquiesce in the decisions of the courts. The cultural salience of a particular right also matters a great deal—if We the People are indifferent or hostile to a particular right, we will not seek recourse to the courts to protect it. Thus, the Third Amendment's proscription against the government quartering troops in private homes is the constitutional equivalent of the human appendix: It's certainly there, but the precise function has been lost in the mists of time.

Absent some means of forcing compliance with a particular human right, enshrining particular human rights in a written constitution will prove to be insufficient, standing alone, as a means of securing them from governmental abridgement. As the chapters that follow will demonstrate, the willingness of judges to take a particular kind of autonomy claim seriously will prefigure the strength (or weakness) of a particular human right far more reliably than whether or not the right is expressly codified and, if codified, precisely how broadly or narrowly the constitution or statute defines the right in question.

This is not to say that text is meaningless or entirely irrelevant. Such a claim would go too far. Text can and often does matter to securing fundamental rights. Australia's example, in particular, suggests that failing to codify a human right can leave that right's existence more open to doubt than would be the case were it written down. Israel, too, provides an example of a constitutional democracy where the failure to protect expressive freedoms overtly and expressly in a codified form arguably has made safeguarding expressive freedoms more difficult for the SCI. Going in the other direction, however, the United Kingdom's example shows that even when a legislature adopts a text, and clearly instructs courts to be particularly solicitous of a particular right (namely, speech and press rights), judges, even in a system whose central defining characteristic is parliamentary sovereignty, will be inclined to chart their own course.

At the end of the day, the ability of text to limit the scope of government action will depend on factors completely independent of the text itself—notably including the existence of an independent judiciary, the salience of the right (or institutional constraint) that the text safeguards within a particular political community,[76] the willingness of the legislature and executive to refrain from violating a particular right, as well as their willingness to respect judicial decisions enforcing a particular right, and the willingness of ordinary people to assert the right—through constitutional litigation if necessary. As the following chapter will demonstrate, the First Amendment's salience in the contemporary United States has far more to do with the general expectation of expressive freedom within the body politic, the reticence of legislators and executive branch officers to be seen as engaged in official censorship of the marketplace of political ideas, and the willingness of courts to issue strong judgments calling out violations when and if they occur, than it does with the amendment's text.

The alacrity with which courts move to disallow government efforts at censorship probably constitutes the most important of these factors. Aggressive judicial protection of expressive freedom both vindicates and reinforces the salience of these freedoms within the body politic. Indeed, it might well be that expressive freedom in the United States would not look much different today if the First Amendment, as such, did not even exist. Australia and Israel demonstrate that courts vested with a power of judicial review can and will protect the marketplace of political ideas based on the inexorable link between free and open public debate and a project of democratic self-government—and a citizenry's expectation of a free and open marketplace of political ideas. In the United States, we have an express textual provision that safeguards speech, but it should not be particularly surprising if the First Amendment's formal text proves to be less important than widely shared sociolegal expectations about the necessity of freedom of expression in a democratic polity. Simply put, if We the People expect and demand a free and open marketplace of political ideas—free of open and obvious forms of government censorship—then judges drawn from the same general sociolegal culture will attempt to meet that expectation in their opinions.[77]

IV. TEXT, JUDGES, AND EXPRESSIVE FREEDOMS—SETTING THE STAGE FOR A COMPARATIVE LEGAL ADVENTURE

The question "Does text really matter?" has a clear answer: "It depends." As the chapters that follow will demonstrate, hopefully persuasively, a text safeguarding expressive freedom can facilitate judicial efforts to protect and safeguard these rights. However, the absence of a relevant text—whether in a constitutional or statutory Bill or Rights—most definitely will not prevent judges from using the power of judicial review to protect speech, press, assembly, and petition. Moreover, the relevance of text pales in comparison to the importance of judges serving on independent courts of law, vested with the power of judicial review, and able to assert their authority successfully against the executive and legislative branches of government.

The first two national systems considered, the United States (Chapter 2) and South Africa (Chapter 3) feature entrenched bills of rights that include explicit protection for expressive freedom. Even so, the Supreme Court of the United States and the Constitutional Court of the Republic of South Africa have not been particularly concerned with reading the text closely and applying the relevant text carefully. The text of the First Amendment, as such, has been largely ignored and the amendment's Free Speech Clause serves as the source of a general rule against government censorship. In South Africa, the drafters of the 1996 Constitution did about all they could to signal the primacy of equality, human dignity, and freedom (meaning proscriptions against unjust arrest, imprisonment, or torture) over other human rights; yet, the Constitutional Court has consistently elevated freedom of speech to a co-equal status with equality, dignity, and human freedom.

The United Kingdom serves as the focus of Chapter 4. It provides an example of a system that lacked an express provision safeguarding expressive freedom that adopted such a provision in relatively recent times. One might predict, if text invariably affects the scope and meaning of rights, rendering them more secure, that codifying a right to freedom of expression would have upgraded and enhanced speech rights in the United Kingdom. In point of fact, things have not worked out this way. Free speech principles remained more or less the same before and after the HRA 98 took legal effect on October 2, 2000.[78] This, of course, does not mean that adopting a text will never lead to the enhancement of judicial protection of the right—but it has not mattered much, to date at least, in the United Kingdom.[79]

In Canada, for example, the 1982 adoption of the Charter of Rights and Freedoms,[80] and in particular Section 2, which expressly safeguards speech and press rights,[81] led to a major change in judicial behavior.[82] Of course, the Canadian Charter did not only codify human rights—it also conveyed an express power of judicial review on the Supreme Court of Canada (SCC).[83] Hence, a "chicken and egg" question arises regarding whether the SCC's reliable and robust enforcement of Charter rights, including expressive freedoms safeguarded under Section 2, was primarily a function of codification of the rights in question, the newly granted power of judicial review, or perhaps some combination of both. The HRA 98, unlike the Canadian Charter, does not expressly vest the Supreme Court of the United Kingdom with the power to invalidate laws that violate human rights protected under the European Convention.

Chapter 5 (Australia) considers a constitutional system in which a written constitution vests courts with the power of judicial review—but lacks any guarantee of speech rights. Chapter 6 (Israel) examines a legal system that lacks a formal written "constitution" as such and instead relies on ordinary statutes, denominated "Basic Laws," to establish Israel's governing institutions and fundamental legal principles. In both places, however, the highest courts, the HCA and SCI, have found that an implied right to freedom of expression exists and proceeded to deploy strong-form judicial review to safeguard it. Whether text would significantly affect judicial behavior in either polity is open to serious doubts.

As Chapter 5 explains in some detail, under a theory of democratic constitutionalism, the HCA generally tries to maintain a low institutional profile; it does not seek to challenge or contest the basic policymaking powers of the elected federal and state parliaments. Given this institutional reticence, the existence of a written guarantee of freedom of expression might well not make much of a difference to the scope and vibrancy of speech rights on the ground. In Israel, however, as discussed in Chapter 6, an express statutory or constitutional warrant for protecting speech might well make a difference—and bring about enhanced judicial protection of expressive freedom in much the same way as Section 2 of the Charter in Canada. The reason for the probable difference in outcomes in Australia versus Israel has far more to with the (very) limited role of the judiciary in making public policy in Australia and the more robust role that courts play in preventing unfair or arbitrary government action in Israel than with the general power of a legal text to command and direct the domestic courts.

The five case studies, all involving democratic polities with strong and long-standing histories of democratic self-government, will show how constitutional (or statutory) text has, at most, a limited role to play in securing expressive freedoms. At the risk of undo repetition, this is not to say, or even to imply, that text never matters or is wholly irrelevant to securing the freedom of speech, press, assembly, and petition. It is to say, however, that the power of text to protect expressive freedoms is very much contingent upon the power of courts within a particular country to issue decisions that disallow policy calls by the legislative and executive branches—as well as on the perceived importance of freedom of expression vis-à-vis other fundamental human rights (such as equality and dignity).

V. CONCLUSION: TEXT MEETS COURTS

One cannot credibly argue that text, whether of a constitutional or statutory stripe, is wholly irrelevant to securing fundamental human rights in general or expressive freedoms in particular. On the one hand, the presence or absence of text can make it easier, or more difficult, for judges to assert a power of judicial review to protect speech rights. On the other hand, however, the widely held view in the United States that text is critically important to securing a particular human right, including speech, seems open to some serious doubts and caveats. Even more deeply ironic, as the next chapter will show in some detail, is the near-complete irrelevance of the First Amendment's text and "original public meaning" to contemporary jurisprudence on expressive freedoms as fundamental human rights.

Across domestic legal systems in industrial democracies that seek to use elections to confer legitimacy on the nation's governing institutions, one will find, if one looks, that judges are the principal expositors of constitutionally protected speech rights. The role and importance of text varies from place to place and from system to system. The role and importance of judges, by way of contrast, proves to be something of a constant. More specifically, judicial culture and the relative power of courts and judges in general serve as better predictors of the security of speech rights than the presence—or absence—of some text that purports to secure expressive freedoms.

2

The United States

THE PROTEAN FIRST AMENDMENT AND
THE (VERY) LIMITED RELEVANCE OF ITS TEXT
TO THE WARP AND WEFT OF EXPRESSIVE FREEDOM

I. THE FIRST AMENDMENT AS A NONTEXTUAL TEXT: THE PROTEAN
NATURE OF THE FIRST AMENDMENT AND THE CRITICAL ROLE OF
JUDGES IN PROTECTING EXPRESSIVE FREEDOM

The First Amendment, like the Greek god Proteus, changes its shape to meet the perceived necessities of safeguarding the ongoing process of democratic deliberation.[1] Despite containing four distinct clauses related to particular forms of expressive freedom[2]—namely, express protections for speech, press, assembly, and petition[3]—the federal courts appear to have "forgotten" three of the amendment's four clauses.[4] Indeed, the First Amendment's text has little, indeed almost nothing, to do with the contemporary metes and bounds of expressive freedom in the United States.

The First Amendment instead stands for the proposition "that debate on public issues should be uninhibited, robust, and wide-open," and consistent with this approach, the public discourse that informs the act of voting on Election Day "may well include vehement, caustic, and sometimes unpleasantly sharp attacks on government and public officials."[5] To serve these constitutional goals, the amendment's meaning depends far less on its language than on its broader and more general purposes. Indeed, the First Amendment's text plays at most a bit part in the Supreme Court's development of "First Amendment" jurisprudence.

Proteus, the son of Poseidon, served as Poseidon's "shepherd of the sea."[6] Homer styles Proteus the "Old Man of the Sea" and also notes that Proteus possessed the gift

---

Free Speech as Civic Structure. Ronald J. Krotoszynski, Jr., Oxford University Press. © Ronald J. Krotoszynski, Jr. 2024.
DOI: 10.1093/9780197662229.003.0002

16 ○‿　　　　　　　　Free Speech as Civic Structure

of prophecy.[7] Thomas Bulfinch explains that in addition to the gift of prophecy, "[h]is peculiar power was that of changing his shape at will."[8] Proteus, as it turns out, was a rather reluctant fortune teller; a person seeking to know the future would have to first catch Proteus and compel him to spill the beans. To avoid capture, Proteus would change his shape and form.[9] From this mythological god comes the modern concept of something being "protean"—meaning changeable rather than fixed in form.

The First Amendment's shape, like that of Proteus, is far from fixed. More broadly, *all* constitutional text is, at least in theory, protean rather than fixed in form. Judge Guido Calabresi, in a strikingly bold but ultimately unsuccessful argument, urged judges to exercise an "updating" role with respect to statutes that they routinely exercise over the common law.[10] Consideration of the First Amendment's departure from a text-based exegesis highlights how federal judges routinely perform an updating role of the sort that Judge Calabresi advocates for statutes[11]—but with respect to the Constitution itself. And, despite decrying "updating" of the Constitution's text, conservative Justices have embraced this practice with real brio in the context of expressive freedom.[12]

The protean nature of the First Amendment is perhaps best exemplified by how little practical or legal effect the actual words of the amendment possess.[13] For starters, an amendment that begins rather specifically, namely, "*Congress* shall make no law,"[14] now applies to all government entities—federal, state, and local—and no one bats an eye at this radical expansion in the amendment's potential scope of application.[15] Indeed, to even raise this point today is to invite being accused of linguistic pedantry of the worst sort.[16]

Yet, the words are unmistakably *there*—and they are unique in *all* the provisions of the Bill of Rights. No other Bill of Rights provision is self-evidently directed solely at the legislative branch of the national government.[17] As Professor David Strauss has observed, the First Amendment could have been written broadly, like other provisions of the Bill of Rights. However, "it wasn't" and "the First Amendment alone singles out Congress."[18] Strauss is surely correct to posit that "[i]f we focus just on the text, the case for protecting free speech against government infringement generally is actually somewhat weak."[19]

The First Amendment's status as an atextual text merely starts with "Congress shall make no law." More generally, an amendment that specifies *four* separate forms of expressive freedom—speech, press, assembly, and petition—has been read and applied as if it contained *only one* (namely, speech). The Supreme Court has essentially ignored the Press, Assembly, and Petition Clauses, analyzing virtually all First Amendment claims through the lens of the Speech Clause.[20] Thus, it turns out that James Madison had no need to bother including the Press, Assembly, and Petition Clauses because, as interpreted and applied by the federal courts, these three clauses are entirely redundant and quite superfluous.

Despite the obsession of many contemporary federal judges with the text and original understanding of the Constitution and Bill of Rights,[21] many of these very same judges are firmly and fiercely committed to giving the First Amendment a dynamic and purposive interpretation.[22] Thus, like Proteus, the form and shape of the First

Amendment bend and change over time—yielding over a dozen three-, four-, and five-part tests that the Justices will deploy to frame and decide cases involving expressive freedom in particular contexts. What's more, the test count is growing—with the Supreme Court adopting new interpretative schemes with each passing term of Court.[23] Strictly speaking, none of these tests have much, if anything, to do with the actual text of the First Amendment.[24]

Of course, this may well be a design feature rather than a bug. Meaning this: if a choice must be made between, on the one hand, a First Amendment tethered in time to 1791, in which each of the specific clauses actually do particular—but largely irrelevant in the twenty-first century—jurisprudential work and, on the other, a world in which the literal language of the First Amendment is taken to represent a more general principle that a just government should not censor "We the People,"[25] with the precise details to be worked out over time by the federal courts through the accumulation of precedents that define the precise metes and bounds of expressive freedom, a very good case can be made in favor of the latter over the former.[26] If our goal is creating and sustaining the conditions necessary for democratic self-government to function, a dynamic First Amendment should be preferred (and strongly) to a static (or statist) First Amendment.

To be clear, I do not suggest that attention to the specific textual clauses should displace the larger and more general understanding of the First Amendment as a bulwark against government censorship. Instead, it is entirely possible, and more desirable normatively, for the federal courts to undertake both projects simultaneously. Taking this approach would enhance and improve the scope and vibrancy of expressive freedom in the contemporary United States.

Nevertheless, there's something deeply incongruous about a judiciary staffed with a great many self-described textualist jurists simply disregarding the First Amendment's plain language when interpreting and applying it. The original understanding of the First Amendment does not fare much better. The Alien and Sedition Acts of 1798, enacted by a Congress that contained a good many delegates from the Federal Convention in Philadelphia and also members personally familiar with Bill of Rights debates of 1789,[27] probably better reflect what the Framers of the First Amendment understood it to mean—perhaps nothing more than Blackstone's construction of freedom of speech as involving only rules against press licensing and prior restraints.[28]

To provide a concrete example of a doctrine that is difficult—indeed probably impossible—to reconcile with the original understanding, consider the robust protection that the Supreme Court has afforded to commercial speech (meaning: advertising to promote the sales of goods and services[29]). The robust protection of commercial speech under the First Amendment simply did not exist from 1791 to 1980 and cannot easily be reconciled with how the generation that wrote the First Amendment understood it and applied it.[30] First Amendment protection of commercial speech seems (very) hard to explain or justify in either originalist or more broadly normative terms.[31]

Other examples abound—for example, the use of the First Amendment to constitutionalize civil service protections and to abolish the spoils system which, since

18 ⌒ Free Speech as Civic Structure

time immemorial, state and local governments used to control access to government employment and contracts.[32] As Justice Lewis Powell observed in *Elrod*, the spoils system constituted "a practice as old as the Republic" and "a practice which has contributed significantly to the democratization of American politics."[33] If political patronage violated the First Amendment, as the framing generation understood it, it's very odd that no one noticed this fact until 1976.

Even if the Constitution's structural provisions may be, as Justice Antonin Scalia so emphatically argued, "dead, dead, dead,"[34] the Free Speech Clause of the First Amendment is very much *alive*—and this is precisely as it should be. But this begs the important question of whether the "living" First Amendment's actual text can and should do more serious work in safeguarding the marketplace of political ideas.[35]

This chapter will proceed in four additional sections. Section II shows how judges play the central role in defining and protecting expressive freedoms in the contemporary United States through an ongoing common law process. Simply put, the First Amendment's actual text is largely irrelevant to "First Amendment" jurisprudence in the contemporary United States. On balance, as section II argues, the central role of federal judges in defining and protecting speech rights constitutes a design feature rather than a bug. Section III posits that sociolegal culture and the expectations of We the People determine the scope of expressive freedom far more reliably than the actual text of the First Amendment; to a large extent, the First Amendment means what we want it to mean. Federal judges use the text as a means of meeting widely held, and deeply seated, legal, cultural, and social expectations within the body politic.

Section IV draws on Chief Justice John Marshall's theory of constitutional interpretation, as well as on Judge Guido Calabresi's theory of judicial "updating," to ground an argument about the centrality of judges in the United States, whose decisions invariably are informed by legal, social, and broader cultural expectations within the broader society, to constitutional law and constitutional interpretation more specifically. Simply put, despite widespread assumptions about the salience of text to constitutions and constitutionalism, constitutional law is fundamentally a species of common, not statutory, law.[36] Advocates of textualism and originalism have failed to engage with this rather basic empirical truth—instead claiming, much like the House of Lords prior to 1966,[37] that courts lack any legitimate power to alter or rescind their prior text-based rulings. Finally, section V offers a brief summary and conclusion.

II. TEXTUALISM AND ORIGINALISM IN CONSTITUTIONAL INTERPRETATION AND ADJUDICATION: THE FIRST AMENDMENT AS AN EXEMPLAR OF COMMON LAW CONSTITUTIONALISM IN ACTION

What is true of constitutional text in general seems to hold doubly true of the First Amendment. As this section will show—ideally with convincing clarity—the scope of expressive freedom in the contemporary United States has little to do with either the precise language and wording of the First Amendment or with the "original intent" of

The United States: The Protean First Amendment —⌒ 19

the Framers of the Bill of Rights. Instead, "the First Amendment" almost entirely consists of rules and doctrines created from whole constitutional cloth by judges engaged in an ongoing project of common law constitutionalism.

Despite its iconic status in the contemporary United States,[38] most federal judges, most of the time, simply ignore the First Amendment's actual text. The full text of the amendment provides:

> Congress shall make no law respecting an establishment of religion, or prohibiting the free exercise thereof; or abridging the freedom of speech, or of the press; or the right of the people peaceably to assemble, and to petition the Government for a redress of grievances.[39]

Focusing for the moment on the language related to the protection of expressive, rather than religious freedoms, the Free Speech Clause is the only provision that routinely does significant doctrinal work today.[40] Indeed, one can count the number of modern Supreme Court cases interpreting and applying the Press, Assembly, and Petition Clauses on the fingers of two hands.[41] The Press Clause has not generated major decisions in decades.[42] A leading scholar (arguably the leading scholar) of the Assembly Clause characterizes the provision as "forgotten."[43]

Lodging a quite similar complaint regarding the Petition Clause, I have lamented "the Supreme Court's unfortunate and highly circumscribed jurisprudence of the Petition Clause, which to date has largely failed to give the clause much, if any, independent legal significance."[44] In fact, the Petition Clause constitutes "little more than a footnote in modern Supreme Court jurisprudence."[45] At worst, it would be fair to say that the Petition Clause does not do any meaningful jurisprudential work to secure expressive freedoms in the contemporary United States; at best, one might credibly posit that it does very little such work. Professor Ash Bhagwat shares this view, observing that "the Petition Clause has disappeared from constitutional litigation."[46] He goes even further, positing that "[p]etitioning is thus dead," at least "as a tool of modern American democracy at the national level."[47]

So, what gives? When federal courts fail to invoke and apply particular constitutional texts, such as the Petition Clause, the provision effectively withers and eventually fades away into total and complete desuetude. To be sure, the language remains in the Constitution—but because it does no jurisprudential work, it ceases to play any meaningful role in our collective constitutional imaginations.[48] For example, with respect to the Petition Clause today, Professor Bhagwat is undoubtedly correct when he balefully posits that "few people even know it exists."[49] And the Press and Assembly Clauses have suffered the same fate as the Petition Clause—these First Amendment provisions have become irrelevant to the scope and meaning of expressive freedom in today's United States.

Thus, federal judges routinely ignore the actual text of the First Amendment— and this behavior should be viewed as problematic for a judiciary staffed with self-proclaimed "textualists."[50] After all, ignoring the text squarely "violates the notion that a court, when interpreting a legal text, should attempt to give legal effect to all provisions of the text."[51] The First Amendment specifies protection not only for "speech" but also for "the press," "assembly," and "petition."[52] And, the elephant in the room—which everyone seems to ignore—the directive that "Congress" shall "make no law."[53]

Chief Justice John Marshall made much of the Bill of Rights lacking the "[n]o state shall" language of Article I, Section 10 (which contains a variety of express limitations on state governments[54]) when holding that the provisions of the Bill of Rights, including the Takings Clause, do not apply to the states.[55] Marshall observed that "[t]he question thus presented is, we think, of great importance, but not of much difficulty."[56] If the absence of "no state shall" language in various provisions of the Bill of Rights provided a clear and conclusive answer to its scope of application vis-à-vis the states, shouldn't the presence of an express scope of application limitation—unique in the entire Bill of Rights—constrain the scope of the provision's application (namely, to the legislative branch, and not to the executive or judicial branches)? Despite the plain wording, today "Congress shall make" for all intents and purposes, on a de facto basis, actually means "no government entity shall make."[57]

For the record, I do not advocate for a general reduction in the First Amendment's institutional scope of application—as a normative matter, any and all government rules that seek to squelch speech based on content or viewpoint cannot be reconciled with a commitment to democratic self-government. Instead, we should probably ask ourselves whether the First Amendment can plausibly be invoked as the source of constitutional protection for particular and differentiated forms of expressive freedom. What is more, if the constitutional protection of expressive freedom really is not a function of the First Amendment's actual text, we should probably be more honest about First Amendment doctrine resting on judge-made constitutional common law rather than on the actual text of the amendment.[58]

It would be possible, of course, to pay more attention to the text and also enhance rather than degrade the scope of expressive freedom. A purposive, but more textualist, approach to interpreting and applying the First Amendment would involve giving all of its clauses meaningful work to do in facilitating the ongoing project of democratic self-government.[59] It would also involve what Professor Akhil Amar calls an "intratextual" reading of the clauses as creating a general rule against government censorship of the marketplace of political ideas.[60]

For the record, this is precisely how a reliable majority of the Supreme Court has approached the First Amendment since it undertook efforts to seriously enforce it.[61] Landmark cases such as *New York Times Co. v. Sullivan*[62] and *Brandenburg v. Ohio*[63] are not exercises in close readings of the First Amendment's text, of the adoption and ratification debates in Congress, or the state legislatures from June 8, 1789 (the date that James Madison introduced what was to become the Bill of Rights in Congress) to December 15, 1791 (the date that the First Amendment, and other provisions of the Bill of Rights, were ratified and entered into force), or the framing generation's understanding of what a commitment to the freedom of expression requires in a democratic republic. The judicially reconstructed provision, instead, represents a more general

The United States: The Protean First Amendment   21

rule against government efforts to engage in viewpoint- or content-based censorship of the marketplace of political ideas. And, in turn, this more general, purposive reading of the First Amendment gives rise to a broader scope of application than the amendment's Framers would likely have foreseen—for example, the protection of commercial speech[64] and graphic forms of pornography.[65]

In sum, the First Amendment provides a poster-child example of a constitutional provision whose literal text does little, if any, serious jurisprudential work and where judicially crafted doctrines bear most, and arguably all, of the jurisprudential weight. Indeed, the First Amendment constitutes a text that is, in many important respects, effectively a nontext. That the First Amendment is a nontextual text should be a source of puzzlement—if not downright consternation. After all, textualism has been a growth stock in U.S. constitutional interpretation since at least the 1980s—and arguably even earlier, with Justice Hugo L. Black advancing strictly textualist arguments in both his judicial opinions[66] and in his academic writings while off the bench.[67] Following in the footsteps of Justice Black, Justice Scalia led a full frontal assault on constitutional doctrines that overtly and transparently rely on judicially crafted legal rules and standards. His concurring opinion in *NASA v. Nelson*[68] provides an instructive example.

Nelson involved a challenge brought by government contractor employees at Caltech's Jet Propulsion Lab (JPL) to the federal government's employee background check program.[69] The JPL employees objected to background questions that the employees deemed unduly invasive and a violation of the right of informational privacy effectively recognized in 1977.[70] A 7–2 majority endorsed and reaffirmed the Supreme Court's assumption of a right of informational privacy as an aspect of the Due Process Clauses.

Justice Samuel A. Alito, Jr. explained that "[w]e assume, without deciding, that the Constitution protects [an informational] privacy right."[71] Nevertheless, the majority found that the federal government's background check program contained sufficient substantive and procedural safeguards and, accordingly, did not implicate the implied right of informational privacy. Given "the protection provided by the Privacy Act's nondisclosure requirement, and because the challenged portions of the forms consist of reasonable inquiries in an employment background check, we conclude that the Government's inquiries do not violate a constitutional right to informational privacy."[72]

The majority's approach rests comfortably within the common law tradition. *Griswold* recognized an unenumerated, yet fundamental, right of privacy derived from penumbras of more specific provisions of the Bill of Rights.[73] In turn, *Whalen v. Roe*'s de facto recognition of a right of informational privacy[74] was a logical and entirely foreseeable extension and application of this more general right of privacy. As Judge Guido Calabresi argues, "the [*Griswold*] Court was, in retrospect, correct" because "[t]he law it struck down was an anachronism held in place solely by inertia."[75]

A fundamentally different approach is, of course, possible. Judges can pretend that they do not perform an updating function with respect to constitutional text. And this is precisely what Justice Scalia, joined by Justice Clarence Thomas, did in *Nelson*.

Justice Scalia agreed that the government employees had failed to state a valid claim—but for a more basic reason. In Scalia's view, "[a] federal constitutional right to 'informational privacy' does not exist"[76] and, accordingly, "[l]ike many other desirable things not included in the Constitution, 'informational privacy' seems like a good idea—wherefore the People have enacted laws at the federal level and in the States restricting government collection and use of information."[77] If the Constitution, as amended, fails to specifically safeguard a particular interest, then the question is entirely up to Congress and the states to decide as they think best. Justice Scalia authored numerous opinions making this argument—most commonly in cases involving substantive due process.[78]

In cases involving provisions of the Bill of Rights, Justice Scalia usually parsed language in a very literal way. For example, the Sixth Amendment's Confrontation Clause means that criminal defendants have the constitutional right to confront their accusers quite literally, "face to face."[79] In other words, the federal judiciary has a duty to enforce strictly the literal words of the Sixth Amendment.

What, then, is one to make of Justice Scalia's failure to strictly enforce the precise language of the First Amendment? "Congress shall make no law" is an express limitation on the scope of the First Amendment—yet Justice Scalia had no objection to applying the Free Speech Clause broadly to executive and judicial officers. For example, Justice Scalia joined Chief Justice John Roberts's majority opinion in *Snyder v. Phelps*,[80] a case that involved judicial application of Maryland's law of tort to permit recovery for an offensive and outrageous targeted protest of Matthew Snyder's funeral and burial services. Snyder was a marine killed while on active duty in Iraq.[81] The legal rule at issue, which permitted Albert Snyder, Matthew Snyder's father, to recover for invasion of privacy, issued from the Maryland state courts—not from Congress or the Maryland state legislature. Moreover, the Maryland courts and a civil jury—not legislative officials—enforced and applied the rule in the case.

In fairness, the Supreme Court's initial consideration of whether the First Amendment's Free Speech and Free Press Clauses should apply against the state governments involved contempt proceedings in the Colorado state courts.[82] Writing for the majority, Justice Oliver Wendell Holmes, Jr. reserved the question of whether the First Amendment applies to the state governments via the Due Process Clause of the Fourteenth Amendment because, in the majority's view, the defendant in the contempt proceedings, a Denver newspaper publisher named Thomas M. Patterson, had failed to raise a valid First Amendment claim. Holmes explained that:

> [E]ven if we were to assume that freedom of speech and freedom of the press were protected from abridgment on the part not only of the United States but also of the States, still we should be far from the conclusion that the plaintiff in error would have us reach.[83]

This result obtained because, in Justice Holmes's view, the First Amendment only prohibited prior restraints—not subsequent punishment for published statements.[84]

A more obvious objection—namely, that the amendment has no application to judicial contempt proceedings at all—did not merit mention (or consideration). Patterson's newspapers had criticized the Colorado Supreme Court, in published editorials and editorial cartoons, regarding a case still technically before the bench; the Colorado Supreme Court's contempt sanctions, on these facts, did not constitute a prior restraint but rather punishment after the fact.[85]

Holmes simply ignored the relevant limiting language that, at least facially, appears to cabin the scope of the amendment's application—namely, that "Congress shall make no law."[86] His interpretation essentially limited the meaning of the amendment to Blackstone's rules against prior restraints and press licensing schemes.[87] This approach, despite giving the amendment a remarkably narrow scope of potential application, nevertheless also failed to take its text seriously or read it carefully.

Justice John Marshall Harlan,[88] in dissent, took note of the First Amendment's application to "Congress," observing that the amendment prohibits "hostile legislation by Congress" but nevertheless concluded that "neither Congress nor any State since the adoption of the Fourteenth Amendment can, by legislative enactments or by judicial action, impair or abridge" the right to free speech and a free press.[89] Of course, modern First Amendment doctrine reflects Harlan's views in *Patterson*—not those of Justice Holmes.

It bears noting that Justice Harlan was an out and proud common law constitutionalist of the first order; he took the view that the Fourteenth Amendment's Privileges or Immunities Clause, Due Process Clause, or both secured fundamental rights against the state governments.[90] Thus, for Harlan, the First Amendment's text did not matter because the right Patterson had invoked arose directly from the Fourteenth Amendment—rather than through literal "incorporation" of the First Amendment against the state governments.[91] Harlan, unlike today's ersatz textualists, was an honest and transparent common law broker. His openness to embracing common law constitutionalism and common law constitutional rights rendered the precise text of the First Amendment entirely irrelevant in a case in which the plaintiff was asserting a free speech and free press claim against a state government. It also meant that even if the First Amendment's scope was limited solely to Congress, the substantive due process liberty interest in expressive freedom under the Fifth Amendment's Due Process Clause was not.[92]

The important point, in both the Holmes and Harlan *Patterson* opinions, is that even in the Supreme Court's first consideration of the First Amendment's potential scope of application to the state governments, "Congress shall make no law" received virtually no consideration as creating a potential limit on the amendment's scope of application. In Holmes's case, the omission seems like a blown call, whereas in Harlan's case, it is simply the natural outgrowth of his overall approach to recognizing and protecting fundamental rights under the rubric of "due process of law" flowing from the Due Process Clauses of both the Fifth and Fourteenth Amendments. Harlan, unlike Holmes, could disregard the specific wording of the First Amendment in favor of a common law approach that took the specific language of the Bill of Rights as reflecting

24 ⌒ Free Speech as Civic Structure

deeply seated human rights commitments, but which also did not construe the absence of specific constitutional language as foreclosing a right running against either the federal or a state government.[93]

The First Amendment's actual words have been irrelevant since before the Supreme Court clearly held that the amendment applied to the states via the Due Process Clause of the Fourteenth Amendment in 1931.[94] To be sure, the Supreme Court, from the 1930s to the 1970s, did make more regular efforts to give meaningful effect to the Press,[95] Assembly,[96] and Petition Clauses.[97] By the 1980s, however, the First Amendment had been reduced to the Free Speech Clause—as a kind of catch-all provision for any and all forms of expressive freedom.[98]

In *Perry Education Association*,[99] decided in 1983, the Justices began using the Free Speech Clause as a synecdoche for the entire First Amendment. After *Perry*, the First Amendment's other clauses were largely judicially orphaned and ceased to generate important new protections for expressive freedom. As Professor John Inazu explains, "[w]ith *Perry*, even cases involving protests or demonstrations could be resolved without reference to assembly."[100] Moreover, the Justices' abandonment of the Press, Assembly, and Petition Clauses went without mention, explanation, or justification. In First Amendment jurisprudence, the new normal became "All Free Speech Clause, all the time."

If one were writing a constitutional free speech guarantee today, it might have made sense to provide only for the protection of "speech." However, this is not what the Framers of the First Amendment actually did—or said. Nor was such a limited text ratified by the state legislatures between 1789 and 1791. The Supreme Court has essentially rewritten the First Amendment and streamlined it; the text is now largely irrelevant to constitutional protection for expressive activities in the contemporary United States. What's more, the interpretation and application of the Free Speech Clause is not (at all) tethered to the Framers' original understanding of that clause's scope or meaning.[101]

Of course, if the text is simply a place holder for the body politic's sense of justice, we should expect the text to be merely a starting point, not the ending point, in the adjudication of constitutional rights.[102] With the passage of time, one would predict that if the plain meaning of the constitutional text departed from the community's values and attitudes regarding the appropriate scope of a particular fundamental right,[103] the text would come to play a less and less important role in the judicial articulation and enforcement of that right.

III. DEEPLY SEATED SOCIOLEGAL NORMS DEFINE THE SCOPE OF FREEDOM OF EXPRESSION MORE RELIABLY THAN CONSTITUTIONAL TEXT—AND THIS MIGHT APPLY TO OTHER SUBSTANTIVE RIGHTS TOO

The First Amendment provides a good starting point for framing the inherent limitations of constitutional text as a way of understanding either a human right or the prescriptive force of a constitutional provision. The federal courts have applied the First

Amendment in a dynamic and purposive fashion—as a "living tree," to use the relevant language from the Supreme Court of Canada.[104] Judicial interpretation and application of the First Amendment are not tethered to the text in any meaningful way, and, moreover, the Framers' understanding of "the" freedom of speech plays little, if any, meaningful role in contemporary First Amendment jurisprudence.

The relevance of constitutional text to the effective protection of constitutional rights in general, and First Amendment rights in particular, is both uncertain and seems to depend on factors wholly unrelated to a constitutional provision's literal text. Although it is commonplace in the United States to assume that constitutional text plays a critically important role in securing fundamental rights, this assumption simply does not bear up to close and considered scrutiny. Does text actually do much work in securing fundamental human rights in general—or the freedom of speech in particular? Or were Madison and Hamilton correct to posit that institutional structure, design, and dynamics are far more important to safeguarding fundamental rights (including expressive freedom)?[105] In the case of expressive freedom, other factors, notably including a general legal culture that values expressive activities, appear to be doing the real work in securing judicial protection for democratic discourse.[106]

The question of whether constitutional text matters is hardly a new one. James Madison famously decried the utility of mere "parchment barriers" to preventing arbitrary government action.[107] In defending the necessity of a system of separation of powers, with a related system of checks and balances among the three branches of the federal government, Madison wrote that "a mere demarcation on parchment of the constitutional limits of the several departments is not a sufficient guard against those encroachments which lead to a tyrannical concentration of all the powers of government in the same hands."[108] Instead, each branch must both possess and be capable of exercising effective tools to check and thwart attempted incursions by the other branches of the federal government—and also have sufficient institutional incentives to protect its own constitutional turf against such encroachments.[109]

Like the separation of powers, the demarcation of fundamental human rights in a written constitution does not, perforce, mean that those words will have any meaningful constraining force on a government that would prefer to disregard constitutionally protected human rights. Indeed, Alexander Hamilton makes precisely this point, at length, in *Federalist No. 84*. Hamilton argues that the inclusion of a written bill of rights would be "not only unnecessary in the proposed Constitution but would even be dangerous."[110] The enumeration of certain rights, Hamilton posits, "would contain various exceptions to powers which are not granted; and, on this very account, would afford a colorable pretext to claim more than were granted."[111] After all, "why declare that things shall not be done which there is no power to do?"[112]

It should therefore be at least mildly surprising that, for most people, most of the time, written guarantees of fundamental rights are thought to be an effective, if not essential, means of securing the enumerated human rights. This certainly proved true in the ratification debates over the U.S. Constitution, when arguments of the sort advanced by Hamilton in *Federalist No. 84* failed to quell potentially fatal objections that the federal government would not be bound to respect fundamental rights.[113] Thus, during the ratification debates over the Constitution, the absence of text designed to secure fundamental human rights mattered—and it mattered a great deal.

The adoption of a bill of rights, however, is not a sufficient condition to ensure that the government will, in practice, respect the enumerated rights. We also know, from the examples of Australia and Israel,[114] that the inclusion of a constitutional provision expressly safeguarding expressive freedom is not even a necessary condition for the exercise of the power of judicial review to invalidate laws that seek to censor or distort the marketplace of political ideas. This does not mean that a written provision is invariably irrelevant—but the force and effect of such a provision will depend critically on a nation's sociolegal culture, the salience of a particular human right within that sociolegal culture, and the institutional ability and willingness of the domestic courts to render binding judgments on the political branches enforcing the right.

Yet, despite these constitutional verities, which can be empirically tested and confirmed,[115] many U.S. legal academics, judges, and lawyers still claim that the text inevitably can and will constrain judicial discretion. The most prominent and influential theory of constitutional interpretation within the federal courts, including the Supreme Court, and advocated consistently and loudly by the Federalist Society, posits that legitimate judicial decisions must be rooted in constitutional text and in the Framers' original understanding of that text. Many—but not all—legal scholars heap scorn on this interpretative methodology as a kind of false faith that does little, if anything, to legitimate judicial decisions granting or withholding relief from particular litigants pressing constitutional claims.[116] Even so, the fact remains that within the Supreme Court and the lower federal courts, textualist originalism, warts and all, presently serves as the most prominent approach to reading and applying the Constitution's provisions.[117]

Moreover, at least some prominent legal academics advocate textualism and the importance of constitutional text to securing fundamental human rights. Akhil Amar is perhaps the most influential (non-Federalist Society) contemporary legal academic who argues that text matters.[118] Amar posits that constitutional text is not only important on its own terms but also should be read dynamically to help lend credence to the idea that judges are enforcing the Constitution (rather than simply imposing their own legal and moral values in the name of the Constitution).[119] For Amar, text has objective meaning, and reliance on this meaning helps to legitimate judicial decisions that enforce the rights set forth in the text.[120] Amar's principal concern relates to the legitimacy of the process of judicial review—and he suggests that text lends legitimacy to judicial decisions enforcing rights.[121] Of course, other prominent public law scholars reject this reasoning as nonsense, arguing that text does not meaningfully constrain judicial discretion and that judicial decision-making is simply another form of ordinary politics.[122]

It is, of course, quite true that text can provide a basis for a judicial decision and can offer a possible answer to the problem of judicial discretion. After all, if "the text" compels a particular outcome, then an individual judge can attempt to disclaim any

The United States: The Protean First Amendment   ⟶ 27

personal responsibility for it.[123] Thus, a textual constitutional provision enables a judge to claim (falsely, of course) that she lacked a free or meaningful choice—the text itself required, indeed compelled, the result.[124] Justice Hugo L. Black, deeply concerned about the legacy of *Lochner*,[125] famously adopted a strict form of textualism as a principal means of trying to limit and effectively constrain judicial discretion.[126] Thus, text and textualism present a way of answering Alexander Bickel's "[c]ounter-[m]ajoritarian [d]ifficulty"[127] by providing a popular mandate for the exercise of judicial review. From this vantage point, textualism responds to problems of discretion and legitimacy associated with judicial review by democratically unaccountable federal judges.

But, at least with respect to expressive freedom in the contemporary United States, the text and textualism plainly constitute a "tin god"—meaning a kind of rhetorical makeweight that does no meaningful jurisprudential work.[128] To invoke text, while paying not the slightest attention whatsoever to the actual words of the text, is to embrace (literally) the jurisprudence of the nonsequitur. The First Amendment's interpretation and application provide a stark example of judges saying one thing while doing quite another; contemporary First Amendment jurisprudence depends critically on judge-made rules and constitutes a clear example of common law constitutionalism in action.[129]

At bottom, the problem is that textualism rests on a false premise—namely, that text actually constrains judges bent on disregarding it. To be sure, text can and does provide political cover for judges.[130] But if we are seriously concerned with effectively securing a particular human right, simply codifying a human right in a constitution will not necessarily get the job done. The Eighteenth Amendment codified a national policy of prohibition, but the amendment did not change either the morality or the drinking habits of the American people. Text can only do so much in the teeth of highly entrenched social customs and habits. Theories of constitutional interpretation need to take this reality into account—but the reigning theory of constitutional interpretation today within the federal courts largely ignores the inability of text to constrain reliably judicial discretion.[131]

Simply making the point that text does not really constrain either governments generally or courts in particular might seem a self-evident observation to more sophisticated scholars of the legal system. But what is true of legal text in a general sort of way holds true of texts—or nontexts—related to the freedom of speech in an unusual, and particularized, kind of way.[132] In the United States, a conservative Supreme Court ostensibly staffed with "textualist-originalist" jurists has essentially ignored the text of the First Amendment in defining and protecting expressive freedom.

Originalism more generally tends to go out the window as well[133]—important precedents protecting commercial speech, for example, enjoy the strong support of the most conservative "textualist-originalist" judges, despite the fact that no evidence exists that the framing generation of the Bill of Rights would have understood commercial advertising to have any protection whatsoever as "speech."[134] Thus, the First Amendment receives a kind of dynamic, or "living tree," purposive interpretation and application, largely shorn of either concerns for giving full effect to the text of the provision or to the Framers' original understanding of the amendment as to its purpose and scope of application.

For the record, this is not necessarily a bad thing. But when we consider how best to secure and safeguard a fundamental right, like expressive freedom, blithely assuming that entrenching a right in a written constitution will get the job done rests on a series of false premises. Text works best when it is in full accord with the settled expectations of the people within a particular political community; common law constitutionalism is the rule, not the exception. Constitutional text will not safeguard a right if the citizenry is either hostile or merely indifferent to a particular freedom or liberty, and omitting constitutional text will not prevent judges from exercising a power of judicial review to protect a right that We the People expect a just and well-ordered government to respect.

Text thus constitutes one input, and admittedly an important input, in a dynamic and ongoing dialectic within both the institutions of government and the body politic on the legitimate scope of the government's coercive powers as measured against an individual citizen's claim to exercise autonomy and to be, in some material respects, self-regulating. Expressive freedom is not cabined by constitutional text in the United States, Australia, or Israel, and probably cannot be effectively defined within any particular linguistic formula. And, contrary to Justice Black's repeated claim that the First Amendment is an "absolute" that permits no exceptions, the legal and constitutional reality is considerably more complex.

Discretion simply cannot be avoided because adjudicating expressive freedom claims will inevitably require courts to strike a balance between the legitimate regulatory aims of a community, as expressed through the institutions of government, and the ability of a lonely dissenter to speak her version of truth to power.[135] Expressive freedom will always involve striking and holding a balance—and that balance will, of necessity, reflect the values and attitudes of the community more reliably and consistently than the precise text of a constitutional free speech guarantee (or, for that matter, the utter absence of such a written constitutional guarantee). It is inherently and intrinsically a common law jurisprudential enterprise.

IV. TURTLES ALL THE WAY DOWN: THE NECESSITY OF COMMON LAW EXEGESIS IN INTERPRETING AND APPLYING CONSTITUTIONAL TEXT

Departure from constitutional text is hardly limited to the First Amendment—or to liberal or progressive judges. Constitutional rights and rules constantly evolve and change, through a process of judicial explication, even though the text remains unchanged. All things considered, it would be better—far better—if federal judges were intellectually honest about this reality and acknowledge the common law nature of the interpretative game that's plainly afoot. Some judges have been open about this reality. Justice Oliver Wendell Holmes, Jr., for example, straightforwardly acknowledges that "[t]he life of the law has not been logic: it has been experience."[136] Common

The United States: The Protean First Amendment — 29

law constitutionalism reflects and incorporates an appreciation of the fact that legitimate judicial decisions must be informed by the lived experience of We the People. To both persuade and endure over time, constitutional decisions must reflect the values and sense of justice of the contemporary body politic.[137]

Chief Justice John Marshall powerfully argued for judges adopting a common law approach to interpreting constitutional text. Perhaps most famously, in *McCulloch v. Maryland*,[138] Marshall posited that federal judges "must never forget[] that it is a constitution we are expounding" with the ultimate goal being "a fair and just interpretation."[139] Any other approach would be untenable because "[a] constitution, to contain an accurate detail of all the subdivisions of which its great powers will admit, and of all the means by which they may be carried into execution, would partake of the prolixity of a legal code, and could scarcely be embraced by the human mind."[140] Such a document "would probably never be understood by the public."[141]

Marshall strongly implies that a constitution inaccessible to We the People would be both illegitimate and ineffectual.[142] Accordingly, a constitution's purpose and nature "require[ ], that only its great outlines should be marked, its important objects designated, and the minor ingredients which compose those objects be deduced from the nature of the objects themselves,"[143] with the precise details to be filled in by the federal courts (albeit with important roles for Congress and the President as well).[144]

When one marries up the interpretative approach Marshall advocates in *McCulloch* with the duty of the federal judiciary to enforce constitutional constraints against the political branches, the necessary conclusion is that the federal courts must, of necessity, perform an updating function that ensures the Constitution, as interpreted and applied, continues to enjoy popular legitimacy.[145] It also bears noting that this is the precisely the same argument that the Privy Council made in *Edwards* when disregarding the plain text of the British North America Act, 1867 (BNA), the original understanding of this text, and consistent practice regarding the constitutional ineligibility of women to serve in Canada's federal Senate—in favor of embracing a "living tree" approach that accommodates "growth and expansion within its natural limits."[146]

The truth is also that ostensible textualist judges have, at best, a mixed record of actually hewing to the text and original understanding—at least when they perceive the stakes to be sufficiently important. Justice Hugo Black, for example, wrote the majority opinion in *Younger v. Harris*,[147] a decision that celebrates "Our Federalism."[148] This decision prohibits a federal court from enjoining ongoing state criminal law proceedings—even if the state law proceedings rest on a clearly unconstitutional state law. Black explains that the basis for this rule is a general principle of respect for the co-sovereignty of the states: "This, perhaps for lack of a better and clearer way to describe it, is referred to by many as 'Our Federalism,' and one familiar with the profound debates that ushered our Federal Constitution into existence is bound to respect those who remain loyal to the ideals and dreams of 'Our Federalism.' "[149]

There's just one problem with Black's *Younger* opinion—it does not cite any provision of the U.S. Constitution for this rule, and it has the effect of delaying, if not denying outright, the ability of criminal defendants in ongoing state court proceedings to access an effective forum in which to vindicate their federal constitutional rights. The *Younger* abstention doctrine lacks any direct textual basis in the Constitution; it is a common law rule fashioned from whole cloth. Under Justice Black's strict textualism, it is a self-evidently illegitimate decision. So much for Justice Black's promise not to add anything to the Constitution precisely as written.[150]

Other examples exist involving more recent members of the Supreme Court. For example, in *Seminole Tribe v. Florida*,[151] the Supreme Court held that Congress could not abrogate state sovereign immunity under the Eleventh Amendment using its powers under the Indian Commerce Clause.[152] Chief Justice Rehnquist explained that "our decisions since *Hans* ha[ve] been equally clear that the Eleventh Amendment reflects 'the fundamental principle of sovereign immunity [that] limits the grant of judicial authority in Art. III.'"[153] Justice Scalia joined the five-Justice majority in *Seminole Tribe* and Chief Justice William H. Rehnquist cites and quotes Justice Scalia's dissent in *Union Gas*,[154] a prior decision that *Seminole Tribe* squarely overrules.[155] *Seminole Tribe*, in turn, constitutes a significant expansion of *Hans v. Louisiana*, an 1890 case that significantly departs from the clear text of the Eleventh Amendment.[156]

Hans radically expands the scope of the Eleventh Amendment by extending it to suits brought against a state government by a citizen of that state—the plain text of the amendment, however, only prohibits suits against state governments brought by citizens of other states or foreign countries.[157] The Eleventh Amendment constitutes a direct response to *Chisholm v. Georgia*, a case that permitted a state to be sued without its consent by the citizens of another state (namely, a citizen of South Carolina).[158] This result followed quite logically, and naturally, from the plain language of Article III, which expressly extended the jurisdiction of the federal courts to reach such actions.[159] The Eleventh Amendment removed specific language in Article III authorizing suits by noncitizens—it was (and remains) entirely silent regarding the ability of citizens to sue their own home states in order to vindicate a federal right. *Hans*, applying a spirit of the laws approach, greatly expanded the scope of the Eleventh Amendment—and *Seminole Tribe* greatly amplified and expanded the scope of *Hans*.

Staking out a normative position on the appropriate scope of state sovereign immunity lies beyond the scope of my present project. My point is this: decisions like *Younger* and *Seminole Tribe* clearly show that conservative judges are no more faithful textualists than progressive jurists. What is more, other salient examples of common law judging in the context of constitutional adjudication exist—for example, the regulatory takings doctrine under the Takings Clause (which Justice Scalia avidly and aggressively supported).[160]

Textualist judges, like Justices Gorsuch, Scalia, and Black, will cry out "bloody murder!" when progressive judges openly deploy common law reasoning and methodology to promote the expansion of individual rights, yet they clearly will embrace this modus operandi, and with real brio, when it suits their jurisprudential agenda.[161] In consequence, their attacks on constitutional common law to secure and protect fundamental rights ring hollow—as it turns out, it's turtles all the way down.

V. CONCLUSION: JUDGES, NOT THE FIRST AMENDMENT'S TEXT, PLAY THE CENTRAL ROLE IN DEFINING AND PROTECTING SPEECH IN THE UNITED STATES

Rather than being defined within the four corners of the First Amendment's text, the constitutional protection of expressive freedom in the contemporary United States, as defined and protected by the federal and state courts, involves a broad general presumption that information markets should be free and open and that government efforts to control or even actively regulate speech markets are inherently distortionary and, hence, constitutionally illegitimate.[162] Rather than a doctrine that hews carefully to constitutional text and the original understanding of it, First Amendment jurisprudence today consists almost entirely of judge-made constitutional common law, mostly dating from the 1960s to the present, that establishes and enforces a rather general constitutional rule against any and all forms of government censorship (and reaches even some private censorship as well[163]).

The First Amendment that many judges, legal academics, lawyers, and ordinary citizens claim to know and cherish has little, if any, relationship to the actual text that the first Congress sent to the states for their consideration and which became part of the Constitution when Virginia ratified the First Amendment on December 15, 1791. This jurisprudential reality cries out for a great deal more notice and commentary than it has received to date. After all, with a Supreme Court bench now packed with purported textualist, originalist judges, it is exceedingly odd that the actual words of the First Amendment would matter so little in the pages of *U.S. Reports*.

At a broader level of analysis, the First Amendment's example should give a thoughtful person serious pause about the ability of text to define and constrain particular human rights. Rather than grounding the protection of expressive freedom in the text of the First Amendment and the practices of the generation that wrote and adopted it, the federal courts have essentially sought to ensure that citizens have the ability to participate freely in the process of democratic deliberation—a process integral to the use of elections as a means of conferring legitimacy on the institutions of government.[164]

On the one hand, this common law approach to safeguarding expressive freedom has much to recommend it. Most judges and legal scholars would agree that it is very difficult to imagine a system of free and fair elections that does not provide some measure of protection for the process of public debate.[165] However, the First Amendment itself simply does not reference the process of democratic deliberation—even if the nexus between speech and democracy is a reasonably self-evident one.[166] The democratic self-government theory of the freedom of speech constitutes a common law "update" of the amendment's text.[167]

On the other hand, however, the fact that very strong normative reasons support the Supreme Court's purposive and dynamic interpretative approach should not—at least for a textualist and originalist judge—serve as a legitimate basis for simply disregarding the text and original understanding of the First Amendment's expressive freedom provisions. That such judges seem to have few, if any, compunctions about

32 ∽ Free Speech as Civic Structure

adopting a purposive and dynamic approach to the First Amendment should also raise serious doubts about the ability of text to constrain even jurists who claim particularly deep and abiding fealty to constitutional text as a central bulwark against unduly broad judicial discretion. Simply put, if judges who proclaim that they will enforce the text as written, nothing more and nothing less, do not actually do this, instead embracing a common law "updating" function,[168] is there any reason to believe that any judges will feel honor-bound to hew closely and exclusively to constitutional text when deciding constitutional cases? And, if they could actually chart such a course, how long would they actually hold it before the pressure for constitutional revision, via either judicial action or amendment, became inexorable?[169]

3

South Africa

RECONCILING THE FREEDOM OF SPEECH WITH
DIGNITY, EQUALITY, AND HUMAN FREEDOM IN
THE LONG SHADOW OF APARTHEID

I. INTRODUCTION: THE CONSTITUTIONAL COURT OF THE REPUBLIC OF SOUTH AFRICA AS THE GUARDIAN OF CONSTITUTIONAL RIGHTS, VALUES, AND STRUCTURES

Chapter 2 demonstrated, in some detail, how and why the actual text of the First Amendment does not play a particularly meaningful role in the U.S. Supreme Court's modern expressive freedom jurisprudence.[1] Rather than taking the actual words of the First Amendment into careful account, the U.S. Supreme Court instead has adopted a broad, purposive "living tree" approach that treats the amendment's text as standing for a rather general constitutional proscription against government efforts to control or even merely to manipulate the marketplace of ideas in general and the marketplace of political ideas in particular.[2]

The same holds true in another country, Australia, where, despite maintaining a written constitution that quite intentionally omits any mention of constitutional rights to the freedom of speech, press, assembly, association, or petition, the High Court of Australia found these expressive activities protected by an "implied freedom of political and government communication" derived from constitutional provisions that require free and fair elections on a regular basis for the nation's governing parliamentary institutions.[3] Thus, in the United States and Australia, the presence of text (United States) and the absence of text (Australia) do not prefigure, at all, the scope

---

Free Speech as Civic Structure. Ronald J. Krotoszynski, Jr., Oxford University Press. © Ronald J. Krotoszynski, Jr. 2024.
DOI: 10.1093/9780197662229.003.0003

and vibrancy of constitutionally protected expressive freedoms—instead judges set the metes and bounds that delimit these rights.

One might well respond: "Well, so what? That text does not matter in those places hardly shows that text does not matter anywhere in defining the scope of free speech." It is certainly true that the limited relevance of constitutional text in the United States and Australia (and one could add to this list Israel[4] and the United Kingdom[5] as well) might be explained in some way that negates my thesis that text does not meaningfully constrain constitutional courts in expressive freedom cases.

As Professor David Strauss has observed, in the United States, "the text of the Constitution will play, at most, a ceremonial role" in most constitutional adjudications.[6] Why is this so? He explains that "American constitutional law is about precedents, and when the precedents leave off, it is about commonsense notions of fairness and good policy."[7] In other words, in the United States, the Constitution provides at most a jumping-off point that frames how legal advocates will make their arguments in the broadest terms—but more granular arguments invariably will rest not on the actual text of the U.S. Constitution, but rather on the Supreme Court precedents that interpret and apply that text.

Perhaps a counterexample exists—a constitutional democracy where the judges hew closely and carefully to the relevant constitutional texts rather than creating constitutional free speech doctrine from whole cloth using a common law methodology over time.[8] After all, the U.S. Constitution dates back to 1787 and the Australian Constitution to 1901. The relatively ancient vintage of both these constitutional instruments might render it necessary for judges to "update" them to an extent that simply would not be necessary in a polity with a constitution of more recent vintage. A contemporary constitutional document should, in theory, better accord with contemporary constitutional, political, social, and moral values.

South Africa provides an excellent example of an industrial democracy with a constitution adopted within the living memory of most judges. The Republic of South Africa adopted its current Constitution in 1996—and the document entered into force on February 4, 1997.[9] The South African Constitution of 1996 was a carefully drafted document that replaced the interim 1993 Constitution. As Professors Judith Geldenhuys and Michelle Kelly-Louw observe, "South Africa has a history of vast inequity along racial lines" which the 1993 Interim Constitution and permanent 1996 Constitution sought to redress.[10] They explain that "[b]efore 1993 a system of parliamentary sovereignty existed, and the South African courts did not have the power to test the validity or fairness of legislation."[11]

The 1996 Constitution places principal faith in the Constitutional Court of the Republic of South Africa (CCSA) to serve as the guardian of constitutional rights and values.[12] It also guarantees citizens effective remedies for any and all constitutional violations proven in open court.[13] The drafters considered numerous constitutional models (old and new) and also took into account transnational human rights instruments, such as the European Convention for the Protection of Human Rights and Fundamental Freedoms[14] and the Universal Declaration of Human Rights.[15]

South Africa's 1996 Constitution reflects a careful process that proceeded in two stages, with an interim 1993 Constitution put in place while a constituent assembly was elected; the constituent assembly, which possessed democratic legitimacy that the apartheid-era legislature that adopted the interim 1993 Constitution utterly and completely lacked, proceeded to draft a permanent constitution, which, to be ratified, required review and final approval by the newly created CCSA (which the interim 1993 Constitution created).[16] Professor Siri Gloppen argues, correctly, that "[t]he 'final' constitution places a heavy burden on the legal system" because of "the relatively weak separation of powers between the executive and legislative arms of government."[17] Gloppen posits that the political branches require a check against unconstitutional behavior, and "the Constitutional Court together with the other 'watchdog' bodies provided for in the constitution, are left with most of the responsibility for keeping the majority in line, at least as long as there is a clear parliamentary majority."[18]

The CCSA was an entirely new juridical entity that stands both outside and above the regular domestic courts. Both the CCSA's design and functions greatly resemble Germany's highest juridical entity, the Federal Constitutional Court (FCC). The framers of Germany's new democratic constitution, the *Grundgesetz* ("Basic Law"), sought to create a new juridical entity that would exist outside and above the existing judicial system, whose legitimacy had been fatally compromised by the courts' complicity in enforcing Nazi-era laws, regulations, and policies (including the "Final Solution").[19] The FCC's role would include protecting Germany's new democratic social order and governing institutions from another meltdown of the sort that took place from 1932 to 1945 under the National Socialist German Workers' Party (commonly called the Nazi Party). The historical parallels are quite obvious between, on the one hand, Germany, following the Allies' defeat of the Axis powers and restoration of genuine democratic self-governance in 1949, with West Germany's adoption of the Basic Law, and, on the other, the end of all-white minority rule in South Africa under the National Party's Herrenvolk democracy and the creation of a new "rainbow" nation (to use Bishop Desmond Tutu's and President Nelson Mandela's preferred turn of phrase[20]).

In post-apartheid South Africa, a clear and pressing need existed for a juridical entity that was untainted by association with the national catastrophe under apartheid and Herrenvolk democracy. As Professor Mark Kende explains, "[t]he general view is that South Africa needed to break from its past including the duplicity of many courts and lawyers under apartheid."[21] The creation of a new and powerful juridical institution, the CCSA, constituted the framers' institutional solution for giving South Africa the best means of achieving a fresh start with an institution that lacked any complicity in either facilitating Herrenvolk democracy or enforcing apartheid.[22]

South Africa's young Constitution necessarily reflects and incorporates contemporary constitutional values and understandings. Moreover, if the vintage of a constitutional text, or the absence of a constitutional text, forces judges to engage in self-help in defining and protecting free speech, a modern, recently adopted constitutional text should, at least in theory, better constrain judges as they go about defining and protecting expressive freedoms. As it turns out, however, constitutional free speech law in

South Africa is no less the product of judicial common law reasoning than free speech rules in Australia, Israel, the United Kingdom, and the United States.

Candor requires acknowledging that the 1996 Constitution gives the CCSA a vast constitutional toolkit with which to undertake its critically important work. The document includes an extensive Bill of Rights,[23] including a number of positive rights, the inclusion of a Holy Trinity of three "foundational values" that should infuse and inform the CCSA's interpretation of the 1996 Constitution's substantive provisions, and express authorizations to consider both international law (which is mandatory)[24] and foreign law (which is merely discretionary).[25] In many respects then, given the express textual authorizations to draw on myriad principles, rights, and external sources of law, the 1996 Constitution goes a very long way toward empowering, rather than limiting, the CCSA's exercise of discretion when interpreting a constitutional clause or provision. This makes the CCSA's fidelity to constitutional text difficult to ascertain with any high degree of confidence; with such an open-ended text to draw upon, virtually any set of judicial conclusions could be said to honor the text and structure of the 1996 Constitution. The framers clearly intended to vest the CCSA with broad discretionary authority in its efforts to interpret and apply the document.[26] That said, the drafters did include some important textual signals about the relative priority of dignity, equality, and certain aspects of human freedom—textual cues that the CCSA has not consistently followed.[27]

To some extent, the Justices (the CCSA consists of a Chief Justice, a Deputy Chief Justice, and nine Associate Justices),[28] all appointed to a fixed-term-of-years-in-office period (up to 15 years of total judicial service and not less than 12 years on the CCSA) coupled with a mandatory retirement at age (members of the CCSA may serve until they reach 75 years of age)[29] can legitimately pick and choose which aspects of the constitutional text to prioritize—and which provisions they will deemphasize (or ignore completely). Even so, however, a good argument exists that, with respect to the freedom of expression, the CCSA has elevated its status beyond the boundaries that several important provisions of the text would support.

In particular, South Africa's 1996 Constitution expressly carves out hate speech from the protection of Section 16.[30] In addition, the text, in Section 1, declares "human dignity, the achievement of equality, and the advancement of human rights and freedoms," along with "non-racialism and non-sexism," and the "supremacy of the constitution and the rule of law" to be the values on which the government of South Africa is based[31]—thereby serving as the nation's apex human rights values.[32] Professor Heinz Klug explains that "the express inclusion of a set of founding provisions in Chapter 1 of the Constitution provides the most explicit source of the principles underlying the final Constitution."[33] The substantive fundamental rights directly aligned with these foundational values arguably should enjoy a relative priority over other fundamental rights that are not so aligned (including the freedom of speech).

Yet, as this chapter will show, he CCSA has not afforded an absolute priority to advancing dignity, equality, and human freedom over the freedom of speech. It has, instead, sought to carefully balance the Constitution's Holy Trinity of apex values

South Africa: Free Speech as a Co-Equal Right —⌒ 37

(again human dignity, equality, and human freedom) with a strong and meaningful commitment to safeguarding the freedom of speech (which obviously facilitates the ongoing process of democratic deliberation that informs the act of voting).[34] In the words of Associate Justice Steven A. Majiedt, this judicial process involves a "delicate balancing exercise between the fundamental right to freedom of expression, dignity, and equality."[35]

Section 37, on the suspension of fundamental rights during times of war or civil unrest, provides the most telling signal of the framers' intention to convey an elevated status on the rights of dignity, equality, and certain aspects of human freedom. Section 37 permits the national parliament to declare a "state of emergency" when "the life of the nation is threatened by war, invasion, general insurrection, disorder, natural disaster or other public emergency" and "the declaration is necessary to restore peace and order."[36] Most of the rights set forth in the Bill of Rights (which comprises Chapter 2 of South Africa's 1996 Constitution) are subject to limitation or complete abrogation under this provision, including the provisions related to expressive freedom (Section 16) and equal rights of participation in the electoral process (Section 19). However, several rights are entirely nonderogable; even in times of national emergency, the government may not suspend these rights incident to efforts to meet the pending national crisis.[37]

And, what rights are entirely nonderogable? Human dignity (Section 10) and life (Section 11) are entirely nonderogable.[38] So, too, Section 9's guarantee of "equality," but only "with respect to unfair discrimination solely on the grounds of race, colour, ethnic or social origin, sex, religion or language."[39] Section 12, which safeguards "freedom and security of the person," is nonderogable with respect to proscriptions against torture (Section 12(1)(d)), the imposition of "cruel, inhuman, or degrading" punishment or treatment (Section 12(1)(e)), and using human beings for "medical or scientific experiments without their informed consent" (Section 12(2)(c)).[40] Section 16, and the other provisions related to expressive freedom, including Sections 17 (freedoms of assembly, demonstrations, picket, and petition), 18 (freedom of association), and 19 (right to vote, form a political party, and participate in the electoral process on a free and equal basis) are derogable—meaning that, with a proper declaration, the government may suspend them entirely during a period of national crisis.

Surely declaring that a right may never be suspended, even in the face of an existential national emergency, and with an obvious and pressing need for so doing, sends a clear and unmistakable signal that those rights are more important, and stand on a higher constitutional rung on the human rights ladder, than rights which may be burdened or suspended entirely. Section 37 provides important, arguably compelling, evidence that the drafters of the 1996 Constitution intended dignity, equality, and human freedom (defined narrowly as freedom from torture or physical abuse) are not merely holistic animating human rights values, but also constitute the apex human rights under South Africa's Constitution.

In other words, despite multiple textual directives in the 1996 Constitution to give particular attention, and priority, to dignity, equality, and freedom (narrowly defined) over other fundamental human rights, the CCSA has instead attempted to harmonize these rights with the freedom of expression (safeguarded under the derogable Section 16)—at least to the extent it is possible to do so successfully.[41] With respect to freedom of expression, as a normative matter this approach makes a great deal of sense—for speech is an essential element of a healthy and well-functioning democracy and multiple provisions of the 1996 Constitution emphasize the central importance of South Africa as a democratic polity.[42] Nevertheless, this consistent practice, clearly reflected in the CCSA's most recent (and arguably most important) hate speech cases,[43] demonstrates that in South Africa, the 1996 Constitution's text has not effectively circumscribed the South African judiciary's discretion by effectively compelling domestic judges to relegate free speech to an inferior constitutional status vis-à-vis human dignity, equality, and freedom.

The following pages will show that, consistent with the CCSA's prevailing balancing approach—an approach that seeks to reconcile freedom of expression with the nation's founding values (which also constitute substantive rights)—the Justices have read hate speech regulations narrowly and carefully circumscribed their scope in order to ensure that the marketplace of political ideas is, to borrow Justice William J. Brennan, Jr.'s iconic turn of phrase from *New York Times Co. v. Sullivan*, "robust, uninhibited, and wide-open."[44] Again, this is not to say that the CCSA's approach to hate speech is objectionable or mistaken—it plainly is not. It is to say, however, that the Justices have not felt constrained to hew closely to the clear signals set forth within the constitutional text to give Parliament a relatively free hand in regulating hate speech as part of its efforts to promote human dignity and equality.

This chapter proceeds in four additional main sections. Section II sets forth the constitutional text arguably relevant to the scope of Parliament's power to regulate hate speech. Repeatedly, the drafters indicate that dignity, equality, and human freedom are to be the lodestar human rights values, as well as the apex constitutional rights, under the 1996 Constitution.[45] Moreover, it bears noting that the 1996 Constitution's free speech guarantee, Section 16, expressly excludes hate speech from its scope of coverage.[46] Accordingly, at least in theory, "no bar [exists] to the enactment of legislation that prohibits such expression."[47] Yet, as section III explains in some detail, the CCSA has defined "hate speech" quite narrowly and indicated, repeatedly and emphatically, that the government may not simply censor hyperbolic political speech because it has attached the label "hate speech" to it.

Section IV seeks to explain why the CCSA, despite the constitutional text that arguably creates an objective order of human rights values that prioritizes dignity, equality, and human freedom, has elevated the freedom of speech to a coequal status as a fundamental right. To be sure, the Justices have made very clear that free speech does not enjoy *priority* over these foundational values—which also constitute substantive rights.[48] Even so, however, the freedom of speech plainly enjoys a coequal constitutional status with these apex rights and is not a subordinate or inferior human right. In section IV, this chapter argues that the explanation lies, at least in part, in the National Party's aggressive and persistent use of government censorship during the apartheid era as a means of silencing advocates of constitutional reform. Section IV posits that this history of government censorship has, to the present day, created a sociolegal culture in South Africa that is highly skeptical of government speech regulations—even when the government claims that it is restricting speech to advance and protect dignity, equality, and human freedom.[49] Finally, section V offers a brief overview of the main claims and arguments and some concluding thoughts and observations.

In sum, rather than breaking the pattern of constitutional courts using a common law methodology to define and protect expressive freedoms, the CCSA's work to reconcile a strong constitutional commitment to free speech with strong and pervasive constitutional commitments to dignity, equality, and freedom fits very nicely with the larger pattern one finds across other constitutional democracies that feature independent courts vested with a power of judicial review engaging in an ongoing, common law process to reconcile conflicting human rights in order to advance sometimes cross-cutting, and conflicting, constitutional objectives. Thus, it turns out that a relatively recent constitutional text is no more efficacious at cabining the judicial role in safeguarding speech than older constitutional instruments. Nor does an interpretative directive to elevate dignity, equality, and certain aspects of human freedom over speech necessarily ensure that judges will follow the directive—an entirely understandable outcome given the essential relationship between speech and democracy.

II. THE SOUTH AFRICAN CONSTITUTIONAL TEXT: DIGNITY, EQUALITY, AND HUMAN FREEDOM AS THE APEX HUMAN RIGHTS AND FOUNDATIONAL CONSTITUTIONAL VALUES

The framers of the 1996 Constitution could not have been any clearer concerning their intentions in regard to the government's broad constitutional authority to regulate, or even to ban, hate speech. Perhaps most important, Section 16, South Africa's analogue to the First Amendment's Free Speech Clause, expressly excludes several categories of speech from constitutional protection. More specifically, Section 16(2) provides that the general protection for free speech set forth in Section 16(1)[50] does not include "propaganda for war," "incitement of imminent violence," or "advocacy of hatred that is based on race, ethnicity, gender or religion, and that constitutes incitement to cause harm."[51] The third exclusion, Section 16(2)(c), provides an express textual warrant for the adoption and enforcement of hate speech regulations; it does not, however, actually define what constitutes "hate speech."

The breadth of the hate speech exclusion could be either quite broad or relatively narrow—meaning that it could allow a fairly wide margin of appreciation for hyperbolic political speech, or, in the alternative, it could provide a constitutional warrant for banning such speech when, in context, it might reasonably be thought to give rise to "bad tendencies" with respect to race relations in South Africa (or relations between the majority and a minority community, however defined).[52] Indeed, one could read the proscription very narrowly, perhaps as excluding from constitutional protection only targeted race-based, sex-based, or religion-based threats. Under this approach,

40 ⌒ Free Speech as Civic Structure

which the CCSA seems to have adopted in its landmark *Qwelane* and *Masuku* decisions, only speech that presents a near-certainty of causing serious social harms would be subject to proscription. Mere offense or hurt feelings would not be sufficient to justify banning speech or expressive conduct.[53]

This is precisely how the U.S. Supreme Court approached a Virginia state law that prohibited cross burnings. Justice Sandra Day O'Connor, writing for a plurality in *Virginia v. Black*,[54] opined that Virginia's statute banning cross burnings could be applied to criminalize cross burnings only when, on the facts presented, the activity communicated a true and targeted threat to a particular person of color.[55] Justice O'Connor explained that "[w]e conclude that while a State, consistent with the First Amendment, may ban cross burning carried out with the intent to intimidate, the provision in the Virginia statute treating any cross burning as prima facie evidence of intent to intimidate renders the statute unconstitutional in its current form."[56] Applying this reasoning, a majority concluded that "Virginia's statute does not run afoul of the First Amendment insofar as it bans cross burning with intent to intimidate."[57]

Justice Clarence Thomas, by way of contrast, took the view that a cross burning, whenever or wherever it occurs, conveys a targeted racialized threat to people of color within the community.[58] He explained that "[i]n our culture, cross burning has almost invariably meant lawlessness and understandably instills in its victims well-grounded fear of physical violence."[59]

Going in the opposite direction, Justice David Souter, joined by Justices Ruth Bader Ginsburg and Anthony Kennedy, would have invalidated the Virginia law as facially inconsistent with the First Amendment.[60] Souter "agree[d] with the majority that the Virginia statute makes a content-based distinction within the category of punishable intimidating or threatening expression" but disagreed "that any exception should save Virginia's law from unconstitutionality under the holding in *R. A. V.* or any acceptable variation of it."[61] From Justice Souter's perspective, general laws prohibiting threats and harassment would be sufficient to punish those who engage in cross burnings to convey threats or harass others.[62] He explained that "[i]t is difficult to conceive of an intimidation case that could be easier to prove than one with cross burning," which renders the Virginia statute "unnecessary to legitimate prosecution of intimidation."[63] Given this state of affairs, the law could not survive strict judicial scrutiny—the standard of review applicable to content-based government speech regulations in the United States.[64]

Black demonstrates how a rule that excludes racialized threats from constitutional protection as "speech" might be construed very broadly (Thomas), narrowly to encompass only targeted threats that cause emotional or psychological harm (O'Connor), or very narrowly to permit only prosecutions that do not take into account at all the content or viewpoint of the speech or expressive conduct used to convey the threat or to harass (Souter). So too with section 16(2)(c)—the provision might be read very broadly to create a general warrant for Parliament to enact hate speech regulations with a free hand, it might be read to authorize some, but not all, proscriptions against hate speech, or it could be read incredibly narrowly, to prohibit only hate speech that actually produces social harms (such as racial unrest or violence).

South Africa: Free Speech as a Co-Equal Right   —∽ 41

An important question of who decides how to construe section 16(2)(c) also requires resolution—Parliament or the courts? As section III will explain in some detail,[65] in South Africa, the courts, and the CCSA in particular, decide how to interpret and apply Section 16(2)(c) and the CCSA has not been particularly deferential to the national legislature's statutory handiwork in this area.[66]

Section 16(2)(c)'s express exclusion of hate speech—whether the provision should be interpreted broadly or narrowly—is only one piece of the puzzle. As noted earlier,[67] South Africa's 1996 Constitution expressly elevates three human rights values above all others—namely, dignity, equality, and human freedom. What is more, it does this repeatedly. At least arguably, courts should construe Section 16(2)(c) in light of these direct interpretative commands to advance the nation's lodestar human rights values (which all constitute substantive constitutional rights as well).

Section 1, one of the Constitution's "Founding Provisions," specifically provides that South Africa's government rests on the values of "[h]uman dignity, the achievement of equality and the advancement of human freedom."[68] Section 7(1) then repeats this directive, providing that "[t]his Bill of Rights is a cornerstone of democracy in South Africa" and "enshrines the rights of all people in our country and affirms the democratic values of *human dignity, equality and freedom*."[69] In the substantive Bill of Rights provisions, the 1996 Constitution goes on to expressly protect equality,[70] dignity,[71] and freedom and security of the person.[72] Thus, equality, dignity, and specified elements of human freedom (freedom from torture, cruel or unusual punishment, or involuntary participation in medical experiments) are not just *values* that should inform the interpretation and application of the 1996 Constitution's provisions—they also constitute expressly enumerated *substantive rights*—as Sections 9(1), 10, and 12(1) and 12(2) make clear beyond peradventure. As Professor Klug observes, "[d]ignity, equality, and freedom play a foundational role in South Africa's post-apartheid Constitution."[73]

Another way of assessing the relative importance of a constitutional right involves whether, and the ease with which, the government may abridge or even abrogate completely specific constitutional fundamental rights. If the elected branches of government may abrogate a right freely in times of war or national crisis, one could conclude that the right in question is subaltern. By way of contrast, if the government may *not* abridge or abrogate a particular fundamental right, even during times of war or national crisis, it stands to reason that it constitutes a foundational or "apex" human right.

Thus, a nonderogable constitutional right would seem to stand, as a matter of text in any event, on a higher rung of a domestic constitutional system's human rights ladder. Denying the government constitutional authority to limit or abrogate a right in order to meet a public emergency is arguably, in fact, the best possible textual signal that the drafters of a national constitution can provide to indicate the relative priority of safeguarding and securing the nonderogable rights vis-à-vis rights that may be limited or suspended during a crisis. Section 37 makes dignity, specified aspects of equality, and specified aspects of human freedom nonderogable;[74] it does not protect either freedom of expression or voting and electoral participation rights in the same way.[75]

If the constitutional text effectively binds South Africa's judiciary, one would expect the CCSA to follow these textual cues and elevate dignity, equality, and human freedom over the other rights set forth in the Bill of Rights when they come into conflict. Yet, this is not how matters have played out. More specifically, the freedom of speech clearly enjoys a coequal status with the apex human rights of dignity, equality, and (defined aspects) of human freedom.[76]

Finally, although the argument is a bit more attenuated, the highly entrenched nature of Section 1, which establishes South Africa's foundational values, also sends an important textual signal about the constitutional centrality of these provisions. Section 74(1) highly entrenches Section 1, requiring "the National Assembly, with a supporting vote of at least 75 per cent of its members" and "the National Council of Provinces, with a supporting vote of at least six provinces,"[77] to approve any amendments to Section 1. This is not to say that the Bill of Rights, set forth in Chapter 2 of the 1996 Constitution, is not highly entrenched: Section 74(2) requires a two-thirds majority to amend a provision of the Bill of Rights.[78] However, a 75% supermajority vote is a higher threshold for amendment than a two-thirds majority requirement.

The higher threshold for amendment of Section 1 provides additional evidence of its fundamental importance. Professor Klug observes that "[t]he status of these founding provisions is further enhanced by the requirement that any amendment to section 1 of the Constitution, which contains these constitutional values, may only be achieved with a 75 per cent majority in the National Assembly and the support of six of the nine provinces."[79] In his view, "[t]his is a level of constitutional entrenchment that requires a degree of electoral support that even the hugely popular ANC led by Nelson Mandela did not come close to reaching."[80] The supermajority requirement thus renders Section 1 effectively unamendable.

To be sure, these constitutional values do not give rise, directly, to judicially enforceable claims of right. As Chief Justice Arthur Chaskalson has explained, "[t]he values enunciated in section 1 of the Constitution are of fundamental importance" because "[t]hey inform and give substance to all the provisions of the Constitution."[81] Despite their importance, "[t]hey do not, however, give rise to discrete and enforceable rights in themselves."[82] He observes that "[t]his is clear not only from the language of section 1 itself, but also from the way the Constitution is structured and in particular the provisions of Chapter 2 which contains the Bill of Rights."[83] By way of contrast, however, "[t]he rights entrenched in the Bill of Rights include equality, dignity, and various other human rights and freedoms"[84] and "[t]hese rights give effect to the founding values and must be construed consistently with them."[85] Thus, because the foundational values are also substantive rights, the fact that the foundational values themselves are not judicially enforceable is of little moment.

The combination of limits on the freedom of speech within the four corners of Section 16 with the 1996 Constitution's multiple interpretative directives to prioritize dignity, equality, and freedom arguably should give Parliament broad discretion to enact laws aimed at promoting these values—even when doing so requires limiting or abridging the freedom of speech. Yet, this is not how things have come to pass.

South Africa: Free Speech as a Co-Equal Right   —◦ 43

It is certainly true, as Justice Kate O'Regan observed in *Khumalo*, that the freedom of expression, although "fundamental in our society," does not constitute a "paramount value."[86] Instead, as she explained, "[i]t must be construed in the context of the other values enshrined in our Constitution" and "[i]n particular, the values of human dignity, freedom and equality."[87] Thus, although freedom of expression does not have priority over dignity, equality, and freedom, it does not hold an *inferior* status either.

Thus, even if free speech is not a "paramount" value, the CCSA has declined to subordinate freedom of expression to dignity, equality, and freedom as a fundamental human right. And, this seems odd—at least as a textual matter. Sections 1, 7, and 37 of the 1996 Constitution provide clear textual signals to the domestic courts that when free speech bumps up against dignity, equality, and freedom, the nonderogable foundational human rights (which are "foundational values" as well) ought to prevail.

As will be explained in section III, however, this is simply not how things work in South Africa. Free speech is a coequal human rights value—not a subordinate human rights value. This state of constitutional affairs demonstrates rather clearly that judges, taking judicial notice of deeply seated sociolegal and cultural values that reflect distrust of government censorship of political speech, have more to do with the warp and weft of South African free speech jurisprudence than the 1996 Constitution's text.[88]

To be sure, the 1996 Constitution does contain text related to voting and elections, including provisions in Section 1, and these provisions related to democracy and elections could provide a strong textual basis for affording expressive freedom related to the electoral process a coequal status with dignity, equality, and human freedom. Section 1 itself repeatedly references the democratic character of South Africa's government, declaring that "[t]he Republic of South Africa is one, sovereign, democratic state"[89] that guarantees to all of its citizens "[u]niversal adult suffrage, a national common voters roll, regular elections and a multi-party system of democratic government, to ensure accountability, responsiveness and openness."[90] Moreover, voting and elections are not merely foundational "values," but also constitute freestanding substantive "rights." Section 19, on "political rights," establishes benchmarks for democracy and democratic participation, including the free formation of political parties, participation in political parties, electioneering activities, the conduct of "free, fair and regular elections for any legislative body established in terms of the Constitution," the right both "to vote in elections for any legislative body established in terms of the Constitution, and to do so in secret" and "to stand for public office and, if elected, to hold office."[91]

The CCSA has, repeatedly, linked constitutional protection of speech to its central role in animating and facilitating the democratic process.[92] As Justice Majiedt explained in *Qwelane*, "[t]he right to freedom of expression, as enshrined in section 16(1) of the Constitution, is the benchmark for a vibrant and animated constitutional democracy."[93] Chief Justice Mogoeng Mogoeng echoes these sentiments in *Economic Freedom Fighters*, observing that "[i]t is no exaggeration to characterise the right to freedom of expression as the lifeblood of a genuine constitutional democracy that keeps it fairly vibrant, stable and peaceful."[94] Thus, "[w]hen citizens are very angry or frustrated, it serves as the virtual exhaust pipe through which even the most venomous of toxicities within may be let out to help them calm down, heal, focus and move on" and "[m]ore importantly, free expression is an indispensable facilitator of a vigorous and necessary exchange of ideas and accountability."[95]

In short, as Justice Johann Kriegler argues in *Mamabolo*, "[f]reedom of expression, especially when gauged in conjunction with its accompanying fundamental freedoms, is of the utmost importance in the kind of open and democratic society the Constitution has set as our aspirational norm."[96] He adds that "[h]aving regard to our recent past of thought control, censorship and enforced conformity to governmental theories, freedom of expression—the free and open exchange of ideas—is no less important [in South Africa] than it is in the United States of America."[97] Indeed, Justice Kriegler posits that "[i]t could actually be contended with much force that the public interest in the open market-place of ideas is all the more important to us in this country because our democracy is not yet firmly established and must feel its way," and, accordingly, "we should be particularly astute to outlaw any form of thought-control, however respectably dressed."[98]

The CCSA's opinions plainly link freedom of expression to the project of democratic self-government—and this provides a basis for elevating speech, at least related to elections and governance, to a coequal status with dignity, equality, and human freedom. At the same time, however, this does not explain why the 1996 Constitution's clear signals, in Sections 1, 7, 9, 16, and 37 regarding the country's constitutional commitments to equality and human dignity do not justify some margin of appreciation, or judicial deference, to legislative enactments that seek to make the marketplace of political ideas open and welcoming to all.

It would be possible to maintain a commitment to democratic self-government concurrently with strong rules that limit the use of language that vilifies or attacks particular groups within the political community.[99] As Professor Alexander Brown posits, "even if incitement to hatred laws do prevent some people from participating in public discourse in an intellectually honest and authentic manner, that is, in a manner of their choosing or in ways that perfectly express who they are as people and what they believe in, and even if this prevention thereby has a detrimental impact on the collective authorization and democratic legitimacy of downstream laws, free and equal people would nevertheless still have grounds to reasonably reject a failure to enact and apply such laws, which is a matter of political legitimacy."[100] From this point of view, the failure to enact and enforce reliably laws against hate speech has the effect of diminishing democracy because it has the potential to banish targeted groups within the community from the process of democratic deliberation.[101]

The CCSA, however, has declined to afford the national legislature much, if any, deference as to the means it uses to enforce Sections 9(4)[102] and 16(2)(c).[103] This approach stands in stark contrast with other constitutional courts, including the Supreme Court of Canada[104] and the European Court of Human Rights (ECtHR).[105] Constitutional courts in other jurisdictions tend to defer more readily and willingly to the national parliament regarding how to define and regulate hate speech. Because such speech has low social value (one might even posit *negative* social value), and arguably constitutes a kind of public nuisance, many national and transnational courts will defer, on an almost reflexive basis, to elected legislators' regulatory efforts. This simply does not hold true in contemporary South Africa.

For example, the ECtHR, in *Norwood*, held that the use of hate speech incident to a public policy discussion (the United Kingdom's immigration policies) did not even fall within the scope of Article 10, but rather constituted an "abuse" of the freedom of speech under Article 17.[106] Article 17 of the European Convention provides that "[n]othing in this Convention may be interpreted as implying for any State, group or person any right to engage in any activity or perform any act aimed at the destruction of any of the rights and freedoms set forth herein or at their limitation to a greater extent than is provided for in the Convention."[107] Section 10(1) of the European Convention provides broad protection for the freedom of speech and other expressive freedoms, subject to a list of limitations in Section 10(2) that involve application of the doctrine of proportionality—meaning that a national government may restrict free speech if the limitation is demonstrably necessary in a free and democratic society, is prescribed by law, and is sufficiently narrowly tailored.[108]

However, in the case of hate speech, the ECtHR has completely excluded the content from Article 10(1)'s scope of application,[109] which means that it will not require a government to defend such regulations under proportionality analysis. Because hate speech does not trigger the application of Article 10(1), a signatory government to the European Convention has no burden of justification for enacting and enforcing a hate speech ban.

The ECtHR has thus embraced a policy of broad judicial deference to national governments with respect to adopting laws and regulations that ban hate speech. Jacob Mchangama and Natalie Alkiviadou complain that "the ECtHR has, in practice, exempted many controversial expressions from the protection of Article 10, by adopting a broad understanding of impermissible hate speech, as the nonexhaustive examples above have shown."[110] They add that "[i]t has also resorted to the use of Article 17, which seriously restricts speech as cases are excluded from the court's consideration without a legal analysis of Article 10."[111] In sum, "the ECtHR is liable to err on the side of restrictiveness" in cases involving hate speech or advocacy of antidemocratic policies and programs.[112] A less pejorative way of stating this point is to say that if the end is legitimate (and eradicating public expressions of hate speech most certainly constitutes a legitimate end in most democratic countries, both in Western Europe and more generally), the ECtHR will allow member state governments broad flexibility when adopting particular means designed to address the adverse social effects of hate speech—rather than aggressively second-guess such measures.

By way of contrast, in South Africa—and as section III will show—the CCSA has not afforded the national parliament much deference as to the means it uses to regulate hate speech. It has, instead, exercised independent judgment regarding whether a particular law, such as the Equality Act, has unduly restricted speech in the name of safeguarding equality and human dignity. I do not claim as a normative matter that the SCC and the ECtHR have things right and the CCSA has them wrong. Very strong theoretical arguments exist in favor of judges serving as honest brokers, or umpires, in reviewing potentially self-serving speech regulations enacted by incumbent politicians (who possess a strong self-interest in regulating speech that could affect their reelection prospects); the national courts *should* serve as a brake on potentially self-serving speech regulations, undertaking a critically important checking function. It is to say, however, that the lack of deference, given the 1996 Constitution's textual signals, is somewhat surprising.

It also merits mention that deep skepticism of hate speech regulations seems considerably less pronounced in South Africa's lower courts than it is in both the CCSA and the Supreme Court of Appeal (SCA). In practice, hate speech charges, of both a civil and criminal stripe, routinely result in convictions in local trial courts. This circumstance closely mirrors the reality in the United States regarding the use of fighting words—and in particular the use of fighting words directed toward law enforcement officers. Despite the U.S. Supreme Court's emphatic and repeated holdings, in a series of First Amendment cases dating back to the early 1970s, that the Free Speech Clause broadly protects profane and opprobrious language in public (and especially when directed toward law enforcement officers), state trial and appellate courts often fail to observe scrupulously the Supreme Court's rulings in this area of First Amendment law. So too, in South Africa, lower court trial judges do not always consistently, fully, and fairly observe the CCSA's constitutional holdings enforcing Section 16.

In sum, more than a little daylight exists between South Africa's formal free speech rules and doctrines and the day-to-day practices of police officers and magistrate judges. My arguments engage South Africa's formal freedom of expression jurisprudence, as the CCSA authoritatively articulates and enforces it, rather than the de facto status of hate speech in contemporary South African society.

III. THE UNDERLYING CONSTITUTIONAL REALITY: FREEDOM OF EXPRESSION AS A COEQUAL CONSTITUTIONAL VALUE IN THE CCSA'S CONSTITUTIONAL JURISPRUDENCE

The 1996 Constitution's text suggests that the nation's foundational human rights values, which are also expressly enumerated constitutional rights, should enjoy a priority over other human rights—including the freedom of speech. However, this is not how matters have come to rest jurisprudentially. The CCSA has repeatedly and consistently rejected affording the freedom of speech an absolute priority over dignity, equality, and human freedom—but this should not be at all surprising. What one might find surprising, however, is the CCSA's emphatic rejection of speech as a subordinate or less pressing human rights value.

Cases involving hate speech and defamation most clearly demonstrate the coequal status of speech with South Africa's foundational human rights values. Two relatively recent CCSA hate speech decisions, as well an older precedent that imposed limits on the scope of hate speech regulations applicable to broadcast television and radio, demonstrate with convincing clarity that the Justices seek to balance, or harmonize, expressive freedom, dignity, equality, and freedom.[113] In addition, the CCSA's landmark *Kuhmalo* decision, South Africa's analogue to *New York Times Co. v. Sullivan*,[114] emphatically rejects affording freedom of speech an absolute priority, but is no less emphatic in rejecting a subordinate status for Section 16 rights. This provides another context in which the Justices have declined to relegate freedom of speech to a second-class, or subordinate, status.

A. *The Hate Speech and Broadcasting Decisions: Speech as a Coequal Constitutional Value*

The Promotion of Equality and Prevention of Unfair Discrimination Act 4 of 2000 (Equality Act) plays a central role in the adjudication of hate speech claims in South Africa. This statute creates civil and criminal penalties for the dissemination of hate speech. Although Section 16(2)(c) withdraws constitutional protection from speech that "advocate[s] hatred that is based on race, ethnicity, gender or religion, and that constitutes incitement to cause harm,"[115] this provision is not self-executing as a ban on hate speech.[116] Instead, Parliament must actually enact laws that limit or proscribe incitements to racial-, religious-, or gender-based hatred in order to create civil or criminal liability for hate speech. As Justice Sisi Khampepe observes, "while section 16(2) may define forms of expression that fall outside of constitutionally protected expression, it is still incumbent on the Legislature, if it so wishes, to enact legislation to regulate these forms of speech."[117]

Thus, neither Section 9, which requires legislation aimed at preventing proscribed forms of discrimination,[118] nor Section 16 "create[s] a prohibition out of thin air."[119] The Equality Act represents Parliament's effort to enforce Section 9 and to operationalize the exclusion of certain hate speech in Section 16. To date, however, the CCSA has responded with deep skepticism toward Parliament's handiwork[120]—and has gone so far as to rewrite the Equality Act to limit its scope of application and thereby provide more breathing room for the freedom of speech.

As Mchangama and Alkiviadou explain, "the South African position on hate speech is more robust and nuanced than its ECtHR equivalent" because, despite "the acknowl-edgment of the evils of the apartheid era," both the CCSA and the SCA (the highest regular court in South Africa) have held that this history serves "as a caution rather than as an invitation to limit freedom of expression."[121] In other words, rather than emphasizing the government's need to censor potentially hurtful or offensive speech, South African courts instead have exhibited a healthy skepticism of government censorship—even when the government argues that censorship is needed to secure human dignity and equality within the community. As the CCSA's landmark *Qwelane* decision emphatically holds, "the expression of unpopular or even offensive beliefs does not constitute hate speech."[122] This rule reflects the jurisprudential reality that "a healthy democracy requires a degree of tolerance towards expression or speech that shocks or offends."[123] Thus, skepticism, rather than deference, characterizes the judicial attitude toward hate speech regulations.

48 ๑—   Free Speech as Civic Structure

More specifically, Section 10 of the Equality Act, as originally enacted, prohibited the public dissemination of words based on certain "prohibited grounds,"[124] which Section 1 defines as including "race, gender, sex, pregnancy, marital status, ethnic or social origin, colour, sexual orientation, age, disability, religion, conscience, belief, culture, language and birth" or "any other ground" that denigrates or degrades based on a characteristic that "perpetuates systemic disadvantage," "undermines human dignity," or "adversely affects the equal enjoyment of a person's rights."[125] As enacted, Section 10 proscribed public utterances that "could reasonably be construed to demonstrate a clear intention" to "be hurtful," "be harmful or to incite harm," and/or "promote or propagate hatred."[126] Section 10(2) provides for civil liability for violations of Section 10(1) and authorizes referrals for criminal prosecutions under Section 21.[127]

The Equality Act clearly goes beyond the categories set forth in Section 16(2), which are limited to "race, ethnicity, gender or religion."[128] This is of little constitutional moment, however, because Section 1 of the Equality Act closely tracks the language of Section 9(3). This may, in part, explain why the CCSA has limited the Equality Act's scope of application under Section 16(1). Strictly speaking, the Equality Act protects against hate speech not covered by Section 16(2)'s categories—meaning, at least in theory, that Section 16(1) must afford some measure of protection to the regulated speech. Resolving the constitutional status of Section 10(1) would involve proportionality analysis under Section 36(1)[129] and judicial harmonization of the Section 9(3) duty to promote equality with Section 16(1)'s protection of freedom of expression. This is only a partial explanation, however, because the CCSA has read the Equality Act narrowly even in cases where the speech at issue directly relates to a form of discrimination that Section 16(2)(c) expressly sets forth.

The facts in *Qwelane* are straightforward. An editorial writer, Jonathan Dubula Qwelane, published an op-ed entitled "Call Me Names—But GAY Is not OK" in the Sunday, July 20, 2008, edition of the "*Sunday Sun*, a national tabloid newspaper."[130] The editorial contained extensive homophobic content and was accompanied by a highly offensive cartoon that drew a material equivalence between same-sex relationships and bestiality.[131]

Numerous complaints arose following publication of the offensive editorial and cartoon. As the Supreme Court explains in its recitation of the facts, "[t]he publication was met with a huge public outcry, with expressions of outrage and disgust."[132] The South African Human Rights Commission (HRC) initiated an investigation that led to an administrative order finding that Mr. Qwelane had engaged in hate speech (which the Equality Court subsequently upheld), in violation of Section 10 of the Equality Act, and required him to issue a "an unconditional public apology" (which the Equality Court also upheld).[133]

Mr. Qwelane appealed the adverse decisions of the HRC and the Equality Court to the SCA. On appeal, the SCA reversed the Equality Court's order, holding that Section 10 of the Equality Act restricted too much speech—including speech not excluded from protection under Section 16(1) by Section 16(2).[134] The SCA concluded that Section 10 of the Equality Act violated Section 16 because it cut too deeply by prohibiting speech more broadly than contemplated by Section 16(2) and was otherwise overbroad and vague.[135] In particular, because Section 10 proscribed merely "hurtful" speech as opposed to only speech that actually inflicts serious harm (such as legitimate fear for a person's safety), it unduly restricted into the freedom of expression—and did so under a legal standard for imposing liability that the SCA declared to be "barely intelligible."[136] The SCA found that a saving construction was not possible and, accordingly, voided Section 10 in its entirety.[137]

The CCSA affirmed in part and reversed in part the SCA's decision. Justice Majiedt performed judicial surgery on Section 10 by excising liability for merely "hurtful" speech, declaring Section 10(a) to be unconstitutional on Section 16(1) grounds.[138] He explained that "[e]xpressions that are merely hurtful, especially when understood in everyday parlance, are insufficient to constitute hate speech."[139] In addition, with respect to the remaining provisions of Section 10 (namely, Sections 10(b) and 10(c)), the CCSA held that they must be applied conjunctively, meaning that to constitute hate speech, the government must show that a speaker or publisher exhibited a "clear intention" to "be harmful or incite harm" *and* to "promote or propagate hatred" based on the proscribed grounds.

This outcome, which was less speech-protective than the SCA's approach but still quite speech protective, was necessary because South Africa's commitment to "pluralism, tolerance, and open-mindedness require[s] that our democracy fosters an environment that allows a free and open exchange of ideas, free from censorship, no matter how offensive, shocking, or disturbing those ideas may be."[140] This means "that the expression of unpopular or even offensive beliefs does not constitute hate speech."[141] Justice Majiedt emphasized that "a healthy democracy requires a degree of tolerance toward expression or speech that shocks or offends."[142]

Hate speech involves more than mere "offense" or hurt feelings—instead, it "travels beyond offensive expression and can be understood as extreme detestation and vilification which risks provoking discriminatory activities against that group."[143] In light of these constitutional free speech principles, "Section 10(1)(a) of the Equality Act [was] declared unconstitutional for vagueness and unjustifiably limiting section 16 of the Constitution."[144] Going forward, a Section 10 violation would require proof that a speaker or publisher possesses an intention to "be harmful or to incite harm" and, also, that the speech in question actually "promote[s] or propagate[s] hatred." Because "the impugned section is reasonably capable of a conjunctive reading,"[145] the CCSA read the statute down to reach only speech that targets a group and actually causes, or has a high probability of causing, tangible harm to members of that group beyond mere offense or hurt feelings.

Applying the revised Section 10 to Mr. Qwelane's op-ed, the CCSA found that he had, in fact, engaged in prohibited hate speech, failed to participate in good faith in the HRC and Equality Court proceedings, and, prior to his death, failed to evince sincere remorse or to issue a public apology for propagating his homophobic viewpoints.[146] Justice Majiedt explained that "[t]here can be no question that Mr Qwelane's statements constitute hate speech" because he "was advocating hatred, as the article plainly

50 ⌒   Free Speech as Civic Structure

constitutes detestation and vilification of homosexuals on grounds of sexual orientation."[147] Moreover, "[t]here is a reasonable apprehension that Mr Qwelane's article fueled the already burning anti-LGBT+ fire (alluded to by the witnesses) and galvanised further discrimination, hostility and violence against the LGBT+ community."[148] In other words, Mr. Qwelane's challenged speech caused cognizable harms to sexual minorities as a group and these harms extended well beyond mere offense or bruised feelings.

Masuku, a case involving arguably antisemitic speech, travels the same middle-of-the-road approach that *Qwelane* traverses. In *Masuku*, Mr. Bongani Masuku made blog posts critical of Israel's treatment of Palestinians. In relevant part, he said:

> [A]s we struggle to liberate Palestine from the racists, fascists, and Zionists who belong to the era of their Friend Hitler! We must not apologise, every Zionist must be made to drink the bitter medicine they are feeding our brothers and sisters in Palestine. We must target them, expose them and do all that is needed to subject them to perpetual suffering until they withdraw from the land of others and stop their savage attacks on human dignity.[149]

This language is obviously problematic—starting with its reference to "Friend Hitler."

Justice Khampepe, applying *Qwelane*, found that the first statement constituted proscribed hate speech, under the modified Section 10 of the Equality Act, but that the remainder of the statement did not.[150] In terms of framing the questions presented, Justice Khampepe explained that South Africa's new democracy rests on "a commitment to building a non-racial and non-sexist society which chooses to celebrate and accommodate our diversity rather than reject it" but "more than 27 years since that constitutional promise was first made, as a country we are still grappling with how to reconcile that promise with our commitment to protecting and promoting freedom of expression and a culture of openness, transparency and healthy democratic dialogue which necessarily means that free expression must have its limits."[151]

On these facts, the first statement, which clearly targeted Jewish people because of their religious identity, was proscribed, whereas the other statements, which were "clearly aimed at Israel and those who support Israel," were not.[152] The CCSA sustained the HRC's finding of an Equality Act violation with regard to the first part of the statement, invoking Hitler, but not with respect to the remainder of Mr. Masuku's statement. In striking this balance, which sought to accommodate extreme or hyperbolic political speech while, at the same time, disallowing calls to racial, gender-based, or religious vilification, Justice Khampepe explained that this "is unlikely to be a straight-forward task, and will involve careful consideration of law and context."[153] The CCSA instructed the lower South African courts to "strik[e] an elusive yet crucial balance between the imperative to regulate hate speech and the importance of fostering 'an environment that allows a free and open exchange of ideas, free from censorship, no matter how offensive, shocking or disturbing these ideas may be.'"[154]

The CCSA's approach in *Qwelane* and *Masuku* was entirely consistent with its earlier 2002 decision in *Islamic Unity Convention*.[155] In this landmark decision, the CCSA held that the Independent Broadcasting Authority could not prohibit the broadcast of language "likely to prejudice relations" between groups within society.[156] Clause 2(a) of the Broadcasting Code, a schedule to the Broadcasting Act, provided, in relevant part, that "[b]roadcasting licensees shall . . . not broadcast any material which is indecent or obscene or offensive to the public morals or offensive to the religious convictions or feelings of any section of a population or likely to prejudice the safety of the State or the public order *or relations between sections of the population.*"[157] The case turned on the last clause—the proscription against broadcasting material, via television or radio, that might "prejudice . . . relations between sections of the population."

The Islamic Unity Convention, accused of airing programming critical of Israel that could prejudice relations between Jewish South Africans and others, argued that the provision was unconstitutionally vague and overbroad—so much so that "the whole clause was unconstitutional."[158] The Independent Broadcasting Authority (IBA) argued that the prohibition on the broadcast of material that could prejudice relations, even if unconstitutional on Section 16(1) grounds, was nevertheless severable from the other provisions of Section 2(a). The CCSA agreed; Deputy Chief Justice Pius Langa limited the CCSA's review to the specific language regarding "prejudice" arising from a broadcast "between sections of the population."[159]

Deputy Chief Justice Langa found that the challenged provision of the Broadcasting Code violated Section 16(1) and could not be saved by application of Section 16(2)(c), which excludes certain forms of hate speech from protection under Section 16(1). He concluded, first, that "[t]he prohibition against the broadcasting of material that is 'likely to prejudice relations between sections of the population' self-evidently limits the right in section 16 of the Constitution."[160] Moreover, this "prohibition clearly goes beyond the categories of expression enumerated in section 16(2)" because the prohibition on broadcasts did not "require that the material prohibited should amount to advocacy of hatred, least of all hatred based on race, ethnicity, gender or religion, nor that it should have any potential to cause harm."[161]

The government attempted to defend the prohibition as "justifiable in the interests of human dignity and equality, which are founding values of the Constitution" or on the basis of "national unity," which implicates Sections 9 and 10 of the Constitution (which safeguard equality and dignity, respectively).[162]

Deputy Chief Justice Langa made short work of the IBA's attempts to justify the prohibition against socially divisive broadcasts. First, "[t]he effect of the limitation in this case is substantial" because it prohibits a wide swath of material and prevents the public from receiving "information, views, and opinions" about a wide range of matters of public concern.[163] Indeed, "[t]here is no doubt that the inroads on the right to freedom of expression made by the prohibition on which the complaint is based are far too extensive and outweigh the factors considered by the Board as ameliorating their impact."[164] The broadcast ban constituted a "serious infraction" of Section 16(1) and the government failed to show "that the very real need to protect dignity, equality, and the development of national unity could not be adequately served by the enactment of a provision which is appropriately tailored and more narrowly focused."[165] In light of these considerations, "the relevant portion of clause 2(a) impermissibly limits the right to freedom of expression and is accordingly unconstitutional."[166] The CCSA invalidated the clause on broadcasts that prejudice relations "between sections of the population" but left the remaining provisions of clause 2(a) in place.[167]

To be sure, the CCSA was clear that "open and democratic societies permit reasonable proscription of activity and expression that pose a real and substantial threat to such values and the constitutional order itself."[168] But the ban on all material that might cause social disquiet simply went too far and banned too much speech directly relevant to the process of democratic self-government. As Langa explained, "[w]here the state extends the scope of regulation beyond expression envisaged in section 16(2), it encroaches on the terrain of protected expression and can do so only if the regulation meets the justification criteria in section 36(1) of the Constitution."[169] Here, the government failed (badly) to meet this burden of justification; Section 16(1) required the enactment of a considerably more narrowly tailored regulation.

As in its later decisions in *Qwelane* and *Masuku*, even as the CCSA acknowledged the constitutionality of the *ends* the government sought to advance (namely, dignity and equality), the Justices declined to grant broad deference to the government as to the *means* it adopted for the achievement of these (constitutional) ends. In all three landmark decisions, the CCSA decided for itself whether the means the government chose were sufficiently narrowly tailored to be justified under the proportionality analysis that Section 36(1) requires after a plaintiff has successfully invoked a provision of the Bill of Rights.

B. Defamation and the Role of a Free Press in a Democratic Polity

The CCSA's hate speech precedents follow a jurisprudential approach presaged in its landmark *Khumalo* decision on reconciling the rights of speech and press with those of personal dignity in the context of reporting on a public official. Like *Qwelane*, *Masuku*, and *Islamic Unity Conference*, *Khumalo* affords the freedoms of speech and press coequal status—rather than subordinate status—with the foundational human rights values of dignity, equality, and freedom. It also demonstrates, once again, the central role of judges in defining the boundary that divides the 1996 Constitution's protection of dignity, equality, and freedom from the freedom of expression.

Khumalo presented an important question of free speech law: under South Africa's common law of torts, should the plaintiff bear the burden of proving that a particular statement was, in fact, false (making it harder for plaintiffs to win defamation actions but increasing the media's breathing room to get things wrong in good faith) or, instead, should the defendant be required to prove truth in order to defeat the plaintiff's cause of action (which obviously has a serious chilling effect on the press). The CCSA, as it usually does, split the difference, declining to place the burden of proving truth squarely on the press, but also declining to place the burden of proving

South Africa: Free Speech as a Co-Equal Right   —⌀ 53

falsity on plaintiffs. Justice Kate O'Regan, writing for a unanimous bench, held that Section 16(1) does not require South Africa's law of torts to place the burden of proving falsity on the plaintiff, but also endorsed a "reasonable publication" defense that the SCA previously had developed that would provide meaningful breathing room for the press.[170]

The case involved a news story about Bantubonke H. Holomisa, "a well-known South African politician and the leader of a political party."[171] The _Sunday World_, a South African newspaper, ran a news story about Holomisa that alleged "amongst other things, that [he] was involved in a gang of bank robbers and that he was under police investigation for this involvement."[172] Holomisa did not allege in his complaint that the story was false—but, under South African common law, he was not obliged to allege, or prove, that the story about him was false. Instead, under the common law of torts, a defendant, in order to avoid liability, had to prove that the story was both true and published in the public interest.[173] At the time Holomisa initiated the lawsuit, "[i]t [was] not an element of the delict in common law that the statement be false."

The _Sunday World_ argued that placing the burden of proving truth on a media defendant unduly chilled the freedoms of speech and press guaranteed under Section 16(1). Thus, the case "raised the question whether, to the extent that the law of defamation does not require a plaintiff in a defamation action to plead that the defamatory statement is false in any circumstances, the law limits unjustifiably the right to freedom of expression as enshrined in section 16 of the Constitution."[174]

Justice O'Regan acknowledged the signal importance of the freedoms of speech and press in a democratic polity: "The importance of the right of freedom of expression in a democracy has been acknowledged on many occasions by this Court, and other South African courts" and "is integral to a democratic society for many reasons."[175] Notably, "without it, the ability of citizens to make responsible political decisions and to participate effectively in public life would be stifled."[176]

Even so, the CCSA squarely rejected the _Sunday World_'s constitutional argument. It did so because, among other things, "although freedom of expression is fundamental to our democratic society, it is not a paramount value."[177] Instead, expressive freedom must be "construed in the context of other values enshrined in our Constitution," including "the values of human dignity, freedom, and equality."[178] Both dignity and equality are core, or "foundational," constitutional values as well as substantive constitutional rights.[179]

The SCA previously has held that a media defendant could defeat an action for libel by showing "reasonable publication"—this would not necessarily require proving a published statement to be true and published in the public interest, but it would require the media defendant to prove that, considering all the facts and circumstances, it had acted reasonably.[180] As Judge Joos Hefer explained the concept in _Bogoshi_, "reasonable publication" means that "the publication in the press of false defamatory allegations of fact will not be regarded as unlawful, if, upon a consideration of all the circumstances of the case, it is found to have been reasonable to publish the particular facts

54 ~   Free Speech as Civic Structure

in the particular way and at the particular time."[181] Relevant factors include whether the plaintiff is a public official or a public figure, "the nature, extent, and tone of the allegations," "the nature of the information on which the allegations were based," "the reliability of the source," and "the steps taken to verify the information."[182] In other jurisdictions, such as Canada and the United Kingdom, this approach is often called a defense of responsible journalism, or communication, on matters of public interest.

Returning to *Khumalo*, it seems reasonably clear that placing a burden of justification on a media defendant, rather than a burden of proving falsity on the plaintiff, will have a significant chilling effect on reportage by the press and mass media. The CCSA's response to this potential objection is that the "chilling effect is reduced considerably by the defense of reasonable publication in the public interest."[183] Justice O'Regan posits that the CCSA's newly-minted defense, first established by the SCA in *Bogoshi*, is constitutionally sufficient for purposes of Section 16(1) because "it permits a publisher who is uncertain of proving the truth of a defamatory statement . . . nevertheless to publish where he or she can establish that it is reasonable."[184] In so holding, the CCSA considered—but squarely rejected—the U.S. approach in *New York Times Co. v. Sullivan*,[185] in which the Supreme Court of the United States held that a public official plaintiff must prove, by clear and convincing evidence, both falsity and actual malice, meaning that the media defendant published a falsehood either with knowledge of its falsity or with reckless indifference as to whether or not the statement was true.[186] Justice O'Regan observes that *Sullivan* arguably constitutes "the high-water mark of foreign jurisprudence protecting the freedom of speech and many jurisdictions have declined to follow it."[187]

The need to protect dignity and personal honor undergirds the CCSA's decision to refuse to impose the burden of proving falsity on the defamation plaintiff.[188] The subjective nature of the "reasonable publication" defense, according to Justice O'Regan, is also a virtue rather than a vice precisely because it facilitates an ad hoc balancing of the competing, and opposed, interests in freedom of speech and the press against human dignity and privacy: "in determining whether publication was reasonable, a court will have regard to the individual's interest in protecting his or her reputation in the context of the constitutional commitment to human dignity" and "will also have regard to the individual's interest in privacy."[189] Shifting the burden of proving falsity to the plaintiff, by way of contrast, "would destabilise the careful balance struck between plaintiffs' and defendants' interests achieved by the Supreme Court of Appeal's development of a defense of reasonable publication."[190]

The defense of reasonable publication necessarily elevates speech and press rights to a coequal status with human dignity. As a normative matter, this position has much to recommend it—for the well-articulated reasons that Justice O'Regan identifies that relate to democratic self-government and the marketplace of ideas.[191] And, although freedom of expression is not a "paramount" value that automatically trumps dignity, equality, or privacy interests, neither is freedom of expression subordinate to these rights; it holds a coequal status and has no more, or less, importance than the rights aligned with the 1996 Constitution's foundational values.

C. Drawing the Line: The Examples of Julius Sello Malema, Vicki Momberg, and the Edgy Art Student as Potential Propagators of Constitutionally Unprotected Hate Speech

Julius Sello Malema and Vicki Momberg both have used racially charged language and been credibly accused of propagating hate speech. A graduate student studying fine arts at the University of Cape Town, Dean Hutton, did not intend to propagate hate speech but instead sought to call out indifference to racial discrimination and social inequality. All three found themselves accused of propagating hate speech. Two of them (Malema and Hutton) successfully defended their speech and, to date, have avoided liability. Momberg, by way of contrast, found herself sentenced to jail for using a directed racial epithet to a Black police officer. The jail time was, to be sure, the result of Momberg refusing to implement in good faith an Equality Court decree to offer a sincere and public apology for her actions.

Julius Malema, the leader of a populist political party known as the Economic Freedom Fighters (EFF), likes to use a protest song that was commonplace during the struggle to end apartheid. "We Shall Overcome" this song is not—it's "Kill the Boer" (or "Awuubula Ibhunu" in Xhosa).[192] Mr. Malema's variations on "Kill the Boer" can be highly creative. In one such variation, Malema changes "Kill the Boer" to "Kiss the Boer" but uses both hands, index finger and thumb, to simulate a pistol as he invokes the modified phrase. The words may have been changed (ever so slightly) but the basic message remained the same.

Malema and the EFF argue that use of the song, and phrase, is merely hyperbolic political speech meant to call attention to the government's failure to enact a meaningful program to reform land ownership in South Africa. On the one hand, Mr. Malema argues that his speech is entitled to the full protection of Section 16(1). AfriForum, on the other hand, argues that Malema's speech seeks to incite hatred against landowning farmers of Dutch ethnic ancestry. As will be explained, at the time of this writing, the matter is currently pending before the SCA, which must decide if, in context, Mr. Malema's use of "Kill the Boer" at EFF events constitutes merely hyperbolic political speech (which would be protected under Section 16(1)) or incitement to racial hatred against White farmers of Dutch ancestry (which would fall outside the scope of Section 16(1) by operation of Section 16(2)).

Without question, "Kill the Boer" has been something of a national *cause célèbre*. For example, Professors Buitendag and van Marle write that "[a] large section of the public followed the press coverage" after Malema led a 2010 rally featuring the song at the University of Johannesburg, an event that triggered "outrage[ ] by the fact that the song had been sung."[193] Right-wing politicians and public intellectuals regularly argue that "Kill the Boer," both the song and the chant, constitute a call to violence against White South Africans of Dutch descent;[194] Mr. Malema, backed by more than a few academics (including historians and political scientists), say that the song is not to be taken literally.[195] No evidence exists of targeted violence flowing directly from an EFF political rally; the claim is that the song and chant contribute to a general culture in which violence against Dutch-ethnic farmers is more probable than it would be in the absence of the song and chant.

Malema was initially hailed before the Equality Court in 2011,[196] which found him guilty of propagating hate speech.[197] Judge Colin G. Lamont explained his merits decision as follows:

> It must never be forgotten that in the spirit of ubuntu this new approach to each other must be fostered. Hence the Equality Act allows no justification on the basis of fairness for historic practices which are hurtful to the target group but loved by the other group. Such practices may not continue to be practised when it comes to hate speech. I accordingly find that Malema published and communicated words which could reasonably be construed to demonstrate an intention to be hurtful to incite harm and promote hatred against the white Afrikaans speaking community including the farmers who belongs to that group. The words accordingly constitute hate speech.[198]

Malema appealed this adverse decision to the SCA. After oral argument, and at the suggestion of the SCA, the parties entered into a mediation. This proceeding resulted in a settlement of the proceeding under which Malema promised to stop using the song, or variations of it, at EFF rallies.[199] Thus, Malema promised to go and sin no more incident to the mediation and settlement agreement.[200] Alas, old habits die hard. Over time, Mr. Malema failed to follow either the letter or the spirit of the consent decree—which led AfriForum to file a new complaint with the Equality Court in 2020—as well as complain that Malema had breached the 2012 settlement from the earlier proceedings.[201]

Accordingly, based on AfriForum's 2020 complaint, Malema faced new hate speech charges associated with his enthusiasm for "Kill the Boer"—but was acquitted by the Equality Court of these charges on August 25, 2022.[202] This decision currently is on appeal before the SCA. Sitting as the Equality Court, Judge Edwin M. Molahlehi first squarely rejected AfriForum's efforts to seek judicial enforcement of the 2012 settlement agreement because that judgment "ha[d] no binding effect" on the Equality Court.[203] He explained that "[t]he judgment is not binding on this court for the simple reason that the test it applied in determining whether the impugned song was hate speech is one that has subsequently been declared unconstitutional by the Constitutional Court in *Qwelane*."[204] Judge Molahlehi was undoubtedly on solid legal ground in reaching this conclusion. *Qwelane* held Section 10(a) of the Equality Act, which created liability for merely "hurtful" speech based on race or ethnicity, violative of Section 16(1) of the Constitution and, accordingly, without legal effect.

Turning to the merits of the 2020 complaint, and applying the reworked provisions of Sections 10(b) and 10(c) of the Equality Act, which both must be met to find a violation after *Qwelane*, Judge Molahlehei concluded that AfriForum had failed to prove that "Kill the Boer," or the variations on it, had actually caused harm or was likely to cause harm.[205] He explained that "[i]t is in the current political situation a song directed at articulating the failure of the current government in addressing the issues of economic power, land reform and distribution."[206] Given this state of play, "declaring the impugned song to be hate speech would significantly alter or curtail freedom of expression."[207] Thus, "in my view, the singing of the impugned song and its lyrics should be left to the political contestations and engagement on its message by the political role players"—not the courts.[208]

In sum, Malema's position, validated in the 2022 Equality Court judgment, is that the phrase should not be taken literally and constitutes a call to better and more efficacious land reform policies—a position that the Equality Court accepted in the 2022 litigation.[209] Under the post-*Qwelane* revised standards of liability under Section 10 of the Equality Act, Judge Molahlehi's legal analysis, based on the facts at bar—and particularly on AfriForum's failure to present any credible evidence of actual or highly probable harm flowing from Malema's performance of the song—seems spot on.

The K-word, or "kaffir," is South Africa's counterpart to the "N-word" in the United States. *New York Times* journalist Norimitsu Onishi characterizes it as "South Africa's most charged epithet, a term historically used by Whites to denigrate Black people and considered so offensive that it is rarely said out loud or rendered fully in print."[210] It is a word simply not used in polite company—and certainly not a word that a White South African would say to the face of a Black South African. As Professors Geldenhuys and Kelly-Louw explain, "[t]he k-word is considered to be so blatantly derogatory that its nature is taken to be established," so much so that "[a] black person can also be guilty of injuring the feelings of another black person by using the k-word."[211]

Vicki Momberg was having a bad day. While driving her car in Johannesburg, on February 3, 2016, she was the victim of a "smash and grab" incident and lost her purse to an aggressive thief.[212] Having been victimized by crime before, she took this particular incident very badly. First, Momberg repeatedly called 10111 (South Africa's equivalent of the 911 emergency response telephone number in the United States). During each of the calls, she verbally abused the 10111 operator, using language such as "'fuckin kaffir,'" "'fuckin bitch,'" and "'useless stupid kaffir.'"[213] These calls were both recorded and verified in open court; Momberg did not contest the accuracy of the 10111 call recordings.[214]

Still driving, Momberg flagged down a police car with three officers inside it. After Momberg and the police "pulled into a nearby parking lot," Momberg's racist tirade continued unabated.[215] When the police attempted to assist her by taking a statement and filing an incident report, Momberg went on another racially tinged tirade against Black South Africans.[216] In her rant, she characterized Black South Africans as "plain and simple useless" before repeatedly dropping the "K-word" on the responding police officers. Momberg also proceeded to utter racist threats to the officers, one of whom was Black.[217]

Momberg was indicted, tried, and convicted of a common law crime—the *crimen injuria*. The Equality Act contemplates criminal referrals from the Equality Courts when circumstances warrant and, given Momberg's lack of cooperation and remorse for her targeted racist ravings, one should not be surprised that the proceedings morphed from the civil Equality Court side of things to a public prosecution for a common law crime. In March 2023, South Africa's General Assembly passed the Prevention

Free Speech as Civic Structure

and Combating of Hate Crimes and Hate Speech Bill, which had been pending since 2018.[218] If ultimately enacted into law, Section 4 of this bill would create a statutory crime for hate speech that, tracking *Qwelane*, "causes harm" (rather than is merely "hurtful" or "offensive"). In the meantime, however, the common law action remains available as a vehicle for bringing criminal hate speech charges against those who use language that vilifies based on a category protected under Section 9 and that causes, or is likely to cause, harm to a member or members of the targeted group. However, criminal law is *not* the preferred vehicle for resolving disputes involving hate speech— instead, Equality Court proceedings, which are civil and do not involve jail time, serve as the primary legal means for addressing hate speech allegations.

Had Momberg accepted responsibility for her actions and offered a sincere public apology, her interaction with the legal system over her intemperate and racist behavior would likely have been over. In general, Equality Act sanctions, based on a model of restorative justice, at least for a repentant offender, extend only to an order requiring the defendant to offer a sincere public apology and perhaps also a requirement to per- form community service. However, Momberg declined to cooperate with the Equality Court's proceedings and refused to express remorse or to apologize. She ended up spending a short time in jail as a consequence of being convicted of the criminal hate speech charges that resulted from her near-total failure to cooperate. (It bears noting that South Africa embraces a restorative justice model for resolving social conflict— and deployed it even for those involved in the worst human rights abuses under apart- heid; if a former member of the state security services appeared before the Truth and Reconciliation Commission, freely admitted their wrongdoing, and offered up a sin- cere public apology, that was the end of the matter and no criminal charges, even for murders, resulted for the most heinous past criminal acts.)

Our third case study involves an edgy art exhibit at one of the Iziko's cultural institutions—more specifically, the South African National Gallery, in Cape Town. The gallery organized an exhibit of "outsider" art entitled "The Art of Disruptions." The exhibition included an installation by Dean Hutton, a graduate art student at the University of Cape Town.[219] Judge Daniel M. Thulare, then the Chief Magistrate, sit- ting as a judge of the Equality Court, explains that "[t]he aim of the 'Art of Disruptions' exhibition was to collect and create dialogue."[220] Hutton's installation prominently featured the phrase "Fuck White People" and "include[d] a multi-media installation which consists of wallpaper mounted on a board, a chair, and golden boots."[221] Judge Thulare adds that "[t]he wallpaper on the board consists of the words 'Fuck', 'White' and 'People' repeatedly written on each line in capital letters."[222]

The artist explains his motivations in the following terms:

> You see, white pain demands attention all the time, while black pain flows con- stantly. So I made a suit to fuck white people. It began as an experiment to see what happens when a white body wears this. It makes people angry, sometimes to the point of violence. But I can do it—that is white privilege. I'm here for

your pain because white people think empathy can cure racism but what we must strive for is complete dismantling of the systems of power that keep white people racist.

Learn to fuck the white in you too. Fuckwhitepeople.org #fuckwhitepeople[223]

Hutton's motivation was not to vilify or encourage violence against White South Africans, but rather constituted a challenge for them to do more, and better, to address long-standing and systemic racial inequalities in contemporary South African society.

Judge Thulare rejected the plaintiff's contention that the installation constituted hate speech: "In my view, properly contexualised and understood, the words complained of by the complainant against respondent, to wit, 'Fuck White People,' is Hutton's main message which viewed in the totality of the work means: **REJECT, CONFRONT AND DISMANTLE STRUCTURES, SYSTEMS KNOWLEDGE, SKILLS AND ATTITUDES OF POWER THAT KEEP WHITE PEOPLE RACIST.'**"[224] Thus, rather than trying to harass, intimidate, or bring about acts of violence against White South Africans, "Hutton is calling for Whites as a race towards a demonstrable change of mindset, a paradigm shift from the old ways."[225] He concluded that "[i]t follows that I am unable to find that the respondent, by dissemination of Hutton's ideas, contravened [the Equality Act]."[226]

More specifically, Judge Thulare ruled that Hutton's installation did not constitute a violation of Section 7 of the Equality Act, which proscribes "dissemination of any propaganda or idea, which propounds the racial superiority or inferiority of any person, including incitement to, or participation in, any form of racial violence."[227] Nor did it violate Section 10, in its pre-*Qwelane* form, which included Section 10(a)'s prohibition of speech that is merely "hurtful."[228] Indeed, even if the installation implicated Section 10, Section 12 of the Equality Act, which protects "*bona fide* engagement in artistic creativity, academic and scientific inquiry, fair and accurate reporting in the public interest or publication of any information, advertisement or notice in accordance with section 16 of the Constitution,"[229] would have precluded any imposition of liability for the gallery's public display of the work. Judge Thulare did not reach the Section 12 question because he did not find that Hutton's work triggered Section 10's proscriptions—but, even if he had concluded that Section 10 was implicated on the facts at bar, "it would be saved from prohibition by the proviso to section 12 of the Act."[230]

In sum, the art museum was free to display Hutton's installation without running afoul of any provision of the Equality Act. As Judge Thulare explained, "[t]he work in general, and the words 'Fuck White People' in particular as used by Dean Hutton in his protest art is not unfair discrimination on the ground of race as envisaged in section 7 of the Act" nor was it "hate speech as prohibited by section 10 of the Act" and "its dissemination, publication and display by the respondent is not prohibited as envisaged in section 12 of the Act."[231]

At first glance, one might think that all three of these cases should have been decided identically. On more careful examination, however, it is possible to draw a plausible line of distinction between these speakers and their speech. The art gallery's display of Hutton's controversial installation provides the easiest case, insofar as Hutton's art clearly was not intended to incite violence against White people, nor was there any realistic probability that it would have that effect. To sustain the imposition of sanctions for its display would have cut very deeply into the freedom of expression, and it would have done so without any obvious prospect of improving race relations within South Africa.

Malema's speech presents a harder case. Having a highly visible populist leader, who heads an active and relatively successful political party, regularly exclaiming "Kill the Boer," "Shoot the Boer!," or "Kiss the Boer!" (with his gun-hands gestures) could cause farmers of Dutch descent to be fearful for their safety.[232] On the other hand, the phrase was used at mass political rallies and was never actually targeted at any particular White farmers. Had Malema trespassed on to a Dutch farmer's vineyard, in Stellenbosch, with a group of his followers, in the dead of night, to lead the chant, a different juridical analysis would apply. But, Malema's polemics were never directly addressed to any White South Africans. Although the SCA, and perhaps the CCSA, will ultimately have to resolve the legality of Malema's chants and sing-alongs, in my view, the Equality Court decision of 2022 gets the matter right—considered in sociolegal context, the use of the phrase is not a true threat but a hyperbolic call to more effective, and more comprehensive, land reform.[233]

Momberg's targeted and highly personalized use of the K-word can easily be distinguished from Hutton's art installation and Malema's (political) war cry. To use that word, on a one-to-one basis with a Black South African, is to impose serious psychological harm and perhaps to provoke a spontaneous, but irrepressible, violent response by the victim. If South Africa has any "fighting" words, to borrow a U.S. First Amendment construct, the K-word belongs at the top of the list.[234] As Justice Frank Murphy, of the U.S. Supreme Court, observed in *Chaplinsky*, "[t]here are certain well-defined and narrowly limited classes of speech, the prevention and punishment of which have never been thought to raise any Constitutional problem,"[235] and "[t]hese include the lewd and obscene, the profane, the libelous, and the insulting or 'fighting' words—those which by their very utterance inflict injury or tend to incite an immediate breach of the peace."[236] Fighting words, as well as these other unprotected types of speech, do not enjoy any First Amendment protection because "such utterances are no essential part of any exposition of ideas, and are of such slight social value as a step to truth that any benefit that may be derived from them is clearly outweighed by the social interest in order and morality."[237]

It seems easy to separate Momberg's racist tirade, which involved directing arguably fighting words at the police responding to her incident, from Hutton's artwork and Malema's political invective. It would, of course, be possible to treat all three forms of speech as proscribable hate speech—and arguably, in Section 10(a) of the Equality Act, South Africa's national parliament indicated its intention to do just that (at least with respect to "hurtful" speech that includes targeted insult or invective based on race, sex, or religion).

Even so, the better view, and the view most consistent with the CCSA's governing precedents, is that hyperbolic speech enjoys full protection as speech under Section 16(1) unless the speaker clearly manifests an intention to vilify or provoke hatred of a particular covered group *and* the speech occurs in a place, and at a time, where members of the group would actually experience fear—or even acts of violence—as a result of the speech activity.[238] Under this approach, Momberg's speech is the only one of the three that merited a response from the legal system—and it is all but certain that the CCSA would not find the targeted use of the K-word to constitute protected speech under Section 16(1).[239] In short, there is a method, and a set of well-conceived principles, at work in the South African lower courts' precedents balancing freedom of expression with dignity, equality, and human freedom.

D. Conclusion: Expressive Freedoms Do Not Hold an Inferior Status as Fundamental Human Rights in Contemporary South Africa

The CCSA's decisions in *Qwelane, Masuku, Islamic Unity Convention,* and *Khumalo* all decline to afford the freedom of speech an absolute priority over the foundational human rights values of dignity, equality, and freedom. Even so, however, all four decisions recognize the inextricable relationship between the freedom of speech and a free press and the maintenance of a well-functioning democratic polity. Even if democracy, as a form of government, is not specifically enumerated in Sections 1, 7, and 37 of the 1996 Constitution, the entire document's core animating purpose is to create and sustain the conditions necessary for successful democratic self-government in the Republic of South Africa. One cannot seriously fault the CCSA for recognizing democratic self-government as a coequal "foundational" human rights value (or commitment).

Freedom of speech is not, to use the language of *Khumalo*, a "paramount" human right that must be reflexively and absolutely protected at the expense of securing and safeguarding other constitutional rights. More specifically, freedom of expression does not enjoy an absolute constitutional priority over dignity, equality, and freedom. That said, however, freedom of expression and other expressive freedoms protected by Section 16(1) plainly hold a coequal constitutional rank.

As a matter of constitutional theory, as well as constitutional practice, affording expressive freedom a coequal status with dignity, equality, and human freedom makes a great deal of sense. South Africa is a democratic polity, and it is quite impossible to have truly free and fair elections in the absence of the freedom of expression, a free press, and the rights to associate, assemble, and petition. To say that the democratic character of South Africa, and the electoral process used to maintain the country's democratic character, are human rights interests of the first order, also enjoys strong textual support in the 1996 Constitution.[240] Even so, however, and conceding that the constitutional text that vests the CCSA with broad discretion to draw upon myriad sources to inform its interpretation and enforcement efforts, one cannot plausibly deny that it is the CCSA, and not the text itself, that draws the boundary lines when

Free Speech as Civic Structure

fundamental rights come into conflict (as freedom of expression so often does with human dignity, equality, and freedom).

IV. THE LONG SHADOW OF APARTHEID AND FREEDOM OF EXPRESSION: LINGERING SOCIAL SKEPTICISM ABOUT EVEN WELL-INTENTIONED GOVERNMENT EFFORTS TO CENSOR POLITICAL SPEECH

Given that the contemporary government of South Africa is freely and fairly elected, should South Africa's judges afford greater deference to the political branches when, in well-intentioned efforts to promote equality and human dignity, they adopt legislation that sets the metes and bounds of political and governmental speech? Properly answering this question, and understanding precisely why the CCSA and SCA have not been particularly deferential to the national parliament's attempts to regulate hate speech, requires recourse to South Africa's fraught history of discrimination and political exclusion—and the overt and strong use of government censorship to maintain an organized system of oppression that subordinated South Africa's people of color for generations. If, within living memory, government censorship served as a tool to manipulate and distort the marketplace of political ideas, a posture of deep skepticism toward government efforts to declare free speech winners and free speech losers would constitute a natural and quite appropriate judicial response.

As previously explained, the CCSA arguably has departed from the 1996 Constitution's formal text by giving freedom of speech a coequal place with the lodestar human rights values of dignity, equality, and freedom. However, in my view, the decision to do so is easily explained by another human rights value that, although not repeated with the same frequency as "dignity," "equality," and "human freedom," was clearly front and center in the minds of the persons who drafted the 1996 Constitution: democratic self-government.

An unstated—but entirely self-evident—premise of South Africa's 1996 Constitution is that South Africa will be a mass participatory democracy in which all citizens are both free and equal as overseers of the government and its actions. Indeed, Section 1, which sets forth the country's founding principles, begins by describing South Africa as "one, sovereign, democratic state."[241] It also identifies founding values typically associated with the traditional features of an electoral democracy, including "universal adult suffrage, a national common voters roll, regular elections and a multi-party system of democratic government, to ensure accountability, responsiveness and openness."[242] One could plausibly renormalize the commitments to dignity, equality, and human freedom as relating to a foundational commitment to creating and then successfully maintaining a mass participatory democracy in which each and every citizen enjoys an equal voice and vote.

As Professor Klug explains, "[t]he national liberation struggle in South Africa was at its core a struggle for democracy, which came to fruition with the 1994 election and the establishment of Nelson Mandela's government as the country's first truly democratically elected government."[243] He argues that "[t]he fundamental sources of the Constitution arose from the particular history and traditions of South Africa's political struggles, legal practices, and culture."[244] To be sure, the text of the Constitution provides a decisional framework that the Justices of the CCSA repeatedly have pledged to respect.[245] That said, however, South Africa's founding principles are not directly enforceable in South Africa's domestic courts—including the CCSA.[246]

Professor Klug observes that "[t]he Constitutional Court has declared that although the 'values enunciated in section 1 of the Constitution are of fundamental importance,' they are not the basis of justiciable rights."[247] Instead, as the CCSA has explained, the founding principles "inform and give substance to all the provisions of the Constitution," but do not give rise to discrete and enforceable rights in themselves."[248] However, substantive provisions, set forth in Section 19 of the 1996 Constitution expressly guarantee universal suffrage and equal citizenship—rendering them not merely "values" but also fundamental "rights" as well.[249] Section 19's guarantees related to the electoral process would therefore provide a sound constitutional basis, in conjunction with democratic self-government as a founding "principle," or value, for elevating the status of expressive activity that relates to, and is essential for, animating and facilitating the electoral process.

If, in fact, creating and then maintaining a truly democratic polity constitutes a bedrock principle of South African constitutionalism, it is simply impossible as both a normative and practical matter to afford expressive freedoms a lower constitutional priority than dignity, equality, and human freedom. Indeed, I am prepared to state the case in even stronger terms: In the absence of a fully free and open marketplace of political ideas, it is simply impossible, over the longer term, to safeguard effectively human dignity, equality, and freedom. The status of these apex rights will depend critically on the ability of the body politic to hold those vested with the reins of government power accountable for their actions—free and open political debate is an essential condition for We the People to perform this most important civic duty.[250]

Professor Alexander Meiklejohn, generally credited with best articulating the democratic self-government theory for protecting the freedom of speech, makes this point in clear and emphatic terms.[251] He explains that "unabridged freedom of discussion is the bedrock on which [the U.S.] government stands."[252] For Meiklejohn, freedom of political expression is an essential constitutive element for the creation and maintenance of a system of democratic self-government. In his view, "the citizens of the United States will be fit to govern themselves under their own institutions only if they have faced squarely and fearlessly everything that can be said in favor of those institutions, everything that can be said against them."[253]

What is true of democratic self-government in the United States holds equally true for democratic self-government in South Africa. Open and robust public debate is essential to empowering voters to render wise electoral judgments. As Meiklejohn makes the point, "[i]n the last resort, it is not our representatives who govern us," but rather "[w]e govern ourselves, using them" and "do so in such ways as our own free

64 ⌒ Free Speech as Civic Structure

judgment may decide."[254] Thus, "[w]hen a free man is voting, it is not enough that the truth is known by someone else, by some scholar or administrator or legislator."[255] Instead, "[t]he voters must have it, all of them."[256]

Free speech and a vigorous public debate are essential to voters possessing the information necessary to render prudent electoral verdicts at the ballot box on election day. Accordingly, compromising the protection of free speech puts at risk the ability of We the People to use the electoral process to hold the government accountable. In light of this underlying reality, any free speech guarantee in a mass participatory democracy— whether Section 16 of South Africa's 1996 Constitution or the U.S. Constitution's First Amendment—exists so that, as Meiklejohn puts it, "all the citizens shall, so far as possible, understand the issues which bear upon our common life."[257] It follows that "no idea, no opinion, no belief, no counter belief, no relevant information, may be kept from them."[258] Government censorship of the marketplace of political ideas is antithetical to the practice of democracy.

Thomas Jefferson makes a largely identical point. In a letter to Charles Yancey, Jefferson observes that "[t]he functionaries of every government have propensities to command at will the liberty and property of their constituents" and, in consequence, "[t]here is no safe deposit for these but with the people themselves; nor can they be safe with them without information."[259] In other words, if voters are to perform their crucial checking function against bad government behavior, they must have the information necessary to render sensible judgments.

Meiklejohn echoes these views, positing that "[i]n my view, 'the people need free speech' because they have decided, in adopting, maintaining and interpreting their Constitution, to govern themselves rather than to be governed by others" and "in order to make that self-government a reality rather than an illusion, in order that it may become as wise and efficient as its responsibilities require, the judgment-making of the people must be self-educated in the ways of freedom."[260] The free flow of information within the body politic is essential because "[u]nder the compact upon which the Constitution rests, it is agreed that men shall not be governed by others, that they shall govern themselves."[261]

Self-education in the ways of freedom requires sufficient breathing room for speech that is "hurtful," "insulting," and produces genuine upset—even outright anger. It need not, however, encompass speech that conveys a true threat or constitutes a form of targeted harassment. Between the two potential polar approaches that the CCSA might embrace—reflexive judicial deference to properly enacted hate speech regulations or reflexive judicial skepticism to such regulations—lies the point that the CCSA seems to be seeking to find and hold. This point would not limit the legislature's regulatory discretion to enact hate speech regulations solely to prohibit speech that would otherwise constitute a free-standing crime regardless of its content (because it threatens or harasses the person or persons to whom it is directed). But, at the same time, it would not give elected officials a completely free hand to manipulate the marketplace of political ideas through the guise of protecting the feelings and sensibilities of members of minority communities (however defined).

South Africa: Free Speech as a Co-Equal Right —⟴ 65

The immediate relevance of these arguments to the necessary scope of Section 16 should be quite obvious. If South Africa is to achieve its larger and overarching democratic ambitions, free speech will have to play a critical role in facilitating prudent oversight of the government by the body politic. This reality animates the CCSA's solicitude for the freedom of speech—even when protecting speech comes into conflict with the foundational values, which are substantive rights as well, of dignity, equality, and freedom.

Cognizance of South Africa's apartheid past also plays an important role in shaping the CCSA's approach to hate speech regulation.[262] During the nation's sad and prolonged apartheid era, ersatz hate speech regulations played an important role in the National Party's efforts to maintain and enforce apartheid. As former Chief Justice Mogoeng quite accurately observes in *Economic Freedom Fighters*, "expression of thought or belief and own worldview or ideology was for many years extensively and severely circumscribed in this country."[263] Thus, "[i]t was visited, institutionally and otherwise, with the worst conceivable punishment or dehumanising consequences."[264]

The former Chief Justice cites "[t]he tragic and untimely death of Steve Biko as a result of his bold decision to talk frankly and write as he liked, about the unjust system and its laws."[265] Efforts by the apartheid government to suppress speech critical of the government, under the rubric of banning pro-democracy advocacy as a form of "hate speech," led to some highly visible—and highly questionable—government censorship decisions. For example, the National Party government banned the broadcast of the made-for-television adaptation of Alex Haley's *Roots* from its release in 1977 to 1984 because the government feared that the broadcast of the miniseries might arouse anger or hatred toward White South Africans.[266] Professors Norvella Carter, Warren Chalklen, and Bhekuyise Zungu explain that "[g]iven *Roots*' portrayal of [the] oppression of black people, the miniseries was banned by the South African government as undesirable."[267] The critically acclaimed and award-winning miniseries could not be tolerated in South Africa because it was "contrary to the ideals of the apartheid government."[268]

The use of government censorship to silence Black voices made it difficult, if not impossible, for people of color to explore and express their racial and personal identities. As Tlhalo Sam Radithalo poignantly writes, in the late apartheid era of the 1970s and 1980s, "th[e] lack of information and books, and the routine banning of progressive newspapers (the authoritative *The World* and *Daily Dispatch* were banned together with others on 19 October 1977), made it difficult for a high school student to seek to know what it meant to be Black in South Africa."[269]

The CCSA repeatedly invokes the apartheid-era government's extensive use of official censorship as a means of political control and, arguably attempted thought control. For example, in *Islamic Unity Convention*, then-Deputy Chief Justice, and later Chief Justice, Pius Langa observes that "[w]e have recently emerged from a severely restrictive past where expression, especially political and artistic expression, was extremely circumscribed by various legislative enactments."[270] During the National Party's reign, under apartheid, "[t]he restrictions that were placed on expression were not only a denial of democracy itself, but also exacerbated the impact of systemic violations of other fundamental human rights in South Africa."[271] Given this history of using official government censorship to deny human dignity, equality, and equal rights of participation in democratic self-government, similar "restrictions [today] would be incompatible with South Africa's present commitment to a society based on a 'constitutionally protected culture of openness and democracy and universal human rights for South Africans of all ages, classes and colors.'"[272]

Chief Justice Mogoeng makes exactly the same point in *Economic Freedom Fighters*,[273] a 2021 decision involving whether hyperbolic speech about land ownership reform policies, made at political events, constituted a true threat (and was therefore a proper basis for imposing criminal punishment).[274] The CCSA found that a provision of South Africa's incitement statute, Section 18(2)(b) of the Riotous Assemblies Act,[275] was fatally overbroad because it failed to distinguish between serious social harms and relatively minor ones and imposed a limiting construction to bring the law within the constitutional boundary line required by Section 16(1).[276] In framing how aggressive the government could be in punishing incitement based on hyperbolic core political speech, the Chief Justice emphasized that pervasive government censorship of such speech existed "for many years" under the National Party-led government, with freedom of expression "extensively and severely circumscribed in this country."[277] Moreover, violations of the apartheid-era government's censorship rules and regulations subjected speakers to "the worst conceivable punishment[s]," punishments that commonly involved "dehumanising consequences."[278]

Precisely because of this highly problematic record of South Africa's government claiming good motives but acting from unadorned, naked self-interest, and as Chief Justice Mogoeng explains, freedom of speech "has to be treasured, celebrated, promoted and even restrained with a deeper sense of purpose and appreciation of what it represents in genuine constitutional democracy, considering our highly intolerant and suppressive past."[279] So too, in *Qwelane*, Justice Majiedt observes that "the stains of our colonial and apartheid past reinforce the point that freedom of expression has a particularly important role to play in our constitutional democracy."[280]

Thus, the necessity of safeguarding hyperbolic political speech seems particularly pressing today because, in the not so distant past, the government's aggressive and effective use of official censorship silenced many, if not most, South African Black voices. Indeed, Radithalo laments that, while growing up in the 1970s in South Africa, "[o]ne had to resort to whatever book shed light on the human condition within and without South Africa."[281] He specifically cites Alex Haley's *Roots*, which was available in his township public library, as a case in point of having to look abroad to get a better understanding and perspective of what was going on at home in South Africa.[282]

In 1987, at the very end of the apartheid era, the U.S. Department of State acidly observed that "South Africa is not any closer in late 1987 to respecting free speech and free political participation by all its citizens than it was 1 year ago."[283] In other words, the apartheid government, under the all-White National Party, used censorship, including bogus hate speech regulations, to attempt to retain its antidemocratic hold on power.

William Faulker once wrote, "The past is not dead. It's not even past."[284] In contemporary South Africa, this holds true. Despite the National Party having left the political scene, and not holding power in Pretoria since the early 1990s, and notwithstanding today's government officers holding their posts by dint of seeking and winning popular election, the apartheid past very much influences the democratic present. Simply put, memories are long and memories of official government censorship during the apartheid era make South Africans from all walks of life skeptical of government efforts to decide what can and cannot be said in the marketplace of political ideas.

South Africa's past makes everyday citizens—as well as the Justices of the CCSA— deeply skeptical of government efforts to police the marketplace of political ideas. South Africa's distinct and unfortunate history with government censorship in general, and hate speech regulations in particular, explains in large measure the contemporary legal culture's deep skepticism toward government hate speech regulations. In this particular area of law, sociolegal culture and cultural memory—rather than constitutional text—seem to play the most important role in shaping the metes and bounds of expressive freedom in today's South Africa.

V. CONCLUSION: FREEDOM OF EXPRESSION AS A COEQUAL CONSTITUTIONAL VALUE WITH DIGNITY, EQUALITY, AND HUMAN FREEDOM

Rather than serving as the exception that proves the rule, the CCSA's approach to enforcing Section 16's protection of expression generally fits the pattern one finds in Australia, Israel, the United Kingdom, and the United States—namely, a constitutional court defining and enforcing the freedom of speech as it deems necessary to safeguard the process of democratic deliberation, fashioning new constitutional free speech doctrines as the necessities of the times may require. Despite clear and express textual signals set forth in the 1996 Constitution that would seem to give the constitutional rights of dignity, equality, and human freedom, which constitute foundational values as well, an absolute priority over other human rights, when these apex human rights come into conflict with other constitutional rights integral to democratic self-government, the CCSA instead has embarked on a program of harmonization. Rather than affording priority to dignity, equality, and freedom over speech rights, the Justices consistently have deployed an approach that seeks to reconcile a strong and robust commitment to the freedom of speech with equally important constitutional commitments to creating and maintaining a society that adheres strictly to a policy of substantive equality among its citizens.[285]

The reasons for this approach are also consistent with the reasoning and approach of other constitutional courts—and particularly with those in Australia and Israel (which both found an implied right to freedom of speech as a necessary corollary

68 ⌒ Free Speech as Civic Structure

to a commitment to democracy featuring free and fair elections). It is quite impossible to conduct free and fair elections without the possibility of an open and wide-ranging debate about the policies that the government should pursue (and those it should abjure). A government empowered to censor core political speech, even if doing so in the name of equality and dignity, presents an existential risk to the process of democratic deliberation. What is more, an inherent conflict of interest arises when those doing the censoring have a vested stake in the outcome of the electoral process. A strong structural need exists for an independent judiciary to play a checking function in order to protect the democratic process from distortion (or worse).[286]

In the end, this puts South Africa and the CCSA in the same boat with the Supreme Court of the United States. South African judges, using a process of common law reasoning, seek to reconcile the 1996 constitutional mandate for the respect of dignity, equality, and human freedom with the imperative nature of a free and open marketplace of political ideas in a democratic polity. The judges, cognizant of South Africa's fraught history with official government censorship, exercise the power of judicial review to ensure that citizens remain free to speak their version of truth to power. To be sure, the Justices routinely credit the legislature's motivation in promoting dignity, equality, and freedom—but they nevertheless exercise independent judgment as to the adequacy of the constitutional balance that the legislature struck in the relevant statute.

In sum, along with dignity, equality, and defined aspects of human freedom, democracy appears among South Africa's foundational values. Indeed, the entire constitutional enterprise exists to help create, maintain, and operationalize a well-functioning, mass participation democracy. Were political speech subject to blanket government censorship whenever the elected branches deemed such censorship necessary to promote dignity, equality, and human freedom, the government's power to distort the operation of the marketplace of political ideas would undermine elections as a means of conferring legitimacy on the government. As the *Qwelane* Court states the proposition, a well-functioning democracy must "foster[ ] an environment that allows a free and open exchange of ideas, free from censorship no matter how offensive, shocking, or disturbing those ideas may be."[287]

4

The United Kingdom

FREE SPEECH AS A SOCIOLEGAL NORM

I. INTRODUCTION: THE UNITED KINGDOM AS A CAUTIONARY TALE ABOUT THE IMPORTANCE OF TEXT—AS OPPOSED TO JUDGES—IN SECURING FUNDAMENTAL RIGHTS

For generations, it was both commonplace and legally correct to observe that the United Kingdom lacked any legally enforceable bill of rights. Although once true, it is no longer so. Since October 2, 2000, the date that the Human Rights Act 1998 (HRA 98) came into effect,[1] the domestic law of the United Kingdom has included a codified bill of rights that includes an express guarantee of freedom of expression. The HRA 98 incorporated the European Convention for the Protection of Human Rights and Fundamental Freedoms (European Convention)[2] into domestic law and instructed the courts in the United Kingdom to take account of the European Convention, as well as decisions of the European Court of Human Rights (ECtHR), when interpreting and applying provisions of domestic law and also when considering the lawfulness of public authorities' actions.

The standard narrative posits that, with respect to the rights codified in the European Convention, the HRA 98 worked a sea change in both the ability and willingness of the British domestic courts to protect fundamental human rights, which, under the European Convention, include freedom of expression.[3] Article 10 expressly protects "freedom of expression" and encompasses "freedom to hold opinions and to receive and impart information and ideas without interference by public authority and

---

Free Speech as Civic Structure. Ronald J. Krotoszynski, Jr., Oxford University Press. © Ronald J. Krotoszynski, Jr. 2024.
DOI: 10.1093/9780197662229.003.0004

regardless of frontiers."[4] Under the HRA 98, this provision, as of October 2, 2000, created a statutory right to protection of expressive freedom in the United Kingdom. However, as a number of commentators have observed, codification of speech and press rights via the HRA 98 has not made much of a difference to their scope of application.[5]

It is fair to say that, as a general matter, the HRA 98 has proven a disappointment to both its supporters and its critics alike.[6] Professor Aileen Kavanaugh observes that advocates of the HRA 98 "claimed that it would transform society for the better, providing us with a fresh set of values for a godless age."[7] HRA 98 skeptics, on both the left and the right of the ideological spectrum, feared the transfer of power from a democratically elected Parliament to the domestic courts, whose members, unlike members of Parliament, are "unelected and unaccountable."[8] Kavanaugh adds, however, that "both admirers and detractors alike seemed to agree on its immense constitutional and institutional significance."[9] In consequence, one cannot gainsay that the HRA 98 greatly empowered the judiciary, arguably at the expense of Parliament, with respect to securing human rights protected under the European Convention.

Even so, however, the HRA 98's impact is more obvious in some areas of human rights law than in others. For example, with regard to procedural due process values, the HRA 98 has emboldened the domestic courts to reject efforts by Parliament to limit or deny fair procedures to individuals, such as asylum seekers, in disputes with the United Kingdom's government.[10] In this context, the HRA 98 plainly has made a significant, positive difference.

Thus, on the one hand, the Supreme Court of the United Kingdom (SCUK), and before it came into existence in 2009, the Appellate Committee of the House of Lords (HOL), have engaged some European Convention rights seriously and used the power to render saving constructions of statutes boldly to essentially rewrite laws that arguably failed to respect rights protected under the European Convention (with respect to due process and a fair trial, Article 6 of the European Convention[11]). On the other hand, however, British decisions involving expressive freedom did not change much, if at all, after the advent of the HRA 98 era—which is something of a puzzle.

In theory, the incorporation of an express free speech guarantee, along with a statutory interpretative mandate to render saving constructions of domestic legal provisions to avoid abridgment of the right,[12] should have led British courts to more forcefully safeguard expressive freedom. Moreover, the HRA 98 includes a specific provision, Article 12(4), that gives an interpretative directive to the domestic courts to have "particular regard" for safeguarding the freedoms of speech and press.[13] Thus, the HRA 98 not only incorporates Section 10(1) of the European Convention but would also appear to make freedom of expression a "preferred freedom," to use a turn of phrase that the U.S. Supreme Court once commonly deployed when describing the relative importance of the freedom of speech.[14] Over two decades later, however, this is not how things have turned out.

Indeed, the HOL held, in 2004, that Section 12(4) actually does not mean what it so clearly and plainly says.[15] As Professor Eric Barendt has observed, "[f]reedom of

The United Kingdom: Free Speech as a Sociolegal Norm 71

expression is not given any pre-eminence by the HRA 1998, but must be balanced against the competing rights and interests recognized by the Convention."[16] Thus, under the HRA 98, speech, although certainly protected, does not enjoy any relative priority over other fundamental rights protected under the European Convention. The HOL, and lower British courts, simply ignored Parliament's directive to prioritize expressive freedom. This adds an important detail to the overall picture; there was a clear textual signal in the HRA 98 to the domestic courts to upgrade and prioritize expressive freedom—but the domestic courts elected to chart a different jurisprudential course.

So, what happened? Why didn't the HRA 98 prove to be a game changer for freedom of expression in the United Kingdom? With regard to expressive freedom, the HRA 98 was the dog that did not bark. It would have been quite reasonable to assume that the enactment of an express statutory right to the freedom of expression, coupled with an interpretative directive to the British domestic courts to have "particular regard" for speech rights,[17] would have led to a significant expansion of the scope of protected speech activity. Almost a quarter century after the HRA 98 came into force, this is not how things have come to pass.

It turns out, with respect to speech rights, that the domestic British courts arguably jumped the gun. As Professor Barendt has persuasively demonstrated,[18] the U.K.'s domestic courts began to invoke freedom of speech as an important social value, if not a formal legal right, in the 1980s, as Sir Anthony Lester and others began to agitate for the adoption of a British bill of rights that would entrench the rights set forth in the European Convention and authorize judicial review to safeguard them.[19] As Lester and his coauthors stated their case in chief, "[t]here is growing concern about the protection of civil liberties in Britain" and "we believe that the time has come to set them out formally in a Bill of Rights and to entrench them as part of a written constitution."[20]

A reasonable observer might conclude that with respect to expressive freedoms, Lester and his allies won the battle but nevertheless lost the war. As this chapter will explain in some detail, free speech as a protected legal interest did not change much, if at all, after the HRA 98 came into force. Courts had already began considering free speech values prior to 2000. Moreover, free speech did not enjoy significantly higher levels of judicial solicitude after the judges possessed a clear textual mandate from Parliament to consider free speech claims when developing and applying the common law or interpreting statutes and regulations. The operative question that cries out to be asked and answered is: "Why?" Does text matter in securing fundamental rights? Or is it the case that, however much or little text matters, judges simply matter more?

The United Kingdom thus presents an interesting test case for the relevance of constitutional or, more precisely, in the United Kingdom, statutory text to the scope and vibrancy of expressive freedom. Prior to October 2000, no textual mandate existed in domestic law either for invalidating or rewriting statutes or regulations because they trenched too deeply on the freedom of speech. Yet, from the 1980s forward, British courts would invoke free speech when interpreting and applying statutes and read statutes down in order to safeguard speech. The Public Order Act 1986 provides an excellent case study of this practice.[21] One might reasonably have predicted that the enactment of the HRA 98, and its coming into force, would lead to enhanced judicial solicitude for expressive freedoms—and this has not happened. With regard to expressive freedoms, Professor Barendt observes that "[i]n fact, it is doubtful whether the change has so far been much more than cosmetic."[22]

Yet, as Professor Stephen Gardbaum lucidly demonstrates in his important book on the "new commonwealth model of constitutionalism,"[23] this has not been the case with respect to other fundamental rights—including rights associated with procedural fairness.[24] Nor does it hold true for privacy rights—privacy as a legal interest expanded significantly after the HRA 98 came into force.[25] The HOL, in its landmark *MGN Ltd. v. Campbell* decision, significantly expanded the tort of breach of confidence to create a de facto Prosser-style tort[26] for the public disclosure of private facts.[27]

It also bears noting that the SCUK has not directly incorporated provisions of the European Convention into domestic British law, instead considering European Convention claims only *after* a litigant has properly invoked an existing legal right under domestic law.[28] Rather than recognizing and then enforcing new European Convention-derived rights directly into British law, the domestic courts have instead considered the European Convention only when construing existing statutory or common law provisions. Thus, before the HRA 98 went into effect, no general right of privacy existed in British law and, to this day, that remains the case[29]—despite a strong argument that Article 8 requires the United Kingdom to provide effective civil law remedies for violations of privacy interests.[30] Instead, as Baroness Brenda Hale explained in *Campbell*, "where existing remedies are available, the court not only can but must balance the competing Convention rights of the parties."[31]

The premise of this chapter is that the HOL and lower courts alike had already largely incorporated the freedom of speech into British law before the HRA 98 came on to the legal scene. As popular political support for a written British bill of rights began to grow in the late 1980s and early 1990s, judges in the United Kingdom took notice and began directly discussing freedom of speech in their published decisions. In fact, statutory construction of laws that directly regulate speech, such as Section 5 of the Public Order Act 1986 (POA 86), routinely took account of the need to strike a balance between maintaining public order and safeguarding the ability of the market-place of political ideas to function. Judges read down laws like the POA 86 in order to protect the freedom of political speech. Accordingly, when the HRA 98 took effect in 2000, courts had already performed judicial surgery on laws that raised the specter of undue government censorship of unpopular dissenting speech. So too, English courts had already started to modify the common law to take account of free speech values well before enactment and enforcement of the HRA 98.[32]

I will argue, and attempt to prove, that by the late 1990s, the U.K.'s domestic courts were already in the habit of using statutory construction techniques to temper the worst potential censorial effects of laws that directly regulate speech. Accordingly, when the HRA 98 took effect, material jurisprudential changes were not really needed in order to give full effect to Article 10 of the European Convention in domestic law.

The United Kingdom: Free Speech as a Sociolegal Norm — 73

Accordingly, Professor Barendt posits that the advent of the HRA 98 did not lead to a renaissance in free speech law in the United Kingdom—but this was because the courts, on their own, had already adopted free speech as a fundamental right and set about protecting it—at least to the extent that they were ready, willing, and able to do so—regardless of whether these judicial efforts enjoyed a direct textual imprimatur from Parliament.

This chapter will proceed in five additional main sections. In theory, courts in the United Kingdom had no warrant in domestic law for considering and vindicating free speech claims before the advent of the HRA 98. However, and as section II will demonstrate, free speech consciousness grew in the United Kingdom despite the absence of a written bill of rights from the 1960s onward—and this cultural shift significantly predated the HRA 98 entering into force. Moving forward, section III will describe and discuss the HRA 98 and its incorporation of the European Convention into British domestic law. Section IV makes the case that judges in the United Kingdom incorporated free speech as a legal value, if not a formal legal "right," well before October 2, 2000 (the effective date of the HRA 98). Section V argues freedom of expression constitutes a common law constitutional right—that is, a right that courts will recognize and protect without regard to whether a clear textual command instructs them to do so because We the People simply expect the right to be vindicated by the courts. Finally, section VI offers a brief summary and conclusion.

The domestic courts of the United Kingdom incorporated free speech as a legally cognizable interest, if not a "right," in response to growing and highly visible public demands for more robust protection of fundamental rights. Exercising their common law powers, and perhaps taking a page from Judge Guido Calabresi's theory of "judicial updating,"[33] judges began to invoke and apply freedom of speech as a basis for reading down statutes that otherwise might have trenched too deeply on the ability of citizens to participate actively in the process of democratic deliberation that ultimately informs the act of voting. Courts also did this, as Professor Barendt observed,[34] with respect to the common law. Thus, when the HRA 98 came onto the scene, with respect to the freedom of speech, it simply "underpinned" the preexisting common law right.[35]

The British example provides empirical support for Professor David Strauss's thesis that, at its heart, all constitutional law constitutes a kind of common law enterprise.[36] If this is so, it raises important questions about the ability of those engaged in constitutional drafting to constrain effectively judicial discretion through text. It also suggests that using broad, open-ended, and adaptable language to frame fundamental human rights commitments to enable, rather than to frustrate and to impede, the ability of judges to render decisions that the citizenry deems legitimate, might best secure such rights.

This is not to say that text is completely irrelevant—important reforms in British law can be traced directly to the enactment and coming into force of the HRA 98. *Campbell* provides a useful exemplar in this regard. Even if the HOL/SCUK did not use the HRA 98 and Article 8 of the European Convention to create a free-standing right of privacy, the scope of privacy rights, under the rubric of breach of confidence, expanded

74 ⌇ Free Speech as Civic Structure

significantly. One cannot gainsay that Article 8 played an important role in getting the HOL to rewrite the tort of breach of confidence to safeguard privacy.

It is to say, however, that, as Chief Justice Charles Evans Hughes, then Governor of New York, once observed, even in a polity that lives under a written constitution, the "Constitution is what the judges say it is."[37] The HRA 98 certainly provides a clear textual warrant for judicial consideration of rights protected under the European Convention. It also provides procedural mechanisms for the vindication of these rights[38] and authorizes effective judicial remedies for violations by public authorities.[39] It would, accordingly, go too far to characterize the HRA 98 as unimportant, much less irrelevant, to the protection of expressive freedom in the contemporary United Kingdom. The HRA 98 ratified the British judiciary's prior efforts to protect freedom of expression and, in a system that places parliamentary sovereignty at the apex of both constitutional and institutional values,[40] put judicial solicitude for speech rights on a firmer constitutional footing.[41] It did not, however, usher in a new Golden Age for the freedom of speech in the United Kingdom.

II. THE PRE-HRA 98 PUSH FOR A BRITISH BILL OF RIGHTS AND GROWING JUDICIAL SOLICITUDE FOR EXPRESSIVE FREEDOM CLAIMS

The expansion of the judicial role in safeguarding human rights in the United Kingdom has been a story of popular agitation and organizing followed by interstitial change— never a human rights revolution, more of an evolutionary process with the government, including Parliament and the courts, adopting modest reforms in response to growing public demands for a judicially enforceable written bill of rights. These small changes at the margins proved to be sufficient to meet the growing popular demands for major constitutional change; efforts to secure large-scale reform instead produced more modest constitutional modifications, but sufficient change to blunt the momentum of more radical changes to Britain's constitutional DNA (which incorporates a strong form of parliamentary sovereignty[42] and judicial self-restraint[43]). The story begins after World War II, with the United Kingdom quickly acceding to the European Convention on Human Rights (formally denominated "The Convention for the Protection of Human Rights and Fundamental Freedoms").

Sir Anthony Lester (1936-2020) spent his entire professional life seeking to advance the cause of civil rights and liberties in the United Kingdom. Along with prominent legal academics, such as Professor Ronald Dworkin, Lester helped generate the political pressure that led Parliament to enact the HRA 98 into law. Lester observed that, "[w]hen I came to the Bar some forty years ago [in 1966] there was no legally enforceable right to free expression in this country."[44] He hastened to add that although "[f]ree speech was a hallowed British political value" it held "an inferior status" as a matter of law "occupying the space left by manifold legal restrictions protecting official secrecy, personal reputation, confidential information, copyright, public decency, public order, and the right to a fair trial."[45] Thus, "[f]ree speech was a

The United Kingdom: Free Speech as a Sociolegal Norm   —◌ 75

weak residuary legatee of the English legal system, an exceptional freedom rather than a positive right."[46]

In the 1960s, "English courts gave too little weight to free speech and too much weight to the restrictions on free speech."[47] Parliament, in Lester's view, was largely indifferent to this state of affairs. Working with others in the civil rights community, he set about trying to upgrade the status of free speech and other fundamental rights in the United Kingdom.

The first step toward reform was the U.K.'s accession to the jurisdiction of the European Commission and the European Court of Human Rights. Before January 1966, British citizens could not bring their complaints to Strasbourg because the British government had refused to accept either the European Commission's or the European Court's jurisdiction over such complaints. Lester posited that the growing number of European Court decisions enforcing Article 10 began to force British judges to take speech claims more seriously. He explained that "a new generation of British judges, unhappy at their inability to give direct effect to Convention rights" instead proved "willing to do so indirectly."[48]

Over time, starting in the 1970s, "English courts gave more latitude to free speech and interpreted restrictions on speech more narrowly."[49] Judges in the United Kingdom engaged not only with decisions of the European Court, but also with case law "from the Supreme Court of the United States interpreting the right to free speech . . . and Commonwealth courts in Australia, Canada, India, New Zealand, and South Africa."[50] Lester cited the important libel decision of the HOL in *Reynolds v. Times Newspapers Ltd*[51] and the decision of the Court of Appeals in *Derbyshire County Council v. Times Newspapers Ltd*[52] as emblematic of the trend toward serious judicial engagement with free speech values.

It bears noting that *Reynolds*, decided in 2001, postdates the HRA 98. By way of contrast, however, *Derbyshire City Council*, which involved a city government attempting to sue a newspaper for libel over reportage critical of the city government, significantly predates the HRA 98. The fact that British courts had regard to European Convention rights in shaping the common law almost a decade before HRA 98 entered the scene is telling. In *Ex Parte Brind*, however, the HOL, in 1991, declared itself powerless to invalidate an administrative regulation that imposed a gag order on the press by banning direct coverage of statements from official representatives of the Irish Republican Army (IRA).[53] The HOL observed that the freedom of speech was of fundamental importance in a democracy, but concluded that it could not bring Article 10 to bear in a challenge to an administrative regulation that prohibited broadcasting content directly from representatives of the IRA.[54] Lester argues that "[t]he *Brind* case illustrated the pressing need for a Human Rights Act that would make the Convention rights part of our law and enable our courts to give effective remedies."[55]

For advocates of an entrenched compendium of fundamental human rights, like Sir Anthony, judicial decisions like *Brind* provided clear evidence, if any additional such evidence was required, that free speech as a legal right needed to be put on a more solid jurisprudential foundation. Lester, joined by prominent legal thinkers like Professor

Ronald Dworkin, continued to press for the adoption of a codified bill of rights that the domestic courts would have the power to enforce. Lester explained that "because of the doctrine of parliamentary supremacy, in the absence of any parliamentary mandate for the judicial use of the Convention, there were limits beyond which our courts refused to go."[56] But this analysis presumes that it was the absence of a parliamentary mandate, rather than a lack of judicial commitment, that explained the relatively weak status of freedom of expression in the United Kingdom. Suppose it was not the absence of a statutory mandate to consider free speech claims on the merits but rather the judicial attitude toward the permissibility and legitimacy of the government's speech regulations that was to blame?

In the 1990s, advocates of the adoption of a bill of rights pressed their case not in the courts of law, but rather in the court of public opinion. *A British Bill of Rights*, published in 1990 by a group of distinguished lawyers and legal academics, presented an extended argument in favor of the adoption of a codified bill of rights in the United Kingdom. As the joint authors stated their case in chief, "[t]o protect fundamental rights and freedoms from erosion by the 'tyranny of convenience,' we believe the time has come to set them out formally in a Bill of Rights and to entrench them as part of a written constitution."[57] Supporters of an entrenched, codified bill of rights, enforced through strong-form judicial review, sought to overturn the centuries-old doctrine of parliamentary sovereignty, a doctrine that holds courts must enforce, rather than second-guess, any statute that Parliament properly enacts. Adoption of this approach to enforcing fundamental human rights would constitute a constitutional revolution— both then and even now.

Acknowledging the highly entrenched British constitutional tradition of adherence to parliamentary sovereignty and reliance on the political process to protect fundamental rights, the joint authors straightforwardly conceded that "[w]e take a radically different view" and instead posited that "[r]epresentative government cannot work fairly or at all without certain agreed prior conditions or 'rules of the game.'"[58] In particular, "[t]here is not much point in holding elections if censorship prevents the electors from making a critical judgment of the government," thus rendering free speech "part of democracy's structure and not just an optional extra."[59]

Advocates of an entrenched, judicially enforceable bill of rights, including an express guarantee of freedom of expression, ultimately succeeded in building sufficient public support for the issue to serve as a central theme in the U.K.'s 1997 national parliamentary elections. The Labour Party's resounding electoral victory sent Tony Blair to No. 10 Downing Street as prime minister with a mandate to "bring human rights home." Figuring out the details of how to reconcile the United Kingdom's deeply rooted and long-standing commitment to parliamentary sovereignty with a new system of entrenched, judicially enforceable fundamental human rights remained to be worked out. Moreover, proponents of a domestic bill of rights probably should have invested more time, energy, and thought into how the existing British judges would approach their new duties under a domestic bill of rights. After all, it is not entirely clear why one could reasonably expect a deeply institutionally conservative institution, the British

The United Kingdom: Free Speech as a Sociolegal Norm   —⌐ 77

judiciary, to issue strikingly bold decisions vindicating European Convention rights. As the saying goes, "you can lead a horse to water, but you cannot make it drink."

III. THE ADVENT OF THE HRA 98: BRINGING FUNDAMENTAL HUMAN RIGHTS, INCLUDING EXPRESSIVE FREEDOMS, HOME

The growing calls for the codification and entrenchment of human rights clearly spurred Parliament to act—but these efforts paid other human rights dividends as well. Perhaps most importantly, organizing in support of domestic human rights reform also plainly caught the attention of judges—at least with respect to expressive freedom. Enactment of the HRA 98 constituted a very clear victory—albeit a *partial* one—for advocates of meaningful constitutional reform in the United Kingdom. Parliament's decision to incorporate the European Convention into domestic law constituted an undeniably important effort to respond to growing public pressure for an entrenched bill of rights that could be enforced in the domestic courts. At the same time, however, the HRA 98 constituted only a *modest* reform. Like earlier efforts by the government, the HRA 98 carefully avoided modifying the bedrock principle of the British constitution—namely, the principle of parliamentary sovereignty.[60]

In 1997, Tony Blair and the Labour Party campaigned, in part, on a pledge to incorporate the European Convention into British domestic law. In the party's electoral platform, the Labour Party argued that "[c]itizens should have statutory rights to enforce their human rights in the U.K. courts"[61] and, accordingly, "[w]e will by statute incorporate the European Convention into U.K. law to bring these rights home and allow our people access to them in their national courts."

The United Kingdom's reluctance to incorporate the European Convention into domestic law until 2000 is somewhat puzzling. The United Kingdom played a central role in the drafting of the European Convention and was the first nation to ratify it on March 8, 1951.[62] The treaty entered into force on September 3, 1953, when Luxembourg provided the tenth ratification.[63] The United Kingdom did not, however, accede to the jurisdiction of the European Commission or the European Court of Human Rights for another fifteen years.[64] K. R. Simmonds, writing contemporaneously about the decision of the British government to accede to the jurisdiction of the European Commission and European Court, observed that "it is a cause for satisfaction that the United Kingdom has at last, although with qualification, accepted the implications of her ratification of the Convention."[65]

Even so, however, the provisions of the European Convention were not formally part of the domestic law of the United Kingdom. As a ratified treaty, the domestic courts could consider its provisions when interpreting an ambiguous statute and, even then, only to the extent that the traditional tools of statutory construction did not preclude an interpretation that harmonized the provision with the requirements of the European Convention. However, as *Ex Parte Brind*[66] made crystal clear, the European Convention was not generally a part of domestic British law and could not directly serve as the basis for judicial protection of European Convention rights in the absence of further parliamentary action.

After securing a parliamentary majority for the Labour Party in the 1997 general elections, Prime Minister Tony Blair quickly made good on the party's promise to "bring home" the human rights secured by the European Convention. Adopted on November 9, 1998, the HRA 98 came into legal force around two years later on October 2, 2000.

The HRA 98 has three principal provisions. First, it instructs the domestic courts "[s]o far as it is possible to do so" to interpret "primary legislation and subordinate legislation" in a fashion "compatible with the Convention rights."[67] This provision does not empower the British courts to exercise a power of judicial review,[68] and instead merely authorizes a court to issue a "declaration of incompatibility" when a statutory directive cannot be reconciled with rights safeguarded under the European Convention.[69]

The HRA 98 also contains a more general provision, Section 6, that declares "[i]t is unlawful for a public authority to act in a way which is incompatible with a Convention right."[70] Once again, however, this provision expressly exempts executive or judicial actions compelled by a properly enacted statutory provision.[71] Nevertheless, Section 6 is highly important because courts constitute "public authorities"[72] and, accordingly, the U.K.'s domestic courts now labor under a duty to interpret and apply the common law in a fashion consistent with European Convention rights. When a public authority (including a court) acts in a way that violates a right safeguarded under the European Convention, a reviewing court "may grant such relief or remedy, or make such order, within its power as it considers just and appropriate."[73]

The HRA 98 contains a provision, Section 12, that, at least on its face, seems to instruct the U.K.'s domestic courts to give enhanced weight and importance to expressive freedom: "The court must have particular regard to the importance of Convention rights to freedom of expression."[74] A largely identical interpretative directive, set forth in Section 13, instructs the courts to "have particular regard" for the rights to "freedom of thought, conscience, and religion."[75] The British courts, however, have declined to interpret either Section 12 or Section 13 as requiring special solicitude for expressive freedom or rights of conscience.

Viewed from one perspective, this outcome is entirely understandable because the European Convention itself does not establish any absolute priority of human rights. Accordingly, when litigants appear at bar asserting conflicting human rights claims under the European Convention, a reviewing court has a duty to give effect to both rights rather than only to one. It is also the case that the HRA 98, in Section 3, instructs the domestic courts to interpret statutes and common law rules in a way that keeps Britain from breaching its European Convention duties—at least when it is possible to do so through a saving construction. Yet, the reason, or reasons, for affording Section 3 an absolute priority over Section 12 are far from self-evident.

Simply put, Parliament was perfectly entitled—and well within its constitutional authority under the doctrine of parliamentary sovereignty—to create a relative priority for selected European Convention-protected rights through domestic legislation. Moreover, it appears that Parliament has done precisely this in Sections 12 and 13 of the HRA 98. Accordingly, this statutory directive should convey a relative priority to speech and press rights, protected under Article 10, over other rights, including privacy rights, protected under Article 8. If taken seriously and applied fairly, the doctrine of parliamentary sovereignty, at least in theory, requires courts to implement in good faith a clear and express statutory directive—even if doing so might risk placing the United Kingdom in breach of its obligations under the European Convention.[76]

Despite possessing a very clear textual warrant—arguably a directive—for affording expressive freedom and rights of conscience a relative priority over other European Convention rights, the domestic British courts have flatly refused to chart this judicial course.[77] This is in and of itself a rather clear demonstration of the fact that text is not always effective at constraining judicial discretion. It bears noting that the courts, invoking the doctrine of the margin of appreciation, could give a relatively higher priority to speech and press rights over conflicting rights (such as privacy), without putting the United Kingdom in breach of its European Convention legal duties and obligations.

To be sure, in the context of the right of privacy, it is simply not possible meaningfully to safeguard the ability of a person to control how their image is disseminated within the community, which the ECtHR has indicated that Article 8 requires a signatory state to do,[78] with an absolute right of the press to publish such images if a newspaper's editorial staff deems the photograph newsworthy.[79] But even if Section 12(4) does not mandate an *absolute* priority (because such a priority would violate Section 3), it would still be quite possible to afford speech and press rights a *relative* priority. Yet, the British courts have not taken this approach. *Campbell v. MGN Limited* provides a particularly telling example of how the British courts have conveyed an absolute priority on enforcing Section 3, which requires U.K. law to be interpreted consistently with the European Convention and the ECtHR's precedents interpreting it, rather than Section 12, which instructs the domestic courts to have "particular regard" to expressive freedom claims.

In *Campbell*, the HOL did not deem the Article 10 speech and press claims as effectively precluding super model Naomi Campbell's ability to assert a privacy claim under Article 8 of the European Convention. Nor did the interpretative directive set forth in Section 12 alter this outcome. As Baron David Hope explained, "[t]he effect of these provisions [Articles 8 and 10] is that the right to privacy which lies at the heart of an action for breach of confidence has to be balanced against the right of the media to impart information to the public."[80] Moreover, "the right of the media to impart information to the public has to be balanced in its turn against the respect that must be given to private life."[81] Accordingly, and despite Section 12(4)'s admonition to the courts to have "particular regard" for expressive freedom, "you cannot have particular regard to article 10 without having equally particular regard at the very least to article 8" because "section 12(4) does not give either article pre-eminence over the other."[82]

This approach—not reading Section 12(4)'s interpretative directive to convey either an absolute or relative priority on speech and press rights over other European Convention rights—now constitutes very well-settled law. This in itself represents

80 ～ Free Speech as Civic Structure

a kind of judicial reconstruction of the HRA 98's text. After all, it would have been entirely plausible to interpret and apply Section 12 to require courts to put a thumb on the scale when a litigant properly invoked Article 10's protection of expressive freedom. Yet, this is not how the British judiciary proceeded. Rather than giving broad effect to Section 12, the courts have instead read the provision down, essentially ignoring it, by holding that it only requires judges to *consider* Article 10 rights—which Section 3 of the HRA 98 would have required of its own force and without the need for Section 12.

This construction renders Section 12(4) entirely superfluous and nugatory—in other words, meaningless. Rather than follow the plain language of the HRA 98's text, the courts instead followed the precedents of the ECtHR that require all rights protected by the European Convention to be taken into account and conflicts between rights to be resolved in a fashion that reconciles, rather than cancels out, the relevant but conflicting provisions. This approach effectively involves judicial amendment of the HRA 98 by rewriting Section 12(4) to require merely "consideration" rather than "particular regard" for speech and press rights safeguarded under Article 10 (language that plainly denotes giving some sort of relative priority for expressive freedom claims over other human rights claims, including privacy rights under Article 8). And, again, it would have been easy to enforce *both* Sections 3 and 12 by simply invoking the doctrine of the margin of appreciation to afford speech and press rights merely a relative or contingent priority—priority within the scope of discretion a European Convention signatory state enjoys to shape particular human rights in order to reflect local legal, cultural, political, and moral values.

One might wonder whether, and to what extent, Brexit has affected the HRA 98.[83] In point of fact, the United Kingdom's withdrawal from the European Union has not affected, at all, the legal status or operation of the HRA 98. To be sure, the Conservative Party, also known as the Tory Party or simply "the Tories," has routinely called for the repeal of the HRA 98 and its replacement with a "British Bill of Rights" that would more or less mirror the provisions of the European Convention. Professor Gardbaum, writing in 2013, noted that during the 2010 general elections, "the Conservative Party had pledged to repeal the HRA and replace it with a 'British bill of rights,' of undisclosed content and status."[84] Prime Minister David Cameron established a study commission to consider this question, but nothing ever came of it. A decade and four prime ministers later, the HRA 98 remains on the statute books. A House of Commons Library white paper details the various repeated (failed) "reform" efforts from 2010 to 2017.[85] Despite multiple efforts to secure passage of a "repeal and replace" bill, successive Conservative Party prime ministers proved unable to secure passage of new fundamental rights legislation.

In December 2021, the government, led by then-Prime Minister Boris Johnson, published a report advocating the repeal and replacement of the HRA 98 with a "British Bill of Rights."[86] The motivations for this review, and the development of a bill to replace the HRA 98 include "a concern that the HRA 98 may have drawn U.K. courts into ruling on issues better suited to political resolution" in addition to "concerns the Act undermines parliamentary sovereignty by requiring the courts to interpret U.K. legislation compatibly with Convention rights where possible."[87] The Johnson government's chancellor, Dominic Raab, made reform of the HRA 98 a priority issue and did his best to move the "reform" effort forward. Toward this end, Johnson's government introduced a bill in the House of Commons that would have replaced the HRA 98 with a purely domestic bill of rights.[88] It bears noting that this legislation would also have weakened the British judiciary's power to enforce European Convention-protected rights through creative saving constructions.

The Tory leadership's primary concerns appear to relate to Article 6 decisions involving procedural due process for noncitizens facing deportation and the use of Section 3 to rewrite statutes, arguably engaging in "judicial amendment of legislation" that involves "the courts displacing Parliament in determining questions of public policy."[89] Complaints about the operation of the HRA 98 also include fuzzier concerns about "the growth of a 'rights culture' that has displaced due focus on personal responsibility and the public interest."[90] Clearly, replacing Section 3 with a narrower power to harmonize domestic statutes with the European Convention and the ECtHR's governing case law has been, and remains, a political goal among some members of the Conservative Party's leadership.

Accordingly, on June 22, 2022, Johnson's government introduced a bill that would have repealed and replaced the HRA 98 with a domestic bill of rights. The Bill of Rights Act, had it been enacted into law, would have repealed Section 3 and reduced the obligation of the SCUK to consider governing ECtHR case law when adjudicating claims arising under the newly minted British Bill of Rights. The net effect of this legislation would have been to weaken the ability of the domestic courts to vindicate European Convention-protected rights by limiting their ability to use saving constructions—which, again, some in the Tory Party view as a form of impermissible judicial legislation. Perhaps ironically, the Bill of Rights Bill would have attempted once again to elevate the freedom of expression as an apex human right[91]—despite the failure of Section 12(4), the Johnson government wanted to try, try, again to upgrade the status of freedom of expression.

History repeated itself, however—after the government introduced the bill on June 22, 2022, and the House of Commons gave it a first reading, the Conservative Party's leadership scuttled the bogus "reform" effort. On September 7, 2022, Prime Minister Liz Truss suspended further proceedings on the pending legislation. Less than a year later, Prime Minister Rishi Sunak's government unceremoniously withdrew the bill from further consideration on June 27, 2023.[92] Weakening judicial protection of fundamental human rights turned out to be a significantly heavier legislative lift than the U.K.'s withdrawal from the European Union. With the withdrawal of the Bill of Rights Bill, the continuing validity of the HRA 98 is no longer open to serious question. To be sure, good arguments exist for indigenizing the rights set forth in the European Convention and also taking greater advantage of the ECtHR's doctrine of the margin of appreciation to localize the scope and meaning of fundamental human rights in the United Kingdom.

The main problem with the failed Bill of Rights Bill inhered in the (numerous) provisions aimed at weakening the judiciary's ability to enforce and protect fundamental rights—rather than with efforts to better tailor those rights to take into account Britain's distinctive sociolegal culture. All of the so-called reform efforts aimed at repealing and replacing the HRA 98 have involved clear efforts to make it harder for judges to enforce protected rights through meaningful remedies. Advocates of the legislation claimed to be doing one thing (localizing human rights and indigenizing them)—but were clearly up to something else (ensuring that members of Parliament, not the judges, enjoy the last word on the meaning of statutes).

The bottom line: For the time being, the HRA 98 and the U.K.'s participation in the European Convention system of safeguarding fundamental human rights have survived Brexit and repeated efforts over time, by five prime ministers and counting, to weaken the role of the courts in protecting human rights under the HRA 98. Moreover, no active effort to repeal and replace the HRA 98 currently is pending before Parliament. Given the various economic and social service crises presently facing the incumbent Sunak government, taking away the people's fundamental rights by weakening the ability of the domestic courts to protect them would seem a misguided legislative priority.

All of the ersatz reform efforts have failed, to date at least, because taking away people's fundamental rights is not a politically popular thing to do in the contemporary United Kingdom. As the Law Society's president, Lubna Shuja, observed after the Sunak government abandoned the most recent 2022–2023 reform effort to repeal the HRA 98 and replace it with a weaker protection for Convention-protected rights in British domestic law, "[s]crapping the Bill is the right decision as it would have created an acceptable class of human rights abuses, weakened individual rights and seen the U.K. diverge from our international human rights obligations."[93] On this front, at least for the time being, the judges clearly hold the stronger hand. It seems likely that the United Kingdom will continue to enforce European Convention rights directly as part of domestic law—and this will include expressive freedom, safeguarded under Article 10(1).

IV. EXPRESSIVE FREEDOM IN THE UNITED KINGDOM AFTER THE HRA 98 COMES INTO FORCE: PLUS ÇA CHANGE, PLUS C'EST LA MÊME CHOSE

The HRA's codification of Article 10 of the European Convention created, for the first time, an express guarantee of freedom of expression. Article 10 provides that:

> Everyone has the right to freedom of expression. This right shall include freedom to hold opinions and to receive and impart information and ideas without interference by public authority and regardless of frontiers. This Article shall not prevent States from requiring the licensing of broadcasting, television or cinema enterprises.[94]

Like all European Convention rights, however, signatory states may burden or even completely abridge protected rights if they can demonstrate a sufficiently important

The United Kingdom: Free Speech as a Sociolegal Norm ⟶ 83

reason for doing so and that the means used to achieve the government's important interest(s) are sufficiently narrowly tailored to achieve it:

> The exercise of these freedoms, since it carries with it duties and responsibilities, may be subject to such formalities, conditions, restrictions or penalties as are prescribed by law and are necessary in a democratic society, in the interests of national security, territorial integrity or public safety, for the prevention of disorder or crime, for the protection of health or morals, for the protection of the reputation or rights of others, for preventing the disclosure of information received in confidence, or for maintaining the authority and impartiality of the judiciary.[95]

Thus, a two-step analysis governs adjudication of European Convention claims. At the first step, a litigant must successfully invoke a Convention-protected right by proving that it has been abridged or denied. At step two, assuming the rights claimant meets this burden of production, the offending government may attempt to show that the restriction or abridgement is permissible. Called "proportionality analysis," this kind of open-ended balancing is commonplace in most of the democratic world (although not in the contemporary United States).[96]

As Professor Vicki Jackson has explained, "[i]f you have not heard of [the proportionality doctrine], that is because the concept has received far more elaboration and evaluation outside the United States."[97] Despite its lack of salience in U.S. human rights jurisprudence, then-Professor and now-Judge Grant Huscroft and his coauthors correctly observe that "[i]t is no exaggeration to claim that proportionality has overtaken rights as the orienting idea in contemporary human rights law and scholarship."[98]

The U.K.'s jurisprudential tradition is actually closer—much closer—to the U.S. approach than to the rest of Europe's approach when it comes to reliance on proportionality analysis. The kind of open-ended balancing of rights and government interests central to the application of proportionality analysis was largely, if not quite completely, foreign to English law before the HRA 98 came into force.[99] The English and Welsh common law, and legal tradition more generally, is much more formal and rule-bound than is typical of much post-World War II continental jurisprudence under both the European Convention and the European Union's Charter of Fundamental Rights.[100]

As Professors P. S. Atiyah and Robert Summers have explained, "English judges typically think of a legal rule as not including the values, purposes, rationales, except insofar as these are (more or less) explicitly incorporated in the rule"[101] and "[t]he version of stare decisis which prevails in England today is somewhat less strict than the version which [once] operated . . . but is still very strict by modern American standards."[102] Having judges engage in open-ended policy analysis is anathema—ascertaining and then reconciling conflicting social, moral, and legal interests is a task for Parliament, not the courts, to undertake.[103]

The POA 86[104] provides a useful case study on how the HRA 98 did not fundamentally change the status of freedom of speech as a constitutional interest in the United

Kingdom. As will be explained in some detail, from a U.S. perspective, the POA 86 is deeply problematic because it empowers police officers to enforce a heckler's veto over unpopular speakers, thereby squelching speech that average citizens find opprobrious.

The POA 86 replaced a prior statute, the Public Order Act 1936. Both laws exist to provide police officers with legal authority to arrest speakers when, under the facts and circumstances, speech seems likely to bring about a breach of the peace. Until 2013, Section 5 of the POA 86 proscribed using "threatening, abusive, or insulting words or behavior"[105] in public or the display of "any writing, sign, or other visible representation which is threatening, abusive, or insulting."[106] The POA 86 includes a *mens rea* element. In order to be guilty of an offense under Section 5(1), the defendant must "intend[ ] his words or behaviour, or the writing, sign or other visible representation, to be threatening, abusive, or insulting" or be "aware that it may be threatening, abusive, or insulting or (as the case may be) he intends his behaviour to be or is aware that it may be disorderly."[107]

A Section 5 offense does not require the government to prove that a person was actually threatened or abused; it is sufficient to show that, were a person belonging to a targeted group present, that person *might* feel threatened or abused.[108] A defendant facing charges under Section 5 may avoid liability if the person can establish that "he had no reason to believe that there was any person within hearing or sight who was likely to be caused harassment, alarm or distress,"[109] that the statement was made or the sign was displayed inside a private home,[110] or "that his conduct was reasonable."[111]

Decisions about whether speech or displays constitute "threatening, abusive, or insulting" speech are questions of fact rather than law.[112] To be sure, the HOL opined in *Brutus* that mere offense was not sufficient to make out a violation of Section 5. The case involved an anti-apartheid protest during the annual Wimbledon tennis match and the defendant's conviction was overturned. However, because the question is purely one of fact, rather than a mixed question of fact and law, it is difficult for a defendant to appeal an adverse determination on this front.[113] Although the *Brutus* interpretation of the scope of Section 5 is speech protective, the characterization of the determination of the defendant's speech as "threatening" or "abusive" as one solely of fact is most definitely *not*.

By way of contrast, in the United States, under the First Amendment's Free Speech Clause, fact questions in First Amendment cases are not uncommonly subject to de novo review on appeal in order to prevent juries from squelching unpopular speech and thereby silencing unpopular speakers.[114] As Justice John Paul Stevens explained in *Bose Corporation*, "[t]he question whether the evidence in the record in a defamation case is of the convincing clarity required to strip the utterance of First Amendment protection is not merely a question for the trier of fact."[115] Instead, "[j]udges, as expositors of the Constitution, must independently decide whether the evidence in the record is sufficient to cross the constitutional threshold that bars the entry of any judgment that is not supported by clear and convincing proof of 'actual malice.' "[116] Unfortunately, however, things do not work in this fashion. Under the POA 86's Section 5, a trial judge's characterization of the speech is, for most intents and purposes, final. Unless the trial court's fact finding is clearly erroneous, an appellate court will disturb it.

The United Kingdom: Free Speech as a Sociolegal Norm 85

To be sure, Section 5 penalties are admittedly far from draconian. The statute does not authorize imprisonment and only permits the imposition of modest fines by way of punishment. Fines for proven Section 5 violations typically run from £100–£300—hardly a bankrupting amount. Thus, no one is being packed off to prison to serve a multiyear sentence for a speech crime under Section 5. That said, the statute's most pernicious effect does not inhere in the potential punishments it authorizes for violations, but rather in the vast, essentially unfettered discretionary authority that the law conveys on police officers to shut down speech activity in public.

In 2013, the HOL sought to strike the words "insulting" from both Sections 5(1) and 6(3).[117] The government agreed to this amendment—largely because the Director of Public Prosecutions informed then-Home Secretary Theresa May that no successful prosecutions existed for "insulting" speech or displays that could not have been successfully prosecuted for being merely "abusive."[118] The current version of the statute accordingly prohibits only "threatening" and "abusive" language and displays. That said, the deletion of merely "insulting" speech from Section 5's coverage was largely cosmetic because "abusive" speech encompasses "insulting" speech as well.

Section 5's arguably most objectionable aspect is that it provides a mechanism for police to arrest public protestors if a police officer believes that speech or displays contain "threatening" or "abusive" content. The statute obviously empowers police to squelch public protest if a cop on the beat deems speech or the display of a sign to present a risk of giving offense. As Professor Barendt explains, even though "[t]he provision was primarily intended to deal with hooligans who, say, pester and alarm people late at night" the statute "can be used to penalize the exercise of protest rights."[119] For example, "[t]he term 'disorderly conduct' could be applied to symbolic speech such as the burning of flags or effigies."[120] This is certainly so; Section 5 has been used to successfully prosecute antiwar protestors who burned paper poppies on Armistice Day proximate to a parade featuring military personnel as well as to a teenager who posted a poppy-burning video on Facebook.[121] Barendt warns that "unless it [Section 5] is appropriately interpreted and applied by the courts in conformity with the right to freedom of expression, the legislation significantly restricts freedom to protest."[122]

Prosecutions under Section 5 after the HRA 98 came into force include charges for displaying signs with homophobic[123] and Islamophobic content.[124] Police arrests, without subsequent prosecution on POA 86 charges, also have taken place based on a drunken college student asking a police officer "if he realized that his horse was gay," a teenager's anti-Church of Scientology protest proximate to the church's London headquarters, and for Innkeepers who allegedly made comments critical of Islam to a guest who belonged to the faith.[125] More recently, Section 5 served as a basis for arresting protestors who sought to disseminate antimonarchy, pro-republic sentiments during public ceremonies marking the death of Queen Elizabeth II[126] and the coronation of King Charles III.[127]

The case of antiwar protestors Mohammad Haque and Emdadur Choudhury is particularly telling. They were arrested, tried, and convicted of violating Section 5 after they chanted "British soldiers burn in hell" on Armistice Day (November 11) in 2010.

86 ⌒ Free Speech as Civic Structure

At the appointed memorial hour of 11:00 AM, they began their chant outside the Royal Geographical Society, in central London, as part of a "Muslims against Crusaders" (MAC) protest.[128] The trial judge, Chief Magistrate Judge Harold Riddle, reports that "[a]fter almost exactly two minutes, what appears to be two large plastic orange poppies are placed at the centre front of the MAC demonstration and set on fire."[129] The government did not present any evidence, at all, of an actual disturbance associated with the MAC protest and poppy burning. Even so, both Haque and Choudhury were convicted of Section 5 offenses because their protest offended the sensibilities of the dominant cultural group in the United Kingdom.

Judge Riddle explains that "[t]he ceasefire at 11am on 11 November 1918 has huge significance for most people in this country" and "[t]he event has been marked annually for the past 90 years or so."[130] Using Poppy Day for an antiwar protest was "bound to be seen as insulting" and "is behavior likely to cause distress" as well as "harassment or alarm."[131] He muses that "[i]t may be that using insulting behavior likely to cause distress when people are gathered publicly to remember the dead is itself justification for invoking the criminal law, to protect the rights of others."[132] Accordingly, "invoking the criminal law to interfere with freedom of expression [was] proportionate" and the conviction of the defendants was consistent with the imperatives of Article 10(1) of the European Convention. Although Parliament amended Section 5 (in 2013) to remove the word "insulting" from the law, it is doubtful that the outcome on the same facts would be any different today; the trial judge would simply have to recharacterize the offending speech as being potentially "abusive" rather than "insulting."

Displaying signs opposing homosexuality or gay marriage is also a basis for a successful Section 5 prosecution.[133] On October 13, 2001, Harry Hammond displayed anti-LGBTQ signs in a public square.[134] These signs bore the messages "Stop Immorality," "Stop Homosexuality," and "Stop Lesbianism."[135] Hammond's protest did generate an angry crowd of "30 to 40 people" who were "arguing and shouting; some people in the crowd were angry, others were aggressive or distressed."[136] Hammond was convicted and this conviction was sustained on appeal by the High Court of Justice.[137]

To be clear, the absence of any public unrest is not a sufficient factor to defeat a Section 5 prosecution.[138] In *Abdul*, police arrested protestors opposed to the United Kingdom's participation in the wars in Iraq and Afghanistan. The protest took place proximate to a military parade in Luton, England, on March 10, 2009. Among the statements that served as the basis for the prosecution were "British soldiers are murderers," "Baby killers," "Rapists all of you," "Terrorists," "British soldiers go to hell," and similar sentiments.[139] The soldiers reported that they "had not been bothered 'one jot' by the demonstration."[140] Even so, the High Court of Justice sustained the Section 5 convictions, reasoning "that the soldiers themselves were, as it happened, broad-shouldered enough not to care one jot does not matter; it was, in any case, unsurprising that attending well-wishers were offended and insulted and provoked."[141] The risk of potential disorder justified silencing the protest and imposing criminal punishment on the protestors.[142]

These judicial outcomes are no different from earlier decisions under Section 5 that predate the advent of the HRA 98. Thus, in the 1990s, anti-abortion protestors were

The United Kingdom: Free Speech as a Sociolegal Norm   —⌒ 87

arrested, tried, and convicted of Section 5 offenses.[143] However, nothing really changed after the HRA 98 entered the scene. As Professor Anthony Geddis observes, "even though the coming into force of the HRA might have been expected to reduce the potential rigour of s. 5 as it applies to individual dissenters, it continues to be used against such expression."[144]

The primary difficulty with Section 5, Professor Geddis posits, is that "expressive behavior by those wishing to challenge established social mores or beliefs, or to make public their views on controversial matters, can easily fall afoul of the provision."[145] Indeed, "a literal reading of s. 5 covers an extraordinarily wide range of potential expression."[146] Accordingly, if a would-be speaker wishes to express "controversial opinions about matters of public interest," that person runs the risk of arrest and prosecution under Section 5.[147] This was true before the HRA 98 came into effect—and unfortunately it remains true today, almost thirty years later. And, at least arguably, Section 12(4) of the HRA 98 mandates a more speech-protective approach than prevailed before the HRA 98 took effect in the context of Section 5 of the POA 86.[148]

One might argue that lower court opinions applying Section 5 of the POA 86 do not serve as sufficient proof that free speech law in the United Kingdom did not shift in favor of would-be speakers after the enactment and coming into force of the HRA 98. However, decisions of the HOL, just like the trial court decisions involving the POA 86, fail to reflect any significant enhancement in the scope or status of freedom of expression. In particular, the HOL's decision in *ProLife Alliance*[149] provides a quite telling example of the legal status of freedom of speech remaining more or less unchanged under the HRA 98. It also provides clear evidence that, after the HRA 98, British courts remained broadly deferential to both Parliament and the executive branch when litigants challenged statutes, regulations, or policies that burdened or completely abridged speech.

ProLife Alliance involved a challenge, on Article 10 free speech grounds, to a U.K. statute that banned the broadcast of offensive speech—more specifically, the Broadcasting Act 1990 prohibited the BBC and other U.K. broadcasters from "include[ing] in its programmes [any content] which offends against good taste or decency or is likely to encourage or incite to crime or to lead to disorder or to be offensive to public feeling."[150] "Good taste or decency" is hardly self-defining; the language provides U.K. broadcasters with broad discretion to censor speech based on its content. In 2003, Parliament repealed and replaced the Broadcasting Act 1990 with the Communications Act 2003.[151] Among the many revisions to U.K. telecommunications law and policy was the adoption of Section 319, which replaced the "good taste or decency" language with a proscription against the broadcast of content that is "offensive and harmful."[152] Advertising, presumably including political advertising, may not be broadcast if it contains material that is "misleading, harmful or offensive."[153]

In *ProLife Alliance*, the HOL had to decide whether the BBC could lawfully refuse to air a political party's election broadcasts because it featured graphic and gruesome depictions of aborted fetuses and therefore would offend the BBC's viewers.[154] ProLife Alliance took the position that, as a recognized political party vested with

88 ☙ Free Speech as Civic Structure

government-sponsored television advertising time, it had the legal discretion to craft and disseminate whatever electoral messages it wished to disseminate. The BBC, by way of contrast, argued that it had a responsibility under the Broadcasting Act 1990 not to air any content, even in an election campaign advertisement, that violated the "good taste" or "decency" restrictions in Section 6.

ProLife Alliance's entire raison d'être involved waging general public and electoral "campaigns for 'absolute respect for innocent human life from fertilisation until natural death'" and "[a]mong its principal policies is the prohibition of abortion."[155] In May 2001, ProLife Alliance qualified for government-sponsored campaign advertising associated with the June 2001 general elections.[156] Lord Nicholls of Birkenhead explained that the party's "transmission was scheduled for a little under five minutes" and "[e]arly in May 2001 ProLife Alliance submitted a tape of its proposed broadcast to BBC, ITV, Channel 4 and Channel 5."[157] The ad "devoted to explaining the processes involved in different forms of abortion, with prolonged and graphic images of the product of suction abortion: aborted foetuses in a mangled and mutilated state, tiny limbs, a separated head, and the like," content that Lord Nicholls characterized as "deeply disturbing" and as "distressing, even harrowing."[158] The BBC refused to air ProLife Alliance's electoral advertisement unless and until the graphic images of the aborted fetuses were excised.[159] ProLife Alliance sued the BBC and, after losing before the trial court, prevailed before the Court of Appeal, which found that the BBC could not, consistent with Article 10 and Section 3 of the HRA, censor ProLife Alliance's core political speech.[160] The HOL granted the BBC leave to appeal and reversed, finding that the BBC's actions not only did not violate Article 10 of the European Convention, but, furthermore, that ProLife Alliance did not even possess a viable claim to the freedom of speech in the first place.[161]

Lord Hoffman observed that "[t]he fact that no one has a right to broadcast on television does not mean that article 10 has no application to such broadcasts" but "[i]nstead of being a right not to be prevented from expressing one's opinions, it becomes a right to fair consideration for being afforded the opportunity to do so; a right not to have one's access to public media denied on discriminatory, arbitrary or unreasonable grounds."[162] This conclusion makes no sense when the government had vested ProLife Alliance with a right to engage in political advertising, using state-owned broadcast facilities, as part of a general election.

Professor Barendt hit the jurisprudential nail on the head when he argues that "[t]he House of Lords decision showed scant regard for freedom of speech."[163] As he explains, even if, as a general matter, no person or organization has a general right to use state-owned broadcast facilities, this "does not mean that freedom of speech is not guaranteed in this context, at least for those who are licensed or given access to broadcast."[164] In his view, "[t]he House of Lords should have construed the broadcasting legislation, as HRA 1998, s 3 requires, not to interfere with freedom of political expression."[165] This was, of course, precisely the approach that the Court of Appeal took—but which the HOL rejected by a 4–1 vote of the panel.[166]

It is difficult to see what difference—if any—the HRA 98 made to the HOL's reasoning and analysis in *ProLife Alliance*. The decision, like the lower court decisions sustaining POA 86 Section 5 convictions based on core political speech,[167] elevates the community's interest in being free of unwanted speech above the interest of would-be speakers in communicating their preferred message to others as they think best. The British courts' willingness to sustain the application of mandatory civility norms did not change, at all, with the advent of the HRA 98. In a democracy, in which a process of democratic deliberation is supposed to facilitate the casting of well-informed ballots on election day, a political party and its members should be free to make their case to the voters in whatever fashion they wish—even if their speech is unlikely to be efficacious in moving public opinion.[168] The government should not be in the position of deciding either what ideas the body politic may lawfully hear or to censor how those ideas are expressed.

V. FREE SPEECH AS A COMMON LAW CONSTITUTIONAL RIGHT IN THE UNITED KINGDOM

The United Kingdom maintains a mass participatory democracy—and the freedom of speech is essential to the process of democratic deliberation that animates the project of self-government. Accordingly, it was probably not possible for the U.K.'s domestic courts to ignore the effects of statutes and regulations on the process of democratic deliberation. As Sir Anthony Lester posits, "[f]ree speech is the lifeblood of democracy."[169] Along similar lines, Helena Kennedy argues that "[f]ree speech is one of the core values in a democracy and it should be championed with a vengeance."[170] It should come as no surprise, then, that judges in the United Kingdom have expressed their solicitude for the freedom of speech in published judicial opinions with great regularity over the past fifty or so years.[171]

This does not mean that litigants with free speech claims invariably win—but they do get a careful hearing and a clear explanation of why the government should prevail in applying a legal rule that inhibits or proscribes speech. More often than not, British courts will sustain speech regulations designed to protect the sensibilities of an involuntary audience—including restrictions on both hate speech and mandatory civility norms. Speaker autonomy regarding how best to convey a message tends to get short shrift—particularly in the context of the POA 86. Highly offensive speech—such as burning paper poppies on Decoration Day—even if clearly political in nature, is not reliably protected in today's United Kingdom.

The mass arrests of antimonarchy protestors by London's municipal police on the day of King Charles III's coronation provided a useful, and telling, exclamation point on this reality[172] and that the police had given a green light to the protests before arresting the pro-republic protestors adds insult to injury. So too, antimonarchy protestors found themselves arrested, rather than tolerated, during Queen Elizabeth II's state funeral. Arrests of protestors advocating abolition of the monarchy and the creation of a constitutional republic are of a piece with the arrests (and convictions) of antiwar protestors burning paper poppies on Decoration Day. Even with the word "insulting" excised from the Section 5 of the POA 86 in 2013, the remaining legal proscriptions against "threatening" and, in particular, "abusive" speech, give law enforcement officers more than sufficient discretion to silence the public expression of unpopular forms of dissenting speech.

It would be unthinkable in the United States for a federal judge to sustain the silencing of a protestor because the judge deemed the speaker's message abusive, and hence unpersuasive, to the targeted audience. Yet, British judges, at all levels of the court system, seem perfectly comfortable advising speakers about how best to frame their arguments to convince their countrymen of the wisdom and righteousness of their respective causes. Even if speech might be entirely counterproductive, as a means of successfully moving public opinion, speaker autonomy constitutes a core component of the constitutional protection of expressive freedom. Contemporary British law does not do a very good job either of recognizing or vindicating this bedrock free speech value. The HRA 98 could have changed this state of affairs—but that is not how things have turned out.

From a U.S. perspective, measures of this sort are deeply problematic because they vest the government with broad, discretionary authority to select free speech winners and losers. Also deeply problematic, again from a U.S. perspective, is the notion that the government can dictate to a would-be speaker how and when to speak their version of truth to power.

This openness to government content- and viewpoint-based speech restrictions has led some U.K. academics to question whether the freedom of speech is adequately protected—particularly for unpopular dissenting voices advocating offensive or controversial public policy positions. For example, Professor Eric Barendt posits that "English law has traditionally taken little or no notice of freedom of speech."[173] And, in many material respects, this claim is unobjectionable if a commitment to freedom of speech means having judges prevent the government from adopting regulations that target speech based on its content and/or viewpoint.

Nevertheless, even Barendt concedes that "the courts in England, particularly over the past thirty years, have sometimes suggested that the common law did recognize the freedom of speech, and have also held that the right could be invoked to shape the interpretation and development of both statutory and common law."[174] He posits that the absence of a formal free speech guarantee made the protection of expressive freedom unpredictable and created an unfortunate chilling effect.[175] Barendt expresses "doubt whether the HRA has had a very radical impact on the legal protection of freedom of expression."[176] By way of explanation, he adds that "we know that legislation rarely brings about the consequences that it intends to achieve."[177]

I think it is probably a mistake to fault the HRA 98 rather than the judges who staff the domestic courts of the United Kingdom for the relatively tepid judicial efforts to safeguard unpopular dissenters. Indeed, it might well be the case that, had Parliament vested the SCUK with a full power of judicial review, the Justices would have either abjured using the power completely or used it very sparingly (like the Supreme Court of Japan[178]). The assumption that judges who do not view it as their business to engage and decide major questions of social policy would respond with alacrity to a newfound statutory grant of power to engage in such behavior fails to take into account the institutional realities of the British judiciary.

Professor Dominic McGoldrick argues that, by the early 1990s, "there had clearly been much greater judicial receptivity" to consideration of fundamental human rights, reflected in "greater weight being accorded to the ECHR and notions of fundamental rights in statutory interpretation, developments in the scope and application of judicial review post-*Brind*, the development of the common law as a reflection of ECHR rights, informing the exercise of judicial discretion, reviewing the exercise of powers conferred for the purpose of bringing the law into line with the ECHR, the 'most anxious scrutiny' applied in cases involving the liberty of individuals, and understanding of the concept of irrationality that took it close to, if not indistinguishable from, one of proportionality, and a striking increase in 'extra-judicial' writings on human rights and in favour of incorporation."[179] In his view, the British courts had effectively domesticated the European Convention before Parliament made things official with the HRA 98.

Despite having a less dyspeptic perspective on the human rights decisions of the U.K. courts, McGoldrick actually arrives, more or less, at the exact same place as Professor Barendt: "To the not insignificant extent that UK courts had been treating the ECHR as *de facto* incorporated, for example, as reflected in the common law and in reviewing the exercise of an administrative discretion which affects the liberty of the individual, then giving 'further effect' will not make much practical difference."[180] Thus, he argues that the British courts had more or less done what they were going to do before the HRA 98 entered into force. This view seems quite plausible based on the consistency of results in free speech cases decided before and after October 2, 2000 (the date that the HRA 98 took effect).

Anthony Lester and his coauthors, in *A British Bill of Rights*, fully anticipated the problem of courts not applying a codified bill of rights in a strong, much less maximalist, fashion. They wrote that "[o]pponents of the incorporation of the European Convention into domestic law, and of the enactment of a free-standing Bill of Rights, often argue that British judges are not qualified by their training or experience to interpret and apply broadly phrased, open-textured documents of this kind."[181] What is more, skeptics posited that "British judges would be likely to adopt restrictive interpretations of basic rights and freedoms, giving too much leeway to governments and public authorities by a loose interpretation of the exception clauses."[182] Lester and his coauthors readily and cheerfully conceded that "[i]t is undoubtedly true that British judges have interpreted the law in significant cases in a way which has restricted individual rights and freedoms."[183]

Turning the argument that British judges would not be much inclined to enforce rights provisions aggressively on its head, Lester and company posit that "[i]t is clearly unlikely that an incorporated Bill of Rights would make the judges any less sensitive to fundamental rights and freedoms than they may now be."[184] At the same time, however, they acknowledged the existence of a "well founded concern that the narrow social and professional base from which the judiciary is drawn would be reflected in the decisions reached on some of the controversial issues likely to be raised under a Bill of Rights."[185] In other words, simply adopting a written bill of rights will not, perforce, lead to a revolutionary transformation in the behavior of judges who are fearful of overstepping their proper institutional role in a constitutional system that embraces parliamentary sovereignty as its highest institutional value.[186] As the saying goes, you can lead a horse to water, but you cannot make the horse drink it.

Writing in 2001, at the dawn of the HRA 98 era, Professor McGoldrick posited that the effects of the incorporation of the European Convention into domestic law "will be shaped, *inter alia*, by accidents of litigation, the personnel who make a significant input to its evolution at critical junctures, the degree to which it enters into the sociocultural consciousness of the community and its constituent parts, the training and education provided to those directly affected by it, and its more general educative role, perhaps in the context of teaching about citizenship."[187] In the absence of a "'sympathetic legal climate,'" simply codifying a laundry list of fundamental human rights will not necessarily result in stronger and more effective protection of those rights.[188] In short, legal culture matters to the efficacy of any particular effort at codifying rights—and the judicial legal culture in the United Kingdom is not particularly receptive to judges enforcing vaguely worded human rights guarantees that also happen to require open-ended balancing exercises when the government seeks to enforce a rule notwithstanding its adverse effects on a right protected under the European Convention.

Lester and his coauthors ultimately share McGoldrick's view that institutional players and design will prefigure, to a great extent, the efficacy of any effort to entrench human rights through codification and judicial enforcement. They explain that "[r]ights can scarcely be enforced or protected unless there is some degree of consensus in support of them."[189] They nevertheless embrace the codification of rights because a bill of rights "will help to make a reality of rights which are now recognized in principle but frequently disregarded in practice."[190] The "Bill of Rights will also be a rallying point for all who care for human freedom" and "British democracy will be strengthened as a result."[191]

However, there's clearly a gap in the syllogism: if judges are hostile or indifferent to enforcing a bill of rights, every reason would exist to predict that it would serve as little more than a mere "parchment barrier" (to use James Madison's excellent turn of phrase). In a letter to Thomas Jefferson, Madison argued that "experience proves the inefficacy of a bill of rights on those occasions when its controul is most needed."[192] He observed that "[r]epeated violations of these parchment barriers have been committed by overbearing majorities in every State" and such violations would likely occur at the federal level as well because "[w]herever the real power in a Government lies, there is the danger of oppression" and "[w]herever there is an interest and power to do wrong,

The United Kingdom: Free Speech as a Sociolegal Norm —o 93

wrong will generally be done."[193] In other words, in the absence of a legal culture that takes rights seriously, simply adopting a written compendium of rights probably will not do much good in securing those rights.

The United Kingdom has a broad and general commitment to protecting the freedom of speech. At the same time, however, it also maintains a serious commitment to creating and enforcing mandatory civility norms. When speech and social norms conflict, social norms more often than not will prevail.[194] This was true before the HRA 98 came into effect and it remains true today. What is more, the British courts have not done a particularly good job of explaining precisely how judges would attempt to reconcile the individual's autonomy interest in self-expression with the community's legitimate authority to treat rude or offensive speech as a kind of public nuisance and then regulate or proscribe it.[195]

Professor Ian Cram, for example, argues that "domestic free speech/public order law lacks in general terms a theorised account in the jurisprudence about why controversial and unpopular forms of expression might be worth protecting."[196] Anthony Geddis makes a very similar point, characterizing the U.K. approach as "pro-civility" and positing that under this approach "the state legitimately can require that anyone wishing to espouse or discuss matter of general public or political interest respect the sensibilities of others, and act in a fashion that preserves a measure of decorum in society as a whole."[197] This understanding of the freedom of political speech writes off offensive and insulting public speech as possessing "limited social utility" and as ineffective in any case because "in practice [such] expression has minimal efficacy as it is not fitted to lead to a large-scale change in attitudes."[198]

One could easily relate the HOL's controversial decision in *ProLife Alliance* to this understanding of the freedom of speech.[199] The HOL, in a 4–1 division, upheld the BBC's decision to refuse to broadcast ProLife Alliance's election-related speech because it would have featured gruesome images of aborted fetuses. The main opinion, by Lord Leonard Hoffman, did not take ProLife's right to speak as it wished as particularly important or as seriously implicating the freedom of speech because no one has an absolute right to use the government's broadcasting facilities to propagate a message.[200] Although the statute regulating content on the BBC subsequently has been amended to use the language "offensive and harmful" rather than "taste and decency," as with the deletion of the word "insulting" from Section 5 of the POA 86, this is largely a distinction without a difference. Mandatory civility norms still govern access to the BBC's broadcast stations and even core electoral speech is subject to censorship if the BBC's producers and editors deem the proposed political broadcast material unduly offensive.

Professor Barendt is strongly critical of the HOL's *ProLife Alliance* decision and argues that a robust commitment to the freedom of speech requires a democratic society to tolerate speech that it deems to be offensive (and even highly so).[201] As he states his case, "[f]reedom of expression is at issue whenever the object of a law or other rule is to suppress or restrict the dissemination of some idea, rather than to achieve some end divorced from the communication of a particular message, say to stop the spread of litter or to preserve the peace of a residential neighborhood."[202] In my view, Barendt's criticisms are well stated and highly persuasive, but this may simply reflect my Americanized understanding of speech—and an analytical approach that essentially zeroes out the social cost of speech when determining whether it should be protected. For what it is worth, within the United States this is the dominant position and embraced with brio by ordinary citizens and federal judges alike.

Thus, in the United States, the Supreme Court has squarely held that "one man's vulgarity is another's lyric."[203] Justice John Marshall Harlan's paean to the freedom of speech in *Cohen v. California*, a case involving Paul R. Cohen wearing a jacket emblazoned with the phrase "Fuck the Draft" while in public at a Los Angeles, California courthouse,[204] serves as perhaps the best and most paradigmatic exemplar of U.S. hostility to government efforts to impose mandatory civility norms to protect the sensibilities of the general public.[205] Based on his idiosyncratic sartorial choice, Cohen was arrested, tried, and convicted under a California statute that prohibited "disturbing the peace"[206]—essentially on grounds that more or less mirror the grounds of a POA 86 Section 5 prosecution in today's United Kingdom. The Supreme Court, by a 5–4 vote, reversed Cohen's conviction on First Amendment grounds.[207] The *Cohen* decision nicely encapsulates a very widely held, and widely shared, U.S. understanding of the central role that free speech plays in a democratic polity.[208]

Justice Harlan opens his opinion by conceding that "[t]his case may seem at first blush too inconsequential to find its way into our books," but immediately hastens to add that "the issue it presents is of no small constitutional significance."[209] In fact, the case involves nothing less than the constitutional authority of the government to prohibit, via criminal sanctions, the use of particular words, and thereby the expression of certain ideas, from the public square. Harlan explains that "[w]e think it is largely because governmental officials cannot make principled distinctions in this area that the Constitution leaves matters of taste and style so largely to the individual."[210] In other words, distrust of government and its officials requires the adoption and enforcement of strong prophylactic free speech rules that will prevent content- and viewpoint-based government censorship of speech. This means that one of the social costs of living in a country that practices democratic self-government includes tolerating rude, uncivil, or offensive speech in the public square whenever such speech relates, even tangentially, to the process of democratic self-government.[211]

Justice Harlan emphasizes the centrality of freedom of expression to the operation of democracy and democratic self-government. Using language that resonates on the same frequencies as George Orwell's dystopian masterpiece *1984*, he observes that:

> [W]e cannot indulge the facile assumption that one can forbid particular words without also running a substantial risk of suppressing ideas in the process. Indeed, governments might soon seize upon the censorship of particular words as a convenient guise for banning the expression of unpopular views. We have been able, as noted above, to discern little social benefit that might result from running the risk of opening the door to such grave results.[212]

The United Kingdom: Free Speech as a Sociolegal Norm   95

The risk of government censorship distorting the marketplace of political ideas is simply too great to tolerate.[213] Even if most people would agree that certain kinds of language, in certain locations, goes beyond the pale, the government may not intervene to proscribe it unless the speech regulation can be renormalized as a regulation of conduct that is wholly unrelated to the message the behavior conveys.[214] Thus, flag burning is protected expressive conduct,[215] as is a targeted funeral protest of a Marine killed while on active duty that prominently features highly offensive hate speech targeting the LGBTQ community.[216]

Professor Alexander Meiklejohn makes this point in an emphatic fashion in his iconic work, *Free Speech and Its Relation to Self-Government*, published during the Red Scare years in 1948. In his view, the government in a democracy cannot attempt to control or delimit the process of democratic deliberation that informs the act of voting and facilitates the use of regular elections as a means of securing government accountability.[217] Democratic self-government means that any idea, any thought, any ideology must be open to discussion and consideration by We the People. Even speech that violates basic social norms of propriety and decency must enjoy protection from government censorship.[218]

Simply put, results of this sort in free speech cases are utterly unthinkable in the British domestic courts—if the government wishes to regulate targeted insults, it may do so and would-be speakers must recalibrate the precise means used to communicate their messages or face civil—and perhaps even criminal—legal consequences. The precise wording of the HRA 98—or Article 10 for that matter—cannot overcome deeply seated British cultural norms that prize civility in public and view government efforts to prevent grossly offensive public protest as both necessary and appropriate. It also bears noting that the British attitude toward uncivil speech and hate speech is commonly shared within Europe and is consistent with the free speech law of France and Germany.[219] The U.S. absolutist approach, which reflects a "free speech over all other values" understanding, simply is not part of the United Kingdom's sociolegal DNA.[220]

Professor Alexander Brown encapsulates the European approach quite well when he explains that:

> I believe that even if incitement to hatred laws do prevent some people from participating in public discourse in an intellectually honest and authentic manner, that is, in a manner of their choosing or in ways that perfectly express who they are as people and what they believe in, and even if this prevention thereby has a detrimental impact on the collective authorization and democratic legitimacy of downstream laws, free and equal people would nevertheless still have grounds to reasonably reject a failure to enact and apply such laws, which is a matter of *political* legitimacy.[221]

This style of argument constitutes the mirror image of the U.S. understanding—an understanding that makes distrust of government the principal object of free speech law and treats efforts to limit or proscribe speech related to government and matters of public concern as inherently distortionary of the democratic process (and, hence, unconstitutional).

In a society that places mandatory civility norms over speaker autonomy (like the United Kingdom and most of contemporary Western Europe, save perhaps for Sweden), content- and even viewpoint-based speech regulations are not only constitutionally acceptable—they are arguably constitutionally *required* to safeguard the dignity and equality of all persons living within the community. As Professor Brown explains, "[i]t seems to me that free and equal people might reasonably look upon the adequate protection of their equal civic dignity, such as via group defamation laws (*sensu strictu*), as a precondition of any notional agreement to joining the political community."[222] In other words, speech must give way to efforts to promote dignity and equality; failing to protect members of minority communities from targeted verbal attacks degrades the legitimacy of a democracy.

Yet it is difficult to square this normative justification with the results on the ground under, for example, the POA 86 or the Broadcasting Act. Using majoritarian offense to squelch antimonarchist protests seems dangerously close to either a form of lèse-majesté or, worse still, seditious libel. Using the ostensible justification of protecting the sensibilities of minority communities as a basis for in reality protecting the moral, political, and aesthetic values of the electoral majority *does not* protect either minority individuals or communities. Instead, it actually protects the sensibilities of the dominant group (which, in a place like the United Kingdom, that observes the doctrine of parliamentary sovereignty, should not be necessary in the first place). If the majority controls the levers of governmental power, why does it need to be protected from uncivil or offensive speech by political minorities who do not? Such laws and policies seem aimed more at protecting the political status quo than at safeguarding the dignity and equality of members of minority communities. Simply put, neither Queen Elizabeth II or King Charles III, nor their friends, relations, and political supporters, should require either lèse-majesté or seditious libel laws to retain either their sense of dignity or self-worth in the contemporary United Kingdom.[223]

Of course, under the First Amendment, the government lacks any legitimate authority to prescribe how a speaker will convey her message.[224] As Justice Robert Jackson so eloquently stated the point, "[i]f there is any fixed star in our constitutional constellation, it is that no official, high or petty, can prescribe what shall be orthodox in politics, nationalism, religion, or other matters of opinion or force citizens to confess by word or act their faith therein."[225] Moreover, he warned that "[i]f there are any circumstances which permit an exception, they do not now occur to us."[226]

By way of contrast, in most of the world, including the United Kingdom, average citizens accept that the government has a legitimate role to play in setting the metes and bounds of acceptable public expression—even in the context of core political speech. As Professor Brown explains, laws that proscribe hate speech "sensibly and properly applied, will not stop the speaker from expressing him or herself in other permissible ways."[227] Thus, "if laws prohibit the use of threatening words or behaviour to stir up hatred, then hate speakers can perform the same speech acts in other ways, using

The United Kingdom: Free Speech as a Sociolegal Norm   —◦ 97

other kinds of words or behaviour"[228] and "narrowly framed laws will curtail only that given form of speech."[229]

Brown then provides two examples of anti-Muslim speech—one of which he deemed proscribable and the other which he deems legally acceptable.[230] The first example, which Professor Brown argues should be legally proscribable: "'You think you can trust Muslims, think again, they are vile, backward, and dangerous people who deserve only our hatred, and when this country is finally united in its hatred of Muslims, *they had better watch out!*'"[231] The second iteration, which a suitably "narrowly framed" law would permit a speaker lawfully to utter in public: "'You think you can trust Muslims, think again, they are vile, backward, and dangerous people who deserve only our hatred.'"[232] The only difference, literally, between the two statements consists of the threat appended to the first iteration—namely, "'they had better watch out!'"

Certainly the inclusion of an express threat, targeting a particular religious minority group, would trigger Sections 4 and 5 of the POA 86 and render the speech criminally punishable in the United Kingdom. But, from the perspective of a Muslim person living in the contemporary United Kingdom, I rather doubt that their sense of offense, or even fear of harm, depends entirely on a speaker's express inclusion of a direct threat. *Both* iterations of the idea would make a Muslim resident of the United Kingdom fearful of her personal safety—and full and equal status within the community. The law would need to proscribe both statements if the goal is creating a welcome and inclusive marketplace of political ideas.

Now, let's consider the problem from the opposite vantage point, namely, that of would-be speakers, who face being silenced by the local constable if they cross the line between permissible hyperbole and impermissible "threatening" or "abusive" hate speech. In my view, a reasonable observer might well question whether a police officer or public prosecutor would actually draw a meaningful distinction between Professor Brown's two formulations of the Islamophobic statements. A cop on the beat would likely view the two statements as equally capable of causing legally cognizable harm— meaning either a threat or abuse—to a member of the targeted group. Note too that the absence of any actual Muslim person proximate to the speaker is entirely irrelevant under the POA 86; if a police officer can hypothesize that, were a Muslim person within sight or hearing of the speaker, that person would feel threatened or abused, the officer may make an arrest under Sections 4 or 5 of the POA 86.

It also bears consideration that, under the HOL's holding in *Brutus v. Cozens*,[233] whether or not speech is "threatening" or "abusive" is a question of *fact* and not *law*. In consequence, appellate courts will review this determination by trial court judges only for a clear abuse of their fact-finding discretion. Thus, when a police officer, a public prosecutor, and a Divisional Court trial judge all agree that a protest included speech that was threatening or abusive, that will be that—appealing any further the factual determination will involve a very heavy lift (and one that most defendants will not be able to meet).

The other obvious problem inheres in having cops on the beat exercising essentially unfettered discretion in making arrests that squelch core political speech in traditional public forums. If all police officers were law professors specializing in free speech law, then perhaps Professor Brown's proposed distinction between permissible and proscribable speech would hold up. Of course, in the real world, they are not. In fact, police officers, often drawn from members of the dominant cultural group (meaning the cultural and political majority), will have to guess, in real time, about whether particular speech constitutes either a "threat" or "abuse." Even when public prosecutors decline to bring charges (as was the case with the pro-republican protestors in 2022 and 2023 London), would-be speakers seeking to communicate a message to a particular audience in real time are effectively silenced when they are arrested and detained (but then subsequently released without being prosecuted).

The scope of a police officer's discretion under Section 5 is both wide and deep—and, again, involves a question of fact rather than law. As Theresa May, then-Home Secretary and later Prime Minister, reported to Parliament, when, in 2013, the government agreed to amend Section 5 of the POA 86 to delete the "insulting" language from the statute's ambit, "[l]ooking at past cases, the Director of Public prosecutions could not identify *any* [cases] where the behaviour leading to a conviction could not be described as 'abusive' as well as 'insulting.'"[234] Accordingly, the Director of Public Prosecutions concluded that "'the word 'insulting' could safely be removed without the risk of undermining the ability of the CPS to bring prosecutions.'"[235] Because deleting "insulting" from Section 5's text would not have any material legal effect on the statute's potential scope of coverage, May explained that "the Government are not minded to challenge the amendment made in the other place [the House of Lords]."[236] At the end of the day, insulting speech and abusive speech amount to the very same thing.

It should be reasonably obvious to a fair-minded observer that when unpopular minorities engage in speech of a dissenting cast, not uncommonly using hyperbole to make their point, police officers can and will deem the speech to be either "threatening" or "abusive." This explains, in part, the mass arrests of entirely peaceful antimonarchy, pro-republic protestors following the death of Queen Elizabeth II and during the coronation events for King Charles III.[237] Wearing a t-shirt, carrying a sign, or raising a banner bearing the message "Not My King" or "Who Voted for Charles?" became a legal basis for mass arrests and subsequent detention of protestors under Section 5 of the POA 86. Moreover, this held true despite the lack of any credible evidence that bystanders attending Queen Elizabeth's state funeral events or the coronation of King Charles felt either "threatened" or "abused."

Vesting the police with broad authority to arrest speakers based on whether a law enforcement officer thinks that public speech activity might lead a hypothetical bystander to feel threatened or abused, without requiring any evidence of an actual bystander taking umbrage, will invariably have a profound chilling effect on the freedom of political speech—and particularly on political speech of a dissenting cast. Those seeking to challenge the sacred cows of contemporary British society must do so at the risk of arrest and detention for having the temerity to speak their version of truth to power.

Professor Brown argues that "surely another, perhaps even more fundamental purpose of a regime of free speech is to ensure that all citizens enjoy at least sufficient real opportunities to participate in public discourse."[238] I quite agree with this sentiment. But the concept of "minority" must encompass not only demographic characteristics but also political, moral, and aesthetic beliefs and commitments. It is far from clear how silencing political minorities seeking to move public opinion in favor of some program of law reform can be reconciled with a meaningful commitment to the process of democratic deliberation essential to using elections as a means of securing government accountability.

What is more, would-be speakers have to bet a great deal (up to and including their freedom) to assume that the local cop on the beat will share Professor Brown's understanding of how Sections 4 and 5 of the POA 86 should be interpreted and applied. Simply put, the chilling effect of having such laws on the books is both inescapable and undeniable. However, in the contemporary United Kingdom, mandatory civility rules take legal precedence over the ability of dissenting voices to say their piece in public venues. Antimonarchy protestors who object to having Charles Windsor serve as an unelected, hereditary head of state, as well as antiwar protestors who express dissent by burning paper poppies on Decoration Day, will find themselves arrested, silenced, and fined—rather than tolerated.

To be clear, I do not seek to mount a normative argument for or against the constitutional wisdom and probity of either mandatory civility laws or hate speech laws. Reasonable arguments exist both in favor of and opposing such measures on free speech grounds. Instead, my point is more basic: adopting a written free speech guarantee in the United Kingdom, thereby incorporating a textual free speech guarantee into British domestic law, did not rewire the general social attitudes regarding the appropriate limits of expressive freedom in the United Kingdom. Both judges and members of the general public view vindicating the individual's autonomy interest in freedom of expression as less pressing, at least in some cases that involve culturally important persons and institutions, than requiring a modicum of decorum in public spaces and places.

Just as failing to adopt a British analogue to the First Amendment's speech, press, assembly, and petition clauses did not prevent judges in the United Kingdom from invoking the free speech principle and applying it when developing the common law and interpreting statutes prior to the HRA 98, adding an express text—and even including a specific interpretative directive to give particular regard to free speech and press rights—failed to alter either the judiciary's or the body politic's understanding of the proper limits of expressive freedom in Great Britain. Indeed, even if Parliament were to adopt a free speech guarantee that mirrors the First Amendment, and that, like the European Communities Act 1972 with respect to European Community law,[239] vests the courts with a duty to give speech an absolute priority over other provisions of domestic law, one suspects that freedom of expression law in the United Kingdom would still permit the creation and enforcement of mandatory civility norms.

This is emphatically *not* to say that the adoption of a text was wholly irrelevant to the status or protection of expressive freedom in the United Kingdom. The HRA 98's incorporation of Article 10 into British domestic law had the effect of legitimating and ratifying the British judiciary's prior work incorporating speech into domestic law as a bedrock constitutional value. Moreover, the HRA 98 also provided a clear procedural mechanism for judicial consideration and resolution of expressive freedom claims. The HRA 98 was, and today remains, an important, indeed watershed, piece of human rights legislation. One cannot reasonably, or plausibly, gainsay its legal and cultural importance.

That said, however, the HRA 98 did not, and probably could not, rewire either the British judiciary's or general public's attitudes regarding the relative importance of speech versus tranquility and social order in public spaces. The HRA 98 took the U.K.'s judges, and citizens, as it found them. Within the governing institutions of the United Kingdom, the courts are the branch of government that is least likely to serve as the harbinger of broad-based, much less radical, social change. If speech was to receive a major upgrade as a legal and sociolegal human rights value, such reform would have to come from Parliament rather than the courts.

Ironically, though, even when Parliament appears to have signaled an intention to give a relative priority to the freedom of expression (in Section 12 of the HRA 98), the judges responded by effectively reading this provision out of the statute. Viewed from this angle, the judicial refusal to expand free speech rights after the HRA 98 entered into force on October 2, 2000, arguably reflects an act of judicial will rather than a standard application of the doctrine of parliamentary sovereignty. A posture of judicial deference to Parliament would have entailed giving full and meaningful effect to both Sections 3 and 12 of the HRA 98—rather than only Section 3.

VI. CONCLUSION: THE JUDICIAL PROTECTION OF THE FREEDOM OF EXPRESSION IN THE UNITED KINGDOM CONSTITUTES COMMON LAW CONSTITUTIONALISM IN ACTION

The emergence of judicial solicitude for expressive freedom as a human rights value in the United Kingdom provides a highly salient example of courts responding—and responding directly—to a clear constitutional expectation that the government will respect, at least to some degree, the people's right to speak their minds freely. Judicial protection of free speech values in the United Kingdom thus provides a useful example of common law constitutionalism in action—judges recognized that contemporary society expected the courts to vindicate some sort of right to freedom of expression, and they responded by issuing judgments that use free speech as a constitutional basis for narrowly reading laws that authorize the government to silence would-be speakers and for modifying common law doctrines to accommodate speech claims as well.

In this specific context, then, Parliament's enactment of the HRA 98 simply ratified the work that courts had already performed—thus validating the judiciary's decision to recognize a de facto right to the freedom of speech in domestic British law even before Article 10 became part of it. The only difference one would expect to see before and after October 2, 2000, the date that the HRA 98 entered in force, is overt discussion of Article 10 as a textual basis for the domestic right to expressive freedom rather than appeals to a more ephemeral and general sociolegal commitment to protect the freedom of speech.[240]

Despite being bound by the doctrine of parliamentary sovereignty and lacking a clear textual mandate for safeguarding expressive freedoms, judges in the pre-HRA 98 era wrote and published decisions that vindicated the constitutional expectations—and values—of the British people regarding the freedom of expression. In so doing, the judges engaged in a form of common law constitutionalism. The judges in the United Kingdom realized that simply ignoring freedom of expression in cases that squarely presented it would have put their handiwork into broad public disfavor.

Judges, almost invariably, want their opinions to be credible with We the People.[241] Moreover, a judicial decision that simply ignores the social expectation of freedom of speech would lack credibility with the citizens of the contemporary United Kingdom. Paradoxically perhaps, judicial efforts to meet the human rights expectations of the body politic likely impeded, and certainly slowed down, the growing momentum within the United Kingdom in the 1980s and 1990s for more fundamental, and more *comprehensive*, constitutional reforms (such as abandoning parliamentary sovereignty completely in favor of a system of entrenched human rights enforced through a process of strong-form judicial review). Britain's judges embraced speech in both their statutory and common law decisions and, in so doing, helped to arrest the growing social and political consensus in favor of adopting a judicially enforceable and entrenched written bill of rights.

In sum, the HRA 98, at least in the context of speech rights, ratified a judicial project that was already well underway—and, in so doing, did not even amplify much, if at all, the right to freedom of expression in the United Kingdom. The HRA 98 certainly vindicated and affirmed the judiciary's prior jurisprudential work—and also established a clear procedure for courts to follow in hearing and deciding expressive freedom claims under Article 10 of the European Convention. The new text made a difference—but the judges themselves made a bigger difference.

British judges, on their own and using the inherent authority of the courts, had already gone a long way toward creating and safeguarding a relatively robust right to expressive freedom. It was the judges, rather than Parliament, who took the initiative in translating the freedom of expression from a general and abstract social value in the United Kingdom into a legally enforceable human right. To this day, the judges still seem to be charting their own course—as the effective repeal of Section 12(4) of the HRA 98 plainly demonstrates. Even when Parliament issued an interpretative directive to the domestic courts to have "particular regard" for HRA 98 claims involving the freedom of speech,[242] the judges instead decided that speech possessed only a coequal value with the other rights set forth in the European Convention and, accordingly, could not be afforded even a relative priority over them.

102 ～   Free Speech as Civic Structure

In conclusion, free speech law in the United Kingdom has been, and likely will remain, primarily the province of the judges rather than the parliamentarians. As in the United States and South Africa, codification of speech rights has had some impact on the work of the judiciary in defining the metes and bounds of protected speech, but the enterprise constitutes, at its core, an exercise in common law constitutionalism.[243]

5

Australia

THE CONSTITUTIONAL PROTECTION OF POLITICAL AND GOVERNMENTAL SPEECH AS AN "IMPLIED FREEDOM" ESSENTIAL TO FACILITATING DEMOCRATIC DELIBERATION, THE ELECTORAL PROCESS, AND DEMOCRACY ITSELF

I. INTRODUCTION: THE ABSENCE OF AN EXPRESS FREE SPEECH PROVISION, JUDICIAL IMPLICATIONS, AND AUSTRALIA'S (PARTIALLY) WRITTEN CONSTITUTION

Australia provides a compelling example of how the presence or absence of constitutional text need not prefigure whether the domestic courts will exercise a power of judicial review to safeguard expressive freedom. Even though Australia lacks a constitutional free speech guarantee, Australia's highest judicial tribunal, the High Court of Australia (HCA), has recognized an "implied freedom" of political and governmental communication as a structural necessity in a polity that practices democratic self-government.[1] This jurisprudential innovation demonstrates with convincing clarity that the absence of a constitutional text safeguarding the freedom of speech, press, assembly, petition, and association need not be an insurmountable obstacle to the exercise of judicial review to protect these expressive freedoms.[2]

The HCA's free speech precedents begin, almost one hundred years after the Commonwealth Constitution[3] took effect on January 1, 1901,[4] with its 1992 landmark decisions in *Australian Capital Television (ACTV)*[5] and *Nationwide News*.[6] The Justices initially enforced the right quite robustly, giving the implied freedom of political and governmental communication (IFPGC) its arguably broadest application in *Theophanous*,[7] decided in 1994. Within three years, however, the HCA reversed course

---

Free Speech as Civic Structure. Ronald J. Krotoszynski, Jr., Oxford University Press. © Ronald J. Krotoszynski, Jr. 2024.
DOI: 10.1093/9780197662229.003.0005

104 ~ Free Speech as Civic Structure

and adopted a posture of very broad judicial deference toward both federal and state laws that burden or abridge the exercise of expressive freedom. After 1997, if a speech regulation advances a legitimate government purpose and features any plausible effort at tailoring, the HCA will likely sustain it.[8] Despite an overall posture of broad judicial deference, the HCA has demonstrated deep skepticism of flat bans on particular kinds of speech, such as speech in public featuring the use of profanity or scatology ("insulting" speech),[9] and generally invalidated flat speech bans.

The HCA's retrenchment—coupled with a general reaffirmation of the slimmed-down IFPGC—commenced with its unanimous 1997 decision in *Lange*[10] and arguably continues to the present. Under the test handed down in *Lange*, which requires only that a burden on the implied freedom be "reasonably appropriate and adapted to serve a legitimate end which is compatible with the maintenance of representative and responsible government,"[11] virtually any law or common law doctrine that advances a legitimate interest with some sort of tailoring will pass judicial review.[12] Thus, despite a relatively robust application of the doctrine from 1992 to 1994, the HCA's overall posture over the past thirty years is one of great deference to the political branches.[13]

Moreover, even today, the justices remain divided regarding the appropriate standard of review to apply in IFPGC cases (with one Justice, Simon Steward, questioning whether the IFPGC should exist at all).[14] The only consistent pattern seems to be that free speech claimants usually lose before the HCA and the government almost always wins—provided that a law contains any plausible effort at tailoring its scope to take account of the freedom of speech.

The HCA's most recent free speech precedents, involving a ban on government employee speech,[15] proscriptions against anti-abortion speech proximate to family planning clinics,[16] and requirements for foreign speakers to register with the government before speaking in Australia,[17] all reflect broad judicial acceptance of the government's legitimate constitutional authority to regulate speech. For example, in *LibertyWorks*, the HCA held that, when applying proportionality analysis, the government's preferred balance between regulation and speech should stand "unless the benefit sought to be achieved by the law is *manifestly outweighed* by the adverse effect on the implied freedom."[18] This balancing exercise veritably exudes judicial deference to the government as to its choice of regulatory means.[19] If the government has a legitimate purpose for regulating speech and adopts *any* sort of tailoring of the speech regulations, then the government regulation will likely pass constitutional muster.[20]

For present purposes, however, the relevant question is not whether the HCA has properly delimited the metes and bounds of expressive freedom via the IFPGC, but rather whether the presence of an express free speech guarantee in the Australian Constitution would necessarily make any difference (at all) to the outcomes in these cases. In my view, it would not. Despite repeated claims that free speech decisions must be grounded in the "text and structure" of the Constitution, the doctrine of democratic constitutionalism provides the most plausible explanation for the relative weakness of the IFPGC (at least when compared to the Free Speech Clause of the First Amendment).

Australia: Free Speech as an Implied Freedom —᠀ 105

Democratic constitutionalism is the first cousin of the United Kingdom's doctrine of parliamentary sovereignty (or "parliamentary supremacy"), which holds that courts have no legitimate power to displace duly enacted legislative policy choices through the exercise of judicial review.[21] The theory is one of judicially imposed self-restraint;[22] it reflects and incorporates the view that elected parliamentarians are better able to assess and protect fundamental human rights than unelected judges.[23] Thus, under democratic constitutionalism, "it is Parliament, not the courts, which should be chiefly responsible for resolving contentious political issues, including those concerning rights."[24]

As Professor Haig Patapan explains, under Australia's theory of democratic constitutionalism, courts take a more limited role in making or revising major social policies because "representative and responsible government [is] essential to human development and progress."[25] He adds, "if we accept this argument, then the [HCA's] rights jurisprudence appears to be consistent with the orthodox constitutionalism in Australia, bringing out and developing notions that are inherent in the idea of responsible government."[26] It is not that the courts should never intervene and prevent enforcement of duly enacted statutes; it is rather that they should only intervene when statutes threaten to distort or prevent the normal operation of the democratic process.[27]

Of course, this approach runs deeply against the grain of post-World War II constitutional design—which almost invariably relies on judicial review as a kind of brake or circuit breaker to protect against arbitrary, unjust, or discriminatory government actions that abridge or deny fundamental human rights.[28] Nevertheless, democratic constitutionalism to this day strongly colors how the HCA views its proper role within Australia's scheme of government.[29]

Although cloaked in the linguistic garb of "legalism" and "textualism,"[30] the HCA's reticence reflects core concerns about the risks that might arise to the court's popular legitimacy were it to overstep the mark by asserting itself too boldly and too regularly into the affairs of the federal and state parliaments. Despite the HCA implying otherwise, the presence of an express constitutional text would probably make little difference—other than ending the debate, most recently rekindled by Justice Steward, regarding the HCA's obligation to consider constitutional expressive freedom claims at all.[31]

Indeed, one could reasonably characterize the Australian approach to the freedom of speech as involving essentially a procedural check to ensure that the legislature has considered the scope of a law that burdens or proscribes expressive activity—with some sort of tailoring as the evidence required to establish that this procedural requirement has been met. Provided that the legislature takes speech rights into account, the HCA will afford the legislature's handiwork broad deference as to the particulars.[32]

Australia's constitutional free speech jurisprudence demonstrates with convincing clarity that the absence of constitutional text does not prevent judges from recognizing free speech as a fundamental right and exercising judicial review to safeguard it. As in the United States, where the Supreme Court has paid scant attention to the

actual text of the First Amendment,[33] Australian judges interpret and apply constitutional free speech principles based on the expectations of "We the [Australian]
People" and do so using a common law process and common law reasoning. In sum,
Australia's Commonwealth Constitution, like the U.S. Constitution, is a living—not
static—document.[34]

This chapter will proceed in four main sections. Section II introduces the IFPGC
and discusses the current tests used to determine whether a law that burdens speech
is constitutional. Section III considers how the HCA goes about framing and deciding IFPGC cases, including positive and negative reliance on foreign legal precedents,
textualism (also known as "legalism" in Australia), and the general reluctance of the
HCA to aggressively superintend the work of the federal and state legislatures. Section
IV considers the arguments for and against the recognition of an implied freedom of
speech—and concludes that the HCA's constitutional logic is quite sound. Simply put,
it is impossible to imagine a popular democracy that fails to protect, to some degree,
the speech required to animate the process of democratic deliberation. Because of this
reality, the presence or absence of an express constitutional text is far less important
than the commitment to democratic self-government as a justification for the exercise
of judicial review in support of expressive freedoms. Section V offers a brief summary
and conclusion.

Australia's example shows that even in a polity which more closely adheres to the
Westminster model for the national courts—meaning that elected legislators, not
judges, are primarily responsible for deciding major questions of social policy[35]—the
Australian people's deep-seated expectation of enjoyment of the freedom of speech led
the HCA to conjure ("imply") a limited freedom of speech as an essential attribute of a
democratic system of government. Notwithstanding the intentional omission of a free
speech guarantee in Australia's written Constitution, the courts found it quite impossible to cast a blind eye on laws that enact speech bans—at least when those bans
would obviously and significantly distort the process of democratic deliberation and
are facially inconsistent with existing cultural free speech traditions and practices.[36]

II. AN INTRODUCTION TO AUSTRALIA'S IMPLIED FREEDOM OF POLITICAL AND GOVERNMENTAL COMMUNICATION

In Australia, the drafters of the federal constitution made a conscious and intentional
decision not to include a written bill of rights.[37] Drawing on the British tradition of
parliamentary sovereignty, they instead created a federal system and divided governing powers between the six states and the federal government.[38] The Constitution does
guarantee a democratic form of government and the right to vote[39]—but it contains
only three specifically enumerated rights-granting provisions.[40] One guarantees the
equal treatment of nonresidents by the states[41]—essentially an analogue to the U.S.
Constitution's Privileges and Immunities Clause (which appears in Article IV, Section
2).[42] Another prohibits religious establishments, prohibits religious oaths for public

office, and protects the free exercise of religion.[43] The Commonwealth Constitution also guarantees trial by jury in criminal cases.[44] Finally, the Australian Constitution contains a weaker form of the U.S. Fifth Amendment's Takings Clause, which prohibits the federal legislature from "acquisition of property" unless it does so "on just terms."[45] This provision neither creates a "right" nor mandates payment of "just compensation," but instead renders legislation that affects an unfair land acquisition invalid.[46]

Australia's Commonwealth Constitution does not contain any provisions safeguarding the freedom of speech, press, assembly, or petition.[47] As Professors Cheryl Saunders and Adrienne Stone note, "the Australian Constitution is directed primarily to establishing the federal system and creating institutions of government for the Commonwealth, but not the State, sphere."[48] The drafters largely left questions concerning fundamental human rights to be decided by democratically elected legislators and protected primarily through the electoral process rather than the courts. This reliance on legislators, not judges, to have primary responsibility for safeguarding fundamental human rights constitutes a cornerstone of "democratic constitutionalism," the animating theory of Australia's constitutional system.[49]

Nevertheless, in the early 1990s the HCA discovered an "implied freedom" of political and governmental communication.[50] The HCA's principal argument—an entirely plausible one—posits that it is simply not possible to have free and fair elections without citizens enjoying the ability to engage with each other in the marketplace of political ideas.[51] As the Justices more recently explained, "[t]he constitutional basis for the implication in the Constitution of a freedom of communication on matters of politics and government is well settled."[52] Indeed, "[t]he freedom is of such importance to representative government that any effective statutory burden upon it must be justified."[53] The IFPGC "is a restriction on legislative power which arises as a necessary implication from ss 7, 24, 64, and 128 and related sections of the *Constitution* and, as such, extends only so far as is necessary to preserve and protect the system."[54]

Thus, the (intentional) omission of an express free speech provision in Australia's Commonwealth Constitution of 1901 has not left freedom of expression entirely to the whim of the federal and state legislatures. Even so, however, Australia's implied right is considerably weaker than the Free Speech Clause of the First Amendment.

First, the HCA consistently has held that the implied freedom does not constitute an individual constitutional "right" that exists to facilitate personal autonomy.[55] Instead, it "operates as a constitutional restriction on legislative power."[56] These doctrinal features have important, and quite negative, implications for the scope of the implied freedom of political and governmental communication. It only applies to speech that is clearly related to politics and government (and not to speech that relates to the arts, literature, science, to commercial speech, or to sexually explicit speech). In this respect, the Australian implied freedom has more in common with Judge Robert Bork's proposed approach to the First Amendment than to current free speech jurisprudence in the United States.[57]

Second, the burden on the government to justify restrictions on the implied freedom is, at best, quite modest. To survive judicial scrutiny, a law that abridges free speech need merely have a "legitimate" purpose (meaning that it must be "compatible with the constitutionally prescribed system of government"), be "proportionate to the achievement of the purpose" (meaning the law constitutes "a rational response to a perceived mischief"), and be "necessary and adequate in its balance" (meaning that it possesses a reasonable fit between its objectives and the means used to achieve them).[58] Most federal and state laws that burden speech—if tailored at all—easily survive this relatively weak form of judicial scrutiny.

The current test for analyzing a free speech claim under the IFPGC involves three steps. The plaintiff bears an initial burden of showing a burden or abridgement of the IFPGC.[59] The second step involves an inquiry into whether a regulation that burdens the IFPGC advances a "legitimate" interest that "does not impede the functioning" of "representative and responsible government."[60] Finally, under "structured" proportionality, a reviewing court must ascertain whether the means used are sufficiently tailored and afford ample alternative channels of communication.[61] It is at this step of assessing means and ends, and whether a speech regulation's breadth is undue, that the HCA's reflexive deference manifests most clearly.

Clubb v. Edwards and *Preston v. Avery*,[62] two cases jointly decided in 2019, demonstrate almost abject deference to state legislatures' choices as to the precise means used to achieve legitimate government objectives—even when the government is directly regulating expressive activity in a traditional public forum (such as a public street or sidewalk). In *Clubb*, Chief Justice Susan Mary Kiefel, joined by Justices Virginia Bell and Patrick Keane, explains that "[t]he issue for the courts is not to determine the correct balance of the law; that is a matter for the legislature."[63] This is an astonishing concession from a U.S. perspective; in the United States, the sufficiency of the tailoring of a speech regulation is very much a judicial, not legislative, task.[64] In Australia, however, "[t]he question is whether the law can be seen to be irrational in its lack of balance in the pursuit of its object."[65] So, "rationality" is the test for the sufficiency of the tailoring of speech regulations. What's more, a strong presumption of validity applies and a court should disallow the balance that the legislature has struck "only where the disproportion is such as to manifest irrationality."[66]

To show "irrationality," a plaintiff challenging a speech regulation must convince the court that the regulation is "'manifestly excessive by comparison to the demands of legitimate purpose.'"[67] Thus, a law need not strike "some ideal balance between competing considerations."[68] Only laws that are "manifestly disproportionate" or where the effect on freedom of expression "manifestly outweigh[s]" the advancement of the government's legitimate interest are subject to judicial invalidation under the IFPGC.[69] Using words like "rational connection" and "manifest disproportion" clearly signals great judicial deference—not beady-eyed judicial scrutiny.

The pejorative phrase "good enough for government work" immediately comes to mind. Under the current doctrinal test, if the government seeks to advance a legitimate purpose (naked censorship for its own sake would not suffice, but almost anything else, it seems, could be sufficient) and adopts sufficient tailoring (meaning *some* tailoring), the government speech regulation is constitutional. Thus, the IFPGC involves little more than rationality review and, in some sense, appears to be merely a procedural check to ensure that the legislature, when it adopts a law that infringes the freedom of speech, indicates some awareness of what it was doing and the potential effects that the statute will have on expressive freedom.[70]

Under this test, then, it was very easy for the HCA to unanimously approve two state laws that banned all protest proximate to persons within sight or hearing distance of a family planning clinic. The HCA explained that "[t]hose wishing to say what they want about abortions have an unimpeded ability to do so outside the radius of the safe access zones."[71] Again, it bears noting that under both state laws, the absolute speech ban on abortion-related speech (and only abortion-related speech) extended for 164 yards (or 150 meters) from a family planning clinic's property lines. This had the effect of making it impossible for would-be protestors to interact in person with clinic staff or patients; the "free speech free zone" rendered in-person communication completely impossible. Moreover, the statutes did this by design; the elimination of anti-abortion protests from within the sight or hearing of clinic staff and patients was a design feature rather than a bug.

The HCA characterizes this as simply a reasonable protection for a "captive audience."[72] Yet, in general, denying a would-be speaker any ability to interact with a particular audience seems fatal to the process of democratic deliberation that the IFPGC ostensibly exists to protect. Because Victoria's protest ban "has a rational connection to its purpose," namely, "seek[ing] to ensure that women seeking a safe termination are not driven to less safe procedures by being subjected to shaming behavior or by the fear of the loss of privacy," the speech ban constitutes "a rational response to a serious public health issue."[73] The same reasoning, and outcome, applied with respect to the Tasmanian statute, which also adopted a 164-yard (or 150 meters) buffer zone and, unlike the Victorian statute, targeted only "protest" for proscription.[74]

Justice Stephen Gageler's concurring opinion in *Preston* is even more remarkable than the plurality opinion authored by Chief Justice Kiefel and joined by Associate Justices Bell and Keane. Justice Gageler argues that the government's rationale for adopting a content-based speech regulation, such as a ban on "protest," "needs to be more than just constitutionally permissible; it needs to be compelling."[75] In addition to a compelling government interest, "the prohibition must be closely tailored to the achievement of that [compelling] purpose."[76] In other words, the regulation "must not burden the freedom of political communication significantly more than is reasonably necessary to do so."[77]

Despite purporting to apply a test that requires a compelling government interest and narrowly tailored means to achieve it, Justice Gageler concludes that the Tasmanian protest ban does not violate the IFPGC. First, "[t]he purpose so identified is unquestionably constitutionally permissible and, by any objective measure, of such obvious importance as to be characterised as compelling."[78] Second, as to the fit between the means and end, "confining the protest prohibition within that 150 m [164-yard] limit leaves enough opportunity for protests to be held at other locations meaningfully proximate to the premises to warrant the conclusion that the burden that the protest prohibition places on political communication, although not insubstantial, is not undue."[79]

Justice Gageler's application of strict scrutiny is more than passing strange to U.S. eyes; if the state government could have achieved its purposes with a 145 m "no protest" zone, under the First Amendment, the 150 m restriction would be unconstitutional. What makes this concurring opinion so telling is that even when a Justice of the HCA purports to apply strict judicial scrutiny, broad deference to elected legislators as to the means used to achieve a government interest creeps back into the constitutional analysis. Australian judges, at least in the context of freedom of expression, do not seem of the mind to place the federal or state legislatures on a short leash.

Nor is the reflexive, arguably abject, deference of *Clubb* and *Preston* unusual or specific to laws that seek to ensure safe and easy access to reproductive health care services. Another 2019 decision, *Comcare v. Banerji*,[80] sustains a federal government policy, implemented via statute and administrative regulations, that makes off-the-clock speech activity by civil service employees a basis for discipline—up to and including discharge—if the government employer deems the employee's speech activity too controversial or otherwise sufficiently embarrassing to the agency.[81] The standards for imposing discipline under the Australian Public Service Act (APSA) and the Australian Public Service Code of Conduct (APSC) were (and remain) extraordinarily broad and vague.[82]

Nevertheless, the HCA sustained against an IFPGC challenge the government's policies imposing a gag on Australian civil servants that barred them from making critical comments about their government employers—whether on or off the clock and whether on an attributed or anonymous basis.[83] The joint opinion, authored by Chief Justice Kiefel and Justices Bell, Keane, and Nettle, concludes that "[t]here can be no doubt that the maintenance and protection of an apolitical and professional public service is a significant purpose consistent with the system of representative and responsible government mandated by the Constitution."[84] Moreover, Section 64 of the Constitution, which provides for the establishment of departments of state, and Section 67, which provides for the appointment and removal of officers of the Executive Government other than Ministers, attest to the significance of the APSC as a constituent part of the system of representative and responsible government mandated by the Constitution."[85] Thus, the imperative that government ministers—elected politicians serving in the national Parliament—have a phalanx of loyal minions overrides any autonomy claim by a government employee; "responsible government" justifies imposing a gag rule on federal civil servants in Australia. Nor is the collective interest in government employees engaging in whistleblowing speech, which facilitates the use of elections to hold elected government officials accountable, so much as mentioned in the joint opinion.

Worse still, the APSC only proscribes *critical* comments by government employees on social media platforms. If a government employee posts comments lauding their employer, no violation will exist. This regulatory scheme this creates not merely a content-based speech ban, insofar as the APSC regulations target only speech related to government offices and officials, but is clearly *viewpoint-based* as well. Ms. Banerji was entirely free to praise the government's immigration policies as terrific and wonderful in every possible way. Her (anonymous) comments about these policies, however, were critical and therefore constituted a violation of the APSC. If Australia seeks truly neutral civil servants, the statute and implementing regulations should impose a universal gag order on government workers. Moreover, a complete ban would arguably better protect government works from being pressured by their politician bosses to serve as sock puppet cheerleaders for government agencies. The *Banerji* majority zeroes out completely the importance of government employee speech to using voting and elections as a means of securing government accountability.

Instead, the majority joint opinion places more emphasis on the importance of the interest of government ministers in enjoying loyal subordinates who do not embarrass them or their department rather than the role of government employees as citizens and, not uncommonly, whistleblowers. Even if Ms. Banerji's speech was not of a whistleblowing cast (and clearly it was directly relevant to matters of great public concern, namely the fairness and rationality of the government's immigration policies[86]), government employee speech can be essential to securing government accountability through regular free and fair elections. One will search the joint *Banerji* opinion in vain for any mention, much less considered analysis, of this other side of the government employee speech coin.

Thus, as in New Bedford, Massachusetts, Australian citizens might have the "freedom" to talk politics, but they do not have the right to work for the federal civil service.[87] Then a member of the Massachusetts state supreme court, Justice Oliver Wendell Holmes, Jr., opined that "[t]here are few employments for hire in which the servant does not agree to suspend his constitutional right of free speech, as well as of idleness, by the implied terms of his contract."[88] Accordingly, "[t]he servant cannot complain, as he takes the employment on the terms which are offered him."[89] It would appear that, in contemporary Australia, persons employed by the federal government should think twice, and very carefully, about whether to make critical public comments about the agencies for which they work.[90] It bears noting that in the contemporary United States, government employees now enjoy significant First Amendment protection when they speak out about matters of public concern (notably including speech critical of their employers); the U.S. Supreme Court has squarely rejected the notion that government employers can silence their employees as a condition of continued employment.

One member of the HCA, Justice James Edelman, goes even further than the *Banerji* majority, suggesting that whatever speech protections a government employer permits an agency's employees are more than the government, historically, had to tolerate. He observes that "[f]or much of the century since Federation, any public expression of political opinion by a Commonwealth public servant could be grounds for termination of employment."[91] This ban, under the APSA and APSC, "has been tempered" and "the Code that now regulates their behavior no longer turns public servants into lonely ghosts."[92]

112 ⌒   Free Speech as Civic Structure

Justice Edelman cheerfully acknowledges that, in the United States, a broad and vaguely worded speech code, of the sort that led to Ms. Banerji's termination from employment, "would be struck down as unconstitutional in a heartbeat."[93] He explains that "unlike in the United States, in Australia, the boundaries of freedom of speech are generally the province of Parliament; the judiciary can constrain the choices of a parliament only at the outer margins for reasons of systemic protection."[94] Thus, government employees in Australia should be grateful for whatever speech rights the federal or state governments choose to bestow upon them.

The failure of every member of the HCA to consider the real systemic effects of permitting a government employer to fire a public employee because their off-the-clock speech is embarrassing to the agency is the most troubling aspect of *Banerji*. Quite often, information about government misconduct and malfeasance—information essential to the use of elections and voting to secure government accountability—will be possessed only by those working within a government agency. If, for example, the prime minister was secretly vesting himself with the powers of multiple cabinet offices (at least five), without informing either members of government or the public of this practice,[95] it could come to light *only* if a staff person within one of the affected ministries blows the whistle. However, given the extreme breadth of the regulations applicable to government employee speech under the APSA and APSC,[96] a public employee would have to be prepared to embrace professional martyrdom in order to blow the whistle.

The HCA's free speech analysis in *Banerji* considers only the government's interest in having a loyal and professional civil service; it fails to take into account (at all) either the importance of government employee whistleblowers to the process of democratic deliberation or the critical relationship between whistleblowing speech and the ability of voters to hold the government, and its officers, accountable for misconduct through the electoral process.[97] Clearly, the other side of the scale should include the potential public benefits that flow from creating a system that protects government employee speech essential to the process of democratic deliberation. *Banerji* sends the clear and unfortunate signal that if government employees wish to keep their civil service jobs, contrary to Justice Edelman's suggestion, their best and most prudent course of action would be to embrace with brio the role of a "lonely [silent] ghost" when they possess information about misconduct or malfeasance within their government agency.

Of course, one might posit that the general weakness of Australia's constitutional protection of freedom of expression demonstrates the importance, rather than the irrelevance, of constitutional text. After all, on the one hand, if freedom of speech enjoyed express constitutional protection under the Commonwealth Constitution of 1901, perhaps the HCA would more vigorously safeguard it. On the other hand, Australia's Constitution *does contain* an express guarantee of the free exercise of religion—Section 116.[98] This has not led to more vigorous judicial protection of the free exercise of religion. The HCA consistently has interpreted this express right quite narrowly and rejected most free exercise claims.[99]

Indeed, despite the existence of Section 116, Australian legal academics have posited that framing free exercise claims as more generic "speech" claims might be a more effective strategy for securing exemptions from neutral laws of general applicability that burden religiously motivated conduct.[100] This would suggest that judicial enforcement of a particular right in Australia is not really a function of whether or not the right is expressly set forth in the Commonwealth Constitution.

Thus, an express constitutional provision, which mirrors another provision of the First Amendment, has not been any more efficacious than the "implied freedom" that serves to protect political and governmental speech—and indeed is arguably *weaker* than the judicially crafted IFPGC. This state of affairs strongly supports an inference that the scope and vibrancy of a fundamental right in Australia does not really depend much—if at all—on whether or not it has been codified (so much for the "text" part of "text and structure"). The controlling constitutional consideration is not the "text" at all but rather the judiciary's fealty to "legalism" in the service of democratic constitutionalism. The judiciary is very much the junior partner of the federal and state legislatures in making public policy choices—including choices about how best to regulate expressive freedom. This structural commitment seems to animate and explain the HCA's minimalist approach to defining and enforcing the IFPGC.

Despite repeated invocations of the central importance of hewing carefully to the "text and structure" of the Australian Constitution,[101] one odd aspect of the HCA's free speech jurisprudence is a consistent and pronounced practice of citing and discussing foreign legal precedents. Given the persistent, and consistent, insistence on close attention to the "text and structure" of the Australian Constitution in IFPGC cases,[102] the HCA's regular engagement with foreign and international law, at least in IFPGC cases, is perplexing. In general, textualism or "legalism," as one variant of textualism is known in Australia,[103] would seem to imply that only *domestic* sources of constitutional meaning should have weight or relevance in construing "implications" of Australia's Constitution—as well as its "structure." Yet, the HCA frequently cites to the precedents of the Supreme Court of the United States—as well as to decisions from Canada, New Zealand, and the United Kingdom. What is yet more surprising: These references to foreign law are never explained.

The HCA has never offered any normative theory, or defense, of deploying comparative constitutionalism to justify its reliance, both positive and negative, on foreign precedents.[104] The HCA's talismanic, and oft repeated, concerns with carefully adhering to the Australian Constitution's "text and structure" comports poorly with the loose comparative legal analysis that the HCA routinely deploys in IFPGC cases. In point of fact, the text of the Commonwealth Constitution seems to be the starting point, not the end point, of the HCA's process of constitutional review in IFPGC cases.

In the United States, the Supreme Court, for a period of time in the early 2000's, adopted a weak and quite tentative practice of citing foreign legal decisions—not as precedent, but rather as merely persuasive authority.[105] This judicial dipping of the toe into the comparative constitutional law pool led to a strong and pronounced political backlash that was, at least to some extent, bipartisan in nature. Thus, after citing foreign legal precedents in *Lawrence*, *Roper*, and *Atkins*, the Justices abandoned the practice after it was a subject of sharp criticism at the confirmation hearings for

Chief Justice John G. Roberts, Jr., and Associate Justices Samuel A. Alito, Jr., Sonia M. Sotomayor, and Elena Kagan.

Consistent with abjuring recourse to foreign law as persuasive authority, in the landmark gay marriage case, *Obergefell v. Hodges*,[106] Justice Anthony M. Kennedy cited not a single foreign precedent or legislative reform that secured marriage equality in a foreign jurisdiction[107]—nor did any other member of the 5–4 majority (notably including Justice Stephen Breyer, who has argued publicly, and at great length, that the Supreme Court should engage with the work of other domestic and transnational juridical bodies in its opinions[108]). Instead, Kennedy appended a lengthy list of lower federal and state court decisions that, after *Windsor*,[109] had concluded that either the Due Process Clause or the Equal Protection Clause requires the states and the federal government to recognize same-sex marriage.[110]

In its free speech cases, the HCA never explains or justifies its citations to U.S., Canadian, and U.K. precedents. The Justices simply cite the cases, discuss them, and adopt or reject their reasoning. Such a practice in the contemporary United States would be unthinkable. There is no textual warrant in the Commonwealth Constitution for the HCA to consider foreign or international law when deciding how to interpret Australia's Constitution. By way of contrast, South Africa's 1996 Constitution requires the Constitutional Court of the Republic of South Africa (CCSA) to consider international law and authorizes it to consider foreign law.[111] Thus, the CCSA, unlike the HCA, has a clear textual warrant for the practice of engaging with foreign judicial precedents and using them to help shape the contours of domestic constitutional rights.

Perhaps recourse to the Privy Council, as the ultimate court of appeal for Australia prior to 1986, created a natural tendency for Australian judges to look abroad when deciding domestic legal questions. To U.S. eyes, however, the alacrity with which virtually all members of the HCA discuss and rely upon foreign law as persuasive authority is highly unusual.

Moreover, invoking foreign law, and engaging foreign precedents, involves at least some risk of professional embarrassment.[112] Some domestic legal systems attempt to correct for this by providing dedicated resources to assist local judges with understanding and applying foreign law. For example, the Constitutional Court of Taiwan has strong and reliable institutional support for comparative legal analysis—and the Constitutional Court of South Korea has a comparative constitutional law research center at its disposal.[113] In the United States, no such resources exist—in fact, federal law currently bars the use of government funds for the employment of foreign law clerks (or at least paying such clerks with such funds for their professional services[114]). In consequence, Justices of the U.S. Supreme Court have sometimes embarrassed themselves by citing foreign law—while clearly misapprehending how foreign law actually works.[115]

To be sure, the Supreme Court of Canada (SCC) also has a settled practice of considering international law and foreign law when interpreting the Canadian Charter of Rights and Freedoms. Like the HCA, the SCC considers foreign legal precedents as persuasive authority despite the lack of any textual warrant, in either the Charter or

Australia: Free Speech as an Implied Freedom —◦ 115

the statute books, for doing so. Yet, if the HCA is trying to define what Australian democracy requires in order to function, by inferring constitutional rules from the Commonwealth Constitution's text and structure,[116] it does seem odd to look to the United States for inspiration (whether positive or negative). Simply put, the contemporary U.S. sociolegal and political culture is not Australia's sociolegal or political culture. Nor are U.S. legal practices and traditions Australian legal practices and traditions.

A national constitutional court, like the HCA, being comparative and cosmopolitan—when construing and applying fundamental rights—is, of course, a good thing and not a bad thing.[117] As I have argued previously, "[i]f a judge can find inspiration in a monograph or law review article, why should she refrain from finding such inspiration in a foreign legal text (even if imperfectly understood)?"[118] Judges can and should credit good juridical ideas—regardless of their local or foreign origins.

Even so, if the HCA is genuinely concerned about "rules being rules" and privileging the Commonwealth Constitution's text, as well as its structure, the Justices' rather casual use of foreign law constitutes a very odd practice. Without a constitutional or statutory warrant for such engagement, the Justices have, it would seem, elected simply to embrace foreign law and legal sources as a source of persuasive authority. At least arguably, the sources that inform domestic constitutional rules require some sort of license within domestic law (whether of a constitutional or a statutory character).[119] In other words, the process that informs the articulation and application of human rights is no less important to the scope and meaning of those rights than their substantive scope of application.

It would be very helpful if the HCA were to explain its reliance on foreign legal precedents, in the context of the IFPGC and more generally, with respect to both positive and negative engagement with foreign legal precedents, and to offer some sort of explanation, if not a formal warrant rooted in the "text and structure" of the Australian Constitution, for this everyday judicial practice. Given that the U.S. Constitution served as a model for the Commonwealth Constitution, some consideration of identical or highly similar provisions might be justified on a genealogical basis.[120] So too, the Westminster model for Australia's national government might justify reliance on U.K. precedents as potentially persuasive sources of legal authority.[121] But, if one or both of these postulations actually hold true for the HCA, it should simply say so.

More generally, the HCA's approach to operationalizing the IFPGC remains something of a work in progress—a kind of judicial construction zone. The HCA has used both an open-ended balancing test (*Lange* and *McCloy*) and more categorical rules in cases raising IFPGC claims (*ACTV* and *Coleman*). For example, in *Coleman*, a case involving intentionally insulting speech, the HCA appeared to use a categorical approach that places a very high burden of justification on government regulations that target speech for proscription based on its content.[122] In other cases, however, the HCA has engaged in proportionality analysis, considering the degree to which a government speech restriction burdens the IFPGC, the reasons the government offers to justify the abridgement, and the "fit" between the regulation and the government's legitimate objectives.

As Professor Adrienne Stone has observed, most legal systems use one approach or the other—not both.[123] Yet, the HCA has toggled between categorical rules and proportionality review with "structured proportionality" currently holding jurisprudential sway.[124]

At least arguably, proportionality review does not really differ from a more formal legal standard approach. Professor Stone, in fact, has advanced precisely this argument.[125] As she posits, one could view the HCA's use of "structured proportionality" in free speech cases as nothing more than "an elaboration of previous law that renders more explicit elements of analysis that were already implicit in the Court's doctrines."[126] Moreover, proportionality review offers an opportunity for a court to take into account particularly objectionable regulatory means, such as content, viewpoint, or speaker-based speech bans (an approach advocated by Justice Stephen Gageler in several recent opinions).

The larger problem, however, is what seems to be a kind of ad hoc approach to both developing and applying the governing legal test—after the HCA's 2021 decision in *LibertyWorks*, "structured proportionality." The test is easy enough to state:

1. Does the law effectively burden freedom of communication about political and governmental matters?
2. If so, does the law advance a legitimate government interest?
3. If so, is the law reasonably appropriate and adapted to advance the legitimate government interest?[127]

The third prong of the test involves analysis of whether the challenged statute is "suitable," "necessary," and "adequate in the balance"—all three of these queries relate to whether the means/end fit between the regulation and the government's objective is sufficiently tailored (meaning rational and not grossly overbroad).[128] Given the HCA's consistent application of the structured proportionality since *McCloy*, "its place in constitutional law is surely settled for the moment."[129]

Even if the use of structured proportionality is now settled, the application of the test does not seem to be so. Proportionality review in some cases has been relatively deferential to the government—whereas in other cases, including those presenting challenges to campaign contribution and expenditure limits, the HCA has been rather demanding of the government, particularly with respect to the fit between the precise means used to achieve the government's ends and the ends themselves. And the HCA's occasional use of per se rules, such as a presumption of invalidity for viewpoint-based and content-based speech regulations, is difficult to reconcile with a test of structured proportionality. After all, in a system that uses proportionality review, the fact that a speech regulation is content-based should *not* necessarily mean that it is per se invalid.[130]

If the government's reasons for adopting a content-based speech ban are sufficiently important, and the speech itself is a social evil, then a targeted ban on particular kinds of speech should be constitutional. This might be one way of understanding the otherwise rather free-speech-indifferent decisions in *Clubb* and *Preston*—if targeted abortion protests aimed at patients and clinic staff are a social evil, like true threats of violence or telemarketing fraud, tailoring regulations that limit or proscribe such speech activity should not be necessary because any legal rule that reduces degrading, stigmatizing, and perhaps frightening interpersonal interactions directly advances the government's compelling interest in avoiding these social harms.[131]

However, viewed in this light, the HCA's case involving insulting speech, *Coleman*, is puzzling. If a form of speech constitutes a social evil, then presumably government should enjoy a relatively free hand to regulate it. Most industrial democracies impose mandatory civility norms on public discourse—including political discourse—on the theory that rude or uncivil speech in public constitutes a social evil. This holds true in Canada, France, Germany, Japan, and South Africa. Most constitutional courts have taken the view that a ban on the public use of highly offensive words or phrases does not preclude the articulation and dissemination of any particular ideas.[132]

Australia's approach, which aligns with the U.S. Supreme Court's approach in a series of cases starting with *Cohen v. California*,[133] and extending to *Hustler v. Falwell*[134] and *Snyder v. Phelps*,[135] protects intentionally abusive or offensive speech. As Justice John Marshall Harlan II explained in *Cohen*, "it is nevertheless often true that one man's vulgarity is another's lyric."[136] It follows from this premise that "because governmental officials cannot make principled distinctions in this area that the Constitution leaves matters of taste and style so largely to the individual."[137] Were a different rule to apply, "governments might soon seize upon the censorship of particular words as a convenient guise for banning the expression of unpopular views."[138] Justice Harlan could "discern little social benefit that might result from running the risk of opening the door to such grave results."[139]

In sum, good normative reasons exist that strongly support this approach. At the same time, however, strong normative arguments also exist that posit that insulting and degrading speech drives citizens away from the marketplace of ideas.[140] The SCC, for example, has embraced this approach—in this constitutional court's view, restrictions on insulting or degrading speech enhance the political marketplace of ideas by rendering it a less toxic place.[141] From a collective right perspective, it is difficult to understand why a ban on opprobrious language should not be seen as consistent with the IFPGC. One could plausibly view mandatory civility norms as a kind of "enhancement regulation" that have the salutary effect of encouraging broader participation in the marketplace of political ideas.

III. DECONSTRUCTING THE IFPGC: A COLLECTIVE INTEREST, A PERSONAL RIGHT, OR A STRUCTURAL CONSTRAINT—OR PERHAPS *ALL THREE*?

There is an irony in the HCA consistently rejecting the argument that the IFPGC constitutes a personal "right," but then proceeding to invalidate campaign contribution and spending limitations.[142] In the United States, where the freedom of speech definitely constitutes a personal civil liberty, much debate exists over the consistency of campaign contribution and spending limits with a strong commitment to the freedom of speech. If the IFPGC is not a personal freedom, it would seem to imply that government should enjoy a freer hand to shape how the process of democratic self-government works. But, the HCA has not taken this approach in the context of campaign finance regulations—it has taken an approach much closer in tone and result to *Citizens United* in the United States.[143]

If one conceptualizes the IFPGC as an aspect of a citizen's right to participate in the process of democratic self-government, it is difficult to understand how this right to engage with other citizens about matters of public concern and candidates for political office does not constitute a personal right. If the IFPGC is a necessary corollary of the right to vote, which surely is an individual right (in fact a legally enforceable *duty* or *obligation* in Australia), how can participating in the process of democratic deliberation really be theorized as solely a "collective" interest and not an individual one as well?

Given that Australia has a system of compulsory voting, dating back to 1918,[144] an obvious necessity arises to create and sustain conditions that make it possible for voters to inform themselves about both candidates and issues of the day. To date, however, the HCA has not made much of Australia's system of compulsory voting in grounding and applying the IFPGC. If the Commonwealth Parliament, and the state parliaments to boot, insist on all eligible citizens registering and voting in federal and state elections, they would seem to have necessarily embraced maintaining a marketplace of political ideas that permits these votes to be well-informed.

A conscientious citizen wholly ignorant of the issues of the day might well conclude that the only responsible course of action would be to refrain from casting a random ballot. To be sure, Australian law technically permits collecting a ballot and then not actually casting a vote on election day—but if a person goes to the time and trouble of collecting a ballot, Australia's public policies clearly would seem to support a citizen actually casting it (and ideally based on a well-informed basis).

Mandatory voting, as much as Sections 7, 24, 64, and 128 of the Australian Constitution, on electing federal parliamentarians and holding plebiscites on constitutional amendments, provides a sound constitutional basis for using the power of judicial review to ensure that citizens are able to access the information necessary to exercise the franchise wisely. To require all citizens to vote, but then to permit government to shut down essential channels of political communication, simply would not make any sense. Such an approach would be perverse—in the *Wednesbury* sense of being something a reasonable regulator could not reasonably do.[145] A policy of mandatory participation in the electoral process by poorly informed, ignorant voters is a prescription for utter and complete national disaster.

Thomas Jefferson once observed that "if a nation expects to be ignorant & free, in a state of civilisation, it expects what never was & never will be."[146] He added that "the functionaries of every government have propensities to command at will the liberty & property of their constituents" and that "there is no safe deposit for these but with the people themselves; nor can they be safe with them without information."[147] Australia

Australia: Free Speech as an Implied Freedom   ⁓ 119

does not merely use elections to select its government—it also *requires all citizens to participate in the electoral process*. This seems a point that deserves greater emphasis in framing the IFPGC than it has received to date in the pages of *Commonwealth Law Reports*.

In sum, the animating theory of the IFPGC simply does not square up with the HCA's insistence that it is not a personal right. Any more than it would make sense to say that the implied rights of access to the courts or due process of law are not "personal" rights that safeguard important individual autonomy and dignity interests. Protecting access to justice and ensuring fair procedures in adjudicative proceedings with the government are as much about protecting an individual's interest in justice as limiting the ability of government to engage in arbitrary action.

Of course, one could plausibly posit that the IFPGC is *both* a collective right (insofar as it exists to facilitate and support the process of democratic deliberation that informs the act of voting) and, at the same time, an individual right (insofar as an individual's participation in the process of democratic deliberation very clearly involves an exercise of personal autonomy). Yet, the HCA, since *Lange* and in all of its most recent IFPGC decisions, goes to great pains, and at considerable length, to characterize the IFPGC as a collective, rather than individual, right. Alternatively, the Justices attempt to renormalize the IFPGC as not even a personal or individual "freedom" at all (much less a "right"), but rather, as nothing more than a kind of structural check or limit on the scope of federal and state regulatory power—akin to federalism and the separation of federal and state authority.

Several IFPGC decisions clearly treat the interest as one related to the autonomy of both individual speakers and groups to engage with the body politic through means, and using language, that they prefer to use.[148] A truly collective right, or a check on government power, should not protect, for example, the use of offensive or opprobrious language to express a political idea that could be expressed without using offensive or opprobrious language. As long as it is possible to express the idea in less offensive terms, the process of democratic deliberation is not really adversely affected.[149]

Perhaps proscribing the expression of an idea is meaningfully different from limiting where, when, or how an idea may lawfully be expressed. From this vantage point, the state laws under review in *Clubb* and *Preston* were consistent with the IFPGC precisely because the would-be speakers remained entirely free to protest abortions—somewhere else. The laws did not, strictly speaking, bar the expression of opposition to abortions. By way of contrast, a flat ban on insulting or opprobrious language, at issue in *Coleman*, necessarily involves the prohibition of the expression of an idea.[150] If, in general, structured proportionality requires some kind of means/end fit, a flat ban on speech activity will be constitutional *only* if the speech, in any and all contexts, constitutes a social harm constitutionally worthy of proscription.

Perhaps the most puzzling aspect of the HCA's construction and articulation of the IFPGC is the freedom's limited scope—it clearly excludes, for example, commercial speech, pornography, and quite possibly speech about literature, arts, and science. For example, in *Clubb*, the Justices expressed substantial uncertainty about how best to characterize speech aimed at preventing abortions (or "terminations," using Australian nomenclature). An attempted intervention with a pregnant woman about her health care choices was arguably not the kind of speech to which the IFPGC applies because it is not self-evidently about politics or government policies.

To be sure, some First Amendment theorists in the United States have argued that only core political speech should be constitutionally protected. Robert H. Bork is probably the most prominent proponent of this view.[151] He argued in an iconic law review article that speech not directly and self-evidently related to the process of elections and governance should be freely regulable by the federal and state governments—subject only to a very limited form of "rationality" review.[152] As he states his case:

> The notion that all valuable types of speech must be protected by the first amendment confuses the constitutionality of laws with their wisdom. Freedom of non-political speech rests, as does freedom for other valuable forms of behavior, upon the enlightenment of society and its elected representatives. That is hardly a terrible fate. At least a society like ours ought not to think it so.[153]

Bork's views constitute a very strict interpretation of the First Amendment theories of Professor Alexander Meiklejohn.[154]

Meiklejohn argued that free speech should not be protected as an abstract autonomy interest, but rather because of its integral, and essential, relationship to the process of democratic self-government. For democratic deliberation to function properly, it is not important that everyone have an unlimited ability to speak, but rather that everything that needs saying gets said.[155] The HCA freely cites academic writings on the freedom of speech—in addition to U.S. free speech case law from the Supreme Court. It is therefore at least somewhat surprising that the Justices have not placed greater reliance on Bork and Meiklejohn in framing and enforcing the IFPGC.[156]

But, here's the rub: Meiklejohn was horrified by the Bork thesis. So much so, in fact, that when legal scholars started to cite his work to justify bans on sexually explicit speech, he wrote an article that expressly disavowed such legal arguments based on his writings.[157] Drawing on arguments made by John Dewey,[158] with roots going back to Thomas Jefferson,[159] Meiklejohn instead argued that the First Amendment had to protect speech essential to creating and maintaining a body politic capable of engaging in—and sustaining—an ongoing process of democratic self-government. Protecting only core political speech, and nothing else, would not do because this would leave government empowered to use enforced ignorance as a means of political control.

Which brings us back to the HCA and its IFPGC. If jurists are going to imply a right to freedom of political and governmental speech, as a necessary incident of a commitment to a mass participatory democracy—and deploy judicial review in defense of this implied right—then why not follow the constitutional logic to where it necessarily leads? A society of illiterates is not capable of making prudent electoral choices or engaging in the kind of democratic deliberation necessary to facilitate making prudent choices.

The 2016 U.S. presidential election and Brexit vote both demonstrated how poorly informed voters can engage in electoral malpractice. Some 72,000 votes in three states (Michigan, Pennsylvania, and Wisconsin) determined the outcome of the 2016 presidential election. Many voters in these states believed that Pope Francis endorsed Donald Trump, Hillary Clinton ran a trafficked child sex-slave brothel located in the basement of a pizza parlor in Washington, D.C., the government of Mexico would pay for a U.S. border wall, and stiff new tariffs on Chinese goods would be paid by the Chinese (rather than U.S. consumers who purchase products imported from China). These are not matters of opinion—these matters all involve empirically verifiable *facts*. Poorly informed voters, no less than misinformed voters, will make very imprudent electoral decisions.

Moreover, Australia does not leave voting up to an individual's conscience. As noted earlier,[160] in Australia, at both the federal and state levels, voting is compulsory. Given that the commonwealth Parliament requires Australian citizens to vote, and that the Constitution requires voting for members of the Commonwealth Senate and House, and also with respect to constitutional amendments, protecting only political communications stops well short of what is plainly required to create a citizenry capable of sustaining the ongoing process of democratic self-government. Yet, to date at least, the HCA has not clearly and cleanly made the same turn as Meiklejohn.

As a general matter, in fact, the HCA has failed to define with precision what constitutes "political" or "governmental" speech. This question was front and center in *Clubb* and *Preston*—but the Justices declined to engage seriously the scope-of-application problem. Instead, a majority simply assumed that some of the speech at issue constituted political or governmental speech. A nontrivial question exists regarding whether or not "sidewalk counseling," which is what Ms. Clubb and Mr. Preston sought to do, constitutes speech covered by the IFPGC.

As a matter of constitutional logic, political and governmental speech should exclude things like advertisements for a luggage sale at a Melbourne department store, but what about an advertisement urging people to stop eating meat because animals possess consciousness and can experience pain and therefore should enjoy legal personhood? Or a campaign advocating safe sex within the gay community? Or an anti-littering campaign? Exactly how broadly does the category of "political" and "governmental" speech extend? The existing case law does not go very far in answering these pressing and important questions. Some thirty years after the HCA first recognized the IFPGC, the precise metes and bounds of "political" and "governmental" speech remain distressingly amorphous.

The concept could, at least in theory, encompass all communications save perhaps commercial and sexually explicit speech. Indeed, one could infer this from the HCA's existing precedents—but it would be helpful for the Justices to state this directly if this is the case. To date, however, they have not done so. The precise boundaries of protected speech under the IFPGC are, under existing precedents, poorly defined. The easiest way, doctrinally, of rejecting Clubb's and Preston's free speech claims would have been to hold that attempts at "sidewalk counseling" to persuade women not to terminate their pregnancies, or clinic staff not to participate in facilitating abortions, constitute private speech and not speech related to politics or public policy.[161]

Justice Potter Stewart, of the U.S. Supreme Court, once quipped of obscenity that he could not provide a workable legal definition of the concept, but that he knew such material when he saw it.[162] Of course, a legal rule based on a single judge's personal intuitions is not really a legal rule at all. Justice Stewart had a professional obligation to provide a governing legal standard to guide lower courts in applying the obscenity exception to the Free Speech Clause of the First Amendment. Perhaps more merit exists in using the king's foot as a governing legal standard than it would seem. Even if this is true, however, such an approach makes the work of lower court judges in a hierarchical system of courts considerably more difficult.

If the HCA were to interpret the IFPGC broadly and more clearly a great deal of speech not directly related to candidates for office or ballot propositions could enjoy constitutional protection. Moreover, in protecting expressive conduct[163] and opprobrious or offensive speech,[164] the HCA seems to have signaled that it is not adopting the Borkian approach.[165] In sum, a clearer statement of the IFPGC's scope would be a very useful development—and would reduce the potential chilling effect that inevitably arises from the current ambiguity over the IFPGC's scope of coverage.

It also bears noting that the HCA consistently has resisted efforts to expand the IFPGC to encompass rights to freedom of the press, assembly, association, and petition. If the basis of the IFPGC rests on the relationship of such speech to the process of democratic self-government, why has the HCA failed to recognize other correlative expressive freedoms that are no less integral to the process of democratic self-government? Isn't collective expression necessary to self-government? And even collective *public* expression? The process of democratic deliberation involves not only individuals interacting with each other, but also groups engaging in collective speech activity as part of efforts to move public opinion toward their positions.[166]

Thus, rights (or "implied freedoms") of assembly, association, and petition, coupled with a free press, also seem quite essential conditions for democracy to function (and, ideally, to flourish). To be sure, the HCA seems to have recognized, implicitly at least, these realities.[167] Even if the IFPGC is not a personal right but rather merely a check on government efforts to undermine the efficacy of the electoral process and freedom of electoral choice, why not also recognize correlated expressive freedoms (including assembly, association, petition, and a free press)? (It bears noting that early twentieth-century HCA cases mentioned an implied right of petition—although the HCA has never exercised the power of judicial review to protect the implied right of petition in the modern era.[168])

Consider, for example, the need for targeted constitutional protections for newsgathering. Activity associated with newsgathering and reporting is not, strictly speaking, "speech"—rather, it is antecedent to speech.[169] A free press is obviously essential to democratic self-government. After all, how can citizens cast well-informed ballots on election day in the absence of truthful and accurate information about the pressing public policy issues of the day? Targeted protection of newsgathering activity would thus seem to constitute a necessary and essential "implication" from the text and structure of the Commonwealth Constitution.[170]

The HCA has recognized that expressive conduct constitutes "speech" for purposes of the IFPGC (in the context of animal rights activists who objected to duck hunting[171])—even as it upheld content-neutral regulations that prohibited interfering with lawful bird hunting. The HCA's refusal to embrace the full logic of the democratic necessity argument to provide express protection for the expressive freedoms of assembly, association, and petition, as well as freedom of the press, is puzzling. If judges are drawing reasonable implications from the election of the members of the Senate, House, and on votes on proposed constitutional amendments (Sections 7, 24, and 128 of the Constitution), why shouldn't collective public speech activity (assembly) and voluntary political associations (association) merit differentiated constitutional protection? Given that the HCA recognized, in obiter dicta, a right of petition, this also seems a very easy and logical extension of the IFPGC. If a strong reason exists for shoe horning all expressive freedoms into "speech" rather than recognizing other distinct and differentiable forms of expressive activity that are integral to the democratic process, it is not self-evident.

In fairness to the HCA, it bears noting that the U.S. Supreme Court has done exactly the same thing. It has used the Free Speech Clause of the First Amendment in circumstances where the Assembly, Petition, or Press Clauses would provide a more logical home for a particular expressive freedom claim. But, this does not explain the failure to build out a fuller, and more complete, account of the expressive freedoms essential to the operation of democracy. And, as Professor Ash Bhagwat has cogently argued, the First Amendment's framers "intended to give citizens—ordinary people—the tools to engage in political debate, to organize themselves in associations, to assemble for a variety of purposes, including consulting together regarding the issues of the day, and to call for action from elected officials through formal petitions."[172] Each modality of expressive freedom serves a distinct purpose—but all four clauses of the First Amendment exist to facilitate the ongoing process of democratic deliberation that is vital to maintaining democratic self-government. Accordingly, each merits differentiated recognition and judicial protection—both in Australia and in the United States.

IV. DOES CONSTITUTIONAL TEXT—OR ITS ABSENCE—REALLY MATTER TO THE SCOPE OF EXPRESSIVE FREEDOMS IN AUSTRALIA?

It would be a mistake—and a big one—to posit that the absence of constitutional text is entirely irrelevant to the scope of expressive freedoms in Australia. Any legal scholar, judge, or practitioner who reads the relevant HCA decisions and academic commentary on them will quickly realize that the implication of this "freedom" makes it considerably harder for judges, particularly in a system that observes a relatively strong form of parliamentary sovereignty as part of its constitutional tradition, to second-guess the legislative handiwork of elected legislators. Thus, the absence of text has probably led the HCA to be more cautious in defining and applying the IFPGC than would have been the case if the Commonwealth Constitution contained an analog to the expressive freedom provisions of the First Amendment—or if the federal parliament enacted a statutory bill of rights with an instruction to the courts to harmonize existing laws and common law doctrines with the guarantees the statutory bill of rights sets forth.

In theory, an express guarantee of freedom of speech might have provided a basis for a bolder, more comprehensive, and more robust exercise of judicial review to protect expressive freedoms (and not just the freedom of *political* speech). Certainly, the HCA itself returns—again and again—to the theme of the absence of an express textual guarantee of the freedom of expression as a basis for judicial reticence in exercising the power of judicial review to protect speech and expressive activities more generally. It would be difficult for the Justices to ignore either a constitutional or statutory provision that expressly safeguards speech, press, assembly, and free association rights.

Yet, the Supreme Court of the United Kingdom (SCUK) has done just that with respect to Section 12(4) of the Human Rights Act 1998 (HRA 98), which instructs the British Courts to "have particular regard to the importance of the Convention right to freedom of expression."[173] Despite this clear and express language, the SCUK has essentially read this provision out of the law and rendered it entirely nugatory, explaining that the European Court of Human Rights (ECtHR) precedents have held that all fundamental rights protected under the European Convention on Human Rights, and thus also under the HRA 98, enjoy equal priority and legal status.[174] If the SCUK can ignore, essentially reading out of the statute, a provision giving express priority to speech and press rights, it stands to reason that the HCA could easily do the same.

Moreover, Australia's Constitution does expressly protect a number of rights, including the right to a jury trial,[175] a principle against federal legislation that enacts uncompensated takings,[176] the right to be free of religious establishments and to the free exercise of religion,[177] and a right to nondiscrimination based on state residency when present in another state.[178] Yet, for decades now, the HCA has interpreted these express rights very narrowly.[179] Simply put, the HCA has not reliably and vigorously enforced the limited number of expressly guaranteed rights set forth in the Commonwealth Constitution. This suggests, perhaps, that the HCA's suggestion of constitutional text having a talismanic effect on the scope of a fundamental right, such as the freedom of expression, might be overstated.

Robust disagreements exist among Australian judges and legal scholars regarding the legitimacy of deploying judicial review in the name of "implied freedoms" that are derived only inferentially from the Constitution's text.[180] With regard to an implied freedom of political communication, some scholars—and HCA jurists as well[181]—object to any use of the power of judicial review to protect speech, whereas others advocate a very broad scope of protection for all forms of expression, including, but not limited to, core political speech. Professor Adrienne Stone's impressive work comes immediately to mind as advocating a relatively expansive approach,[182] whereas Jeffrey Goldsworthy's work reflects a position of near total opposition to the HCA deploying judicial review in the name of an implied freedom of political and governmental

Australia: Free Speech as an Implied Freedom — 125

communication.[183] Indeed, some disagreement seems to exist even over the precise nomenclature used to describe Australia's free speech guarantee.[184]

In opinion after opinion issued since 1992, members of the HCA have lamented that, if only the Constitution contained a textual guarantee of the freedom of speech, so much more would be jurisprudentially possible. This seems to be the predicate for Justice Steward's objection to continued recognition of the IFPGC in *LibertyWorks*.[185] As he states his case, "with the greatest of respect, it is arguable that the implied freedom does not exist" because it is "insufficiently supported by the text, structure, and context of the *Constitution* and, because of the continued division within this Court about the application of the doctrine of structured proportionality, it is still not yet settled law."[186]

Scholarly critics of the HCA's decisions in the IFPGC cases, such as Professor Stone, have repeatedly challenged the HCA to offer up a more complete, nuanced, and thoughtful normative account of the reasons why speech merits judicial solicitude, which should include a more systematic and coherent account of what the IFPGC actually encompasses and what it excludes—and the reasons why particular kinds of speech fall into one category or the other. Meanwhile, the HCA continues to cite, and sometimes follow, but other times rejects, U.S. Supreme Court decisions arising under the First Amendment. The HCA has held that expressive conduct about public policies counts as speech—but, on the other hand, also has held that restrictions on the right of free association by persons previously convicted of criminal activity either is not a restriction on speech at all or, if it is, the government's interest in banning such persons from meeting, for any and all purposes, overbears the speech rights of convicted felons.[187]

Accordingly, it is not implausible to ask whether the HCA's invocation of the absence of text as a basis for judicial caution in protecting the freedom of speech is entirely candid (rather than a rhetorical makeweight). Instead, in a system that generally respects the principle of parliamentary sovereignty, or supremacy, it is perhaps more accurate to suggest that the HCA is cautious because it views its appropriate role in setting social policy as being quite limited. Would an express textual provision in Australia's Constitution prevent the HCA from applying a deferential form of proportionality analysis to government regulations that burden speech? All of the available evidence suggests that the answer is "no." It is perhaps somewhat easier for the HCA to tread cautiously in the absence of an express text—but one should take with a grain (or two) of salt the proposition that a preexisting (as opposed to newly adopted) express general guarantee of freedom of speech, or expressive freedoms more generally, would necessarily result in a broader scope of judicial protection for expressive freedom in Australia.

Despite the HCA's oft-repeated claim that it is simply enforcing a restriction on the scope of government power to restrict speech related to government and public policies, the HCA seems to be taking into account the sociopolitical culture of Australia in setting the metes and bounds of the IFPGC.[188] The proscription against the use of insulting or opprobrious language had little obvious effect on the scope or vibrancy of political debate in contemporary Australia. It did, however, impose a gag on a kind of speech that has been commonplace in Australian political and public culture. It would certainly be plausible to posit that the cultural expectation of the freedom of speech, rather than the obvious relationship of a particular kind of speech to democratic self-government, undergirded the HCA's *Coleman* decision.

Moreover, vindicating the citizenry's expectations of what a constitution means can be essential, indeed integral, to public approval of a nation's judiciary. In the United States, the Supreme Court's public approval rating has reached historical lows in the aftermath of *Dobbs v. Jackson Women's Health Organization*,[189] the decision that overturned *Roe v. Wade*,[190] thereby abolishing a fundamental constitutional right that women in the United States had enjoyed for almost half a century. In the immediate aftermath of *Dobbs*, only 35% of respondents held a favorable opinion of the Supreme Court—whereas 42% of Americans held a negative view.[191] What is more, and arguably worse for the Justices, 37% of respondents report "very little or no confidence" in their work. This is a sea change from the results of an identical 2019 poll, which found 39% of respondents had high confidence and only 17% of respondents reported low confidence in the U.S. Supreme Court.

Nor is this public opinion poll an outlier. Another similar public opinion poll, undertaken by Marquette University Law School in early July 2022, found public approval of the Supreme Court as a governing institution fell from 60% of respondents pre-*Dobbs* to only 38% post-*Dobbs*.[192] The same Marquette Law School July 2022 poll found that disapproval of the Supreme Court increased after *Dobbs* from 39% in July 2021 to 61% in July 2022.[193]

Simply put, since *Dobbs*, the Supreme Court's standing with the American people has taken a shellacking. The *Dobbs* decision is deeply unpopular with a majority of the U.S. public. This is not to say that a constitutional court should hew closely to public opinion. But, it would suggest that judicial legitimacy is, at least in part, a function of whether a constitutional court's decisions comport with the expectations of what the citizenry believes a constitution should (or does) mean.

If the Australian people expect to enjoy the freedom of speech, a legitimacy problem does not really arise if the HCA meets this expectation by imposing a common law gloss on the Australian Constitution's electoral provisions. On the contrary, the greater risk to the perceived legitimacy of the judiciary would arise from *not* recognizing such a right. In other words, if the HCA seeks to vindicate widely held sociolegal and cultural expectations, the absence of an express text should not really matter much, if at all, to the outcome of individual free speech cases. Squaring a commitment to parliamentary sovereignty, in its Australian garb of democratic constitutionalism, with entrenched, judicially enforceable rights will require judges to zig and zag—far more so than would be the case in a system that practices judicial supremacy and lacks a strong political commitment to the doctrine of parliamentary sovereignty (such as Germany or the United States).[194]

At the end of the day, a deep irony arises from the HCA's reliance on U.S. cases and on its persistent and consistent drawing of a firm and clear line of distinction between

Australia: Free Speech as an Implied Freedom   127

the IFPGC and the U.S. First Amendment. And, it is this: The U.S. Supreme Court, over the past forty or so years, has read most of the language of the First Amendment out of it.[195] These days, the Free Speech Clause does virtually all the jurisprudential and doctrinal work in the United States.[196] Indeed, one could count the number of contemporary Press Clause and Petition Clause cases on the fingers of two hands.[197] So too, the Assembly Clause has not seen much action since the days of the civil rights movement in the 1960s—and under the Warren Court.[198] Thus, the First Amendment is a text that is largely *ignored* by the U.S. Supreme Court in developing a coherent and overarching theory of the freedom of expression.

In fact, the United States also has an "implied" expressive freedom not contained in the First Amendment itself—the right to freedom of association.[199] This implied expressive freedom is commonly invoked, often successfully, by groups that seek to avoid the application of public accommodation and antidiscrimination laws such as Title II, Title IV, and Title VII of the Civil Rights Act of 1964, as well as state and local laws seeking to advance identical objectives.[200] Thus, even with a written provision that sets forth expressly four distinct forms of expressive freedom (the rights of speech, press, assembly, and petition), the U.S. Supreme Court found it necessary to "imply" a fifth expressive freedom, freedom of association, in order to fully realize the central purposes of the First Amendment.

To be sure, the First Amendment obviously has a kind of talismanic effect—it serves as a kind of judicial totem (or fetish) that justifies the exercise of judicial review in the name of safeguarding the freedom of speech. But for most intents and purposes, the actual text of the First Amendment does very little, if any, meaningful work. Indeed, the text is problematic from the get-go because unlike other provisions of the Bill of Rights, which simply prohibit the federal government from doing things like imposing excessive fines,[201] taking private property for a public purpose without just compensation,[202] or quartering troops in private homes,[203] the First Amendment, strictly speaking, applies *only* to Congress. It states, plainly, that "Congress shall make no law."

On its face, then, it should have no application to either executive or judicial actions that burden the freedom of speech. Yet, those words—"Congress shall make no law"—have not been so much as a speed bump to judicial efforts to prevent executive and judicial authorities from burdening speech.[204] The First Amendment's actual text simply does not support the jurisprudential scope of what the contemporary First Amendment does—and the current members of the U.S. Supreme Court seem completely sanguine about this state of (jurisprudential) affairs.

The other irony is that a democratic self-government justification for protecting the freedom of speech could easily support a broader and more general theory of freedom of expression that proscribes government efforts to control information flows among and between citizens. Perhaps the best articulation of this argument comes from Professor Marty Redish, a prolific First Amendment scholar who, earlier in his academic career, pioneered the legal and normative arguments that led the Supreme Court to afford serious First Amendment protection to commercial speech.[205]

128 ◦— Free Speech as Civic Structure

Professor Redish seeks to reconceptualize the normative and doctrinal implications of adopting a democratic self-government theory of the freedom of expression. Redish deploys the democratic self-government justification for the protection of speakers and audiences to support a more general theory of speaker and audience autonomy.[206] In his view, the First Amendment is a structural check on the powers of the federal and state governments to use their regulatory powers to create forced ignorance among voters.[207] He argues, with considerable persuasive force, that any serious account of voter autonomy has to respect a voter's individual interest in information—regardless of the precise character of that information.[208]

Government cannot be allowed to adopt paternalistic laws aimed at shaping, or controlling, the thought process and expressive activities of "We the People." Redish objects to civic republican theories of the freedom of speech,[209] which are overtly collective and communitarian in cast, because they "incoherently exclude[ ] speech from the First Amendment's scope despite the fact that it directly facilitates democracy."[210] Individual autonomy, accordingly, is a value that falls within the ambit of the democratic self-government theory of the freedom of speech.

Redish's approach essentially collapses the "political/nonpolitical" dichotomy that the HCA has embraced since 1992. In my view, his arguments have significant persuasive force. One can say that "commercial speech" is not relevant to the process of democratic discourse, but isn't the price of milk and bread an issue for voters to consider? If not milk and bread, how about prescription medicines? Or gasoline? If general conditions of human flourishing and happiness are fair subjects for democratic discourse, it is not plausible for a court committed to protecting the process of democratic deliberation to say, "Well, price information about prescription drugs lacks a sufficiently direct connection to elections and electioneering to be constitutionally protected."[211] What about speech related to fundamental autonomy interests—such as reproductive freedom? Is truthful, nonmisleading speech about the availability of abortion services or contraception to be unprotected because in part the speaker hopes to sell medical goods or services?[212]

How about laws banning particular kinds of sexually explicit speech because it propagates the wrong ideas about the equality of the sexes?[213] Is the sale of books merely commercial activity? Is speech related to the sale of Hillary Clinton's *It Takes a Village*[214] or Barack Obama's *Dreams from My Father*[215] merely "commercial" speech for purposes of the IFPGC?[216] And on what possible principled basis could a court find speech about one book to be protected but speech about another, say *Heather Has Two Mommies*,[217] to be unprotected? Simply put, and as Professor Redish argues, a serious commitment to the process of democratic deliberation requires that government permit citizens to exercise agency in deciding what information they deem necessary to make prudent electoral choices.[218] Citizens, not the government, should get to decide how best to make and support their electoral arguments to their fellow citizens, using whatever information and ideas that they deem to possess persuasive force.

This takes us from Redish, by a very direct path, back to Meiklejohn, who argued in instrumental terms that speech related to arts, literature, and science, of whatever

Australia: Free Speech as an Implied Freedom — 129

stripe, had to enjoy robust First Amendment protection if ordinary people were to be capable of using the electoral process to hold the agents and institutions of government accountable on election day. Redish provides a more robust, and direct, argument for protecting audience autonomy as a necessary incident of a properly functioning marketplace of political ideas.[219] And, like the HCA, he sees the First Amendment as being primarily about establishing limits on the exercise of government authority to circumscribe the process of democratic deliberation that is essential to the process of democratic self-government.[220]

In sum, the autonomy of voters to seek and obtain the information that *they deem most relevant* must rest at the center, or "core," of the freedom of expression under the democratic self-government justification for protecting speech. To permit the government to adopt and enforce paternalistic regulations that limit the ability of voters to obtain information that they believe to be relevant to their electoral choices is flatly inconsistent with the use of elections as a means of securing government accountability. As Justice Anthony M. Kennedy stated the matter in *Citizens United*, "[p]remised on mistrust of governmental power, the First Amendment stands against attempts to disfavor certain subjects or viewpoints or to distinguish among different speakers, which may be a means to control content."[221] Moreover, "[p]rohibited, too, are restrictions distinguishing among different speakers, allowing speech by some but not others."[222]

Thus, once one agrees with the proposition that the freedom of speech is essential to the operation of a democratic polity, and, more specifically, to the conduct of genuinely free and fair elections, there is really no principled basis for the government telling citizens what ideas or information are fit for consumption—and which ideas and information are not. Moreover, a speaker's motive for providing information and ideas to a willing audience is often entirely irrelevant to the value of that information to the audience.[223]

Just as the HCA found that government cannot be permitted to control the precise articulation of a political idea,[224] the same logic should also make it difficult, if not impossible, for the government to decide what ideas are fit for the voters to hear and consider. As Meiklejohn explained with some force, "To be afraid of ideas, any idea, is to be unfit for self-government."[225] Moreover, "[a]ny such suppression of ideas about the common good, the First Amendment condemns with its absolute disapproval."[226] Simply put, "[t]he freedom of ideas shall not be abridged."[227]

Alexander Meiklejohn is widely considered the foremost proponent of the democratic self-government theory of the freedom of expression. Even in its original formulation, however, it was rather clear that the Meiklejohn theory of freedom of speech precluded the use of government regulatory power to cut off lines of inquiry by voters because the government sought to protect them from "bad ideas." Voters "must be made as wise as possible" because "the welfare of the community requires that those who decide issues shall understand them."[228] Both wise and unwise ideas must have a hearing because government censorship of ideas is a "*mutilation of the thinking process of the community against which the First Amendment to the Constitution is directed.*"[229]

130 ⌒— Free Speech as Civic Structure

I will not belabor the point. It suffices to observe that a theory of the freedom of speech rooted in the relationship of speech to the process of democratic self-government really does not have, and cannot legitimately ever have, an artificially truncated scope of application. Any effort by the government to limit or control speech in order to tilt the electoral playing field is inconsistent with a fully realized conception of the relationship of the freedom of speech to the ongoing process of democratic self-government.

Accordingly, the HCA should abandon its efforts to limit the scope of protected expression and instead frankly and forthrightly acknowledge that it is no more the business of judges than it is of legislators to decide what the people should hear and discuss. By way of contrast, however, it most certainly is the business of judges to decide whether the government has proffered a sufficiently compelling justification to permit a law to stand despite the fact that it impinges on the exercise of expressive freedoms. And, in this respect, an approach that double checks the legislature's handiwork to ensure that some attention was paid to free speech values is certainly preferable to an approach in which judges have no role whatsoever to play in second-guessing laws that restrict or completely abridge the freedom of speech.

Of course, if the HCA is inclined to use proportionality analysis in its free speech jurisprudence—as a current majority seems to be doing[230]—no good reason exists to impose artificial limitations on the scope of protected speech. If clear differences in the social importance of speech exist—for example, most reasonable judges would find a ban on discussing socialism requires a much higher burden of justification than a ban on sexually explicit speech featuring the images of minors—this will be accounted for in the balancing exercise that proportionality analysis requires.[231] Thus, proportionality analysis provides a very direct means for bringing sociolegal and cultural values to bear in applying a fundamental rights regime. Even if the Justices were to expand the scope of IFPGC's coverage, however, the larger problem with the scope of judicial deference that the HCA consistently affords the balances that legislators strike when regulating speech and expressive activity more generally would still remain.[232] Again, it would appear that if a legislature makes any meaningful effort whatsoever at tailoring a speech regulation—"sufficient" tailoring one might call it—the government will win if the statutory provision is subjected to a judicial challenge.

Australia, like the United States and the United Kingdom, comes from a long, proud, and deep-seated common law legal tradition. Under the common law, judges may legitimately draw upon the traditions and practices of the We the People in both shaping and enforcing legal norms.[233] And, from time to time, the HCA's free speech decisions reflect and incorporate this approach.[234] Using widely held, and shared, sociolegal understandings to shape and develop the IFPGC would stand squarely within this pre-existing and long-standing common law tradition.

As Professor David Strauss explains, common law is an "ancient kind of law" that has been "built not on an authoritative, foundational, quasi-sacred text like the [U.S.] Constitution," but instead rests on "precedents and traditions that accumulate over time."[235] Moreover, "[a] common law constitution is a 'living' constitution"[236] that has the ability to "protect fundamental principles against transient public opinion."[237] This is not to say that constitutional text is irrelevant to the ongoing process of the exegesis of constitutional meaning; it is to say that the text constitutes merely the starting point, not the end point, of making a persuasive constitutional argument.

Strauss posits that contemporary free expression principles do not flow (at all) from the "text and structure" of the First Amendment, or constitutional provisions related to elections and voting, but rather from "the living, common law Constitution."[238] Thus, U.S. free speech principles "were hammered out over time in fits and starts, in a series of judicial decisions and extrajudicial developments over the course of the twentieth century."[239] The process involves a kind of dialectic process: "The story of the emergence of the American constitutional law of free speech is a story of evolution and precedent, trial and error—a demonstration of how the living Constitution works."[240] Moreover, there is nothing fundamentally inconsistent with using proportionality analysis in a common law system of constitutional exegesis and adjudication.

Proportionality analysis also invites a kind of dialogue between courts and legislatures through a judicially mandated legislative second look. Even when courts conclude that long-standing legal restrictions unduly burden the freedom of speech in a mass participatory democracy, proportionality analysis leaves legal and policymaking space for legislators to adopt more narrowly tailored rules that better reconcile the freedom of speech with the concerns that led the government to regulate expressive activity in the first place. Proportionality analysis also allows courts to take all relevant factors into account—this is arguably its principal virtue.[241]

To be sure, proportionality analysis is not a panacea. The open-ended nature of the judicial balancing that it requires creates a risk that judges will overestimate the potential social cost of speech activity and fail to protect dissenting speech in times of national crisis or tumult.[242] As a general matter, categorical rules provide more reliable protection to unpopular speakers in times of national crisis than open-ended balancing tests.[243] On the other hand, however, proportionality review seems potentially very well-suited to addressing the HCA's concerns about overstepping its institutionally appropriate role in second-guessing judgments by the federal parliament or the state parliaments that sufficiently pressing and important reasons exist for restricting the freedom of expression in a particular context. The point remains that a broader conception of the freedom of expression would not necessarily imply a more robust judicial role in second-guessing reasonable legislative judgments.

At the same time, courts have an important, indeed essential, role to play in forcing legislators to consider how statutes will affect the process of democratic deliberation. In the absence of judicial review under the IFPGC, the federal and state governments would have an unfettered ability not only to adopt laws that overtly seek to distort the process of democratic deliberation, but also, and arguably no less problematic, completely disregard the effects of legislative enactments on the process of democratic deliberation. Even if the IFPGC is a distant cousin of the U.S. First Amendment— and a relatively weak one that grants broad, but not infinite, deference to legislative judgments about how best to reconcile speech with legitimate government regulatory objectives—the possibility of judicial review plays an important role in, if not forcing, then certainly incenting, legislators to consider carefully how new statutes will impact the freedom of speech about matters of public concern.[244]

In the end, then, the precise labels or tests are far less important to the process of interstitial constitutional exegesis of Australia's free speech principles than the process of common law evolution itself. And, if in the Australian constitutional tradition, invocation of the "text and structure," and "implications" from the text and structure, enjoy broad popular legitimacy as rhetorical tropes within both the legal establishment (judges, legislators, lawyers) and the body politic, then the HCA's use of these constitutional tools makes eminent sense. Moreover, if structured proportionality analysis advances rather than impedes this common law process of interstitial, rather than wholesale, legal change, the HCA's embrace of structured proportionality as a test constitutes a quite logical jurisprudential course.

V. CONCLUSION: THE ABSENCE OF TEXT MATTERS IN AUSTRALIA, BUT THE PRESENCE OF AN EXPRESS GUARANTEE OF EXPRESSIVE FREEDOMS WOULD NOT NECESSARILY WORK A CONSTITUTIONAL REVOLUTION

The HCA's recognition of the IFPGC in 1992 certainly drew meaningfully upon the "text and structure" of Australia's Constitution. And, grounding the IFPGC in the Commonwealth Constitution's text and structure no doubt rendered the creation of a constitutional interest in freedom of expression less objectionable; implications from the text and structure have a long and deep history in Australian constitutional law, dating back to the HCA's 1920 decision in the *Engineers' Case*.[245] Yet, the HCA's decision to create a limited right to freedom of speech, as a constitutional interest to be protected through judicial review, probably had as much, if not more, to do with the expectations of the Australian people by the early 1990s as with the intentions of the Australian Constitution's framers in 1900. Simply put, ordinary citizens expect a justly ordered polity to respect the freedom of speech.

Even if Australia's constitutional framework draws deeply and strongly on the Westminster model, with elected legislatures having authority to make social policy rather than the courts,[246] by 1992 it would have been difficult, if not impossible, for the HCA to cast a blind constitutional eye on statutory speech bans that featured absolutely no effort to tailor burdens on speech to limit their distortionary effect on the process of democratic deliberation. It was not plausible, as a matter of constitutional, or even merely legal, logic for the HCA's Justices to credibly claim that Australia was a democratic polity, with free and fair elections, in the absence of *any* constitutional protection for expressive freedoms. It also bears noting that the HCA's embrace of common law constitutionalism draws on a sociolegal tradition that is equally deeply seated with the principle of parliamentary sovereignty. The idea that judges, through the common law, will adapt legal rules as needed to vindicate the community's sense of fairness and justice, rests at the very heart of the common law tradition.

Australia: Free Speech as an Implied Freedom   —⌐ 133

It is true that the HCA has exhibited very broad deference to both the national and state legislatures when deciding free speech cases over the more than three decades that have now passed since it decided *ATV*. However, the relative weakness of the IFPGC, at least if compared and contrasted to the U.S. First Amendment, has far more to do with the Australian judiciary's view of its own proper role within the structure of democratic self-government, and in particular to respecting the imperatives of democratic constitutionalism, than it does with the absence of an express free speech provision in the Commonwealth Constitution. Even if the Australian Constitution were to be amended, to include an express guarantee of freedom of expression, it seems highly unlikely that free speech law in Australia would look much different than it does at present under the IFPGC.

Simply put, even if a written constitutional or statutory free speech guarantee existed, Australia's courts would very likely continue to afford broad deference to elected legislatures' policymaking choices, even when those choices directly involve speech activities related to elections and voting. Democratic constitutionalism, as a theory of constitutional interpretation, means that a reviewing court should defer to the legislature's views regarding the constitutionality of particular public policies—as well as the precise means the legislature adopted to achieve them. *Clubb* and *Preston* provide good exemplars of how this doctrine works in practice. If a state legislature decides that a 150-meter (164 yards) buffer zone is necessary to safeguard the privacy and dignity of patients and staff at reproductive health care facilities, then judges should not insist on a 145-meter buffer zone instead because judges deem it equally efficacious in achieving the government's stated objectives. In short, judges owe deference as to both legislative *ends* and *means*. The presence of a written free speech guarantee in Australia's Constitution would not change this longstanding structural feature of Australia's constitutional arrangements.

Going forward, the HCA must decide if it actually means what is has been saying since 1992 (and *ATV*) about the necessary relationship between the freedom of speech (and presumably other expressive freedoms) and the practice of democratic self-government. If expressive freedoms are, in fact, essential to maintaining free and fair elections, then the IFPGC should be expanded and extended to reach any and all communications that help facilitate informed and engaged citizenship by voters and expressly reach any and all forms of expressive activity (including speech, but also including assembly, association, petition, and a free press) that voters seek to utilize. If the relationship of expressive freedom to the operation of democracy is both inexorable and inescapable, as the HCA repeatedly argues, then the Justices should embrace with alacrity the doctrinal reforms presently needed to protect fully the process of democratic deliberation in Australia.

The prospects for such an expansion of the IFPGC are rather dim because the HCA does not seem much inclined to aggressively superintend the work of the federal and state legislatures. Under Australia's constitutional structure and long-standing institutional practices, the judiciary is very much the junior partner to the legislative and executive branches (which also holds true in the United Kingdom[247]). Accordingly, a major expansion in the scope of the IFPGC is very unlikely to occur absent a clear signal from the national legislature that it wants courts to more aggressively protect expressive freedom (which is equally unlikely to happen). Even so, it is surely better to have weak or limited judicial review to safeguard speech related to the process of democratic self-government than to leave the foxes (elected politicians) entirely free to guard the henhouse (the process of democratic deliberation that informs the act of voting).

6

Israel

COMMON LAW CONSTITUTIONALISM, DEMOCRACY, AND DIGNITY

⌒ ───

I. INTRODUCTION: COMMON LAW CONSTITUTIONALISM AND THE JUDICIAL ROLE IN SECURING AND SAFEGUARDING FUNDAMENTAL RIGHTS (INCLUDING FREEDOM OF EXPRESSION)

In 1953, a mere five years after Israel's founding in 1948, the Supreme Court of Israel (SCI) formally recognized expressive freedom (including the freedom of speech, but also including freedom of the press, and ultimately the freedoms of assembly, association, and petition) as a fundamental right that constitutes an essential part of the warp and weft of Israel's status as a democratic polity. In its 1953 landmark decision in *Kol Ha'am* ("Voice of the People"),[1] the SCI embraced—and with real brio—a process of common law constitutional reasoning to identify, define, and protect fundamental human rights that includes, but is not limited to, the freedom of expression.[2]

The SCI exercises both weak-form judicial review (reading statutes and regulations down to reconcile a government policy with a fundamental right) as well as strong-form judicial review (a formal judicial power to declare properly enacted statutes constitutionally invalid and unenforceable).[3] Moreover, unlike the constitutional courts in the United States, South Africa, Australia, and even the United Kingdom, all discussed in previous chapters, the SCI has done so without the benefit of a text that expressly recognizes freedom of expression as a fundamental right or, for that matter, a written provision that unambiguously authorizes the exercise of the power of judicial review.

Free Speech as Civic Structure. Ronald J. Krotoszynski, Jr., Oxford University Press. © Ronald J. Krotoszynski, Jr. 2024.
DOI: 10.1093/9780197662229.003.0006

136 ᴑ— Free Speech as Civic Structure

Accordingly, Israel provides a highly salient example of how judges, using a process of common law constitutionalism,[4] can effectively define and safeguard fundamental rights without the benefit of a written constitution or, as is the case in the United Kingdom and New Zealand, a statutory bill of rights that includes freedom of expression. It is, of course, impossible to say with certainty whether the presence of a formal, written constitutional text would have emboldened the SCI to enforce fundamental human rights—including the freedom of speech—even more aggressively than the Justices have done so to date. But, good evidence, associated with the enactment of the Basic Law: Human Dignity and Liberty, in 1992, exists that would suggest that a written text would not have made a significant difference either to the scope of human rights in Israel or to the SCI's efforts to enforce them.

In *Kol Ha'am*, Justice Shimon Agranat, who later served as the SCI's President (the title given to Israel's Chief Justice), invalidated as unlawful the Minister of the Interior's temporary suspension of two Israeli pro-Communist Party newspapers' press licenses. The minister took this measure as a form of punishment for the newspapers publishing editorials highly critical of Israel's government. At a time when the Supreme Court of the United States effectively upheld the criminalization of the Communist Party, deploying a "bad tendencies" approach to interpreting and applying the First Amendment,[5] the SCI struck out on a very different path—a path that reflects a considerably higher degree of civic courage and confidence in the process of democratic deliberation than the U.S. Supreme Court's highly problematic decision in *Dennis*.[6]

The First Amendment did not prevent the U.S. Supreme Court from falling prey to unjustified fear and social hysteria; so too, the utter absence of a relevant constitutional or statutory text did not prevent the SCI from upholding a fundamental right that is essential to the project of democratic self-government.[7] The juxtaposition of *Kol Ha'am* with *Dennis* provides a powerful and quite telling lesson regarding the real-world limits of constitutional text as a means of effectively safeguarding human rights in general—and freedom of expression in particular.

Unfortunately, the First Amendment counted for precious little in a period of widespread social panic over the (largely imagined) threat of communism to the United States and its governing institutions.[8] One can mount a highly persuasive normative argument that posits, during times of mass panic and irrational fear, that the courts have a particularly strong institutional duty, indeed a constitutional obligation, to stand firm and to vigorously enforce constitutional rights (and particularly the freedom of speech).[9] Yet, *Dennis*, unlike *Kol Ha'am*, reflects the opposite judicial approach (namely, the judiciary throwing its lot in with the frightened mob).

The methodological contrast between *Kol Ha'am* and *Dennis*, judicial decisions rendered at roughly the same moment in time, also demonstrates the importance of an independent judiciary that is demonstrably committed to safeguarding both democratic self-government and the process of democratic deliberation that informs it. As Ronald Dworkin has eloquently argued, some sort of check on poorly conceived majoritarian impulses does not degrade democracy but instead enhances it.[10]

This chapter will proceed in six additional sections. Section II discusses Israel's "constitution," which does not feature a single written document but instead a series of Basic Laws, enacted between 1958 and 2018, that establish the institutions of government, govern the conduct of elections for public offices (including Israel's national legislature, the Knesset), and codify some, but not all, of the fundamental rights that Israeli residents enjoy (and that the SCI protects). Section III then focuses with greater specificity on constitutional protection for freedom of expression, with particular attention to the SCI's 1953 landmark decision *Kol Ha'am Co. Ltd. v. Minister of the Interior*, in which the Justices found an individual right to freedom of expression in the absence of a constitutional text. In that case, the Court also laid the foundation for its future role in the review of legislative and executive actions that infringe upon individual rights. Section III goes on to describe the effect that the *Kol Ha'am* decision had on freedom of expression in Israel from 1953 to 1992.

Section IV examines the Knesset's 1992 enactment of Basic Law: Freedom of Occupation and Basic Law: Human Dignity and Liberty with a particular focus on the latter. The section begins by reviewing and describing the contents of the law and its effect on the SCI's institutional role in the Israeli constitutional scheme. It also describes and analyzes how the SCI—now relying on a "constitutional" provision guaranteeing human dignity—has evaluated some, but not all, expressive freedom claims as implicating aspects of human dignity covered by the Basic Law: Human Dignity and Liberty.

Section V argues that the presence of an express free speech guarantee would probably not significantly alter the scope and vibrancy of expressive freedoms in Israel. This is because the SCI, using a process of common law constitutionalism, has afforded expressive freedoms the same scope of application, and judicial solicitude, as the rights expressly set forth in Basic Law: Human Dignity and Liberty. To be sure, a written text might serve as a framing device for expressive freedom going forward; it would likely also resolve any residual doubts regarding whether courts may exercise strong-form judicial review to protect speech that is not clearly related to human dignity (such as commercial speech or hate speech). But, given the SCI's broad definition of protected speech, coupled with its use of proportionality review and balancing, it seems doubtful that a written free speech guarantee would work a revolution in Israel's freedom of expression law.

Section VI presents a sustained argument in favor of the necessity of a democratic state creating and maintaining independent courts vested with a meaningful power to define and protect fundamental human rights. It posits that elected politicians cannot be trusted to act altruistically when regulating speech related to elections, government accountability, and the democratic process more generally. When foxes guard hen houses, things often turn out badly for the chickens. Because of this reality—which holds true across jurisdictions—judges must play an important *structural* role in safeguarding speech related to democratic self-government to prevent efforts to distort the operation of the marketplace of political ideas. Finally, section VII offers a brief summary of the main points and arguments and a conclusion.

138 ⌒ Free Speech as Civic Structure

The domestic courts in Israel, like the domestic courts in the United States, South Africa, the United Kingdom, and Australia, play an essential role in safeguarding democracy. This project involves sustained and ongoing judicial efforts to protect the process of democratic deliberation from efforts by incumbent politicians to use the state's regulatory powers to distort or disrupt it. Such efforts are probably inevitable; they recur routinely in almost all democratic polities. Because of this fact of democratic life, courts must serve as a kind of umpire, or an honest broker, by thwarting efforts to impede or prevent voters from informing themselves about the issues of the day, debating the merits of candidates for public office and their proposed public policies, and, ultimately, casting well-informed ballots on election day. Israel's example provides an important case study on how judges and courts in a democratic polity inevitably and invariably will reach the conclusion that they must embrace and perform an institutional checking function to safeguard democratic self-government and the process of democratic deliberation that animates it.

II. ISRAEL'S CONSTITUTIONAL ARCHITECTURE:
A FOUNDING WITHOUT A CONSTITUTION

When Israel was established in 1948 after the partition of Palestine, the nation's founders did not enact a formal, written constitution.[11] Instead, Israel's government was formed under a temporary arrangement established in Israel's Declaration of Independence.[12] Among other things, the Declaration provided that a temporary body would govern until elections for a Constituent Assembly could be held. In theory, the elected Assembly would draft and arrange for the implementation of a permanent constitution by October 1, 1948.[13] Things did not go as planned.

Although Israel held national elections in early 1949, the nation found itself engulfed in a war "that sought to undermine the emerging Jewish state"; this rendered quite impossible drafting, debating, and ratifying a formal written constitution.[14] Accordingly, the temporary representative body quickly transferred both general legislative and constitutional "constituent assembly" authority to the newly elected Assembly, which would soon declare itself "the Knesset."[15] It was not until 1950, when circumstances permitted sustained attention to the problem of drafting a formal written constitution, that the Knesset turned its collective attention to the question of whether to enact a formal, written constitution for Israel.[16]

Despite "intensive constitution-making activity" in Israel, these debates did not lead to the implementation of a comprehensive written document.[17] Proponents wanted a constitution primarily "to protect democracy and human rights."[18] Opponents, though, had a "fear of limits on the powers of government and the legislature" and a "fear of judicial review over laws."[19] Moreover, the Israeli people were divided over how much influence the Jewish religion should have on the new government.[20] Simply put, it was impossible to achieve a consensus about the appropriate form and structure for a formal, written, entrenched Israeli constitution.

Israel: Democracy and Dignity   —⌒ 139

Unable to resolve these tensions, the parties reached a compromise known as the *Harari Resolution*. Under that agreement, instead of enacting an entire constitution at one time, the Knesset would enact a series of laws, to be known as "Basic Laws," that would provide a blueprint for Israel's government and governing institutions. The Basic Laws, once the Knesset had enacted them, would then form Israel's constitution.[21] Under this approach, Israel's constitution would be *written*, but neither *entrenched* nor *comprehensive*, and comprised of a number of free-standing, separately enacted "Basic Laws."

As of today, Israel has enacted fourteen Basic Laws, which address a variety of constitutional topics.[22] The majority of them deal with the structure of the government.[23] Only two—originally enacted in 1992—directly address individual rights. They are Basic Law: Freedom of Occupation and Basic Law: Human Dignity and Liberty.[24] These laws explicitly enumerate certain rights, but "freedom of expression" does not appear among them.[25] Indeed, today—seventy-four years after the Harari Resolution—there are still "many constitutional topics" that are not explicitly regulated by a Basic Law, "and Israel is therefore one of the few countries in the world to have no comprehensive constitution."[26]

The Knesset last enacted new Basic Laws in 2018 (Basic Law: Nation-State) and 2014 (Basic Law: Referendum). That said, however, it has not amended the 1992 Basic Laws since 1994. Given this state of play, at least arguably, the Knesset has simply acquiesced in the SCI's assertion of a specific power of judicial review under the Basic Law: Human Dignity and Liberty and Basic Law: Freedom of Occupation. On the other hand, the role of the SCI in reviewing and invalidating laws the Knesset enacts has been consistently contested in some quarters and the Israeli public appears to be badly divided on this question.

To be sure, the Knesset's failure to protect freedom of expression in a constitutional text has not prevented the SCI from affording expressive freedom broad constitutional protection. In its initial weak form, this power involved interpreting both statutes and regulations to avoid conflicts, whenever possible, with the freedom of speech, press, assembly, association, and petition. After 1992, as section IV explains, some aspects of expressive freedom, namely, those connected to the concept of human dignity, receive strong-form judicial review and the SCI will invalidate laws that unjustifiably restrict speech related to human dignity. In both cases, the Knesset has been aware of the SCI's recognition of expressive freedom as an implied fundamental right since 1953 and *Kol Ha'am* but (to date) has not directly legislated to abolish or even to significantly restrict the SCI's efforts to safeguard expressive freedom in Israel.

The Knesset's failure to act, for a period of seventy years, arguably constitutes a form of legislative acquiescence (at least with respect to weak-form judicial review to safeguard expressive freedom). On the other hand, however, neither has the Knesset expressly *ratified* the SCI's handiwork. It also bears noting that since the SCI's decision in *Kol Ha'am*, some segments of the Israeli electorate consistently have objected to the SCI's assumption of a power of judicial review and characterized the SCI's use of that power (whether in strong or weak form) as unauthorized and illegitimate. Thus, the

140 ～　　　　　　　　　　Free Speech as Civic Structure

picture is mixed, with plausible cases to be made both in favor of and against the SCI's precedents recognizing and protecting fundamental but unenumerated human rights (including freedom of expression).

III. FREEDOM OF EXPRESSION AS AN UNENUMERATED, YET NEVERTHELESS FUNDAMENTAL, CONSTITUTIONAL RIGHT

The SCI's initial approach to safeguarding speech involved weak-form judicial review; the courts had an obligation to protect speech, when possible, by reading a statute or regulation in a way that respected the ability of ordinary people to speak their version of truth to power. This approach continues to this day, although the SCI has held that the enactment, in 1992, of Basic Law: Human Dignity and Liberty, authorized it to deploy strong-form judicial review to invalidate laws when a speech regulation involves speech related to human dignity.[27]

A. Kol Ha'am Co. Ltd. v. Minister of the Interior

In its 1953 decision in *Kol Ha'am*, the Supreme Court of Israel held that despite the absence of a Basic Law enumerating individual rights citizens nevertheless enjoyed the right to freedom of expression.[28] At issue in the case were the comments of two Communist Party newspapers criticizing the Israeli Prime Minister's "anti-Soviet" and "anti-national" policies.[29] According to the newspapers, the alleged policies—which contemplated Israel's providing 200,000 troops to aid the United States in the event of a war with the Soviet Union—"speculat[ed] in the blood of Israel['s] youth."[30] At the time, the Minister of the Interior was empowered by statute to suspend the publication of any newspaper that published any "matter . . . likely to endanger the public peace."[31] The minister exercised this authority in suspending both of the papers, *Kol Ha'am* for ten days and *Al-Ittihad* for fifteen days.[32] Both newspapers challenged the suspension in the SCI, sitting as the High Court of Justice, arguing that it conflicted with the newspapers' right to freedom of expression.[33] The minster claimed the suspension was necessary to maintain public security.[34]

In the opinion for the SCI, Justice Shimon Agranat began by holding that freedom of expression—even though unwritten in a constitutional text—was a basic social value in Israel and, as such, also comprised part of Israel's unwritten constitution. Under this reasoning and approach, freedom of expression constitutes an unenumerated, yet fundamental, human right that Israel's courts, at all levels, have a duty to protect. Justice Agranat explained that because Israel is a democracy, it necessarily must protect the freedom of expression: "The principle of freedom of expression is closely bound up with the democratic process."[35] Moreover, a "simple understanding of the democratic regime inevitably leads . . . to the enforcement of the principle of freedom of expression in every state where such a form of government exists."[36]

Israel: Democracy and Dignity ⎯ 141

Freedom of expression "serves as a means and instrument for the purpose of investigating th[e] truth, since only by considering 'all' points of view and a free exchange of 'all' opinions is that 'truth' likely to be arrived at."[37] Further, Israel's Declaration of Independence based the State "'on the foundations of freedom' and the securing of freedom of conscience," leading to the conclusion that "Israel is a freedom-loving State."[38] Freedom of expression, then, was nonnegotiable in a polity dedicated to practicing democratic self-government.

At the same time, however, Justice Agranat emphasized that the right to freedom of expression has limits. The SCI made clear that where the right conflicts with the government's goals in achieving important state and security interests, courts would need to "weigh competing interests in the balance, and, after reflection, select those which, in the circumstances, predominate."[39] Under Justice Agranat's approach, the SCI had to reconcile a statute that expressly allowed the minister to infringe on the newspapers' freedom of expression if the matter to be published was "likely to endanger the public peace"[40] with the constitutional right to freedom of expression. In interpreting the term "likely" while being mindful of the newspapers' rights, the Court concluded that in order to suspend publication, the minister had to determine that it was "probable that as a consequence of the publication, a danger to the public peace" would occur.[41] A "bare tendency in that direction" was not sufficient, and even in the event the minister deemed the resulting harm to be "probable," that harm had to be "so grave" as to justify suspending the newspapers' freedom of expression.[42]

The SCI charted a very different constitutional course than the U.S. Supreme Court's weak-kneed approach in *Dennis* in reconciling freedom of expression with national security concerns . The SCI, unlike the U.S. Supreme Court, emphasized the need to hold would-be government censors to an appropriately short leash in order to protect public criticism of the government. Justice Agranat's well-reasoned opinion squarely rejects the idea that the government could enact laws that punish seditious libel.[43] *Dennis*, by way of contrast, embraces seditious libel by permitting the government to criminalize speech if that speech threatens grave social harm—without requiring the government to produce even a scintilla of evidence establishing the existence of a realistic prospect of that serious social harm actually occurring.

In 1951, despite the First Amendment facially proscribing Congress from banning speech, the U.S. Supreme Court sustained the criminalization of the Communist Party of the United States of America (CPUSA). The reasoning in *Dennis* also supported banning speech merely *sympathetic* to the CPUSA or to its objectives. This mode of constitutional analysis obviously would have a serious and predictable chilling effect on core political speech.

In contrast, *Kol Ha'am*, when engaging in a balancing exercise to determine if the government could punish the newspapers for publishing the editorials at issue, required a specific and highly particularized evidentiary showing of harm. The SCI concluded that, even if the editorials *might* have produced social harm, the government's evidence failed to show that any potential social harm flowing from the newspapers' editorial

142 ~ Free Speech as Civic Structure

speech was sufficiently "probable" to justify the imposition of postpublication punishment.[44] The minister's suspension order was therefore reversed as unconstitutional.[45]

There are three main takeaways from the *Kol Ha'am* decision. First, the SCI declared that the existence and meaning of "freedom of expression" does not depend on any constitutional, or even statutory, text. Second, the SCI showed its willingness to invalidate, based on an unenumerated yet fundamental right to freedom of expression, executive action not expressly authorized by statute. Third, and finally, the SCI held that where freedom of expression and important state interests collide, the "probability test" governs—and a "bad tendency" toward producing a social harm does not constitute a sufficient legal justification to sustain government censorship of speech.[46]

It is important to note that in *Kol Ha'am*, the SCI did not purport to possess the full power of judicial review of statutes passed by the Knesset. Nowhere in the opinion did the Court question the validity of the statute itself.[47] Instead, the SCI based its decision on its interpretation of the word "likely," within the relevant statute and it read that term against the backdrop of an implied constitutional right to freedom of expression.[48] As Professor Pnina Lahav explains, "without a written constitution, either to articulate the constitutional principles or, explicitly or implicitly, to allow for judicial review, 'usurpation' of any powers of judicial review was impossible."[49]

Over the years, the SCI has adhered to this view and accepted the doctrine of parliamentary supremacy. As Justice Menachem Elon wrote in 1995, "the validity of a law enacted by the Knesset is not subject to judicial review."[50] Accordingly, the SCI "can interpret legislation in a manner consistent with constitutional norms, but if there is a clear contradiction between a judicially-identified norm and a statute, the statute prevails."[51] As mentioned, no law protected—either explicitly or implicitly—the right to freedom of expression until 1992. So until that time, when a statute passed by the Knesset violated an individual's right to freedom of expression, the key question was whether it did so with sufficient explicitness to preclude the SCI deploying a saving construction[52] that would reduce the adverse effects of the law on the operation of the marketplace of political ideas.

B. *Freedom of Expression from* Kol Ha'am *to 1992*

Though *Kol Ha'am* unequivocally found that citizens have a right to freedom of expression and that the "probable danger" test governs when a statute vested the executive with discretion to take actions that burden or abridge the freedom of speech, subsequent cases, particularly a number of problematic SCI decisions handed down from the late 1960s to the late 1980s,[53] appear to be plainly inconsistent with *Kol Ha'am*.[54] More precisely, they either fail to recognize a viable expressive freedom claim or, if they recognize a claim, give it short shrift by failing to apply the probable danger test with appropriate rigor—the same rigor reflected in the SCI's earlier and later free expression precedents. Simply put, since *Kol Ha'am*, the SCI has not consistently held the government to a high burden of proof that government censorship of speech was absolutely essential to meet a pressing and important public need.[55]

Writing in 1986, Professor Norman Cantor observes that "[d]uring all this time, the Court has not questioned the basic vitality of the clear probability standard to guide decisions relating to dangerous speech."[56] From this, however, he cautioned that "[w]hether the Court has been consistent in applying that standard is more debatable."[57] Professor Cantor's concerns possess considerable merit.

First, in some instances, the SCI has failed to consider the key holding of *Kol Ha'am* that the right to freedom of expression necessarily limits executive authority. Take, for example, *Forum Films v. Cinematic and Plays Review Board*[58] and *Itzhaki v. Minister of Justice*,[59] in which, according to Professor Lahav, the SCI "failed to recognize that the principle of free expression was [even] implicated."[60] In *Forum Films*, the Cinematic Board decided to issue a permit to screen a documentary only if the script of the documentary—which was in German—was instead read in Hebrew. The SCI upheld this conditional permit, stating that it was not prepared to second-guess the board's decision that the German language was "unfit" for a film about Israel.[61] Along similar lines, in *Itzhaki*, the Minister of Justice withheld a permit to publish a book about Israeli military efforts in 1948. In Lahav's view, the SCI upheld the minister's authority "without consideration of the right to free expression."[62]

In addition, the SCI did not always adhere to the "probable danger" test as formulated in *Kol Ha'am*.[63] In *Yeredor*, for example, the SCI considered whether the Knesset's Central Elections Committee had the power to exclude a group of candidates from running in the 1965 elections.[64] The candidates at issue were members of "El Ard," a Palestinian-friendly group that—at least according to the Elections Committee—sought to "deny the integrity of the State of Israel and its very existence."[65] Notably, before this case reached the SCI, the Minister of Defense had declared El Ard an unlawful organization and the SCI had sustained the denial of a permit for the group to form an association.[66]

In reviewing the committee's power to exclude candidates from elections, the SCI explicitly stated that it would *not* review (1) "the Committee's finding that the candidates on this list are indeed members of the El Ard group," and (2) the committee's finding that "the members of this group 'undermine the very existence of the State, or in any event undermine its territorial integrity.'"[67] In other words, the SCI determined that the issue before it was a pure question of law: whether the committee had the power to exclude.[68]

President Agranat and Justice Sussman concluded that although no statute explicitly gave the Elections Committee the power to exclude candidates for public office based on their political views, El Ard's alleged commitment to undermine the existence of the Jewish state was enough to justify excluding members of that group from standing for public office.[69] President Agranat distinguished *Kol Ha'am*, noting that the speech at issue in that case did not involve a credible threat to the idea that Israel was "founded as a Jewish state in the Land of Israel."[70] Israel is a "sovereign, independent, freedom-loving state," but it also has a Jewish national identity.[71] To conclude that members of El Ard—which sought to undermine Israel's Jewish identity—could occupy seats in the Knesset "would constitute a complete disregard for the two wars

144 ◇— Free Speech as Civic Structure

fought by the State of Israel since its founding in order to prevent its annihilation by hostile Arab states" and a "complete denial of the history of the Jewish people and its yearnings," including the Jewish people's suffering during the Holocaust.[72] The SCI therefore dismissed the appeal.[73]

As Professor Lahav points out, in *Yeredor* the SCI failed to follow, and thereby weakened, the probable danger test from *Kol Ha'am*. Indeed, the SCI seemed to embrace and then to employ the "bad tendency" test that *Kol Ha'am* ostensibly had rejected.[74] Because allowing El Ard party members to join the Knesset if elected might lead to the undermining of the Jewish state, the government could constitutionally infringe the El Ard members' freedom of expression and association. This was true despite the fact that the Knesset had not enacted a statute that expressly allowed for such an infringement of the would-be candidates' and their supporters' constitutional rights. Nor, for that matter, was it clear from the record that the El Ard candidates were personally committed to promoting antidemocratic laws if elected (as was the case with members of the Communist Party USA). An abstract commitment to revolution does not necessarily mean that a group presents an immediate and palpable danger to the security of the state.[75] For example, in the United States, most members of the Communist Party USA held only a theoretical commitment to seeking the violent overthrow of the national government and the creation of a dictatorship of the proletariat.

Justice Oliver Wendell Holmes, Jr.'s well-known dissenting opinion in *Abrams v. United States*[76] provides one of the most iconic expressions of the centrality of speech to the process of democratic self-government. Holmes argues that "when men have realized that time has upset many fighting faiths, they may come to believe even more than they believe the very foundations of their own conduct that the ultimate good desired is better reached by free trade in ideas—the best test of truth is the power of the thought to get itself accepted in the competition of the market, and that truth is the only ground upon which their wishes safely can be carried out."[77] He posits, "[t]hat at any rate is the theory of our Constitution," which constitutes "an experiment, as all life is an experiment."[78] In Justice Holmes's view, "[w]hile that experiment is part of our system I think that we should be eternally vigilant against attempts to check the expression of opinions that we loathe and believe to be fraught with death, unless they so imminently threaten immediate interference with the lawful and pressing purposes of the law that an immediate check is required to save the country."[79] Based on Justice Holmes's constitutional logic in *Abrams*, the government lacks any legitimate constitutional authority to ban a political party, and prohibiting its candidates from standing for public office, in the absence of overwhelming evidence of both its antidemocratic aims *and* its intention to carry out those antidemocratic objectives. In Holmes's view, such ham-fisted government efforts to manipulate the electoral process cannot be reconciled with a serious commitment to democratic self-government.

Applying these principles to *Yeredor*, the decision appears to be deeply problematic because it permits the complete exclusion of candidates for public office without a strong evidentiary showing that their theoretical commitments to the violent overthrow of the government represent a serious and immediate threat to the security of the state and its people. No reasonable person would contest that the nature of the threat was a serious one, but a proper constitutional assessment requires considering not only the seriousness of a particular threat but also its probability.

Before criticizing the SCI's commitment to baseline principles of the freedom of speech and association, one should keep in mind that not only the United States, but Germany as well, has banned anti-democratic parties, and their members, from participating in the democratic process. More specifically, Germany's Basic Law *expressly excludes* parties that seek to overthrow the existing democratic social order from constitutional protection. As a general matter, Article 21 provides that "[p]olitical parties shall participate in the formation of the political will of the people" and that "[t]hey may be freely established."[80] However, this provision also expressly states that "[p]arties that, by reason of their aims or the behaviour of their adherents, seek to undermine or abolish the free democratic basic order or to endanger the existence of the Federal Republic of Germany shall be unconstitutional,"[81] and vests Germany's Federal Constitutional Court (FCC) with the power to approve bans against the participation of antidemocratic parties in any and all German elections.[82] So too, Article 9, the Basic Law's guarantee of the freedom of association, features an express limitation that provides "[a]ssociations whose aims or activities contravene the criminal laws or that are directed against the constitutional order or the concept of international understanding shall be prohibited."[83]

As I have noted previously, "Article 21(2) and Article 9 . . . limit[ ] the full freedom of association, whether by political parties or other groups, in order to safeguard the democratic social order."[84] Accordingly, "[a]lthough the Basic Law establishes a democratic constitutional order, its framers did not intend to tolerate any and all political agendas."[85] Germany is thus a "militant democracy" that features an entrenched, written constitution that explicitly excludes antidemocratic parties, and candidates for public office, from the electoral process.[86]

Yeredor's approach—and outcome too—would seem to be consistent with the German Basic Law and the FCC's decisions interpreting and applying it. One also should keep in mind that Germany (like Israel) has banned antidemocratic parties in the past (namely, the Communist Party[87] and the Socialist Reich Party[88]). Given these facts, unless one is prepared to say that Germany is insufficiently democratic because it excludes antidemocratic parties and associations from the electoral process, one cannot object to Israel taking an identical constitutional approach.

Even if, as a normative matter, it is entirely feasible to have a system of free and fair elections that excludes antidemocratic parties and candidates from participating, what explains the SCI making such a bold and obvious departure from *Kol Ha'am*'s insistence on the importance of freedom of expression and proof of an immediate, serious threat to justify government censorship in the form of a party and candidate ban? Professor Lahav observes that "unquestionably, Israel's vulnerability in terms of national security triggered the Court's aversion to" speech undermining Israel's existence.[89] Similarly, Ilan Saban points to "historical trauma" in explaining the holding in *Yeredor*.[90] The fact that the United States and, even more so, Germany, have enacted bans on antidemocratic political parties and associations also bears consideration when assessing *Yeredor*'s consistency with a robust regime of constitutional protection for expressive freedoms.

If Germany concluded that toleration of antidemocratic parties presents too great a social risk to tolerate, enshrining this rule repeatedly in its Basic Law, one cannot criticize the SCI too harshly for taking the same approach. Even so, banning candidates and entire political parties from standing for election cannot easily be reconciled with another one of Justice Holmes's famous free speech constructs: The marketplace of ideas metaphor. He best explicated his marketplace of ideas metaphor in his renowned *Gitlow* dissent.[91] Holmes thundered that "[i]f in the long run the beliefs expressed in proletarian dictatorship are destined to be accepted by the dominant forces of the community, the only meaning of free speech is that they should be given their chance and have their way."[92] Even so, however, Holmes almost immediately hedges his bet, observing that "[i]f the publication of this document had been laid as an attempt to induce an uprising against government at once and not at some indefinite time in the future it would have presented a different question."[93] For Holmes, then, the question should turn on the immediacy of the threat that an antidemocratic party presents— rather than solely on the fact that it theoretically seeks to bring about antidemocratic outcomes.

Despite the SCI's failure to follow *Kol Ha'am* consistently from the 1950s to the 1980s, the opinion unquestionably influenced later free speech decisions. Professor Guy Carmi notes that, "after several decades of dormancy," the SCI "rediscovered" *Kol Ha'am* and embarked on a new jurisprudential course that rejected "the speech-restricting rulings of the early years of the establishment of Israel."[94] In this period, which arguably extends to the present, freedom of expression became "one of the most powerful rights, if not the most powerful one" and the SCI employed a variety of "strict scrutiny tests in cases of infringement of the right of freedom of expression."[95] Freedom of expression went from something of an afterthought to an apex human right. The SCI, in *Kidum Entrepreneurship and Publishing Limited*, went so far as to opine that "freedom of expression stands at the top of the liberties upon which our democratic regime is founded."[96] Thus, as Carmi observes, "[a]lthough freedom of expression has never been considered an absolute right, the Court clearly positioned it at the top of the array of protected rights."[97]

For example, in *Schnitzer v. Chief Military Censor*,[98] decided in 1989, the SCI interpreted a regulation allowing the Military Censor to prohibit the publication of material that "in his opinion, would be, or be likely to be or become, prejudicial to the defence of the state, public safety or public order."[99] The censor exercised this power when a newspaper published an article criticizing Mossad leadership and publicizing the date on which the leader of the agency would be replaced.[100]

Writing for the SCI, once again sitting as the High Court of Justice, then-Justice, and later President, Aharon Barak explained that in cases where state security concerns and freedom of expression squarely conflict, "it is legitimate to restrain freedom of expression, as a last resort, only when there exists a near-certainty of substantial

Israel: Democracy and Dignity   —ↄ 147

damage to State security and public order."[101] With regard to the criticism of Mossad leadership, the SCI held that the government failed to prove with convincing clarity that the probability of harm justified censoring the publication. In fact, at best the record established only a "remote possibility—a 'harmful tendency' "[102] of serious social harm.

Because "freedom of expression is also freedom of criticism," the newspaper had the right to publish its story.[103] With regard to the date on which Mossad leadership was to be replaced, the potential harm was "merely speculative."[104] As can be seen from this case, *Kol Ha'am's* probable danger test remained an important part of Israel's constitutional freedom of expression jurisprudence. Its restoration and enforcement in the late 1980s shows that *Yeredor* constitutes an exception, or temporally limited departure, rather than a new constitutional rule.

Finally, although *Kol Ha'am* dealt explicitly with political speech, the SCI has made clear that its "approach to the question of the scope of freedom of expression is a broad one."[105] Unlike the implied freedom of political and governmental communication in Australia that the High Court of Australia recognized in 1992,[106] in Israel the freedom of expression "applies to every expression, whether political, literary, commercial or any other, and whether verbal or behavioural (symbolic or otherwise) such as demonstrations."[107] Indeed, no categorical exceptions apply; the free speech principle reaches—and protects—racist expressions, falsehoods, expression that offends "religious sentiments," and obscenity.[108] Coverage, however, does not necessarily mean that the government cannot regulate speech when it possesses a sufficiently important reason for doing so. For example, the SCI has upheld the use of Israel's sedition law, Section 136 of the Penal Code, to prohibit the dissemination of hate speech because such speech threatens the ability of a diverse population to live and work constructively together.[109]

Because the SCI embraces proportionality review and balancing, successfully invoking the right to freedom of expression is only the first step in a two-step process—albeit a necessary one. The fact that particular speech enjoys coverage does not mean that the Israeli courts will invariably prohibit government regulation, up to and including proscription, of it.[110] First, the government may infringe on an individual's freedom of expression if the balancing exercise favors the government's claim that speech must be burdened or even proscribed. If the government can show a substantial risk of serious social harm associated with particular speech, thereby meeting the probable danger test, the government's speech regulation will stand.

Second, and no less important, not all forms of expression are equally protected. The social value of speech will significantly affect the balancing exercise. As the SCI has observed, "political freedom of expression is not equivalent to its commercial counterpart."[111] Accordingly, the government could overcome the constitutional protection of speech more readily if the social value of the speech is particularly low—as is the case with obscenity, libel, and hate speech.

Third, and finally, not all harms arising from speech stand on equal ground. For example, "[h]arm to state security is not on the same footing as harm to the freedom

148 ⌒   Free Speech as Civic Structure

of movement."[112] This factor also informs the outcome of the balancing exercise. The more serious the potential social cost of speech activity, the stronger the government's case will be for regulating or even banning it.

In short, balancing means that context matters—and it matters a great deal. One should note that this approach, known more generally as proportionality review, is quite commonplace in the larger world. Indeed, some legal academics argue that it is now the most important constitutional concept in framing and enforcing fundamental human rights.[113]

To account for these nuances, the SCI has developed "an extensive system of balances between freedom of expression and the values and principles with which it clashes."[114] A reviewing court must "horizontally" balance between the rights of two people. It also must "vertically" balance between "the individual freedom and the public interest."[115] The weaker the alleged harm arising from the speech at issue and the more social value particular speech possesses, the more strongly protected that speech will be. In a similar vein, the less vital and valuable to society in general and to facilitating democratic self-government in particular the specific speech at issue (e.g., commercial speech or obscene pornography), the more latitude the government will possess in restricting, or even banning, it based on a lower-threshold showing of social harm.[116] This balancing exercise provides a structure and framework that permits courts to consider the nature of the government's interest, the burden placed on both individual and collective interests in expression, and the "fit" between the government's preferred means of achieving its stated objective and the actual attainment of that objective.

Ultimately, the constitutional protection of the freedom of speech, as well as other expressive freedoms (press, assembly, petition, and association), serves not so much as a means for empowering individual autonomy and self-realization (although it certainly advances this value as well—in addition to the search for truth[117]), but rather as a kind of structural bulwark meant to safeguard and protect the maintenance of democratic self-government. If incumbent politicians can regulate speech to suit their electoral interests, history teaches that they will seek to distort the process of democratic deliberation in order to further their chances of being reelected. Because of this structural conflict of interest, a politically neutral outside institution that lacks any direct interest in the outcome of contested partisan elections is needed to assess fairly and impartially the merit and necessity of government laws and regulations that burden or suppress speech. In Israel, to date at least, the SCI has performed this crucial civic function.

This is a long and perhaps unduly round about way of suggesting that the SCI got matters right in 1953 when, in *Kol Ha'am*, it found that it simply could not avoid reviewing government efforts to censor speech to ensure that the government's stated reasons were both constitutionally sufficient as well as the actual reasons for the attempted censorship. Performance of this structural checking role requires the SCI to assume a concomitant duty to weigh the government's objectives against the burden that the means selected to achieve these objectives impose on freedom of expression. An honest broker is essential to performing this task, and politicians suffer from an

Israel: Democracy and Dignity   —⌒ 149

obvious self-interest problem. In sum, safeguarding speech is a constitutional necessity, and a constitutional duty, for judges in a democratic polity.[118]

IV. THE ADVENT OF A TEXT—BASIC LAW: HUMAN DIGNITY AND LIBERTY

In 1992, Israeli constitutional law underwent a "revolution,"[119] when the Knesset enacted
Basic Law: Human Dignity and Liberty[120] and Basic Law: Freedom of Occupation.[121]
Aharon Barak argues that "[b]y virtue of this basic legislation, human rights in Israel
have become legal norms of preferred constitutional status."[122] In his view, these laws
empowered Israel's judiciary to embark on a new project of rights creation and rights
protection.[123]

Barak's arguments have significant persuasive force. After all, these Basic Laws
were the first in Israel that directly addressed individual human rights.[124] But the
answer to the question of whether Basic Law: Human Dignity and Liberty and Basic
Law: Freedom of Occupation conveyed, or were intended to convey, the power of judicial review on the SCI to invalidate laws that conflicted with them remained, and arguably still remains, an open one.

This uncertainty held especially true with respect to freedom of expression, which
neither of the new Basic Laws specifically enumerated—and despite Basic Law: Human
Dignity and Liberty containing a long list of specifically enumerated human rights. To
this day, any attempted answer to these questions generates significant controversy
about the proper role of the SCI vis-à-vis the Knesset. Of course, the nature of Basic
Laws had long been in question, and the SCI would now have to grapple with the fact
that the 1992 Basic Laws do not specifically include the right to freedom of expression.
Despite these obstacles, however, the SCI ultimately concluded that Basic Law: Human
Dignity and Liberty conferred a strong form of judicial review on the Israeli courts
(including, but not limited to, the SCI) and also elevated expressive freedom, including the freedom of speech and press, to true constitutional status (at least when the
expressive activity at issue implicates human dignity).

A. *The Status of Basic Laws in General*

Before delving into the contents of the rights-based Basic Laws passed in 1992, one
must understand how the Knesset adopts Basic Laws—as well as how the SCI has
defined the normative status of Basic Laws in comparison to the status of ordinary
statutes. These matters are complicated and not free from controversy.

The Knesset enacts Basic Laws in exactly the same way as it enacts ordinary statutes;
a majority *of the members voting* may pass a new law.[125] That is, no "special majority"
(i.e., an absolute majority of the 120 total members of the Knesset or 61 members) is
needed. In other words, "[a] law is called a 'Basic Law' if the Knesset chooses to give it
that title."[126] Given the unextraordinary process required to enact a Basic Law, it makes

150 ⌒   Free Speech as Civic Structure

sense that a Basic Law does not automatically enjoy a higher status than another duly enacted statute not denominated as a "Basic Law" simply because it carries that designation.[127] Nor does designation of a statute as a "Basic Law" automatically give the SCI the power to strike down "ordinary" statutes that conflict with it.[128]

Rather, in order to invalidate a statute that conflicts with a provision of a Basic Law, the SCI generally has required that the provision of the Basic Law be "entrenched"— that is, the Knesset must explicitly state within the four corners of the Basic Law that it can be contravened only by a statute passed a special majority of 61 members of the 120-member Knesset.[129]

Two important cases addressed the SCI's constitutional authority to exercise a power of judicial review to invalidate statutes that conflict with the entrenched provisions of a Basic Law. In *Bergman v. Minister of Finance*,[130] the petitioners claimed that an elections financing law violated Basic Law: The Knesset, which contained "entrenched" provisions that the Court interpreted to require equality in elections.[131] Although the SCI addressed the question only indirectly due to a concession from the government, the Justices concluded that the elections financing law conflicted with the Basic Law and was thus invalid because it had not been enacted with the requisite sixty-one votes.[132] In doing so, the SCI explicitly stated that if the Knesset wished for the law to be sustained, it could "reenact the financing provisions in the Financing Law . . . if the majority required under sections 4 and 46 of the Basic Law is mustered—that is, if the Knesset complied with the entrenched provisions."[133]

The second case, *Le'or Movement v. Chairman of the Knesset*, required the SCI to confront directly this issue.[134] Similar to the issue in *Bergman*, the petitioners claimed that an elections financing law violated the "entrenched" sections 4 and 46 of Basic Law: The Knesset.[135] Notably, all three Justices agreed that the SCI, sitting as the High Court of Justice, had the power to disregard statutes that conflicted with entrenched provisions of a Basic Law.[136] As summarized by Professor Ivan Rothman, the SCI concluded that although, in general, it could not strike down laws under a theory of judicial review, an "exception" to this rule exists when the content of laws passed by the Knesset "contravened the entrenched provisions of one of the basic laws."[137] The Knesset was under an "obligation—which it had imposed upon itself—to enact" the law "in the manner laid down by the basic law in question."[138]

As Professor Marcia Gelpe points out, these decisions did not "greatly augment the power of the Court" because few Basic Laws had entrenched provisions, and "those clauses that were entrenched were not of great breadth."[139] Notably, no Basic Law before 1992 even addressed individual rights. However, it is nevertheless important to note that in *Le'or*, the SCI did claim the power of judicial review despite no law explicitly conferring that power on it. In other words, nowhere in Basic Law: The Knesset did the legislature say, in so many words, that the SCI was to review either previously or subsequently enacted statutes for conflicts with the Basic Law.

Instead, the Justices decided this issue for themselves, and on the SCI's institutional authority alone. *Bergman* and *Le'or* laid the jurisprudential framework for the SCI's invocation of a similar power with regard to the two Basic Laws that the Knesset enacted in 1992. Professor Gelpe argues that this approach led to a "much greater

Israel: Democracy and Dignity   ➝ 151

expansion of the Court's power."[140] Moreover, this expansion of the SCI's authority proved controversial. To this day, in fact, the legitimacy of the SCI's assertion of a power of strong-form judicial review remains highly contested.

However, the SCI's decisions asserting a power of judicial review predated the Knesset's enactment of the 1992 Basic Laws and the Knesset's members arguably knew that the SCI would likely interpret the inclusion of an entrenchment provision, or giving express textual priority to provisions of a particular Basic Law, or both, as authorizing the exercise of strong-form judicial review—unless and until the Knesset amended the Basic Law in question to remove this power. Thus, it is entirely plausible to posit that including entrenchment provisions in the 1992 Basic Laws, against the existing legal and constitutional backdrop, constituted tacit or de facto acceptance by the Knesset of the SCI deploying judicial review to enforce the new Basic Laws. Certainly, members of the Knesset could not have been shocked or genuinely surprised when the SCI held that the entrenchment provisions authorized strong-form judicial review.

With that said, and even if one might question the proper scope of the SCI's general authority to invalidate or read down legislation to promote unenumerated, yet fundamental rights, it seems reasonably clear that a constitutional court in a democracy possesses very powerful arguments for the exercise of such a power in the specific context of speech and expressive freedom more generally. Elected politicians, when regulating speech related to elections and democratic deliberation, labor under a clear structural conflict of interest—whereas unelected judges do not. Because of this fact of institutional life, judges, rather than legislators, are better positioned to serve as honest brokers in deciding whether particular restrictions on speech, and particularly on speech related to government and elections, advance sufficiently important government objectives, and impair expressive freedoms in a sufficiently narrow and targeted way, to be constitutionally justified.

Indeed, the SCI embraced precisely this reasoning in 2024, when it invalidated the Knesset's ersatz "reforms" to the Basic Law: The Judiciary. The statute, Basic Law: The Judiciary (Amendment No. 3), purported to strip the SCI of its authority, sitting as the High Court of Justice, to review the "reasonableness" of executive branch actions (including both substantive decisions and the appointment of executive branch officers). The case, *Movement for Quality Government v. Knesset*,[141] required the SCI to decide whether it possessed the constitutional authority to invalidate an amendment to a Basic Law if the proposed amendment contravened the fundamental principles, or "core identifying characteristics," of Israel as a democratic polity.[142]

On July 24, 2023, the Knesset, acting as the Constituent Assembly, enacted Basic Law: The Judiciary (Amendment No. 3). This law entered into force and effect on July 26, 2023 (after publication in the *Official Gazette*).[143] In relevant part, it provided:

> Notwithstanding the provisions of this basic law, those who have jurisdiction by law, including the Supreme Court sitting as the High Court of Justice, will not consider the reasonableness of a decision of the government, the prime minister, or any other minister, and shall not issue an order in this regard. In this section,

"decision" means any decision, including regarding appointments or a decision to refrain from exercising any authority.[144]

Shortly after the amendment's adoption, eight parties filed petitions with the SCI, invoking its jurisdiction as the High Court Justice, seeking judicial invalidation of the newly enacted limits on the SCI's traditional oversight powers.[145]

The Justices, stting en banc as a fifteen-member bench for the first time in Israel's history, ruled that a law inconsistent with the fundamental principles of democracy is null, void, and without any legal effect; they did so by a margin of 12-3.[146] A law, including an amendment to a Basic Law, cannot be inconsistent with Israel's existence as a Jewish and democratic polity (which constitute Israel's "core identifying characteristics").[147] President Esther Hayut explains that "the power of the Knesset wearing its constituent authority hat is not unlimited and it is not authorized to deny—in law or in practice—the core identifying characteristics of Israel as a Jewish and democratic state."[148] Thus, *Movement for Government Quality* holds that the SCI possesses a power of judicial review to protect these "core identifying characteristics."[149]

On the more specific question of whether the statute amending Basic Law: The Judiciary was, in fact, inconsistent with the fundamental principles of a democratic nation, the Justices were closely divided. They held, by an 8-7 margin, that the judicial "reform" amendments, if allowed to stand, would prevent the SCI from performing its constitutional duty to enforce the rule of law and separation of powers, through judicial invalidation of unreasonable government actions; accordingly, the new law was inconsistent with the fundamental principles of a democratic government.[150]

President Hayut explains that "judicial review over the legislative and executive branches in Israel is the only effective mechanism that can serve to limit the centralized power of the majority in any real way."[151] Irrational, arbitrary, and unjust government actions are inconsistent with the fundamental principles of democracy; yet, without judicial review of the actions of the political branches, irrational, arbitrary, and unjust government actions would inevitably occur, undermining both the rule of law and the separation of powers. In the process, Israel's core identifying characteristic as a democratic polity would be seriously compromised (and perhaps lost entirely).[152] Accordingly, Amendment No. 3 constituted "an extreme, exceptional amendment" with "no parallel in [Israel's] constitutional history," thereby "strik[ing] head-on at the heart of two of the core characteristics of the State of Israel as a democratic state."[153] Given these circumstances, the only adequate remedy that would restore the balance of powers, and thereby secure the rule of law and the principle of the separation of powers, was judicial invalidation of Amendment No. 3.[154]

This decision, in both its constitutional logic and policy analysis, clearly reflects both the letter and the spirit of *Kol Ha'am*, which in many respects serves as Israel's counterpart to the U.S. Supreme Court's landmark decision in *Marbury v. Madison*,[155] which established the doctrine of judicial review in defense of constitutional rules and values in the United States. *Movement for Quality Government* constitutes a significant milestone in Israeli constitutional development. And, if the Knesset and Israeli people

Israel: Democracy and Dignity —⟡ 153

ultimately accept it as legitimate, the decision will secure the role of the SCI as the principal guardian of the rule of law, as well as the separation of powers, within Israel's system of democratic self-government.

B. Basic Law: Human Dignity and Liberty and Basic Law: Freedom of Occupation—Judicial Review and Freedom of Expression

Dubbed a "constitutional revolution" by Justice Aharon Barak,[156] the enactment of the two rights-based Basic Laws in 1992 made several fundamental changes to Israeli constitutional law. First, both laws explicitly granted citizens fundamental rights. Basic Law: Freedom of Occupation provides that "[e]very citizen or inhabitant of the State is entitled to engage in any occupation, profession or trade."[157] Particularly relevant to this chapter, Basic Law: Human Dignity and Liberty[158] provides that no person shall violate "the life, body, or dignity" of another.[159] A person's property shall not be violated,[160] and one is entitled to "protection of their life, body, and dignity."[161] Moreover, a person in Israel enjoys freedom from "deprivation or restriction of their liberty . . . by imprisonment, arrest, extradition, or by another other means."[162] Residents of Israel also enjoy "the right to privacy and intimacy"[163]—which includes freedom from arbitrary government searches of the person or one's home.[164] In addition, every person is free to leave Israel, and every Israeli citizen is entitled to return.[165] A 1994 amendment to the Basic Law: Human Dignity and Liberty added Section 7A, which explains that "[t]he purpose of this Basic Law is to protect human dignity and liberty, in order to establish in a Basic Law the values of the State of Israel as a Jewish and democratic state."[166] It bears noting that this language tracks closely the language of Justice Agranat's decision in *Kol Ha'am* and arguably constitutes a legislative ratification of it.

Both laws also place restrictions on how and for what reason subsequent laws can violate the rights expressed therein. Specifically, the Basic Laws cannot be violated "save by means of a law that corresponds to the values of the State of Israel, which serves an appropriate purpose, and to an extent that does not exceed what is required."[167] Scholars have dubbed this clause the "limitation clause."[168] Basic Law: Freedom of Occupation also explicitly provides that "[t]his Basic Law is not to be changed save by a [Basic Law] that was adopted by a majority of the Knesset Members"—that is, it is fully "entrenched."[169] Basic Law: Human Dignity and Liberty has no such provision expressly requiring sixty-one votes for any legislation amending or repealing it.

Focusing now on freedom of expression in particular, the Court almost immediately had to answer two important questions regarding the scope of Basic Law: Human Dignity and Liberty. First, was the SCI finally granted the power of judicial review by virtue of that Basic Law, despite no explicit grant of such authority from the Knesset and even though this particular Basic Law was not entrenched? Moreover, even if the Basic Law granted the SCI the power of judicial review, insofar as another law or regulation violates "the values of the State of Israel" as defined and explicated by the SCI, did "human dignity and liberty" encompass freedom of expression—and if so, to what extent?

In 1995, the SCI answered the first question in *United Mizrahi Bank Ltd. v. Migdal Cooperative Village*.[170] The issue in that case was: "Does the Family Agricultural Sector (Arrangements) (Amendment) Law . . . violate the provisions of Basic Law: Human Dignity and Liberty, and should it therefore be regarded as void."[171] In other words, one of the main issues before the SCI was whether it had the power to strike down ordinary statutes that conflicted with the Basic Law.

A panel of nine Justices—each writing a separate opinion—held that, under the Basic Law, the SCI could declare a statute that did not comply with the limitation clause void.[172] Justice Meir Shamgar summarized the SCI's holding by stating: "Basic Law: Human Dignity and Liberty does not contain a supremacy clause, but it refers expressly to the validity of infringing legislation and thereby designates a mandatory route and binding standards."[173] Moreover, "[i]n [section] 8, this Basic Law defines the boundaries of possible infringement and therefore impliedly establishes its supremacy relative to infringing legislation."[174]

Thus, if a statute infringes on the rights guaranteed by the Basic Law yet fails to meet the conditions of the Basic Law's limitation clause, the SCI has the authority to disregard the infringing statute. All nine Justices agreed.[175] Justice Barak, speaking through a law review article written after the decision, explains that "[s]ince [*United Mizrahi Bank*] was handed down, the Supreme Court, sitting in various panels, has repeated that approach."[176]

The Basic Law: Human Dignity and Liberty works in more or less the same way as the United Kingdom's European Communities Act 1972,[177] which instructed the British domestic courts to follow European Economic Community, and later European Union, law over any conflicting provisions of domestic law.[178] In this way, the European Communities Act enjoyed superior status over other British statutes—but Parliament did not vest the House of Lords with a general power of judicial review. And, as a statute, Parliament retained the power to amend or repeal it.[179] Of course, this statute, unlike Basic Law: Human Dignity and Liberty, contained an express direction to harmonize domestic British law with European Union law.[180] In this respect, the European Communities Act 1972 provided a clearer mandate to disregard conflicting statutes than does the Basic Law: Human Dignity and Liberty.

To be sure, though, not everyone agreed—or even today agrees—that Basic Law: Human Dignity and Liberty grants the SCI the power of judicial review. Legal scholars have noted that in enacting the Basic Law, the Knesset never "really and deliberately made" the decision to "confer supremacy on the courts."[181] No statute in Israel explicitly provided for judicial review, much less Basic Law: Human Dignity and Liberty.

This objection does carry some persuasive force: Why would the Knesset include an entrenchment provision in Basic Law: Freedom of Occupation—but not include one in Basic Law: Human Dignity and Liberty—if it meant for it to have preemptive effect? A sound response exists: absent judicial review, what import does the Basic Law's limitation clause possess? As President Barak observes, "a court must review the government because if there is no court—there is no law."[182] Moreover, as Professor Gelpe argues, a legislature bound only by itself cannot seriously be said to be bound at all.[183]

The debates surrounding the expanding power of the SCI have persisted over time. In January 2023, the Netanyahu administration released a plan that would allow the Knesset to override by a simple majority "almost any revocation of parliamentary legislation by the Supreme Court."[184] The plan, in essence, would strip the SCI of the power of judicial review, without requiring any special procedures or obstacles to be followed by the Knesset in doing so.[185] Of course, given the SCI's emphatic ruling in *Movement for Quality Government*,[186] invalidating the Knesset's reasonableness limitation amendment to Basic Law: The Judiciary, that sought to deny the SCI of its longstanding authority to review executive branch actions (including appointments within the executive branch) for "reasonablemenss," it seems very likely that a broader attack on the SCI's ability to enforce and protect the fundamental rights that are constitutive of a democratic policy would also be unconstitutional—and thus without legal effect.

The SCI faced the second major question—whether "human dignity and liberty" included a right to freedom of expression—shortly after the enactment of the Basic Law. *Golan v. Prisons Service*[187] is a good example of the Justices' debates on this issue. In *Golan*, a maximum-security prisoner requested permission to publish a personal column in a newspaper.[188] In this column, the prisoner planned to describe his "life at Ashmoret Prison."[189] Prison officials denied his request, claiming that allowing the prisoner to publish articles would hinder the prison's ability to maintain order, discipline, and security in the facility.[190] The prisoner filed suit, claiming that the prison officials had violated his right to freedom of expression.

A three-judge panel of the SCI, sitting as the High Court of Justice, held that the prison officials had impermissibly violated the prisoner's freedom of expression. Even so, the Justices were divided on whether Basic Law: Human Dignity and Liberty included a right to freedom of expression per se and whether the prison officials' actions in this case violated the limitation clause of that Basic Law. Justice Eliahu Mazza concluded that the Basic Law encompassed the right to freedom of expression.[191] He explained that although Basic Law: Human Dignity and Liberty "does not mention freedom of speech, nor does it define it expressly as a basic right," the Basic Law "enshrined the [past] case-law recognition of the constitutional status of freedom of speech."[192] From this vantage point, freedom of expression is implicit in the concept of human dignity: "For what is human dignity without the basic liberty of an individual to hear the speech of others and to utter his own speech; to develop his personality, to formulate his outlook on life and realize himself?"[193]

Justice Dalia Dorner disagreed. In her view, "[f]reedom of speech is a central basic human right and I do not believe that in Israel it can be regarded as being part of the right to dignity."[194] To be sure, if the prison violated Golan's freedom of speech *"because he is a prisoner,"* that would implicate the Basic Law's protection of dignity.[195] But because not every infringement of freedom of expression involves "humiliation," such an infringement is not per se a violation of the "dignity" guaranteed by the Basic Law.[196] According to Justice Dorner, the Court should evaluate freedom of expression claims that do not implicate dignity independent of the Basic Law.

156 ⌒ Free Speech as Civic Structure

Finally, Justice Mishael Cheshin declined to take a definitive position on the issue but stated that he would "not deny that there are other possible interpretations" of the Basic Law besides concluding that it includes the freedom of expression.[197] Echoing Justice Dorner's position, he explained that the answer to the question depended not only on the meaning of "human dignity" in a linguistic sense, but also "the meaning of the concept *in the special context*" of the Basic Law itself.[198]

When it came to applying the law to the facts, Justices Mazza and Dorner agreed that the prison impermissibly infringed on Golan's freedom of expression, whereas Justice Cheshin concluded that the prison's actions were constitutionally permissible. Notably, the Basic Law's limitation clause did not seem to change the test Justice Mazza used to evaluate freedom of expression claims. Although taking account of the special conditions that must exist in a prison, all three Justices employed the "probability test" or "near certainty" test that the Supreme Court had established approximately forty years earlier in *Kol Ha'am*.[199]

As can be seen by the Court's discussion in *Golan*, the precise scope of the word "dignity" was unclear. Justice Barak, in both his opinions and public appearances and speeches, advocated for a broad reading of the term.[200] And over the years, the Court appears to have followed his lead.[201] On the other side of the equation, though, are views represented by Justice Dorner in *Golan*. In defending her position in *Golan* that human dignity did not necessarily mean freedom of expression, she placed particular emphasis on the fact that in 1993 and 1994, members of the Knesset had thrice submitted drafts of a law called "Basic Law: Freedom of Speech and Assembly."[202] And all three times, the Knesset failed to adopt them.[203] This, coupled with the fact that nowhere in Basic Law: Human Dignity and Liberty did the Knesset mention "freedom of expression" or "freedom of speech," led to the "apparent" conclusion that "the national consensus required for enshrining freedom of speech in a Basic Law had not yet been reached."[204]

C. *Freedom of Expression after* United Mizrahi Bank *and* Golan

Over time, Justice Dorner's views on the incorporation of freedom of expression into Basic Law: Human Dignity and Liberty do not appear to have entirely prevailed. In particular, the SCI "chose partial incorporation of freedom of expression via the Human Dignity Clause" in *Matee Harov v. Israeli Police*.[205] In that case, the petitioners applied for a license from the police commissioner to hold a march in the city of Tel Aviv.[206] The police commissioner conditioned the issuance of the license on petitioners' agreement to cover the costs of, among other things, security personnel, cordons, and fire and ambulance services.[207] Petitioners sued, alleging that the police commissioner's conditions violated their freedom of expression. In their view, section 4 of Basic Law: Human Dignity and Liberty created an obligation on the State to "allocate the resources that are required in order to allow the realization of the right of freedom of speech and demonstration."[208]

Holding that the police commissioner's conditions on the license violated the petitioners' right to freedom of expression, Justice Barak, joined by Justice Miriam Naor, explained that even though the Basic Law included no explicit reference to the freedom of expression, "the Basic Law also includes the freedom of speech."[209] However, the SCI set an important limitation on the scope of incorporation:

> [N]ot all the aspects of the right of freedom of speech are included in the constitutional right to human dignity, but only those aspects [of freedom of speech] that are derived from human dignity and are closely related to those rights and values that lie at the heart of human dignity as expressing a recognition of the autonomy of the individual will, the freedom of choice, and the freedom of action of the individual as a free agent . . . or those aspects that are found in the heart of the right to human dignity.[210]

Justice Barak then concluded that a demonstration that "has a political or social background is an expression of the autonomy of the individual will, freedom of choice and freedom of action."[211] Thus, Basic Law: Human Dignity and Liberty protected the demonstration and section 4 of that law required the State to guarantee the petitioners' right to freedom of demonstration.

Although the majority of the three-Justice panel adopted a partial-incorporation theory, the majority defined "human dignity" more broadly than Justice Dorner would have in *Golan*. Indeed, in *Golan*, Justice Dorner stated explicitly that she did not "believe that in Israel [freedom of speech] can be regarded as being part of the right to dignity."[212] Rather, the only way freedom of speech could be protected under the Basic Law was if there was "a violation of a prisoner's freedom of speech *because he is a prisoner*."[213] The Court in *Matee Harov* disagreed and hinted that any form of expression that "has a political or social background"—and surely a political demonstration meets this criterion—is protected under the Basic Law.[214]

Once it was settled that the Basic Law incorporated some aspects of the freedom of expression, the SCI had to decide a related, subsequent question: whether it had an obligation to invalidate portions of a law that infringed on the freedom of expression—and thus Basic Law: Human Dignity and Liberty. In the 2015 case of *Avneri v. Knesset*,[215] the SCI answered this question in the affirmative. At issue in *Avneri* was Israel's "Prevention of Harm to the State of Israel by Means of Boycott Law," which, inter alia, imposed civil liability on any person who knowingly called for a boycott against the State of Israel.[216] Section 2(c) in particular imposed what the SCI characterized as "punitive damages" on those found to be in violation of the statute.[217] According to Justice Hanan Melcer, "the imposition of a regime of unlimited punitive damages in regard to the boycott tort *deviates, in my opinion, from the bounds of proper proportionality*."[218] Thus, the punitive damages provision failed to satisfy the limitation clause of the Basic Law and was, in consequence, void and of no legal effect.

Instead of reading down this provision, weakening it, to avoid as great an infringement on the freedom of expression, the SCI instead simply struck down this section of the law. *Avneri* presents the SCI at the height of its power deploying judicial review to protect expressive freedom as long as the "freedom of expression" that the petitioner claims falls within the scope of human dignity. Thus, under settled precedent, the SCI currently enjoys the power to invalidate any and all ordinary laws that unduly infringe on expressive freedom—provided that the expressive activity plausibly implicates human dignity. In circumstances where human dignity is not plausibly implicated, such as cases involving corporate speech or commercial speech, strong-form judicial review is *not* available under Basic Law: Human Dignity and Liberty, but weak-form judicial review, under *Kol Ha'am*, could be used to justify the use of a saving construction of a problematic statutory provision or regulation to reduce the conflict between the offending provision and constitutionally protected forms of expressive freedom (including the freedoms of speech and press).

V. THE (LIMITED) RELEVANCE OF A TEXT TO THE PROTECTION OF FREEDOM OF EXPRESSION IN ISRAEL

The evolution of Israeli jurisprudence with respect to freedom of expression and judicial review can be divided into two halves. During the first half, from 1953 to 1992, no textual guarantee of freedom of expression existed in Israeli law. The right to freedom of expression rested on the SCI's common law reasoning in *Kol Ha'am*. However, during the second time period, from 1992 to the present, a text has existed that—at least arguably—protects freedom of expression. Thus, in some respects, the answer to the question whether a text would have mattered in Israeli freedom of expression jurisprudence can be found by comparing and contrasting the periods before and after the Knesset's 1992 enactment of Basic Law: Human Dignity and Liberty.

It is evident that a text guaranteeing citizens freedom of expression was not necessary for the SCI to recognize that citizens nevertheless did enjoy that freedom. *Kol Ha'am* proves this point beyond peradventure. Despite the absence of an express textual provision—either statutory or constitutional—prohibiting the government from arbitrarily silencing citizen speech, the SCI drew on fundamental principles of democracy and freedom to hold that political speech was protected under Israeli law.[219]

The SCI's labors did not end there. Although *Kol Ha'am* established that *political speech* fell within the ambit of protected expression, subsequent cases established that *all forms* of expression—not only political or governmental speech—also enjoyed constitutional protection. Later precedents make crystal clear that judicial protection of freedom of expression does not depend on whether the expression at issue is political or governmental in nature.[220] Indeed, as *Universal City Studios* highlighted, "such freedom applies to every expression, whether political, literary, commercial. . . . [It] extends to every expression, whatever its content, influence, or style."[221]

The SCI arrived at all these conclusions without the help of any constitutional or statutory text.[222] Instead, it acted as a common law court, drawing on the Israeli people's well-settled, and oft-exercised, expectation that the government could not legitimately claim an unlimited power to censor speech and ban expressive activities. Indeed, the fact that the Knesset has not attempted to directly attack or overrule *Kol Ha'am*, some seventy years after the SCI held that the freedom of expression

Israel: Democracy and Dignity   —◦ 159

constitutes a judicially enforceable right in Israel, speaks volumes to the public's settled expectation that each and every Israeli citizen remains free to speak their version of truth to power. As Professor Carmi observes, "[t]his common law development of freedom of expression doctrines was not constitutionally anchored and was partially concealed due to the manner of its formation."[223]

A key question, then, is what changed after the enactment of Basic Law: Human Dignity and Liberty? What effects did that law have on either freedom of expression or judicial review of statutes infringing on freedom of expression? At least arguably, the primary change involves the SCI's holdings in *United Mizrahi Bank*[224] and in cases like *Avneri*.[225]

In *United Mizrahi Bank*, the SCI reasserted its power to disregard statutes that conflict with Basic Laws. In *Avneri*, the SCI suited word to deed by striking down a statutory provision the Knesset had enacted because it impermissibly infringed on the freedom of speech and thus also infringed on Basic Law: Human Dignity and Liberty. The most important change represented by these cases is straightforward. Whereas before Basic Law: Human Dignity and Liberty, the Court was constrained to *interpreting* a statute, if possible, to avoid improper infringement on freedom of expression,[226] after enactment of the 1992 Basic Law, the SCI determined that it had a newfound power to *invalidate* statutes that infringed on freedom of expression.[227]

But this could easily prove to be a distinction without a real difference; a sufficiently determined court can conduct judicial surgery on a statute that violates a fundamental right, essentially rewriting it, and then declare the law does not reach the conduct at issue. This approach is arguably the essence of weak-form judicial review as practiced, for example, by the Supreme Court of the United Kingdom.[228] It is also the Supreme Court of Japan's preferred approach to reconciling statutes that the Diet enacts with the rights guarantees set forth in Japan's Constitution of 1947[229]—despite possessing an express, textual power of judicial review set forth in Japan's Constitution.[230]

To be sure, one could plausibly posit that, had the Knesset passed a Basic Law that expressly protected the freedom of expression and also included in that Basic Law either an entrenchment or limitation clause (rather than considering but rejecting such a Basic Law in 1993 and again in 1994), Israel's post-1992 freedom of expression jurisprudence might have been even more robust. As mentioned above, after the enactment of the 1992 Basic Law, the SCI and scholars debated whether it protected freedom of expression at all.[231]

Moreover, in *Matee Harov*, the SCI explicitly held that not all aspects of freedom of expression are included in the Basic Law—rather, only those aspects that are sufficiently connected to human dignity enjoy coverage.[232] Consequently, it follows that only in some freedom of expression claims (i.e., those sufficiently related to human dignity) does the Court have the formal power to strike down laws (under the Basic Law) instead of simply interpreting them to avoid impermissible infringement (under *Kol Ha'am*). The significance of this divergence, of course, depends on the facts of each case. That said, however, the Knesset could avoid this oddity—that some freedom of expression claims have to pass more and higher hurdles than others—if it simply enacted a Basic Law: Freedom of Expression that expressly provides for judicial review in free speech cases. To be sure, the probability of such action today seems, at best, quite remote, but times change and governments come and go with the next election.

Then again, it is not at all clear, given balancing and proportionality, that the concrete results in free expression cases would shift radically in favor of would-be speakers and against the government were the Knesset to adopt such a law. Even in cases that are not covered by the Basic Law: Human Dignity and Liberty, the resolution of speech disputes in Israel seems to be highly fact specific and to depend on the perceived social value of the speech, the strength of the government's case that it has a pressing and substantial reason for regulating the speech activity at issue, and the overall "fit" between the government's stated objectives and its choice of means.

Cases decided after 1992 involving conflicts between privacy, an expressly enumerated right, and speech, an unenumerated right, do not reflect a clear priority in favor of enumerated rights. Thus, when a group of protestors sought to protest in or near a residential apartment building where a public figure resided, the SCI, sitting as the High Court of Justice, did not reflexively favor privacy over speech (because it is an expressly enumerated right), but instead engaged in a careful effort to reconcile the conflicting fundamental rights to give meaningful effect to both.[233] If speech held an inferior place on Israel's human rights ladder, in such a case the enumerated right would receive priority—but it is very clear that speech and expressive activity more generally enjoy an equal, not inferior, constitutional status with rights expressly set forth in Basic Law: Human Dignity and Liberty.

It also bears noting that the SCI began applying strict scrutiny to laws, regulations, and policies that burden speech well before the 1992 enactment of the Basic Law: Human Dignity and Liberty. The SCI began to reverse decisions of the Board for Film and Theater Review, official censors of public film and theatrical performances, in 1986.[234] The SCI's 1989 decision in *Schnitzer*,[235] overruling the Chief Military Censor's decision to proscribe a news article discussing the Mossad and a pending change of leadership in the agency,[236] clearly demonstrates that heightened judicial solicitude for expressive freedom antedates the enactment of the Basic Law: Human Dignity and Liberty. *Schnitzer* relies on the "near certainty" of harm approach first established in *Kol Ha'am* and requires the government to show, "based on clear, unequivocal and convincing evidence" that absent government censorship of a news story "there will be a near certainty of substantial injury to the security of the State."[237] It thus seems clear that even if the Basic Law: Human Dignity and Liberty provided a clear textual hook on which the SCI could rest its recognition of expressive freedom as a fundamental right (as a constituent element of human dignity), the Justices had already gone a great way toward elevating the freedom of speech as a judicially enforceable right prior to 1992.

This is not to say that the new text was irrelevant to the scope or vibrancy of freedom of expression in Israel. Plainly, the new Basic Law provided the SCI with a stronger basis for exercising a power of judicial review in the strong form—rather than a weak-form power that allowed the Justices to read down statutes or regulations to safeguard speech (the approach in *Schnitzer*). It is to say, however, that freedom of expression was already well-established, and routinely protected, by the late 1980s. Text facilitated the expansion of this jurisprudential project, and perhaps also accelerated it—but the project was already afoot. It also seems unlikely that, in the absence of the Basic Law: Human Dignity and Liberty, freedom of expression in Israel would be significantly weaker than it is today.[238]

VI. FREE SPEECH AND DEMOCRACY: THE ESSENTIAL ROLE OF A CONSTITUTIONAL COURT AS THE GUARDIAN OF THE DEMOCRATIC PROCESS (INCLUDING DEMOCRATIC DELIBERATION)

Israeli legal scholars are badly divided about the legitimacy of the SCI's assertions of a power of judicial review. Some public law scholars take the view that Barak's "Constitutional Revolution" constitutes a necessary, perhaps even an essential, step that helps to sustain, rather than undermine, democratic self-government in Israel.[239] Other legal scholars, with no less conviction, argue that the SCI has gone too far and inserted itself too deeply, and too frequently, into matters most appropriately left for the Knesset and executive officers to decide.[240]

As Professor Gelpe observes, "[t]he debate is conducted both in the popular press, in academia, and in the Knesset."[241] The SCI's use of common law reasoning, and substantial reliance on its precedents recognizing fundamental, yet unenumerated, rights permits the Justices to "defend both democracy and human rights in a strong and meaningful manner."[242] But, there's another side of the coin; some worry that a "danger [exists] of having the Court operate without effective checks and balances" and that performance of its circuit-breaker (or checking) function "endangers the system of separation of powers and threatens to place the decision on political issues in the hands of a body that has no formalized tie to the people and is divorced from all political actors."[243]

It cannot be gainsaid, as Professor Gelpe argues, that "[t]he Supreme Court of Israel is a very powerful body."[244] Moreover, as former Justice Haim Cohn has observed, "[t]he question whether, and to what extent, the Court should adopt the 'activist' position and grant a remedy whenever good cause is shown, or whether it should exercise 'judicial restraint' and confine its jurisdiction to matters to be defined as properly justiciable, has for some time been—and still is—highly controversial and the subject of much agitated discussion."[245]

Providing a very thoughtful analysis and offering a carefully calibrated, balanced approach, Professor Ruth Gavison acknowledges that "[i]t has become fashionable to see courts as the central players and custodians of a democratic constitution."[246] And, it is certainly true that the courts "are indeed crucial partners in the maintenance of a robust constitutional regime."[247] She observes that some caution is requisite because "[l]egislatures and government are central constitutional actors, as important as are courts, each in its own sphere of activity and responsibility."[248] Thus, legislative and executive officers, no less than judges, have a role to play in respecting and realizing democratic values and securing and protecting fundamental human rights.

Professor Gavison posits that "*if* there is a constitution in Israel, it is primarily a judge-made constitution" because "[t]he decision to confer supremacy on the courts was never really and deliberately made by any popular organ acting as either a regular legislature or a constituent assembly" or, for that matter, "ratified by the people themselves."[249] Because neither the Knesset nor the voters have ever formally ratified the SCI's assertion of a power of judicial review, the legitimacy of judicial review remains strongly contested with "that power beyond the reach of both legislation and constitutional amendment itself!"[250] She concludes that "[a]ll we can say at the moment is that the debate is still with us showing no serious signs of abating.[251]

Today, of course, the proper role of the SCI within Israel's system of democracy could not be more vigorously contested. The baseline normative question, then, is whether and to what extent the judiciary should undertake, on its own initiative or with incomplete authorization from either the legislature or the people themselves, a project of defining and defending fundamental rights—including expressive freedom. Whether or not the SCI has been too aggressive in asserting a power of judicial review, as well as a power to read statutes and regulations down in order to reconcile them with fundamental rights, extremely good arguments exist for courts performing a circuit-breaker, or checking, function to ensure that the rights of minorities (however defined) are not unduly burdened or abridged. Drawing on the work of Ronald Dworkin, John Hart Ely, and Alexander Meiklejohn, the next section will argue that although the proper scope of the judiciary's checking function is open to debate, the existence of that function, in order to legitimate democracy and democratic self-government, is not.

A. Dworkin: Unfettered Democracy Is Fundamentally Unjust

To Ronald Dworkin "there's nothing inherently fair, and nothing that provides for genuine self-government for all, simply in the fact that more people favor one decision than favor another."[252] Dworkin argues that "[m]ajority rule is fair only when certain conditions are met—only, for example, when people have a genuine and equal right to participate in the public debate that produces the majority decision, and only when issues of distinct importance to individuals, like the choice of religious commitment, are exempt from majoritarian dictate altogether."[253] For majority rule to be just, it must be "majority rule under appropriate conditions."

From this vantage point, judicial review in the service of protecting fundamental rights, and particularly fundamental rights associated with human dignity, equality, and democracy, must be secured against arbitrary abridgement by majoritarian institutions—like elected legislatures. Under Dworkin's theory of "genuine democracy," judicial review can enhance and improve democratic self-government rather than undermine it. As he states his thesis, "[w]e must look to see whether the consequence of that power [judicial review] is in fact greater democracy because it has

Israel: Democracy and Dignity —ᴏ 163

helped to achieve a more genuine realization of the conditions that genuine democracy requires."[254]

It might once have been plausible to rely on what Dworkin calls "parliamentary conscience" to serve as a reliable check against the worst majoritarian impulses. After all, "Parliament is at once the voice and conscience of the people" and is tasked with "pursu[ing] the general interest."[255] Dworkin observes that "[t]he nineteenth century answer, across Europe (and even, for much of the century, in the United States), was that parliamentary sovereignty—unlimited power in the hands of the elected representatives of the people—would provide an adequate guarantee of individual rights against the people."[256] It bears noting that, even today, this view seems to predominate in contemporary Australia, which features a constitution that lacks a bill of rights and a judiciary that is not much inclined to disallow policymaking decisions by the national and state legislatures—including with respect to speech regulations.[257]

This faith in the fundamental decency of parliamentary bodies did not survive the twentieth century's two world wars. Thus, today the "parliamentary model now seem[s] less attractive,"[258] in large part because "the horrifying tyrannies of the short but terrible twentieth century . . . shattered the complacent Whig assumption that the developing political traditions and sensibilities of industrial nations would naturally produce decent government."[259] In other words, parliamentary democracy failed, and failed catastrophically, to meet reliably the conditions precedent for "genuine democracy" (which include respect for individual autonomy and self-definition, concepts that rest at the very heart of any plausible constitutional concept of human dignity).

When elected popular governments, vested with general authority to regulate, produced fascism and tyranny, it seemed self-evident that some sort of check was necessary to ensure that governmental powers would not be systematically abused. That is why, increasingly, democratic societies turned to courts and judges to serve as a "brake" on the worst tendencies of those empowered by electoral majorities. Judges would serve as a kind of circuit breaker to protect against utterly arbitrary or fundamentally unjust laws. But why judges?

Dworkin argues that judges, unlike elected politicians "are expected to do nothing that they cannot justify in principle."[260] He cautions that "[w]e have no guarantee that the political principles that our judges deploy will be the right or best ones, or that they will articulate those principles consistently or coherently."[261] Even so, the essence of the judicial task is reasoned analysis and explanation based on preexisting legal rules and principles. As Dworkin states the point, judges are "expected, as a matter of institutional responsibility, to set out, or at least presuppose, a body of principle that justifies what they do in each case and contains an articulation of the ground of judgment."[262]

Of course, judges are not perfect. For example, they are not, and cannot be, entirely objective and free from all partisan and ideological biases. That said, however, the judicial task is overtly nonpartisan in virtually all constitutional democracies. What is more, in most places, judicial decisions are not subject to direct forms of majoritarian control or constraint. Accordingly, "[d]emocracy adjusted to include judicial moralizing in order to protect individual rights . . . is an improvement on pure democracy."[263]

In sum, "there is nothing good, even *pro tanto*, about majority rule in itself" and "[t]he fact that more people favor one solution over another in itself counts as no justification for the community forcing that decision through coercive means on those who dissent from it."[264] Accordingly, judicial review enhances and perfects democracy, rather than undermining it. Dworkin posits that "on the whole, in the nations with which we are all familiar, judges having the power and responsibility [of protecting fundamental rights from majority overreach] has made the nation more, rather than less, democratic."[265] This holds true, according to Dworkin, as a general matter, and in my view, the SCI has been quite correct to embrace and act on Dworkin's constitutional logic.

B. *Ely: Judges Have a Duty to Reinforce Democracy and Democratic Institutions Using the Power of Judicial Review*

John Hart Ely famously argued that judicial review should be used to help correct the systematic failures of democracy.[266] Ely called his theory of judicial review, expounded in his classic book, *Democracy and Distrust*, a "representation-reinforcing" approach. He observes that "unlike an approach geared to the judicial imposition of 'fundamental values,' the representation-reinforcing orientation whose contours I have sketched and will develop further is not inconsistent with, but on the contrary is entirely supportive of, the American system of representative democracy."[267] Ely's baseline is that elected government officials should be able to set social and economic policies free and clear of judicial intervention because "rule in accord with the consent of a majority of those governed is the core of the American governmental system."[268] He cautions, that "[j]ust as obviously, however, that cannot be the whole story, since a majority with untrammeled power to set governmental policy is in a position to deal itself benefits at the expense of the remaining minority even when there is no relevant difference between the two groups."[269] Thus, "[t]he tricky task has been and remains that of devising a way or ways of protecting minorities from majority tyranny that is not a flagrant contradiction of the principle of majority rule."[270]

In Ely's view, judges should abstain from trying to identify and protect fundamental human rights (which makes his theory a poor fit for the contemporary SCI and, for that matter, most other constitutional courts around the world today as well).[271] Ely argues that judicial review should exist in two principal areas: to review and, if necessary, invalidate laws when : (1) "the ins are choking off the channels of political change to ensure that they will stay in and the outs will stay out," and (2) "though no one is actually denied a voice or a vote, representatives beholden to an effective majority are systematically disadvantaging some minority out of simple hostility or a prejudiced refusal to recognize commonalities of interest, and thereby denying that minority the protection afforded other groups by a representative system."[272] The first point, obviously, directly implicates legislation aimed at distorting or disrupting the process of democratic deliberation that informs the act of voting.

Thus, under Ely's representation-reinforcing theory of judicial review, judicial interventions are essential to perfect democracy. Unlike Dworkin, however, he does

Israel: Democracy and Dignity   165

not necessarily have a romantic view of judges or judicial decision-making. Instead, Ely's approach seems to draw on concepts associated with comparative institutional advantage,[273] of the necessity and desirability of judicial review as a means of representation reinforcement to correct for systemic failures of the democratic process. Representation reinforcement in the service of protecting the process of democratic self-government plainly requires judges to review speech regulations that could distort, disrupt, or even disable the operation of democratic self-government. Simply put, legislators selected via popular election are too self-interested to be given *carte blanche* authority to regulate speech in general or political and governmental speech in particular. Ely's theory obviously and strongly supports the SCI's approach in *Kol Ha'am*, which seeks to correct for the government's tendency to overregulate speech related to matters of public concern (which would include Israel's foreign policy commitments).

C. *Meiklejohn: Freedom of Speech Constitutes an Essential Condition for the Maintenance of Democratic Self-Government*

Alexander Meiklejohn is arguably the foremost proponent of the democratic self-government theory of the freedom of speech. He posits that a commitment to self-government necessarily requires the courts to protect the freedom of political speech and argues that the First Amendment both authorizes and requires federal judges to safeguard the operation of the marketplace of political ideas.[274] In his view, "[t]he principle of the freedom of speech springs from the necessities of the program of self-government"[275] and constitutes "a deduction from the basic American agreement that public issues shall be decided by universal suffrage."[276]

In Meiklejohn's view, limits on the freedom of expression inherently and inevitably distort the process of democratic deliberation. He explains that "[w]hen men govern themselves, it is they—and no one else—who must pass judgment upon unwisdom and unfairness and danger."[277] It necessarily follows that "unwise ideas must have hearing as well as wise ones, unfair as well as fair, dangerous as well as safe, un-American as well as American."[278] Government efforts to control or censor the marketplace of political ideas cannot be reconciled with the operational necessities of a project of democratic self-government. Meiklejohn was particularly concerned with government efforts to censor ideas. He posits that "[t]o be afraid of ideas, any idea, is to be unfit for self-government."[279] Moreover, "[a]ny such suppression of ideas about the common good, the First Amendment condemns with its absolute disapproval."[280]

It is easy to see how Meiklejohn's democratic self-government theory of the freedom of speech requires judges to serve as umpires, or referees, by ensuring that those who happen to hold the reins of government power today do not abuse that authority by attempting to silence public criticism or opposition to the incumbent government's policies. Indeed, although Justice Agranat does not cite Meiklejohn in his foundational *Kol Ha'am* opinion, the ideas he expresses, and the arguments he mounts, about the integral relationship of freedom of speech and democracy are fully and entirely consonant with Meiklejohn's democratic self-government theory of the freedom of speech.

166 *Free Speech as Civic Structure*

Under Meiklejohn's approach, a system of self-government that vests elected government officials with unconstrained authority to censor speech cannot legitimately be called a democracy. Citizens must be free to access information and share ideas freely.[281] It necessarily follows that "[t]he primary purpose of the First Amendment is, then, that all citizens shall, so far as possible, understand the issues which bear upon the common life."[282] Government may not legitimately attempt to protect voters from bad ideas—"[N]o idea, no opinion, no doubt, no belief, no counterbelief, no relevant information, may be kept from them."[283]

If a nation claims to be a democracy, and its institutions obtain their mandate from the people, that mandate is legitimate only if elections are free and fair. Elections cannot be free and fair in the absence of an open and inclusive process of democratic deliberation in which the voters can engage with each other about candidates, policies, and issues of central importance to the community. Thus, if a nation purports to be a democracy but vests its legislature with an unlimited and unchecked power to censor political speech, it is a democracy in name only. In reality, it cannot be deemed truly democratic because those holding power do not possess it through the freely expressed will of the voters.

D. Judicial Review Facilitates, Rather than Impedes, the Operation of Democratic Self-Governance

Taken together, Professors Dworkin, Ely, and Meiklejohn provide a compelling case in favor of a significant judicial role in safeguarding the process of democratic deliberation. Whether because majority rule, without some sort of check or brake, creates too great a risk of unjust governance (Dworkin), because of the structural need to protect the processes of democracy from self-interested incumbent office holders (Ely), or because a commitment to democracy is radically incomplete in the absence of a free and open marketplace of political ideas (Meiklejohn), all three roads take us to the same place. In a constitutional democracy, it is essential that judges have the power to police self-interested legislation and regulations that seek to distort or control the operation of democratic self-government.

Viewed from this perspective, then, the SCI's assertion of a power of judicial review, whether in the weak-form or strong-form stripe, constitutes a justified and essential assertion of institutional authority to serve as a check on the Knesset. Moreover, regardless of arguments over judicial review in other contexts, judicial review to safeguard the process of democratic deliberation is plainly essential to using elections as a means of rendering the government accountable to the people—and this means courts must deploy judicial review to protect expressive freedom. In a democracy, judicial review in this specific area of law is plainly essential to using elections as a means of conferring legitimacy on government institutions. It might be better, all things considered, if the Knesset had enacted a Basic Law: Expressive Freedom and Democracy. And, the fact that the Knesset considered, but rejected, a Basic Law protecting freedom of expression in 1993 and, again, in 1994, should be borne in mind when considering the appropriate role of the Israeli courts in protecting the freedom of speech (and other expressive freedoms).

Even absent an express text authorizing the use of judicial review, whether in strong or weak form, to protect speech and related forms of expressive activity (press, assembly, association, petition), Israel's commitment to democratic self-government provides a clear and convincing basis for a significant judicial role in this area of law. Elected parliamentarians labor under a clear conflict of interest—the desire to seek and obtain reelection—and accordingly an outside check, an honest broker, is needed to ensure that speech regulations are designed and enforced to advance legitimate government objectives. Justice Agranat well understood this reality with respect to institutional competence and wrote an elegant and persuasive opinion that explains, and justifies, a significant judicial role in protecting the process of democratic deliberation that is essential to the proper functioning of a project of self-government.

VII. CONCLUSION: THE SUPREME COURT OF ISRAEL PLAYS AN ESSENTIAL AND NECESSARY ROLE IN FACILITATING THE OPERATION OF DEMOCRATIC SELF-GOVERNMENT

Although Israel does not have a formal, comprehensive, entrenched, written constitution, it nevertheless recognizes and respects fundamental human rights, including freedom of speech and expressive freedom more generally. The constitutional commitment to human rights in general, and to the freedom of speech in particular, constitute cornerstone features of Israel's existing constitutional order. These commitments do not disrupt or impede democratic self-government and democracy in Israel; on the contrary, they enable and legitimate Israel's experiment in democratic self-governance.

Despite the absence of any written text, constitutional or statutory, that directly conveys legal protection on speech and other expressive freedoms, residents of Israel have enjoyed these fundamental rights since 1953 and the SCI's decision in *Kol Ha'am*. Using a process of common law constitutionalism, over seven decades, Justices of the SCI have built a thoughtful, nuanced, and largely successful jurisprudential bulwark that protects freedom of expression from efforts at government censorship. Indeed, as recent events associated with the Netanyahu government's proposed "judicial reforms" demonstrate with convincing clarity, public protest and civic engagement are very much alive and well in contemporary Israel.

A text guaranteeing freedom of expression could provide Israel's courts with a more secure anchor for the judicial protection of speech, as well as a more robust system of enforcement mechanisms (e.g., strong-form judicial review for all freedom of expression claims). But such a text, absent specific, highly detailed provisions probably would not materially change the scope of expressive freedom in Israel very much—and perhaps not at all. This is so because, at least since the 1990s, the SCI consistently has exhibited great vigilance in protecting speech. Moreover, it has taken this approach because of the clear relationship of free speech to human dignity (as a form of autonomy, self-expression, and self-empowerment), its relationship to the ongoing search for truth, and, perhaps most important, because of its inextricable relationship to the project of democratic self-government.[284]

The SCI, drawing on implications from Israel's status as a democratic polity and from the traditions and expectations of the Israeli people, has performed a circuit-breaker, or checking, function that has helped to ensure that elected politicians cannot distort or disrupt either democratic self-government or the process of democratic deliberation that informs it. Indeed, free and open democratic deliberation constitutes an essential precondition for the holding of truly free and fair elections—and using elections to confer legitimacy on the institutions of government and those who staff those institutions has been a core feature of Israel's government since its founding in 1948. Viewed from this vantage point, ongoing judicial efforts to safeguard expressive freedoms significantly enhance and enable, rather than undermine, democratic self-government in Israel. Clearly, these efforts should not be disrupted—much less ended.

As Alexander Meiklejohn eloquently has argued,[285] democratic self-government simply is not possible without an ongoing process of public engagement and debate. He observed that, in a democracy, "[w]e need the truth as a basis for our actions" but warned that "the truth is better attained if men trade ideas freely than it is if each man stays within the limits of his own discoveries."[286] Constitutional free speech guarantees exist in order "to give every voting member of the body politic the fullest possible participation in the understanding of those problems with which citizens of a self-governing society must deal."[287] And, as Justice William Brennan, Jr., famously wrote in *New York Times Company v. Sullivan*,[288] in order to meet the necessities of democratic self-government, "debate on public issues should be uninhibited, robust, and wide-open" and often will "include vehement, caustic, and sometimes unpleasantly sharp attacks on government and public officials."[289]

Whatever the merits of criticisms of the SCI's role in deciding major questions of public policy in contemporary Israel, its critical institutional role in safeguarding speech cannot plausibly be gainsaid. When government seeks to censor speakers and banish ideas from the marketplace of political ideas, it distorts and corrupts the process of democratic deliberation and renders chimerical the use of elections to confer legitimacy on the institutions of government. A constitutional court in a democratic polity has an essential role, as well as a constitutional duty, to safeguard the process of democratic deliberation from efforts to control, suppress, or disrupt it.

7

Conclusion

COMMON LAW CONSTITUTIONALISM IN THE SERVICE OF EXPRESSIVE FREEDOMS CONSTITUTES A GLOBAL RULE RATHER THAN AN EXCEPTION

I. TEXT OR NO TEXT, JUDGES SET THE METES AND BOUNDS OF EXPRESSIVE FREEDOM

At the end of the day, some constitutional rights cannot be effectively provisioned or circumscribed by textual limitations. Like the Greek god Proteus, these rights can and will change their form and shape over time. The question for those drafting constitutional language then becomes identifying which rights can be more successfully codified—and which rights, because of their deeply seated sociolegal salience, are relatively impervious to efforts to limit or constrain them through particular verbal formulae. Make no mistake, however: constitutional law is a species of common law, meaning that judges, not legislators, are its principal guardians.[1] As Justice Oliver Wendell Holmes, Jr. observed in his iconic book, *The Common Law*, "[t]he felt necessities of the time, the prevalent moral and political theories, intuitions of public policy, avowed or unconscious, even the prejudices which judges share with their fellow men, have had a good deal more to do than the syllogism in determining the rules by which men should be governed."[2]

In the preceding chapters, I have demonstrated how text does not play a significant role in contemporary "First Amendment" litigation.[3] Despite the presence of a majority of self-proclaimed "textualist-originalist" judges on the Supreme Court of the United States, free speech jurisprudence in the United States has little to do with any of the four specific speech-related clauses in the text of the First Amendment.

Free Speech as Civic Structure. Ronald J. Krotoszynski, Jr., Oxford University Press. © Ronald J. Krotoszynski, Jr. 2024.
DOI: 10.1093/9780197662229.003.0007

Moreover, the situation is little different in South Africa, where the Justices of the Constitutional Court of South Africa (CCSA) have elevated the freedom of speech to a coequal status with the apex South African human rights, and values, of equality, dignity, and human freedom. This holds true despite the recent vintage of South Africa's Constitution (adopted in 1996) and clear interpretative directives to give equality, dignity, and human freedom a relative priority when interpreting *any* and *all* provisions of the Bill of Rights (including Section 16, which safeguards the freedom of expression).[4]

In the United Kingdom, free speech rights did not change significantly after the adoption of a statutory bill of rights that called on the domestic courts to have "particular regard" for the freedom of expression. The judges had embarked on their own course before the Human Rights Act 1998 (HRA 98) came onto the legal scene, and they continued to chart their own way after it entered into legal effect.[5] Prior to the HRA 98, the British judiciary had gone a long way toward incorporating the freedom of speech and press into domestic law; the incorporation of Article 10 of the European Convention for the Protection of Human Rights and Fundamental Freedoms did not much move the needle in favor of broader protection for expressive freedom.

Finally, Australia and Israel show that the intentional exclusion of freedom of speech from either a constitutional instrument (Australia[6]) or a statutory compendium of rights (Israel[7]) will not prevent courts from recognizing freedom of expression as a fundamental right and then deploying judicial review to safeguard it. In both jurisdictions, judges implied a right to freedom of expression from legal provisions that declare Australia and Israel to be democratic polities, on the theory that democratic self-government requires protection for the freedom of speech.

Judges, not legislators or constitution drafters, play the leading role in setting the metes and bounds of protected expression in a democracy. The question that remains to be asked and answered is why this is so. In this brief concluding chapter, I set forth some tentative ideas and conclusions about why expressive freedom is difficult to codify—and difficult to ignore as well. More specifically, in Section II, this chapter considers whether text can effectively codify speech rights in a democracy (it cannot), Section III takes up whether judges in democratic polities can avoid undertaking the work of defining for themselves the scope of expressive freedom and then safeguarding these rights in the service of democratic self-government (they cannot), Section IV analyzes whether this critically important judicial work exceeds the proper bounds of judicial authority (it does not), and Section V offers a brief conclusion.

II. EXPRESSIVE FREEDOM, CONSTITUTIONAL TEXT, AND THE PRACTICE OF DEMOCRATIC SELF-GOVERNMENT

To say that constitutional text guaranteeing expressive freedom is inevitably and invariably irrelevant would plainly be wide of the mark. Text can and does matter; government actors, including but not limited to judges, feel obliged to consider constitutional text and to respond on the merits to arguments premised on the text. But

Conclusion: Common Law Constitutionalism ⟶ 171

text matters far less than courts and judges to safeguarding the freedom of speech, press, assembly, association, and petition. If one were forced to choose between an entrenched constitutional guarantee of expressive freedom, but without independent courts vested with a power of judicial review, on the one hand, and independent courts that exercise judicial review, but in the context of a legal system that lacks a constitutional or statutory text that explicitly guarantees expressive freedom, on the other, the system with independent courts but without a written guarantee is likely to enjoy stronger and broader protection of expressive freedom.

Of course, if it is possible for a nation's domestic law to meet *both* conditions, as is the case in the United States and South Africa, and elsewhere too (e.g., in Canada and in the jurisprudence of the European Court of Human Rights and the Court of Justice of the European Union), so much the better. But if one values speech rights and faces making a hard choice between a constitutional system that resembles Australia and Israel versus a system modeled on China or Cuba, the credited response is obvious. Securing human rights in a democratic polity from arbitrary, but highly popular, government actions requires independent courts and governments that respect the rule of law (including acquiescence in the legal judgments of courts).

Elected politicians labor under a clear conflict of interest when they adopt speech regulations that impact the operation of the marketplace of political ideas. In a democracy, any and all government regulations of speech even *arguably* related to the electoral process, including the system of democratic deliberation that informs the act of voting on election day, and including *all* speech relating to matters of public concern,[8] are potentially distortionary. This is not to say that legislators cannot and will not ever adopt fundamentally fair speech regulations related to elections and self-government. It is to say that having a structural check on the abuse or misuse of this power is arguably essential.

History teaches that elected politicians will seek to enact rules that will make their reelection easier to accomplish rather than more difficult. The extreme use of partisan gerrymandering in the contemporary United States provides a highly salient example of this phenomenon.[9] It is also a practice that—unlike speech regulations targeting would-be speakers based on their identity, their viewpoint, or the content of their message—the Supreme Court has sustained against constitutional attack (including First Amendment-based challenges).[10] In this context, then, meaningful judicial review serves as an essential brake on the worst tendencies of the elected branches of government to feather their own nests.[11] And, even weak or relatively tepid judicial review, of the sort practiced in Australia under its implied freedom of political and governmental communication,[12] is likely better than no judicial review at all. The possibility of judicial review should make legislators more careful and attentive when enacting laws that burden or completely abridge the freedom of political speech.

Stating a general rule is relatively easy to do. That said, the effect of text on the operationalization of human rights, including but not limited to expressive freedom, is nonlinear, is complex, and varies from legal system to legal system.[13] Thus, the problem with textual analysis merely begins with understanding the substance of rights. It

III. COMMON LAW CONSTITUTIONALISM, IN THE CONTEXT OF JUDICIAL PROTECTION OF THE EXPRESSIVE FREEDOM, IS INEVITABLE AND UNIVERSAL

In the United States, we reflexively assume that constitutional text matters—that it has a constraining force on legal actors, that its authors had some sort of discernible intent, and that the intent of the text's Framers should have some contemporary relevance when interpreting and applying the text.[15] These assumptions fare badly— very badly—in the specific context of the First Amendment, where the Justices of the Supreme Court of the United States appear to pay virtually no attention either to the express language of the First Amendment or to the original public meaning of that text.[16]

Instead, ostensibly textualist-originalist judges have adopted a "spirit of the law" approach that generalizes the First Amendment's four clauses into a generic rule against government censorship of speech based on a speaker's identity, viewpoint, or the content of the speech itself. And, the First Amendment's most inconvenient textual provision, "Congress shall make no law,"[17] gets totally ignored and has no limiting effect on the scope of the First Amendment at all.[18]

Should this state of affairs be seen as problematic or troubling? Should courts recognize and then enforce rights, through effective remedies, when they conclude such action is essential to securing fundamental constitutional objectives—such as a commitment to democratic self-government? Courts arguably have an institutional duty to secure fundamental constitutional commitments—and to provide reliable, efficacious remedies equal to the task at hand.

Rights are of course effective only if they are backed up with effective remedies. Chief Justice John Marshall famously argued that efficacious enforcement mechanisms for legal rights, including a meaningful remedy, are mandatory elements in a constitutional democracy that claims to practice the rule of law.[19] He observed that "[t]he very essence of civil liberty certainly consists in the right of every individual to claim the protection of the laws, whenever he receives an injury" and "[o]ne of the first duties of government is to afford that protection."[20] Indeed, even the British Crown is subject to the rule of law.[21] It follows, accordingly, that although "[t]he government of the United States has been emphatically termed a government of laws, and not of men," it cannot claim to observe the rule of law "if the laws furnish no remedy for the violation of a vested legal right."[22]

Marshall's observations lead, by a direct route, to important questions involving the structural mechanisms that exist for permitting ordinary citizens to assert their constitutional rights against the government. The structures that delineate the powers and duties of government institutions, in conjunction with the mechanisms associated

Conclusion: Common Law Constitutionalism —○ 173

with asserting and vindicating textually enumerated human rights matter—and they matter a great deal. Yet, in too many comparative constitutional law projects, legal scholars, here in the United States but also abroad, tend to focus exclusively on the scope and substance of substantive rights. Rights matter, of course, but so do the institutions and procedures associated with enforcing them.

As Professor Mark Tushnet has astutely observed, "constitutional systems are *systems*, so that even if one has a good grasp on the way another constitutional system deals with a particular problem, one might not fully understand the way in which that solution fits together with other aspects of the constitutional system."[23] It is not enough to study only substantive constitutional rights, even in a careful and contextual way, without also paying serious attention to issues of the institutional design and operation of the polity's governing institutions (and particularly the domestic courts).[24] A text that guarantees a particular fundamental human right is largely meaningless in the absence of an ability to enforce that right.[25]

In the context of the First Amendment, of course, the federal courts, including the Supreme Court, are doing a rather poor job of suiting word to deed with regard to judges following strictly the letter of the Constitution's text. Whether or not this should be seen as deeply problematic (or not) presents a more difficult question. After all, other legal cultures take a radically different view on the relevance of both the constitutional text and original intent as a constraint on the scope and meaning of a constitutional provision. They are more self-consciously and transparently open to embracing common law constitutionalism, which involves judges adapting constitutional text to the necessities of the times.

For example, for almost one hundred years, the Supreme Court of Canada has generally ignored textualist originalism and instead interpreted constitutional text in a dynamic and purposive fashion. Under the "living tree" model of constitutional interpretation, text serves merely as a starting point, not the ending point, in analyzing, defining, and applying constitutional rights.[26] What is more, the Supreme Court of Canada seems quite comfortable embracing common law constitutionalism.[27] Yet, in the United States, textualist originalism has retained, as a formal matter at least, an outsized role in constitutional interpretation—both in the federal courts and in popular commentary on the Constitution and Bill of Rights.[28]

A pattern of limited textual relevance to the scope and meaning of constitutional rights repeats in other jurisdictions. Australia provides a salient example. In Australia, the drafters of the federal constitution made a conscious and intentional decision not to include a written Bill of Rights.[29] Drawing on the British tradition of parliamentary sovereignty, they instead created a federal system and divided governing powers between the six states and the federal government. The Constitution does guarantee a democratic form of government and the right to vote—but it contains only three specifically enumerated rights-granting provisions. Section 117 guarantees the equal treatment of nonresidents by the states[30]—essentially an analogue to the Privileges and Immunities Clause of Article IV, Section 2.[31] Another clause, Section 80, safeguards the right to a jury trial in all criminal cases.[32] Finally, Section 116, which mirrors some, but not all of the U.S. First Amendment, prohibits religious establishments, prohibits religious oaths for public office, and protects the free exercise of religion.[33] Australia's Commonwealth Constitution does not contain any provisions safeguarding the freedom of speech, press, assembly, or petition. Evidently, the provisions of the First Amendment related to protecting expressive freedoms did not make the cut with the drafters of Australia's Commonwealth Constitution.

Nevertheless, as explained in some detail in Chapter 4, the High Court of Australia (HCA), discovered an "implied freedom" of political and governmental communication in a pair of decisions handed down in 1992.[34] The argument—an entirely plausible one—posits that it is simply not possible to have free and fair elections without citizens enjoying the ability to engage in a process of democratic deliberation. As the Justices more recently have explained, "[t]he constitutional basis for the implication in the Constitution of a freedom of communication on matters of politics and government is well settled."[35] Indeed, "[t]he freedom is of such importance to representative government that any effective statutory burden upon it must be justified."[36]

Thus, the (intentional) omission of an express free speech provision in Australia's Commonwealth Constitution of 1901 has not left freedom of expression to the whim of the federal and state legislatures. The judges could not bring themselves to say that, in the absence of a relevant constitutional or statutory text conveying a right to freedom of political and governmental communication, questions about whether to permit or criminalize speech activity integral to using voting and elections to hold the government accountable were entirely up to the federal and state legislatures to decide for themselves (and as the incumbent officeholders think best).

Indeed, the laws before the HCA in 1992 prohibited flatly third-party political broadcasts via television and radio, effectively giving existing recognized political parties an absolute monopoly on the use of television and radio for electioneering purposes. The conflict of interest inherent in such regulations is self-evident; incumbent members of Parliament, associated with well-established political parties, sought to prevent the use of television and radio by others. This prohibition, of course, was entirely self-serving for the benefit of the incumbent politicians who enacted it.

On these facts, it is quite easy to understand how and why the Justices of the HCA recognized a constitutional obligation to address this situation in order to safeguard truly free and fair elections. They felt compelled to do something to prevent an obvious distortion of the democratic process—and they did.[37] Even so, Australia's implied right is considerably weaker than the Free Speech Clause of the First Amendment. This weakness, however, has far more to do with the place of the HCA, and the courts more generally, within the structure of Australia's government than with the absence of a relevant constitutional provision, or statute, that expressly guarantees the freedom of expression.[38]

One might attempt to generalize from Australia's example the premise that if a domestic legal system lacks a text safeguarding expressive freedoms, the right will inevitably and invariably be weaker as a result. Such a claim would be open to serious doubts given the example that the Supreme Court of Israel's (SCI) free speech jurisprudence provides.

Whereas Australia has a written constitution, which came into force in 1901, as discussed in some detail in Chapter 6, Israel lacks a formal constitution as such. Instead, the SCI has held that a number of statutory enactments, termed "Basic Laws," enjoy quasi-constitutional status.[39] In addition to making it procedurally more difficult to amend or abolish these statutes, by requiring an absolute majority in the Knesset (Israel's parliament), rather than a majority of a quorum to amend or repeal them, the SCI also has found that freedom of speech and equality are "implied" fundamental rights that are essential corollaries of Israel's commitment to democratic self-government.[40]

Professor Neta Ziv observes that "[b]asic rights and liberties such as freedom of assembly and speech, equality, and freedom of religious worship became part of Israel's unwritten constitutional properties."[41] Equality and speech rank among the most important of these implied human rights.[42] Rather than judicial usurpation of legislative powers, Israeli judges argue that the implication of fundamental rights is essential to the legitimacy of a democratic state and also an implicit component of human dignity (which is expressly safeguarded under the Basic Law: Human Dignity and Liberty, which the Knesset enacted in 1992). Thus, as former President (also colloquially known as the "Chief Justice") Aharon Barak posits, "[t]here is no (real) democracy without recognition of values" and these implied values are "based on human dignity, equality, and tolerance."[43]

Since recognizing an implied freedom of speech in *Kol Ha'Am*,[44] decided in 1953, as an implication of Israel's commitment to democratic self-government, the SCI has issued numerous precedents over the years vindicating the implied freedom of speech and has invoked personal autonomy and the search for truth as additional reasons for judicial protection of free expression.[45] Avi Weitzman, a U.S. commentator, observes that "[w]ithout a constitution to rely on, Israeli judges have had to ground free speech jurisprudence in Israel's democratic nature."[46] The Israeli courts have repeatedly invalidated government policies that trench too deeply on freedom of expression: "A broad range of speech is protected for a variety of governmental, social, and personal functions."[47]

Speech is integral to the maintenance of a functioning democracy; in consequence, the judiciary must protect it against government abridgments through the power of judicial review.[48] Thus, even though other human rights values also animate the SCI's protection of expressive freedom—including both individual autonomy and the search for truth—the inexorable relationship of the freedom of speech to a functioning democracy provided the main justification for implying a right to freedom of speech in the first place (in the *Kol Ha'am* decision).

To borrow the catchphrase of the *Jurassic Park* movies, even in the absence of a constitutional text, speech, like nature, "finds a way"—at least in some jurisdictions. Yet, we also see the opposite trend at work. Otherwise democratic polities that feature a written constitution with an entrenched bill of rights, including a guarantee of freedom of expression, read the free speech clause in a limited or minimalist way that permits the government to censor even core political speech when a sufficiently important cultural value is at stake. Spain, for example, maintains and has regularly enforced statutory provisions that criminalize public criticism of the monarchy (including members of the royal family beyond the sovereign).[49] Lèse-majesté laws represent, quite literally, a form of seditious libel, a kind of criminal speech regulation long rejected in the United States as fundamentally incompatible with freedom of political speech.[50]

To be sure, there are places where the constitutional text seems to tell readers something useful about the scope and relative importance of the freedom of speech. Germany and South Africa arguably provide relevant examples. As explained earlier in Chapter 3, however, it is debatable whether South Africa actually departs from rather than follows the rule that constitutional protection for expressive freedom invariably constitutes a constitutional common law project (meaning that judges, not constitutional framers, take the lead role in defining the metes and bounds of free expression rights).[51] Although, given that both nations feature relatively recent constitutions, it may simply be that these texts better correspond with prevailing social norms than constitutions of less recent vintage. In other words, the counterexamples of constitutions where the text does seem to prefigure the scope and vibrancy of expressive freedoms might simply better reflect prevailing social norms about how a commitment to freedom of speech should be operationalized in a democratic polity.[52]

Thus, it is not that the text in these jurisdictions better constrains the judges—rather, the constitutional text itself simply is stronger and in better accord with the prevailing cultural norms that are widely shared within the citizenry, which relieves local judges from the felt necessity of "updating" it through the process of common law constitutionalism. When text aligns with sociolegal culture, text appears to do more meaningful work than when a constitutional text either dates back to a different time and place or when a new text attempts to establish a norm that does not fit very well with prevailing constitutional understandings within the body politic of what a meaningful commitment to expressive freedom requires a just society to tolerate.

In either case, however, it is shared human rights values within the community, and not the constitutional text, that are doing the real work. This explains why the First Amendment's text fails to define much, if at all, the scope of expressive freedom in the contemporary United States. It also explains why the constitutional courts in Australia and Israel have recognized an implied freedom of speech, derived from constitutional and statutory guarantees of free and fair elections, despite the utter and complete absence of constitutional text guaranteeing freedom of expression in these jurisdictions.

Because ordinary citizens in Australia and Israel expect the government to respect the freedom of political speech, elected politicians have accepted, rather than contested, the judiciary's assertion of a power of judicial review in this context (again, despite the absence of a textual constitutional mandate). Indeed, were Australia or Israel to go about drafting new constitutions, these new constitutional texts would almost certainly include express free speech guarantees—precisely because the people of those polities already both expect and demand constitutional protection for freedom of speech (and get it).[53]

Conclusion: Common Law Constitutionalism 177

It also explains why the HRA 98 did not effect a free speech revolution in the United Kingdom. Simply put, such a revolution would have to be preceded by a revolution in the institutional role and function of the judiciary and judges within the United Kingdom's system of government. Indeed, even if Parliament had expressly authorized the domestic courts to exercise an overt power of judicial review to enforce European Convention rights in the HRA 98, it is doubtful whether the British courts would have embraced such authority either with alacrity or brio.

In the United Kingdom, the judiciary is very much the junior partner in relation to both Parliament and the executive branch; British judges are not accustomed to gainsaying Parliament's policymaking choices—and this holds especially true for major or important policy choices. Despite this institutional reticence, however, the U.K.'s domestic courts conjured a right to freedom of expression from British sociolegal values, societal traditions, and shared cultural understandings. The judges also drew quite directly on the inexorable relationship between the freedom of speech and the project of democratic self-government. Simply put, it is not possible to have free and fair elections in places where the incumbent politicians exercise a general censorial power over political speech.

The U.K.'s domestic courts had imported free speech as a legal value well before the HRA 98 came on to the legal scene. The judges, recognizing the people's general expectation of a right to freedom of expression, delivered it to them—and did so starting in the 1980s (meaning well before the HRA 98 entered into force on October 2, 2000). However, in so doing, they fashioned a legal principle that kept the domestic courts well inside their lane vis-à-vis Parliament. The judicially crafted legal principle of freedom of expression was fully consistent with the very limited policymaking role the British courts enjoy under the United Kingdom's (largely unwritten) constitutional structure.

Finally, South Africa fits the overall pattern of judges fashioning free speech rules and principles to suit the expectations of the body politic. The Constitutional Court disregarded repeated textual cues within the 1996 Constitution and elevated speech rights to a coequal status with the apex constitutional values[54]—which are also express constitutional rights.[55] Given that the National Party, all-White government, during the apartheid era, used speech regulations, including hate speech regulations, as a means of social control and as part of a larger project to distort the operation of the marketplace of political ideas, it should not be surprising that South African citizens today—as well as South African jurists—are quite wary of government censorship of speech related to democratic self-government. Culture and the collective memory of the South African people have a more powerful role in determining the meaning of Section 16 of South Africa's Constitution than other express provisions within that document's text.

What one finds, upon careful consideration, is a complex and ongoing process of judicial construction and revision of the rules governing the exercise of expressive freedom. To be sure, the presence or absence of text plays a role in this process. This role, however, is limited and circumscribed in relation to the outsized role of a nation's sociolegal

178 ᴗ Free Speech as Civic Structure

and cultural traditions, coupled with the institutional role of the courts within a particular democratic polity's governing institutions. Practices, values, and expectations shape the scope and meaning of constitutional protection for speech-related rights far more regularly, and reliably, than the precise wording of a free speech guarantee (or the absence of such a guarantee within the four corners of a nation's constitution).

IV. EXPRESSIVE FREEDOM, FUNDAMENTAL RIGHTS MORE GENERALLY, AND JUDGE-MADE LAW: THE CRITICAL ROLE OF JUDGES IN A CONSTITUTIONAL DEMOCRACY

Expressive freedom is the domain of judges, who serve as "umpires" in the game of democracy. Using a common law process to develop and shape legal doctrines that facilitate and maintain the process of democratic deliberation, judges seek to protect the democratic process from ham-fisted efforts to distort or disrupt it. This judicial project is essential to any plausible system of democratic self-government.

Are other fundamental rights equally the primary domain of judges—rather than legislators or constitution drafters? In a sense, one could posit that judges, as expositors of the meaning of constitutional text, always get to have the last word. Viewed from this vantage point, one could posit that Chief Justice John Marshall, in *Marbury*,[56] and Alexander Hamilton, in *The Federalist No. 78*,[57] properly appreciated the critical role of judges in enforcing constitutional constraints. Hamilton's thoughts and observations regarding the necessary role of judges in a constitutional democracy are highly relevant to answering the question of whether judges may legitimately conjure specific fundamental rights from a more general commitment to democratic self-government.

In a system with a written constitution, judges will determine what government actions fall inside, and outside, the relevant constitutional lines. Writing in *The Federalist No. 78*, Alexander Hamilton explains that:

> It is not otherwise to be supposed, that the Constitution could intend to enable the representatives of the people to substitute their WILL to that of their constituents. It is far more rational to suppose, that the courts were designed to be an intermediate body between the people and the legislature, in order, among other things, to keep the latter within the limits assigned to their authority. The interpretation of the laws is the proper and peculiar province of the courts.[58]

In the absence of a judicial referee, or umpire, a written constitution constitutes little more than a "parchment barrier" (to borrow James Madison's wonderful turn of phrase[59]).

Hamilton further posits that a written constitution is effectively meaningless if a legislature is free to decide for itself whether to observe, or ignore, constitutional limitations on its own powers. He explains that "[t]he complete independence of the courts of justice is peculiarly essential in a limited Constitution."[60] Hamilton adds

Conclusion: Common Law Constitutionalism ⟶ 179

that "[b]y a limited Constitution, I understand one which contains certain specified exceptions to the legislative authority; such, for instance, as that it shall pass no bills of attainder, no ex-post-facto laws, and the like."[61] In his view, "[l]imitations of this kind can be preserved in practice no other way than through the medium of courts of justice, whose duty it must be to declare all acts contrary to the manifest tenor of the Constitution void" and "[w]ithout this, all the reservations of particular rights or privileges would amount to nothing."[62]

Self-interest on the part of legislators, coupled with their natural tendency to do that which is most politically expedient, means that courts must serve as a brake, exercising a checking function, to ensure that the legislature does not overflow the banks of its constitutional authority. The accuracy of this proposition seems self-evident. But, Hamilton does not address the potential problem of judges rewriting constitutional limitations, or ignoring them, because of the perceived exigencies of the times. On the one hand, a risk of constitutional infidelity always exists—regardless of the branch of government vested with the last word on the document's meaning. On the other hand, however, federal judges in the United States, who serve for life ("during good behavior") and enjoy constitutional protection against Congress slashing their salaries in retaliation for issuing decisions that members of Congress dislike,[63] seem institutionally well-suited to serving as honest brokers who will enforce, in good faith, constitutional strictures.

Unlike elected members of Congress, Article III judges are not as clearly, or inexorably, self-interested with regard to their constitutional interpretations as are the politicians who populate Congress. This does not mean that judges do not make, and will not make, blown calls—but it does mean that they have less incentive to embrace intellectual dishonesty than do elected officeholders who must seek and obtain popular reelection to retain their offices (and, hence, their power).

All five jurisdictions surveyed in this book purport to be democracies with all citizens enjoying an equal right to participate in the process of democratic deliberation and to vote. All five nations feature constitutional or statutory instruments (most have both) that safeguard voting rights and require regular elections as the means by which public officials, save the judges, gain and hold office. If a government proclaims itself to be a democracy, and to use elections as the principal mechanism through which voters will secure government accountability, judges have an obvious and important role to play in keeping the elected branches of government honest. And, this reality has led judges in the United States, South Africa, the United Kingdom, Australia, and Israel to deploy judicial review to block efforts to distort the process of democratic deliberation through self-serving speech regulations.

Other rights probably also require judges to serve as honest brokers as well—guarantees of equal citizenship come readily to mind. In a democracy, legislatures sometimes target minorities (of whatever stripe) for adverse treatment by the government. In other instances, legislatures featuring members drawn from the majority, and elected by the majority, simply ignore or disregard the rights and interests of minority groups within the community.

Free Speech as Civic Structure

In either case, a structural problem exists that courts, and likely only courts, can meaningfully address and correct.[64] Accordingly, one might expect to see judges playing a more active role in recognizing and enforcing what in the United States would constitute equal protection rights.[65] When the normal processes of democracy feature a structural flaw, such as majorities failing to take into account the interests of minority groups within the community, judges will likely feel a duty to act[66]—and they will act regardless of the precise wording of a constitutional text or the original public meaning of that text.[67]

It lies beyond the scope of this project to catalogue each and every human rights accoutrement that a meaningful commitment to democratic self-government requires—but clearly freedom of expression, and allied expressive freedoms, belong on this list. And, without belaboring the point, I would posit that protection of the equal rights of all persons living within the community constitutes another.[68] Whether a particular human right can be implied from a commitment to democratic self-government, or not, would need to be worked out on a case-by-case basis. That said, however, when a right is self-evidently essential to the maintenance of democracy, and the practice of democratic self-government, judges can and will find a way to vindicate We the People's expectation that the government will recognize, and respect, that right.

At the end of the day, then, a constitution means what We the People believe that it means. And, judges will seek to recognize and vindicate We the People's expectations—subject to the structural limitations of the courts within a particular system of government vis-à-vis the legislative and executive branches of government. This is not to say that judges desire and seek out the general public's approbation or high opinion (or should do so). Rather, it is to say that, when judges sign their names to judicial opinions, they will attempt to muster reasons in support of their decisions that are reasonably persuasive to the body politic. It is also to say that, all things being equal, most judges, most of the time, will strive mightily to avoid giving reasons that are widely viewed within the community as either odious or fundamentally unjust.[69]

Judges, as Professor Ronald Dworkin elegantly argues, are in the business of offering reasons in support of their judgments—and, in general, they seek to offer *persuasive* reasons.[70] As he states his case, "responsibility for articulation is the nerve of adjudication" and "[j]udges are supposed to do nothing that they cannot justify in principle, and to appeal only to principles that they thereby undertake to respect."[71]

This institutional commitment to reason-giving explains, in no small part, the consistency of judges, across national domestic courts, engaging in serious judicial review of speech regulations. To simply hold, in a nation that purports to be a democracy, that the incumbent politicians have an unfettered ability to tilt the playing field in their favor, effectively rigging elections and rendering them less than free and fair, through the use of highly targeted speech regulations, would not constitute a particularly persuasive, much less compelling, reason for refusing to exercise the power of judicial review. What is more, to rely on the accident of constitutional text—on its presence or its absence—as a reason for simply defaulting on the judiciary's general constitutional duty to serve as an honest broker regarding maintaining conditions that permit a fair electoral fight between the contesting political forces within a democratic society, would also not constitute a particularly compelling justification for judicial abstention.[72]

The common law, at its heart, should serve as a reflection of the people's sense of fair play and fundamental justice. Common law judging, accordingly, involves judges who identify social values and then translate them into legal rules capable of reliable enforcement. In the context of expressive freedom, what one finds, if one looks, is judges, across democracies, seeking to find and hold the constitutional line regarding speech regulations that have the potential to disrupt, distort, or destroy the process of democratic deliberation that animates democratic self-government. Rather than a cause for alarm about judges usurping the powers of the elected branches, this behavior instead should be viewed as judges simply undertaking, in good faith, their institutional duty to serve as a circuit breaker when the elected branches seek to manipulate and distort the electoral process.

V. CONCLUSION: THE PROTEAN FIRST AMENDMENT

The scope and meaning of expressive freedom within a particular legal system will, like Proteus, change shape and form, evolving over time, as the felt necessities of democratic self-government require. In consequence, efforts to cabin expressive freedom through constitutional or statutory text—through inclusion but also through exclusion—seem doomed to failure. Judges, across national and transnational jurisdictions, will shape and reshape the doctrines associated with the protection of expressive freedom as necessary to enable them to craft judicial opinions that they believe will be credible—reasonably persuasive—to the general political community. And, in the context of expressive freedom, judges undertake this work as the guardians of democracy and the democratic process. This task is, and probably must be, an exercise in common law judging. The First Amendment, and its foreign cousins as well, are protean—and our understanding of how constitutions work would be significantly improved if we invested more time and energy in trying to understand precisely why this is so.

NOTES

CHAPTER 1

1. In this chapter and in subsequent chapters, I use the phrase "expressive freedom," in addition to "expressive freedoms," as a shorthand for the various, and differentiable, forms of expressive activity that the First Amendment, at least on its face, protects—including the freedoms of speech, press, assembly, and petition. All four activities involve distinct modalities of expression—communication—and all of them contribute in important and distinctive ways to the process of democratic deliberation (which is essential to the project of democratic self-government). As Professor Ash Bhagwat persuasively argues, the First Amendment "was intended to give citizens—ordinary people—the tools to engage in political debate, to organize themselves in associations, to assemble for a variety of purposes including consulting together regarding the issues of the day, and to call for action from elected officials through formal petitions." ASHUTOSH BHAGWAT, OUR DEMOCRATIC FIRST AMENDMENT 161–62 (2020). Free speech is an important but hardly the only form of expressive freedom necessary to sustain democratic deliberation. *See generally* CASS SUNSTEIN, REPUBLIC.COM 153 (2001) (arguing that "the free speech principle should be read in light of the commitment to democratic deliberation," meaning that "a central point of the free speech principle is to carry out that commitment").

2. U.S. CONST. amend. I (providing that "Congress shall make no law . . . abridging the freedom of speech, or of the press; or the right of the people peaceably to assemble, and to petition the Government for a redress of grievances").

3. *See* JOHN D. INAZU, LIBERTY'S REFUGE: THE FORGOTTEN FREEDOM OF ASSEMBLY 61–62 (2012) (noting that the Supreme Court, since 1983, has relied exclusively on the Free Speech Clause to decide major cases involving expressive freedom and adding that "[t]he Court, in fact, has not addressed a freedom of assembly claim in thirty years"); *see also* BHAGWAT, *supra* note 1, at 3–4 (observing that "essentially all of modern discourse and modern law focuses on

only one provision of the First Amendment, the Free Speech Clause," noting that "[t]he rest have been almost entirely forgotten," and arguing that this state of affairs "is tragic because these forgotten provisions—freedom of the press, assembly, and petition—hold the key to understanding why the First Amendment matters").

4. 4 WILLIAM BLACKSTONE, COMMENTARIES ON THE LAWS OF ENGLAND 151–53 (1769).

5. Alien Act, ch. 66, 1 Stat. 577 (July 6, 1798); Sedition Act, ch. 74, 1 Stat. 596 (July 14, 1798).

6. 3 JOSEPH STORY, COMMENTARIES ON THE CONSTITUTION OF THE UNITED STATES §§ 1885–86 (1833) (discussing the Alien and Sedition Acts and observing that the Sedition Act's "constitutionality was deliberately affirmed by the courts of law," as well as "in a report made by a committee of congress" and "by a majority" of state governments).

7. See U.S. CONST. art. I, § 2, cl. 1 ("The House of Representatives shall be composed of Members chosen every second Year by the People of the several States, and the Electors in each State shall have the Qualifications requisite for Electors of the most numerous Branch of the State Legislature."); id., amend. XV, § 1 ("The right of citizens of the United States to vote shall not be denied or abridged by the United States or by any State on account of race, color, or previous condition of servitude."); id., amend. XVII, § 1 (providing for the direct election of members of the U.S. Senate and stipulating that "[t]he electors in each State shall have the qualifications requisite for electors of the most numerous branch of the State legislatures"); id., amend. XIX, § 1 ("The right of citizens of the United States to vote shall not be denied or abridged by the United States or by any State on account of sex."); id., amend. XXIV, § 1 ("The right of citizens of the United States to vote in any primary or other election for President or Vice President, for electors for President or Vice President, or for Senator or Representative in Congress, shall not be denied or abridged by the United States or any State by reason of failure to pay any poll tax or other tax."); id., amend. XXVI, § 1 ("The right of citizens of the United States, who are eighteen years of age or older, to vote shall not be denied or abridged by the United States or by any State on account of age."). Each of these constitutional provisions anticipates the use of elections to select members of the U.S. House, Senate, and Presidential Electors; if freedom of speech is essential to the conduct of free and fair elections, then these provisions mandating elections for federal offices could plausibly serve as a basis for implying a right to freedom of political and governmental speech. This, in fact, is how the High Court of Australia (HCA) recognized a judicially enforceable "freedom of political and governmental communication." See Australian Capital Television Pty. Ltd. v. Commonwealth, (1992) 177 C.L.R. 106 (Austl.); Nationwide News Pty. Ltd. v. Wills, (1992) 177 C.L.R. 1 (Austl.). Since first recognizing the implied freedom in 1992, the HCA has regularly heard and decided cases involving the implied freedom of political and governmental communication. See, e.g., LibertyWorks Inc. v. Commonwealth, (2021) H.C.A. 18 (Austl.); Comcare v. Banerji, (2019) H.C.A. 23 (Austl.).

8. New York Times Co. v. Sullivan, 376 U.S. 254, 270 (1964).

9. ALEXANDER MEIKLEJOHN, FREE SPEECH AND ITS RELATION TO SELF-GOVERNMENT 88–91 (1948) (discussing the importance of information and engagement to the electoral process and thus to self-government by We the People).

10. Moore v. East Cleveland, 431 U.S. 494, 503 (1977) (explaining that "the Constitution protects the sanctity of the family precisely because the institution of the family is deeply rooted in this Nation's history and tradition"); see Dobbs v. Jackson Women's Health Org., 142 S. Ct. 2228, 2246 (2022) (holding that when deciding whether to recognize an unenumerated fundamental right, the federal courts inquire into "whether the right is deeply rooted in [our] history and tradition and whether it is essential to our Nation's scheme of ordered liberty")

Notes to pages 2–3

(internal quotations and citations omitted); Washington v. Glucksberg, 521 U.S. 702, 710 (1997) ("We begin, as we do in all due process cases, by examining our Nation's history, legal traditions, and practices.").

11. In re Winship, 397 U.S. 358, 377 (1970) (Black, J., dissenting) ("I realize that it is far easier to substitute individual judges' ideas of 'fairness' for the fairness prescribed by the Constitution, but I shall not at any time surrender my belief that that document itself should be our guide, not our own concept of what is fair, decent, and right."); Griswold v. Connecticut, 381 U.S. 479, 509–10 (1965) (Black, J., dissenting) (opining that "I get nowhere in this case by talk about a constitutional 'right of privacy' as an emanation from one or more constitutional provisions" and explaining that "I like my privacy as well as the next one, but I am nevertheless compelled to admit that government has a right to invade it unless prohibited by some specific constitutional provision"); Hugo L. Black, A Constitutional Faith 3–11, 23–31 (1968).

12. Black, supra note 11, at 8.

13. *Id.*

14. Antonin Scalia, A Matter of Interpretation: Federal Courts and the Law 24–25 (1997) (objecting to the use of the Due Process Clauses of the Fifth and Fourteenth Amendments to recognize unenumerated fundamental rights, a form of "freewheeling lawmaking" and observing that "it may be or may not be a good thing to guarantee additional liberties, but the Due Process Clause quite obviously does not bear that interpretation"); *see also id.* at 39 ("Never mind the text that we are supposedly construing; we will smuggle these new rights in, if all else fails, under the Due Process Clause (which, as I have described, is textually incapable of containing them).").

15. Robert H. Bork, The Tempting of America: The Political Seduction of the Law 179–85 (1990) (objecting to the judicial recognition and protection of unenumerated rights as part of an effort to update the Constitution). Judge Bork argues that "[w]hen all else is said, however, it is inconceivable that men who viewed the judiciary as a relatively insignificant branch could have devised, without even discussing the matter, a system, known nowhere else on earth, under which judges were given uncontrolled power to override the decisions of the democratic branches by finding authority outside the written Constitution." *Id.* at 185. *But cf.* Stephen Breyer, Active Liberty: Interpreting Our Democratic Constitution 131–32 (2005) ("Literalism has a tendency to undermine the Constitution's efforts to create a framework for democratic government—a government that, while protecting basic individual liberties, permits citizens to govern themselves, and to govern themselves effectively. Insofar as a more literal interpretive approach undermines this basic objective, it is inconsistent with the most fundamental original intention of the Framers themselves.").

16. Korematsu v. United States, 323 U.S. 214, 216 (1944).

17. *See id.* ("It should be noted, to begin with, that all legal restrictions which curtail the civil rights of a single racial group are immediately suspect. That is not to say that all such restrictions are unconstitutional. It is to say that courts must subject them to the most rigid scrutiny. Pressing public necessity may sometimes justify the existence of such restrictions; racial antagonism never can.").

18. *See* Trump v. Hawaii, 138 S. Ct. 2392, 2423 (2018) ("The dissent's reference to *Korematsu*, however, affords this Court the opportunity to make express what is already obvious: *Korematsu* was gravely wrong the day it was decided, has been overruled in the court of history, and—to be clear—has no place in law under the Constitution.") (internal quotations and citations omitted).

186 ⸱◠   Notes to pages 3–4

19. 347 U.S. 483, 495 (1954) ("Separate educational facilities are inherently unequal. Therefore, we hold that the plaintiffs and others similarly situated for whom the actions have been brought are, by reason of the segregation complained of, deprived of the equal protection of the laws guaranteed by the Fourteenth Amendment.").

20. *See* Bolling v. Sharpe, 347 U.S. 497, 499 (1954) (holding that "[c]lassifications based solely upon race must be scrutinized with particular care, since they are contrary to our traditions and hence constitutionally suspect" and citing *Korematsu* in support of this rule).

21. *Id.* at 500 ("In view of our decision that the Constitution prohibits the states from maintaining racially segregated public schools, it would be unthinkable that the same Constitution would impose a lesser duty on the Federal Government. We hold that racial segregation in the public schools of the District of Columbia is a denial of the due process of law guaranteed by the Fifth Amendment to the Constitution."). Justice Black joined this opinion in full—despite its overt reliance on the Due Process Clause of the Fifth Amendment to "reverse incorporate" the Equal Protection Clause of the Fourteenth Amendment (which applies only to *state* governments and not the federal government). *See* U.S. CONST. amend. XIV, § 1 (providing that "[n]o state shall . . . deny to any person within its jurisdiction the equal protection of the laws.").

22. *See, e.g.*, Snyder v. Phelps, 562 U.S. 443, 447–49, 456–61 (2011) (protecting the use of offensive homophobic speech proximate to the funeral and burial services of Matthew Snyder, a deceased Marine killed while on active duty); Hustler Magazine, Inc. v. Falwell, 485 U.S. 46, 52–55 (1988) (holding protected, as caricature and parody, an offensive fake Campari ad in *Hustler Magazine* that suggested Rev. Jerry Falwell, Sr.'s first sexual experience was a drunken rendezvous with his mother in an outhouse); Brandenburg v. Ohio, 395 U.S. 444, 447–48 (1969) (holding that the First Amendment protects the public use of racial epithets at a mass gathering, coupled with calls for racialized violence at some indefinite time in the future because "the constitutional guarantees of free speech and free press do not permit a State to forbid or proscribe advocacy of the use of force or of law violation except where such advocacy is directed to inciting or producing imminent lawless action and is likely to incite or produce such action").

23. RICHARD DELGADO & JEAN STEFANCIC, MUST WE DEFEND NAZIS?: WHY THE FIRST AMENDMENT SHOULD NOT PROTECT HATE SPEECH AND WHITE SUPREMACY 3–19 (2018) (discussing and describing various social harms inflicted on members of minority communities by hate speech).

24. U.S. CONST. AMEND. I (providing that "*Congress* shall make no law" abridging expressive freedoms) (emphasis added).

25. *See infra* Chapter 2.

26. *See infra* Chapter 3.

27. *See infra* Chapter 4.

28. *See infra* Chapter 5.

29. *See infra* Chapter 6.

30. Human Rights Act 1998, ch. 42 (U.K.) (enacted Nov. 9, 1998 and entered into force Oct. 2, 2000) [hereinafter HRA]. For a general discussion of the enactment of the HRA, see Clive Walker & Russell L. Weaver, *The United Kingdom Bill of Rights 1998: The Modernisation of Rights in the Old World*, 33 U. MICH. J. L. REFORM 497 (2000).

31. European Convention for the Protection of Human Rights and Fundamental Freedoms, Nov. 4, 1950, 213 U.N.T.S. 222, 224 [hereinafter European Convention].

32. HRA § 3. The HRA also requires all "public authorities," including the domestic courts, to respect European Convention rights. *See* HRA § 6(1) ("It is unlawful for a public authority to act in a way which is incompatible with a Convention right.").

Notes to pages 4–6   —◦ 187

33. HRA § 12(4).

34. *See* ADAM CHILTON & MILA VERSTEEG, HOW CONSTITUTIONAL RIGHTS MATTER (2020).

35. *See infra* Chapter 4.

36. Ruth Gavison, *Legislatures and the Quest for a Constitution: The Case of Israel*, 11 REV. CONST. STUD. 345, 365–66 (2006).

37. HCJ 73/53, Kol Ha'am Co., Ltd. v. Minister of the Interior, 7 PD 871 (1953) (Isr.), *translated in Translated Opinions*, VERSA, https://versa.cardozo.yu.edu/sites/default/files/upload/opinions/Kol%20Ha%27am%20Co.%2C%20Ltd.%20v.%20Minister%20of%20the%20Interior.pdf.

38. *See, e.g.*, NEIL M. GORSUCH, A REPUBLIC, IF YOU CAN KEEP IT 25 (2019) ("Originalism is simply the idea that when interpreting the Constitution, we should look to text and history and how the document was understood at the time of its ratification. For your constitutional rights should not be subject to judicial revision."). Justice Gorsuch is engaged in clever constitutional legerdemain; a litigant does not possess a right unless and until a judge, sitting here and now, so rules. *See* CHARLES EVANS HUGHES, ADDRESSES OF CHARLES EVANS HUGHES: 1906–1916, at179, 185 (2d ed. 1916) (address of May 3, 1907, to the Elmira Chamber of Commerce) (observing that "[w]e are under a Constitution, but the Constitution is what the judges say it is").

39. It is entirely possible that text might matter more in some contexts than in others. My claim is that, with respect to the freedom of speech and other core expressive freedoms, text, whether constitutional or statutory in nature, does not seem to be doing much significant jurisprudential work.

40. *See, e.g.*, U.S. CONST. amend III ("No Soldier shall, in time of peace be quartered in any house, without the consent of the Owner, nor in time of war, but in a manner to be prescribed by law."). The Third Amendment to the U.S. Constitution appears front and center in the Bill of Rights. Even so, federal judges have long ignored it, and it plays no meaningful role in contemporary U.S. human rights jurisprudence. Clearly, however, James Madison and the legislators who drafted the Bill of Rights viewed the involuntary housing of troops in private homes as a pressing and important problem in need of a solution. Problems that seem pressing and important to one generation may not present as problems at all to subsequent generations. When this happens, entrenching a right in a constitutional instrument will be largely meaningless.

41. *See* MICHAEL J. KLARMAN, FROM JIM CROW TO CIVIL RIGHTS: THE SUPREME COURT AND THE STRUGGLE FOR RACIAL EQUALITY (2004) (arguing that the Warren Court's decision in *Brown* reflected public opinion within the legal community and helped to solidify preexisting support for meaningful enforcement of the Fourteenth Amendment's Equal Protection Clause to disallow government-sponsored racial discrimination but also served as a catalyst for the "Massive Resistance" movement in the South).

42. *See infra* Chapter 2.

43. *See* John F. Manning, *Separation of Powers as Ordinary Interpretation*, 124 HARV. L. REV. 1939, 1943–49, 2005–17, 2021–24, 2040 (2011) (arguing that the federal courts should more strictly enforce specific structural requirements and rules than more general provisions, such as the Vesting Clauses of Articles I, II, and III that allocate powers among the three branches of the national government). Of course, whether even structural provisions provide effective constraints will depend on whether independent courts exist that have the institutional strength to enforce them against backsliding political branches. *See* Ronald J. Krotoszynski, Jr. & Atticus DeProspo, *Against Congressional Case Snatching*, 62 WM. & MARY L. REV. 791,

188 ⌒ Notes to pages 6–7

806 & 806 n.48 (2021) (arguing that specific limits "on the structure and function of the three branches presuppose[ ] a federal judiciary able and willing to make its judgments stick" and positing that "specific constitutional strictures" will actually limit how Congress and the President behave only if the Article III courts have the institutional power to enforce those limits).

44. *See* STANLEY FISH, IS THERE A TEXT IN THIS CLASS?: THE AUTHORITY OF INTERPRETIVE COMMUNITIES 13–16 (1980); HUGHES, *supra* note 38, at 185.

45. Letter from James Madison to Thomas Jefferson (Oct. 17, 1788), https://founders.archi ves.gov/documents/Madison/01-11-02-0218 [https://perma.cc/82RA-QG6R].

46. *Id.*; *see also* FISH, *supra* note 43, at 13–17 (arguing that words have meaning only within the context of specific interpretative communities and that meaning results from a process of contesting meaning that possesses both objective and subjective elements but is neither entirely objective or subjective in character).

47. Letter from James Madison to Thomas Jefferson, *supra* note 45.

48. *See id.* (arguing that "the limited powers of the federal Government and the jealousy of the subordinate Governments, afford a security which has not existed in the case of the State Governments").

49. Even this claim is highly contestable. *See* DAVID A. STRAUSS, THE LIVING CONSTITUTION 132–36 (2010) (explaining that the direct election of U.S. senators significantly antedated the ratification of the Seventeenth Amendment and that "[b]eginning in the 1830s . . . people who wanted to be elected to the Senate began appealing directly to the voters of the state to vote, in state legislative elections, for candidates who were pledged to support them for the Senate"). In other words, constitutional change, with direct popular input on the persons who would serve in the federal Senate, came about through state law reform prior to April 8, 1913 (the Seventeenth Amendment's date of ratification). Thus, "[b]y 1911, a year before the Seventeenth Amendment was proposed, over half the states had adopted the Oregon system," which involved public pledges by candidates for the state legislature to support particular U.S. Senate candidates. *Id.* at 133–34.

50. ALFRED H. KELLY, WINFRED A. HARBISON, & HERMAN BELZ, THE AMERICAN CONSTITUTION: ITS ORIGINS AND DEVELOPMENT 129–31 (6th ed. 1983) (describing and discussing the fierce debate between Alexander Hamilton and Thomas Jefferson, as members of George Washington's cabinet, over the federal government's authority to charter and maintain a national bank).

51. *Id.* at 147–50 (discussing the Louisiana Purchase and Jefferson's initial belief that a constitutional amendment would be necessary to render it lawful and his ultimate acceptance of a common law approach to the Constitution under which "the power to acquire territory was inherent in the very existence of the United States as a sovereign nation—a proposition that challenged the [Democratic-]Republican theory of the Union as a compact among the states"). Professors Kelly, Harbison, and Belz posit that the Louisiana Purchase, and the constitutional arguments that it engendered within the ostensibly "strict construction[ist]" Jefferson Administration, reflect the salience of "new theories and principles" that "embody values in the political culture"—and also perhaps a "cautionary reminder that practice must temper theory." *Id.* at 148–50. Even in the early years of the Republic, a "distinctively American form of constitutional politics" arose, one "based on rhetoric and principles that have the power to influence public opinion because they express fundamental values." *Id.* at 150. In a word, constitutional practice in the United States has traveled the common law methodological path for a very long time—dating back to the Washington and Jefferson Administrations.

Notes to pages 7–8   —◌ 189

52. The Seventeenth Amendment provides an instructive example. Direct election of U.S. senators in a great many states antedated its ratification. *See* STRAUSS, *supra* note 49, at 133–34. As Strauss puts it, "[t]he Seventeenth Amendment . . . did not bring about the direct election of senators; it ratified a practice of de facto direct election that had been instituted by other means." *Id.* at 135. In other words, a common law evolution occurred that had effectively re-written the *structural* rules governing how most members of the U.S. Senate would come to hold that office—"[t]he living Constitution was the real agent of change" rather than the formal amendment process. *Id.* at 136.

53. THE FEDERALIST NO. 84, at 510, 513–14 (Alexander Hamilton) (Clinton Rossiter ed., 1961).

54. *Id.* at 514.

55. *Id.* at 513.

56. *Id.*

57. McCulloch v. Maryland, 17 U.S. (4 Wheat.) 316, 431 (1819) (observing that "the power to tax involves the power to destroy" and that "the power to destroy may defeat and render useless the power to create"). *But cf.* Panhandle Oil Co. v. Knox, 277 U.S. 218, 223 (1928) (Holmes, J., dissenting) ("The power to tax is not the power to destroy while this Court sits.").

58. *See, e.g.*, United States v. Kahriger, 345 U.S. 22 (1953) (upholding a plainly regulatory enactment to impose confiscatory federal taxes on commercial gambling operations). Provided that a federal tax could produce some revenue, a regulatory purpose and effect will not render the "tax" unconstitutional. *See id.* at 28 & 28 n.4; United States v. Sanchez, 340 U.S. 42, 44–45 (1950) (upholding confiscatory taxes on marijuana sales); Sonzinsky v. United States, 300 U.S. 506, 513 (1937) (upholding usurious taxes on the sale of sawed-off shotguns in part because "[e]very tax is in some measure regulatory"). *But cf.* Bailey v. Drexel Furniture (Child Labor Tax Case), 259 U.S. 20, 36–38 (1922) (invalidating a "tax" collected by the Department of Labor that appeared to function as a direct proscription against the use of child labor); *Kahriger*, 345 U.S. at 38 (Frankfurter, J., dissenting) (arguing in dissent that "when oblique use is made of the taxing power as to matters which substantively are not within the powers delegated to Congress, the Court cannot shut its eyes to what is obviously, because designedly, an attempt to control conduct which the Constitution left to the responsibility of the States, merely because Congress wrapped the legislation in the verbal cellophane of a revenue measure").

59. U.S. CONST. art. I, § 8, cl. 1; *see* NFIB v. Sebelius, 567 U.S. 519, 563–74 (2012) (opinion of Roberts, C.J.) (upholding the individual mandate as a constitutionally valid exercise of the taxing power).

60. BHAGWAT, *supra* note 1, at 6–7 (explaining the history behind the ratification conventions in New York and Virginia).

61. *See* GERARD N. MAGLIOCCA, THE HEART OF THE CONSTITUTION: HOW THE BILL OF RIGHTS BECAME THE BILL OF RIGHTS 32–34 (2018) (discussing the compromise that permitted ratification to proceed and observing that Madison and other proponents of ratification "wisely concluded that ratification would occur only if the Virginia convention was allowed to propose" a bill of rights that would be considered expeditiously in the first meeting of Congress); *see also* KELLY ET AL., *supra* note 50, at 110 ("Unwilling to appear less solicitous of liberty than their opponents, Federalists in several states informally agreed to accept subsequent inclusion of a bill of rights as a condition of ratification.").

62. AKHIL REED AMAR & LES ADAMS, THE BILL OF RIGHTS PRIMER: A CITIZEN'S GUIDEBOOK TO THE AMERICAN BILL OF RIGHTS 38 (2013) (discussing the Antifederalists' suspicion of the broad powers given to the federal government).

Notes to pages 8–9

63. *See* KELLY ET AL., *supra* note 50, at 121–22 (explaining that "Federalists had won in several states by promising a series of constitutional amendments embodying a bill of rights," that "[m]any members of the first Congress now felt a moral obligation to fulfill these promises," and, accordingly, "[i]n September 1789 Congress submitted twelve proposed amendments to the states").

64. 1 ANNALS OF CONG. 440–60 (1789) (Joseph Gales ed., 1834) (explaining the importance of this amendment to James Madison); *see* MAGLIOCCA, *supra* note 61, at 38 (noting that James Madison introduced a resolution on June 8, 1789, that set forth the proposed amendments that would come to comprise the Bill of Rights). Madison had collected a file of proposed amendments from the state ratifying conventions, as well as state legislatures, and attempted to propose amendments that were responsive to most of the requests and, in particular, to requests supported by multiple states. *See* AMAR & ADAMS, *supra* note 62, at 39–40; *see also* 2 BERNARD SCHWARTZ, THE BILL OF RIGHTS: A DOCUMENTARY HISTORY 983 (Leon Friedman et al. eds., 1971). As Professors Amar and Adams explain, "Madison had begun work with a file of nearly one hundred suggested amendments (not counting duplications) proposed by eight states to be considered for inclusion in a bill of rights." AMAR & ADAMS, *supra* note 62, at 40.

65. *See* THE FEDERALIST NO. 84, *supra* note 53, at 513–14 (arguing that "bills of rights, in the sense and to the extent in which they are contended for, are not only unnecessary in the proposed Constitution, but would even be dangerous").

66. The United Kingdom's constitution reflects this approach—it relies on structure rather than text to safeguard liberty. The contemporary U.K. lacks a judicially enforceable Bill of Rights and acts of Parliament are not subject to judicial review by the Supreme Court of the United Kingdom. *See* RONALD J. KROTOSZYNSKI, JR., PRIVACY REVISITED: A GLOBAL PERSPECTIVE ON THE RIGHT TO BE LEFT ALONE 117–20 (2016) (explaining how the Parliament has the authority to make any laws). To this day, "the doctrine of parliamentary sovereignty (or supremacy) remains an important, if no longer absolutely defining, characteristic of the British constitution." *Id.* at 120.

67. ROBERT L. MADDEX, CONSTITUTIONS OF THE WORLD vii (3d ed. 2008) ("The governments of China, Cuba, North Korea, and Vietnam remain single-party dictatorships, and Saudi Arabia remains an absolute monarchy."); SUE VANDER HOOK, COMMUNISM 131 (Holly Saari et al. eds., 2011) (observing that "[t]he constitutions of Cuba, North Korea, and Vietnam all promise similar freedoms and human rights" but cautioning that "[m]any historians and human rights advocates have proclaimed Communist constitutions as mere propaganda."); *see* Tom Ginsburg, Nick Foti, & Daniel Rockmore, *"We the Peoples": The Global Origins of Constitutional Preambles*, 46 GEO. WASH. INT'L L. REV. 305, 314 (2014) (noting "the relative importance of the constitution as a symbol, as opposed to a legally operative text, in socialist countries"); Ronald J. Krotoszynski, Jr., *The Irrelevant Wasteland: An Exploration of Why* Red Lion *Doesn't Matter (Much) in 2008, the Crucial Importance of the Information Revolution, and the Continuing Relevance of the Public Interest Standard in Regulating Access to Spectrum*, 60 ADMIN. L. REV. 911, 919–20 n.27, 936–37 (2008) (discussing official state censorship in China, Cuba, and North Korea despite constitutional guarantees that ostensibly safeguard freedom of speech and press in these nations).

68. *See* Kim Lane Scheppele, *Autocratic Legalism*, 85 U. CHI. L. REV. 545, 549–52, 562, 568, 570 (2018) (exploring how antiliberal autocrats deconstruct constitutional curtailments); Kim Lane Scheppele, *The Rule of Law and the Frankenstate: Why Governance Checklists Do Not Work*, 26 GOVERNANCE: AN INT'L J. OF LAW, POL'Y, ADMIN. & INSTS. 559, 560–61 (2013) (explaining

Notes to pages 9–10   —⌒ 191

how Hungary's Prime Minister, Viktor Orbán, with 34% of the popular vote from the 2010 election, could and did fundamentally change the Hungarian constitutional structure).

69. CLIFFORD GEERTZ, THE INTERPRETATION OF CULTURES 28–29 (1973) (reprising the cosmic turtle meme and reporting that "'it is turtles all the way down'").

70. *See* GORSUCH, *supra* note 38, at 25 (arguing that "your constitutional rights should not be subject to judicial revision" and "[t]hey should mean the same today as they did then and they should never be diminished by courts or judges"); *id.* at 28 (arguing that "in our system of separated powers, the judge's job is to enforce the laws as the legislature writes them"). The sleight of hand, of course, involves the fact that judges today are empowered to tell us what the text supposedly meant "then." Simply put, there's no meaningful text-based constraint on a judge's discretion to pick and choose what authorities she will consult, and then credit, in ascertaining and then pronouncing the text's meaning. A judge's interpretation of the text, here and now today, whether characterized as long-standing or newly minted, constitutes the law (at least for this day and train). Meaningful constraints on judicial discretion exist, of course, but constitutional text would likely appear rather far down the list of efficacious constraints on judicial discretion.

71. Marbury v. Madison, 5 U.S. (1 Cranch) 137, 177 (1803) ("It is emphatically the province and the duty of the judicial department to say what the law is. Those who apply the rule to particular cases, [sic] must of necessity expound and interpret that rule.").

72. *See* OLIVER WENDELL HOLMES, JR., THE COMMON LAW 36–37 (1881) (arguing that the law "will become entirely consistent only when it ceases to grow" and positing that common law judges "have a right to reconsider the popular reasons, and, taking a broader view of the field, to decide anew whether those reasons are satisfactory" when deciding whether to maintain, amend, or abolish a common law rule). Justice Holmes is remarkably explicit in his legal realist account of the common law process: "The felt necessities of the time, the prevalent moral and political theories, intuitions of public policy, avowed or unconscious, even the prejudices which judges share with their fellow-men, have had a good deal more to do than the syllogism in determining the rules by which men should be governed." *Id.* at 1.

73. GUIDO CALABRESI, A COMMON LAW FOR THE AGE OF STATUTES 3–4, 52 (1982) (noting the power of common law courts to modify common law rules and observing that "there is an important common law, judicial, function in the updating of outworn laws").

74. *See, e.g.,* Griswold v. Connecticut, 381 U.S. 479, 484–85 (1965) (observing that "specific guarantees in the Bill of Rights have penumbras, formed by emanations from those guarantees that help give them life and substance" and invoking the First, Third, Fourth, Fifth, and Ninth Amendments to require judicial recognition of a "zone of privacy created by several fundamental constitutional guarantees"). Many commentators have criticized Justice William O. Douglas's invocation of "penumbras" from specific provisions of the Bill of Rights as deeply unpersuasive. *See, e.g.,* CALABRESI, *supra* note 73, at 8 (arguing that "the *constitutional* basis for its [the Connecticut statute] invalidity was tenuous, to say the least, especially at the time the decision was made" and explaining that "[p]enumbras of constitutional prohibitions and rights to privacy were much mentioned, but these concepts had not been, and were not soon to be, applied by the Court in principled fashion in other closely related cases"). Regarding *Griswold*'s constitutional predicate, Calabresi posits that "[i]n the end, the case was its own justification." *Id.* at 9.

75. HUGHES, *supra* note 38, at 185 (noting that the meaning of constitutional text depends critically on judicial interpretation and is not self-enforcing).

76. For example, do citizens expect government to respect a particular fundamental right or are they more or less indifferent to whether the government burdens or abridges a particular right?

77. Of course, this works in reverse as well; if a society is indifferent to government speech restrictions, judges are likely to be uninterested in using judicial review to fend off government efforts at censorship (even censorship of core political speech). To a significant, perhaps surprising, degree, a constitution means what a particular political community believes that it means.

78. *See infra* Chapter 4.

79. *See id.*

80. *See* Part I of the Constitution Act, 1982, Canada Act, 1982, ch. 11, sch. B, art. 2, § 1 (U.K.) (containing the Canadian Charter of Rights and Freedoms) [hereinafter Canadian Charter]; *see also* KROTOSZYNSKI, *supra* note 66, at 42–43 ("Prior to 1982, the Canadian judiciary lacked a general power of judicial review."); RONALD J. KROTOSZYNSKI, JR., THE FIRST AMENDMENT IN CROSS-CULTURAL PERSPECTIVE: A COMPARATIVE LEGAL ANALYSIS OF THE FREEDOM OF SPEECH 26–29 (2006) (discussing Canada's adoption of the Charter of Rights and Freedoms).

81. Canadian Charter § 2(b) (protecting "freedom of thought, belief, opinion and expression, including freedom of the press and other media of communication"); *see id.*, § 2(c) (protecting "freedom of peaceful assembly"); *id.* § 2(d) (protecting "freedom of association"). Like the U.S. First Amendment, Section 2 is the first rights-granting provision of the Canadian Charter. Section 1 provides for proportionality analysis, which requires courts to balance the infringement of protected rights against the government's stated justifications for the restrictions. *See id.* § 1 ("The Canadian Charter of Rights and Freedoms guarantees the rights and freedoms set out in it subject only to such reasonable limits prescribed by law as can be demonstrably justified in a free and democratic society."); *see also* R. v. Oakes, [1986] 1 S.C.R. 103 (Can.) (providing the rules governing proportionality analysis under the Canadian Charter).

82. KROTOSZYNSKI, *supra* note 80, at 30–92 (discussing and critiquing the SCC's free expression precedents under Section 2(b) of the Canadian Charter).

83. Canadian Charter § 24(1) ("Anyone whose rights or freedoms, as guaranteed by this Charter, have been infringed or denied may apply to a court of competent jurisdiction to obtain such remedy as the court considers appropriate and just in the circumstances.").

CHAPTER 2

1. Although multiple theories exist for extending strong legal protection to expressive activities, the dominant and most enduring account rests on the relationship of speech, assembly, association, petition, and a free press to the ongoing process of democratic self-government. *See* ALEXANDER MEIKLEJOHN, FREE SPEECH AND ITS RELATION TO SELF-GOVERNMENT 26 (1948) ("The principle of the freedom of speech springs from the necessities of the program of self-government."); *see also* CASS R. SUNSTEIN, DEMOCRACY AND THE PROBLEM OF FREE SPEECH 18 (1993) (positing that a "well-functioning system of free expression" is essential to achieving "the central constitutional goal of creating a deliberative democracy").

2. As noted in Chapter 1, I will use the term "expressive freedom" to refer to various forms of individual and collective expressive activity, including the freedoms of speech, press, assembly, association, and petition. It is commonplace in the contemporary United States to use the "freedom of speech" or the "freedom of expression" as shorthand for any and all forms of

Notes to pages 15–16   —◦ 193

communication. However, as Professor Ash Bhagwat persuasively argues, each form of expressive activity can be—and should be—differentiated because each possesses distinct attributes and characteristics. ASHUTOSH BHAGWAT, OUR DEMOCRATIC FIRST AMENDMENT 3–4 (2020). Moreover, each one arguably serves a particularized function in facilitating the process of democratic deliberation that animates the process of democratic-self-government. *Id.* at 3–9.

3. U.S. CONST. amend. I.

4. BHAGWAT, *supra* note 2, at 4.

5. N.Y. Times Co. v. Sullivan, 376 U.S. 254, 270 (1964); *see* Snyder v. Phelps, 562 U.S. 443, 460–61 (2011) (acknowledging that "[s]peech is powerful" and "can stir people to action, move them to tears of both joy and sorrow and—as it did here—inflict great pain" but that it is better "to protect even hurtful speech on public issues" than to "stifle public debate").

6. CHARLES L. "PIE" DUFOUR, KREWE OF PROTEUS: THE FIRST HUNDRED YEARS 5 (1981) (describing Proteus as the "'shepherd of the sea'" and explaining that he was "the herdsman of Poseidon's seals"); *see also* EDITH HAMILTON, MYTHOLOGY 38 (1942) (discussing Proteus and the god's powers).

7. MAUREEN ALDEN, PARA-NARRATIVES IN THE ODYSSEY: STORIES IN THE FRAME 23 (2017) (noting that Proteus was known as the "Old Man of the Sea"); DUFOUR, *supra* note 6, at 5 (describing Proteus as "the Old Man of the Sea"); *see* HOMER, THE ODYSSEY 56–57 (George H. Palmer trans. 1892) (noting that Proteus was the son of Poseidon and the "old man of the sea").

8. THOMAS BULFINCH, BULFINCH'S MYTHOLOGY 173 (1913); HAMILTON, *supra* note 6, at 42.

9. *See* BULFINCH, *supra* note 8, at 191 ("Proteus, waking and finding himself captured, immediately resorted to his arts, becoming first a fire, then a flood, then a horrible wild beast, in rapid succession."); HAMILTON, *supra* note 6, at 299 ("But to hold him—that was another matter. [Proteus] had the power of changing his shape at will, and there in our hands he became a lion and a dragon and many other animals, and finally even a high-branched tree.").

10. GUIDO CALABRESI, A COMMON LAW FOR THE AGE OF STATUTES 3–5, 178–80, 190–91 (1982).

11. *Id.* at 163–71.

12. I should emphasize that I am not referring to monumental shifts in constitutional meaning, of the scope associated with Professor Bruce Ackerman's "constitutional moments," but instead I am claiming that judicial construction of constitutional meaning constitutes a quotidian judicial activity. *See* BRUCE ACKERMAN, WE THE PEOPLE, VOLUME 2: TRANSFORMATIONS 4–17, 408–21 (1998) (describing and discussing the concept of "constitutional moments," which are points of inflection when the Supreme Court ratifies a major de facto amendment of the U.S. Constitution presaged by strong, empirically observable shifts in the nation's political life, beliefs, and constitutional commitments). In a sense, any construction of language necessarily involves ascribing meaning to particular words, and words only have meaning in the context of a particular interpretative community. *See* STANLEY FISH, IS THERE A TEXT IN THIS CLASS?: THE AUTHORITY OF INTERPRETIVE COMMUNITIES 14 (1980) ("Indeed, it is interpretive communities, rather than either text or the reader, that produce meanings and are responsible for the emergence of formal features."). Even if a judge claims that they are merely following the "plain meaning" or "the original understanding" of a particular constitutional turn of phrase, that exercise involves *that judge*, and *no one else*, conjuring legal effects from the words. *See id.* at 13–16. Fish explains that:

> An interpretive community is not objective because as a bundle of interests, of particular persons and goals, its perspective is interested rather than neutral; but by the

194 ◦— Notes to page 16

very same reasoning, the meanings and texts produced by an interpretive community are not subjective because they do not proceed from an isolated individual but from a public and conventional point of view.

Id. at 14.

13. *See* BHAGWAT, *supra* note 2, at 3 (arguing that "essentially all of modern discourse and modern law focuses on only one of the remaining provisions, freedom of speech").

14. U.S. CONST. amend. I (emphasis added); *see* ERIC BARENDT, FREEDOM OF SPEECH 49 (2d ed. 2005) ("Textual arguments have been ignored in other respects. The First Amendment literally only applies to the laws of Congress, but it has never seriously been suggested that executive and police orders are immune from judicial review."); *see also* DAVID A. STRAUSS, THE LIVING CONSTITUTION 9 (2010) ("And then there is the first word of the First Amendment, which is 'Congress'; so the courts, or the president, or the City of Chicago can freely abridge my freedom of speech? That can't be right, and, under clearly established law, it is not right."). Professor Barendt quite accurately notes that "[r]arely has such an apparently simple legal text produced so many problems of interpretation." BARENDT, *supra*, at 48. Making a related but distinct point, Professor Strauss characterizes the Supreme Court's free speech jurisprudence as "a tremendous success story in American constitutional law" but cautions that "these successful principles" are the product of a "the living, common law Constitution" rather than the text or original understanding. STRAUSS, *supra*, at 52–53.

15. *See infra* text and accompanying notes 75 to 102; *see also* STRAUSS, *supra* note 14, at 56 (observing that "[t]he first word of the amendment is 'Congress'" but noting that "[n]o one today would suggest that the president or the courts may infringe free speech").

16. *See, e.g.*, SANFORD LEVINSON & JACK M. BALKIN, DEMOCRACY AND DYSFUNCTION 145 (2019) (lamenting that "[i]t is now regarded as simply naïve to point to the text of the Constitution and its assignment to Congress of the power to 'declare war'"). The First Amendment's "Congress shall make no law" language has become even less relevant than the express textual assignment of the war power to Congress. That said, however, the growth of the imperial presidency, despite clear textual guardrails meant to forestall such a development, clearly constitutes a blown constitutional call by the nation's governing institutions. Indeed, Professor Sandy Levinson argues that things have reached an absolute nadir today, such that insisting on paying attention to the Constitution's specific assignment of joint responsibility for the war power to both Congress and the president provokes yawns rather than concern from the law faculty at a leading (arguably *the* leading) national law school. *See id.* at 173–75.

17. *See* STRAUSS, *supra* note 14, at 56 (noting that the text of the First Amendment "could have been drafted" broadly and "without limiting the prohibition to a certain branch of the government" to better resemble literally *all* the other rights-granting provisions of the Bill of Rights).

18. *Id.*

19. *Id.*

20. BHAGWAT, *supra* note 2, at 3 (lamenting that "essentially all of modern discourse and modern law focuses on only one" of the First Amendment's clauses, namely "freedom of speech"). Professor Bhagwat accurately observes that the Press, Assembly, and Petition Clauses "have been almost entirely forgotten." *Id.*

21. For an iconic illustrative example, *see* ANTONIN SCALIA, A MATTER OF INTERPRETATION: FEDERAL COURTS AND THE LAW 23–25, 37–47 (1997). Justice Scalia strenuously objects to "The Living Constitution," an approach that he describes as embracing the idea that the Constitution "grows and changes from age to age, in order to meet the needs of

Notes to page 16 —◌ 195

a changing society" and argues that the only legitimate approach to constitutional interpretation involves consideration of "the original meaning of the text." *Id.* at 38. *But cf.* STEPHEN G. BREYER, ACTIVE LIBERTY: INTERPRETING OUR DEMOCRATIC CONSTITUTIONS 115–20, 127–32 (2005) (rejecting originalism and textualism, characterizing both approaches pejoratively as forms of "literalism," arguing that literalist constitutional interpretation is both antidemocratic and suffers from "inherently subjective elements" that undermine this approach's ability to generate predictable, principled results, and positing that courts would better advance constitutional values by engaging in dynamic and purposive constitutional interpretation that reads constitutional text in a way that best enables the process of democratic self-government). Using considerably more direct language to make this same point, Scalia quipped, incident to a law school lecture, that the Constitution is "not a living document" but rather is "dead, dead, dead." Katie Glueck, *Scalia: The Constitution Is "Dead,"* POLITICO (Jan. 29, 2013, 8:26 AM EST), https://www.politico.com/story/2013/01/scalia-the-constitution-is-dead-086853 [https://perma.cc/ZE8Q-UFL5].

22. *See* Laurence H. Tribe, *Comment, in* A MATTER OF INTERPRETATION, *supra* note 21, at 65, 79–82 (observing that despite Justice Scalia's claim that the First Amendment "ought to be read as a still-photo command that Congress not abridge such speech rights of Englishmen as were then extant" and positing that Scalia's approach to deciding First Amendment cases "has in fact been guided by a conception of the First Amendment more like my own," meaning an approach that "evolve[s] over time"). Professor Tribe is assuredly correct when he asserts that Justice Scalia "has not interpreted the freedom of speech as a mere codification of the memories (or perhaps the 'memories,' mixing hope and desire with actual recollection)" strictly tied to "a certain moment in the late eighteenth century." *Id.* at 81. Such a conception would surely not have encompassed protection for violent video games, for example—something that would have constituted commercial entertainment rather than speech well into the twentieth century. *Compare* Brown v. Ent. Merchs. Ass'n, 564 U.S. 786, 799 (2011) (invalidating a ban on selling violent video games to minors "[b]ecause the Act imposes a restriction on the content of protected speech") *with* Mutual Film Corp. v. Indus. Comm'n of Ohio, 236 U.S. 230, 243–44 (1915) ("We immediately feel that the argument is wrong or strained which extends the guaranties of free opinion and speech to the multitudinous shows which are advertised on the bill-boards of our cities and towns and which regards them as emblems of public safety . . . and which seeks to bring motion pictures and other spectacles into practical and legal similitude to a free press and liberty of opinion."). *Mutual Film Corporation's* refusal to extend any First Amendment protection to motion pictures, assimilating them with "the theatre, the circus, and all other shows and spectacles" and rejecting the film company's argument that all of these entertainments must enjoy "the same immunity from repression or supervision as the public press," *Mutual Film Corp.*, 236 U.S. at 243, surely reflected a well-settled and long-standing understanding of the First Amendment's proper scope of application. Accordingly, Justice Scalia's purposive application of the amendment to invalidate California's child-protection law was inconsistent with more than 150 years of Supreme Court precedent limiting the amendment's scope to political or ideological speech. *See, e.g.*, Valentine v. Chrestensen, 316 U.S. 52, 55 (1942) (refusing to afford any First Amendment protection to a flyer that, in part, promoted a submarine tourist attraction). Indeed, as late as 1949, a thoughtful lawyer would have believed a dormant Commerce Clause challenge more likely to succeed as a basis for invalidating a ban on commercial advertisements on panel trucks than the First Amendment's Free Speech or Free Press Clauses. *See, e.g.*, Ry. Express Agency, Inc. v. New York, 336 U.S. 106, 111 (1949) (addressing the litigant's argument that a local regulation banning commercial

196 ⌐ Notes to pages 16–17

advertisement violates the Commerce Clause). Justice Scalia, by way of contrast, had no problem with affording commercial speech broad and deep constitutional protection. *See, e.g.*, City of Cincinnati v. Discovery Network, Inc., 507 U.S. 410, 428–31 (1993) (featuring Justice Scalia joining a sweeping majority opinion holding that commercial speech cannot be regulated more aggressively than noncommercial speech unless it contributes to a regulatory problem in a distinctive way that noncommercial speech does not).

23. The Supreme Court's 2021 decision on the speech rights of public-school students while off campus provides an illustrative example. *See* Mahanoy Area Sch. Dist. v. B.L., 141 S. Ct. 2038 (2021). Rather than apply any of its preexisting precedents and tests involving student speech rights, Justice Stephen Breyer, writing for the majority, fashioned a completely new test to govern whether public school authorities could impose discipline on a student for speech activity taking place off campus, but directed toward an audience comprised largely of students, faculty, and staff members at the public school:

> Given the many different kinds of off-campus speech, the different potential school-related and circumstance-specific justifications, and the differing extent to which those justifications may call for First Amendment leeway, we can, as a general matter, say little more than this: Taken together, these three features of much off-campus speech mean that the leeway the First Amendment grants to schools in light of their special characteristics is diminished.

Id. at 2046.

The general governing test for on-campus student speech, *Tinker*, merited mention in applying this open-ended balancing test, *see id.* at 2047–48, but only insofar as the majority concluded that the disruption associated with B.L.'s social media rant did not seriously affect or impede the Mahanoy Area Public High School's regular operations.

24. *See* STRAUSS, *supra* note 14, at 9, 52–56 (arguing that the First Amendment's literal text and the Framers' original understanding of it have been equally irrelevant to the development of First Amendment doctrine). Rather than text or the original understanding, Strauss argues that "[w]e owe these [expressive freedom] principles to the living, common law Constitution" and First Amendment jurisprudence rests almost exclusively on "a series of judicial decisions and extrajudicial developments, over the course of the twentieth century." *Id.* at 53; *see* Eric J. Seagall, *The Constitution Means What the Supreme Court Says It Means*, 129 HARV. L. REV. F. 176, 186 (2016) (arguing that "if policy considerations and prior cases truly generate results in most constitutional cases, just should not hide behind the textual and historical considerations that do not drive decisions and are merely window dressing").

25. *See* SUNSTEIN, *supra* note 2, at 157–58 (positing that, under the First Amendment, "government's burden is greatest when it is regulating political speech" because regulations of political speech are most likely to reflect "illegitimate considerations, such as self-protection, or giving assistance to powerful private groups" and are therefore both "biased" and "harmful"). As Sunstein states the proposition, "[c]ontrols on public debate are uniquely damaging, because they impair the process of deliberation that is a precondition for political legitimacy." *Id.* at 158.

26. *See* Tribe, *supra* note 22, at 79–82 (arguing that the First Amendment should be read to establish a general principle of freedom of expression and expressive activity rather than as a highly circumscribed guarantee tethered entirely to government practices regarding toleration of expressive freedoms in 1791).

27. Alien Act, ch. 66, 1 Stat. 577 (July 6, 1798); Sedition Act, ch. 74, 1 Stat. 596 (July 14, 1798); *see* 3 JOSEPH STORY, COMMENTARIES ON THE CONSTITUTION OF THE UNITED STATES

Notes to page 17   —◌ 197

§§ 1885–86 (1833) (discussing the Alien and Sedition Acts and observing that the Sedition Act's "constitutionality was deliberately affirmed by the courts of law," as well as "in a report made by a committee of congress" and "by a majority" of state governments).

28. BHAGWAT, *supra* note 2, at 16–17, 25; *see* 4 WILLIAM BLACKSTONE, COMMENTARIES ON THE LAWS OF ENGLAND 151–53 (1769) ("The [l]iberty of the [p]ress is indeed essential to the nature of a free state: but this consists in laying no *previous* restraints upon publications, and not in freedom from censure for criminal matter when published."); *id.* (opining that "[t]o subject the press to the restrictive power of a licenser, as was formerly done, both before and since the revolution, is to subject all freedom of sentiment to the prejudices of one man, and make him the arbitrary and infallible judge of all controverted points in learning, religion, and government" but cautioning that "to punish (as the law does at present) any dangerous or offensive writings, which, when published, shall on a fair and impartial trial be adjudged of a pernicious tendency, is necessary for the preservation of peace and good order, of government and religion, the only solid foundations of civil liberty"); STORY, *supra* note 27, §§ 1878, 1883–89 (discussing the limited scope of "the freedom of the press" under the First Amendment and its relation to Blackstone's conception of press freedom); Citizens United v. Fed. Election Comm'n, 558 U.S. 310, 335 (2010) (holding that the a Federal Election Commission's (FEC) administrative review process of political advertising "function[ed] as the equivalent of prior restraint by giving the FEC power analogous to licensing laws implemented in 16th- and 17th-century England, laws and governmental practices of the sort that the First Amendment was drawn to prohibit").

29. *See* Bolger v. Youngs Drug Prods. Corp., 463 U.S. 60, 66–68 (1983) (holding that the "core notion" of commercial speech relates to expression that "does no more than propose a commercial transaction") (internal citations and quotations omitted); Ohralik v. Ohio State Bar Ass'n, 436 U.S. 447, 455–56 (1978) (declining to set forth a clear analytical framework for deciding when a lawyer's speech is commercial rather than noncommercial in nature and positing that the distinction rests on little more than the application of "commonsense"); *see also* Ronald J. Krotoszynski, Jr., *Into the Woods: Broadcasters, Bureaucrats, and Children's Television Programming*, 45 DUKE L.J. 1193, 1212–13 (1996) ("Although the Supreme Court has a well-developed jurisprudence with which to analyze governmental burdens on 'commercial' speech, it never has defined precisely what constitutes commercial speech, nor has it provided a set of analytical tools one can use to accurately and efficiently separate commercial speech from non-commercial speech.").

30. *See supra* note 22.

31. GREGORY P. MAGARIAN, MANAGED SPEECH: THE ROBERTS COURT'S FIRST AMENDMENT 50–57 (2017). Professor Magarian argues that "[t]he *Lochner* era and the commercial speech doctrine converge because First Amendment limits on commercial speech regulations might seem to resurrect *Lochner*." *Id.* at 53; *see* Leslie Kendrick, *First Amendment Expansionism*, 56 WM. & MARY L. REV. 1199, 1206–09 (2015) (discussing "First Amendment opportunism" and positing that a growing proportion of contemporary First Amendment "claims mirror *Lochner*-era claims in their structure" because "they posit a constitutional right, held by business interests (be they sole proprietors or corporate entities), which immunizes them from government regulation, often regulation that relies upon state interests in public health, safety, and welfare"); *see also* Frederick Schauer, *Commercial Speech and the Perils of Parity*, 25 WM. & MARY BILL RTS. J. 965 (2017) (criticizing the broad protection afforded commercial speech under contemporary First Amendment doctrine and arguing against the expansion of the First Amendment rights of commercial speakers).

198 ⌒   Notes to pages 18–19

32. Heffernan v. City of Paterson, 578 U.S. 266, 268 (2016) ("The First Amendment generally prohibits government officials from dismissing or demoting an employee because of the employee's engagement in constitutionally protected political activity."); *see* Branti v. Finkel, 445 U.S. 507, 517 (1980) (prohibiting the discharge, based on their political beliefs and associations, of government employees who lack policy-making authority or process confidential information); *see also* Elrod v. Burns, 427 U.S. 347, 349 (1976) (holding, for the first time, that the First Amendment generally prohibits a government employer from making an employee's partisan identity a basis for hiring and firing decisions).

33. *Elrod*, 427 U.S. at 376 (Powell, J., dissenting).

34. *See supra* note 22. Note that the relatively static interpretation of structural provisions in the Constitution is more a function of judicial common law practice than of the text itself. If my thesis that all constitutional interpretation is more common law than statutory in nature is correct, the specificity of the text or its relationship to rights versus structure simply is not the controlling, or even the most important, factor in informing judicial decision making and reason giving. Instead, the behavior of judges is the most dispositive factor in determining the relevance, or irrelevance, of constitutional text.

35. *See* BHAGWAT, *supra* note 2, at 4–9.

36. *See* STRAUSS, *supra* note 14, at 33–34 (explaining that in most cases presenting constitutional questions "the text of the Constitution will play, at most, a ceremonial role" because "American constitutional law is about precedents, and when the precedents leave off, it is about commonsense notions of fairness and good policy"). Strauss argues that "[t]he common law is a system built not on an authoritative, foundational, quasi-sacred text like the Constitution" but instead rests on "precedents and traditions that accumulate over time." *Id.* at 3.

37. *See* [1966] 1 Weekly L.R. 1234 (H.L.) (Eng.); *see also* CALABRESI, *supra* note 10, at 185–86 n.12 (discussing the House of Lords announcing that it could, contrary to its past claims to the contrary, alter or abolish prior precedents and would take such action going forward); W. Barton Leach, *Revisionism in the House of Lords: The Bastion of Rigid Stare Decisis Falls*, 80 HARV. L. REV. 797, 798–99, 803 (1967) (discussing and describing the House of Lords's change of heart regarding its power to overturn prior precedents and observing that "the House of Lords with grace and dignified simplicity has removed the artificial block to judicial law reform set up by its predecessors").

38. Under the "preferred position" doctrine, the Supreme Court has held that the federal courts have a special obligation to enforce the First Amendment with particular vigilance. *See* Thomas v. Collins, 323 U.S. 516, 530 (1945) (noting "the preferred place given in our scheme to the great, the indispensable democratic freedoms secured by the First Amendment"); Murdock v. Pennsylvania, 319 U.S. 105, 115 (1943) ("Freedom of press, freedom of speech, freedom of religion are in a preferred position."). Writing in *Thomas*, Justice Wiley Rutledge explained that the First Amendment's "priority gives these liberties a sanctity and a sanction not permitting dubious intrusions." *Thomas*, 323 U.S. at 530. The Supreme Court's use of the "preferred position" characterization has waned in more recent opinions, but it still appears from time to time. *See, e.g.*, Emp. Div., Dep't of Hum. Res. v. Smith, 494 U.S. 872, 895 (1990) (O'Connor, J., concurring in part and dissenting in part) ("The compelling interest test effectuates the First Amendment's command that religious liberty is an independent liberty, *that it occupies a preferred position*, and that the Court will not permit encroachments upon this liberty, whether direct or indirect, unless required by clear and compelling governmental interests of the highest order[.]") (emphasis added) (internal quotations omitted) (citing Wisconsin v. Yoder, 406 U.S. 205, 215 (1972)), *superseded by statute as stated in* Ramirez v. Collier, 142 S. Ct. 1264 (2022).

Notes to pages 19–20   —☞ 199

39. U.S. CONST. amend. I.

40. BHAGWAT, *supra* note 2, at 3–6 (explaining the central importance of the Free Speech Clause in contemporary First Amendment jurisprudence and discussing the Supreme Court's exclusive reliance on the Free Speech Clause in constitutional litigation today).

41. *See id.* at 4 (describing the Assembly Clause as "irrelevant" and noting that "it has not been relied upon by the Supreme Court since 1983!"); JOHN D. INAZU, LIBERTY'S REFUGE: THE FORGOTTEN FREEDOM OF ASSEMBLY 61–62 (2012) (describing the right to assemble as "largely forgotten" and observing that "[t]he Court, in fact, has not addressed a freedom of assembly claim in thirty years"); *see also* Perry Educ. Ass'n v. Perry Local Educators' Ass'n, 460 U.S. 37, 45, 55 (1983) (featuring a few passing references to the Assembly Clause in a decision that rests primarily on the Free Speech Clause). Professor Inazu correctly posits that "[w]ith *Perry*, even cases involving protests or demonstrations could now be resolved without reference to assembly." INAZU, *supra*, at 62. In point of fact, that is precisely how things have come to rest. The First Amendment protects collective public protests not as instantiations of the right "to assemble" but rather as just another form or species of "speech." The federal courts' studied neglect of the Assembly Clause largely corresponds to a concomitant lack of sufficient legal protection for collective speech activity (aka "assembly") in public. *See* Tabatha Abu El-Haj, *The Neglected Right of Assembly*, 56 UCLA L. REV. 543, 564–65 (2009) (discussing and strongly criticizing the Supreme Court's failure to enforce and protect the right to assemble as a freestanding and independent expressive freedom).

42. RonNell Andersen Jones & Sonja R. West, *The U.S. Supreme Court's Characterizations of the Press: An Empirical Study*, 100 N.C. L. REV. 375, 391–92 (2021) (documenting, explaining, and critiquing the steep decline in references to the First Amendment's Press Clause in the Supreme Court's published decisions from 1820 to 2015); RonNell Andersen Jones & Sonja R. West, *The Fragility of the Free American Press*, 112 NW. U. L. REV. 567, 579 (2017) (criticizing the Supreme Court's abject failure to make any serious jurisprudential efforts to enforce the Press Clause and observing that "[t]he United States Supreme Court has also grown less interested in press protections" over time).

43. INAZU, *supra* note 41, at 7–10, 149–53, 185–86.

44. RONALD J. KROTOSZYNSKI, JR., RECLAIMING THE PETITION CLAUSE: SEDITIOUS LIBEL, "OFFENSIVE" PROTEST, AND THE RIGHT TO PETITION THE GOVERNMENT FOR A REDRESS OF GRIEVANCES 156 (2012).

45. *Id.* at 153.

46. BHAGWAT, *supra* note 2, at 79.

47. *Id.*

48. The Guarantee Clause and the Third Amendment both provide useful examples of constitutional provisions that have fallen largely, if not completely, into a state of desuetude. *See* Baker v. Carr, 369 U.S. 186, 293–98 (1962) (Frankfurter, J. dissenting) (discussing the nonenforcement of the Guaranty Clause); Griswold v. Connecticut, 381 U.S. 479, 484 (1965) (providing a rare, and passing, reference to the Third Amendment as advancing a privacy interest in the home).

49. BHAGWAT, *supra* note 2, at 4.

50. NEIL M. GORSUCH, A REPUBLIC, IF YOU CAN KEEP IT 25–28, 110–25 (2019) (advocating strict adherence to textualism and originalism and arguing that "living constitutionalism" serves as a convenient device for judges implementing their personal moral and policy preferences on the American people).

51. KROTOSZYNSKI, *supra* note 44, at 158.

200 ⌒ Notes to pages 20–21

52. U.S. CONST. amend. I.

53. *Id.*

54. *See* U.S. CONST. art. I, § 10.

55. Barron v. Baltimore, 32 U.S. (7 Pet.) 243, 247–51 (1833), *superseded by constitutional amendment*, U.S. CONST. amend XIV, *as recognized in* Dobbs v. Jackson Whole Women's Health Org., 141 S. Ct. 2228 (2022).

56. *Barron*, 32 U.S. at 247.

57. *See generally* BARENDT, *supra* note 14, at 48–49 (discussing the limited relevance of the First Amendment's text to its contemporary legal meaning and significance).

58. *See* STRAUSS, *supra* note 14, at 9–12, 51–56, 104–11 (opposing crude forms of textualist originalism and positing that judges, lawyers, and legal academics alike should forthrightly acknowledge the common law nature of almost all important constitutional law adjudication). Professor Strauss argues that "[o]ur living constitution includes precedents and traditions that have developed over time" and that "[i]t is impossible to understand American constitutional law without recognizing as much." *Id.* at 99.

59. *See* BHAGWAT, *supra* note 2, at 6–9 (arguing that each provision of the First Amendment has important work to do, at least potentially, in advancing the project of democratic self-government). Professor Bhagwat is surely correct when he argues that "[i]t is now time to return to those 'other' provisions" in order to facilitate the process of democratic deliberation essential to a successful project of democratic self-government. *Id.* at 9.

60. Akhil Reed Amar, *Intratextualism*, 112 HARV. L. REV. 747, 788–802 (1999) (arguing that persuasive constitutional interpretation requires reading particular clauses dynamically, purposively, and with careful consideration of the context that other words, phrases, and clauses located within the document provide). Amar explains that "[p]erhaps the greatest virtue of intratextualism is [that] it takes seriously the document as a whole rather than as a jumbled grab bag of assorted clauses." *Id.* at 795.

61. *See* Terminiello v. Chicago, 337 U.S. 1, 4–6 (1949) (invalidating, on First Amendment grounds, a state court breach of peace conviction because to allow the conviction to stand would be to empower a so-called heckler's veto because the arrest and conviction stemmed from the audience's hostile reaction to the speech); Hague v. Comm. for Indus. Org., 307 U.S. 496, 512–19 (1939) (invalidating, on First Amendment grounds, a New Jersey city ordinance that prohibited labor organizations from meeting whether on public or private property); Near v. Minnesota *ex rel.* Olson, 283 U.S. 697, 721–723 (1931) (invalidating, on First Amendment grounds, a Minnesota statute that imposed liability for the publication of "lewd" or "scandalous" material).

62. 376 U.S. 254, 269, 270, 282–83, 292 (1964) (restricting the scope of Alabama defamation law to facilitate public criticism of public officials even if such criticism happens to contain unintentional factual errors).

63. 395 U.S. 444, 447–49 (1969) (per curiam) (holding that Ohio could not punish calls to unlawful action "except where such advocacy is directed to inciting or producing imminent lawless action and is likely to incite or produce such action" and explaining that "[a] statute which fails to draw this distinction impermissibly intrudes upon the freedoms guaranteed by the First and Fourteenth Amendments").

64. *See* Cent. Hudson Gas & Elec. Co. v. Pub. Serv. Comm'n, 447 U.S. 557, 566, 571–72 (1980) (holding that the First Amendment's Free Speech Clause protects commercial advertising and applying a form of intermediate scrutiny to government regulations of commercial speech); *see also* Alex Kozinski & Stuart Banner, *Who's Afraid of Commercial Speech?*, 76 VA. L. REV. 627,

Notes to page 21   —☙ 201

628 (1990) (advocating for the extension of First Amendment protection to commercial speech and arguing that constitutional protection of commercial speech should be no less rigorous and robust than the protection afforded to core political speech because the First Amendment exists to protect and facilitate both speaker and audience autonomy). Arguably, Professor Marty Redish should receive credit—or blame—for firing the opening shot in the effort to convince the federal courts to extend robust First Amendment protection to commercial advertising. *See* Martin H. Redish, *The First Amendment in the Marketplace: Commercial Speech and the Values of Free Expression*, 39 GEO. WASH. L. REV. 429 (1971). Redish's article set forth a holistic argument favoring the autonomy of readers, listeners, and viewers—rather than the government—to determine the value of particular kinds of expression. *See id.* at 433–34, 438–40 (arguing that because "advertising performs a significant function for its recipients, its values are better viewed with the consumer, rather than the seller, as the frame of reference" and proposing that a persuasive theory of the freedom of speech must empower individual citizens to pursue "rational self-fulfillment" that necessarily must encompass the right to "participate actively in decisions that significantly affect him") (quoting PETER BACHRACH, THE THEORY OF DEMOCRATIC ELITISM, A CRITIQUE 98 (1967)) (internal quotation marks omitted). Redish's audience-autonomy-based theory of the freedom of speech ultimately carried the day and, accordingly, contemporary First Amendment doctrine affords broad and deep protection to commercial speech.

65. *See* United States v. Playboy Ent. Grp., Inc., 529 U.S. 803, 827 (2000) (invalidating, on First Amendment grounds, a federal statute that imposed special, burdensome rules on sexually explicit cable programming because the regulation was content-based and did not meet the requirements of strict scrutiny review, meaning that it did not advance a compelling government interest in a sufficiently narrowly tailored way); *see also* Amy Adler, *The Perverse Law of Child Pornography*, 101 COLUM. L. REV. 209, 271–73 (2001) (arguing that First Amendment protection of sexually explicit speech should encompass not only materials featuring adult actors but also some materials featuring minors); Andrew Koppelman, *Is Pornography "Speech"?*, 14 LEGAL THEORY 71, 72, 74, 77, 88–89 (2008) (arguing that viewer or reader autonomy adequately justifies First Amendment protection of sexually explicit forms of communication in the absence of more convincing proofs that pornography causes material social harms).

66. *See In re* Winship, 397 U.S. 358, 377–78 (1970) (Black, J., dissenting) (noting that "nowhere in [the Constitution] is there any statement that conviction of crime requires proof of guilt beyond a reasonable doubt," positing that the "document itself should be our guide," and arguing that "the words of the written Constitution itself" should be preferred to "the shifting, day-to-day standards of fairness of individual judges"); Griswold v. Connecticut, 381 U.S. 479, 510 (1965) (Black, J., dissenting) ("I like my privacy as well as the next one, but I am nevertheless compelled to admit that government has a right to invade it unless prohibited by some specific constitutional provision."); *id.* at 527 (opining that because "Connecticut's law as applied here is not forbidden by any provision of the Federal Constitution as that Constitution was written" the federal courts have no power to invalidate it).

67. Hugo L. Black, *The Bill of Rights*, 35 N.Y.U. L. REV. 865, 867 (1960) ("It is my belief that there *are* 'absolutes' in our Bill of Rights, and that they were put there on purpose by men who knew what words meant, and meant their prohibitions to be 'absolutes.'") [hereinafter *The Bill of Rights*]; *see* HUGO L. BLACK, A CONSTITUTIONAL FAITH 19–20, 23–24, 35–36 (1968) (arguing that federal judges must strictly enforce the "absolute" commands set forth in the Bill of Rights and Fourteenth Amendment and positing that judges cannot legitimately either

202 ⌒ Notes to pages 21–22

add or subtract from the rights expressly set forth in the Constitution itself) [hereinafter A CONSTITUTIONAL FAITH].

68. 562 U.S. 134, 159–61, 165 (2011) (Scalia J., concurring) ("Thirty-three years have passed since the Court first suggested that the right [to informational privacy] may or may not, exist. It is past time for the Court to abandon this Alfred Hitchcock line of our jurisprudence.").

69. *Id.* at 138–42.

70. *See* Whalen v. Roe, 429 U.S. 589, 598–600, 605 (1977) (rejecting a privacy-based constitutional challenge to a New York state law that imposed special record-keeping requirements for certain highly addictive prescription medicines because the challenged law included constitutionally adequate procedural and substantive safeguards on the collection, storage, and use of the sensitive personal medical data, cautioning that the Due Process Clauses of the Fifth and Fourteenth Amendments protect a right to informational privacy, and warning that the government must not collect or disclose sensitive personal information without a legitimate reason and adequate safeguards against unwarranted disclosures).

71. *Nelson*, 562 U.S. at 138; *see id.* at 147 ("As was our approach in *Whalen*, we will assume for present purposes that the Government's challenged inquiries implicate a privacy interest of constitutional significance.").

72. *Id.* at 159.

73. Griswold v. Connecticut, 381 U.S. 479, 484 (1965) (recognizing a "right of privacy" and explaining that this unenumerated, yet nevertheless fundamental, right springs from "specific guarantees in the Bill of Rights [that] have penumbras, formed by emanations from those guarantees that help give them life and substance" and these "[v]arious guarantees create zones of privacy").

74. *Whalen*, 429 U.S. at 599, 605–06; *see* NASA v. Nelson, 562 U.S. 134, 138 (2011) ("We assume, without deciding, that the Constitution protects a privacy right of the sort mentioned in *Whalen* and *Nixon*."). For a general overview of how the lower federal courts have operationalized the important dicta in *Whalen*, *see* Mary D. Fan, *Constitutionalizing Informational Privacy by Assumption*, 14 U. PA. J. CONST. L. 953, 954, 956 (2012), and Scott Skinner-Thompson, *Outing Privacy*, 110 NW. U. L. REV. 159, 161 (2015). Professor Skinner-Thompson reports that most lower federal and state courts have recognized a constitutional right to informational privacy post-*Whalen*: *See* Skinner-Thompson, *supra*, at 184. Professor Fan concurs in this assessment. *See* Fan, *supra*, at 956–57; *see also* Larry J. Pittman, *The Elusive Constitutional Right to Informational Privacy*, 19 NEV. L.J. 135, 156–57, 160 (2018) (arguing that *Whalen* effectively established a constitutional right to informational privacy and reporting that, even post-*Nelson*, "substantially all of the federal circuit courts of appeals presently cite *Whalen* as definitively establishing a constitutional right to informational privacy").

75. CALABRESI, *supra* note 10, at 11.

76. *Nelson*, 562 U.S. at 160 (Scalia, J., concurring).

77. *Id.* at 159–60.

78. *See, e.g.*, Planned Parenthood of Se. Pa. v. Casey, 505 U.S. 833, 980 (1992) (Scalia, J., concurring in part and dissenting in part) (opining that "[t]he issue is whether [abortion] is a liberty protected by the Constitution of the United States" and observing that "I am sure it is not" because "the Constitution says absolutely nothing about it"). Other members of the Supreme Court, notably including Justices Samuel Alito and Clarence Thomas, had adopted a similar approach that privileges text over common law constitutional precedents. *See, e.g.*, Dobbs v. Jackson Women's Health Org., 142 S. Ct. 2228, 2243–45 (2022) (opining that "[t]he Constitution makes no express reference to a right to obtain an abortion, and therefore those

Notes to pages 22–23   ⟶ 203

who claim that it protects such a right must show that the right is somehow implicit in the constitutional text" and concluding that because abortion is neither expressly mentioned in the text nor supported by longstanding historical and legal tradition, *Roe* and *Casey* should be overruled); *id.* at 2304 (Thomas, J., concurring) (opining that "we should follow the text of the Constitution, which sets forth certain substantive rights that cannot be taken away, and adds, beyond that, a right to due process when life, liberty, or property is to be taken away" and arguing that because "[s]ubstantive due process conflicts with that textual command and has harmed our country in many ways" the doctrine "should [be] eliminate[d] from our jurisprudence at the earliest opportunity) (internal quotations and citations omitted).

79. Coy v. Iowa, 487 U.S. 1012, 1016–20 (1988); *see also* Maryland v. Craig, 497 U.S. 836, 860–61 (1990) (Scalia, J., dissenting) (objecting that "[s]eldom has this Court failed so conspicuously to sustain a categorical guarantee of the Constitution against the tide of prevailing current opinion," arguing that "[t]he Sixth Amendment provides, with unmistakable clarity, that '[i]n all criminal prosecutions, the accused shall enjoy the right . . . to be confronted with the witnesses against him,'" and categorically rejecting the "subordination of explicit constitutional text to currently favored public policy").

80. 562 U.S. 443 (2011).

81. *Id.* at 447–50.

82. Patterson v. Colorado, 205 U.S. 454 (1907).

83. *Id.* at 462.

84. *Id.* (observing that "the main purpose of such constitutional provisions is 'to prevent all such *previous restraints* upon publications as had been practiced by other governments,' and they do not prevent the subsequent punishment of such as may be deemed contrary to the public welfare" and, accordingly, "subsequent punishment may extend as well to the true as to the false").

85. *See* David M. Rabban, Free Speech in Its Forgotten Years, 1870-1920, at 130–34, 148–49, 164–65 (1997) (discussing *Patterson* and its legal reasoning in some detail and offering a generally critical analysis of Justice Holmes's majority opinion). Professor Rabban explains that "Holmes believed that Blackstone's reasoning, developed in the context of the common law of criminal libel, was particularly applicable to contempts of court." *Id.* at 134.

86. *See* Barendt, *supra* note 14, at 49 (observing that "[t]he First Amendment literally only applies to the laws of Congress"). It is odd that Justice Holmes did not consider the amendment's facially limited scope in rejecting a claim challenging a judicial contempt proceeding.

87. *But cf.* Rabban, *supra* note 85, at 132 ("A significant number of state court decisions, in contrast to Justice Holmes's opinion for the Supreme Court in *Patterson*, vigorously rejected Blackstone and the English common law as guides to American constitutional provisions on speech.").

88. The first Justice Harlan is perhaps most well-known for his dissenting opinion in *Plessy*, in which he opined that "[o]ur Constitution is color-blind, and neither knows nor tolerates classes among citizens" and "[i]n respect of civil rights, all citizens are equal before the law." Plessy v. Ferguson, 163 U.S. 537, 559 (1896) (Harlan, J., dissenting).

89. *Patterson*, 205 U.S. at 464–65 (Harlan, J., dissenting).

90. *See* Chicago B. & Q. R.R. Co. v. Chicago, 166 U.S. 226, 235–37, 241 (1897) (finding that due process imposes a rule against uncompensated takings by state governments). Justice Harlan's majority opinion expressly grounds the recognition of a substantive due process right against uncompensated takings on foundational common law principles. *See id.* at 236 ("The requirement that the property shall not be taken for public use without just compensation is

204 ‿ Notes to pages 23–24

but "an affirmance of a great doctrine established by the common law for the protection of private property. It is founded in natural equity, and is laid down by jurists as a principle of universal law."). Of course, Harlan's view regarding the application of rights set forth in the Bill of Rights to the states did not carry the day. Instead, the doctrine of selective, but complete, incorporation ultimately prevailed. Under the doctrine of selective-but-complete incorporation, specific provisions of the Bill of Rights are either "in" or "out" as against the states and, if incorporated, will then apply identically against the state governments as they apply against the federal government. *See* Duncan v. Louisiana, 391 U.S. 145, 147–50, 149 n.14 (1968). It bears noting that the second Justice Harlan, John Marshall Harlan II, vigorously objected to this approach and was a steadfast proponent of the theory of independent, due process-based fundamental rights arising wholly separately from any specific provision of the Bill of Rights. *See* Williams v. Florida, 399 U.S. 78, 117–19, 130–33 (1970) (Harlan, J., dissenting). He consistently opposed both "total incorporation" and "selective incorporation" of particular provisions of the Bill of Rights in favor of recognizing free standing, and wholly independent, fundamental, unenumerated rights. *See id.* at 131 n.14 (listing Harlan's numerous opinions making this argument). The due process approach to protecting fundamental rights against the states, quite ably advocated by both the first and second Justice Harlan, is self-evidently an exercise in common law reasoning and adjudication; it draws directly on the traditions and customs of the people to ascertain the existence and scope of a fundamental right. *See* Poe v. Ullman, 367 U.S. 497, 541–42 (1961) (Harlan, J., dissenting).

91. *See, e.g.,* O'Neil v. Vermont, 144 U.S. 323, 370–71 (1892) (Harlan, J., dissenting) (recognizing a substantive due process right to be free of cruel and unusual punishments inflicted by the state governments). The first Justice Harlan grounded all fundamental rights running against the states in the Due Process Clause of the Fourteenth Amendment and argued that most rights set forth in the Bill of Rights, as well as unenumerated yet fundamental rights, applied against the state governments as either "privileges and immunities" or aspects of "due process of law." *See* Maxwell v. Dow, 176 U.S. 581, 613–14 (1900) (Harlan, J., dissenting); Hurtado v. California, 110 U.S. 516, 540–43, 547–50 (1884); *see also* Maxwell, 176 U.S. at 614 ("The Fourteenth Amendment does not in terms refer to the taking of private property for public use, yet we have held that the requirement of 'due process of law' *in that Amendment* forbids the taking of private property for public use without making or securing just compensation.").

92. *Hurtado,* 110 U.S. at 547–48 (Harlan, J., dissenting).

93. *Id.* at 542–58.

94. Stromberg v. California, 283 U.S. 359, 368–69 (1931); Near v. Minnesota, 283 U.S. 697, 723 (1931); *see* RABBAN, *supra* note 85, at 373–75 (discussing the incorporation of the First Amendment against the state governments under the Due Process Clause of the Fourteenth Amendment).

95. *See, e.g.,* Mills v. Alabama, 384 U.S. 214 (1966); Murdock v. Pennsylvania, 319 U.S. 105 (1943); Grosjean v. Am. Press Co., 297 U.S. 233 (1936).

96. *See, e.g.,* Edwards v. South Carolina, 372 U.S. 229 (1963); Thomas v. Collins, 323 U.S. 516 (1945).

97. *See, e.g.,* California Motor Transp. Co. v. Trucking Unlimited, 404 U.S. 508 (1972); Mine Workers v. Pennington, 381 U.S. 657 (1965); NAACP v. Button, 371 U.S. 415 (1963); Eastern R.R. Presidents Conf. v. Noerr Motor Freight, Inc., 365 U.S. 127 (1961). For a helpful discussion and overview of the *Noerr-Pennington* doctrine, which exempts petitioning of legislative or executive branch officials, even via mass media or billboard public campaigns, from serving as a basis for imposing antitrust liability on the speaker, as an incident of the First Amendment's

Notes to pages 24–25

Petition Clause, see Joseph B. Maher, Comment, *Survival of the Common Law Abuse of Process Tort in the Face of a* Noerr-Pennington *Defense*, 65 U. CHI. L. REV. 627, 630–33 (1998).

98. *See* BHAGWAT, *supra* note 2, at 3–6; INAZU, *supra* note 41, at 61–62.

99. Perry Educ. Ass'n. v. Perry Local Educators' Ass'n, 460 U.S. 37, 45–47 (1983) (framing the expressive freedom claim at bar *solely* in terms of the Free Speech Clause and ignoring both the Assembly and Petition Clauses as a potential basis for decision); *see* INAZU, *supra* note 41, at 61 ("In 1983, the Court swept the remnants of assembly within the ambit of free speech law in *Perry Education Association v. Perry Local Educators' Association*.").

100. INAZU, *supra* note 41, at 62.

101. *See supra* text and accompanying notes 74 to 101.

102. Hurtado v. California, 110 U.S. 516, 547–50 (1884) (Harlan, J., dissenting) (positing that the express inclusion of a particular right in the Bill of Rights *does not* mean and *should not* mean that it is not constitutive of "due process" or the antecedent and synonymous clause in Magna Carta, the "law of the land").

103. For example, the British North America Act, 1867 (BNA), Canada's constitution, used exclusively male pronouns ("he") to describe both the qualifications for serving in the Senate and also the conditions that would justify removal of a sitting senator from office. BNA §§ 23 & 31. The question arose if the plain text of these provisions precluded women from serving in the federal Senate. Adopting a "living tree" approach, the Privy Council, Canada's highest appellate court at the time, departed from the BNA's plain text, original understanding, and consistent practice from 1867 to 1930, and held that the use of male pronouns *did not* preclude women from serving as senators. *See* Edwards v. Att'y Gen. of Canada, [1930] A.C. 124, 136 (PC) (appeal taken from S.C.C.) (Lord Sankey) ("The British North America Act planted in Canada a living tree capable of growth and expansion within its natural limits. The object of the Act was to grant a Constitution to Canada."). In so doing, it overruled the contrary holding of the Supreme Court of Canada. It was highly likely, given the absence of female suffrage in both the United Kingdom and Canada in 1867, that the use of male pronouns in the BNA was not accidental but rather intentional. Even so, the Privy Council was quite right to "update" the BNA by reading the language inclusively rather than literally—and without regard to the original intent of the drafters of the BNA. *See id.* ("Their Lordships do not conceive it to be the duty of this Board—it is certainly not their desire—to cut down the provisions of the Act by a narrow and technical construction, but rather to give it a large and liberal interpretation so that the Dominion to a great extent, but within certain fixed limits, may be mistress in her own house, as the Provinces to a great extent, but within certain fixed limits, are mistresses in theirs."); *see also* CALABRESI, *supra* note 10, at 2–3, 163–71, 178–81 (arguing that courts should exercise an "updating" power over statutes "as if they were no more and no less than part of the common law").

104. Edwards v. Att'y Gen. of Canada, [1930] A.C. 124, 136 (P.C.) (Can.).

105. *See supra* text and accompanying notes 46 to 62.

106. *See supra* text and accompanying notes 74 to 101.

107. THE FEDERALIST NO. 48, at 308, 313 (James Madison) (Clinton Rossiter ed., 1961).

108. *Id.* at 313.

109. *See id.* at 308–13. (discussing how demarcating each branch of government's powers in writing is not enough to thwart abuse of their power and encroachment onto the powers of the other branches).

110. THE FEDERALIST NO. 84, *supra* note 107, at 513 (Alexander Hamilton).

111. *Id.*

206 ⌒   Notes to pages 25–26

112. *Id.*

113. *See* GERARD MAGLIOCCA, THE HEART OF THE CONSTITUTION: HOW THE BILL OF RIGHTS BECAME THE BILL OF RIGHTS 32–34 (2018) (discussing the political necessity of promising to adopt written rights guarantees in order to secure ratification of the draft Constitution); *see also* ALFRED H. KELLY, WINFRED A. HARBISON, & HERMAN BELZ, THE AMERICAN CONSTITUTION: ITS ORIGINS AND DEVELOPMENT 121–22 (6th ed. 1983) noting that proponents of the Constitution secured ratification in several states "by promising a series of constitutional amendments embodying a bill of rights").

114. *See infra* text and accompanying notes 144 to 173.

115. *See, e.g.,* ADAM CHILTON & MILA VERSTEEG, HOW CONSTITUTIONAL RIGHTS MATTER (2020) (using empirical methods to deduce how constitutional rights in different countries define and delimit the rights of individuals practically); *see also* Mila Versteeg, Cosette Cramer, & Kevin Cope, *Empirical Studies of Human Rights Law*, 15 ANN. REV. L. & SOC. SCI. 155 (2019) (discussing an empirical study on the effects of codified human rights and constitutional rights).

116. *See* Mitchell N. Berman, *Originalism is Bunk*, 84 N.Y.U. L. REV. 1, 8 (2009) (arguing that originalism "is not merely false but pernicious as well" and exists primarily as a means of "bolster[ing] the popular fable that constitutional adjudication can be practiced in something close to an objective and mechanical fashion" and warning that "originalism threatens to undermine the judiciary's unique and essential role in our system of government"); Mark Seidenfeld, *Textualism's Theoretical Bankruptcy and Its Implication for Statutory Interpretation*, 100 B.U. L. REV. 1817, 1819 (2020) (arguing that "while some might reasonably argue that textualism embodies attractive attributes for the practice of statutory interpretation, its theoretical footing is essentially bankrupt"). Although Seidenfeld's immediate focus is textualism in statutory interpretation, his theoretical critique is equally applicable to textualism in constitutional interpretation as well with respect to its potential efficacy in constraining and controlling judicial discretion. *See id.* at 1840–48.

117. *See* JOHN O. MCGINNIS & MICHAEL B. RAPPAPORT, ORIGINALISM AND THE GOOD CONSTITUTION 1 (2013) (observing that originalism "has been an important principle of constitutional interpretation since the early Republic," which still presently enjoys "prominent adherents on the Supreme Court," and emphasizing that "[l]egal academics across the political spectrum espouse some form of originalism"); *see also* BREYER, *supra* note 21, at 115–32 (offering a thoughtful discussion and critique of originalism as an interpretative approach to the constitutional text).

118. *See* AKHIL REED AMAR, THE BILL OF RIGHTS: CREATION AND RECONSTRUCTION (1998) (providing a comprehensive, arguably epic, overall interpretation of the Bill of Rights); Akhil Reed Amar, *The Bill of Rights as a Constitution*, 100 YALE L.J. 1131 (1991) (providing a textual and structural overview of the Bill of Rights).

119. Amar, *supra* note 60, at 788–91.

120. *Id.* at 796 (arguing that "[e]mphasis on the Constitution's writtenness—its general textuality and its specific textual provisions—has certain democratic values" that notably include "constitut[ing] a democratic focal point" that serves to "structure the conversation of ordinary Americans as they ponder the most fundamental and sometimes divisive issues in our republic of equal citizens"); *see* SANFORD LEVINSON, CONSTITUTIONAL FAITH 9–15 (1988) (positing that a kind of generalized reverence for the Constitution, without much attention to its specifics, is a deeply embedded feature of U.S. political culture and observing that "'[v]eneration' of the Constitution has become a central, even if sometimes challenged, aspect of the American political tradition" and serves as a kind of "'civil religion'").

Notes to pages 26–27 — 207

121. Amar, *supra* note 60, at 765 ("There are many arguments for judicial review, but perhaps the most elegant and forceful is the simple two-pronged notion that the Constitution is supreme law, and that judges must apply this law in cases within their jurisdiction."); *see id.* at 795–99 (arguing that intratextual constitutional interpretation renders judicial decision-making less objectionable and helps to reduce the counter majoritarian difficulty by grounding judicial decisions in a document that itself possesses democratic legitimacy even if Article III judges do not). Oddly enough, Amar himself follows the modern practice of both ignoring the First Amendment's facially limited scope of application (it purports to restrict only Congress, not the executive or judicial branches) and failing to apply his intratextual interpretative methodology to the First Amendment's clauses that secure expressive freedom. *See id.* at 812–18. At least arguably, an intratextualist approach to the First Amendment itself would take the specific examples set forth (speech, press, assembly, petition) to stand for a larger, and more general, guarantee of expressive freedom. However, Amar does not propose this interpretative approach. I agree with Amar that "[g]ood interpreters need to know how to read between the lines" but they also need to be able to extrapolate larger meanings from those lines as well. *Id.* at 827.

122. *See* Bruce Ackerman, *The New Separation of Powers*, 113 HARV. L. REV. 633, 667 (2000) (positing that "[p]art of the problem is cultural: Do lawyers and judges take the process of legal interpretation seriously?"); *see also* Bruce Ackerman & David Fontana, *Thomas Jefferson Counts Himself to the Presidency*, 90 VA. L. REV. 551, 630–31 (2004) (arguing that "even textualists should accord substantial weight to subsequent practice in resolving constitutional indeterminacies").

123. *See, e.g.*, Texas v. Johnson, 491 U.S. 397, 420–21 (1989) (Kennedy, J., concurring). Justice Anthony Kennedy offered an apologia for his vote to apply the First Amendment to disallow a viewpoint-based state law that prohibited the burning of a U.S. flag to express disagreement with government policies—but permitted the retirement of a flag from use by burning it:

> The hard fact is that sometimes we must make decisions we do not like. We make them because they are right, right in the sense that the law and the Constitution, as we see them, compel the result. And so great is our commitment to the process that, except in the rare case, we do not pause to express distaste for the result, perhaps for fear of undermining a valued principle that dictates the decision. This is one of those rare cases.

Id.

124. *See id.* at 421 ("I do not believe the Constitution gives us the right to rule as the dissenting Members of the Court urge, however painful this judgment is to announce . . . . It is poignant but fundamental that the flag protects those who hold it in contempt.").

125. *See* Lochner v. New York, 198 U.S. 45, 53–54, 58–60, 64 (1905) (invalidating, under the doctrine of substantive due process's protection of a right to "liberty of contract," a New York state law that limited the maximum hours per day and per week that a baker could lawfully work).

126. *See* BLACK, A CONSTITUTIONAL FAITH, *supra* note 67, at 3–11, 20–21, 23–31, 35–36 (1969) (advocating strict textualism and arguing that federal judges have no legitimate power to recognize and enforce enumerated fundamental rights); Black, *The Bill of Rights*, *supra* note 67, 866–67, 874–75 (arguing that the Bill of Rights imposes "absolute" restrictions on the government and that the purpose of the Bill of Rights "was to withdraw from the Government all power to act in certain areas—whatever the scope of those areas may be"). For an illuminating

208   *Notes to page 27*

discussion of the relationship between Justice Black's textualism and Justice Antonin Scalia's textualist originalism, along with a persuasive critique of both, see Michael J. Gerhardt, *A Tale of Two Textualists: A Critical Comparison of Justices Black and Scalia*, 74 B.U. L. REV. 25 (1994).

127. ALEXANDER M. BICKEL, THE LEAST DANGEROUS BRANCH: THE SUPREME COURT AT THE BAR OF POLITICS 16 (1962).

128. Kisor v. Wilkie, 139 S. Ct. 2400, 2448 (2019) (Gorsuch, J., concurring) ("If today's opinion ends up reducing *Auer* to the role of a tin god—officious, but ultimately powerless—then a future Court should candidly admit as much and stop requiring litigants and lower courts to pay token homage to it.").

129. *See* STRAUSS, *supra* note 14, at 52–53 (observing that "[t]he First Amendment was part of the Constitution for a century and a half before the central principles of the American regime of free speech, as we now know it, became established in the law" and positing that "[w]e owe [these] principles . . . to the living, common law Constitution").

130. *See, e.g.*, Texas v. Johnson, 491 U.S. 397, 420–21 (1989) (Kennedy, J., concurring); *see also supra* text and accompanying note 123.

131. Indeed, Justice Elena Kagan argues that "we're all textualists now." Harvard Law School, *The 2015 Scalia Lecture: A Dialogue with Justice Kagan on the Reading of Statutes*, YOUTUBE, at 8:29 (Nov. 25, 2015), https://www.youtube.com/watch?v=dpEtszFT0Tg [https://perma.cc/ EE2B-2MPD]. If this is truly so, then the vexing problem of judicial discretion constitutes a "buy" stock.

132. For a cogent critique of the Supreme Court's failure to develop an independent jurisprudence of the right to assemble, and for some persuasive suggestions on what a reanimated Assembly Clause jurisprudence might look like, see INAZU, *supra* note 41. For a sustained and thoughtful argument that the Supreme Court should give independent force and effect to the Press Clause, see Sonja West, *Press Exceptionalism*, 127 HARV. L. REV. 2434 (2014); Sonja West, *Awakening the Press Clause*, 58 UCLA L. REV. 1025 (2011). For the most part, the Rehnquist and Roberts Courts have rolled constitutional protection of all expressive freedoms into the Free Speech Clause—which is a very odd thing for ostensibly textualist-originalist judges to do.

133. *See, e.g.*, Janus v. Am. Fed'n of State, Cnty. & Mun. Emps., Council 31, 138 S. Ct. 2448, 2469–71 (2018) (rejecting out of hand an originalist argument for sustaining mandatory union collective bargaining fees in favor of enforcing "decades of landmark precedent," dating to 1968 rather than 1791, instead).

134. *See* Frederick Schauer, *Commercial Speech and the Architecture of the First Amendment*, 56 U. CIN. L. REV. 1181, 1182 (1988) (arguing that commercial speech, although "previously taken to be outside the coverage of the first amendment," has nonetheless been admitted into its coverage); *see also* Frederick Schauer, *The Politics and Incentives of First Amendment Coverage*, 56 WM. & MARY L. REV. 1613 (2015) [hereinafter Schauer, *First Amendment Coverage*] (arguing that the Supreme Court has defined the First Amendment's scope of coverage far too broadly to encompass a wide variety of commercial and noncommercial activities having little to do with core First Amendment values). Schauer posits that "[w]hat is most interesting about these various claims and arguments [for very broad application of the First Amendment to various forms of often commercial conduct] is not merely that some of them have been taken seriously," but rather that "they have been advanced at all . . . ." *Id.* at 1616. He explains that "a generation ago . . . the suggestion that the First Amendment was even applicable to some of these activities would far more likely have produced judicial laughter or incredulity, if not Rule 11 sanctions." *Id.* at 1616.

Notes to pages 28–29   —◌ 209

135. STEVEN F. SHIFFRIN, DISSENT, INJUSTICE, AND THE MEANINGS OF AMERICA 110–18, 124–30 (1999) (arguing that "protecting and supporting" dissenters and facilitating the public expression of dissenting viewpoints should be "at the center of the First Amendment tradition" and generally rejecting the marketplace of ideas metaphor because it overprotects speech that has at best a marginal relationship to the public expression of dissenting voices); *see* Robert C. Post, *The Constitutional Concept of Public Discourse: Outrageous Opinion, Democratic Deliberation, and* Hustler Magazine v. Falwell, 103 HARV. L. REV. 601, 624–32, 668–70 (1990) (arguing that just as government may not directly censor speech without undermining the process of democratic deliberation essential to a meaningful project of democratic self-government, the government must not be permitted to do so indirectly through the imposition of civil liability for offensive speech and emphasizing that "every issue that can potentially agitate the public is also potentially relevant to democratic self-governance").

136. OLIVER WENDELL HOLMES, JR., THE COMMON LAW 1 (1881); *see* Lum v. Fullaway, 42 Haw. 500, 502–03 (1958) (observing that "the genius of the common law, upon which our jurisprudence is based, is its capacity for orderly growth" through the "vehicle" of "judge-made law.").

137. Professor Michael Klarman, a well-regarded legal historian, persuasively argues that most major constitutional decisions involving equal protection and racial justice were, and presumably still are, squarely within the metes and bounds of contemporary public opinion. *See* MICHAEL J. KLARMAN, FROM JIM CROW TO CIVIL RIGHTS: THE SUPREME COURT AND THE STRUGGLE FOR RACIAL EQUALITY (2004). My claim is that judges will work to keep their decisions within acceptable bounds more generally, even when doing so requires creative judicial interpretation of constitutional text or even outright departure from the text as written. *See generally* CALABRESI, *supra* note 10, at 199 n.18 (positing that judges should update a statute that "is out of phase" and explaining that this circumstance "neither entails nor requires that the statute be old, in terms of the number of years since its enactment" but instead means that the law "no longer fits in with the legal landscape, and it can become out of phase upon the advent of social, technological, or political changes.").

138. 17 U.S. (4 Wheat.) 316 (1819).

139. *Id.* at 407.

140. *Id.*

141. *Id.*

142. *Id.*

143. *Id.*

144. *See* Marbury v. Madison, 5 U.S. (1 Cranch) 137, 177–78 (1803) (holding that "[i]t is emphatically the province and duty of the judicial department to say what the law is" and this means that "if a law be in opposition to the constitution" then "the court must determine which of these conflicting rules governs the case."). Marshall characterizes the power of judicial review to enforce constitutional constraints as "the very essence of judicial duty." *Id.* at 178.

145. *See generally* CALABRESI, *supra* note 10, at 3–5, 19–21, 161–73 (arguing that courts must play an "updating" function to ensure that legal rules keep pace with the evolving sense of justice and fair play within the political community).

146. Edwards v. Att'y Gen. of Canada, [1930] A.C. 124, 136 (PC) (appeal taken from Canada); *see* BERNARD SCHWARTZ, THE SUPREME COURT: CONSTITUTIONAL REVOLUTION IN RETROSPECT 19 (1957) ("The Constitution must be capable of adaptation to needs that were wholly unforeseen by the Founding Fathers; else, it is less a document intended to endure through the ages than a governmental suicide-pact.").

210 ᧈ— Notes to pages 29–30

147. 401 U.S. 37 (1971).

148. *Id.* at 43–45.

149. *Id.* at 44.

150. BLACK, A CONSTITUTIONAL FAITH, *supra* note 67, at 20 ("When I get to the other meaning of 'judicial activist,' however, namely, one who believes he should interpret the Constitution and statutes according to his own belief of what they ought to prescribe instead of what they do, I tell you at once I am not in that group. The courts are given power to interpret the Constitution and laws, which means to explain and expound, not to alter, amend, or remake."). In light of Justice Black's opinion in *Younger*, which lacks *any* textual basis for its paean to "Our Federalism," the most charitable conclusion one can draw is that Justice Black's admonition against judicial activism must be of the "do as I say, not as I do" stripe despite his firm conviction that "[j]udges take an oath to support the Constitution as it is, not as they think it should be." *Id.* at 20–21.

151. 517 U.S. 44 (1996).

152. *Id.* at 47, 63–65; *see* U.S. CONST. art. I, § 8, cl. 3 (providing that Congress has the power "[t]o regulate Commerce with foreign Nations, and among the several States, and *with the Indian Tribes*") (emphasis added).

153. *Seminole Tribe*, 517 U.S. at 64 (citing and quoting Pennhurst State Sch. & Hosp. v. Halderman, 465 U. S. 89, 97–98 (1984)).

154. Pennsylvania v. Union Gas Co., 491 U.S. 1, 38 (1989) (Scalia, J., dissenting) (opining that "'the entire judicial power granted by the Constitution does not embrace authority to entertain a suit brought by private parties against a State without consent given'") (citing *Ex Parte New York*, 256 U.S. 490, 497 (1921)).

155. *Seminole Tribe*, 517 U.S. at 65–73.

156. 134 U.S. 1, 13–15 (1890).

157. U.S. CONST. amend. XI ("The Judicial power of the United States shall not be construed to extend to any suit in law or equity, commenced or prosecuted against one of the United States by Citizens of another State, or by Citizens or Subjects of any Foreign State.").

158. Chisholm v. Georgia, 2 U.S. (2 Dall.) 419, 461 (1793) (Wilson, J.) (rejecting "the haughty notions of state independence, state sovereignty and state supremacy" because vindicating Georgia's claims would permit "the state [to] assum[e] a supercilious pre-eminence above the people who have formed it").

159. U.S. CONST. art. III, § 2, cl. 1 (providing that "[t]he judicial Power shall extend . . . to Controversies . . . between a State and Citizens of another State . . . and between a State, or the Citizens thereof, and foreign States, Citizens or Subjects").

160. The Supreme Court created the regulatory takings doctrine during the *Lochner* era; its first appearance occurs in *Pennsylvania Coal v. Mahon*, 260 U.S. 393 (1922). In an opinion by Justice Holmes, the Supreme Court voids a Pennsylvania law that conditions the exploitation of mineral rights on the consent of the owner of surface rights, where mining operations could cause damage to surface structures. *See id.* at 415–16. Holmes writes that:

> The general rule at least is, that while property may be regulated to a certain extent, if regulation goes too far it will be recognized as a taking. It may be doubted how far exceptional cases, like the blowing up of a house to stop a conflagration, go—and if they go beyond the general rule, whether they do not stand as much upon tradition as upon principle.

Id.

Notes to pages 30–32 —◌ 211

This rule was cut from whole constitutional cloth; from 1791 to 1922, a Takings Clause claim required government expropriation and possession of a property interest. Even so, Justice Scalia was a strong proponent of the regulatory takings doctrine. *See* Lucas v. S.C. Coastal Council, 505 U.S. 1003, 1027–31 (1992) (holding that a land use regulation that renders land valueless constitutes a "per se" regulatory taking).

161. *Bolling v. Sharpe*, 347 U.S. 497 (1954) provides another example of Justice Black's selective approach to textualism. The Supreme Court, with Black's vote, "reverse incorporated" the Equal Protection Clause against the federal government. *See id.* at 500. The Fourteenth Amendment contains both a Due Process Clause and an Equal Protection Clause; a serious textualist would be very hard pressed to explain this redundancy if the concept of due process necessarily implies a right to equal protection of the law.

162. *See* Jane Bambauer, *Is Data Speech?*, 66 STAN. L. REV. 57, 118 (2014) ("The First Amendment is, in many ways, an experiment that hinders the government from deciding what speech, and what thoughts, are good, even if most levelheaded people could agree on the matter. After all, a benevolent dictator is still a dictator.").

163. *See* Marsh v. Alabama, 326 U.S. 501, 506 (1946) (holding that the First Amendment applies to a company-owned town because the operation of a municipal corporation constitutes an exclusive government function); *see also* Amalgamated Food Emp. Union Loc. 590 v. Logan Valley Plaza, Inc., 391 U.S. 308, 325 (1968) (holding that private ownership of a local shopping center does not preclude the imposition of First Amendment duties on the property's owners because the mall was the modern-day functional equivalent of a traditional town square and therefore an essential locus for democratic deliberation). Although the Supreme Court ultimately overruled the holding of *Logan Valley Plaza*, *see* Hudgens v. NLRB, 424 U.S. 507, 518 (1976), it has held that Congress, state legislatures, or the state courts can impose free speech duties on private property owners. *See* PruneYard Shopping Ctr. v. Robins, 447 U.S. 74, 85–88 (1980). In fact, the Supreme Court implicitly reaffirmed *PruneYard* in 2021. *See* Cedar Point Nursery v. Hassid, 141 S. Ct. 2063, 2076–77 (2021) (distinguishing the shopping center at issue in *PruneYard* from an agricultural work site and explaining that "the PruneYard was open to the public, welcoming some 25,000 patrons a day" unlike the nursery which was "closed to the public").

164. *See* Citizens United v. Fed. Elections Comm'n, 558 U.S. 310, 339 (2010) (opining that "[s]peech is an essential mechanism of democracy, for it is the means to hold officials accountable to the people" and positing that "[t]he right of citizens to inquire, to hear, to speak, and to use information to reach consensus is a precondition to enlightened self-government and a necessary means to protect it").

165. *See e.g.*, MEIKLEJOHN, *supra* note 1, at 25–27, 89–91 (arguing that freedom of speech is an essential and non-negotiable precondition for any society committed to a meaningful project of democratic self-government).

166. *See* BHAGWAT, *supra* note 2, at 9, 81–98, 160–63 (noting instances where democratic deliberation and democracy are interconnected and emphasizing the central importance of democratic deliberation to self-government under the U.S. Constitution).

167. *See supra* text and accompanying notes 93 to 99.

168. *See* CALABRESI, *supra* note 10, at 163–71.

169. *See* ACKERMAN, *supra* note 12, at 4–17, 87–88, 248, 408–20; *see also* BRUCE ACKERMAN, WE THE PEOPLE: FOUNDATIONS 266–67 (1991).

CHAPTER 3

1. *See supra* Chapter 2.

2. *See* Ronald J. Krotoszynski, Jr., *Common Law Constitutionalism and the Protean First Amendment*, 25 U. PA. J. CONST. L. 1, 4–11 (2023).

3. *See infra* Chapter 5.

4. *See infra* Chapter 6.

5. *See infra* Chapter 4.

6. DAVID A. STRAUSS, THE LIVING CONSTITUTION 33 (2010).

7. *Id.* at 34.

8. *See id.* at 2–11, 52–56 (arguing that all constitutional law is, at some level, judge-made common law rather than a form of statutory law and making this case with particular vigor in the context of the First Amendment); *see also* GUIDO CALABRESI, A COMMON LAW FOR THE AGE OF STATUTES (1982) (arguing that judges possess both the duty and the power to "update" statutory texts that have fallen into "desuetude" through legislative neglect).

9. President Nelson Mandela promulgated the new Constitution of the Republic of South Africa in Sharpeville, on December 10, 1996, after the Constitutional Court gave its final approval to the revised text on December 4, 1996. *See* Thomas M. Franck & Arun K. Thiruvengadam, *Norms of International Law Relating to the Constitution Making Process, in* FRAMING THE STATE IN TIMES OF TRANSITION: CASE STUDIES IN CONSTITUTION MAKING 10 (Laurel E. Miller ed., 2010); *see also* Hassen Ebrahim, THE SOUL OF A NATION: CONSTITUTION-MAKING IN SOUTH AFRICA 224–46 (1998) (discussing, describing, and critiquing the final process associated with the ratification of the final text of the 1996 Constitution). The 1996 Constitution became legally effective on February 4, 1997. *See* The Constitutional Court of the Republic of South Africa, *The Constitution: The Certification Process*, http://www.constitutionalcourt.org.za/site/theconstitution/thecertificationprocess.htm (last visited Feb. 23, 2022). The common practice of South African courts and legal scholars is to refer to the post-apartheid final Constitution as the "1996 Constitution" or "Constitution, 1996," and I have generally followed this convention.

10. Judith Geldenhuys & Michelle Kelly-Louw, *Hate Speech and Racist Slurs in the South African Context: Where to Start?*, 23 PER/PELJ 1, 4 (2020).

11. *Id.*

12. CONSTITUTION OF REPUBLIC OF SOUTH AFRICA, 1996, Act No. 108, § 167(5) ("The Constitutional Court makes the final decision whether an Act of Parliament, a provincial Act or conduct of the President is constitutional, and must confirm any order of invalidity made by the Supreme Court of Appeal, the High Court of South Africa, or a court of similar status, before that order has any force.") [hereinafter CONSTITUTION].

13. *Id.* § 38 (providing that "the court may grant appropriate relief, including a declaration of rights" to anyone "alleging that a right in the Bill of Rights has been infringed or threatened").

14. Convention for the Protection of Human Rights and Fundamental Freedoms, Nov. 4, 1950, 213 U.N.T.S. 222, 224 [hereinafter European Convention]. The European Convention entered into force on September 3, 1953.

15. *See* HEINZ KLUG, THE CONSTITUTION OF SOUTH AFRICA: A CONTEXTUAL ANALYSIS (2010); *see also* MARK KENDE, CONSTITUTIONAL RIGHTS IN TWO WORLDS: SOUTH AFRICA AND THE UNITED STATES 87–90 (2009) (discussing models that the drafters of South Africa's Constitution embraced and rejected, including the U.S. Constitution of 1787).

Notes to pages 35–36   —⌀ 213

16. KLUG, *supra* note 15, at 46–58 (discussing the two-step process that resulted in the adoption of the 1993 Interim Constitution, the election and work of the Constituent Assembly, and the ultimate adoption of the new, permanent, 1996 Constitution).

17. SIRI GLOPPEN, SOUTH AFRICA: THE BATTLE OVER THE CONSTITUTION 226 (1997).

18. *Id.*

19. *See* DONALD P. KOMMERS & RUSSELL A. MILLER, THE CONSTITUTIONAL JURISPRUDENCE OF THE FEDERAL REPUBLIC OF GERMANY 7–10 (3d ed. 2012); *see also* RONALD J. KROTOSZYNSKI, JR., THE FIRST AMENDMENT IN CROSS-CULTURAL PERSPECTIVE: A COMPARATIVE LEGAL ANALYSIS OF THE FREEDOM OF SPEECH 93 (2006) ("Following the end of World War II, the portion of Germany under the control of the Western Alliance worked to establish a functioning constitutional democracy. One of the primary bulwarks of this new democratic order was the adoption of the Basic Law.").

20. President Nelson Mandela, Inaugural Address, May 10, 1994, https://www.africa.upenn.edu/Articles_Gen/Inaugural_Speech_17984.html (last visited Sept. 10, 2023) ("We enter into a covenant that we shall build the society in which all South Africans, both black and white, will be able to walk tall, without any fear in their hearts, assured of their inalienable right to human dignity—a rainbow nation at peace with itself and the world.").

21. KENDE, *supra* note 15, at 45.

22. *Id.* at 45–46.

23. CONSTITUTION §§ 7–39. Sections 7 to 39 of the 1996 Constitution comprise Chapter 2, the Bill of Rights. It includes both negative (for example, freedom of speech, safeguarded by Section 16(1)) and also positive, or affirmative, fundamental rights (including, for example, rights to housing, *id.*§ 26(1), "[h]ealth care, food, water, and social security," *id.* § 27(1), and education, *id.* § 29(1)).

24. CONSTITUTION § 39(1)(b) ("When interpreting the Bill of Rights, a court, tribunal, or forum . . . must consider international law."). Note this obligation does not require the CCSA to harmonize domestic law with public international law; instead, it is a procedural requirement that mandates consideration of relevant international law principles.

25. *Id.* § 39(1)(c) ("When interpreting the Bill of Rights, a court, tribunal, or forum . . . may consider foreign law.").

26. *See generally* McCulloch v. Maryland, 17 U.S. (4 Wheat.) 159, 206 (1819) ("Let the end be legitimate, let it be within the scope of the constitution, and all means which are appropriate, which are plainly adapted to that end, which are not prohibited, but consist with the letter and spirit of the constitution, are constitutional.") Although Chief Justice John Marshall was writing about the scope of Congress's discretion under Article I, Section 8 of the U.S. Constitution of 1787, a careful review of South Africa's 1996 Constitution would lead a reasonable reader to conclude that the framers sought to empower the CCSA rather than restrict it. *See* KLUG, *supra* note 15, at 119–27 (discussing the CCSA's broad and dynamic approach to interpreting and enforcing the Bill of Rights).

27. *See infra* text and accompanying notes 114 to 191.

28. CONSTITUTION § 167(1) ("The Constitutional Court consists of the Chief Justice of South Africa, the Deputy Chief Justice and nine other judges.").

29. CONSTITUTION § 176(1). The Judges Act extends the maximum term of office from twelve to fifteen years and the mandatory retirement age from age seventy to age seventy-five. Judges' Remuneration and Conditions of Employment Act, 2001, No. 47 of 2001, § 4.

30. CONSTITUTION § 16(2)(c).

31. *Id.* § 1.

32. KLUG, *supra* note 15, at 107–10 (discussing the role and importance of Section 1's "founding principles").

33. *Id.* at 107.

34. *See id.*

35. Qwelane v. South African Hum. Rts. Comm'n (CCT 13/20), 2021 (6) S.A. 579 (CC), para. 2.

36. CONSTITUTION § 37(1).

37. *Id.* § 37(5)(c) (prohibiting "any derogation from a section mentioned in column 1 of the Table of NonDerogable Rights, to the extent indicated opposite that section in column 3 of the Table").

38. *Id.* § 37(5) Table of NonDerogable Rights.

39. *Id.* This is a less extensive, and inclusive, list than appears in Section 9, which provides:

> The state may not unfairly discriminate directly or indirectly against anyone on one or more grounds, including race, gender, sex, pregnancy, marital status, ethnic or social origin, colour, sexual orientation, age, disability, religion, conscience, belief, culture, language and birth.

CONSTITUTION § 9(3). In times of national emergency, the government may discriminate based on pregnancy, marital status, sexual orientation, age, disability, conscience, belief, culture, or birth. One can understand excluding some of these categories, such as perhaps "age" and "disability." In a military draft, the government would presumably seek to enlist younger adults without major physical disabilities for induction into South Africa's armed forces. Other exclusions, however, seem harder to understand—for example, green-lighting government discrimination based on sexual orientation.

40. *Id.* § 37(5) Table of NonDerogable Rights.

41. *See infra* text and accompanying notes 114 to 119.

42. *See* CONSTITUTION §§ 1 & 1(d) ("The Republic of South Africa is one, sovereign, democratic state founded on the following values . . . Universal adult suffrage, a national common voters roll, regular elections and a multi-party system of democratic government, to ensure accountability, responsiveness and openness."), 7(1) (providing that "[t]his Bill of Rights is a cornerstone of democracy in South Africa" and that "[i]t enshrines the rights of all people in our country and affirms the *democratic values* of human dignity, equality and freedom") (emphasis added), and 39(1) (providing that "[w]hen interpreting the Bill of Rights, a court, tribunal or forum . . . must promote the values that *underlie an open and democratic society* based on human dignity, equality and freedom") (emphasis added).

43. South African Hum. Rts. Comm'n v. Masuku and Another (CCT 14/19), 2022 (4) S.A. 1 (CC); Qwelane v. South African Hum. Rts. Comm'n (CCT 13/20), 2021 (6) S.A. 579 (CC).

44. New York Times Co. v. Sullivan, 376 U.S. 254, 270 (1964) ("Thus we consider this case against the background of a profound national commitment to the principle that debate on public issues should be uninhibited, robust, and wide open, and that it may well include vehement, caustic, and sometimes unpleasantly sharp attacks on government and public officials.").

45. *See, e.g.*, Minister of Fin. v. Van Heerden (CCT 63/03), 2004 (6) S.A. 121 (CC), para. 22 ("The Constitution commands us to strive for a society built on the democratic values of human dignity, the achievement of equality, the advancement of human rights and freedom. Thus the achievement of equality is not only a guaranteed and justiciable right in our Bill of Rights but also *a core and foundational value*; a standard which *must inform all law and against which all law must be tested for constitutional consonance.*" (emphasis added)).

Notes to pages 38–39   —∽ 215

46. *See* Islamic Unity Convention v. Indep. Broadcasting Auth'y (CCT 36/01), 2002 (4) S.A. 294 (CC), paras. 32–36 (discussing the meaning and scope of Section 16(2)(c) of the 1996 Constitution).

47. *Id.* para. 33.

48. *Qwelane*, 2021 (6) S.A. 579 (CC), para. 74 (observing that "pluralism, tolerance, and open-mindedness require that our democracy fosters an environment that allows a free and open exchange of ideas" that is "free from censorship no matter how offensive, shocking, or disturbing these ideas may be" but cautioning that "this does not mean that freedom of expression enjoys superior status in our law"); Khumalo v. Holomisa (CCT 53/01), 2002 (5) S.A. 401 (CC), para. 25 (holding that "although freedom of expression is fundamental to our democratic society, it is not a paramount value" and "must be construed in the context of the other values enshrined in our Constitution" including "the values of human dignity, freedom and equality").

49. Both here and in the title to this chapter, I have ordered the lodestar human rights as "dignity, equality, and human freedom." I have taken this approach because the 1996 Constitution consistently orders these rights as "dignity, equality, and human freedom." However, the CCSA, in its recent landmark hate speech precedents, *Masuku* and *Qwelane*, adopts the order "equality, dignity, and freedom." *See* South African Hum. Rts. Comm'n v. Masuku (CCT 14/19),, 2022 (4) S.A. 1 (CC), para. 1 ("These rights—the rights to equality, human dignity, and the right to freedom of speech and expression—are rights that carry unique and troubled pasts interwoven into the fabric of apartheid history."); Qwelane v. South African Hum. Rts. Comm'n (CCT 13/20), 2021 (6) S.A. 579 (CC), para. 49 ("Through this prism, section 10 [of the Equality Act] is located at the confluence of three fundamental rights: equality, dignity, and freedom of expression, and we ought to navigate an interpretation of that section within this terrain."); *id.* para. 67 ("Is it not only the rights to equality and dignity that our Constitution seeks to protect. The right to free speech is equally protected."). Thus, although the 1996 Constitution consistently sequences the apex human rights as "human dignity, equality, and freedom," see CONSTITUTION § 7(1), the CCSA frequently reorders them in the context of hate speech cases—which one can understand when it is interpreting and applying a statutory instrument called "The Equality Act." This is perhaps a distinction without a difference because equality and dignity arguably constitute two sides of the same coin in South African human rights jurisprudence. The animating purpose and idea, if not ideal, is the creation of a polity in which all citizens enjoy a meaningful form of equal citizenship. *See Qwelane, supra*, para. 58 ("Our jurisprudence is resolute that the type of equality underpinning our constitutional framework is not mere formal equality, but in order to give meaning to the right to dignity, also substantive equality."). Simply put, human dignity is an essential condition for the achievement of substantive equality. *See* RONALD J. KROTOSZYNSKI, JR., PRIVACY REVISITED: A GLOBAL PERSPECTIVE ON THE RIGHT TO BE LEFT ALONE 112 (2016) ("Essentially, the South African Constitution seeks to elevate the status of the individual person and safeguard all persons from unfair, arbitrary, or irrational government treatment. Recognizing the inherent worth and value of all human beings—dignity—presents the first line of defense against the gross abuses that characterized South Africa's long period of Herrenvolk democracy."). In other words, "the state may not treat human beings as objects rather than subjects." *Id.*

50. Section 16(1) empowers South African courts to review government actions that abridge four distinct expressive freedoms:

1. Everyone has the right to freedom of expression, which includes—
   a. freedom of the press and other media;
   b. freedom to receive or impart information or ideas;

216 ꝏ— Notes to pages 39–41

    c. freedom of artistic creativity; and

    d. academic freedom and freedom of scientific research.

CONSTITUTION, § 16(1). Other expressive freedoms enjoy constitutional protection as well, including freedom of assembly and petition, *id.* § 17, freedom of association, *id.* § 18, and political rights of participation, *id.* § 19. Finally, Section 15 safeguards "[f]reedom of religion, belief, and opinion." *Id.* § 15.

51. *Id.* § 16(2)(a)–(c).

52. *See* Dennis v. United States, 341 U.S. 494, 509 (1951) (holding that the First Amendment permits criminalization of the advocacy of communist doctrines because the First Amendment "cannot mean that before the Government may act, it must wait until the *putsch* is about to be executed, the plans have been laid and the signal is awaited" and observing that "[i]If Government is aware that a group aiming at its overthrow is attempting to indoctrinate its members and to commit them to a course whereby they will strike when the leaders feel the circumstances permit, action by the Government is required"). The *Dennis* majority held that "success or probability of success" was not required for the government to punish speech if that speech related to a sufficiently grave harm and would have a bad tendency toward bringing that harm about. *See id.* at 509–11.

53. *Qwelane*, 2021 (6) S.A. 579 (CC), para. 76 ("These dictates of pluralism, tolerance and open-mindedness require that our democracy fosters an environment that allows a free and open exchange of ideas, free from censorship no matter how offensive, shocking or disturbing these ideas may be."); v. Indep. Broadcasting Auth. (CCT 36/01), 2002 (4) S.A. 294 (CC), paras. 26–28 (emphasizing that Section 16 generally protects speech and ideas that are shocking *or* upsetting provided that they do not cross the line into targeted threats of racial, gender, or religious violence).

54. 538 U.S. 343 (2003).

55. *Id.* at 347–48, 361–62.

56. *Id.* at 347–48.

57. *Id.* at 362.

58. *See id.* at 388 (Thomas, J., dissenting) ("In my view, whatever expressive value cross burning has, the legislature simply wrote it out by banning only intimidating conduct undertaken by a particular means.").

59. *Id.* at 391.

60. *Id.* at 380–81 (Souter, J., concurring in part and dissenting in part).

61. *Id.*

62. *Id.* at 386–88.

63. *Id.* at 387–88.

64. *See id.* at 388 (opining that "the statute under which all three of the respondents were prosecuted violates the First Amendment, since the statute's content-based distinction was invalid").

65. *See infra* text and accompanying notes 114 to 240.

66. *See* Maria E. Marais, *A Duty Perspective on the Hate Speech Prohibition in the* Equality Act, 24 PER/PELJ 1, 21–29 (2021) (arguing that Supreme Court of Appeal failed to afford sufficient importance to the 1996 Constitution's commitments to equality and dignity when it voided Section 10 of the Equality Act and "failed to recognise the state's obligation in terms of section 9(4) of the Constitution to enact legislation to prohibit and prevent unfair discrimination on the grounds in section 9(3))." Professor Marais was, strictly speaking, writing about the

Supreme Court of Appeal's (SCA) decision in *Qwelane* rather than the CCSA's decision. Even so, however, the CCSA's decision, although leaving a significantly narrowed Section 10 in place, essentially places the same emphasis on freedom of expression that the SCA's decision voiding Section 10 outright reflects and incorporates. Both the CCSA and the SCA tend to read hate speech proscriptions narrowly—although the lower trial courts in South Africa, including the Equality Court, "tend to attach higher weight to dignity and equality than freedom of expression, when these values are seen to clash." Jacob Mchangama & Natalie Alkiviadou, *South Africa the Model?: A Comparative Analysis of Hate Speech Jurisprudence of South Africa and the European Court of Human Rights*, 1 J. FREE SPEECH L. 542, 577 (2022).

67. *See supra* text and accompanying notes 23 to 35.

68. CONSTITUTION § 1(a).

69. *Id.* § 7(1) (emphasis added).

70. *Id.* § 9(1) ("Everyone is equal before the law and has the right to equal protection and benefit of the law."). Proscribed grounds of discrimination under Section 9 include "race, gender, sex, pregnancy, marital status, ethnic or social origin, colour, sexual orientation, age, disability, religion, conscience, belief, culture, language and birth." *Id.* § 9(3). It bears noting that this list is far more inclusive than the exclusion of hate speech in Section 16, which is limited to "race, ethnicity, gender or religion." *Id.* § 16(2)(c). Section 9 creates an affirmative duty on the government's part to protect against proscribed forms of discrimination. *See id.* § 9(4) ("National legislation must be enacted to prevent or prohibit unfair discrimination."). At least arguably, this duty to prevent "unfair discrimination" might also serve as a basis for prohibiting targeted forms of hate speech based on any of the proscribed grounds. *But cf.* Islamic Unity Convention v. Indep. Broadcasting Auth. (CCT 36/01), 2002 (4) S.A. 294 (CC), paras. 34–36, 51 (invalidating an IBA regulation that prohibited the broadcast of material "likely to prejudice relations between sections of the population" without specifying the particular grounds of such compromised social relations because it went far beyond the grounds for regulating hate speech set forth in Section 16(2)(c) and was not otherwise a justified infringement of the freedom of speech). It is unclear whether a law or regulation that tracks compromised relations on the grounds elaborated in Section 9(3) would be constitutionally permissible. At least arguably, such a law or regulation could be distinguished from the regulation at issue in *Islamic Unity Convention* and would constitute and enforcement measure under Section 9(4).

71. CONSTITUTION § 10 ("Everyone has inherent dignity and the right to have their dignity respected and protected.").

72. *Id.* § 12(1) (providing that "[e]veryone has the right to freedom and security of the person" which encompasses interests associated with bodily control, personal liberty, freedom of movement, and prohibitions against torture or medical experimentation). Section 12 corresponds to the Canadian Charter of Human Rights provision that safeguards "life, liberty, and security of the person." *See* Constitution Act, 1982, ch. 11, Schedule B, Part 1, Canadian Charter of Rights and Freedoms, § 7 [hereinafter Canadian Charter].

73. KLUG, *supra* note 15, at 127.

74. CONSTITUTION § 37(1) & (5).

75. *See supra* text and accompanying notes 36 to 43.

76. Qwelane v. South African Hum. Rts. Comm'n (CCT 13/20), (2021) 6 S.A. 579 (CC), para. 2 ("Central to the issue before us is a delicate balancing exercise between the fundamental rights to freedom of expression, dignity, and equality."); Khumalo v. Holomisa (CCT 53/01), 2002 (5) S.A. 401 (CC), para. 25 (observing that "although freedom of expression is fundamental to our democratic society, it is not a paramount value" but, instead, "must be construed in the

context of the other values enshrined in our Constitution," notably including "the values of human dignity, freedom, and equality").

77. CONSTITUTION § 74(1)(a) & (b).

78. *Id.* § 74(2).

79. KLUG, *supra* note 15, at 107.

80. *Id.*

81. Minister of Home Affairs v. Nat'l Inst. for Crime Prevention and the Re-Integration of Offenders (NICRO) (CCT 03/04), 2005 (3) S.A. 280 (CC), para. 21.

82. *Id.; see* KLUG, *supra* note 15, at 108–11 (discussing the relevance and importance of the founding values of dignity, equality, and human freedom).

83. *NICRO*, 2005 (3) S.A. 280, para. 21.

84. *Id.* para. 23.

85. *Id.*

86. Khumalo v. Holomisa (CCT 53/01), 2002 (5) S.A. 401 (CC), para. 25.

87. *Id.*

88. *See generally* CONSTITUTION § 167 (vesting the Constitutional Court of South Africa with an express power of judicial review).

89. CONSTITUTION § 1.

90. *Id.* § 1(d).

91. CONSTITUTION § 19(1)–(3).

92. It bears noting the democracy and voting *does* appear in the South African Constitution among the "founding principles." Section 1 provides that the Constitution exists, in part, in order to secure "[u]niversal adult suffrage, a national common voters roll, regular elections and a multi-party system of democratic government, to ensure accountability, responsiveness and openness." *Id.* § 1(d). This provision could serve as a textual "hook" for elevating the freedom of political speech to a coequal status with dignity, equality, and freedom. However, to date, the Constitutional Court has not invoked Section 1(d) when relating Section 16's protection of freedom of speech to the project of self-government.

93. Qwelane v. South African Hum, Rts. Comm'n (CCT 13/20), 2021 (6) S.A. 579 (CC), para. 67.

94. Economic Freedom Fighters & Another v. Minister of Justices (CCT 201/19), 2021 (2) S.A. 1(CC), para. 1.

95. *Id.*

96. S. v. Mamabolo (CCT 44/00), 2001 (3) S.A. 409 (CC), para. 37.

97. *Id.*

98. *Id.*

99. *See* Alexander Brown, *Hate Speech Laws, Legitimacy, and Precaution: A Reply to James Weinstein,* 32 CONST. COMMENT. 599, 613–14 (2017).

100. *Id.* at 609.

101. *See* RICHARD DELGADO & JEAN STEFANCIC, MUST WE DEFEND NAZIS?: WHY THE FIRST AMENDMENT SHOULD NOT PROTECT HATE SPEECH AND WHITE SUPREMACY 1–20 (2018) (arguing that hate speech targeting minorities diminishes democratic deliberation because it leads members of minority groups to withdraw from the political process rather than expose themselves to the trauma associated with targeted racial vilification).

102. CONSTITUTION § 9(4) ("National legislation must be enacted to prevent or prohibit unfair discrimination.").

103. *Id.* § 16(2)(c) (providing that constitutional protection of freedom of expression does not apply to "advocacy of hatred that is based on race, ethnicity, gender or religion, and that constitutes incitement to cause harm").

Notes to pages 44–48

104. *See* R. v. Keegstra, [1990] 3 S.C.R. 697 (Can.).

105. *See* Féret v. Belgium, App. No. 15615/07 (ECtHR July 16, 2009), *English-language summary*, https://hudoc.echr.coe.int/eng-press#{%22itemid%22:[%22003-2800730-3069797%22]} (last visited Sept. 16, 2023).

106. Norwood v. United Kingdom, App. No. 23131/03, at 4 (ECtHR Nov. 16, 2004).

107. European Convention art. 17.

108. *Id.* art. 10(1) & (2).

109. *See* Mchangama & Alkiviadou, *supra* note 66, at 556–60.

110. *Id.* at 560.

111. *Id.*

112. *Id.*

113. *See, e.g.*, South African Hum. Rts. Comm'n v. Masuku (CCT 14/19), 2022 (4) S.A. 1 (CC), para. 171 ("In dealing with the delicate relationship between the fundamental rights at stake in a matter like this, the ends of our constitutional democracy are served by striking an elusive yet crucial balance between the imperative to regulate hate speech and the importance of fostering 'an environment that allows a free and open exchange of ideas, free from censorship, no matter how offensive, shocking, or disturbing these ideas may be.'" (quoting *Qwelane, infra*, para. 74)): Qwelane v. South African Hum. Rts. Comm'n (CCT 13/20), 2021 (6) S.A. 579 (CC), para. 2 ("Central to the issue before us is a delicate balancing exercise between the fundamental rights to freedom of expression, dignity and equality.").

114. 376 U.S. 254, 269–70, 283–84 (1964) (holding that the First Amendment prohibits states from imposing tort liability on a media defendant for defamation of a public official under a legal standard less demanding that actual malice, meaning the public official must prove with clear and convincing evidence publication of a false and damaging fact either with actual knowledge of its falsity or with reckless indifference to its truth or falsity).

115. CONSTITUTION § 16(c)(2).

116. *Masuku*, 2022 (4) S.A. 1 (CC), paras. 99–100.

117. *Id.* para. 100.

118. The government's duty to act to address hate speech arguably arises through the conjunction of Section 7, which provides that "[t]he state must respect, protect, promote and fulfill the rights in the Bill of Rights," CONSTITUTION § 7(2), and Section 9(4), which states that "[n]o person may unfairly discriminate directly or indirectly against anyone on one or more grounds in terms of subsection (3)" and mandates the enactment of "[n]ational legislation . . . to prevent or prohibit unfair discrimination," *id.* § 9(4). *See Qwelane*, 2021 (6) S.A. (CC) 579, paras. 50–51. Justice Majiedt explains that "[t]he ambit of this obligation is both positive and negative" and "requires of the State not only to refrain from infringing on fundamental rights, but also to take positive steps to ensure that these rights are realised." *Id.* para. 51. Professors J.L. Pretorious and Maria E. Marais explain that "[s]ubsections 9(3) and (4) of the *Constitution* require the state to enact national legislation to prevent or prohibit unfair discrimination." Maria E. Marais & J.L. Pretorious, *A Contextual Analysis of the Hate Speech Provisions of the Equality Act*, 18 PER/PELJ 901, 904 (2015).

119. *Masuku*, 2002 (4) S.A. 1 (CC), para. 100.

120. *See* Mchangama & Alkiviadou, *supra* note 66, at 565–74.

121. *Id.* at 577.

122. *Qwelane*, 2021 (6) S.A. 579 (CC), para. 79.

123. *Id.*

124. The Promotion of Equality and Prevention of Unfair Discrimination Act 4 of 2000, § 10(1) [hereinafter Equality Act].

125. *Id.* § 1.

126. *Id.* §10(1)(a) to (c).

127. *Id.* § 10(2); *see also id.* § 21(2)(n) (authorizing an Equality Court to refer a matter to the Director of Public Prosecutions for criminal charges and prosecution).

128. CONSTITUTION § 16(2)(c).

129. *Id.* § 36(1) (providing that "[t]he rights in the Bill of Rights may be limited only in terms of law of general application to the extent that the limitation is reasonable and justifiable in an open and democratic society based on human dignity, equality and freedom, taking into account all relevant factors" which include "the nature of the right," "the importance of the purpose of the limitation," "the nature and extent of the limitation," "the relation between the limitation and its purpose," and the potential existence of "less restrictive means to achieve the purpose").

130. Qwelane v. South African Hum. Rts. Comm'n, 2020 (2) SA 124 (SCA), para. 4.

131. *Id* paras. 4–5. The cartoon "appeared on the same page as the column, depicting a man on his knees alongside a goat, appearing in front of a priest to be married. The caption above the man and the goat reads: 'When human rights meet animal rights'." *Id.* para. 5.

132. *Id.* para. 6.

133. *Id.* para. 34.

134. *Id.* para. 95.

135. *See id.* paras. 67–74.

136. *Id.* para. 68.

137. The SCA's decision to void Section 10 completely provoked widespread criticism within the South African legal academy. *See, e.g.*, Marais, *supra* note 64, at 28–30 (strongly criticizing the SCA's decision in *Qwelane* and accusing the judges of that bench of having "failed to recognize the state's obligation in terms of section 9(4) of the Constitution to enact legislation to prohibit unfair discrimination on the grounds in section 9(3)").

138. *Qwelane*, 2021 (6) S.A. 579 (CC), paras. 102–4.

139. *Id.* para. 103.

140. *Id.* para. 74.

141. *Id.* para. 79.

142. *Id.*

143. *Id.* para. 81 (internal quotations omitted).

144. *Id.* para. 195.

145. *Id.* para. 104.

146. *See id.* paras. 182–195.

147. *Id.* para. 182.

148. *Id.* para. 188.

149. South African Hum. Rts. Comm'n v. Masuku (CCT 14/19), 2022 (4) S.A. 1 (CC), para. 3.

150. *See id.* paras. 165–66.

151. *Id.* para. 96.

152. *Id.* para. 165.

153. *Id.* para. 171.

154. *Id.* (quoting Qwelane v. South African Hum. Rts. Comm'n (CCT 13/20), 2021 (6) S.A. 579 (CC), para. 74).

155. Islamic Unity Convention v. Indep. Broadcasting Auth. (CCT 36/01), 2002 (4) S.A. 294 (CC).

156. Act 153 of 1993, schd. 1, cl. 2(a)

157. *Id.* (emphasis added).

158. *Islamic Unity Convention*, 2002 (4) S.A. 294 (CC), para. 23.

159. *Id.* para. 24.

160. *Id.* para. 35.

161. *Id.*

162. *See id.* para. 49.

163. *Id.* para. 50.

164. *Id.* para. 51.

165. *Id.*

166. *Id.*

167. *See id.* para. 57.

168. *Id.* para. 29.

169. *Id.* para. 34.

170. Khumalo v. Holomisa (CCT 53/01), 2002 (5) S.A. 401 (CC), paras. 41–45.

171. *Id.* para. 1.

172. *Id.*

173. *See id.* paras. 4–5, 18.

174. *Id.* para. 4.

175. *Id.* para. 21.

176. *Id.*

177. *Id.* para. 25.

178. *Id.*

179. *See id.* paras. 26–27.

180. *See* Nat'l Media Ltd. v. Bogoshi, 1998 (4) S.A. 1196 (SCA).

181. *Id.* at 1212.

182. *Id.* at 1212–13.

183. *Khumalo*, 2002 (5) S.A. 401 (CC), para. 39.

184. *Id.*

185. 376 U.S. 254 (1964).

186. *Id.* at 269–70, 279–80.

187. *Khumalo*, 2002 (5) S.A. 401 (CC), para. 40.

188. *See id.* para. 41 ("In deciding whether the common law rule complained of by the applicants does indeed constitute an unreasonable limitation of section 16 of the Constitution, sight must not be lost of other constitutional values and in particular, the value of human dignity.").

189. *Id.* para. 43.

190. *Id.* para. 44.

191. *See id.* paras. 21–24.

192. Kgaugelo Masweneng, *AfriForum Tells SCA Malema Violated an Agreement on 'Kill the Boer' from 11 Years Ago*, TIMES LIVE (Sept. 4, 2023) https://www.timeslive.co.za/news/south-africa/2023-09-04-afriforum-tells-sca-malema-violated-an-agreement-on-kill-the-boer-from-11-years-ago/ (last visited Sept. 8, 2023).

193. Nico Buitendag & Karen van Marle, AfriForum v. Malema: *The Limits of Law and Complexity*, 17 PER/PELJ 2893, 2894 (2014).

194. *See id.* at 2894–95.

195. *See* John Eligon, *"Kill the Boer" Song Fuels Backlash in South Africa and U.S.*, N.Y. TIMES (Aug. 2, 2023), https://www.nytimes.com/2023/08/02/world/africa/south-africa-kill-boer-song.html.

Notes to pages 56–59

196. AfriForum v. Malema (EC20968/2010), 2011 (6) S.A. 240 (EqC). For a discussion of Mr. Malema and his political activities, first as the leader of the ANC's Youth League and later as the head of the EFF, and his regular use of "Dubula bhulu," which is Xhosa for "Kill the Boer," see Buitendag & van Marle, *supra* note 193, at 2894–96.

197. *AfriForum*, 2011 (6) S.A. 240 (EqC), paras. 108–9.

198. *Id.* para. 108.

199. Eligon, *supra* note 195.

200. Masweneng, *supra* note 192.

201. *See* AfriForum v. Economic Freedom Fighters & Julius Sello Malema (EQ 04/2020), 2022 (6) SA 357 (GJ), paras. 2–7 (discussing the 2010 case, its resolution via the mediation process, and the settlement agreement of November 1, 2012, which AfriForum alleges that Melma and the EFF proceeded to serially violate) [hereinafter *AfriForum II*].

202. Tania Broughton, *Judge Rules that "Kill the Boer—Kill the Farmer" Is Not Hate Speech*, Ground Up (Aug. 25, 2022), https://www.groundup.org.za/article/judge-rules-kill-boer---kill-farmer-not-hate-speech/.

203. *AfriForum II*, 2022 (6) SA 357 (GJ), para. 98.

204. *Id.*

205. *Id.* paras. 111–12.

206. *Id.* para. 111.

207. *Id.*

208. *Id.* para. 112.

209. *See id.* (reporting on the decision of Judge Edwin Molahlehi, who found that Malema's use of the contested phrase "does not constitute hate speech and deserves to be protected under the rubric of freedom of speech" because it "articulates the failure of the current government to address issues of economic empowerment and land division").

210. Norimitsu Onishi, *Jail Time for Using South Africa's Worst Racial Slur?*, N.Y. Times (Oct. 17, 2016), https://www.nytimes.com/2016/10/28/world/africa/south-africa-hate-speech.html.

211. Geldenhuys & Kelly-Louw, *supra* note 10, at 26–27. Moreover, the CCSA "is patent in regarding its denunciation of using the k-word inside or outside the workplace." *Id.* at 26.

212. Momberg v. S. (A206/2018), 2019 (2) SACR 505 (GJ) (28 June 2019), para. 5.

213. *Id.*

214. *See id.* paras. 6–7.

215. *Id.* para. 8.

216. Onishi, *supra* note 210.

217. *Momberg*, 2019 (2) SACR 505 (GJ), para. 11. Her racial threats included "'If I see a kaffir I will drive over him.'" and "'If I had a gun I will shoot everybody.'" *Id.*

218. Prevention and Combating of Hate Crimes and Hate Speech Bill, Bill No. 9B-2018; *see* Esther Rose, *South Africa: National Assembly Passes Bill to Criminalise Hate Speech and Hate Crimes*, AllAfrica (Mar. 15, 2023), https://allafrica.com/stories/202303150396.html (last visited Sept. 12, 2023).

219. In the Matter between Cape Party-Kaapse Party and Iziko-South African National Gallery, Case No. EC02/2017 (July 4, 2017), at 1–2.

220. *Id.* at 2.

221. *Id.* at 4.

222. *Id.*

223. *Id.* at 3.

224. *Id.* at 5 (all capitalization in the original).

225. *Id.* at 6.

226. *Id.*

227. Equality Act § 7(a).

228. *Id.* § 10.

229. *Id.* § 12.

230. *In the Matter between Cape Party-Kaapse Party*, Case No. EC02/2017, at 7.

231. *Id.* at 8.

232. Judith Geldenhuys & Michelle Kelly-Louw, *Demystifying Hate Speech under the PEPUDA*, 23 PER/PELJ 1, 14 (2020) ("Where and to whom the utterance is made may determine whether it constitutes hate speech or only rude or distasteful speech.").

233. It also bears noting that South African legal academics suggest that, under the doctrine of "substantive equality," which means that courts should take into account social and economic disparities among various groups within South Africa when applying Section 9, members of disempowered groups might have greater leeway to use hyperbolic speech that leans in on race, sex, or religion. *See id.* at 14 (observing that "[i]n South Africa, as in other jurisdictions, if the alleged perpetrator is a member of a previously disadvantaged group which was subject to historical oppression, offensive speech is tolerated more readily") [hereinafter Demystifying Hate Speech]. Thus, "South Africa, like other jurisdictions, is more lenient to perpetrators belonging to groups which has suffered previous disadvantage." *Id.* at 36. However, Professors Geldenhuys and Kelly-Louw caution that "it appears in South Africa this leniency is abused and even raised as a defence against hate speech charges." *Id.*

234. *See* Chaplinsky v. New Hamphsire, 315 U.S. 568 (1942).

235. *Id.* at 571–72.

236. *Id.* at 572.

237. *Id.*

238. *See generally* Joanna C. Botha & Avinash Govindjee, *Hate Speech Provisions and Provisos: A Response to Marais and Pretorius and Proposals for Reform s*, 20 PER/PELJ 1, 17 (2017) (arguing that "[a]n objective test should be applied to determine" if particular speech meets the legal threshold for constituting "hate speech" and that "[i]mportant factors include the identity and status of both speaker and audience; the mode and reach of the speech; the content and purpose of the speech; the vulnerability of the group; historical patterns of discrimination against the group; and relevant social and political circumstances").

239. Indeed, it is far more likely that the CCSA would find the intentional, targeted deployment of the K-word in a face-to-face encounter with a Black South African person to fall within Section 16(2)'s exclusion of speech that seeks to foment racial resentments and hatred.

240. *See, e.g.,* CONSTITUTION § 1(d) (declaring "[u]niversal adult suffrage, a national common voters roll, regular elections and a multi-party system of democratic government," all in order to secure government "accountability, responsiveness, and openness" as founding constitutional values); *id.* § 7(1) ("This Bill of Rights is a cornerstone of democracy in South Africa. It enshrines the rights of all people in our country and affirms the democratic values of human dignity, equality, and freedom.").

241. *Id.* § 1.

242. *Id.* § 1(d); *see* KLUG, *supra* note 15, at 107–10 (discussing the foundational values of the 1996 Constitution).

243. KLUG, *supra* note 15, at 5.

244. *Id.* at 83.

245. *See id.* at 72–74; *see also* S. v. Zuma & Others (CCT 5/94), 1995 (2) S.A. 642, para. 17 ("While we must always be conscious of the values underlying the Constitution, it is nonetheless our task to interpret a written instrument."). Justice Sydney Kentridge, writing for the CCSA in *Zuma*, explains that he is "well aware of the fallacy of supposing that general language must have a single 'objective' meaning" and admits "[n]or is it easy to avoid the influence of one's personal intellectual and moral preconceptions." *Id.* Nevertheless, he emphasizes that "it cannot be too strongly stressed that the Constitution does not mean whatever we might wish it to mean." *Id.*

246. KLUG, *supra* note 15, at 108.

247. *Id.* (citing Minister of Home Affairs v. Nat'l Inst. for Crime Prevention and the Re-Integration of Offenders (NICRO) (CCT 03/04), 2005 (3) S.A. 280 (CC), para. 21).

248. *NICRO*, 2005 (3) S.A. 280 (CC), para. 21.

249. CONSTITUTION § 19.

250. See ALEXANDER MEIKLEJOHN, FREE SPEECH AND ITS RELATION TO SELF-GOVERNMENT 22–27, 37–39, 88–91, 94 (1948).

251. *Id.* at 26-27, 88-89.

252. *Id.* at 20.

253. *Id.* at 91.

254. *Id.* at 37.

255. *Id.* at 88.

256. *Id.*

257. *Id.* at 88–89.

258. *Id.* at 89.

259. Letter from Thomas Jefferson to Charles Yancey, Jan. 6, 1816, *reprinted in* 9 PAPERS OF THOMAS JEFFERSON, RETIREMENT SERIES, SEPTEMBER 1815 TO APRIL 1816, at 328, 330 (J. Jefferson Looney ed., 2013).

260. Alexander Meiklejohn, *The First Amendment Is an Absolute*, 1961 SUP. CT. REV. 245, 263.

261. *Id.* at 89.

262. *See* IAIN CURRIE & JOHAN DE WAAL, BILL OF RIGHTS HANDBOOK 141 (6th ed. 2013) (observing that South Africa's past plays in important, but incremental, role in the CCSA's approach to interpreting the 1996 Constitution and Bill of Rights).

263. Economic Freedom Fighters & Another v. Minister of Just. & Corr. Servs. (CCT 201/19), 2021 (2) S.A. 1 (CC), para. 2.

264. *Id.*

265. *Id.*

266. *See* Norvella P. Carter, Warren Chalklen, & Bhekuyise Zungu, *Re-Rooting* Roots: *The South African Perspective, in* RECONSIDERING *ROOTS*: RACE, POLITICS, AND MEMORY 165–80 (Erica L. Ball & Kellie Carter Jackson eds., 2017).

267. *Id.* at 168.

268. *Id.* at 166; *see also* Tlhalo Sam Radithalo, *Disgrace, Historical Trauma, and the Extreme Edge of Civility, in* TRAUMA, MEMORY, AND NARRATIVE IN THE CONTEMPORARY SOUTH AFRICAN NOVEL: ESSAYS 243–44 (Ewald Mengel & Michela Borzaga eds., 2012) (discussing the pervasive use of state-censorship during apartheid to silence Black voices and noting the government's ban on *Roots* as well as other works of fiction that engaged issues of race, such as Mongane Wally Serote's *To Every Birth in Blood*).

269. Radithalo, *supra* note 268, at 244.

270. Islamic Unity Convention v. Indep. Broadcasting Auth. (CCT 36/01), 2002 (4) S.A. 294 (CC), para. 25.

Notes to pages 66–69   —◦ 225

271. *Id.*

272. *Id.* (quoting Shabalala and Others v. Att'y Gen., Transvaal and Another, 1996 (1) S.A. 725 (CC), para. 26).

273. *Economic Freedom Fighters*, 2021 (2) S.A. 1 (CC).

274. *See id.* paras. 6–9 (discussing Julius Sello Malema's statements calling for self-help in redistribution of land ownership rights in 2014, 2016, and 2017, which served as the basis for criminal charges under Section 18(2)(b) of the Riotous Assemblies Act).

275. Riotous Assemblies Act 17 of 1956, § 18(2)(b).

276. *See Economic Freedom Fighters*, 2021 (2) S.A. 1, paras. 55–67.

277. *Id.* para. 2.

278. *Id.*

279. *Id.*

280. Qwelane v. South African Hum. Rts. Comm'n (CCT 13/20), 2021 (6) S.A. 579 (CC), para. 75.

281. Radithalo, *supra* note 268, at 244.

282. *See id.* at 243–45.

283. 87 Dep't of State Bulletin, Issue No. 2129, at 34 (December 1987).

284. William Faulkner, Requiem for a Nun 73 (Vintage ed. 2011).

285. Kende, *supra* note 15, at 91 ("Substantive equality requires that the courts favor the disadvantaged class. In contrast, formal equality presumes that the courts should treat everyone the same."). Professor Kende explains that "South African laws assisting the historically disadvantaged receive judicial deference because the Constitutional Court supports 'substantive equality' as opposed to the American concept of 'formal equality,' in which everyone must be treated the same." *Id.* at 163. In his view, South Africa's doctrine of substantive equality encompasses three main constitutive elements: "a group-oriented equality norm," "an anti-dominance principle," and "a pragmatic interpretive philosophy." *Id.* at 93.

286. *See* John Hart Ely, Democracy and Distrust: A Theory of Judicial Review 6–19, 42–43, 101–5 (1980).

287. Qwelane v. South African Human Rights Comm'n (CCT 13/20), 2021 (6) S.A. 579 (CC), para. 74.

CHAPTER 4

1. The Human Rights Act 1998 (Commencement No. 2) Order 2000, 2000 No. 1851 (c. 47) ("The day appointed for the coming into force of those provisions of the Human Rights Act 1998 that are not already in force is 2nd October 2000."); *see* The Human Rights Act 1998, ch. 42, § 22 (U.K.) (enacted November 9, 1998 and entered into force on Oct. 2, 2000) (permitting the effective date of the HRA 98 to be set by order) [hereinafter HRA].

2. Council of Europe, European Convention for the Protection of Human Rights and Fundamental Freedoms, 4 November 1950 (ETS 5), 213 U.N.T.S. 222 [hereinafter European Convention]. The Council of Europe published the European Convention on November 4, 1950 and the treaty entered into force on September 3, 1953.

3. *See, e.g.,* Sir Jeffrey Jowell, *Judicial Deference and Human Rights, in* Law and Administration in Europe: Essays in Honor of Carol Harlow 67, 68 (Paul P. Craig & Richard Rawlings eds., 2003) (praising Parliament's wisdom in enacting the HRA 98 and characterizing the law as "a higher order framework, a constitutional order, which constrains all public institutions and is expected to constrain even the elected legislature itself"); Sir William

226 — Notes to pages 69–70

Wade, *Human Rights and the Judiciary*, 1998 EUR. HUM. R. L. REV. 520, 532 (1998) (arguing that enactment of the HRA 98 constitutes "one of our great constitutional milestones" and "marks a quantum leap into a new legal culture of fundamental rights and freedoms").

4. European Convention, art. 10(1).

5. *See* Eric Barendt, *Freedom of Expression in the United Kingdom Under the Human Rights Act 1998*, 84 IND. L.J. 851, 866 (2009) (opining that "I doubt whether the HRA has had a very radical impact on the legal protection of freedom of expression" and positing that "in terms of the decided cases I do not think it has been as substantial as it might have been"). *But cf. id.* (observing that "[o]n the other hand, freedom of expression arguments have been taken seriously in circumstances when I doubt they would even have been raised before the enactment of the HRA").

6. *See* AILEEN KAVANAUGH, CONSTITUTIONAL REVIEW UNDER THE HUMAN RIGHTS ACT 1–3 (2009).

7. *Id.* at 1.

8. *Id.* at 1–2.

9. *Id.* at 2. Professor Kavanaugh's excellent book provides a comprehensive and quite thoughtful overview of how the HRA 98 has disrupted, at least to some degree, the operation of the doctrine of parliamentary sovereignty in the United Kingdom. Her work builds a highly persuasive normative framework that attempts to reconcile the expanded role of the domestic courts in defining and protecting fundamental rights with the United Kingdom's historical and near-absolute commitment to the doctrine of parliamentary sovereignty. *See id.* at 338–419.

10. Sec'y of State for the Home Dep't v. AF (No. 3), [2009] U.K.H.L. 28 (U.K.); Sec'y of State for the Home Dep't v. MB, [2007] U.K.H.L. 46 (U.K.); A and Others v. Sec'y of State for the Home Dep't, [2004] U.K.H.L. 56 (U.K.).

11. *See* STEPHEN GARDBAUM, THE NEW COMMONWEALTH MODEL OF CONSTITUTIONALISM: THEORY AND PRACTICE 169–73 (2013) (arguing that the SCUK/HOL have creatively interpreted domestic statutes, abandoning traditional principles of statutory construction, in order to protect procedural fairness and regularity in civil and criminal trials within the United Kingdom). *But cf.* James Bird, *Article 6 in the Supreme Court: Conflicting Views on the Right of Confrontation*, 6 PLYMOUTH L. & CRIM. JUSTICE REV. 107 (2014) (arguing persuasively that the SCUK has not faithfully followed the ECtHR's Article 6 precedents requiring that a criminal defendant be able to confront witnesses against him in a criminal trial and has, in fact, blatantly disregarded ECtHR precedents on this point).

12. HRA 98, § 3 ("So far as it is possible to do so, primary legislation and subordinate legislation must be read and given effect in a way which is compatible with the Convention rights."). The House of Lords (HOL) squarely held that this statutory directive authorizes the courts to creatively interpret statutes to harmonize them with European Convention rights and the decisions of the ECtHR. *See* Ghaidan v. Godin-Mendoza, [2004] U.K.H.L. 30, [2004] 2 A.C. 557, paras. 33, 49, 110–13, 116 (U.K.) (holding that, under Section 3 of the HRA 98, a reviewing court should render a saving construction of a statute that otherwise would violate a European Convention-protected right even if doing so requires the bench to abandon traditional rules of statutory construction, including probative evidence of Parliament's intent as to the meaning of a particular statutory provision); *see also* Sheldrake v. Dir. of Pub. Prosecutions, [2004] U.K.H.L. 43, [2005] 1 A.C. 364 , para. 28 (U.K.) (Lord Bingham) (opining that the "interpretative obligation under section 3 [of the HRA 98] is a very strong and far reaching one, and *may require the court to depart from the legislative intention of Parliament*" (emphasis added)).

Notes to pages 70–72 — 227

13. HRA 98, § 12(4) (providing that "[t]he court must have particular regard to the importance of the Convention right to freedom of expression").

14. Thomas v. Collins, 323 U.S. 516, 530 (1945) (noting "the preferred place" of rights protected under the First Amendment and opining that the First Amendment's "priority gives these liberties a sanctity and a sanction not permitting dubious intrusions"); Murdock v. Pennsylvania, 319 U.S. 105, 115 (1943) ("Freedom of press, freedom of speech, freedom of religion are in a preferred position.").

15. Campbell v. MGN Ltd., [2004] 2 A.C. 457, paras. 55 (Lord Hoffman), 111 (Lord Hope) & 138–41 (Baroness Hale) (H.L.) (appeal taken from Eng.).

16. ERIC BARENDT, FREEDOM OF SPEECH 44 (2d ed. 2005).

17. HRA 98, § 12(4).

18. BARENDT, *supra* note 16, at 39–48.

19. For a good overview and explanation of the proposal that Anthony Lester (among others) advocated in the late 1980s, see ANTHONY LESTER ET AL., A BRITISH BILL OF RIGHTS (Institute for Public Policy Research 1990).

20. *Id.* at 5.

21. *See infra* text and accompanying notes 105 to 147.

22. BARENDT, *supra* note 16, at 39.

23. GARDBAUM, *supra* note 11, at 41–46.

24. *Id.* at 169–74.

25. RONALD J. KROTOSZYNSKI, JR., PRIVACY REVISITED: A GLOBAL PERSPECTIVE ON THE RIGHT TO BE LEFT ALONE 120–32 (2016). Privacy rights have definitely expanded in the United Kingdom since 2000, although the SCUK has not created a broad or general right of privacy— instead, it has enhanced privacy protections at the margins, for example, by rewriting the tort of breach of confidence to safeguard the ability of an individual to prevent publication of her image or confidential medical information. *See id.* at 125–31. In the context of privacy, the British courts have taken a cautious, incremental, approach—but it cannot be gainsaid that judicial solicitude for privacy as a legal interest in greater in 2024 than it was in 1999. *See id.* at 132–42.

26. William L. Prosser, *Privacy*, 48 CALIF. L. REV. 383, 392–98 (1960) (discussing a privacy tort for public disclosure of private facts and explaining that the tort "consists of public disclosure of embarrassing private facts about the plaintiff" where the disclosure "would be offensive and objectionable to a reasonable man of ordinary sensibilities" with "[t]he interest protected [being] that of reputation, with the same overtones of mental distress that are present in libel and slander"). Of course, unlike defamation torts, public disclosure of private facts involves the dissemination of truthful, but embarrassing, information about the plaintiff. For a general discussion of Dean Prosser's contributions to the development of privacy law, see Daniel J. Solove & Neil M. Richards, *Prosser's Privacy Law: A Mixed Legacy*, 98 CALIF. L. REV. 1887 (2010).

27. *See* Campbell v. MGN, Ltd., [2004] 2 A.C. 457, para. 132–33 (H.L.) (Baroness Hale) (appeal taken from Eng.); *see also* KROTOSZYNSKI, *supra* note 25, at 127–28 (discussing the holding and reasoning in *Campbell* in some detail).

28. *See* Wainwright v. Home Office, [2003] U.K.H.L. 53, paras. 29, 34–35, 62 (appeal taken from Eng.).

29. *Id.* para. 29; *see Campbell*, [2004] A.C. 457, para. 133 (Baroness Hale) (observing "that case [*Wainwright*] indicates that our law cannot, even if wanted to, develop a general tort of invasion of privacy").

228 ꙮ Notes to pages 72–74

30. X & Y v. Netherlands, App. No. 8978/80, 8 Eur. H.R. Rep. 235, 239–40, para. 23, 241, para. 27, 242, para. 30 (1985) (holding that Article 8 of the European Convention for the Protection of Human Rights and Fundamental Freedoms may require signatory states to adopt "measures designed to secure respect for private life even in the sphere of the relations of individuals between themselves").

31. *Campbell*, [2004] 2 A.C. 457, para. 133 (Baroness Hale).

32. *See, e.g.*, Derbyshire Cnty. Council v. Times Newspapers Ltd, [1992] Q.B. 770 (C.A.); [1993] A.C. 534 (H.L) (appeal taken from Eng.) (holding that, under the common law of England, a local government could not sue for defamation based on critical public comments on the entity's actions and policies and relating such public criticism of the government and its officers to the process of democratic self-government).

33. GUIDO CALABRESI, A COMMON LAW FOR THE AGE OF STATUTES 2–3, 82–83, 161–71 (1982). Judge Calabresi posits that common law courts "can (without resort to constitutions or passive virtues or strained interpretations) alter a written law or some part of it in the same way (and with the same reluctance) in which they can modify or abandon a common law doctrine or even a whole complex set of interrelated doctrines." *Id.* at 82.

34. *See* Barendt, *supra* note 5, at 852–55 (noting that the HOL had already recognized the freedom of speech as an important common law right prior to the advent of the HRA 98). Professor Barendt posits that "[i]t may be that in these [pre-HRA 98] decisions, the House of Lords was deliberately anticipating the impact of incorporation of the ECHR" and "claiming for the common law an attachment to freedom of speech that earlier decisions did not strictly warrant." *Id.* at 854.

35. R. v. Shayler, [2003] 1 A.C. 247, para. 22 (Lord Bingham) (appeal taken from Eng.).

36. DAVID A. STRAUSS, THE LIVING CONSTITUTION (2010).

37. CHARLES EVANS HUGHES, ADDRESSES BY CHARLES EVANS HUGHS: 1906-1916, at 179, 185 (2d ed. 1916) (address of May 3, 1907 to the Elmyra Chamber of Commerce) (observing that "[w]e are under a Constitution, but the Constitution is what the judges say it is").

38. *See* HRA 98 §§ 3, 4, & 6.

39. *Id.* § 8(1) ("In relation to any act (or proposed act) of a public authority which the court finds is (or would be) unlawful, it may grant such relief or remedy, or make such order, within its powers as it considers just and appropriate.").

40. *See* A.V. DICEY, INTRODUCTION TO THE STUDY OF THE LAW OF THE CONSTITUTION 39-40, 42, 107 (1885). As Dicey explains the concept of parliamentary sovereignty, also known as parliamentary supremacy, Parliament has "the right to make or unmake any law whatsoever." *Id.* at 39–40; *see* P. S. ATIYAH & ROBERT S. SUMMERS, FORM AND SUBSTANCE IN ANGLO-AMERICAN LAW: A COMPARATIVE STUDY OF LEGAL REASONING, LEGAL THEORY, AND LEGAL INSTITUTIONS 55 ("It is elementary that no question of constitutional validity arises with respect to duly enacted statutes.").

41. *See* BARENDT, *supra* note 16, at 39 (noting that "[t]he appearance of the law is clearly different, in that courts examine rulings of the European Human Rights Court and sometimes explain their own decisions in term of the Convention").

42. Legal scholarship, both in the United States and the United Kingdom, deploys both "parliamentary sovereignty" and "parliamentary supremacy" to describe the British constitutional rule that, in a conflict between the judiciary and Parliament over the wisdom of a particular legal rule, the courts must defer to Parliament's legislative judgment—provided that Parliament expressed its policy preference through a procedurally correct means (viz, via a statute passed consistently with the rules of the House of Commons). These phrases

are completely synonymous and mean precisely the same thing. In this article, however, I will use "parliamentary sovereignty" to describe this vitally important British constitutional principle rather than "parliamentary supremacy." For clarity and in deference to the practice of British judges, lawyers, and legal scholars, save for quoted material, I will use "parliamentary sovereignty" because within the United Kingdom, in both judicial decisions and legal scholarship, authors most often use "parliamentary sovereignty" to refer to this constitutional principle. (As the saying goes, "When in Rome, do as the Romans.") That said, it bears noting that U.S. legal scholarship tends to use "parliamentary supremacy" to identify this bedrock principle of the U.K.'s "unwritten" constitution.

43. ATIYAH & SUMMERS, *supra* note 40, at 109 ("The English view is that most policy issues (and especially very controversial policy issues) raise substantive questions which are for the legislature to settle.").

44. Anthony Lester, *Free Speech, Religious Freedom and the Offence of Blasphemy*, in FREE EXPRESSION IS NO OFFENSE 211, 212 (Lisa Appignanesi ed., 2006).

45. *Id.*

46. *Id.*

47. *Id.*

48. *Id.* at 214.

49. *Id.*

50. *Id.*

51. [2001] 2 A.C. 127 (H.L) (appeal from Eng.).

52. [1992] Q.B. 770 (C.A.); [1993] A.C. 534 (H.L) (appeal from Eng.).

53. *See* R. v. Sec'y of State for the Home Dep't, Ex Parte Brind, [1991] 1 A.C. 696 (H.L.) (appeal from Eng.). Home Secretary Douglas Hurd promulgated an administrative regulation that prohibited television and radio stations from broadcasting "any matter which consists of or includes—any words spoken, whether in the course of an interview or discussion or otherwise, by a person who appears or is heard on the programme in which the matter is broadcast where—(a) the person speaking the words represents or purports to represent an organisation specified in paragraph 2 below or (b) the words support or solicit or invite support for such an organisation, other than any matter specified in paragraph 3 below." Directive of the Home Secretary (Oct. 19, 1988), *reprinted in Brind*, [1991] 1 App. Cas. at 711 (C.A.). The organizations covered by the regulation included "any organisation which is for the time being a proscribed organization for the purposes of the Prevention of Terrorism (Temporary Provisions) Act 1984 or the Northern Ireland (Emergency Provisions) Act 1978; and (b) Sinn Fein, Republican Sinn Fein and the Ulster Defence Association." *Id.*

54. *Id.* at 748–49, 757–58; *see* Ronald J. Krotoszynski, Jr., Brind & Rust v. Sullivan: *Free Speech and the Limits of a Written Constitution*, 22 FLA. ST. U. L. REV. 1, 11–14 (1994).

55. Lester, *supra* note 44, at 215.

56. *Id.*

57. LESTER ET AL., *supra* note 19, at 5.

58. *Id.*

59. *Id.*

60. *See* ATIYAH & SUMMERS, *supra* note 40, at 55–56, 227–29, 245, 267–70 (discussing the deeply embedded nature of the doctrine of parliamentary sovereignty and the British judiciary's reflexive deference to Parliament under this doctrine). Professors Atiyah and Summers explain that "English jurists were very slow to wake to the realization that the unlimited nature of Parliament's legislative powers was not a necessary truth, derived from the inherent

230 ᧥ Notes to pages 77–79

nature of a sovereign legislature, and that the United States Constitution illustrated a political society in which the law itself defined and limited the authority of law-making and law-applying bodies." *Id.* at 245.

61. Labour Party Manifesto (1997), http://www.labour-party.org.uk/ manifestos/1997/ 1997- labour-manifesto.shtml (last visited Feb. 22, 2022).

62. A. W. BRIAN SIMPSON, HUMAN RIGHTS AND THE END OF EMPIRE: BRITAIN AND THE GENESIS OF THE EUROPEAN CONVENTION 808 (2001).

63. *Id.*

64. Letters from E.B. Boothby to the Secretary General, Council of Europe (January 14, 1966) *reprinted in* K. R. Simmonds, *The United Kingdom and the European Convention on Human Rights*, 15 INT'L & COMP. L.Q. 539, 539–41 (1966); *see* Government White Paper, Rights Brought Home: The Human Rights Bill, CM 3782, para. 1.2 (Oct. 1997) ("In 1966 the United Kingdom accepted that an individual person, and not merely another State, could bring a case against the United Kingdom in Strasbourg (the home of the European Commission of Human Rights and Court of Human Rights, which were established by the Convention). Successive administrations in the United Kingdom have maintained these arrangements.") [hereinafter Rights Brought Home].

65. Simmonds, *supra* note 64, at 541.

66. R. v. Sec'y of State for the Home Dep't, [1991] 1 App. Cas. at 748–51.

67. HRA § 3.

68. *Id.* § 3(2)(b) (noting that the HRA 98 "does not affect the validity, continuing operation, or enforcement of any incompatible primary legislation").

69. *Id.* § 4(2) & (4).

70. *Id.* § 6(1).

71. *See id.* § 6(2).

72. *Id.* § 6(3)(a).

73. HRA § 8(1).

74. *Id.* § 12(4).

75. *Id.* § 13(1).

76. For example, the U.S. Supreme Court has squarely held that it must interpret and apply an international treaty independently for purposes of domestic law—even when a treaty expressly declares that a particular transnational juridical institution, such as the International Court of Justice (ICJ), will have the final word on the treaty's meaning. The Vienna Convention on Consular Relations (Vienna Convention) expressly vests the ICJ with interpretative primacy over its meaning—yet the U.S. Supreme Court has repeatedly held that it will interpret this treaty on its own for purposes of U.S. domestic law. *See* Medellin v. Texas, 552 U.S. 491, 514–19 (2008) (holding that the Supreme Court will decide for itself whether the Vienna Convention requires foreign nationals facing criminal charges in the United States to enjoy pretrial access to their country's consul and rejecting an ICJ ruling, which actually involved the very same litigant, that interpreted the Vienna Convention to mandate such consular access on a pretrial basis). Chief Justice John G. Roberts, Jr. explained that "whether the treaties underlying a judgment are self-executing so that the judgment [of an international tribunal like the ICJ] is directly enforceable as domestic law in our courts is, of course, a matter for this Court to decide." *Id.* at 519; *see* Sanchez-Llamas v. Oregon, 548 U.S. 331, 353–54 (2006) ("If treaties are to be given effect as federal law under our legal system, determining their meaning as a matter of federal law 'is emphatically the province and duty of the judicial department,' headed by the 'one supreme Court' established by the Constitution.") (internal citations omitted). It is ironic

Notes to pages 79–81 — 231

that the U.S. Supreme Court has repeatedly refused to defer to ICJ's interpretations of the Vienna Convention, instead insisting that it must interpret the Vienna Convention independently as a form of domestic law, whereas the SCUK has instead ignored Section 12(4)'s plain command that the domestic courts give "particular regard" to speech and press rights under the Article 10 of the European Convention because doing so might put the United Kingdom in breach of its European Convention duties. Simply put, the HRA 98's full text should be controlling on the British domestic courts—and this text includes Section 12.

77. *See* BARENDT, *supra* note 16, at 43–44 (noting that the domestic courts have effectively read Section 12(4) out of the HRA 98 and explaining that "[f]reedom of expression is not given any pre-eminence by the HRA 1998" despite "[t]his subsection . . . appear[ing] to give some priority to freedom of expression over competing rights"); *see also* Douglas v. Hello!, [2001] Q.B. 367, paras. 133–35 (holding that Section 3's directive to harmonize British domestic law with the European Convention and the ECtHR's case law interpreting it prevents affording freedom of expression even a relative priority over other European Convention-protected rights).

78. *See* Von Hannover v. Germany (No. 1), Application No. 59320/00, 40 EUR. H.R. REP. 1 (2005) (decided June 24, 2004). *But cf.* Von Hannover v. Germany (No. 2), Applications No. 40660/ 08 & 60641/08 (decided Feb. 7, 2012), http:// hudoc.echr.coe.int/sites/eng/pages/ search.aspx?i=001109029#{%22itemid%22:[%22001109029%22]} (holding that German domestic courts unduly restricted publication of photographs of Princess Caroline of Monaco, a person of apparently endless fascination to the German general public).

79. *See* Campbell v. MGN Ltd., [2004] A.C. 457 (Eng.); *see also* N. A. Moreham, *Privacy in Public Places*, 65 CAMBRIDGE L.J. 606, 617 (2006) (arguing that under English tort law "it is possible to have an expectation of privacy in public places").

80. *Campbell*, [2004] A.C. 457, para. 105 (opinion of Lord Hope).

81. *Id.*

82. *Id.* para. 111; *see* Douglas v Hello! Ltd, [2001] Q.B. 967, 1003, paras. 133, 137 (opining that, under the European Convention, no one right has a "presumptive priority" over another and that it necessarily follows that Section 12(4) "cannot, consistently with section 3 and article 17, give the article 10(1) right of free expression a presumptive priority over other rights"). As Lord Sedley explained in *Douglas*, Section 12(4) simply "require[s] the court to consider article 10(2) along with article 10(1), and by doing so to bring into the frame the conflicting right to respect for privacy." *Douglas*, [2001] Q.B., para. 137.

83. The United Kingdom ended its membership in the European Union on January 31, 2020, under the terms of a 2018 law implementing the United Kingdom's 2016 Brexit vote. *See* European Union (Withdrawal) Act 2018, 2018 ch. 16 (June 26, 2018).

84. GARDBAUM, *supra* note 11, at 156.

85. *Id.* at 11–15.

86. Joanna Dawson, Report 9406, House of Commons Library, Reform of the Human Rights Act 1998 (Dec. 21, 2021).

87. *Id.* at 5.

88. Bill of Rights Bill, Bill No. 117, 2022–23 (introduced June 22, 2022), https://bills.parliam ent.uk/bills/3227 (last visited Aug. 6, 2023).

89. Dawson, *supra* note 86, at 31.

90. *Id.* at 29.

91. Bill of Rights Act, § 4(1) ("When determining a question which has arisen in connection with the right to freedom of speech, a court must give great weight to the importance of protecting the right.").

232 ❧ Notes to pages 81–84

92. Bill of Rights Bill, UK Parliament, https://bills.parliament.uk/bills/3227 (last visited Aug. 7, 2023); The Law Society, *Human Rights Act Reforms and the Bill of Rights Bill*, https://www.lawsociety.org.uk/topics/human-rights/human-rights-act-reforms (last visited Aug. 8, 2023) ("On 27 June 2023, it was announced that the government will not be proceeding with the Bill of Rights Bill.") [hereinafter The Law Society, *Human Rights Act Reforms*].

93. The Law Society, *Human Rights Act Reforms, supra* note 92.

94. European Convention, art. 10(1).

95. *Id.* art. 10(2).

96. *See* Grant Huscroft et al., *Introduction, in* PROPORTIONALITY AND THE RULE OF LAW: RIGHTS, JUSTIFICATION, AND REASONING 1, 1–4 (Grant Huscroft et al. eds., 2014); *see also* AHRON BARAK, PROPORTIONALITY: CONSTITUTIONAL RIGHTS AND THEIR LIMITATIONS 32, 131–33 (Doron Kalir trans., 2012).

97. Vicki C. Jackson, *Being Proportional About Proportionality*, 21 CONST. COMMENT. 803, 803 (2004).

98. Huscroft et al., *supra* note 96, at 1.

99. ATIYAH & SUMMERS, *supra* note 40, at 54–55, 227–29. The doctrine of parliamentary sovereignty goes a long way toward explaining the reticence of most British judges to embrace policy-oriented reasoning and analysis. *See id.* at 55 (explaining that "[s]tatutes are of paramount authority, and any conflict between a statute and a judicial decision must be decided in favour of the statute" and "[i]t is elementary that no question of constitutional validity arises with regard to duly enacted statutes").

100. Charter of Fundamental Rights of the European Union, 2012/C 326/02 (Oct. 26, 2012), https://eur-lex.europa.eu/legal-content/EN/TXT/?uri=CELEX:12012P/TXT.

101. ATIYAH & SUMMERS, *supra* note 40, at 103.

102. *Id.* at 119.

103. *See id.* at 109 (noting that "the English view is that most policy issues (and especially very controversial policy issues) raise substantive questions which are for the legislature to settle").

104. Public Order Act 1986, 1986 ch. 64 (enacted Nov. 7, 1986 and entered into force on Apr. 1, 1987) (U.K.) [hereinafter POA 86].

105. *Id.* § 5(1)(a).

106. *Id.* § 5(1)(b).

107. *Id.* § 6(4).

108. Percy v. Dir. of Pub. Prosecutions, [2001] E.W.H.C. (Admin.) 1125, para. 34 (U.K.) (observing that "it is plain from the wording [of] section 5(1)—that the prosecution do not have to prove that the display of the poster in fact caused anyone harassment, alarm, or distress"). *Percy* involved the public display of a poster bearing the messages "Islam out of Britain" and "Protect the British people" and featuring an image of a burning World Trade Tower and a crescent star with a cancellation red slash over it. *See id.* para. 6.

109. POA 86 § 5(3)(a).

110. *Id.* § 5(3)(b).

111. *Id.* § 5(3)(c).

112. Brutus v. Cozens, [1973] A.C. 854 (appeal from Eng.), [1972] U.K.H.L. 6.

113. *Cf.* Bose Corp. v. Consumers Union of United States, Inc., 466 U.S. 485, 499 (1984) (explaining that "in cases raising First Amendment issues we have repeatedly held that an appellate court has an obligation to 'make an independent examination of the whole record' in order to make sure that 'the judgment does not constitute a forbidden intrusion on the field

Notes to pages 84–86

of free expression.' *New York Times Co. v. Sullivan*, 376 U. S. at 284-286."). Thus, in the United States under the First Amendment, an appellate court must review de novo adverse findings of fact when a public official or public figure libel plaintiff prevails against a media defendant.

114. *See id.* at 510–11 ("The requirement of independent appellate review reiterated in *New York Times Co. v. Sullivan* is a rule of federal constitutional law. It emerged from the exigency of deciding concrete cases; it is law in its purest form under our common-law heritage. It reflects a deeply held conviction that judges—and particularly Members of this Court—must exercise such review in order to preserve the precious liberties established and ordained by the Constitution.").

115. *Id.* at 511.

116. *Id.*

117. *See* Crime and Courts Act 2013, 2013 ch. 22, § 57 (2) & (3) (U.K.).

118. Patrick Strickland & Diana Douse, Library of the House of Commons, Standard Note SN/HA/5760, *"Insulting words or behaviour": Section 5 of the* Public Order Act 1986, at 15.

119. BARENDT, *supra* note 16, at 300.

120. *Id.*

121. Crown Prosecution Serv. v. Haque & Choudhury (Mar. 7, 2011) (Westminster Magistrates' Court), http://www.europeanrights.eu/public/sentenze/JEW7mar.pdf (last visited July 24, 2023); *see* BBC, *Man Guilty of Burning Poppies at Armistice Day Protest*, BBC News (Mar. 7, 2011), https://www.bbc.com/news/uk-england-london-12664346; Reuters Staff, *Muslim Men "Burned Poppies" in Anti-Army Demo*, REUTERS (Feb. 23, 2011, 8:14 AM), https://www.reuters.com/arti cle/uk-britain-poppies-idUKTRE71M45G20110223; *Police Accused of Over-Zealous Reaction to Poppy Burning*, THE GUARDIAN (Nov. 12, 2012, Nov. 13, 2012, 00:26), https://www.theguardian. com/uk/2012/nov/12/teenager-arrested-burning-poppy-facebook.

122. BARENDT, *supra* note 16, at 302.

123. Hammond v. Dir. of Pub. Prosecutions, [2004] E.W.H.C. 69, paras. 19, 21, 31–33 (Admin.).

124. Percy v. Dir. of Pub. Prosecutions, [2001] E.W.H.C. 1125 (Admin.); [2002] Crim. L. Rep. 835, paras. 4, 28–33.

125. Strickland & Douse, *supra* note 118, at 5–6 (collecting and citing cases and contemporary news coverage of arrests without subsequent prosecution).

126. *See* Annabelle Timsit, *Police Arrest Anti-Monarchy Protesters at Royal Events in England, Scotland*, WASH. POST (Sept. 13, 2022, 10:37 AM EDT), https://www.washingtonpost.com/ world/2022/09/13/queen-elizabeth-death-protests-arrest-police/ ("Lawyers and free-speech activists are ringing alarm bells after reports emerged in recent days of police detaining, moving and in some cases even arresting protesters at the events marking the death of Queen Elizabeth II and the accession of her eldest son, Charles.").

127. Emma Bubola & Megan Specia, *The London Police, with New Powers against "Serious Disruption," Arrest Dozens of Protesters*, N.Y. TIMES (May 6, 2023), https://www.nytimes.com/ 2023/05/06/world/europe/coronation-protests-arrests.html ("London's Metropolitan Police said they arrested 52 people on Saturday, most for offenses that appeared connected to the coronation of Charles III, including public order offenses, breach of the peace and conspiracy to cause a public nuisance. In the afternoon, the police said that all those arrested remained in custody."). The protestors were mainly affiliated with Republic, "the leading anti-monarchy group in Britain." *Id.*

128. Crown Prosecution Serv. v. Haque & Choudhury, *supra* note 121, at 1.

129. *Id.*

130. *Id.* at 3.

234 ✑ Notes to pages 86–88

131. *Id.* at 4.

132. *Id.* at 6.

133. *See* Hammond v. Dep't of Public Prosecutions, [2004] E.W.H.C. 69 (Admin.) (Eng.).

134. *Id.* para. 4.

135. *Id.*

136. *Id.*

137. *Id.* paras. 32–34.

138. *See* Adbul & Others v. Dir. of Pub. Prosecutions, [2011] E.W.H.C. (Admin.) 247 (U.K.).

139. *Id.* paras. 2, 16–18.

140. *Id.* para. 19.

141. *Id.* para. 61 (Lord Davis).

142. *See id.* (opining that "for purposes of the qualification contained in Article 10, it can properly be said, in this particular case, that prosecution and conviction was proportionate in pursuit of a legitimate aim not only of the prevention of disorder (although that of course is capable of being sufficient in itself) but also of the protection of the reputation or rights of others.").

143. *See, e.g.,* Morrow v. Dir. of Pub. Prosecutions, [1994] Crim. L. Rep. 58 (D.C.) (U.K.); Dir. of Pub. Prosecutions v. Clarke, Lewis, O'Connell & O'Keefe, [1992] Crim. L. Rep. 60 (D.C.) (U.K.); Dir. of Pub. Prosecutions v. Fidler, [1991] 94 Ct. App. R. 286 (C.A.) (U.K.).

144. Andrew Geddis, *Free Speech Martyrs or Unreasonable Threats to Social Peace?—"Insulting" Expression and Section 5 of the Public Order Act 1986,* 2004 PUB. L. 853, 857.

145. *Id.* at 856.

146. *Id.*

147. *Id.* at 857.

148. *See supra* text and accompanying notes 75 to 83.

149. R. (on the application of ProLife Alliance) v. BBC, [2004] 1 A.C. 185 (H.L.) (appeal from Eng.), [2003] U.K.H.L. 23.

150. Broadcasting Act 1990, 1990 ch. 42, pt. 1, ch. 1, § 6(1)(a) [hereinafter Broadcasting Act 1990].

151. Communications Act 2003, 2003 c. 21.

152. *Id.* § 319(2)(c).

153. *Id.* § 319(2)(h).

154. R. (on the Application of ProLife Alliance) v. BBC, [2004] 1 A.C. 185, [2003] U.K.H.L. 23, paras. 2–3; *see* BARENDT, *supra* note 16, at 46–47 (discussing and strongly criticizing the House of Lord's decision to uphold the ban against the political advertisements).

155. *ProLife Alliance,* [2003] U.K.H.L., para. 2.

156. *Id.*

157. *Id.* paras. 2–3.

158. *Id.* para. 3.

159. *Id.*

160. R. (on the Application of ProLife Alliance) v. BBC, [2002] 3 W.L.R. 1080, 1097-99 (C.A.) (app. from Eng.) (Laws, J.).

161. *ProLife Alliance,* [2003] U.K.H.L. 23, paras. 56–57 (Lord Hoffman) (opining that "[i]n the present case, that primary right was not engaged" because "[t]here is no human right to use a television channel").

162. *Id.* para. 58.

163. BARENDT, *supra* note 16, at 47.

Notes to pages 88–89 —∽ 235

164. *Id.*

165. *Id.*

166. Richard Scott, Lord Scott of Foscote, dissented from the HOL majority's decision to reverse the judgment of the Court of Appeal. *See ProLife Alliance*, [2003] U.K.H.L. 23, paras. 83–100 (Lord Scott). In his view, "[t]he conclusion to which the broadcasters came could not, in my opinion, have been reached without a significant and fatal undervaluing of two connected features of the case: first, that the programme was to constitute a party election broadcast; second, that the only relevant criterion for a justifiable rejection on offensiveness grounds was that the rejection be necessary for the protection of the right of homeowners not to be subjected to offensive material in their own homes." *Id.* para. 83. On the facts presented, and applying Article 10 of the European Convention and Section 3 of the HRA 98, the BBC's officials exceeded the lawful scope of their discretion in refusing to broadcast ProLife Alliance's electoral speech. *Id.* para. 100 (opining that "the decision of the BBC and the other broadcasters to refuse to transmit the Alliance's desired programme was, in my opinion, a decision to which no reasonable decision maker, applying the standards prescribed by paragraphs 5.1(d) of the BBC Agreement and section 6(1)(a) of the 1990 Act, and properly directing itself in accordance with Article 10, could have come.").

167. *See supra* text and accompanying notes 124 to 149.

168. *But cf. ProLife Alliance*, [2003] U.K.H.L.23, para. 68 (Lord Hoffmann) ("Although it may be said that all questions of social and economic policy are open to discussion in a general election, the Alliance PEB was quite unrelated to the specific policy of encouraging an informed choice at the ballot box. Their views were of electoral concern, at any rate theoretically, to the voters in only six of the Welsh constituencies."). Lord Hoffman seems to be saying that because it was unlikely that the ProLife Alliance's political speech would be effective at moving public opinion, the government's case for censoring it was stronger. The whole point of a legal provision like Article 10 of the European Convention, or the First Amendment, is to protect speech that most voters find distressing or offensive. Simply put, speakers seeking to propagate messages that are broadly popular seldom face the prospect of official government censorship. Thus, even if, as Lord Hoffman posits, ProLife Alliance's political advertisement would have been "of concern to very few of those voters," it is up to a would-be speaker, not the government, to fashion her message.

169. Lester, *supra* note 44, at 234.

170. Helena Kenney, *Postscript, in* Free Expression is No Offence 240, 245 (Lisa Appignanesi ed., 2006).

171. *See, e.g.*, Brutus v. Cozens, [1973] A.C. 854, [1972] U.K.H.L. 6, [1972] 56 Crim. App. 799 (H.L.) (appeal from Eng.) (imposing a limiting construction on Section 5 of the Public Order Act and holding that speech which is merely annoying or offensive is not subject to criminal prosecution under Section 5). Viscount Reginald Dilhorne explains that "[b]ehaviour which evidences a disrespect or contempt for the rights of others does not of itself establish that that behaviour was threatening, abusive or insulting." *Id.* at 810 (Viscount Dilhorne). Indeed, "[s]uch behaviour may be very annoying to those who see it and cause resentment and protests but it does not suffice to show that the behaviour was annoying and did annoy for a person can be guilty of annoying behaviour without that behaviour being insulting." *Id.* Lord James Reid expressly discusses the freedom of speech as a countervailing legal value and observes that "[i]t would have been going much too far to prohibit all speech or conduct likely to occasion a breach of the peace because determined opponents may not shrink from organising or at least threatening a breach of the peace in order to silence a speaker whose views they detest."

Id. at 805 (Lord Reid). This is obviously an implicit embrace of the U.S. free speech doctrine that prohibits a "heckler's veto." *See* HARRY KALVEN, JR., THE NEGRO AND THE FIRST AMENDMENT 140–41, 145 (1965). Professor Kalven is commonly credited with coining the phrase "heckler's veto" and then explicating a free speech theory that prohibits the government from permitting a hostile audience to silence an unpopular speaker. *See* Owen M. Fiss, *Free Speech and Social Structure*, 71 IOWA L. REV. 1405, 1412–16 (1986) (crediting Professor Kalven with originating the concept of the heckler's veto) . However, the concept's origins can be traced back to Justice William O. Douglas's majority opinion in *Terminiello* and Justice Hugo L. Black's dissenting opinion in *Feiner. See* Feiner v. New York, 340 U.S. 315, 326–29 (1951) (Black, J., dissenting); Terminiello v. Chicago, 337 U.S. 1, 4–6 (1949).

172. Niamh Kennedy et al., *"Something Out of a Police State": Anti-Monarchy Protesters Arrested ahead of King Charles' Coronation*, CNN.COM (May 6, 2023, 9:38 PM EDT), https://www.cnn.com/2023/05/06/uk/king-charles-anti-monarchy-protest-arrests-ckc-gbr-intl/index.html ("London's Metropolitan Police said it made 52 arrests during the coronation of King Charles III on Saturday, as the force faces growing scrutiny over its attitude toward anti-monarchy demonstrators."). Those arrested were released without being prosecuted—but the arrests had their intended effect, which was to stifle dissent associated with the coronation of Charles Windsor as the United Kingdom's new head of state and to render this dissent quite literally invisible. *See* Sean Seddon, *Coronation: Met Expresses "Regret" over Arresting Six Anti-Monarchy Protesters*, BBC.COM (May 9, 2023), https://www.bbc.com/news/uk-65527007 (reporting on arrests of members of Republic, including the group's leader, Graham Smith, when they attempted to engage in anti-monarchy speech the day of Charles Windsor's coronation ceremony at King Charles III); Daniel Boffey & Nicola Slawson, *Police Accused of "Alarming" Attack on Protest Rights After Anti-Monarchist Leader Arrested*, THE GUARDIAN (May 6, 2023, 19:46 EDT), https://www.theguardian.com/uk-news/2023/may/06/head-of-uks-leading-anti-monarchy-group-arrested-at-coronation-protest (reporting comments by Peter Tachell, a human rights activist in the United Kingdom, and one of the frustrated would-be protesters who complained that the police failed to honor promises to permit peaceful, non-violent protest during the coronation ceremony and celebrations "by arresting the head of Republic, seizing their placards and megaphones, submitting those here to photographic surveillance").

173. Barendt, *supra* note 5, at 851. It bears noting that Barendt's views about the efficacy of the HRA 98 are not universally shared within the U.K.'s legal academy. *See, e.g.,* Dominic McGoldrick, *The United Kingdom's Human Rights Act 1998 in Theory and Practice*, 50 INT'L & COMP. L.Q. 901, 901 (2001) ("The HRA of 9 November 1998 was a significant development in legal and political culture. It was imaginative and, in a sense, *revolutionary*.").

174. Barendt, *supra* note 5, at 851.

175. *See id.* at 851–52.

176. *Id.* at 866.

177. *Id.*

178. *See* RONALD J. KROTOSZYNSKI, JR., THE FIRST AMENDMENT IN CROSS-CULTURAL PERSPECTIVE: A COMPARATIVE LEGAL ANALYSIS OF THE FREEDOM OF SPEECH 141-43, 175-78, 181 (2006) (observing that the Supreme Court of Japan has invalidated national legislation very infrequently, but often uses creative interpretation of statutory language to reconcile statutes with the Constitution's guarantee of freedom of expression).

179. McGoldrick, *supra* note 173, at 904.

180. *Id.* at 949-50.

181. LESTER ET AL., *supra* note 19, at 11.

Notes to pages 91–94   ─◌ 237

182. *Id.*

183. *Id.*

184. *Id.* at 13.

185. *Id.*

186. *See* Michael Skold, Note, *The Reform Act's Supreme Court: A Missed Opportunity for Judicial Review in the United Kingdom?*, 39 U. CONN. L. REV. 2149, 2152 (2007) ("Dicey's conception of Parliamentary sovereignty has until quite recently been accepted in British legal, political and social circles as the foundation of British constitutionalism."); *see also id.* ("Austin's version of positivism . . . became the dominant tradition in England and so thoroughly influenced English lawyers and judges that it became almost literally inconceivable that the judges could ever have power to question the authority of Acts of Parliament.").

187. McGoldrick, *supra* note 173, at 952.

188. *Id.*

189. LESTER ET AL., *supra* note 19, at 25.

190. *Id.*

191. *Id.*

192. Letter from James Madison to Thomas Jefferson, Oct. 17, 1788, *available at* https://founders.archives.gov/documents/Madison/01-11-02-0218 (last visited June 30, 2021); *see also* RICHARD LABUNSKI, JAMES MADISON AND THE STRUGGLE FOR THE BILL OF RIGHTS 104-05, 160-64 (2006). It was left to Alexander Hamilton to defend the omission of a Bill of Rights to the public. *See* THE FEDERALIST NO. 84, at 510, 512-14 (Alexander Hamilton) (Clinton Rossiter ed., 1961).

193. James Madison's Letter to Thomas Jefferson, *supra* note 192.

194. For an excellent general explanation of how cultural values and expectations can exert significant and important influence over legal, and even constitutional norms, and analysis of how socio-legal culture profoundly shapes the law of constitutional privacy, see James Q. Whitman, *The Two Western Cultures of Privacy: Dignity Versus Liberty*, 113 YALE L.J. 1151, 1153-60 (2004). As Professor Whitman cogently explains, "[p]rivacy law is not the product of logic" nor is it "the product of 'experience' or of supposed 'felt necessities' that are shared in all modern societies." *Id.* at 1219. Instead, privacy law rules are "the product of local social anxieties and local ideals." *Id.* Socio-legal norms and expectations, rather than some universal, transcendent understanding of "privacy" as a fundamental human right, prefigures the scope and meaning of constitutional privacy protections within a particular domestic legal system. This would seem to hold true in the United Kingdom with respect to expressive freedom.

195. Hammond v. Dir. Pub. Prosecutions, [2004] EWHC 69 (Admin.) (U.K.) (convicting an street preacher of violating Section 5 based on the display of signs with anti-LGBTQ messages); Norwood v. Dir. of Pub. Prosecutions, [2003] E.W.H.C. 1564 (Admin.) (U.K.) (upholding a Section 5 conviction for the public display of a poster featuring "Islam out of Britain").

196. Ian Cram, *Coercing Communities or Promoting Civilised Discourse?: Funeral Protests and Comparative Hate Speech Jurisprudence*, 12 HUM. RTS. L. REV. 455, 468 (2012).

197. Geddis, *supra* note 144, at 869.

198. *Id.* at 870.

199. R. (on the application of Prolife Alliance) v. British Broad. Co., [2004] 1 App. Cas. 185 (appeal taken from Eng.).

200. *Id.* at paras. 56–59 (Hoffman).

201. *See* Barendt, *supra* note 5, at 858–59.

202. *Id.* at 859.

238

Notes to pages 94–95

203. Cohen v. California, 403 U.S. 15, 25 (1971) ("For, while the particular four-letter word being litigated here is perhaps more distasteful than most others of its genre, it is nevertheless often true that one man's vulgarity is another's lyric.").

204. *Id.* at 16–17.

205. Ronald J. Krotoszynski, Jr., Cohen v. California: *"Insignificant" Cases and Larger Legal Principles*, 74 TEX. L. REV. 1251, 1254 (1996) ("By distinguishing the question of full and free public debate from the particular content of the message (or the nature of the messenger), Justice Harlan vindicated the individual citizen's right to hold and share political views within the marketplace of ideas, and to communicate those ideas in unconventional—or even patently offensive—ways.").

206. *Cohen*, 403 U.S. at 16–17; *see* Cal. Penal Code § 415 (prohibiting "maliciously and willfully disturb[ing] the peace or quiet of any neighborhood or person . . . by . . . offensive conduct" and further providing that anyone convicted under this provision "is guilty of a misdemeanor, and upon conviction by any Court of competent jurisdiction shall be punished by fine not exceeding two hundred dollars, or by imprisonment in the County Jail for not more than ninety days, or by both fine and imprisonment, or either, at the discretion of the Court").

207. *Cohen*, 403 U.S. at 26.

208. Krotoszynski, *supra* note 205, at 1255 ("In language easily understood by most citizens, Justice Harlan explains—over the course of fewer than a dozen pages—why the First Amendment precludes the state from prohibiting a particular form of political expression. In this respect, the opinion is akin to a medieval morality play in which Everyman meets Free Expression.").

209. *Cohen*, 403 U.S. at 15.

210. *Id.*

211. *See* Snyder v. Phelps, 562 U.S. 443, 460–61 (2011) ("Speech is powerful. It can stir people to action, move them to tears of both joy and sorrow, and—as it did here—inflict great pain. On the facts before us, we cannot react to that pain by punishing the speaker. As a Nation we have chosen a different course—to protect even hurtful speech on public issues to ensure that we do not stifle public debate."). *Snyder* involved a highly offensive, targeted protest of the funeral mass and internment service of Marine Lance Corporal Matthew Snyder, who was killed in Iraq while on active duty. *See id.* at 448. Bearing signs with slogans including "God Hates the USA/ Thank God for 9/11," "God Hates Fags," and "Thank God for Dead Soldiers," Fred Phelps, the leader of the Westboro Baptist Church, based in Topeka, Kansas, targeted Matthew Snyder's funeral service and burial in the hope that their outrageous and offensive behavior attracting the attention of the mass media—and they succeeded in this ambition. *See id.* at 448–49.

212. *Cohen*, 403 U.S. at 26.

213. *See* ALEXANDER MEIKLEJOHN, FREE SPEECH AND ITS RELATION TO SELF-GOVERNMENT 24–27 (1948) (arguing the freedom of expression is integral to creating and sustaining a project of democratic self-government).

214. *See* Virginia v. Black, 538 U.S. 343 (2003) (holding that Ku Klux Klan cross burnings constitute constitutionally protected speech unless, on the facts and circumstances of the activity, the cross burning conveyed, on a targeted basis, a true threat).

215. Texas v. Johnson, 491 U.S. 397 (1989).

216. Snyder v. Phelps, 562 U.S. 442 (2011).

217. MEIKLEJOHN, *supra* note 213, at 88–91.

218. Alexander Meiklejohn, *The First Amendment Is an Absolute*, 1961 SUP. CT. REV. 245, 262 (arguing that "the authority of citizens to decide what they shall write and, more fundamental,

Notes to pages 95–101   239

what they shall read and see, has not been delegated to any of the subordinate branches of government").

219. *See* Martin Kwan, *Should There Be a Tort for Section 4A of the Public Order Act 1986?*, 1 J. RTS. & JUST. 4, 22–24 (2020).

220. *See* Alexander Brown, *Hate Speech Laws, Legitimacy, and Precaution: A Reply to James Weinstein*, 32 CONST. COMMENT. 599 (2017).

221. *Id.* at 609.

222. *Id.*

223. *But cf.* Boffey & Slawson, *supra* note 172 (reporting on thwarted Republic protesters, whom police in the United Kingdom arrested en masse on the day of King Charles III's coronation and noting that a frustrated protester believed that the arrests and seizure of the group's signs took place "so that the king would not see the protest as he passed by on the way to the palace"). After his arrest on coronation day, Republic's leader, Graham Smith, ruefully observed that "I have been told many times the monarch is there to defend our freedoms" but "[n]ow our freedoms are under attack in his name." *Id.*

224. *See* West Va. Bd. of Educ. v. Barnette, 319 U.S. 624 (1943).

225. *Id.* at 642.

226. *Id.*

227. Brown, *supra* note 220, at 614.

228. *Id.*

229. *Id.*

230. *See id.*

231. *Id.* (emphasis added).

232. *Id.*

233. [1973] A.C. 854 (H.L), [1972] U.K.H.L. 6 (U.K.).

234. Strickland & Douse, *supra* note 118, at 15 (emphasis added).

235. *Id.*

236. HC Deb. January 14, 2013 c 642.

237. Harrison Jones, *Coronation Arrests: Republic Leader Graham Smith Takes Legal Action*, BBC.COM, News (Sept. 12, 2023), https://www.bbc.com/news/uk-66786938 (reporting on the arrest of Republic protesters, including the group's leader, Graham Smith, and subsequent litigation challenging the legality of the arrests): Archie Bland, *Wednesday Briefing: How the Police Overstepped with Republican Protests*, THE GUARDIAN (Sept. 14, 2022, 01:52 EDT), https://www.theguardian.com/world/2022/sep/14/wednesday-briefing-the-police-response-to-displays-of-royal-dissent (reporting on arrests of pro-republic, anti-monarchy protestors at events associated with Queen Elizabeth's funeral services and on broad-based public criticism of the police for overreacting, noting that "[v]ery few observers were ready to defend police conduct over the arrests, with criticism from left and right over what many saw as a free speech issue").

238. Brown, *supra* note 220, at 615.

239. European Communities Act, 1972 ch. 68 (Oct. 17, 1972), § 2(1), *repealed by* European Union (Withdrawal) Act 2018, 2018 ch. 16 (June 26, 2018).

240. *See* R. v. Sec'y of State for the Home Dep't, Ex Parte Brind, [1991] 1 A.C. 696, 748–49 (H.L.) (concurring opinion of Lord Roskill) ("But again, this surely does not mean that in deciding whether the Secretary of State, in the exercise of his discretion, could reasonably impose the restriction he has imposed on the broadcasting organisations, we are not perfectly entitled to start from the premise that any restriction of the right to freedom of expression

240 ℘   Notes to pages 101–103

requires to be justified and that nothing less than an important competing public interest will be sufficient to justify it.").

241. *See* Frederick Schauer, *Giving Reasons*, 47 STAN. L. REV. 633, 635 (1995) ("When lawyers argue and when judges write opinions, they seek to justify their conclusions, and they do so by offering reasons."). Schauer explains that "[h]aving given a reason, the reason-giver has, by virtue of an existing social practice, committed herself to deciding those cases within the scope of the reason in accordance with the reason." *Id.* at 656. He warns that although "there are things we can think but cannot write down," this fact would not justify a judge in "believ[ing] an outcome to be correct when it could not be explained by a reason." *Id.* at 652.

242. HRA 98 § 12(4).

243. *See* STRAUSS, *supra* note 36, at 9 (explaining how little relevance the actual text of the First Amendment has to the warp and weft of "First Amendment" doctrine and jurisprudence). In the United States, Professor Strauss observes, the constitutional protection of expressive freedom, which he characterizes as "a tremendous success story" constitutes the product of "a living, common law Constitution." *Id.* at 52–53; *see* Eric J. Segall, *The Constitution Means What the Supreme Court Says It Means*, 129 HARV. L. REV. F. 176 (2016) (arguing that constitutional text matters far less than judges in resolving difficult constitutional questions and positing "that difficult and controversial constitutional problems are best decided by debating today's values and priorities, not contested interpretations of value and often outdated constitutional text); *see generally* Jud Campbell, *Natural Rights and the First Amendment*, 127 YALE L.J. 246, 256 (2017) (observing that "to the extent that Founding Era elites originally understood the First Amendment as imposing determinate limits on Congressional power, these limits were delineated by accepted common-law rules and by the inalienable nature right to make well-intentioned statements of one's thoughts).

CHAPTER 5

1. *See* Leanne Griffiths, *The Implied Freedom of Political Communication: The State of the Law Post Coleman and* Mulholland, 12 JAMES COOK U. L. REV. 93, 93 (2005) ("Although Australian law does not have an express guarantee of free speech, the High Court has acknowledged in various decisions that an implied freedom of communication exists under the Constitution in relation to political and governmental matters.").

2. *Cf.* U.S. CONST. amend. I ("Congress shall make no law . . . abridging the freedom of speech, or of the press; or the right of the people peaceably to assemble, and to petition the Government for a redress of grievances.").

3. Commonwealth of Australia Act, 1900 (Imp), 63 & 64 Victoria, c. 12, § 9 (U.K.), https://www.aph.gov.au/constitution (last visited May 5, 2023) [hereinafter AUSTRALIA CONST.].

4. The Australian Commonwealth Constitution entered into force on January 1, 1901, a date set by Queen Victoria on September 17, 1900. *See* SIR JOHN QUICK & SIR ROBERT RANDOLPH GARRAN, THE ANNOTATED CONSTITUTION OF THE AUSTRALIAN COMMONWEALTH 250–51 (1901). Quick and Garran explain that "[t]he prevailing opinion was in favour of the 1st January, 1901, the first date of the twentieth century—a dramatic and significant date for the birth of Australian nationhood." *Id.* at 250. A practical reason also existed, namely, that "the 1st January was the beginning of a financial half-year in all the colonies." *Id.*

5. Australian Capital Television Pty. Ltd. v. Commonwealth, (1992) 177 C.L.R. 106 (Austl.).

6. Nationwide News Pty Ltd v. Wills, (1992) 177 C.L.R. 1 (Austl.).

7. Theophanous v. Herald & Weekly Times Ltd., (1994) 182 C.L.R. 104 (Austl.).

Notes to page 104 ～241

8. Justice Michael Kirby, in *Levy*, suggests that the overarching question a reviewing court should ask and answer is "does the law which is impugned have the effect of preventing or controlling communication upon political and governmental matters in a manner which is inconsistent with the system of representative government for which the Constitution provides?" Levy v. Victoria, (1997) 1 C.L.R. 520, 646 (Kirby, J., concurring). A complete ban on speech obviously has the immediate and obvious effect of "preventing" and "controlling" communication related to democratic deliberation. Tailored speech regulations, on the other hand, are far less likely to completely "prevent" or "control" a citizen's ability to express an idea.

9. *See* Coleman v. Power, (2004) 220 C.L.R. 1, para. 105 (Austl.) (reading down Section 7(1)(d) of the Queensland Vagrants Act, which prohibits the use of "insulting" language in public, as trenching too deeply on the IFPGC absent a narrowing construction because "insults are a legitimate part of the political discussion protected by the Constitution" and "[a]n unqualified prohibition on their use cannot be justified as compatible with the constitutional freedom") (McHugh, J.). In his concurring opinion, Justice Kirby explains that "[f]rom its earliest history, Australian politics has regularly included insult and emotion, calumny and invective, in its armoury of persuasion" and, accordingly, "[t]hey are part and parcel of the struggle of ideas." *Id.* para. 239 (Kirby, J.).

10. Lange v. Australian Broadcasting Corp., (1997) 189 C.L.R. 520 (Austl.).

11. *Id.* at 566–68. For a relevant discussion and critique of this decision, see Adrienne Stone, *The Constitution and the Common Law: A Reply*, 26 MELB. U. L. REV. 646 (2002).

12. Indeed, the Justices have been quite explicit that the question for the judiciary is *not* whether the federal or a state government has enacted the most narrowly tailored, or even a carefully tailored, means to advance its legitimate purpose. Instead, a reviewing court should afford broad deference to the legislature's choice of means with respect to tailoring and invalidate a speech regulation only if it is patently unreasonable. *See Levy*, (1997) 1 C.L.R. at 598 (opining that "[u]nder our Constitution, the courts do not assume the power to determine that some more limited restriction than that imposed by an impugned law could suffice to achieve a legitimate purpose" and holding that "[t]he courts acknowledge the law-maker's power to determine the sufficiency of the means of achieving the legitimate purpose, reserving only a jurisdiction to determine whether the means adopted could reasonably be considered to be appropriate and adapted to the fulfilment of the purpose") (Brennan, C.J.). In other words, any "reasonable" means adapted to securing the government's "legitimate" purpose will suffice. Although the formal test for analyzing claims under the IFPGC now relies on something called "structured proportionality," the level of scrutiny under this test appears to be more or less exactly the same—and it constitutes a form of rationality review.

13. In the view of some Australian legal academics, the HCA's posture of broad deference is entirely appropriate. *See* Caroline Henckels, *Proportionality and the Separation of Powers in Constitutional Review: Examining the Role of Judicial Deference*, 45 FED. L. REV. 181, 182 (2017) (arguing that "the prospect of judges substituting their own views for those of the other branches of government in relation to factual assessments made by other branches of government raises significant concerns about the proper boundary of the judicial role"). However, it bears noting that this point of view is not universal. *See* Diana Sedgwick, *The Implied Freedom of Political Communication: An Empty Promise?*, 7 U. W. SYDNEY L. REV. 35, 55–56 (2003) ("It is my opinion that the wide margin of appreciation that courts have accorded Parliament since the 1992 decisions, where a relatively narrow margin of appreciation was employed, has resulted in a very loose standard of review being applied."). Professor Henckels warns that if judges

engage in evaluative reasoning when applying the IFPGC, they risk assuming a "de facto" legislative power. *See id.* at 185. She observes that the HCA has demonstrated a "concern that judges would be drawn into political or policy questions that were rightly the domain of the legislature" if the Justices "engage in evaluative reasoning and substitute their decisions for factual assessments made by other branches of government." *Id. But cf.* Marbury v. Madison, 5 U.S. (1 Cranch) 137, 177 (1803) ("It is emphatically the province and duty of the judicial department to say what the law is. Those who apply the rule to particular cases, must of necessity expound and interpret that rule. If two laws conflict with each other, the courts must decide on the operation of each."). Thus, from a U.S. perspective, the judicial duty under a constitutional system with judicially enforceable, entrenched rights *requires* and indeed *demands* that judges second-guess the policy choices of legislators when those choices abridge protected rights. *See, e.g.,* Cooper v. Aaron, 358 U.S. 1, 18 (1958) (holding that "the federal judiciary is supreme in the exposition of the law of the Constitution, and that principle has ever since been respected by this Court and the Country as a permanent and indispensable feature of our constitutional system" and that "[i]t follows that the interpretation of the Fourteenth Amendment enunciated by this Court . . . is the supreme law of the land, and Art. VI of the Constitution makes it of binding effect on the States").

14. *See* Rosalind Dixon, *Calibrated Proportionality*, 48 FED. L. REV. 92, 92 (2019) ("The High Court applies two broad tests to determine whether laws impermissibly burden the implied freedom of political communication ('IFPC') under the *Commonwealth Constitution*: a test of "structured proportionality" and a more traditional test, which asks whether a law is 'reasonably appropriate and adapted' to achieving a legitimate end in a manner compatible with the constitutionally prescribed system of representative and responsible government ('reasonably appropriate and adapted') formula.").

15. Comcare v. Banerji, (2019)] H.C.A. 23, paras. 17, 35–38, 42 (Austl.) (Kiefel, C.J., Bell, Keane, & Nettle, JJ.) (upholding a statute and implementing regulations that prohibit criticism of the government, if a government employer objects to an employee's off-the-clock private speech as "unreasonably or harshly critical" of the government).

16. Clubb v. Edwards & Preston v. Spencer, (2019) H.C.A. 11, paras. 100–102 (*Clubb*) & paras. 126–29 (*Preston*) (Austl.) (Kiefel, C.J., Bell & Keane, JJ.) (upholding unanimously flat speech bans on anti-abortion protests within a 164-yard radius of property associated with a reproductive care clinic).

17. LibertyWorks Inc. v. Commonwealth, (2021) H.C.A. 18, paras. 74–85 (Austl.) (Kiefel, C.J., Keane & Gleeson, JJ.) (upholding mandatory registration requirements for foreign speakers under the Foreign Influence Transparency Scheme Act 2018).

18. *Id.* para. 85 (emphasis added).

19. *See* Sedgwick, *supra* note 13, at 55 ("This raises the question as to why our legislators should be accorded the respect of being provided with real and qualitative analyses of legislation proven to be invalid, while the individual, who has taken action on the basis that they believe their constitutional right has been infringed, is often treated with disrespect."). Professor Sedgwick goes so far as to posit that, prior to the adoption of structured proportionality review, "the restrictive impact the impugned legislation may be having on the individual's right to speak freely on political matters, is often discounted or not even examined." *Id.* at 55. Even though the effect of laws on would-be speakers is now part of the formal legal analysis under the *McCloy* formulation of structured proportionality, the results have not changed one whit—at least arguably, this has the unfortunate effect of degrading, rather than elevating, an individual's interest in speaking her version of truth to power.

Notes to pages 104–105 243

20. *Clubb* and *Preston*, the abortion protest cases, are particularly instructive. The HCA sustained a ban on any "protest" activity within 150 meters of a family planning clinic. *Clubb*, (2019) H.C.A. 11, paras. 100–102, 126–28. It bears noting that 150 meters is equivalent to 164 yards—or more than an entire U.S. football field (by 44 yards). The state of Victoria claimed that such a ban, which encompassed 70,000 square meters, was essential to protecting the dignity and safety of clinic patients and staff. This is obviously an important, indeed compelling, government interest. And, it certainly bears noting that the Supreme Court of the United States has upheld, against First Amendment challenges, targeted regulations that limit speech activities proximate to family planning clinics. *See* McCullen v. Coakley, 573 U.S. 464 (2014); Hill v. Colorado, 530 U.S. 703 (2000); Schenck v. Pro-Choice Network of W. N.Y., 519 U. S. 357 (1997); Madsen v. Women's Health Ctr., Inc., 512 U.S. 753 (1994). Under these precedents, a buffer zone of thirty-six feet, or eleven meters, is constitutionally permissible to secure free access to a family planning clinic—but a three-hundred-foot (or ninety-one meter) buffer zone is not.

In Australia, by way of contrast, a flat ban on protest activity over a football field away is evidently consistent with the IFPGC. It would also be possible, quite easily, to restrict approaching staff and patients with a "bubble" of something like ten yards, or thirty feet, that would prevent any direct harassment or intimidation. The purpose—and effect—of these state laws was to deny entirely the ability of anti-abortion protestors to communicate within the sight or hearing of family planning clinic staff or patients. This would seem to constitute a flat ban on communication of this kind—at least if the IFPGC encompasses the ability to deliver a message to a particular target audience. In consequence, *Clubb* and *Preston* would suggest that the IFPGC *does not* include the right to interact with a particular audience. This is quite odd if the purpose of the IFPGC is to facilitate democratic deliberation, an interest that arguably requires access to specific voters in order to convince them to change their views about a particular question of public policy.

21. *See* P. S. Atiyah & Robert Summers, Form and Substance in Ango-American Law: A Comparative Study of Legal Reasoning, Legal Theory, and Legal Institutions 55 (1987) (explaining that in the United Kingdom "[s]tatutes are of paramount authority, and any conflict between a statute and a judicial decision must be decided in favor of the statute").

22. Haig Patapan, Judging Democracy: The New Politics of the High Court of Australia 41–50, 59–65 (2000).

23. Lisa Burton Crawford, Patrick, & Dale Smith, *Introduction, in* Law under a Democratic Constitution: Essays in Honour of Jeff Goldsworthy 1–3 (Lisa Burton Crawford, Patrick Emerton & Dale Smith eds., 2019).

24. *Id.* at 1. Professor Jeff Goldsworthy is a primary expositor and advocate of Australia's principal reliance on elected politicians, rather than unelected judges, to serve as the primary guardians of fundamental rights. *See, e.g.*, Jeffrey Goldsworthy, Parliamentary Sovereignty: Contemporary Debates 9–13 (2010) (offering a spirited defense of parliamentary sovereignty and Australia's local species of this approach to safeguarding human rights). Indeed, Professor Richard Ekins describes Goldsworthy as "the foremost scholar" of the doctrine of parliamentary sovereignty, which serves as "the centrepiece of the British constitutional order," compares his work on the subject favorably to that of A. V. Dicey, and argues that "[t]he significance of Goldsworthy's work lies not only in its painstaking exposition of the historical and jurisprudential foundations of the doctrine, but also in its measured yet forceful defence of entrusting Parliament with responsibility for final lawmaking choice." Richard Ekins, *Models of (and Myths About) Rights Protection, in* Crawford et al., *supra* note 23, at 227.

244   Notes to page 105

Professor Goldsworthy argues that "ordinary people have a right to participate on equal terms in the political decision-making that affects their lives as much as anyone else's, and should be presumed to possess the intelligence, knowledge and virtue needed to do so." Goldsworthy, *supra*, at 9–10. He believes that under majoritarian rule, "clear injustices will be relatively rare, and that in most cases, whether or not the law violates someone's rights will be open to reasonable disagreement." *Id.* at 10. The rather obvious problem with this model: Adolph Hitler and Benito Mussolini came to power through the democratic process and, after coming to power, the "clear injustices" that they perpetrated were not addressed—save by the Allied troops that deposed their governments.

25. PATAPAN, *supra* note 22, at 60.

26. *Id.*

27. John Hart Ely's structural approach to judicial review, under which courts should not attempt to identify or protect fundamental rights (whether enumerated or not), but rather should adopt a "representation-reinforcing orientation" that "recognizes the unacceptability of the claim that appointed and life-tenured judges are better reflectors of conventional values than elected representatives" and, consistent with the approach to judicial review, should focus on "policing the mechanisms by which the system seeks to ensure that our elected representatives will actually represent." JOHN HART ELY, DEMOCRACY AND DISTRUST: A THEORY OF JUDICIAL REVIEW 101–03 (1980). This approach seems quite consistent with Australia's theory and practice of democratic constitutionalism.

28. *See* Ronald Dworkin, *The Secular Papacy*, in JUDGES IN CONTEMPORARY DEMOCRACY: AN INTERNATIONAL CONVERSATION 67, 76–77, 83 (Robert Badinter & Stephen Breyer eds., 2004) (discussing the demise of "the old parliamentary model" after the "horrifying tyrannies of the short but terrible twentieth century" that "shattered the Whig assumption that the developing political traditions and sensibilities of industrial nations would naturally produce decent government" and rendered untenable the premise that "parliamentary sovereignty—unlimited power in the hands of the elected representatives of the people—would provide an adequate guarantee of individual rights against the people"). Professor Dworkin argues that the radical breakdown of democratic self-government into totalitarian dictatorship rendered untenable faith in the idea of "naturally good people reasoning together and collectively developing, out of their innate sense of justice, a governing ethos that disciplines the successful development of civil society." *Id.* at 83. In most constitutional democracies, after World War II, thoughtful citizens understood "it was no longer true (if it ever was) that their elected leaders were statesmen with a noble calling" rather than "politicians bent on re-election above all else." *Id.* at 77. Dworkin also posits that the "increasing ethnic and cultural pluralism of nation states, together with the increasing association of those nation states in larger and inevitably culturally diverse political communities like the European Union, made the old assumptions about social convergence on a moral sense newly implausible." *Id.* These historical facts, and social trends, "help to explain why people began to distrust the parliamentary model and were tempted by the different (and in some respects older) idea of Montesquieu and of the eighteenth-century American formation—that it is a mistake to use one lever for both ideals of good government and that the moral brake should be separated from the social accelerator." *Id.* Under the new paradigm, "judges, among all the institutional possibilities" now "hold the brake" and "express and guard a political conscience." In contemporary Australia, if indeed the judges "hold the brake," they do not seem much of a mind to use it either with great frequency or force—at least in the specific context of protecting expressive freedom.

Notes to page 105 ⎯⌀ 245

29. *See* Sedgwick, *supra* note 13, at 40 ("In Australia, our courts are wary about assessing the legitimacy of government objectives.").

30. Cheryl Saunders & Adrienne Stone, *Introduction, in* THE OXFORD HANDBOOK OF THE AUSTRALIAN CONSTITUTION 1, 10 (Cheryl Saunders & Adrienne Stone eds., 2018) (observing that "[t]he prevailing approach to constitutional reasoning, widely accepted as appropriate, is often described as 'Australian legalism'" an approach that "gives priority to constitutional text and structure and generally eschews express reliance on external considerations but nevertheless allows for some flexibility in outcomes, drawing on judicial techniques honed in the development of the common law") [hereinafter THE OXFORD HANDBOOK TO THE AUSTRALIAN CONSTITUTION].

31. Of course, if, counterfactually, the federal parliament proposed an amendment that explicitly protects the freedom of speech, and Australia's voters were to ratify that amendment, it is possible that the HCA would take notice—just as Canada's Supreme Court adopted a more aggressive stance vis-à-vis the national parliament in Ottawa after the Charter of Rights and Freedoms came into force in 1982. The Charter fundamentally reshaped and expanded the role of the Supreme Court of Canada in defining and safeguarding fundamental human rights. Although even this prediction could be contested with regard to the HCA. After all, the U.K.'s House of Lords, and currently the Supreme Court of the United Kingdom, did not deploy the United Kingdom's Human Rights Act 1998 to bring about a fundamental revolution in the relationship of the British courts and Parliament in defining and safeguarding the fundamental rights set forth in the European Convention for the Protection of Human Rights and Fundamental Freedoms; the addition of an express textual warrant for the domestic U.K. courts to recognize and protect fundamental rights did not change the pre-existing judicial culture in the United Kingdom. *See supra* Chapter 3. The judicial culture in the Australia, which closely mirrors that of the United Kingdom's Supreme Court, at least with respect to the limited role for judges and courts in making or changing major social policies, might well carry the day in Australia despite the adoption of a constitutional amendment expressly safeguarding expressive freedoms. Even before the advent of the Charter of Rights and Freedoms, Canada's Supreme Court was a less reticent juridical body—for example, claiming and then exercising the power of judicial review in defense of federalism—than either the HCA or the Supreme Court of the United Kingdom. The minimalist judicial enforcement of the few existing rights in Australia's 1901 Constitution would suggest that codification might not make a significant difference in the willingness of the Justices to invalidate duly enacted statutes.

32. *See* James B. Thayer, *The Origins and Scope of the American Doctrine of Constitutional Law*, 7 HARV. L. REV. 129, 129, 144–48, 151–56 (1893) (arguing that courts should use judicial review sparingly to invalidate statutes and should, generally, defer to a legislature's reasonable judgment that a law complies with constitutional constraints but cautioning that courts have a duty to invalidate plainly or patently unconstitutional enactments); *see also Symposium, One Hundred Years of Judicial Review: The Thayer Centennial Symposium*, 88 NW. U. L. REV. 1 (1993) (discussing and critiquing Thayerian constitutional review). For an excellent and detailed examination of the virtues and potential vices of the Thayerian model of judicial review, using a comparative analytical lens, see Mark Tushnet, *Policy Distortion and Democratic Debilitation: Comparative Illumination of the Countermajoritarian Difficulty*, 94 MICH. L. REV. 245 (1995). The HCA's construction and contemporary enforcement of the IFPGC appears to adhere very closely to Thayer's rule that only a "clear error" can justify judicial refusals to implement properly enacted statutes. *See* Thayer, *supra*, at 144 (arguing that judicial invalidation of a properly enacted statute should not take place unless "those who have the right to

make laws have not merely made a mistake, but have made a very clear one—so clear that it is not open to rational question").

33. *See* Ronald J. Krotoszynski, Jr., *Common Law Constitutionalism and the Protean First Amendment*, 25 U. Pa. J. Const. L. 1 (2023).

34. *See* David A. Strauss, The Living Constitution 34 (2010) (observing that "when a case involves the Constitution, the text routinely gets no attention" and arguing that "[o]n a day-to-day basis, American constitutional law is about precedents, and when the precedents leave off, it is about commonsense notions of fairness and good policy"). Professor Strauss warns that "[n]o nation can survive for as long as ours has, and can live through so much, without learning, changing, and adapting." *Id.* at 139. The common law process of reasoning is the means through which courts facilitate and implement this process of interstitial change and adaptation. *See* Krotoszynski, *supra* note 33, at 51–58.

35. Adrienne Stone, *Expression*, in Saunders & Stone eds., The Oxford Handbook of the Australian Constitution *supra* note 30, at 952, 956–57 ("That is, Australian judges, more than any of their counterparts in the common law world, adhere to the idea that judges should, so far as possible, decide cases by reference only to *legal* materials and without reference to ideas, concepts, or values without a firm legal basis."). There is, however, an inherent tension between this conception of a constitutional court's proper role and the theory and practice of common law legal reasoning—which draws, in no small part, on the traditions and conceptions of justice that hold sway within a particular socio-legal community.

36. *Id.* at 973, 975 (noting the relevance of history and tradition to the outcome of major IFPGC decisions).

37. Luke Beck, Australian Constitutional Law: Concepts and Cases 18, 24–25 (2020); *see* Scott Stephenson, *Rights Protection in Australia*, in The Oxford Handbook of the Australian Constitution Saunders & Stone, eds., *supra* note 30, at 905–15 (discussing in some detail the conscious decision to omit a bill of rights from the Australian Constitution). Professor Stephenson explains that "[t]he initial decision not to include a bill of rights in the Constitution was grounded in a belief in the capacity of representative democracy to protect rights and a fear that a bill of rights would prevent the States from enacting racially discriminatory legislation." Stephenson, *supra*, at 906. Thus, although the Australian drafters borrowed many design elements from the U.S. Constitution, they declined to include a written bill of rights. *See* Beck, *supra*, at 18 ("While they rejected the presidential system of government and a comprehensive Bill of Rights, in other respects they found in the American system, what Sir Owen Dixon described as 'an incomparable model.'").

38. *See* Sedgwick, *supra* note 13, at 40–41. Professor Sedgwick explains that "[u]nder the British system, Parliament was given unlimited power because it was believed that the individual would not be harmed by this wide power," *id.* at 40, presumably because democratic elections (admittedly with very restricted voting rights for most British citizens for a very long period of time) would ensure that government would not adopt manifestly unjust laws.

39. Australia Const. §§ 7, 24, 64, & 128 (providing for elections and voting for the federal parliament and for amendments to the Commonwealth Constitution).

40. *Id.* §§ 80 (trial by jury), 116 (religious freedom and freedom from a state-established church), 117 (nondiscrimination against citizens of other states).

41. Australia Const. § 117 ("A subject of the Queen, resident in any State, shall not be subject in any other State to any disability or discrimination which would not be equally applicable to him if he were a subject of the Queen resident in such other State.").

Notes to pages 106–107

42. U.S. CONST. art. IV, § 2, cl. 1 ("The Citizens of each State shall be entitled to all Privileges and Immunities of Citizens in the several States.").

43. AUSTRALIA CONST. § 116 ("The Commonwealth shall not make any law for establishing any religion, or for imposing any religious observance, or for prohibiting the free exercise of any religion, and no religious test shall be required as a qualification for any office or public trust under the Commonwealth.").

44. *Id.* § 117.

45. *Id.* § 51(xxxi) (authorizing the "acquisition of property on just terms from any State or person for any purpose in respect of which the Parliament has power to make laws").

46. Commonwealth v. Tasmania, (1983) 158 C.L.R. 1, 289 (Austl.) (Deane, J) ("The effect of the paragraph is that a law providing for an acquisition of property for the purposes of the Commonwealth otherwise than on just terms is invalid."). The HCA will also grant broad discretion to the federal parliament to decide what constitutes "just terms." *See id.* (holding that "[i]t is implicit in s 51(xxi) that it is for the Parliament to determine what is the appropriate compensation in respect of an acquisition. If that compensation satisfies the requirement of 'just terms,' the Court will not declare the terms unjust and the law in excess of power for the reason that the Court entertains an opinion that other terms would have been fairer or more appropriate").

47. Saunders & Stone, *supra* note 30, at 8 (observing that "[t]he Australian Constitution is thin, in terms of substance rather than status" and explaining that "[m]ost notably, it provides little direct protection for rights; on one view of the jurisprudence, no protection at all, if rights can be distinguished from limits on power").

48. *Id.*

49. *See* GOLDSWORTHY, *supra* note 24, at 9–16, 77–83 (arguing that elected legislators, rather than judges, should be the principal expositors and defenders of fundamental human rights because they, unlike judges, possess an electoral mandate that validates their moral judgements); *see also* Crawford et al., *supra* note 23, at 2–3 (discussing the theory and practice of democratic constitutionalism in Australia).

50. Australian Capital Television Pty Ltd v. Commonwealth, (1992) 177 C.L.R. 106 (Aus.); Nationwide News Pty Ltd v. Wills, (1992) 177 C.L.R. 1 (Aus.). The High Court has regularly heard and decided cases involving the implied freedom of political and governmental communication since recognizing the implied right in 1992. *See, e.g.*, LibertyWorks Inc. v. Commonwealth, , (2021)H.C.A. 18 (Austl.); Comcare v. Banerji, (2019) H.C.A. 23 (Austl.). That said, however, at least one member of the High Court rejects the recognition of fundamental rights, including freedom of speech, through implications from other constitutional clauses. *See LibertyWorks*, [2021] H.C.A. 18, para. 249 (Steward, J., concurring) (opining that "it is arguable that the implied freedom does not exist" and positing that the implied freedom "may not be sufficiently supported by the text, structure and context of the Constitution"). Justice Simon Steward argues that "because of the continued division within this Court about the application of the doctrine of structured proportionality, it is still not yet settled law." *Id.* At present, however, these views do not command a majority at the HCA. Instead, a clear and strong majority stands by the precedents recognizing the implied freedom of political and governmental communication; on the other hand, disagreement exists among the Justices over the precise constitutional standard of review that should govern in free speech cases.

51. Stone, *supra* note 35, at 955 ("Stated in brief, the High Court reasoned that freedom of political communication is 'indispensable' to the proper operation of these aspects of the Constitution [the electoral provisions]."). Stone explains that "freedom of political

248 ⌒ Notes to pages 107–108

communication ensures that the choice of representatives exercised by voters under section 7 and 24 is a 'true choice.'" *Id.*

52. *LibertyWorks*, (2021) H.C.A. 18, para. 44.

53. *Id*. para. 45.

54. Comcare v. Banerji, (2019) H.C.A. 23, para. 20 (Austl.) (Kiefel, C.J., Bell, Keane & Nettle, JJ.).

55. *Id*. para. 44. *But cf*. MARTIN H. REDISH, THE ADVERSARY FIRST AMENDMENT: FREE EXPRESSION AND THE FOUNDATIONS OF AMERICAN DEMOCRACY 31–33, 71–74 (2013) (arguing that free expression can best be understood as empowering individuals to seek out information and ideas that enable them to be well-informed and engaged citizens). Professor Redish posits that "[t]he adversary theory of democracy emphasizes individual autonomy as theoretically and practically interwoven into the process of collective self-government." *Id*. at 5. Redish's theoretical framework is essentially the mirror image of the HCA's approach; he explains that "[a]dversary theory thus contrasts sharply with exclusively participatory versions of democratic theory because those theories systematically marginalize pure exercises of individual autonomy, considering individual autonomy to be relevant to democracy only to the extent it facilitates collective autonomy." *Id*. at 11.

56. *LibertyWorks*, (2021) H.C.A. 18, para. 44.

57. *See* Robert H. Bork, *Neutral Principles and Some First Amendment Problems*, 47 IND. L.J. 1, 28 (1971) (arguing that "[t]he notion that all valuable types of speech must be protected by the first amendment confuses the constitutionality of laws with their wisdom" and positing that protection of non-political expression "rests, as does freedom for other valuable forms of behavior, upon the enlightenment of society and its elected representatives" which is "hardly a terrible fate"). *But cf*. Alexander Meiklejohn, *The First Amendment Is an Absolute*, 1961 SUP. CT. REV. 245, 262 ("Shall the government establish a censorship to distinguish between 'good' novels and 'bad' ones? And, more specifically, shall it forbid the publication of novels that portray sexual experiences with a frankness that, to the prevailing conventions of our society, seems 'obscene'? The First Amendment seems to me to answer that question with an unequivocal 'no.'"). Meiklejohn emphatically rejects the Bork approach, arguing with considerable force that "[i]t is 'reserved to the people,' each deciding for himself to whom he will listen, whom he will read, what portrayal of the human scene he finds worthy of his attention." Meiklejohn, *supra*, at 262.

58. *LibertyWorks*, (2021) H.C.A. 18, paras. 45–46.

59. Clubb v. Edwards & Preston v. Spencer, (2019) H.C.A. 11, para. 41 (Austl.) (Kiefel, C.J., Bell & Keane, JJ.) ("The first step in applying the *McCloy* test is to ask whether the communication prohibition burdens the implied freedom. To answer that question, it is necessary to consider the terms, legal operation and practical effect of the statute.").

60. *Id*. para. 44.

61. *See id*. paras. 61–84.

62. *Id*. paras. 100–102 (*Clubb*) & 126-129 (*Preston*).

63. *Id*. para. 66.

64. *See, e.g.*, McCullen v. Coakley, 573 U.S. 464 (2014) (invalidating, in part, provisions of a Massachusetts state law because the Supreme Court deemed the state's protest restrictions overly broad and insufficiently narrowly tailored to pass constitutional review).

65. *Clubb*, (2019) H.C.A., para. 66.

66. *Id*.

67. *Id*. at 69 (quoting Brown v. Tasmania, (2017) 261 C.L.R. 323, 422–23).

Notes to pages 108–112   249

68. *Id.*

69. *Id.* para. 70.

70. It bears noting that some legal scholars support the HCA's posture of broad deference as to means as necessary to respect the separation of powers. *See* Henckels, *supra* note 13, at 197 ("To afford a measure of deference to the other branches of government in situations of normative or empirical uncertainty is to respect the democratic legitimacy or the greater institutional competence or expertise of another branch of government, when those characteristics make the opinion or judgment of the branch more reliable than that of the judiciary.").

71. *Clubb*, (2019) H.C.A., para. 83.

72. *Id.*

73. *Id.* para. 84.

74. *See id.* para. 116–17 (holding that differences between the Victorian and Tasmanian state laws "do not warrant a different result in the Preston appeal").

75. *Id.* para. 184 (Gageler, J.).

76. *Id.*

77. *Id.*

78. *Id.*

79. *Id.* para. 213.

80. (2019) H.C.A. 23 (Austl.).

81. *See id.* para. 42 (Kiefel, CJ, Bell, Keane & Nettle JJ) (holding that "the impugned provisions . . . present as a plainly reasoned and focussed response to the need to ensure that the requirement of upholding the APS Values and the integrity and good reputation of the APS trespasses no further upon the implied freedom than is reasonably justified").

82. *See id.* paras. 16–17.

83. *Id.* paras. 31–36.

84. *Id.* para. 31.

85. *Id.*

86. *See id.* para. 2.

87. McAuliffe v. Mayor of City of New Bedford, 155 Mass. 216, 220, 29 N.E. 517, 517 (1892) ("The petitioner may have a constitutional right to talk politics, but he has no constitutional right to be a policeman.").

88. *Id.*

89. *Id.*

90. By way of contrast, in the United States, the First Amendment affords meaningful protection to government employees who speak out, whether on or off the clock, about matters of public concern. *See* Pickering v. Bd. of Educ., 391 U.S. 563, 568–69, 572–75 (1968) (holding that the Free Speech Clause of the First Amendment protects government employees from discharge for speaking out as citizens about matters of public concern, unless the government can show that the employee's presence in the workplace would be unduly disruptive).

91. *Banerji*, [2019] H.C.A. 23, para. 164 (Edelman, J.).

92. *Id.*

93. *Id.*

94. *Id.*

95. Josh Butler & Sarah Martin, *Scott Morrison Secretly Appointed to Five Ministries, Including Treasury and Home Affairs, Says PM*, THE GUARDIAN (Aug. 16, 2022, 06:02 EDT), https://www.theguardian.com/australia-news/2022/aug/16/scott-morrison-five-more-secret-ministries-minister-portfolio-ministry-including-treasury-home-affairs ("The prime minister, Anthony

250 ~ Notes to pages 112–113

Albanese, says Scott Morrison was appointed to five additional ministries, including Treasury and home affairs, labelling his predecessor's actions an 'unprecedented trashing of our democracy'.").

96. *See Banerji*, (2019) H.C.A. 23, para. 17 (describing grounds for discipline as including "comment made on public or social issues" in the mass media if the comment would raise questions about "bias" on the part of an employee, if the comment is "so harsh or extreme in its criticism of the government, a member of Parliament or other political party" as to "call into question the employee's ability to work professionally, efficiently, or impartially," if the comment "could disrupt the workplace," or is "unreasonably or harshly critical of departmental stakeholders, their clients or staff"). The proscription against "critical" comments about a public employee's government agency are extraordinarily broad and also quite ambiguous ("overbroad" and "vague" in the parlance of U.S. First Amendment doctrine).

97. *See* Ronald J. Krotoszynski, Jr., *Whistleblowing Speech and the First Amendment*, 93 IND. L.J. 267 (2018).

98. AUSTRALIA CONST. § 116.

99. Section 116 has been limited in its scope to legislation (as opposed to executive and judicial actions) and, even with respect to legislation, provides very limited protection against neutral laws of general applicability. *See* Mitchell Landrigan, *Can the Implied Freedom of Political Discourse Apply to Speech by or about Religious Leaders?*, 34 ADELAIDE L. REV. 427, 433 (2014) ("The High Court has not given a broad interpretation to the free exercise provision or s 116 more generally.").

100. *See id.* at 432–35.

101. McGinty v. W. Australia, (1996) 186 C.L.R. 140, 140, 168 (Brennan, C.J) (Austl.) ("Implications are not devised by the judiciary; they exist in the text and structure of the Constitution and are revealed or uncovered by judicial exegesis. No implication can be drawn from the Constitution which is not based on the actual terms of the Constitution, or on its structure."); *see id.* at 232 (McHugh, J.) (arguing that "it is not legitimate to construe the Constitution by reference to political principles or theories that are not anchored in the text of the Constitution or are not necessary implications from its structure"). *But cf.* Adrienne Stone, *The Limits of Constitutional Text and Structure: Standards of Review and the Freedom of Political Communication*, 23 MEL. U. L. REV. 668, 704 (1999) (positing that "reasoning about the freedom of political communication *will* involve reference to values that are external to the *Constitution* and the High Court can only choose whether to express those values in rules or whether to allow them to remain unexpressed through the use of an incompletely theorised text") [hereinafter Stone, *Text and Structure*].

102. *LibertyWorks*,(2021), H.C.A. 18, para. 199 ("The parties and the interveners proceeded upon the now accepted approach for analysing whether legislative provisions are incompatible with the freedom of political communication that is implied from the text and structure of the Constitution."); *id.* para. 200 ("Each of the three tests reflects the roots of the freedom of political communication as an implication derived as a matter of necessity from the text and structure of the Constitution: '[t]he nature and extent of the freedom is governed by the necessity which requires it.'") (quoting APLA Ltd v. Legal Serv. Comm'r (NSW), (2005) 224 C.L.R. 322, 350); *Clubb*, (2019)] H.C.A. 11, para. 467 (Edelman, J.) ("At each stage the application of proportionality testing in Australia must be tied to the purpose for which it is employed, namely to ensure only that which is necessary for the effective functioning of representative and responsible government manifested in the structure and text of the Constitution, particularly ss 7, 24 and 128, and ss 62 and 64."); Lange v. Australian Broad. Corp., (1997) 189 C.L.R. 520, 566–67 (Austl.)

Notes to pages 113–114   251

("Since *McGinty* it has been clear, if it was not clear before, that the Constitution gives effect to the institution of 'representative government' only to the extent that the text and structure of the Constitution establish it. . . . Although some statements in the earlier cases might be thought to suggest otherwise, when they are properly understood, they should be seen as purporting to give effect only to what is inherent in the text and structure of the Constitution.").

103. *See generally* Sir Owen Dixon, *Address Upon Taking the Oath of Office in Sydney as Chief Justice of the High Court of Australia* (Apr. 21, 1952), *reprinted in* JESTING PILATE AND OTHER PAPERS AND ADDRESSES 247, 249 (Severin H. Z. Woinarski ed., 2d ed. 1997) (arguing that "the Court's sole function is to interpret a constitutional description of power or restraint upon power and say whether a given measure falls on one side of a line consequently drawn or the other, and that it has nothing whatever to do with the merits or demerits of the measure"). Chief Justice Dixon observes that "close adherence to legal reasoning is the only way to maintain the confidence of all parties in federal conflicts" and posits that "[t]here is no other safe guide to judicial decisions in great conflicts than a 'strict and complete legalism." *Id.; see* BRENDAN LIM, AUSTRALIA'S CONSTITUTION AFTER WHITLAM 163–65 (2017) (discussing the "'strict and complete legalism'" that prevailed in the HCA's jurisprudence for much of the twentieth century and observing that this institutionally conservative approach to the HCA's role in the structure of government under the Commonwealth Constitution "persisted in Australia for a surprisingly long time").

104. *See* Roger P. Alford, *In Search of a Theory of for Constitutional Comparativism*, 52 UCLA L. REV. 639, 640–42, 644, 713 (2005) (arguing that the U.S. Supreme Court has failed to provide any plausible theory of comparative constitutional law that would justify its use when interpreting and applying the U.S. Constitution). *But cf.* David Fontana, *Refined Comparativism in Constitutional Law*, 49 UCLA L. REV. 539, 550–52, 557–59 (2001) (offering up several justifications, some practical and others theoretical, for U.S. courts using foreign legal precedents as a form of persuasive legal authority).

105. *See* Roper v. Simons, 543 U.S. 551 (2005); Lawrence v. Texas, 539 U.S. 558 (2003); Atkins v. Virginia, 536 U.S. 304 (2002).

106. 576 U.S. 644 (2015).

107. *See generally id. passim.* By way of contrast, Justice Kennedy references favorably federal and state lower court decisions finding that the US Constitution requires recognition of same-sex marriage—as well as state statutes that legalized same sex marriage. *See id.* at 662–63.

108. *See* STEPHEN BREYER, THE COURT AND THE WORLD: AMERICAN LAW AND THE NEW GLOBAL REALITIES (2015). For somewhat trenchant reviews, see Ronald J. Krotoszynski, Jr., *Linnaean Taxonomy and Globalized Law*, 115 MICH. L. REV. 865 (2017); Eric A. Posner, *A Review: The Court and the World: American Law and the New Global Realities*, 126 YALE L.J. 504 (2016).

109. United States v. Windsor, 570 U.S. 12 (2013).

110. *Obergefell*, 576 U.S. at 681–86.

111. CONST. OF REPUBLIC OF SOUTH AFRICA § 39(b) & (c) (1996).

112. *See* Mark Tushnet, *The Possibilities of Comparative Constitutional Law*, 108 YALE L.J. 1225, 1228, 1230–32 (1999) (observing that "U.S. courts can sometimes gain insights into appropriate interpretation of the U.S. Constitution by a cautious and careful analysis of constitutional experience elsewhere" but cautioning against uncareful or ill-considered reliance on foreign legal precedents and reasoning); *see also* Roger P. Alford, *Misusing International Sources to Interpret the Constitution*, 98 AM. J. INT'L L. 57, 64–69 (2004) (warning against poorly informed, haphazard use of international and foreign law in domestic constitutional interpretation).

Notes to pages 114–115

113. *See* David S. Law, *Judicial Comparativism and Judicial Diplomacy*, 163 U. PA. L. REV. 927, 964–73, 980–82 (2015).

114. *See id.* at 1016 ("Nor is it easy to import the necessary expertise, as Congress has by statute barred the hiring of foreign lawyers as law clerks."); *see also* Consolidated Appropriations Act of 2010, Pub. L. No. 111-117, § 704, 123 Stat. 3034, 3205–06 (2009) (prohibiting the use of federal funds "to pay the compensation of any officer or employee of the Government of the United States" unless the employee is a (1) citizen, (2) a permanent resident "seeking citizenship," (3) a refugee who plans to pursue citizenship, or (4) "a person who owes allegiance to the United States").

115. *See, e.g.*, Printz v. United States, 521 U.S. 898, 576–78 (1995) (Breyer, J., dissenting) (arguing that the United States should adopt Germany's practice of requiring state governments to implement federal laws). *But cf.* Mark Tushnet, *When Is Knowing Less Better Than Knowing More?: Unpacking the Controversy over Supreme Court Reference to Non-U.S. Law*, 90 MINN. L. REV. 1275, 1294 (2006) ("The most cogent criticism of references to non-U.S. law in constitutional interpretation is surely that such references are likely to be wrong."). Professor Tushnet observes, quite correctly, that Justice Breyer failed to take into account important structural differences between the German and U.S. versions of federalism and, more specifically, the greater role of the German state governments in the enactment of federal laws. *See id.* at 1294–95. Because of these institutional differences, "what Justice Breyer asserted was a 'common legal problem' [of having state governments enforce federal laws] was not in fact a single problem faced by two systems, but two distinct problems." *Id.* at 1295.

116. *See* Amalgamated Soc'y of Eng'rs v. Adelaide Steamship Co Ltd (*Engineers' Case*), (1920) 28 C.L.R. 129, 155 (Austl.) (holding that the text and structure of the Commonwealth Constitution may give rise to "implications" that the Australian courts may enforce and protect); *see also* Australian Capital Television Pty Ltd v. Commonwealth, (1992) 177 C.L.R. 106, 135, 209–10 (Austl.) (applying the *Engineers' Case* principle to imply a freedom of political and governmental communication); Melbourne Corp. v. Commonwealth, (1947) 74 C.L.R. 31, 83 (Austl.) (invoking and applying the *Engineers' Case* principle of constitutional rules arising from penumbras of the Australian Constitution's text and structure). For examples of the repeated invocation of the "text and structure" requirement for judicial recognition of implied constitutional principles, see *supra* notes 101 & 102.

117. *See generally* TIMOTHY ZICK, THE COSMOPOLITAN FIRST AMENDMENT: PROTECTING TRANSBORDER EXPRESSIVE AND RELIGIOUS LIBERTIES (2012).

118. Ronald J. Krotoszynski, Jr., *"I'd Like to Teach the World to Sing (in Perfect Harmony)": International Judicial Dialogue and the Muses—Reflections on the Perils and the Promise of International Judicial Dialogue*, 104 MICH. L. REV. 1321, 1357 (2006).

119. *See* Alford, *supra* note 104, at 641–44.

120. Fontana, *supra* note 104, at 550 ("In a system of genealogical comparativism, a court indicates that it looks to comparative constitutional law because some relationship exists between the lender country—the country supplying the idea or fact the American court is considering borrowing—and the United States.").

121. *See id.* at 572–74 (describing and discussing genealogical constitutional comparativism and advocating its use when a constitution's text has roots in an antecedent foreign legal system's constitution); *see also* Saunders & Stone, *supra* note 30, at 4 ("The Australian Constitutions collectively provide parliamentary representative democracy nationally and in each of the States and territories, organized around the principles and practices of responsible government originally developed at Westminster."). Professor Fontana explains that

Notes to pages 115–118   —◌ 253

"[g]enealogical comparativism makes sure to note that one of the central reasons that the American court looks to comparative constitutional law is because of the historical, legal, and/ or cultural relationship between that country and the United States." Fontana, *supra* note 104, at 550.

122. Coleman v. Power, (2004) 220 C.L.R. 1 (Austl.).

123. *See* Stone, *Text and Structure*, *supra* note 101, at 696–705.

124. *See* LibertyWorks Inc. v. Commonwealth, (2021) H.C.A. 18, paras. 48, 76–85 (Austl.) (Kiefel, C.J., Keane & Gleeson, JJ.).

125. Adrienne Stone, *Proportionality and Its Alternatives*, 48 FED. L. REV. 123, 148 (2020) (arguing that "the merits of proportionality and of the 'reasonably appropriate and adapted' test are much closer than first appears" and positing that "proportionality has so far not changed the outcome in any case before the Court"). Professor Stone quite accurately observes that "judges rejecting proportionality have reached the same results as the majority who accept it." *Id.* If two (or more) legal tests produce the same outcomes, over time and across a wide range of free speech questions, there must not be all that much daylight between them.

126. *Id.* at 125.

127. Brown v. Tasmania, (2017) 261 C.L.R. 328.

128. *See* McCloy v. New South Wales, (2015) 257 C.L.R. 178, 194–95 (Austl.). Professor Stone provides a useful overview of how the governing test has evolved from *Lange* to *McCloy*. *See* Stone, *supra* note 125, at 126–28.

129. Stone, *supra* note 125, at 124.

130. In Germany, for example, the Federal Constitutional Court has sustained bans on Holocaust denial and on pro-Nazi speech and symbols. *See* RONALD J. KROTOSZYNSKI, JR., THE FIRST AMENDMENT IN CROSS-CULTURAL PERSPECTIVE: A COMPARATIVE LEGAL ANALYSIS OF THE FREEDOM OF SPEECH 126-30 (2006).

131. Justice Gageler seems to have adopted this reasoning. *See* Clubb v. Edwards & Preston v. Spencer, (2019) H.C.A. 11, paras. 184–85, 197, 212 (Austl.) (Gageler, J.) (purporting to apply a form of strict judicial scrutiny to the Tasmanian abortion protest ban, but finding that the 164-yard ban on abortion protest to be narrowly tailored to achieve a compelling government interest).

132. *But cf.* Cohen v. California, 403 U.S. 15, 26 (1971) ("We cannot sanction the view that the Constitution, while solicitous of the cognitive content of individual speech, has little or no regard for that emotive function which, practically speaking, may often be the more important element of the overall message sought to be communicated.").

133. *See id.* at 24–26.

134. 485 U.S. 46 (1988).

135. 562 U.S. 443 (2011).

136. *Cohen*, 403 U.S. at 25.

137. *Id.*

138. *Id.* at 26.

139. *Id.*

140. *See Language as Violence v. Freedom of Expression: Canadian and American Perspectives on Group Defamation*, 37 BUFF. L. REV. 337 (1988/1989).

141. *See* R. v. Butler, [1992] 1 S.C.R. 452 (Can.); R. v. Keegstra, [1990] 3 S.C.R. 697 (Can.).

142. Unions of NSW v. New South Wales, (2013) 252 C.L.R. 530 (Austl.).

143. *See* Citizens United v. Fed. Elec. Comm'n, 558 U.S. 310, 339 (2010) (observing that "[s]peech is an essential mechanism of democracy, for it is the means to hold officials

254 ◦— Notes to pages 118–120

accountable to the people" and holding that "[t]he right of citizens to inquire, to hear, to speak, and to use information to reach consensus is a precondition to enlightened self-government and a necessary means to protect it"). Justice Kennedy adds that, because of the centrality of free speech to the process of democratic self-government, "political speech must prevail against laws that would suppress it, whether by design or inadvertence." *Id.* at 340–41.

144. Commonwealth Electoral Act of 1918 § 245 (making voting in federal elections compulsory and fining persons AUD $20 for failing to vote in a national election).

145. Associated Provincial Picture Houses Ltd. v. Wednesbury Corp., [1948] 1 K.B. 223, 229 (UK) (appeal from Eng.) (devising and applying a test for administrative regulations that asks whether a reasonable administrator could reasonably have adopted a particular regulatory measure).

146. Letter from Thomas Jefferson Letter to Col. Charles Yancey (Jan. 6, 1816) <https://founders.archives.gov/documents/Jefferson/03-09-02-0209>.

147. *Id.*

148. Coleman v. Power, (2004) C.L.R. 1 (Austl.) (holding that a state government may not ban the use of offensive or opprobrious language in public); *see also* Monis v. The Queen, (2013) 249 C.L.R. 92 (Austl.) (presenting an evenly divided HCA on the question of whether a federal law that banned sending offensive letters violated the IFPGC). As Professor Stone observes, with some persuasive force, "[i]f this line of reasoning is developed further, it might be that [in] its scope, the freedom of political communication is not much different from constitutional rights and guarantees that protect 'expression' or 'speech.'" Stone, *supra* note 35, at 970. For the relevant U.S. case on this point, *see* Cohen v. California, 403 U.S. 15 (1971). I view *Cohen* as possibly the most foundational U.S. free speech cases in the canon—the power to censor the precise means of expressing an idea entails the power to actually suppress the idea itself. *See* Ronald J. Krotoszynski, Jr., Cohen v. California: *"Insignificant" Cases and Larger Legal Principles*, 74 TEX. L. REV. 1251 (1996). The right of an individual to choose the precise terms used to express a thought or idea cannot plausibly be characterized as anything other than an individual right. In my view, *Coleman's* reasoning and outcome are simply irreconcilable with the notion that the IFPGC is not a personal right.

149. The Supreme Court of Canada has taken this view—the government may proscribe the use of offensive or opprobrious language, but it may not ban the expression of political ideas (even objectively false ones, such as Holocaust denial). *Compare* R. v. Keegstra, [1990] 3 S.C.R. 697 (Can.) (upholding as proportionate and justified a ban on hate speech that vilifies another person based on race, sex, religion, or other status-based characteristics) *with* R. v. Zundel, [1992] 2 S.C.R. 731 (Can.) (invalidating a statute used to criminalize Holocaust denial because the government lacks the power to declare objective truth in the political marketplace of ideas).

150. *See Cohen*, 403 U.S. at 24–26.

151. Bork, *supra* note 57, at 26–28.

152. Rationality review of social and economic legislation in the United States, at least since 1937, requires the party challenging the validity of a state or federal law to show that no set of facts exists under which a rational legislator could find the law bears a rational relationship to a legitimate state interest. (It is more or less the same as *Wednesbury* review of administrative regulations in the United Kingdom. *See* Associated Provincial Picture Houses Ltd. v. Wednesbury Corp., [1948] 1 K.B. 223 (C.A) (appeal from Eng.).) Thus, under true rationality review, the government has no burden of production or persuasion—and the challenger must

Notes to pages 120–122

essentially prove a negative. *See* Federal Commc'ns Comm'n v. Beach Commc'ns, Inc., 508 U.S. 307 (1993).

153. Bork, *supra* note 57, at 28.

154. *See* ALEXANDER MEIKLEJOHN, FREE SPEECH AND ITS RELATION TO SELF-GOVERNMENT (1948).

155. *Id.* at 25–26.

156. It bears noting that, unlike the Justices of the HCA, Australian legal academics *have* noted and engaged the consanguinity of Bork and Meiklejohn to the HCA's normative account of the IFPGC. *See, e.g.*, Adrienne Stone, *The Limits of Constitutional Text and Structure Revisited*, 28 U.N.S.W. L.J. 842, 848–49 (2005) (discussing the potential relevance of the Meiklejohn theory to defining the scope of the IFPGC and positing that some sort of overarching normative theory of how freedom of speech facilitates democracy is necessary because invoking "text and structure" by itself does not provide any useful answers, or guidance, regarding hard questions about the government's power to regulate, or even proscribe, speech).

157. *See* Meiklejohn, *supra* note 57, at 262–66.

158. *See* JOHN DEWEY, DEMOCRACY AND EDUCATION (1916).

159. *See supra* text and accompanying notes 145 to 146.

160. *See supra* text and accompanying notes 142 to 144.

161. *See* Connick v. Myers, 461 U.S. 138, 147–48 (1983) (holding that government employee speech about matters of private concern, including the terms and conditions of a worker's employment, constitute speech about a matter of private rather than public concern that does not trigger First Amendment protection and explaining that "[o]ur responsibility is to ensure that citizens are not deprived of fundamental rights by virtue of working for the government" and this responsibility "does not require a grant of immunity for employee grievances").

162. Jacobellis v. Ohio, 378 U.S. 184, 197 (1964) (Potter, J., concurring) ("I shall not today attempt further to define the kinds of material I understand to be embraced within that shorthand description [of obscenity]; and perhaps I could never succeed in intelligibly doing so. But I know it when I see it, and the motion picture involved in this case is not that.").

163. Levy v. Victoria, (1997) 189 C.L.R. 579 (Austl.).

164. Coleman v. Power, (2004) 220 C.L.R. 1 (Austl.).

165. The current general test for non-content based speech restrictions appears in McCloy v. New South Wales, (2015) 257 C.L.R. 178 (Austl.). The test places the initial burden of showing an infringement of the IFPGC on the person or entity challenging the government speech regulation. If this burden of production is met, the analysis shifts and the government bears the burden of showing that "the means adopted to achieve that purpose [are] legitimate," meaning "compatible" with the IFPGC, and the government must show that the means used to achieve its objective are "reasonably appropriate and adapted to advance that legitimate object." The test looks quite similar to the Supreme Court of Canada's proportionality test under *R. v. Oakes*, [1986] 1 S.C.R. 103, 138–40 (Can.). For a useful, comprehensive, and quite thoughtful discussion of the salience of proportionality review in contemporary human rights adjudication, see Vicki C. Jackson, *Constitutional Law in an Age of Proportionality*, 124 YALE L.J. 3094 (2015).

166. *See* RONALD J. KROTOSZYNSKI, JR., RECLAIMING THE PETITION CLAUSE: SEDITIOUS LIBEL, "OFFENSIVE" PROTEST, AND THE RIGHT TO PETITION THE GOVERNMENT FOR A REDRESS OF GRIEVANCES 50–52, 122–28, 212–14 (2012).

167. *See* Unions of New South Wales v. New South Wales, (2013) 252 C.L.R. 530. *But cf.* McCloy v. New South Wales, (2015) 257 C.L.R. 178 (sustaining a law aimed at preventing

256   Notes to pages 122–124

"undue influence" over the electoral process). For a relevant discussion of so-called "enhance-ment regulations" aimed at leveling the political playing field, see Stone, *supra* note 35, at 972–73. Stone observes, correctly, that "if one accepted the American view of the propensity of regulation to distort political debate, one could readily conclude that such laws undermined the electoral choice guaranteed by the Constitution." *Id.* at 973.

168. *See* R. v. Smithers; Ex parte Benson, (1912) 16 C.L.R. 99, 109-10 (1912) (Austl.) (holding that "the creation of a federal union with one government and one legislature in respect of national affairs assures to every free citizen the right of access to the institutions, and of due participation in the activities of the nation").

169. *See* Ashutosh Bhagwat, *Producing Speech*, 56 WM. & MARY L. REV. 1029 (2015). Professor Bhagwat posits that "[t]he question that obviously arises is whether, and if so to what extent, the First Amendment protects the antecedent act of producing speech, not just the eventual communication." *Id.* at 1034. He argues that the Press Clause of the First Amendment can and should be deployed to protect information that takes place before reportage and is necessary to facilitating it. *See id.* at 1058–65.

170. *See id.* at 1080 ("The First Amendment does not only protect speech, meaning an act of communication. It also protects the creation of communicative materials—in other words, producing speech.").

171. Levy v. Victoria, (1997) 189 C.L.R. 579 (Austl.).

172. ASHUTOSH BHAGWAT, OUR DEMOCRATIC FIRST AMENDMENT 161–62 (2020).

173. Human Rights Act 1998, ch. 42, § 12(4) (U.K) (adopted Nov. 9, 1998 and entered into force Oct. 2, 2000).

174. Campbell v. MGN Ltd., [2004] A.C. 457 (Eng.), para. 111 (Lord Hope) (opining that "you cannot have particular regard to article 10 without having equally particular regard at the very least to article 8" because "section 12(4) does not give either article pre-eminence over the other"); *see* Douglas v. Hello! Ltd, [2001] Q.B. 967, 1003, paras. 133, 137 (opining that, under the European Convention, no protected right enjoys a "presumptive priority" over any other and, accordingly, Section 12(4) "cannot, consistently with section 3 and article 17, give the article 10(1) right of free expression a presumptive priority over other rights"). In theory, how-ever, Parliament is quite free to depart from ECtHR precedents when establishing a domestic human rights regime for the United Kingdom—it is, after all, possessed of sovereignty and may legislate as it wishes with respect to the priority of one human right over another. *See* ATIYAH & SUMMERS, *supra* note 21, at 227–29, 267–70.

175. AUSTRALIA CONST. § 80.

176. *Id.* § 51(xxxi).

177. *Id.* § 116.

178. *Id.* § 117.

179. For example, the HCA has given a very narrow construction to section 116 of the Australian Constitution—limiting it to legislation (as opposed to executive and judicial actions) and not giving the provision a particularly robust scope of application. Landrigan, *supra* note 99, at 433 ("The High Court has not given a broad interpretation to the free exercise provision or s 116 more generally."); *see* Attorney-General (Victoria); Ex rel. Black v. Commonwealth, (1981) 146 C.L.R. 559 (reading the anti-establishment provision to relate solely to an official national church); Adelaide Company of Jehovah's Witnesses Inc. v. Commonwealth, (1943) 67 C.L.R. 116 (reading the free exercise provision to protect only belief and not conduct man-dated by religious belief). Section 116 is an express guarantee of the free exercise of religion, but Australian academics have suggested that framing free exercise claims as more generic

Notes to pages 124–125

"speech" claims might be a more effective strategy at securing exemptions from laws that burden religiously-motivated conduct. *See* Landrigan, *supra* note 99, at 432–35. This would suggest that judicial enforcement of a particular right in Australia is not really a function of whether or not the right is expressly set forth in the Commonwealth Constitution. For a relevant discussion of the case law imposing limited glosses on these express rights provisions—glosses that reflect broad judicial deference to the national legislature—see TONY BLACKSHIELD & GEORGE WILLIAMS, AUSTRALIA CONSTITUTIONAL LAW & THEORY: COMMENTARY AND MATERIALS 987–1054 (2d ed. 1998).

180. Interestingly, the HCA claimed in *Australian Capital Television* that the Supreme Court of Canada (SCC) had recognized an implied right to the freedom of speech. This is not, strictly speaking, entirely true. Prior to the enactment of a statutory bill of rights, in 1960, the SCC had noted that the Canadian system of government included a principle of freedom of speech. However, unlike Australia's implied freedom of political and governmental communication, the Canadian free speech principle did not involve the exercise of a power of judicial review. Nor did the 1960 Canadian statutory Bill of Rights authorize Canadian courts to decline to apply lawfully enacted statutes. *See* PETER W. HOGG, CONSTITUTIONAL LAW OF CANADA 430 (1st ed. 1977) ("A difficulty with this line of reasoning [involving judicial recognition and enforcement of implied rights] is that the central feature of the Constitution of the United Kingdom, and of its Parliament in 1867, and still is, parliamentary sovereignty."); Peter H. Russell, *The Growth of Canadian Judicial Review and the Commonwealth and American Experiences*, in COMPARATIVE JUDICIAL REVIEW AND PUBLIC POLICY 29, 33 (Donald W. Jackson & C. Neal Tate eds., 1992) (noting that prior to the enactment of the Canadian Charter of Rights and Freedoms in 1982, "the federal division of powers was the only constitutional limitation on legislative power in Canada"). Thus, Canada's "implied freedom" of speech was merely a general canon of statutory and regulatory interpretation—when a court could construe a statute or regulation in way that promoted free speech values, it would do so. This was also the mandate of the Bill of Rights Act of 1960—fundamental rights, including the freedom of speech, would serve as principles of statutory interpretation. *See* Hogg, *supra*, at 197–98, 429–30 (noting that policing the boundaries of provincial and federal authority was the only basis for judicial review under the British North America Act of 1867). Thus, the SCC lacked any power of judicial review with respect to the freedom of speech until 1982 and the advent of the Canadian Charter of Rights and Freedoms. Because the Australian implied freedom entails the exercise of the power of judicial review to invalidate federal and state laws, it is very different from Canada's pre-Charter implied freedom. *See generally* Ex Parte Brind, [1991] App. Cas. 696 (H.L) (appeal from Eng.) (holding that freedom of speech is a legal principle that judges should take into account when interpreting statutes and regulations because it is a background sociolegal principle of British law).

181. LibertyWorks Inc. v. Commonwealth, (2021) H.C.A. 18, para. 249 (Austl.) (Steward, J., concurring) (questioning the wisdom of recognizing the IFPGC and positing that continued disagreements within the HCA's members over how to interpret and apply the implied freedom means "it is not yet settled law").

182. *See* Adrienne Stone, *supra* note 35, at 953 ("The argument that freedom of expression is essential for, or intrinsic too, democratic self-government is one of the most influential ideas in liberal political thought. Freedom of expression is valued because it allows citizens to get information about their government; to hold their government accountable to them, and to exercise choice as to who governs them.").

183. Jeffrey Goldsworthy, *Constitutional Implications and Freedom of Political Speech*, 23 MONASH U. L. REV. 362 (1997).

258 ‿ Notes to pages 125–126

184. Academic commentators do not even agree about the correct nomenclature. Professor Stone uses the phrase "freedom of political communication," which sounds more robust than the nomenclature more conservative members of the HCA use, namely, "an implied freedom of political and governmental communication." Dropping "implied" in my view makes the right sound more robust—the word "implied" connotes "junior varsity" if not "ersatz." I agree with Professor Stone that more robust nomenclature is needed if the HCA is serious about using judicial review to ensure that the deliberative discourse necessary to sustain a project of democratic self-government can and will take place. Indeed, when I began my work on this chapter, I initially used the phrase "freedom of political speech," which better aligns the concept with contemporary understandings of the First Amendment.

185. *See LibertyWorks*, [2021] H.C.A. 18, paras. 249, 298–300, 304 (Steward, J., concurring).

186. *Id.* para. 249.

187. *See* Tajjor v. New South Wales, [2014] HCA 35 (Austl.). The irony is deep—suppose that persons who had been convicted of crimes sought to meet and organize political support for criminal justice reform efforts aimed at reducing recidivism. The law in question was both overbroad (it applied to both licit and illicit associational activity) and vague (its scope of application would not have been reasonably clear to a person of normal intelligence). *See* Anthony Gray, *Freedom of Association in the Australian Constitution and the Crime of Consorting*, 32 U. TASMANIA L. REV. 149 (2015).

188. *See* Stone, *supra* note 35, at 973 (positing that "values deep within the Australian political tradition . . . were determinative [in the campaign finance cases] rather than the 'text and structure' of the Constitution"); *see id.* at 975–77 (discussing how cultural values play an important and distinctive role in major IFPGC decisions). As Professor Stone states her point, "[i]f the long history of political insult to which Justice McHugh and Kirby refer, exists alongside a long history of regulation of insulting behaviour, it is necessary to explain why one practice rather than the other had priority in determining the content of the freedom of political communication." *Id.* at 976.

189. 142 S. Ct. 2228 (2022).

190. 410 U.S. 113 (1973).

191. Chuck Todd et al., *Public's Opinion of Supreme Court Plummets after Abortion Decision*, MTP FIRST READ (Aug. 26, 2022), https://www.nbcnews.com/meet-the- press/first-read/publics-opinion-supreme-court-plummets-abortion-decision-rcna44962.

192. Charles Franklin, *Detailed Results of the Marquette Law School Supreme Court Poll-July 5-12, 2022*, Marquette L. Sch. (July 21, 2022), https://law.marquette.edu/poll/2022/07/21/detailed-results-of-the-marquette-law-school-supreme-court-poll-july-5-12-2022/.

193. *Id.* CNN political reporter Devan Cole observes that "[t]he findings [of the Marquette Law School July 2022 poll] demonstrate the rapid collapse of support by Americans for the high court, which has historically received higher marks than Congress and the White House." Devan Cole, *60% of Americans Approved of the Supreme Court Last July. Now, It's 38%, According to a New Poll*, CNN.COM (5:03 AM, July 20, 2022), https://www.cnn.com/2022/07/20/politics/supreme-court-job-approval-marquette-poll/index.html.

194. In this respect, Professor Stone's suggestion that the HCA should use the common law as an indirect means of safeguarding the freedom of speech has much to recommend it. *See* Adrienne Stone, *Freedom of Political Communication, the Constitution, and the Common Law*, 26 FED. L. REV. 219 (1998). The interstitial nature of common law development, and the dialogue that exists between courts and legislatures in maintaining and amending common law rules, make the common law approach much more compatible with a commitment to the doctrine of

Notes to pages 126–128   ⟶ 259

parliamentary sovereignty. *See generally* GUIDO CALABRESI, A COMMON LAW FOR THE AGE OF STATUTES (1985).

195. *See* Krotoszynski, *supra* note 33, at 20–24.

196. *See id.* at 32–34. Indeed, since the 1980s, "[i]n First Amendment jurisprudence, the new normal became 'All Free Speech Clause, all the time.'" *Id.* at 33.

197. *Id.* at 21 (observing that "the Free Speech Clause is the only provision that routinely does significant doctrinal work today. Indeed, one can count the number of modern Supreme Court cases interpreting and applying the Press, Assembly, and Petition Clauses on two hands.").

198. *See* JOHN D. INAZU, THE FORGOTTEN FREEDOM OF ASSEMBLY (2012); Tabatha Abu El-Haj, *The Neglected Right of Assembly*, 56 UCLA L. REV. 543 (2009).

199. *See* NAACP v. Button, 371 U.S. 415 (1963); NAACP v. Alabama ex rel. Patterson, 357 U.S. 449 (1957).

200. Boy Scouts of Am. v. Dale, 530 U.S. 640 (2000); Hurley v. Irish-Am. Gay, Lesbian, and Bisexual Group of Boston, Inc., 515 U.S. 557 (1995). Such claims do not inevitably prevail, however—the group seeking to use the First Amendment to shield itself from a federal, state, or local antidiscrimination law must show that class-based discrimination is integral to its expressive mission. *See* Christian Legal Soc'y Chapter v. Martinez, 561 U.S. 661 (2010); Hishon v. King & Spaulding, 467 U.S. 69 (1984); Roberts v. United States Jaycees, 468 U.S. 69 (1984).

201. U.S. CONST. amend. VIII ("Excessive bail shall not be required, nor excessive fines imposed, nor cruel and unusual punishments inflicted.").

202. *Id.* amend. V (providing that "nor shall private property be taken for public use, without just compensation").

203. *Id* amend. III ("No Soldier shall, in time of peace be quartered in any house, without the consent of the Owner, nor in time of war, but in a manner to be prescribed by law.").

204. STRAUSS, *supra* note 34, at 9 ("And then there is the first word of the First Amendment, which is 'Congress'; so the courts, or the president, or the City of Chicago can freely abridge the freedom of speech? That cannot be right, and, under clearly established law, it is not right.").

205. *See* Martin H. Redish, *The First Amendment in the Marketplace: Commercial Speech and the Values of Free Expression*, 39 GEO. WASH. L. REV. 429, 431 (1971); *see also* Martin H. Redish, *Commercial Speech, First Amendment Intuitionism and the Twilight Zone of Viewpoint Discrimination*, 41 LOY. L.A. L. REV. 67, 69–71 (2007).

206. REDISH, *supra* note 55, at 27–31, 179–81.

207. *See id.* at 27–31, 176–81.

208. *See id.* at 27 ("Even at its worst, a First Amendment grounded in principles of adversary democracy is far preferable to a logically flawed or deceptively manipulative appeal to democratic and expressive theories grounded in some vague notion of the pursuit of 'the common good' as a basis for selective suppression of unpopular ideas.").

209. *See, e.g.,* CASS R. SUNSTEIN, DEMOCRACY AND THE PROBLEM OF FREE SPEECH xviii–xx, 7–11, 17–52 (1993). Professor Sunstein argues that "[w]e should not reflexively invoke 'the freedom of speech' in order to invalidate reforms that would serve Madisonian goals." *Id.* at xix.

210. REDISH, *supra* note 55, at 31.

211. *See* Va. Bd. of Pharmacy v. Virginia Consumer Council, Inc., 425 U.S. 748 (1976).

212. *See* Bolger v. Youngs Drug Prods. Corp., 463 U.S. 60 (1983); Bigelow v. Virginia, 421 U.S. 809 (1975); Griswold v. Connecticut, 381 U.S. 479 (1965).

213. American Booksellers Ass'n, Inc. v. Hudnut, 771 F.2d 323 (7th Cir. 1985), *summarily aff'd*, 475 U.S. 1001 (1986).

214. Hillary Rodham Clinton, It Takes a Village: And Other Lessons Children Teach Us (2012).

215. Barack Obama, Dreams from My Father: A Story of Race and Inheritance (1995).

216. The HCA has clearly held that commercial speech does not fall within the scope of the IFPGC. *See* APLA Ltd v. Legal Servs. Comm'r (NSW), (2005) 224 C.L.R. 322 (Austl.) (rejecting argument that the implied freedom of political and governmental communication reaches lawyer advertising).

217. Lesléa Newman, Heather Has Two Mommies (1989).

218. Redish, *supra* note 55, at 27–31.

219. *Id.* at 3–5, 31, 176–81.

220. *See id.* at 176 (arguing that a plausible theory of the First Amendment grounded in the relationship of the freedom of speech to democratic self-government must "leave[] to the individual speaker the decision of whether to pursue whatever concerns she seeks to advance in a cooperative or confrontational manner").

221. Citizens United v. Federal Elec. Comm'n, 558 U.S. 310, 341 (2010).

222. *Id.*

223. *See id.* at 339–42.

224. Coleman v. Power, (2004) 220 C.L.R. 1 (Austl.).

225. Meiklejohn, *supra* note 154, at 27.

226. *Id.*

227. *Id.*

228. *Id.* at 25.

229. *Id.* at 26 (emphasis in the original).

230. *See* LibertyWorks Inc. v. Commonwealth, , (2021) H.C.A. 18, paras. 48, 76–85 (Kiefel, C.J., Keane & Gleeson, JJ.).

231. *See* Stone, *Proportionality and Its Alternatives, supra* note 125, at 143 (arguing that "[o]ne virtue of proportionality lies in the flexibility and context sensitivity of its method" which means that this approach to framing and deciding free speech claims "keeps to the fore the question of whether the exercise of power is justified" and thus "is able to respond to the particulars of the case and better placed to expose unreasonable exercises of police [power] authority").

232. Whether this should be characterized as a bug or a design feature constitutes a disputed question. For example, Professor Henckels argues that the HCA's "circumspect approach" is necessary to vindicate the separation of powers. *See* Henckels, *supra* note 13, at 195–97. She explains that "[i]n many cases, it will be appropriate for judges to take into account the institutional competence or expertise of government in determining the suitability and necessity of a challenged measure: for example, by relying on [the] government's argument that no alternative measures were reasonably available to achieve the law's objective." *Id.* at 197. Taking such an approach, however, ultimately means that the legislature, not the courts, are deciding what the Commonwealth Constitution requires. From an American perspective, this disrupts the entire purpose of judicial review—which is to ensure that the political branches stay within constitutionally prescribed limits. If a legislature gets to define constitutional limits because judges are reflexively deferential, it is the legislature, not the courts, who are saying "what the law means." *Cf.* Marbury v. Madison, 5 U.S. (1 Cranch) 137, 177 (1803). As Chief Justice John Marshall states this point, "[s]o if a law be in opposition to the constitution; if both the law and the constitution apply to a particular case, so that the court must either decide that case conformably to the law, disregarding the constitution; or conformably to the

Notes to pages 130–132   ∽ 261

constitution, disregarding the law; the court must determine which of these conflicting rules governs the case." *Id.* at 178. Marshall emphasizes that undertaking this task "is of the very essence of judicial duty." *Id.*

233. *See* STRAUSS, *supra* note 34, at 2–5 (discussing the common law legal tradition and positing that "[t]he written Constitution is a central part of our law, but it is only a part"). Strauss argues "precedent and past practices are, in their own way, as important as the written U.S. Constitution itself." *Id.* at 3. Of course, embracing openly this kind of broad, open-ended policy making authority is largely, if not entirely anathema to the Australian theory and practice of constitutionalism, which goes to great lengths to minimize—if not deny entirely—the broad and deep discretion that courts possess to recognize, shape, and enforce legal rights. *See* Dixon, *supra* note 103, at 249–51. Regularly repeated denials of judicial discretion in interpreting and applying both written and unwritten constitutional norms does not alter the fact that, at the end of the day, that the Commonwealth Constitution means precisely what the HCA says it means. *See* CHARLES EVANS HUGHES, ADDRESSES BY CHARLES EVANS HUGHES: 1906–1916, at 179, 185 (2d ed. 1916) (address of May 3, 1907 to the Elmyra Chamber of Commerce) (observing that "[w]e are under a Constitution, but the Constitution is what the judges say it is").

234. *See, e.g.*, Coleman v. Power, (2004) 220 C.L.R. 1, para. 105 (Austl.) (rendering a saving construction of a state law that criminalized the use of "insulting" language in public because "insults are a legitimate part of the political discussion protected by the Constitution").

235. STRAUSS, *supra* note 34, at 3.

236. *Id.*

237. *Id.*

238. *Id.* at 53.

239. *Id.*

240. *Id.*

241. *See* AHARON BARAK, PROPORTIONALITY: CONSTITUTIONAL RIGHTS AND THEIR LIMITATIONS (Doron Kalir trans., 2012).

242. *See* STEVEN H. SHIFFRIN, DISSENT, INJUSTICE, AND THE MEANINGS OF AMERICA (1999); Vincent Blasi, *The Pathological Perspective and the First Amendment*, 85 COLUM. L. REV. 449 (1985).

243. *See* Blasi, *supra* note 242, at 466–84; Christina E. Wells, *Fear and Loathing in Constitutional Decision-making*, 2005 WIS. L. REV. 115, 214–22.

244. Social psychology has established that the mere possibility of review by an outside entity can significantly reduce various kinds of decisional bias and improve the overall quality of decision making. *See* Mark Seidenfeld, *Cognitive Loafing, Social Conformity, and Judicial Review of Agency Rulemaking*, 87 CORNELL L. REV. 486, 508 (2002) ("Psychological studies suggest that accountability, if properly structured, can significantly improve the quality of decisionmaking in the sense of minimizing the extent to which individuals unthinkingly rely on inappropriate decisionmaking rules or fall prey to psychological biases."). Professor Seidenfeld explains that "[o]ne mechanism for avoiding careless or improper reliance on such shortcuts is to hold the decisionmaker accountable for her choice." *Id.* at 547. Thus, "[i]f structured properly, accountability can attenuate many of the systematic biases that flow from improper use of decisionmaking shortcuts." *Id.* The IFPGC creates a form of third-party oversight for federal and state laws that abridge or deny the freedom of speech; as such, social psychology studies suggest that the IFPGC probably enhances the quality of lawmaking regarding these statutes.

245. Amalgamated Soc'y of Eng'rs v. Adelaide Steamship Co. Ltd., (1920) 28 C.L.R. 129 (Austl.).

Notes to pages 132–136

246. Sedgwick, *supra* note 13, at 40 ("The caution exhibited by the Australian courts may be traced to the origins of our Constitution and the strength of our original ties with the British system of government.").

247. *See supra* Chapter 4.

CHAPTER 6

1. HCJ 73/53, Kol Ha'am Co., Ltd. v. Minister of the Interior, 7 PD 871 (1953) (Isr.), *translated in Translated Opinions*, VERSA, https://versa.cardozo.yu.edu/sites/default/files/upload/opinions/Kol%20Ha%27am%20Co.%2C%20Ltd.%20v.%20Minister%20of%20the%20Interior.pdf (last visited Mar. 7, 2024).

2. Implied fundamental rights in Israel include equality (broadly defined), the presumption of innocence, freedom of speech, association, assembly, and press, freedom of conscience, privacy, dignity, property ownership, bodily integrity, freedom of movement, and procedural due process. *See* Marcia Gelpe, *Constraints on Supreme Court Authority in Israel and the United States: Phenomenal Cosmic Powers; Itty Bitty Living Space*, 13 EMORY INT'L L. REV. 493, 507–08 (1999); *see also* H.C. 680/88, Schnitzer v. Chief Military Censor, 42(4) P.D. 617, 627–69, *translated in* 9 SELECTED JUDGMENTS OF THE SUPREME COURT OF ISRAEL 77, 88–90 (1977–1990); H.C. 953/87, Poraz v. Mayor of Tel Aviv-Yaffo, 42(2) P.D. 309, 330–31. Although the SCI recognized these fundamental rights, drawing upon a variety of domestic and international law sources, in addition to Israel's status as a free and democratic state, the Basic Law: Human Dignity and Liberty, enacted in 1992 and amended in 1994, expressly codifies many, but not all, of these fundamental rights. *See* Basic Law: Human Dignity and Liberty §§ 2–7 (conferring express protection on life, bodily integrity, dignity, property, freedom from arbitrary arrest and/or imprisonment, freedom of movement, privacy, and intimacy). Moreover, it also provides that "[t]here shall be no violation of rights under this Basic Law except by a law befitting the values of the State of Israel, enacted for a proper purpose, and to an extent no greater than required, or by regulation enacted by virtue of express authorization of such law." *Id.* § 8. This provision, at least arguably, authorizes Israeli courts to give priority to rights safeguarded under the Basic Law: Human Dignity and Liberty over the enforcement of ordinary statutes or regulations that, if applied, would burden or abridge the rights set forth in the Basic Law. *See infra* text and accompanying notes 156 to 204.

3. For an extended discussion of "weak form" and "strong form" judicial review, and the differences between these two models, see STEPHEN GARDBAUM, THE NEW COMMONWEALTH MODEL OF CONSTITUTIONALISM: THEORY AND PRACTICE 1–17, 23–47 (2013). Weak-form judicial review generally withholds the formal power of judicial review from the domestic courts but mandates that judges undertake reasonable efforts to harmonize statutes and regulations that conflict with the rights set forth in a statutory bill of rights (such as the United Kingdom's Human Rights Act 1998). By way of contrast, strong-form judicial review vests the judiciary with a formal power to strike down laws that conflict with fundamental human rights.

4. *See* DAVID A. STRAUSS, THE LIVING CONSTITUTION 33–34 (2010) (explaining that, in the United States, in most constitutional cases "the text of the Constitution will play, at most, a ceremonial role" because "American constitutional law is about precedents, and when the precedents leave off, it is about commonsense notions of fairness and good policy"). In this sense, then, the adjudication of constitutional rights in the United States is not really all that different from the process in Israel—despite the United States having a written constitution and Israel lacking one. Professor Strauss explains that, in the United States, "[o]ur living

Notes to page 136   ⟿ 263

constitution includes precedents and traditions that have developed over time." *Id.* at 99. In his view, "[i]t is impossible to understand American constitutional law without recognizing as much." *Id.*

5. *See* Dennis v. United States, 341 U.S. 494 (1951). The Supreme Court of the United States upheld convictions under the Smith Act, a 1940 law that Congress enacted to prevent the Communist Party from organizing and operating in the United States. *See* The Smith Act of 1940, Pub. L. 76-670, 54 Stat. 670, 671 (June 28, 1940) (subsequently codified at 18 U.S.C. § 2835). Section 1 of the Smith Act prohibited the advocacy "of overthrowing or destroying any government in the United States by force or violence, or by the assassination of any officer of any such government." 18 U.S.C. § 2385. Section 2, in turn, criminalized publication and distribution of materials advocating the violent overthrow of the government, and Section 3 banned "organiz[ing]" or "helping to organize" a "society, group, or assembly of persons who teach, advocate, or encourage the overthrow or destruction of any government in the United States by force or violence" and this proscription encompassed merely "becom[ing] a member of, or affiliate with, any such society, group, or assembly of persons." *Id.* Thus, the Smith Act sought to proscribe advocacy of Stalinist-Leninist communism, printing and distributing materials sympathetic to communism, or organizing a political party or other organization aimed at advancing these ideas. It was, in short, a viewpoint-based ban on speech and did not require any showing of a serious probability of actual harm in order for criminal liability to attach to mere abstract advocacy. Even so, the Supreme Court upheld the law, embracing a "bad tendencies" approach. *See Dennis,* 341 U.S. at 509–11. Writing for a plurality, but a 6–2 majority counting the concurring opinions of Justices Felix Frankfurter and Robert Jackson, Chief Justice Fred M. Vinson opined that "[i]f the ingredients of the reaction are present, we cannot bind the Government to wait until the catalyst is added," despite the absence of any proof, whatsoever, that the defendants had undertaken any concrete steps to overthrow the U.S. government. *Id.* at 510.

6. The *Dennis* decision reflects a serious lack of the civic courage that the First Amendment, at least in theory, is supposed to reflect and incorporate. *See* Vincent A. Blasi, *The First Amendment and the Ideal of Civic Courage: The Brandeis Opinion in* Whitney v. California, 29 WM. & MARY L. REV. 653 (1988). *Dennis* also plainly reflects and amplifies a kind of social panic regarding the threat of communism that unfortunately was quite widespread in the United States during the late 1940s and 1950s. *See* Christina E. Wells, *Fear and Loathing in Constitutional Decision Making,* 2005 WIS. L. REV. 115 (discussing, critiquing, and placing into sociolegal and historical context the Smith Act prosecutions of the leaders of the Communist Party of the United States of America (CPUSA) in *Dennis* and the Supreme Court's unfortunate decision to uphold these convictions against First Amendment objections). As Professor Wells cogently observes, "*Dennis* is an extreme example of judicial capitulation to fear and prejudice, but it hardly stands alone in history." *Id.* at 226. She warns that "[t]he frequency with which courts have faced national security threats and the current post-September 11th atmosphere suggests that courts may again find themselves in the difficult position of balancing free speech and national security." *Id.*

7. *See* ALEXANDER MEIKLEJOHN, FREE SPEECH AND ITS RELATION TO SELF-GOVERNMENT 26–27 (1948). As Meiklejohn states the point, "[t]he principle of the freedom of speech springs from the necessities of the program of self-government." *Id.* at 26. Moreover, the absolute necessity of protection for freedom of speech as a component of any credible program of self-government constitutes "a deduction from the basic American agreement that public issues shall be decided by universal suffrage." *Id.* at 27; *see Kol Ha'am, translated in Translated Opinions,*

Notes to pages 136–139

VERSA, at 6–7 ("The principle of freedom of expression is closely bound up with the democratic process" and "in a state with a democratic regime—that is, government by the 'will of the people'—the 'rulers' are looked upon as agents and representatives of the people who elected them, and the latter are entitled, therefore, at any time, to scrutinize their political acts.").

8. *See* Wells, *supra* note 6, at 127–56 (discussing the widespread fear of communism and the Communist Party in the United States in the mid-twentieth century). Wells explains that "[d]espite the lack of evidence supporting anticommunist charges, Americans' beliefs about the CPUSA nevertheless persisted, in large part because of anticommunists' continuous, vivid portrayals of CPUSA members as secretive disciples loyal to Joseph Stalin's every command." *Id.* at 137.

9. *See* Vincent A. Blasi, *The Pathological Perspective and the First Amendment*, 85 COLUM. L. REV. 449 (1985). Professor Blasi posits that "the overriding objective at all times should be to equip the first amendment to do maximum service in those historical periods when intolerance of unorthodox ideas is most prevalent and when governments are most able and most likely to stifle dissent systematically." *Id.* at 449. Under this approach, judges should enforce the First Amendment most stringently in times of national tumult and crisis. *See id.* at 450 ("The first amendment, in other words, should be targeted for the worst of times.").

10. *See* Ronald Dworkin, *The Secular Papacy in* JUDGES IN CONTEMPORARY DEMOCRACY: AN INTERNATIONAL CONVERSATION 67, 74 (Robert Badinter & Stephen Breyer eds., 2004) (arguing that "there is nothing inherently fair, and nothing that provides genuine self-government for all, simply in the fact that more people favor one decision than favor another" and positing that some sort of brake or circuit breaker is essential because such a mechanism "does not compromise but rather protects democracy").

11. Ruth Gavison, *Legislatures and the Quest for a Constitution: The Case of Israel*, 11 REV. CONST. STUD. 345, 365–66 (2006).

12. *Id.* at 366. The document's official title is "'The Declaration of Establishment of the State of Israel,' but it is popularly referred to as the Declaration of Independence." Pnina Lahav, *American Influence on Israeli Law: Freedom of Expression, in* ISRAEL AND THE UNITED STATES: SIX DECADES OF US-ISRAELI RELATIONS 210 n.15 (Robert O. Freedman ed., 2012); *see* *Declaration of Independence*, THE KNESSET, https://m.knesset.gov.il/en/about/pages/declaration.aspx (last visited Jan. 16, 2023) (providing an English translation).

13. *Declaration of Independence*, THE KNESSET, https://m.knesset.gov.il/en/about/pages/declaration.aspx (last visited Jan. 16, 2023).

14. Gavison, *supra* note 11, at 366.

15. *Id.*

16. *Id.*

17. Assaf Likhovski, *The Rise and Demise of Constitutional Duties in Israel*, 61 AM. J. LEG. HIST. 90, 95 (2021).

18. Gavison, *supra* note 11, at 366–37.

19. *Id.* at 366 n.48.

20. Likhovski, *supra* note 17, at 95.

21. *Id.*; Gavison, *supra* note 11, at 367.

22. *Basic Laws*, THE KNESSET, https://m.knesset.gov.il/en/activity/pages/basiclaws.aspx (last visited Jan. 16, 2023).

23. Gelpe, *supra* note 2, at 501.

24. *Id.*

Notes to pages 139–142

25. Basic Law: Freedom of Occupation, 5754-1994, S.H. 90, *translated in Basic Laws*, THE KNESSET, https://m.knesset.gov.il/EN/activity/documents/BasicLawsPDF/BasicLawOccupat ion.pdf (last visited Jan. 16, 2023); Basic Law: Human Dignity and Liberty, 5752-1992, S.H. 150, *translated in Basic Laws*, THE KNESSET, https://m.knesset.gov.il/EN/activity/documents/Basic LawsPDF/BasicLawLiberty.pdf (last visited Jan. 16, 2023).

26. Likhovski, *supra* note 17, at 95.

27. *See infra* text and accompanying notes 205 to 218.

28. HCJ 73/53, Kol Ha'am Co., Ltd. v. Minister of the Interior, 7 PD 871 (1953) (Isr.), *translated in Translated Opinions*, VERSA, https://versa.cardozo.yu.edu/sites/default/files/upload/opinions/Kol%20Ha%27am%20Co.%2C%20Ltd.%20v.%20Minister%20of%20the%20Interior.pdf (last visited Mar. 7, 2024).

29. *Id.* at 4–5.

30. *Id.*

31. *Id.* at 3.

32. *Id.*

33. *See id.* at 1, 6. The Supreme Court's jurisdiction is "twofold." First, it sits as the Court of Appeals of last resort, hearing appeals from all civil and criminal cases. Second, it sits as the "High Court of Justice," exercising jurisdiction "in such matters as are not within the jurisdiction of any other court and are necessary to be decided for the administration of justice." Haim H. Cohn, *The First Fifty Years of the Supreme Court of Israel*, 24 J. SUP. CT. HIST. 3, 8 (1999).

34. *See Kol Ha'am, translated in Translated Opinions*, VERSA, at 12.

35. *Id.* at 6.

36. *Id.* at 7.

37. *Id.* at 8.

38. *Id.* at 18. President Agranat explained that even though the Declaration was not a legal document purporting to define the rights and duties of the government and citizens, the Court is "bound to pay attention to the matters set forth in it when we come to interpret and give meaning to the laws of the State." *Id.*

39. *Id.* at 11.

40. *Id.* at 14

41. *Id.* at 29.

42. *Id.* Put another way, "the state may restrict the freedom of speech to protect public safety only if there is a near certainty that unrestricted speech would severely compromise public safety." Aharon Barak, *A Judge on Judging: The Role of a Supreme Court in a Democracy*, 116 HARV. L. REV. 19, 95–96 (2002).

43. *See* Harry Kalven, Jr., *The New York Times Case: A Note on "The Central Meaning of the First Amendment,"* 1964 S. CT. REV. 191, 204–09 (discussing the concept of seditious libel, in the context of the Sedition Act of 1798, and arguing that proscriptions against seditious libel cannot be reconciled with either the freedom of speech or the concept of democratic self-government). Professor Kalven argues that, after *Sullivan*, "[t]he touchstone of the First Amendment has become the abolition of seditious libel and what that implies about the function of free speech on public issues in American democracy." *Id.* at 209.

44. *Id.* at 30–36.

45. *Id.* at 36.

46. *See* Pnina Lahav, *American Influence on Israel's Jurisprudence of Free Speech*, 9 HASTINGS CONST. L.Q. 21 (1981) (providing a detailed discussion of the SCI's holding in *Kol Ha'am* and its effects on Israeli freedom-of-expression jurisprudence in the following years).

Notes to page 142

47. *Kol Ha'am, translated in Translated Opinions*, VERSA, at 30 (implying that the Court was not questioning the validity of the statute itself by noting that "the High Court of Justice will not interfere with [the Minister of the Interior's] discretion unless . . . he has departed from" the test set out by the Court).

48. *See id.* at 14.

49. Lahav, *supra* note 46, at 32; *see also* Aharon Barak, *Freedom of Speech in Israel: The Impact of the American Constitution*, 8 TEL AVIV U. STUD. L. 241, 243 (1988) ("Without a constitution, we cannot declare a statute unconstitutional. But we can, and in fact we must, interpret th[e] statute.").

50. HCJ 142/89, Laor Movement v. Speaker of the Knesset, 44(3) PD 529, 555 (1995) (Isr.), *quote translated in* Zeev Segal, *Israel Ushers in a Constitutional Revolution: The Israeli Experience, the Canadian Impact*, 6 CONST. F. 44, 44 (1995).

51. Gelpe, *supra* note 2, at 509; *see also* Gavison, *supra* note 11, at 367 (citing HCJ 10/48, Ziv v. Governick, 1 PD 33 (1948)) ("Violations of human rights would only be validated if explicitly authorized by a law.").

52. *See* Edward J. DeBartolo Corp. v. Fla. Gulf Coast Bldg. & Constr. Trades Council, 485 U.S. 568, 575 (1988) (holding that "where an otherwise acceptable construction of a statute would raise serious constitutional problems, the Court will construe the statute to avoid such problems unless such construction is plainly contrary to the intent of Congress" and explaining that this practice "not only reflects the prudential concern that constitutional issues not be needlessly confronted, but also recognizes that Congress, like this Court, is bound by and swears an oath to uphold the Constitution"); *see also* Richard H. Fallon, Jr., *Facial Challenges, Saving Constructions, and Statutory Severability*, 99 TEX. L. REV. 215, 250–54 (2020) (discussing the use of saving constructions that interpret federal statutes to avoid potential constitutional invalidity); Adrian Vermeule, *Saving Constructions*, 85 GEO. L.J. 1945, 1947–49 (1997) (discussing the use of saving constructions to avoid having to invalidate a federal statute on constitutional grounds).

53. *See* Illan Ben-Ami, *Artistic Censorship in Israel: 1949-1991*, 16 CONTEMP. JEWRY 3, 6–12 (1995) (discussing SCI decisions, sitting as the HCJ, reviewing and declining to overturn decisions of the Israeli Board for Film and Theater Review from 1960 to 1986). Professor Ben-Ami explains that "[o]fficial governmental censorship of all films and plays was imposed for Israel for over four decades." *Id.* at 3. This censorship of film and theatrical productions involved speech associated with "sacred cows," that included "anti-religion material," "anti-Israeli propaganda, especially if directed at its Arab citizens," "material that could possibly jeopardize Israeli national security or foreign affairs," "issues related to the Israeli Defense Forces (IDF)" and "bereavement, i.e., anything related to those killed in Israel's wars or to their families, and to anything related to the Holocaust and Nazi era." *Id.* at 5–6. He reports that "[i]t was not until 1986, almost forty years after the Board for Films and Theater Review was established, that the Israeli High Court for Justice finally changed [course and] rejected a Board decision" thereby "allow[ing] the performance of a highly controversial play." *Id.* at 10. The play, "Efraim Is Back in The Army," involved two "sacred cows," namely, "the Israeli army and Nazism." *Id.*; *see* HCJ 14/86, Laor v. Bd. for Film and Theater Censorship, 41(1) IsrSC 421 (Isr.) (observing that "[f]reedom of expression is the freedom to write plays and to present them" and includes "the freedom to produce any piece of work, whether it has an elevated artistic value, or it has not artistic value at all") (translated, in part, in Ben-Ami, *supra*). Unfortunately, no English-language translation of the SCI's complete *Laor v. Board* decision presently exists.

Notes to pages 142–143   267

54. Professor Ben-Ami observes that "during all of its more than four decades of existence, the Board for Film and Theater Review, as well as the Israeli Supreme Court in rulings dealing with the Board's decisions, were two venues in which Israel's 'sacred cows' were reflected and strengthened." Ben-Ami, *supra* note 53, at 12. These "sacred cows" were "so widely respected in Israeli society that even the democratic ethos was pushed aside when confronted by them and official censorship of films and plays practiced." *Id.* It bears noting that many scholars of Israel's free expression jurisprudence concur in the view that *Kol Ha'am* was not consistently followed from the 1950s to the mid-1980s. *See, e.g.,* Lahav, *supra* note 46, at 65–68 (discussing the SCI's inconsistent application of *Kol Ha'am* in the 1960s and 1970s and noting that a sizeable cohort of SCI cases exist "in which the Court failed to recognize that the principle of free expression was implicated"). Writing in 1981, before the SCI began issuing strong free speech decisions on a consistent basis, Professor Lahav lamented that "Israeli free speech law is still struggling for self-identity" and "[t]ransplantation of American law . . . has been less than successful." *Id.* at 108.

55. *See* Guy E. Carmi, *"Dignitizing" Free Speech in Israel: The Impact of the Constitutional Revolution on Free Speech Protection*, 57 McGill L.J. 791, 796 ("The landmark *Kol Ha'am* case in 1953 is perhaps the most important free speech ruling in the history of the Israeli Supreme Court. But the 1950s-1970s were not characterized by a robust protection of free speech."); Lahav, *supra* note 46, at 65–69 (discussing cases in which the SCI failed to cite and apply the probable danger test and, in consequence, sustained various burdens on freedom of expression against constitutional objections); *see generally* Gelpe, *supra* note 2, at 506–10 (discussing *Kol Ha'am*, its constitutional logic, and its test).

56. Norman L. Cantor, *On Clear and Present Danger, Clear Probability, and Free Speech Standards in Israel*, 16 Isr. Y.B. Hum. Rts. 260, 276 (1986).

57. *Id.*

58. HCJ 260/60, 15 PD 611 (1960), summarized in English in Lahav, *supra* note 12, at 65 n. 203.

59. 28(2) PD 692 (1973), summarized in English in Lahav, *supra* note 12, at 65 n. 203.

60. Lahav, *supra* note 46, at 65.

61. *Id.* at 65 n.203.

62. *Id.*

63. *See id.*; *see also* EA 1/65, Yeredor v. Central Elections Comm. for the Sixth Knesset, 19(3) PD 365 (1965) (Isr.), *translated in Translated Opinions*, Versa, https://versa.cardozo.yu.edu/sites/default/files/upload/opinions/Yeredor%20v.%20Chairman%20of%20the%20Central%20Elections%20Committee%20for%20the%20Sixth%20Knesset.pdf (last visited Nov. 5, 2023).

64. *Yeredor, translated in Translated Opinions*, Versa, at 7 (Cohn, J., dissenting).

65. *Id.* at 2.

66. *Id.*; *id.* at 19 (opinion of Agranat, President) (citing HCJ 253/64, Jerias v. Dist. Comm'r of Haifa, 18(4) PD 673 (1964) (Isr.)).

67. *Id.* at 7 (Cohn, J., dissenting).

68. *Id.*; *see also id.* at 19 (opinion of Agranat, President).

69. *Id.* at 22 (opinion of Agranat, President); *id.* at 24 (opinion of Sussman, J.) ("Just as one need not consent to be killed, so a state need not agree to be annihilated and wiped off the map.").

70. *Id.* at 20 (opinion of Agranat, President).

71. *Id.*

Notes to pages 144–147

72. *Id.* at 20–21.

73. *Id.* at 23.

74. Lahav, *supra* note 46, at 66–67.

75. *But cf.* Abrams v. United States, 250 U.S. 616, 630 (1919) (Holmes, J., dissenting) (arguing that censorship of political speech can be reconciled with democratic self-government only when speech presents an immediate risk of causing serious social harm and the government can convincingly prove that the risk is real and palpable rather than merely hypothetical). The SCI's assumption seems to be that permitting El Ard candidates to seek election to the Knesset would present an existential risk to Israel's existence—but the record did not disclose any immediate plans for unlawful action by the candidates or the party's members.

76. *Id.* at 624–31.

77. *Id.* at 630.

78. *Id.*

79. *Id.*

80. Grundgesetz [Basic Law], art. 21(1) (F.R.G.) [hereinafter Basic Law].

81. *Id.* art. 21(2).

82. *See id.* art. 21(4).

83. *Id.* art. 9(2).

84. Ronald J. Krotoszynski, Jr., The First Amendment in Cross-Cultural Perspective: A Comparative Legal Analysis of the Freedom of Speech 125 (2006).

85. *Id.*

86. *See id.* at 124–26 (discussing in some detail the concept of "militant democracy" in German expressive freedom jurisprudence).

87. *See* Communist Party, 5 BVerfGE 85 (1986).

88. *See* Socialist Reich Party, 2 BVerfGE 1 (1952).

89. Lahav, *supra* note 46, at 67.

90. Ilan Saban, *Offensiveness Analyzed: Lessons for Comparative Analysis of Free Speech Doctrines*, 2 Chi.-Kent J. Int'l & Comp. L. 60, 66 & n. 9 (2002).

91. Gitlow v. New York, 268 U.S. 652, 672–73 (1925) (Holmes, J., dissenting).

92. *Id.* at 673.

93. *Id.*

94. Carmi, *supra* note 55, at 797.

95. *Id.* at 798.

96. HCJ 606/93, Kidum Entrepreneurship and Publ'g Ltd v. Broad. Auth., [1994] IsrSC 48(2) 1, 9 (Isr.), *translated in* Carmi, *supra* note 55, at 796 n. 9.

97. Carmi, *supra* note 55, at 799.

98. HCJ 680/88, 42(4) PD 617 (1989) (Isr.), *translated in Translated Opinions*, Versa, https://versa.cardozo.yu.edu/sites/default/files/upload/opinions/Schnitzer%20v.%20Chief%20Military%20Censor.pdf (last visited Mar. 19, 2024).

99. *Id.* at 32.

100. *Id.* at 50.

101. *Id.* at 32.

102. *Id.* at 52.

103. *Id.* at 53.

104. *Id.* at 57.

105. HCJ 806/88, Universal City Studios Inc. v. Films & Plays Censorship Bd., 43(2) PD 22 (1989) (Isr.), *translated in Translated Opinions*, Versa, at 15, https://versa.cardozo.yu.edu/

Notes to pages 147–148   ⟶ 269

sites/default/files/upload/opinions/Universal%20City%20Studios%20Inc.%20%20v.%20
%20Films%20and%20Plays%20Censorship%20Board.pdf (last visited Apr. 11, 2023).

106. *See* Austl. Cap. Television Pty. Ltd. v. Commonwealth, (1992) 177 C.L.R. 106 (Austl.); Nationwide News Pty. Ltd. v. Wills, (1992) 177 C.L.R. 1 (Austl.). For a relevant general discussion of Australia's implied freedom of political and governmental communication, see Adrienne Stone, *The Limits of Constitutional Text and Structure Revisited*, 28 U.N.S.W. L.J. 842 (2005).

107. HCJ 806/88, Universal City Studios, *translated in Translated Opinions*, Versa, at 15.

108. *Id.; see also* HCJ 4804/94, Station Film Co. v. Film Review Bd., 50(5) PD 661 (1997) (Isr.), *translated in Translated Opinions*, Versa, at 17, https://versa.cardozo.yu.edu/sites/default/files/upload/opinions/Station%20Film%20Co.%20v.%20Film%20Review%20Board.pdf (last visited Apr. 11, 2023) (holding that freedom of expression "extends to cinematic expression the content of which is pornographic").

109. CrimFH 1789/89, State of Israel v. Kahane, 54(5) PD 195 (2000) (Isr.), *translated in Translated Opinions*, Versa, at 22, https://versa.cardozo.yu.edu/sites/default/files/upload/opinions/State%20of%20Israel%20v.%20Kahane.pdf (last visited July 17, 2023) ("The value of 'social cohesiveness' according to the stated meaning is of particular importance against the background of a society with a varied social mosaic like the State of Israel, in which minorities, and members of various religious sects, live side by side and in which the differences between the various population groups that live in it are significant."); *see* Penal Code 5737-1977 § 136 (Isr.) (proscribing speech and publications that promote the violent overthrow of the government, in addition to speech and publications that "promote discontent or resentment among the inhabitants of the land" or that "promote feelings of strife and enmity between different segments of the population"). Writing for a 5–2 majority of a seven-member panel of the SCI, sitting as the HCJ, Justice Theodor Or sustained the conviction of Binyamin Kahane for sedition because his anti-Arab speech activity, including campaign publications calling for violence against Arab residents, risked causing social unrest within Israel, thereby threatening the stability of the state and its governing institutions. Justice Or explained that "[i]ncitement which is directed against a population or group on the basis of a racist or ideological background which incites enmity against it and calls for violence against it as a group, using violent means, constitutes a violation of the same value of social cohesiveness in the sense described [and covered by Section 136]." *Kahane*, Versa, at 21–22. Accordingly, "[p]ublic discourse, which is at the foundation of democracy, is not to be allowed to be turned into a double-edged sword, and to sabotage the public order." *Id.* at 22–23. Thus, sedition, under Israeli law, encompasses not just attempts to overthrow the state or its governing institutions, but also includes "promot[ing] feelings of ill-will and enmity between different sections of the population." Miriam Gur-Arye, *Can Freedom of Expression Survive Social Trauma: The Israeli Experience*, 13 Duke J. Comp. & Int'l L. 155, 162–63 (2003). Hate speech is thus protected as "speech," but the government has a sufficiently compelling justification to regulate it—or even to ban it.

110. *Universal City Studios, translated in Translated Opinions*, Versa, at 16.

111. *Station Film Co., translated in Translated Opinions*, Versa, at 16.

112. *Id.*

113. *See* Grant Huscroft, Bradley W. Miller & Grégoire Webber, *Introduction*, in Proportionality and the Rule of Law: Rights, Justification, Reasoning 1, 1 (Grant Huscroft, Bradley W. Miller & Grégoire Webber eds., 2014) ("To speak of human rights is to speak of proportionality. It is no exaggeration to claim that proportionality has overtaken rights as the orienting idea in contemporary human rights law and scholarship."). To be sure,

270 ☙ Notes to pages 148–150

"there is no consensus on its methodology" and use of proportionality review to analyze and decide constitutional human rights claims does not "guarantee consensus on substantive rights provisions." *Id.* at 2. The main virtue of proportionality review is the "promise [of] a common analytical framework, the significance of which is not in its ubiquity, but in how its structure influences (some would say controls) how courts reason to conclusions in many of the great moral and political controversies confronting political communities." *Id.*

114. *Station Film Co.*, translated in Translated Opinions, VERSA, at 16.

115. HCJ 6126/94, Szenes v. Broad. Auth., 53(3) PD 817 (1999) (Isr.), *translated in Translated Opinions*, VERSA, at 15, https://versa.cardozo.yu.edu/sites/default/files/upload/opinions/Szenes%20v.%20Matar_0.pdf (last visited Apr. 11, 2023).

116. Obviously, a flat ban on particular speech would call for a higher-order justification from the government than a regulation that merely limits or constrains the speech. For example, limits on residential picketing to protect privacy would be easier for the government to justify than restricting protests proximate to government buildings and offices. *See* HCJ 2481/93, Dayan v. Wilk, 48(2) PD 456 (1994) (Isr.), *translated in Translated Opinions*, VERSA, at 27 https://versa.cardozo.yu.edu/sites/default/files/upload/opinions/Dayan%20v.%20Wilk.pdf (last visited Feb. 9, 2023). Then-Vice-President Barak, in *Dayan*, explained that "[t]he right to hold an assembly, procession or picket in the city streets and the right to the privacy of a person's home are constitutional rights in Israel" and "they are cherished by Israeli democracy." *Id.* However, neither right has an absolute priority: "Neither of them is preferable to the other." *Id.*

117. *See* HCJ 4804/94, Station Film Co. v. Film Review Bd., 50(5) PD 661 (1997) (Isr.), *translated in Translated Opinions*, VERSA, at 13–14, https://versa.cardozo.yu.edu/sites/default/files/upload/opinions/Station%20Film%20Co.%20v.%20Film%20Review%20Board.pdf (last visited Apr. 11, 2023) (explaining that Israeli constitutional law protects freedom of expression "to expose the truth, to advance and secure "human self-fulfillment," and constitutes a "prerequisite for democracy").

118. *See infra* text and accompanying notes 239 to 283.

119. *See* Aharon Barak, *A Constitutional Revolution: Israel's Basic Laws*, 4 CONST. F. 83, 83 (1993).

120. Basic Law: Human Dignity and Liberty, 5752-1992, S.H. 150 (Isr.), *translated in Basic Laws*, THE KNESSET, https://m.knesset.gov.il/EN/activity/documents/BasicLawsPDF/BasicLawLiberty.pdf (last visited Jan. 16, 2023).

121. Basic Law: Freedom of Occupation, 5754-1994, S.H. 90 (Isr.), *translated in Basic Laws*, THE KNESSET, https://m.knesset.gov.il/EN/activity/documents/BasicLawsPDF/BasicLawOccupation.pdf (last visited Jan. 16, 2023). Note that Basic Law: Freedom of Occupation was originally passed in 1992 and amended in 1994.

122. Barack, *supra* note 119, at 83.

123. *See id.* ("The principal organ of state that must pour content into the majestic generalities, and must resolve the inherent conflicts, is the judiciary—primarily the Supreme Court.").

124. Gelpe, *supra* note 2, at 501.

125. *Id.* at 504; *see also* § 24, Basic Law: The Knesset, 5718-1958, 12 L.S.I. 85 (Isr.), *translated in Basic Laws*, THE KNESSET, https://m.knesset.gov.il/EN/activity/documents/BasicLawsPDF/BasicLawTheKnesset.pdf (last visited Feb. 8, 2023) (stating that the Knesset "shall hold debates and adopt resolutions with the participation of any number of Members").

126. Gelpe, *supra* note 2, at 503.

127. *Id.*

Notes to pages 150–152   —◌ 271

128. *Id.*

129. *See* Segal, *supra* note 50, at 44 (noting that the Supreme Court of Israel, as of 1995, had voided statutes on the basis that they conflicted with Basic Laws in only four cases, all of which involved a statute that violated an entrenched provision of a Basic Law without being passed by a special majority of the Knesset).

130. HCJ 98/69, Bergman v. Minister of Finance 23(1) P.D. 693 (1969) (Isr.), *translated in Translated Opinions*, VERSA, https://versa.cardozo.yu.edu/sites/default/files/upload/opini ons/Bergman%20v.%20Minister%20of%20Finance.pdf (last visited Feb. 8, 2023).

131. *Id.* at 4–5.

132. *Id.* at 10.

133. *Id.*

134. HCJ 142/89, 44(3) PD 529 (1990), summarized in English in Ivan Rothman, *A Digest of Selected Judgments of the Supreme Court of Israel*, 26 ISR. L. REV. 250, 258 (1992).

135. *Id.*

136. *Id.* at 260.

137. *Id.*

138. *Id.*

139. Gelpe, *supra* note 2, at 516.

140. *Id.* at 517.

141. HCJ 5648/23, Movement for Quality Gov't v. Knesset, VERSA: OPINIONS OF THE SUPREME COURT OF ISRAEL (Jan. 1, 2024) (Isr.), https://versa.cardozo.yu.edu/sites/default/ files/upload/opinions/Movement%20for%20Quality%20Government%20v.%20The%20Knes set.pdf.

142. *Id.* paras. 1–2, 176–83.

143. Basic Law: The Judiciary (Amendment No. 3) (Isr.); *see Movement for Quality Gov't*, VERSA, paras. 16–26 (providing a legislative history of Basic Law: The Judiciary (Amendment No. 3)); *see also* Rush Levush, *Israel: Legislation Abolishes Reasonableness as a Standard for Judicial Review of Government's Decisions*, LIBR. OF CONG. (Oct. 25, 2023), https://www.loc.gov/ item/global-legal-monitor/2023-10-24/israel-legislation-abolishes-reasonableness-as-a-stand ard-for-judicial-review-of-governments-decisions/(discussing in some detail the Knesset's adoption of the amendment to Basic Law: The Judiciary that sought to abolish the SCI's authority to review executive branch actions for reasonableness and discussing the SCI's use of reasonableness review to invalidate arbitrary, unjust, and irrational government actions).

144. Basic Law: The Judiciary (Amendment No. 3) (Isr.).

145. *Movement for Quality Gov't*, VERSA, para. 2.

146. *Id.* para. 64.

147. *Id.*

148. *Id.*

149. *Id.* paras. 64–66.

150. *See id.* paras. 158–79. Whether the margin should be deemed 8-7 or 10-5 is open to question. Two members of the SCI, Justices Alex Stein and Gila Canfy Steinitz, wrote a concurring opinion that held the SCI possessed the inherent authority to void the amendment abolishing reasonableness review, but concluded that the proper remedy involved reading down the amendment, to limit its effect on the ability of the SCI to review executive branch actions, rather than to invalidate it entirely. *See* Jeremy Sharon, *In Historic Ruling, High Court Strikes Down Key Judicial Overhaul Legislation*, TIMES OF ISRAEL (Jan. 1, 2024, 10:57 PM), https://www. timesofisrael.com/in-historic-ruling-high-court-strikes-down-key-judicial-overhaul-legislat

272 ◦ Notes to pages 152–154

ion/ (discussing the concurring opinion authored by Justices Stein and Steinitz and reporting that they preferred to impose a limiting construction on Amendment No. 3 rather than invalidate it completely). Of course, the practical difference between voiding a statute and interpreting it very narrowly to prevent an unconstitutional outcome often can prove to be astonishingly small. Thus, a clear majority of the SCI, comprising ten of the fifteen justices, have made plain that the Knesset does not possess unfettered discretion to abolish the SCI's authority to safeguard Israel's democratic character (and, more specifically, rule of law and separation of powers values).

151. *Id.* para. 114.

152. *Id.* paras. 114–116

153. *Id.* para. 176.

154. *See id.* para. 183 ("In the absence of another remedy that might provide a response to the unprecedented harm to the nuclear characteristics of the State of Israel a[s] a democratic state as a result of Amendment [N]o. 3 to Basic Law: The Judiciary, I am of the opinion that there is no recourse but to declare the Amendment void.").

155. 5 U.S. (1 Cranch) 137, 177, 180 (1803) (observing that "[i]t is emphatically the province and duty of the judicial department to say what the law is" and holding that "a law repugnant to the constitution is void").

156. Barak, *supra* note 119, at 83.

157. Basic Law: Freedom of Occupation, 5754-1994, S.H. 90, § 3 (Isr.), *translated in Basic Laws*, THE KNESSET, https://m.knesset.gov.il/EN/activity/documents/BasicLawsPDF/BasicLawOccupation.pdf (last visited Jan. 16, 2023).

158. Basic Law: Human Dignity and Liberty, 5752-1992, S.H. 150 (Isr.), *translated in Basic Laws*, THE KNESSET, https://m.knesset.gov.il/EN/activity/documents/BasicLawsPDF/BasicLawLiberty.pdf (last visited Jan. 16, 2023).

159. *Id.* § 2.

160. *Id.* § 3.

161. *Id.* § 4.

162. *Id.* § 5.

163. *Id.* § 7(a).

164. *Id.* § 7(b).

165. *Id.* § 6(a).

166. *Id.* § 7A.

167. *Id.* § 8; *see also* Basic Law: Freedom of Occupation, 5754-1994, S.H. 90, § 4 (Isr.), *translated in Basic Laws*, THE KNESSET, https://m.knesset.gov.il/EN/activity/documents/BasicLawsPDF/BasicLawOccupation.pdf (last visited Jan. 16, 2023).

168. *See, e.g.*, Segal, *supra* note 50, at 45.

169. Basic Law: Freedom of Occupation, 5754-1994, S.H. 90, § 7 (Isr.), *translated in Basic Laws*, THE KNESSET, https://m.knesset.gov.il/EN/activity/documents/BasicLawsPDF/BasicLawOccupation.pdf (last visited Jan. 16, 2023).

170. CA 6821/93, 49(4) PD 221 (1995) (Isr.), *translated in Translated Opinions*, VERSA, https://versa.cardozo.yu.edu/sites/default/files/upload/opinions/United%20Mizrachi%20Bank%20v.%20Migdal%20Cooperative%20Villiage_0.pdf (last visited Feb. 8, 2023).

171. *Id.* at 18.

172. *See id.*; *see also* Lahav, *supra* note 12, at 201 (attributing this "idea" to Justice Aharon Barak).

173. *United Mizrahi Bank*, VERSA, at 92.

Notes to pages 154–155

174. *Id.*

175. *See id.*; *see also* Gelpe, *supra* note 2, at 518–19.

176. Aharon Barak, *Human Rights in Israel*, 39 Isr. L. Rev. 12, 18 (2006) (citing HCJ 1030/99, Oron v. Chairman of the Knesset, 56(3) PD 640 (2002)); *see also* Gavison, *supra* note 11, at 372 & n.70 (noting that the Supreme Court, using the approach in *United Mizrahi Bank*, has struck down laws that violated Basic Law: Human Dignity and Liberty, one of which was *Oron*, where the Court "invalidated a law legitimating some unauthorized radio stations").

177. European Communities Act, 1972 ch. 68 (Oct. 17, 1972) [hereinafter ECA], *repealed by* European Union (Withdrawal) Act 2018, 2018 ch. 16 (June 26, 2018).

178. ECA § 2(1) ("All such rights, powers, liabilities, obligations and restrictions from time to time created or arising by or under the Treaties, and all such remedies and procedures from time to time provided for by or under the Treaties, as in accordance with the Treaties are without further enactment to be given legal effect or used in the United Kingdom shall be recognised and available in law, and be enforced, allowed and followed accordingly; and the expression 'enforceable Community right' and similar expressions shall be read as referring to one to which this subsection applies."). As Baroness Brenda Hale explained, before the United Kingdom's official exit from the European Union, on January 31, 2020, "Parliament has . . . for the time being at least, limited its own powers by the European Communities Act 1972 and, in a different way, by the Human Rights Act 1998." Jackson v. Att'y Gen, [2006] 1 A.C. 262, para. 159 (Eng.) (Baroness Hale); *see* Regina v. Sec'y of State for Transp., ex parte Factortame Ltd. (No. 2), [1991] 1 App. Cas. 603 (H.L.) (app. from Eng.) (holding that, because the ECA provides that European Union law should preempt domestic British law in the event of a conflict, an injunction should issue so the Court of Justice of the European Union could provide an authoritative construction of European Union law on fishing rights despite a 1988 Act of Parliament that directly addressed the legal question at bar); *see also* Anne-Marie Slaughter, *Judicial Globalization*, 40 Va. J. Int'l L. 1103, 1106 (2000) ("British courts overturned the sacrosanct doctrine of parliamentary sovereignty and issued an injunction blocking the effect of a British law pending judicial review at the European level.").

179. P. S. Atiyah & Robert S. Summers, Form and Substance in Anglo-American Law: A Comparative Study of Legal Reasoning, Legal Theory, and Legal Institutions 54–55 (1987) (acknowledging that the ECA 72 gave preemptive effect to European Community law over British domestic law, but cautioning that Parliament remained free to limit or repeal the preemptive effect of EU law within British domestic law).

180. *See* ECA § 2(1).

181. Gavison, *supra* note 11, at 392 ("I share the view of those who think that *if* there is a constitution in Israel, it is primarily a judge-made constitution.").

182. Barak, *supra* note 49, at 245.

183. Gelpe, *supra* note 2, at 556–59.

184. Patrick Kingsley, *Netanyahu Surges Ahead With Judicial Overhaul, Prompting Fury in Israel*, N.Y. Times (Jan. 12, 2023), https://www.nytimes.com/2023/01/12/world/middlee ast/netanyahu-israel-judicial-reform.html?smid=nytcore-ios-share&referringSource=artic leShare.

185. *See id.*

186. HCJ 5648/23, Movement for Quality Gov't v. Knesset, Versa: Opinions of the Supreme Court of Israel (Jan. 1, 2024) (Isr.), https://versa.cardozo.yu.edu/sites/default/ files/upload/opinions/Movement%20for%20Quality%20Government%20v.%20The%20Knes set.pdf.

274 ⌒— Notes to pages 155–157

187. PPA 4463/94, 50(4) PD 136 (1996) (Isr.), *translated in Translated Opinions*, Versa, https://versa.cardozo.yu.edu/sites/default/files/upload/opinions/Golan%20v.%20Pris ons%20Service.pdf (last visited Feb. 8, 2023); *see also* Barak, *supra* note 176, at 22 (citing *Golan* and stating that human dignity includes the freedom of expression).

188. *Id.* at 5.

189. *Id.*

190. *Id.* at 5, 11.

191. *See id.* at 18.

192. *Id.* at 18.

193. *Id.* Justice Mazza, in reaching this conclusion, cited to Justice Barak's decisions in CA105/ 92, Re'em Contracting Eng'rs Ltd. v. Upper Nazareth Municipality, 47(5) PD 189 (1993) (Isr.), and HCJ 2481/93, Dayan v. Wilk, 48(2) PD 456 (1994) (Isr.), *translated in Translated Opinions*, Versa, https://versa.cardozo.yu.edu/sites/default/files/upload/opinions/Dayan%20v.%20W ilk.pdf (last visited Feb. 9, 2023). In *Dayan*, Justice Barak stated: "I am prepared to assume, without deciding the matter, that the law does not compel us to prefer one basic right to the other merely because one [i.e., freedom of demonstration] is not mentioned expressly in the Basic Law whereas the other [i.e., protection of property] is mentioned." *Id.* at 35.

194. *Golan, translated in Translated Opinions*, Versa, at 63 (opinion of Dorner, J.).

195. *Id.* at 62.

196. *Id.* at 65 (opining that a "violation of commercial expression, for example by banning an advertisement, does not usually involve humiliation" and that therefore such a ban could not violate the Basic Law).

197. *Id.* at 58 (opinion of Cheshin, J.).

198. *Id.*

199. *See id.* at 19–20 (opinion of Mazza, J.); *id.* at 49–51 (opinion of Cheshin, J.) (balanc- ing the right of the prisoner with the security concerns of the prison); *id.* at 66 (opinion of Dorner, J.) ("Most certainly we cannot conclude from past experience that there is a near cer- tainty that publishing the appellant's articles will significantly and seriously disrupt prison discipline.").

200. *See* Gavison, *supra* note 11, at 374.

201. *Id.* at 374–75 (explaining that the SCI has found that the Basic Law includes the right of equality and covers basic welfare rights, despite no mention of either in the Basic Law itself).

202. *Golan, translated in Translated Opinions*, Versa, at 64.

203. *Id.*

204. *Id.*

205. Guy E. Carmi, *Dignity—The Enemy From Within: A Theoretical and Comparative Analysis of Human Dignity as a Free Speech Justification*, 9 U. Pa. J. Const. L. 957, 975 n.87 (2007) (citing HCJ 2557/05, Matee Harov v. Israeli Police, 62(1) PD 200 (2006) (Isr.), *translated in Translated Opinions*, Versa, https://versa.cardozo.yu.edu/sites/default/files/upload/opinions/Major ity%20Camp%20v.%20Israel%20Police.pdf (last visited Apr. 11, 2023)).

206. *Matee Harov, translated in Translated Opinions*, Versa, at 4.

207. *See id.* at 4–5.

208. *See id.* at 5–6, 13.

209. *Id.* at 11.

210. *Id.* at 12.

211. *Id.*

212. *Golan, translated in Translated Opinions*, Versa, at 63 (opinion of Dorner, J.).

213. *Id.* at 62.

214. *See Matee Harov, translated in Translated Opinions*, VERSA, at 12.

215. HCJ 5239/11, 2015 Isr. L. Rep. 159 (2015) (Isr.), *translated in Translated Opinions*, VERSA, https://versa.cardozo.yu.edu/sites/default/files/upload/opinions/Avneri%20v.%20Knesset.pdf (last visited Apr. 11, 2023).

216. *Id.* at 7–8.

217. *Id.* at 53.

218. *Id.* at 54.

219. *See generally* HCJ 73/53, Kol Ha'am Co., Ltd. v. Minister of the Interior, 7 PD 871 (1953) (Isr.), *translated in Translated Opinions*, VERSA, https://versa.cardozo.yu.edu/sites/default/files/upload/opinions/Kol%20Ha%27am%20Co.%2C%20Ltd.%20v.%20Minister%20of%20the%20Interior.pdf (last visited Mar. 7, 2024).

220. HCJ 806/88, Universal City Studios Inc. v. Films & Plays Censorship Bd., 43(2) PD 22 (1989) (Isr.), *translated in Translated Opinions*, VERSA, at 15, https://versa.cardozo.yu.edu/sites/default/files/upload/opinions/Universal%20City%20Studios%20Inc.%20%20v.%20%20Films%20and%20Plays%20Censorship%20Board.pdf (last visited Apr. 11, 2023).

221. *Id.* at 14–15.

222. *See* Carmi, *supra* note 55, at 799 (arguing that, prior to 1992's Basic Law: Human Dignity and Liberty, constitutional protection for freedom of expression ha[d] become an integral part of the Israeli legal ethos" but "was created solely by the Supreme Court's rulings").

223. *Id.*

224. CA 6821/93, United Mizrahi Bank Ltd. v. Migdal Coop. Vill., 49(4) PD 221 (1995) (Isr.), *translated in Translated Opinions*, VERSA, https://versa.cardozo.yu.edu/sites/default/files/upload/opinions/United%20Mizrachi%20Bank%20v.%20Migdal%20Cooperative%20Village_0.pdf (last visited Feb. 8, 2023).

225. HCJ 5239/11, Avneri v. Knesset, 2015 Isr. L. Rep. 159 (2015) (Isr.), *translated in Translated Opinions*, VERSA, https://versa.cardozo.yu.edu/sites/default/files/upload/opinions/Avneri%20v.%20Knesset.pdf (last visited Apr. 11, 2023).

226. Barak, *supra* note 49, at 243 ("Without a constitution, we cannot declare a statute unconstitutional. But we can, and in fact we must, interpret th[e] statute."); *see also* Lahav, *supra* note 46, at 32 ("[W]ithout a written constitution, either to articulate the constitutional principles or, explicitly or implicitly, to allow for judicial review, 'usurpation' of any powers of judicial review was impossible.").

227. *See generally Avneri, translated in Translated Opinions*, VERSA.

228. *See* GARDBAUM, *supra* note 3, at 41–46, 156–203 (discussing weak-form judicial review in the United Kingdom under the HRA 98). Professor Gardbaum acknowledges that the Supreme Court of the United Kingdom's aggressive use of its HRA Section 3 power to "interpret" statutes and regulations to avoid conflicts with European Convention rights arguably has created "a major gap between form and substance, theory and practice, or between how the HRA seems and what it really is." *Id.* at 180. More specifically, this critique posits that "the formal restraints on the judiciary have become largely illusory" and, in consequence, "the theoretical distinction between strong-form judicial review, as in Germany and the US, and the HRA's weak-form judicial review has proven itself to be just that: a theoretical distinction without much of a difference in the real world." *Id.* at 181. To be sure, the question of when rendering a saving construction via "interpretation" and "harmonisation" ends, and wholesale judicial amendment of an act of Parliament begins, may largely be in the eyes of the beholder. *See id.* at 191 ("Indeed, it is probably accurate and candid to describe the judicial function under

section 3 as including limited modifications of statutes to protect rights rather than merely interpretation.").

229. *See* KROTOSZYNSKI, *supra* note 84, at 155–56, 175–77 (discussing the Supreme Court of Japan's routine practice of rendering saving constructions to avoid conflicts between statutes and constitutional rights).

230. NIHONKOKU KENPŌ [Constitution of Japan] art. 81 ("The Supreme Court is the court of last resort with power to determine the constitutionality of any law, order, regulation or official act.").

231. *See supra* notes 119 to 124 & 187 to 204 and accompanying text.

232. *See* HCJ 2557/05, Matee Harov v. Israeli Police, 62(1) PD 200 (2006) (Isr.), *translated in Translated Opinions*, VERSA, at 12, https://versa.cardozo.yu.edu/sites/default/files/upload/opinions/Majority%20Camp%20v.%20Israel%20Police.pdf (last visited Apr. 11, 2023).

233. *See* HCJ 2481/93, Dayan v. Wilk, 48(2) PD 456 (1994) (Isr.), *translated in Translated Opinions*, VERSA, at 27–28, https://versa.cardozo.yu.edu/sites/default/files/upload/opinions/Dayan%20v.%20Wilk.pdf (last visited Feb. 9, 2023) ("We are concerned with two human rights of equal standing, and the balance between them must therefore find expression in a reciprocal waiver whereby each right must make a concession to the other in order to allow the coexistence of both."); *id.* at 29–30 (opining that when "hold[ing] an assembly or picket next to the house of a public figure" the courts must find and maintain "a proper balance . . . between a person's right to hold an assembly or picket and the right of the public figure and his neighbors to their privacy in their apartments").

234. Ben-Ami, *supra* note 53, at 10–12.

235. HCJ 680/88, Schnitzer v. The Chief Military Censor, 42(4) PD 617 (1989) (Isr.), *translated in* VERSA, https://versa.cardozo.yu.edu/sites/default/files/upload/opinions/Schnitzer%20v.%20Chief%20Military%20Censor.pdf (last visited Mar. 19, 2024).

236. *Id.* at 32 ("Precisely because of the implications for the life of the nation contained in decisions of a security nature, the door should be opened to a free exchange of opinions on matters of security. In this connection it is particularly important that the press be free to serve as a forum for the exchange of opinions and for criticism in matters of vital interest to the public and the individual.").

237. *Id.* at 39; *see id.* at 49 ("Publication of criticism of the functioning of the head of the Mossad does not create a near certainty of substantial harm to the security of the State. We have here a remote possibility—'a bad tendency' in the words of Justice Agranat in H.C. 73/53 [7]—which has no place in our system of law."); *id.* at 54 ("The possibility that publication of the date of the forthcoming replacement of the head of the Mossad would increase the danger to his security appears to me to be purely speculative. No data whatever were brought before us—save for the above evaluation—which support this claim.").

238. *But cf.* Carmi, *supra* note 55, at 794 (arguing that "[f]or free speech to be adequately protected, it needs to be explicitly enumerated within the constitutional documents in a manner that buttresses its standing and grants it the protection it deserves"). With all due respect to Professor Carmi, the fact that the SCI deployed judicial review so dramatically, around 1986, six years before the Knesset adopted Basic Law: Human Dignity and Liberty, suggests that a written text was *not* essential. Helpful? Certainly. But, "helpful" is simply not the same as a condition precedent to meaningful judicial protection of expressive freedoms.

239. *See, e.g.,* Eli M. Salzberger, *Judicial Appointments and Promotions in Israel: Constitution, Law, and Politics, in* APPOINTING JUDGES IN AN AGE OF JUDICIAL POWER: CRITICAL PERSPECTIVES FROM AROUND THE WORLD, 241, 251–53 (Kate Malleson & Peter H. Russell

Notes to pages 161–164   —◌ 277

eds., 2006) (arguing that the SCI plays a critical role in safeguarding basic human rights and, in so doing, enhances rather than undermines the authority and legitimacy of the political branches of Israel's government and democratic values more generally).

240. *See* Reuven Rivlin, *Who Is Sovereign?: A Constitutional Revolution or a Regime Putsch?*, NEWS FIRST CLASS (May 22, 2003), https://www.news1.co.il/archive/003-D-2694-00.html?tag= 13-04-08 (Hebrew) (objecting that a single, low-level judge, such as a justice of the peace, may invalidate a law the Knesset has duly enacted); *see also* Malvina Halberstam, *Judicial Review, A Comparative Perspective: Israel, Canada, and the United States*, 31 CARDOZO L. REV. 2393, 2397 (2010) (presenting and summarizing critical perspectives on the scope of the SCI's authority vis-à-vis the Knesset).

241. MARCIA GELPE, THE ISRAEL LEGAL SYSTEM 85 (2013).

242. *Id.*

243. *Id.*

244. *Id.*

245. Cohn, *supra* note 33, at 10.

246. Gavison, *supra* note 11, at 364.

247. *Id.*

248. *Id.*

249. *Id.* at 392.

250. *Id.*

251. *Id.* at 388.

252. DWORKIN, *supra* note 10, at 74.

253. *Id.*

254. *Id.*

255. *Id.* at 75.

256. *Id.* at 83.

257. *See supra* Chapter 5.

258. DWORKIN, *supra* note 10, at 76.

259. *Id.* at 77.

260. *Id.* at 78.

261. *Id.*

262. *Id.* at 85.

263. *Id.* at 79.

264. *Id.* at 82.

265. *Id.*

266. JOHN HART ELY, DEMOCRACY AND DISTRUST: A THEORY OF JUDICIAL REVIEW 15–22 (1980).

267. *Id.* at 101–02.

268. *Id.* at 7.

269. *Id.*

270. *Id.* at 7–8.

271. *See id.* at 42–72 (criticizing the Supreme Court's human rights jurisprudence in general and its use of the doctrine of substantive due process in particular).

272. *Id.* at 103; *see* United States v. Carolene Prods. Co., 304 U.S. 144, 152–53 n. 4 (1938) (opining that courts should not defer to legislative policy making when legislation reflects animus toward "discrete and insular minorities" or burdens fundamental rights). Ely is far more enthusiastic about the use of judicial review to advance the first objective than he is about

278 ⌒ Notes to pages 164–171

efforts to advance the second. *See* ELY, *supra* note 266, at 43–72 (questioning the legitimacy and ability of federal judges to identify and protect fundamental rights in general and unenumerated fundamental rights in particular).

273. *See* NEIL K. KOMESAR, IMPERFECT ALTERNATIVES: CHOOSING INSTITUTIONS IN LAW, ECONOMICS, AND PUBLIC POLICY 5–9, 19–22, 139–49 (1997) (discussing how some governing tasks are best suited to one branch of government over another because of the nature of the task and the competencies and abilities of one branch of government relative to the others).

274. MEIKLEJOHN, *supra* note 7, at 22–27.

275. *Id.* at 26.

276. *Id.* at 27.

277. *Id.* at 26.

278. *Id.*

279. *Id.* at 27.

280. *Id.*

281. *See id.* at 88 ("When a free man is voting, it is not enough that the truth is known by someone else, by some scholar or administrator or legislator. The voters must have it, all of them.").

282. *Id.* at 88–89.

283. *Id.* at 89.

284. HCJ 4804/94, Station Film Co. v. Film Review Bd., 50(5) PD 661 (1997) (Isr.), *translated in Translated Opinions*, VERSA, at 13–14, https://versa.cardozo.yu.edu/sites/default/files/upl oad/opinions/Station%20Film%20Co.%20v.%20Film%20Review%20Board.pdf (last visited Apr. 11, 2023) (discussing the "[t]hree rationales [that] form the basis for recognizing freedom of expression as a fundamental right" which include "expos[ing] the truth," "the need for human self-fulfillment," and safeguarding and securing democracy).

285. *See* MEIKLEJOHN, *supra* note 7, at 88–91.

286. *Id.* at 88.

287. *Id.*

288. New York Times Co. v. Sullivan, 376 U.S. 254 (1964).

289. *Id.* at 270.

CHAPTER 7

1. *See* GUIDO CALABRESI, A COMMON LAW FOR THE AGE OF STATUTES 3–5 (1982).

2. OLIVER WENDELL HOLMES, JR., THE COMMON LAW 1 (1881).

3. *See supra* Chapter 2.

4. *See supra* Chapter 3.

5. *See supra* Chapter 5.

6. *See supra* Chapter 4.

7. *See supra* Chapter 6.

8. *See* Snyder v. Phelps, 562 U.S. 443, 553 (2011) ("Speech deals with matters of public concern when it can 'be fairly considered as relating to any matter of political, social, or other concern to the community,' *Connick*, *supra*, at 146, or when it 'is a subject of legitimate news interest; that is, a subject of general interest and of value and concern to the public,' *San Diego*, *supra*, at 83–84"). In *Snyder*, Chief Justice John G. Roberts, Jr., writing for the majority, explained that "[i]n considering content, form, and context, no factor is dispositive, and it is

Notes to page 171   —꙳ 279

necessary to evaluate all the circumstances of the speech" to determine whether it addresses a matter of public concern. *Id.* at 454. The speech at issue in *Snyder* was fairly far removed from intelligent and well-informed public discourse about matters of government policy— and instead consisted of unhinged homophobic, religiously bigoted, and anti-military rants. *See id.* ("The placards read 'God Hates the USA/Thank God for 9/11,' 'America is Doomed,' 'Don't Pray for the USA,' 'Thank God for IEDs' 'Fag Troops,' 'Semper Fi Fags,' 'God Hates Fags,' 'Maryland Taliban,' 'Fags Doom Nations,' 'Not Blessed Just Cursed,' 'Thank God for Dead Soldiers,' 'Pope in Hell,' 'Priests Rape Boys,' 'You're Going to Hell,' and 'God Hates You.'"). Despite the meager social value of the Westboro Baptist Church's ravings, the Supreme Court, by an 8–1 margin, found that the messages clearly related to matters of public concern. *See id.* ("While these messages may fall short of refined social or political commentary, the issues they highlight—the political and moral conduct of the United States and its citizens, the fate of our Nation, homosexuality in the military, and scandals involving the Catholic clergy—are matters of public import. The signs certainly convey Westboro's position on those issues, in a manner designed, unlike the private speech in *Dun & Bradstreet*, to reach as broad a public audience as possible.").

9. *See* Rucho v. Common Cause, 139 S. Ct. 2484 (2019) (sustaining, against First Amendment and Fourteenth Amendment objections, an extreme partisan gerrymander adopted by Wisconsin's state legislature that permitted a minority of Wisconsin voters to elect a supermajority of the state legislature on a more-or-less permanent basis).

10. *See id.* at 2506–08 (holding that partisan gerrymanders do not present a justiciable question because the federal courts lack reasonable objective standards to decide how much partisanship is too much and explaining that "we have no commission to allocate political power and influence in the absence of a constitutional directive or legal standards to guide us in the exercise of such authority").

11. *See* Mark Seidenfeld, *Cognitive Loafing, Social Conformity, and Judicial Review of Agency Rulemaking*, 87 CORNELL L. REV. 486, 508 (2002) (exploring and explaining cognitive science studies that establish that the prospect of outside review can significantly improve the quality of decision-making and help to keep decision makers honest). Professor Seidenfeld, writing in the specific context of federal administrative agencies engaged in policy making endeavors, explains that external review of work product "can attenuate many of the systematic biases that flow from improper use of decisionmaking shortcuts." *Id.* at 547.

12. *See, e.g.*, LibertyWorks Inc. v. Commonwealth, (2021) H.C.A. 18, paras. 74–85 (Austl.) (Kiefel, C.J., Keane & Gleeson, JJ.) (upholding against an implied freedom of political and governmental communication challenge the Foreign Influence Transparency Scheme Act 2018's imposition of mandatory registration requirements for foreign speakers); Comcare v. Banerji, (2019) H.C.A. 23, paras. 17, 35–38, 42 (Austl.) (Kiefel, C.J., Bell, Keane, & Nettle, JJ.) (upholding vague and amorphous statutory and regulatory provisions that authorize a federal government employer to impose discipline on government employees—up to and including discharge—if an employee engages in public criticism of the government employer that it deems "unreasonably or harshly critical"); Clubb v. Edwards & Preston v. Spencer, (2019) H.C.A. 11, paras. 100–102 (*Clubb*) & paras. 126–29 (*Preston*) (Austl.) (Kiefel, C.J., Bell & Keane, JJ.) (upholding unanimously a 164-yard free speech-free zone around family planning clinics as necessary to protect the safety and dignity of clinic patients and employees and flatly refusing to consider requiring a more carefully, a narrowly tailored speech ban).

13. The *process* of constitutional adjudication also varies widely from place to place and clearly affects the effective scope of constitutional rights. *See* Vicki C. Jackson, *Constitutional*

280 ~   Notes to pages 171–172

Law in an Age of Proportionality, 124 YALE L.J. 2680, 3094 (2015) (discussing the doctrine of proportionality, which many foreign constitutional courts use to provide methodological, structured, and transparent balancing of individual rights against government claims that abridge or deny a particular constitutional right on the facts presented, as both necessary and justified).

14. *See* Mark V. Tushnet, *Interpreting Constitutions Comparatively: Some Cautionary Notes, with Reference to Affirmative Action*, 36 CONN. L. REV. 649, 650–55 (2004) (arguing that the substance of constitutional rights, such as freedom of speech or equality, is often entwined with institutional constraints that delimit how courts go about protecting those rights). Professor Tushnet cautions that when engaging in comparative constitutional analysis, one "must be aware of the way in which institutional and doctrinal contexts limit the relevance of comparative information." *Id.* at 662.

15. Bostock v. Clayton Cnty., Ga., 140 S. Ct. 1731, 1737 (2020) ("When the express terms of a statute give us one answer and extratextual considerations suggest another, it's no contest. Only the written word is the law, and all persons are entitled to its benefit."). *But cf.* DAVID R. STRAUSS, THE LIVING CONSTITUTION 8–10, 34–38, 53, 56 (2010) (arguing that strict adherence to the text of the First Amendment cannot support a great deal of the Supreme Court's jurisprudence on expressive freedom, observing that "[t]he central features of the First Amendment were hammered out in fits and starts, in a series of judicial decisions and extrajudicial developments, over the course of the twentieth century," and warning that "[i]f we focus just on the text, the case for protecting free speech against government infringement generally is actually somewhat weak"); Eric J. Seagall, *The Constitution Means What the Supreme Court Says It Means*, 129 HARV. L. REV. F. 176, 176–78, 185–86 (2016) (arguing that judges almost never rely solely on text to decide hard constitutional cases and that it is highly disingenuous of them to claim otherwise). Justice Neil Gorsuch's approach to a textualist analysis of Title VII drew a stinging rebuke from Justice Samuel Alito, Jr. Alito objected that Gorsuch's approach "is like a pirate ship" because "[i]t sails under a textualist flag, but what it actually represents is a theory of statutory interpretation that Justice Scalia excoriated—the theory that courts should 'update' old statutes so that they better reflect the current values of society." *Id.* at 1755–56 (Alito, J., dissenting).

16. *See supra* Chapter 2.

17. U.S. CONST. amend. I ("*Congress shall make no law* . . . prohibiting the free exercise thereof; or abridging the freedom of speech, or of the press; or the right of the people peaceably to assemble, and to petition the Government for a redress of grievances.") (emphasis added).

18. *See* STRAUSS, *supra* note 15, at 9 (noting that "there is the first word of the First Amendment, which is 'Congress'," which implies that "the courts, or the president, or the City of Chicago can freely abridge my freedom of speech?," which Strauss argues "can't be right, and, under clearly established law, it is not right").

19. Marbury v. Madison, 5 U.S. (1 Cranch) 137, 163 (1803).

20. *Id.*

21. *Id.* ("In Great Britain the king himself is sued in the respectful form of a petition, and he never fails to comply with the judgment of his court.").

22. *Id.*; *see* Ronald J. Krotoszynski, Jr. and Caprice L Roberts, *Reimagining First Amendment Remedies*, 109 IOWA L. REV. 911, 913–16 (2024) (arguing that the Supreme Court has paid insufficient attention to the efficacy of First Amendment remedies in enabling a would-be speaker to speak and positing that "First Amendment rights are only as secure as the remedies

Notes to pages 172–173 · 281

available to protect them when the government oversteps the mark and unconstitutionally censors speech").

23. Tushnet, *supra* note 14, at 663.

24. *See id.* at 650–55, 662–63.

25. *Marbury*, 5 U.S. (1 Cranch) at 162–63.

26. Edwards v. Att'y Gen. of Canada, [1930] A.C. 124, 136, 143 (PC) (appeal taken from S.C.C.) (holding that the term "person" encompasses both men and women for purposes of federal Senate appointments and explaining that the framers of the British North America Act 1867 (BNA Act) "planted in Canada a living tree capable of growth and expansion within its natural limits"); *see also* PETER W. HOGG, 2 CONSTITUTIONAL LAW OF CANADA § 36.8(a) (5th ed. 2007) (discussing the Supreme Court of Canada's adoption of the "living tree" metaphor to describe its approach to interpreting the Canadian Charter of Rights and Freedoms and the BNA Act). The Supreme Court of Canada has taken pains to emphasize that the "living tree" approach flatly rejects originalism as an interpretative methodology: "[t]he 'frozen concepts' reasoning [original intent] runs contrary to one of the most fundamental principles of Canadian constitutional interpretation: that our Constitution is a living tree which, by way of progressive interpretation, accommodates and addresses the realities of modern life." Reference re Same Sex Marriage, [2004] 3 S.C.R. 698, para. 22 (Can.).

27. *See* Carter v. Canada (Attorney General), [2015] 1 S.C.R. 331, paras. 70, 147 (Can.) (invoking s. 7 of the Canadian Charter of Rights and Freedoms, which expressly safeguards "life, liberty, and security of the person" and invalidating a federal ban on physician assisted suicide as an unreasonable constraint on "security of the person").

28. *See* ANTONIN SCALIA, A MATTER OF INTERPRETATION: FEDERAL COURTS AND THE LAW 39–47 (1997) (arguing against dynamic or "living tree" interpretation of the Constitution and positing that it empowers judges to impose their own moral preferences over those of elected legislators who enjoy a democratic imprimatur to make social policies); *see also* ROBERT H. BORK, THE TEMPTING OF AMERICA: THE POLITICAL SEDUCTION OF THE LAW 251–59 (1990) (positing that *only* textualist originalism can constrain judges from imposing their own moral preferences and therefore is the only legitimate approach to interpreting and applying constitutional text). Of course, many of these jurists ultimately prove out to be ersatz textualist-originalists and embrace dynamic "living tree" interpretative approaches when doing so is essential to safeguarding an important constitutional value—like the freedom of expression in the context of democratic self-government.

29. LUKE BECK, AUSTRALIAN CONSTITUTIONAL LAW: CONCEPTS AND CASES 18, 24–25 (2020); *see* Scott Stephenson, *Rights Protection in Australia*, in THE OXFORD HANDBOOK OF THE AUSTRALIAN CONSTITUTION 906–15 (Cheryl Saunders & Adrienne Stone eds., 2018) (discussing in some detail the conscious decision to omit a bill of rights from the Australian Constitution). Professor Stephenson explains that "[t]he initial decision not to include a bill of rights in the Constitution was grounded in a belief in the capacity of representative democracy to protect rights and a fear that a bill of rights would prevent the States from enacting racially discriminatory legislation." Stephenson, *supra*, at 906. Thus, although the Australian drafters borrowed many design elements from the U.S. Constitution, they declined to include a written bill of rights. *See* BECK, *supra*, at 18 ("While they rejected the presidential system of government and a comprehensive Bill of Rights, in other respects they found in the American system, what Sir Owen Dixon described as 'an incomparable model.'").

30. Commonwealth of Australia Act, 1900 (Imp), 63 & 64 Victoria, c. 12, § 117 (U.K.), https://www.aph.gov.au/constitution (last visited May 5, 2023) ("A subject of the Queen,

282 ⌒ Notes to pages 173–174

resident in any State, shall not be subject in any other State to any disability or discrimination which would not be equally applicable to him if he were a subject of the Queen resident in such other State.") [hereinafter AUSTRALIA CONST.].

31. U.S. CONST. art. IV, § 2, cl. 1 ("The Citizens of each State shall be entitled to all Privileges and Immunities of Citizens in the several States.").

32. AUSTRALIA CONST. § 80 ("The trial on indictment of any offence against any law of the Commonwealth shall be by jury, and every such trial shall be held in the State where the offence was committed, and if the offence was not committed within any State the trial shall be held at such place or places as the Parliament prescribes.").

33. *Id.* § 116 ("The Commonwealth shall not make any law for establishing any religion, or for imposing any religious observance, or for prohibiting the free exercise of any religion, and no religious test shall be required as a qualification for any office or public trust under the Commonwealth.").

34. Australian Capital Television Pty. Ltd. v. Commonwealth, (1992) 177 C.L.R. 106 (Austl.); Nationwide News Pty. Ltd. v. Wills, (1992) 177 C.L.R. 1 (Austl.). The High Court has regularly heard and decided cases involving the implied freedom of political and governmental communication since recognizing the implied right in 1992. *See, e.g.,* LibertyWorks Inc. v. Commonwealth, (2021) H.C.A. 18 (Austl.); Comcare v. Banerji, (2019) H.C.A. 23 (Austl.). That said, however, at least one member of the High Court rejects the recognition of fundamental rights, including freedom of speech, through implications from other constitutional clauses. *See LibertyWorks,* (2021) H.C.A. 18, para. 249 (Steward, J., concurring) (opining that "it is arguable that the implied freedom does not exist" and positing that the implied freedom "may not be sufficiently supported by the text, structure and context of the Constitution"). Justice Simon Steward argues that "because of the continued division within this Court about the application of the doctrine of structured proportionality, it is still not yet settled law." *Id.* At present, however, these views do not command a majority at the HCA. A clear and strong majority stands by the precedents recognizing the implied freedom of political and governmental communication; even so, serious disagreements exist among the justices over the precise constitutional standard of review that should govern in free speech cases.

35. *LibertyWorks,* (2021) HCA 18, para. 44.

36. *Id.* para. 45.

37. *See* JOHN HART ELY, DEMOCRACY AND DISTRUST: A THEORY OF JUDICIAL REVIEW 7–8, 15–22, 101–05 (1980). Professor Ely argues, with some force and at length, that judges have a duty to intervene when necessary to protect the process of democracy from legislative self-dealing—he calls his theory of judicial review "representation reinforcing," meaning that it seeks to ensure the smooth and fair functioning of the democratic process. *See id.* at 103 (arguing that judges must intervene and, if necessary invalidate duly enacted legislation, when either "the ins are choking off the channels of political change to ensure that they will stay in and the outs will stay out" or "though no one is actually denied a voice or a vote, representatives beholden to an effective majority are systematically disadvantaging some minority out of simple hostility or a prejudiced refusal to recognize commonalities of interest, and thereby denying that minority the protection afforded other groups by a representative system").

38. *See* Adrienne Stone, *The Limits of Constitutional Text and Structure Revisited,* 28 U.N.S.W. L.J. 842, 847–49 (2005) (discussing and explaining the limited scope of Australia's implied freedom of political and governmental communication); *see also* Adrienne Stone, *Rights, Personal Rights and Freedoms,* 25 MELB. U. L. REV. 374, 378–89 (2001) (analyzing and critiquing the High

Notes to pages 174–175

Court of Australia's failure to define protected speech clearly and explaining the limited, but ambiguous, scope of the implied freedom of political and governmental communication).

39. GIDEON SAPIR, THE ISRAELI CONSTITUTION: FROM EVOLUTION TO REVOLUTION 54–58, 69–71 (2018) (discussing the judicial recognition of Basic Laws and explaining how the Supreme Court of Israel (SCI) has conveyed limited entrenchment on these statutory enactments and used them as a basis for exercising a power of judicial review).

40. *See id.* at 58–66, 132, 144–46 (discussing these implied freedoms, including the freedom of speech and explaining that the SCI embraced "[a]n expanded reading of the right to dignity as including such rights as equality, freedom of speech, and freedom of religion" and brought these rights into Israeli law "through the window" meaning by judicial fiat, rather than the "front door," meaning via legislative recognition); *id.* at 19–29, 63–64 (discussing the implied principle of equality in conjunction with several other dignity-based rights, including freedom of speech and religion); *see also* Amal Jamar, *The Hegemony of Neo-Zionism and the Nationalizing State in Israel—The Meaning and Implications of the Nation-State Law, in* DEFINING ISRAEL: THE JEWISH STATE, DEMOCRACY, AND THE LAW 153–71 (Simon Rabinovitch ed., 2018) (discussing the implied principle of equality and judicial enforcement of it). For a discussion of the Supreme Court of Israel's bold assertion of a power of judicial review to enforce implied constitutional rights, including speech and equality, see SAPIR, *supra* note 39, at 31–48, 109–51.

41. Neta Ziv, *Combining Professionalism, Nation Building and Public Service: The Professional Project of the Israeli Bar 1928-2002,* 71 FORDHAM L. REV. 1621, 1639 (2003).

42. Former SCI President Aharon Barak has explained that "[e]quality is one of the State of Israel's fundamental values." HCJ 6698/95 Ka'adan v. Israel Land Admin., 54(1) PD 258 (2000) (Isr.). However, freedom of speech is no less essential than equality in Israeli human rights jurisprudence. Aharon Barak, *Foreword: A Judge on Judging: The Role of a Supreme Court in a Democracy,* 116 HARV. L. REV. 19, 85–93 (2002) (discussing "fundamental principles" of a democracy, notably including equality of all persons and freedom of expression); Aharon Barak, *Human Rights in Israel,* 39 ISR. L. REV. 12 (2006) (discussing the normative basis for judicial protection of fundamental principles of justice in Israel, including freedom of speech and equality); Aharon Barak, *The Role of a Supreme Court in a Democracy, and the Fight Against Terrorism,* 58 U. MIAMI L. REV. 125, 127 (2003) (explaining that "[r]eal democracy is not just the law of rules and legislative supremacy" but instead "is a multidimensional concept" that includes "the supremacy of values, principles and human rights") [hereinafter *Role of the Supreme Court*].

43. Barak, *Role of the Supreme Court, supra* note 42, at 127.

44. HCJ 73/53 Kol Ha'am v. The Minister of Interior, 7(2) PD 871, *translated in* SELECTED JUDGMENTS OF THE SUPREME COURT OF ISRAEL 90 (1953). Other relevant cases establishing an implied freedom of speech as a necessary element of democratic self-government include HCJ 14/86 Laor v. Theatre Review Bd., 41(1) PD 421; and HCJ 680/88 Schnitzer v. Chief Military Censor, 42(4) PD 617. In 1962, the Supreme Court of Israel recognized an implied constitutional right to freedom of conscience. *See* HCJ 262/62 Peretz v. Local Council of Kfar Shmaryahu, 16(3) PD 2101.

45. Avi Weitzman, *A Tale of Two Cities: Yitzhak Rabin's Assassination, Free Speech, and Israel's Religious-Secular Kulturkampf,* 15 EMORY INT'L L. REV. 1, 25 n. 98 (2001) (listing relevant cases).

46. *Id.* at 24.

47. *Id.* at 25.

48. Aharon Barak, *Freedom of Speech in Israel: The Impact of the American Constitution,* 8 TEL AVIV U. STUD. L. 241, 246–47 (1988).

284 ～ Notes to page 176

49. CÓDIGO PENAL [C.P.] [CRIMINAL CODE] §§ 490–91 (Spain); *see* Clarisse Loughrey, *Rapper Jailed for Three and Half Years after Criticising the Royal Family*, THE INDEPENDENT (London, UK) (Feb. 24, 2018), https://www.independent.co.uk/arts-entertainment/music/news/ rap-per- jailed-lyrics-spanish-royal-family-valtonyc-josep-miquel-arenas-beltran-a8226421.html. [https://perma.cc/SYU4-LRJS]; *see generally* OSAC, Lèse Majesté: Watching What You Say (and Type) Abroad, https://www.osac.gov/Content/Report/e48a9599-9258-483c-9cd4-169f9 c8946f5 [https://perma.cc/WZU3-9JNJ] ("Several European monarchies, including Belgium, Denmark, Sweden, Spain, Netherlands, and Monaco still have *lèse majesté* laws on the books. The laws tend to carry harsher criminal penalties than other types of defamation and insult laws, though the charges are typically not as extreme as in other regions of the world.").

50. *See* Hustler Magazine, Inc. v. Falwell, 485 U.S. 46, 50–56 (1988) (observing that criticizing political figures is among the most valuables forms of speech protected by the First Amendment); New York Times Co. v. Sullivan, 376 U.S. 254, 268–86 (1964) (noting that the ability of citizens to openly criticize public officials constitutes a core purpose of the First Amendment and is fundamental to the process of democratic self-government).

51. *See supra* Chapter 3.

52. It bears noting, however, that South Africa's Constitutional Court has been more skeptical of hate speech regulations than the text of the 1996 Constitution might warrant, given the express elevation of dignity, equality, and human freedom as the nation's "foundational" constitutional values. CONST. OF THE REPUBLIC OF SOUTH AFRICA, 1996, Act No. 108, § 1(a); *see id.* § 7(1) (providing that "[t]his Bill of Rights is a cornerstone of democracy in South Africa" and "enshrines the rights of all people in our country and affirms the democratic values of *human dignity, equality and freedom*") (emphasis added). The free speech provision, Section 16, expressly excludes from protection "propaganda for war," "incitement of imminent violence," and "advocacy of hatred that is based on race, ethnicity, gender or religion, and that constitutes incitement to cause harm." *Id.* § 16(2)(a) to (c). Moreover, the equality provision, Section 9, requires the government to advance and security the equality of all persons. *See id.* § 9(4) ("National legislation must be enacted to prevent or prohibit unfair discrimination."). Finally, the provision on the abrogation of fundamental rights, Section 37, declares the substantive provisions safeguarding dignity, equality, and human freedom (as liberty of the person in Section 12) to be nonderogable; all other rights in the Bill of Rights, including the freedom of speech, are subject to legislative suspension in times of war or national emergency. *See id.* § 37(1) & (5). Even so, the Constitutional Court has invalidated national legislation aimed at punishing and deterring hate speech. *See* S. Afr. Hum. Rts. Comm'n v. Masuku, 2022 (5) S.A. 1 (CC) (S. Afr.); Qwelane v. S. Afr. Hum. Rts. Comm'n, 2021 (6) S.A. 579 (CC) (S. Afr.). Thus, the Constitutional Court's approach to hate speech regulations appears to be in at least some tension with the express text of the Constitution—suggesting perhaps that South Africa *follows* the more general pattern of constitutional courts going their own way when deciding free speech cases, through a process of common law adjudication, rather than *departs from* this model.

53. The European Union (EU), for example, included an express privacy protection for personal data—in addition to a more generic privacy guarantee—when writing and adopting the European Charter of Fundamental Rights. Charter of Fundamental Rights of the European Union, 2012/C 326/02, art. 8(1) ("Everyone has the right to the protection of personal data concerning him or her."). Data protection is a central concern among the citizens of the EU—as reflected by the GDPR. It was, accordingly, entirely foreseeable that the Charter would include an express guarantee of this particular aspect of privacy—in addition to a

more general provision that tracks the privacy clause of the European Convention on Human Rights. *See id.* art. 7 ("Everyone has the right to respect for his or her private and family life, home and communications.").

54. CONST. OF THE REPUBLIC OF SOUTH AFRICA § 7(1) ("This Bill of Rights is a cornerstone of democracy in South Africa. It enshrines the rights of all people in our country and affirms the democratic values of *human dignity, equality and freedom.*" (emphasis added)); *see also id.* § 1(a) ("The Republic of South Africa is one, sovereign, democratic state founded on the following values . . . [h]uman dignity, the achievement of equality and the advancement of human rights and freedoms.").

55. *See id.* § 9(1) ("Everyone is equal before the law and has the right to equal protection and benefit of the law."); *id.* § 10 ("Everyone has inherent dignity and the right to have their dignity respected and protected."); *id.* § 12(1)(a) to (e) (providing that "[e]veryone has the right to freedom and security of the person" and then detailing specific instantiations of this general principle, including the right "not to be deprived of freedom arbitrarily or without just cause," "not to be detained without trial," "to be free from all forms of violence from either public or private sources," "not to be tortured in any way," and "not to be treated or punished in a cruel, inhuman or degrading way").

56. Marbury v. Madison, 5 U.S. (1 Cranch) 137, 177–78 (1803) (positing that judges must interpret and apply the provisions of a written constitution because "[i]t is emphatically the province and duty of the judicial department to say what the law is").

57. THE FEDERALIST NO. 78, at 464, 467 (Alexander Hamilton) (Clinton Rossiter ed., 1961) ("If it be said that the legislative body are themselves the constitutional judges of their own powers, and that the construction they put upon them is conclusive upon the other departments, it may be answered, that this cannot be the natural presumption, where it is not to be collected from any particular provisions in the Constitution.").

58. *Id.* at 467.

59. THE FEDERALIST NO. 48, at 308, 313 (James Madison) (Clinton Rossiter ed., 1961).

60. THE FEDERALIST NO. 78, *supra* note 57, at 466.

61. *Id.*

62. *Id.*

63. U.S. CONST. art. III, § 1 ("The Judges, both of the supreme and inferior Courts, shall hold their Offices during good Behaviour, and shall, at stated Times, receive for their Services, a Compensation, which shall not be diminished during their Continuance in Office.").

64. *See* Ely, *supra* note 37, at 101–11.

65. U.S. CONST. amend. XIV, § 1 (providing that "[n]o State shall . . . deny to any person within its jurisdiction the equal protection of the laws").

66. *See* United States v. Carolene Prods. Co., 304 U.S. 144, 152-53 n.4 (1938) (arguing that judicial review should be stricter when legislation targets "particular religious" or "racial minorities" because "prejudice against discrete and insular minorities may be a special condition, which tends seriously to curtail the operation of those political processes ordinarily to be relied upon to protect minorities, and which may call for a correspondingly more searching judicial inquiry").

67. The Equal Protection Clause of the Fourteenth Amendment provides a highly useful exemplar. The Supreme Court, less than a decade after the Fourteenth Amendment's ratification, conclusively held that it did not have any application, whatsoever, to gender-based classifications. *See* Minor v. Happersett, 88 U.S. (21 Wall.) 162, 175–79 (1872) (holding that Missouri could deny women the right to vote based on their sex without violating the Fourteenth

Amendment); Bradwell v. Illinois, 83 U.S. 130, 139 (1872) (holding that Illinois could categorically prohibit women from becoming members of the bar without violating the Fourteenth Amendment). By the 1970s, however, this approach was no longer tenable; the attitude of average citizens in the United States regarding gender-based discrimination had emphatically changed and imposing burdens or withholding benefits based on sex was no longer viewed as something that a justly ordered polity would do. *See* Reed v. Reed, 404 U.S. 71, 76–77 (1971) ("To give a mandatory preference to members of either sex over members of the other, merely to accomplish the elimination of hearings on the merits, is to make the very kind of arbitrary legislative choice forbidden by the Equal Protection Clause of the Fourteenth Amendment; and whatever may be said as to the positive values of avoiding intrafamily controversy, the choice in this context may not lawfully be mandated solely on the basis of sex."). After a period of debate and contestation among the Justices, by the 1990s, every member of the Supreme Court accepted the general constitutional principle that gender-based classifications required heightened judicial scrutiny and were presumptively invalid. *See* United States v. Virginia, 518 U.S. 515, 532–33 (1996) ("Focusing on the differential treatment or denial of opportunity for which relief is sought, the reviewing court must determine whether the proffered justification is 'exceedingly persuasive.' The burden of justification is demanding and it rests entirely on the State.").

68. In this context, it bears noting that the Supreme Court of Israel implied a general right to equal status under the law from Israel's democratic character. *See* Barak, *Role of the Supreme Court*, *supra* note 42, at 126–27.

69. Arthur Miller, the playwright, powerfully emphasizes this point in his seminal work, *The Crucible*. When the trial judge asks John Proctor why he will not cooperate with the authorities, and (falsely) admit to conduct that he did not engage in, Proctor explains that he does not wish to preserve his life at the cost of murdering his honor and, by implication, his human dignity:

> Because it is my *name*! Because I cannot have another in my life! Because I *lie* and sign myself to lies! Because I am not worth the dust on the feet of them that hang! How may I live without my name? I have given you my soul; leave me my name!

ARTHUR MILLER, THE CRUCIBLE 90 (1952). Judges, at least in places like the United States that generally identify an opinion's authoring judge by name, necessarily associate themselves, both professionally and personally, with the outcomes of the cases they decide—in addition to the reasons that they invoke to support those outcomes. *See* Frederick Schauer, *Giving Reasons*, 47 STAN. L. REV. 633, 652–53, 658 (1995) (arguing that a judge has a moral and professional duty to give reasons in support of outcomes and to respect those reasons in similar cases going forward). Professor Schauer is surely correct when he posits that "[although] there are things we can think but cannot write down," a judge may not legitimately "believe an outcome to be correct when it could not be explained by a reason." *Id.* at 652.

70. Ronald Dworkin, *The Secular Papacy*, in JUDGES IN CONTEMPORARY DEMOCRACY: AN INTERNATIONAL CONVERSATION 67, 78 (Robert Badinter & Stephen Breyer eds., 2004) [hereinafter *Secular Papacy*]; *see also* RONALD DWORKIN, LAW'S EMPIRE 190 (1986) (arguing that a legitimate judicial decision must be supported by sincere and transparent reasons offered in support of it).

71. Dworkin, *Secular Papacy*, *supra* note 70, at 78.

72. *See* ELY, *supra* note 37, at 7–9, 101–05. *But cf.* Rucho v. Common Cause, 139 S. Ct. 2484, 2506–08 (2019) (holding that the federal courts will not police extreme partisan gerrymanders

under either the First or Fourteenth Amendments because "we have no commission to allocate political power and influence in the absence of a constitutional directive or legal standards to guide us in the exercise of such authority"). The Supreme Court simply defaulted in *Rucho* and rendered a decision that permits an incumbent majority in a state legislature to maintain its majority power, more or less permanently, while garnering only a minority of votes in consecutive general elections. Extreme partisan gerrymanders present a compelling case for judicial intervention. The *Rucho* decision, accordingly, lacks legitimacy because the majority opinion, authored by Chief Justice John G. Roberts, Jr., fails to offer up persuasive reasons for abject judicial deference in the face of efforts to distort the democratic process.

INDEX

For the benefit of digital users, indexed terms that span two pages (e.g., 52–53) may, on occasion, appear on only one of those pages.

abortion
    anti-abortion speech
        Australia, in, 109–10, 116–17, 243n.20
        UK, in, 87–89, 93
        US, in, 243n.20
    sociolegal culture and, 126
Ackerman, Bruce, 193–94n.12
Adams, John, 1–2
adversary theory of democracy, 248n.55
AfriForum, 55, 56–57
Agranat, Shimon, 136, 140–41, 143–44, 265n.38
Albanese, Anthony, 249–50n.95
Alito, Samuel A., Jr., 21, 113–14, 202–3n.78, 280n.15
Alkiviadou, Natalie, 45, 47
Amar, Akhil Reed, 8, 20, 26, 200n.60
antidiscrimination principle
    South Africa, in, 214n.39, 217n.70
    US, in, 3–4, 185nn.17–21, 209n.137
antisemitism, 50–52
apartheid. *see* South Africa
art exhibits, 58–59
Atiyah, P.S., 83, 229–30n.60

Australia
    Canada compared, 257n.180
    commercial speech in, 128
    common law constitutionalism in, 130–31, 132, 258–59n.194
    Commonwealth Constitution
        generally, xiii
        free exercise of religion under, 106–7, 112, 247n.43, 256–57n.179, 282n.33
        jury trial under, 106–7, 124, 282n.32
        lack of explicit guarantee of freedom of expression in, 106–7
    comparative law analysis in, 113, 114–15, 126–27
    compulsory voting in, 118–19, 121
    constitutional text, importance of, 10
    democratic constitutionalism in, xiii, 12–13, 105
    democratic process, importance of implied freedom of political and governmental communication to, 106
    express guarantee of freedom of expression as having limited potential impact, 132–34
    Foreign Influence Transparency Scheme Act 2018, 279n.12

Index

Australia (*cont.*)
free exercise of religion in, 106–7, 112, 247n.43, 256–57n.179, 282n.33
fundamental rights in, 282n.34
implied freedom of political and governmental communication (IFPGC), 106–17
generally, 12, 33–34, 103, 106, 170, 174, 176
anti-abortion speech and, 109–10, 116–17, 243n.20
attempts to expand, 122–23
collective right, as, 117–23
deference to government, 103–4, 108–9, 133, 241nn.12–13, 249n.70
defining political and governmental communication, 121–22
democratic process, importance to, 106
election law and, 174
expressive conduct and, 123
gag order on government employees and, 110–12
"insulting" speech and, 117, 241n.9
judicial review and, 131–32, 171
judicial scrutiny, 107–8
limited scope of, 119–20
newsgathering and, 122–23
non-content based restrictions, 255n.165
origins of, 103–4
personal right, as, 117–23
rationality review, 108–9, 242n.14
sociolegal culture, impact of, 125–26, 132
structural constraint on legislature, as, 107, 117–23
structured proportionality and, 104, 115–16, 130, 242n.14
use of term, 258n.184
weakness of, 103–4, 133–34
Israel compared, 147
judicial culture in
generally, 245n.31
judge-made law, xv
judicial review in
generally, xiii, 4–5, 12
implied freedom of political and governmental communication and, 131–32, 171
lack of explicit guarantee of freedom of expression not impediment to, 26
limited role of judiciary, 12–13
jury trial in, 106–7, 124, 282n.32

lack of explicit guarantee of freedom of expression in, 103–6
generally, 4–5, 12, 33–34, 174
express guarantee as having limited potential impact, 104, 132–34
judicial review, not impediment to, 26
relevance to scope of freedom of expression, 112–13, 123–32, 174
legalism in, 105, 106, 113
limited relevance of constitutional text in, 12–13, 173–74
Privy Council and, 114
Public Service Act (APSA), 110, 111
Public Service Code of Conduct (APSC), 110, 111
separation of powers in, 260–61n.232
South Africa compared, 114
textualism in, 105, 106, 113
UK compared, 105
US compared, 105–7, 111, 117, 123, 126–27, 133, 173–74, 243n.20

Barak, Aharon, 146–47, 149, 153, 154, 156–57, 161, 175, 270n.116, 274n.193
Barendt, Eric, 70–73, 85, 88, 90, 93–94, 194n.15, 228n.34
BBC, 87–88, 93
Bell, Virginia, 108, 109, 110
Ben-Ami, Illan, 266nn.53–54
Bhagwat, Ash, 19, 183n.1, 192–93n.2, 194n.20, 200n.59, 256n.169
Biko, Steve, 65
Black, Hugo L., 2–4, 21, 28, 29–30, 185n.11, 207–8n.126, 210n.150, 211n.161
Blackstone, William, 1–2, 17, 23
Blair, Tony, 76–77, 78
Blasi, Vincent A., 264n.9
Bork, Robert H., 3, 107, 120, 122, 185n.15, 248n.57
boycotts, 157–58
Brennan, William J., xiv, 38, 168
Breyer, Stephen G., 185n.15, 194–95n.21, 196n.23, 252n.115
broadcasting, 47–52, 87–89
Brown, Alexander, 44, 95, 96–98, 99
Bulfinch, Thomas, 15–16

Calabresi, Guido, 16, 18, 21, 73, 191n.74, 228n.33
Cameron, David, 80
Campbell, Naomi, 79

Index

Canada
Australia compared, 257n.180
Bill of Rights Act of 1960, 257n.180
British North America Act of 1867, 205n.103, 281n.26
Charter of Rights and Freedoms, 12, 192n.81, 192n.83, 245n.31, 281nn.26–27
civility norms in, 117
comparative law analysis in, 114–15
freedom of expression in, 44–45, 171
"living tree" approach in, 173, 281n.26
political speech versus offensive language, 254n.149

Cantor, Norman, 143
Carmi, Guy E., 146, 158–59, 276n.238
Carter, Norvella, 65
censorship
democratic process and, 129, 165–66, 268n.75
Israel, in
judicial opposition to, 142
national security and, 141, 146–47, 160
judicial opposition to, 11, 20–21, 95
South Africa, in
apartheid, under, 65–66
judicial opposition to, 47, 67–68, 177
UK, in
generally, 177
anti-abortion speech, 53–54, 57–58
US, in (see United States)

Chalken, Warren, 65
Charles III, 85, 89–90, 96, 98, 233n.127, 233n.128, 236n.172, 239n.223
Chaskalson, Arthur, 42
Cheshin, Michael, 156
China, written constitution in, 8–9, 171
Choudhury, Emdadur, 85–86
civility norms
generally, 117
common law constitutionalism versus, 93, 95, 96
Clinton, Hillary, 121, 128
Cohen, Paul R., 94
Cohn, Haim, 161
commercial speech
Australia, in, 128
US, in, 17, 197n.29, 197n.31, 200–1n.64, 208n.134
common law, judge-made law as, 10
common law constitutionalism
generally, xiv

Australia, in, 130–31, 132, 258–59n.194
inevitability of, 172–78
Israel, in, xv, 135–38, 158
limited role of constitutional text and, 6–9
South Africa, in, 35–36
UK, in (see United Kingdom)
universality of, 172–78
US, in
First Amendment as, 18–24
necessity of common law interpretation, 28–30
originalism as less important, 18–24
structural provisions, interpretation of, 198n.34
textualism as less important, 18–24

Communists
Israel, in, 136–37, 140–42
US, in, 136, 141, 263nn.5–6
comparative analysis, 11–13
compulsory voting, 118–19, 121
"constitutional moments," 193–94n.12
constitutional text
generally, xv
arguments against written guarantees of rights, 6–9
common law constitutionalism, limited role of constitutional text and, 6–9
democratic process, relevance to, 170–72
facilitating judicial enforcement, as, 5
human rights, relation to, 1–6, 25–26
judicial interpretation of, 191n.70
limited relevance of (see limited relevance of constitutional text)
limiting government action, as, 10–11
"parchment barriers," 8, 9, 25, 92–93, 178
structural provisions versus rights provisions, 7, 187–88n.43

Cosmic Turtle metaphor
generally, xiv
judge-made law and, 9–11
Cram, Ian, 93
cross burnings, 40
The Crucible (play), 286n.69
Cuba, written constitution in, 8–9, 171, 190n.67

defamation, 228n.32
democratic constitutionalism, xiii, 12–13
democratic process
censorship and, 129, 165–66, 268n.75
constitutional text, relevance of, 170–72

292   Index

democratic process (*cont.*)
  freedom of expression, importance of, 127–
    30, 133, 165–66, 170–72, 260n.220
  Israel, in (*see* Israel)
  judge-made law, importance of, 178–81
  judicial culture, importance of, 178–81
  South Africa, in, 43–44, 62–65
democratic self-government theory, 63–64, 129
Dewey, John, 120
Dilhorne, Reginald, 235–36n.171
discretion, 28
Dixon, Owen, 251n.103
Dorner, Dalia, 155–56, 157
Douglas, William O., 191n.74
Dworkin, Ronald, 74–76, 136, 162–64, 166,
    180, 244n.28

Edelman, James, 111–12
election law
  Australia, in, 174
  Germany, in, 145, 146
  Israel, in, 143–46, 268n.75
Elizabeth II, 85, 89–90, 96, 98, 233n.127
Elkins, Richard, 243–44n.24
Ely, John Hart, 162, 164–65, 166, 244n.27,
    277–78n.272, 282n.37
European Commission, 75
European Convention for the Protection
    of Human Rights and Fundamental
    Freedoms (ECHR)
  generally, 83
  freedom of expression under, 45, 82–83
  privacy under, 228n.30
  South Africa Constitution incorporating, 34
  UK accession to, 74, 77–78
  UK Human Rights Act incorporating, 4, 69,
    70–71, 72, 73, 74, 78–80, 91, 100, 124,
    170, 186n.32, 226n.12
European Court of Human Rights (ECtHR)
  freedom of expression and, 44–46
  hate speech and, 44–46, 47
  UK accession to jurisdiction of, 75, 77
  UK Human Rights Act and, 4
European Union
  Charter of Fundamental Freedoms, 83,
    284–85n.53
  Court of Justice, 171
  privacy in, 284–85n.53

Faulkner, William, 67

Federalist Papers, 7, 25–26, 178
Federalist Society, 26
Fish, Stanley, 193–94n.12
Fontana, David, 252–53n.121
France, civility norms in, 117
Francis (Pope), 121
freedom of association, 127
free exercise of religion, 106–7, 112, 247n.43,
    256–57n.179, 282n.33

Gageler, Stephen, 109–10, 116
Gardbaum, Stephen, 72, 80, 275–76n.228
Gavison, Ruth, 161–62
Geddis, Anthony, 86–87, 93
Geldenhuys, Judith, 34, 57
Gelpe, Marcia, 150–51, 154, 161
gender discrimination, 285–86n.67
"genuine democracy" theory, 162–63
Germany
  civility norms in, 117
  election law in, 145, 146
  Federal Constitutional Court (FCC), 35
  Grundgesetz (Basic Law), 35, 145, 146
  Holocaust denial in, 253n.130
  Israel compared, 145, 146
  pro-Nazi speech in, 253n.130
  relevance of constitutional text in, 176
gerrymandering, 171, 279nn.9–10,
    286–87n.72
Ginsburg, Ruth Bader, 40
Gloppen, Siri, 35
Goldsworthy, Jeffrey, 124–25, 243–44n.24
Gorsuch, Neil, 30, 187n.38, 280n.15

Hale, Brenda, 72, 273n.178
Haley, Alex, 66
Hamilton, Alexander, 7–8, 25–26, 178–79
Hammond, Harry, 86
Haque, Mohammad, 85–86
Harlan, John Marshall, 23–24, 94, 117,
    203n.88, 203–4nn.90–91, 238n.205,
    238n.208
hate speech
  ECtHR and, 44–46, 47
  South Africa, in (*see* South Africa)
  UK, in, 95–97
Hayut, Esther, 151–52
Hefer, Joos, 53
Henckels, Caroline, 241–42n.13, 260–61n.232
Hoffman, Leonard, 88, 93, 235n.168

Index

Holmes, Oliver Wendell, Jr., 7–8, 22, 23–24, 28–29, 111, 144, 146, 169, 191n.72, 203n.85, 203nn.86–87, 210–11n.160
Holomisa, Bantubonke H., 53
Homer, 15–16
Hope, David, 79
Hughes, Charles Evans, 74
human rights
  freedom of expression as, 180
  proportionality analysis and, 269–70n.113
  relation to constitutional text, 1–6, 25–26
Hungary, written constitution in, 9
Hurd, Douglas, 229n.53
hurtful speech, 49
Huscroft, Grant, 83
Hutton, Dean, 58–60

Inazu, John, 24
incitement, 200n.63, 216n.52
"insulting" speech
  Australia, in, 117, 241n.9
  UK, in, 85, 89–90, 98
International Court of Justice (ICJ), 230–31n.76
Islamic Unity Convention, 51
Islamophobic speech, 97
Israel
  Australia compared, 147
  Basic Law: Freedom of Occupation
    generally, 137, 139, 149
    enactment of, 153
    freedom of expression and, 153, 154
    limitation clause, 153
  Basic Law: Human Dignity and Liberty
    generally, xii, 137, 139, 149
    boycotts and, 157–58
    enactment of, 153
    freedom of expression under, 153–56, 159–60
    judicial review and, 153–54, 157–58, 159
    limitation clause, 153, 154
    political protest and, 156–57
    post-*United Mizrahi/Golan* law, 156–58
  Basic Law: Judiciary, 150–53, 155
  Basic Law: Judiciary (Amendment No. 3), 150–53, 155
  Basic Laws
    generally, 137, 139, 175
    enactment of, 149–50
    "entrenched" provisions, 150, 151
    judicial review and, 149–53, 155, 271n.129
    status of, 149–51

  Board for Film and Theater Review, 160, 266nn.53–54
  censorship in
    judicial opposition to, 142
    national security and, 141, 146–47, 160
  Central Elections Committee, 143–44
  Chief Military Censor, 146, 160
  Cinematic Board, 143
  common law constitutionalism in, xv, 135–38, 158
  core identifying characteristics, 150–52
  Declaration of Independence, 138, 141
  democratic process, freedom of expression and
    generally, 137–38, 161–62
    essential condition, freedom of expression as, 165–66
    judicial review and, 164–65, 166–67
    role of courts, 167–68
    unfettered democracy as fundamentally unjust, 162–64
  El Ard, 143–44, 268n.75
  Family Agricultural Sector (Arrangements) (Amendment) Law, 154
  fundamental principles of democracy, 151–52
  fundamental principles of democracy and judicial review, 151–52, 155
  Germany compared, 145, 146
  Harari Resolution, 139
  implied fundamental rights in, 262n.2
  judicial culture in, 135–38
  judicial review in
    generally, xii, 4–5
    attempts to curtail, 150–53, 155, 167
    Basic Law: Human Dignity and Liberty and, 153–54, 157–58, 159
    Basic Law: Judiciary, 150–53, 155
    Basic Law: Judiciary (Amendment No. 3), 150–52, 155
    Basic Laws and, 149–53, 155, 271n.129
    democratic process, importance to, 164–65, 166–67
    lack of explicit guarantee of freedom of expression not impediment to, 26
    robust role of judiciary, 12–13
    strong-form judicial review, 135, 150–51, 159
    weak-form judicial review, 135
  lack of explicit guarantee of freedom of expression in, 138–40
    generally, 4–5, 12, 135

294 ⌒   Index

Israel (*cont.*)
    judicial review, not impediment to, 26
    unenumerated yet fundamental
        constitutional right, effect on, 142
    limited relevance of constitutional text in,
        12–13, 137, 158–61
    Mossad, 146–47
    Movement for Quality Government, 150–
        53, 155
    parliamentary supremacy in, 142, 150–53, 155
    Penal Code, 147
    privacy in, 160, 276n.233
    rule of law in, 151–53
    sedition in, 269n.109
    separation of powers, 151–53
    strength of freedom of expression in, 5
    UK compared, 154, 159
    unenumerated yet fundamental
        constitutional right, freedom of
        expression as
      generally, 12, 140, 170, 175, 176
      balancing tests, 147–48
      Communists and, 136–37, 140–42
      election law and, 143–46, 268n.75
      executive action, invalidation of, 142, 143
      Kol Ha'am case, 136–37, 140–42
      lack of explicit guarantee of freedom of
        expression, effect of, 142
      legislative acquiescence to, 139–40
      Mossad and, 146–47, 160, 276n.237
      other than political speech, 158
      post-*Kol Ha'am* law, 142–49
      "probable danger" test, 142, 143, 144,
        146, 147, 148
      proportionality analysis and, 147, 160
      US compared, 136, 141–42, 262–63n.4

Jackson, Robert, 96
Jackson, Vicki, 83
Japan
    civility norms in, 117
    freedom of expression in, 236n.178
    judicial review in, 159
Jefferson, Thomas, 6, 64, 92–93, 118–19, 120,
    188n.51
Johnson, Boris, 80–81
judge-made law
    generally, xii
    Australia, in, xv
    common law, as, 10

Cosmic Turtle metaphor and, 9–11
democratic process, importance to, 178–81
judicial independence, importance of,
    10–11
UK, in, xiii, 10
judicial culture
    generally, xiii
    Australia, in
      generally, 245n.31
      judge-made law, xv
    democratic process, importance to, 178–81
    equal citizenship guarantees and, 179–80
    freedom expression, as setting bounds of,
      169–70
    Israel, in, 135–38
    judicial independence, importance of,
      10–11
    legislative self-interest versus, 178, 282n.37
    UK, in (*see* United Kingdom)
    US, in (*see* United States)
judicial discretion, 28
judicial independence, importance of, 10–11
judicial review
    Australia, in (*see* Australia)
    freedom of expression and, 245–46n.32
    Israel, in (*see* Israel)
    social psychology and, 261n.244
    South Africa, in
      Constitution, in conjunction with, 171
      Constitutional Court, in, 212n.12
    strong-form judicial review, 135, 150–51,
      159, 262n.3
    structural approach, 244n.27
    UK, in
      Human Rights Act, under, 12,
      275–76n.228
      weak-form judicial review, 159
    US, in (*see* United States)
    weak-form judicial review, 135, 159, 262n.3
judicial "updating," 18, 73, 176

Kagan, Elena, 113–14
Kahane, Binyamin, 269n.109
Kalven, Herry, Jr., 265n.43
Kavanaugh, Aileen, 70, 226n.9
Keane, Patrick, 108, 109, 110
Kelly-Louw, Michelle, 34, 57
Kende, Mark, 35, 225n.285
Kennedy, Anthony M., 40, 114, 129, 207n.123,
    251n.107, 253–54n.143

Index

Kennedy, Helena, 89
Kentridge, Sydney, 224n.245
Khampepe, Sisi, 50
Kiefel, Mary, 108, 109, 110
"Kill the Boer" (song), 55–57, 60
Kirby, Michael, 241nn.8–9, 258n.188
Klarman, Michael, 209n.137
Klug, Heinz, 36, 41, 42, 62–63
Kriegler, Johann, 44

Lahav, Pnina, 142, 143, 144
Lamont, Colin G., 56
Langa, Pius, 51–52, 65–66
legalism, 105, 106, 113
lèse-majesté laws, 96, 175–76
Lester, Anthony, 71, 74–76, 89, 91–92
limited relevance of constitutional text
    Australia, in, 12–13, 173–74
    Israel, in, 12–13, 137, 158–61
    South Africa, in, xv, 11–12, 170, 176
    UK, in (see United Kingdom)
    US, in (see United States)
"Living Constitution," 131
"living tree" approach
    Canada, in, 173, 281n.26
    US, in, 24–25, 27–28, 29, 33, 205n.103,
        281n.28
Long, Huey P., 7–8

Madison, James, 6–9, 16, 20–21, 25, 92–93,
        178, 190n.64
Majiedt, Steven A., 36–37, 43–44, 49–50, 66,
        219n.118
Malema, Julius Sello, 55–57, 60, 225n.274
Mandela, Nelson, 35, 42, 62–63, 212n.9
Marais, Maria E., 216–17n.66
"marketplace of ideas" metaphor, 95, 146,
        209n.135
Marshall, John, 7–8, 18, 20, 29, 172–73, 178,
        213n.26, 260–61n.232
Masuku, Bongani, 50
May, Theresa, 85, 98
Mazza, Eliahu, 155, 156
McGoldrick, Dominic, 91, 92
Mchangama, Jacob, 45, 47
McHugh, Michael, 258n.188
Meiklejohn, Alexander, 63, 64, 95, 120, 121,
        128–29, 162, 165–66, 168, 248n.57,
        263–64n.7
Melcer, Hanan, 157

Miller, Arthur, 286n.69
Mogoeng, Mogoeng, 43–44, 65, 66
Molahlehi, Edwin, 56, 222n.209
Momberg, Vicki, 55, 57–58, 60–61
Morrison, Scott, 249–50n.95

Naor, Miriam, 156–57
Netanyahu, Benjamin, 155, 167
Nettle, Geoffrey, 110
newsgathering, 122–23
New Zealand, freedom of expression in, 136
Nichols, Donald, 88
North Korea, written constitution in, 8–9,
        190n.67

Obama, Barack, 128
O'Connor, Sandra Day, 40
Onishi, Norimitsu, 57
Or, Theodore, 269n.109
O'Regan, Kate, 52–53, 54
originalism
    generally, xi
    common law constitutionalism as more
        important, 18–24
    First Amendment, 31–32
    infrequency of use, xii
    prominence of, 26, 173, 206n.117
    Protean nature of First Amendment
        versus, 16–17
    "spirit of the law" approach, 172
Orwell, George, 94
"Our Federalism," 29, 210n.150

"parchment barriers," 8, 9, 25, 92–93, 178
parliamentary sovereignty, 228–29n.42,
        232n.99
parliamentary supremacy, 142, 228–29n.42
Patapan, Haig, 105
Patterson, Thomas M., 22, 23
Phelps, Fred, 238n.211
Poland, written constitution in, 9
police discretion, 97–99
political protest
    Israel, in, 156–57
    UK, in, 85–86
Powell, Lewis, 17–18
"Preferred Position" Doctrine, 198n.38
privacy
    ECHR, under, 228n.30
    European Union, in, 284–85n.53

Index

privacy (*cont.*)
  Israel, in, 160, 276n.233
  UK, in, 73–74, 79, 227nn.25–26
  US, in, 21–22, 202n.70
procedural due process, 70
ProLife Alliance, 87–88, 93
proportionality analysis
  generally, 131, 260n.231
  Australia, structured proportionality in,
     104, 115–16, 130, 242n.14
  human rights and, 269–70n.113
  Israel, in, 147, 160
  UK, in, 83
protest songs, 55–57
Proteus, 15–17, 169

Qwelane, Jonathan Dubula, 48–49

Raab, Dominic, 80–81
Rabban, David M., 203n.85
racial discrimination
  South Africa, in, 34
  US, in, 285n.66
Radithalo, Tlhalo Sam, 65, 66, 224n.268
rationality review, 254–55n.152
Redish, Martin H., 127–29, 200–1n.64, 248n.55
regulatory takings, 210–11n.160
Rehnquist, William, 30
"reverse incorporation," 211n.161
Riddle, Harold, 85–86
Roberts, John G., Jr., 22, 113–14, 278–79n.8,
    286–87n.72
Roots (television series), 65, 66
Rothman, Ivan, 150
rule of law, 172
Russia, written constitution in, 9

Saban, Ilan, 145–46
Saunders, Cheryl, 107
Scalia, Antonin, 3, 18, 21–22, 30, 185n.14, 194–
    95nn.21–22, 207–8n.126, 280n.15, 281n.28
Schauer, Frederick, 240n.241, 286n.69
Scott, Richard, 235n.166
Sedgwick, Diana, 242n.19
sedition, 269n.109
Seidenfeld, Mark, 261n.244, 279n.11
selective-but-complete incorporation, 203–4n.90
sexually explicit speech, 201n.65
sexual orientation, 48–50
Shamgar, Meir, 154

Shuja, Lubna, 82
Simmonds, K.R., 77
Snyder, Albert, 22
Snyder, Matthew, 22, 238n.211
sociolegal culture
  Australia, in, 125–26, 132
  importance in protecting freedom of
    expression, xiv, 10–11, 176
  US, in (*see* United States)
Sotomayor, Sonia M., 113–14
Souter, David, 40
South Africa
  antidiscrimination principle in, 214n.39,
    217n.70
  apartheid in
    censorship under, 65–66
    Constitutional Court as break from, 35
    freedom of expression and, 65–67
  Australia compared, 114
  Bill of Rights, 214n.42, 220n.129, 285n.54
  Broadcasting Code, 51
  censorship in
    apartheid, under, 65–66
    judicial opposition to, 47, 67–68, 177
  civility norms in, 117
  common law constitutionalism in, 35–36
  comparative analysis, 39
  Constitution (1996)
    generally, xii
    adoption of, 34
    amendments to, 42
    hate speech exclusion, 37–38, 39–40,
      41, 47
    interpretation of, 41
    judicial review in conjunction with, 171
    other human rights in, 11–12, 39–46, 67–68
    racial discrimination and, 34
  Constitutional Court
    generally, 34
    creation of, 35
    expansion of role, 36
    guardian of rights, as, 33–39
    interpretation of Constitution and, 41
    judicial review in, 212n.12
  defamation in, 52–54
  dignity, equality, and human freedom as
    constitutional values, 39–46
    generally, 215n.49, 285nn.54–55
    elevated constitutional status of, 36–37,
      41, 67–68, 170

Equality Act and, 216–17n.66
non-derogability of, 37, 41, 43
Economic Freedom Fighters (EFF), 55, 56
ECtHR compared, 44–46
explicit protection of freedom of
expression in, 11–12
freedom of expression as coequal
constitutional value
generally, 46–47, 67–68, 170
apartheid and, 65–67
broadcasting and, 47–52
defamation and, 52–54
delineation of rights, 215–16n.50
democratic process and, 43–44, 62–65
elevation to coequal status, 38–39, 42,
43, 177
hate speech and, 47–52
not inferior status, 61–62
freedom of press in, 52–54
hate speech in
generally, 284n.52
antisemitism, 50–52
art exhibits, 58–59
broadcasting, in, 51–52
Constitutional exclusion, 37–38, 39–40,
41, 47
exception from protection, 36
freedom of expression as coequal
constitutional value, 47–52
hurtful speech distinguished, 49
"K-word," 57–58
objective test for, 223n.238
protest songs, 55–57
sexual orientation and, 48–50
Human Rights Commission (HRC), 48
Independent Broadcasting Authority, 51
interim Constitution (1993), 34, 35
Judges Act, 213n.29
judicial review
Constitution, in conjunction with, 171
Constitutional Court, in, 212n.12
limited relevance of constitutional text in,
xv, 11–12, 170, 176
National Party, 35, 38–39, 65–67, 177
Parliament
freedom of expression and, 42–43,
45–46
interpretation of Constitution and, 41
Prevention and Combating of Hate Crimes
and Hate Speech Bill, 57–58

Promotion of Equality and Prevention of
Unfair Discrimination Act (Equality
Act), 45–46, 47, 48–50, 56–57, 59
Riotous Assemblies Act, 66, 225n.274
substantive equality in, 223n.233, 225n.285
Truth and Reconciliation Commission, 58
US compared, 54, 63–64, 68
voting rights in, 218n.92
South Korea, comparative law analysis in, 114
sovereign immunity, 30
Spain, lèse-majesté laws in, 175–76
spoils system, 17–18
Stephenson, Scott, 246n.37, 281n.29
Stevens, John Paul, 84
Steward, Simon, 104, 105, 125, 247n.50, 282n.34
Stewart, Potter, 122
Stone, Adrienne, 107, 116, 124–25, 247–48n.51,
253n.125, 254n.148, 258n.184, 258n.188
Story, Joseph, 1–2
Strauss, David A., 16, 34, 73, 130–31, 194n.15,
196n.24, 198n.36, 200n.58, 240n.243,
246n.34, 261n.233, 262–63n.4, 280n.18
students, speech rights of, 196n.23
substantive due process, 203–4n.90, 207n.125
Summers, Robert, 83, 229–30n.60
Sunak, Rishi, 81, 82
Sunday World, 53
Sunstein, Cass R., 196n.25, 259n.209

Taiwan, comparative law analysis in, 114
taxing power, 7–8, 189n.58
tenure of judges, 285n.63
text. see constitutional text
textualism
generally, 2–4
Australia, in, 105, 106, 113
common law constitutionalism as more
important, 18–24
constraint on judges, not serving as, 27–28
false premise of, 27, 28
First Amendment, 31–32
inconsistency in, 26–27, 29–31
prominence of, 173
Protean nature of First Amendment
versus, 16–17
"spirit of the law" approach, 172
Thayer, James B., 245–46n.32
Thomas, Clarence, 21–22, 40, 202–3n.78
"threatening" and "abusive" speech, 85, 89–
90, 97, 98

298   Index

Thulare, Daniel M., 58, 59

treaties, 230–31n.76

Tribe, Laurence H., 195–96n.22

Trump, Donald, 121

Truss, Liz, 81

Turkey, written constitution in, 9

Tushnet, Mark, 173, 252n.115, 280n.14

Tutu, Desmond, 35

United Kingdom
- anti-monarchy protests in, 85, 89–90, 96, 98, 233nn.126–127, 236n.172, 239n.223
- Australia compared, 105
- Bill of Rights, efforts to enact
  - generally, 71
  - common law constitutionalism versus, 91–93
  - freedom of expression and, 74–77
  - Human Rights Act, in lieu of, 80–82
- Brexit, 80, 82, 121
- Broadcasting Act 1990, 87, 96
- censorship in
  - generally, 177
  - anti-abortion speech, 53–54, 57–58
- common law constitutionalism, freedom of expression and, 89–100
  - generally, 73, 100–2, 177
  - anti-abortion speech and, 93
  - Bill of Rights versus, 91–93
  - civility versus, 93, 95, 96
  - hate speech and, 95–97
  - Islamophobic speech and, 97
  - limited recognition of, 90
  - police discretion and, 97–99
  - pre-Human Rights Act, 72–73
- Communications Act 2003, 87
- defamation in, 228n.32
- ECHR, accession to, 74, 77–78
- ECtHR, accession to jurisdiction of, 75, 77
- European Communities Act 1972, 99, 154, 273n.178
- House of Lords, 198n.37
- Human Rights Act 1998
  - generally, xiii
  - anti-abortion speech and, 87–89
  - Bill of Rights in lieu of, efforts to enact, 80–82
  - broadcasting and, 87–89
  - common law constitutionalism prior to, 72–73

- ECHR incorporated into, 4, 69, 70–71, 72, 73, 74, 78–80, 91, 100, 124, 170, 186n.32, 226n.12
  - freedom of expression under, 77–82
  - fundamental human rights under, 77–82
  - judicial review under, 12, 275–76n.228
  - limited impact on protection of freedom of expression, 69–74, 82–89, 177
  - limited relevance of constitutional text, xv, 12, 100–1, 170
  - "particular regard" for freedom of expression, 70–71, 124
  - procedural due process under, 70
  - protection of freedom of expression prior to, 75, 228n.34
  - Public Order Act, impact on, 83–84, 86–87
- Israel compared, 154, 159
- judicial culture in
  - generally, xiii, 10, 245n.31
  - freedom of expression, as more important regarding, 101–2
  - judge-made law, xiii, 10
  - junior role of judiciary, 177
- judicial review in
  - Human Rights Act, under, 12, 275–76n.228
  - weak-form judicial review, 159
- lack of explicit guarantee of freedom of expression in
  - generally, 12
  - guarantee of freedom of expression in spite of, 73
- limited relevance of constitutional text in
  - freedom of expression versus other rights, 72
  - Human Rights Act, xv, 12, 100–1, 170
  - Public Order Act, 71–72
  - structure versus constitutional text, 190n.66
- Northern Ireland (Emergency Provisions) Act 1978, 229n.53
- parliamentary sovereignty in, 228–29n.42, 232n.99
- parliamentary supremacy in, 228–29n.42
- Prevention of Terrorism (Temporary Provisions) Act 1984, 229n.53
- privacy in, 73–74, 79, 227nn.25–26
- proportionality analysis in, 83
- Public Order Act 1986
  - generally, 71–72, 96
  - Human Rights Act, impact of, 83–84, 86–87

Index

"insulting" speech, 85, 89–90, 98
limited relevance of constitutional text, 71–72
political protest and, 85–86
punishment under, 84
"threatening" and "abusive" speech, 85, 89–90, 97, 98
US compared, 83, 84, 89, 90, 94
United States
abortion in, 126
Affordable Care Act, 7–8
Alien and Sedition Acts, 1–2, 17
anti-abortion speech in, 243n.20
antidiscrimination principle in, 3–4, 185nn.17–21, 209n.137
Article III judicial power, 210n.159
Australia compared, 105–7, 111, 117, 123, 126–27, 133, 173–74, 243n.20
Bill of Rights
"absolute" restrictions on government in, 207–8n.126
adoption of, 8–9
"penumbras," 191n.74
censorship in
First Amendment and, 4, 17, 20–21, 95, 172
judicial opposition to, xi, 2, 20–21, 31, 94–95
"ceremonial" role of Constitution in, 34
Civil Rights Act of 1964, 127, 280n.15
commercial speech in, 17, 197n.29, 197n.31, 200–1n.64, 208n.134
common law constitutionalism in
First Amendment as, 18–24
necessity of common law interpretation, 28–30
originalism as less important, 18–24
structural provisions, interpretation of, 198n.34
textualism as less important, 18–24
comparative law analysis in, 113–14
Confrontation Clause, 22, 203n.79
cross burnings, 40
Due Process Clause, 3–4, 21, 22, 23–24, 202n.70, 204n.91, 211n.161
Eighteenth Amendment, 27
Eleventh Amendment, 30
Equal Protection Clause, 3–4, 187n.41, 211n.161, 285–86n.67
explicit protection of freedom of expression in, 11–12

Fifth Amendment, 3–4, 23–24, 191n.74, 202n.70
First Amendment
Assembly Clause, 16, 19–20, 24, 123, 126–27, 199n.41, 208n.132
"atextual text," as, xv, 15–18
censorship and, 4, 17, 20–21, 95, 172
commercial speech under, 17, 197n.29, 197n.31, 200–1n.64, 208n.134
common law constitutionalism and, 18–24
Communists and, 136, 141, 263nn.5–6
Congress, as applying to, 4, 16, 19–20, 194n.15, 194n.16
de novo review, 84, 232–33n.113
expansive view as implication of voting provisions of Constitution, 2, 184n.7
Free Speech Clause as synecdoche for entire First Amendment, 24
general purposes of, 15
government employees and, 249n.90, 255n.161
ignoring of text, xi, 11–12, 17, 172, 173
incitement and, 200n.63, 216n.52
judicial review in conjunction with, 171
limited relevance of text, 127, 169, 176
limited view of, 1–2
Petition Clause, 16, 19–20, 24, 123, 126–27
"Preferred Position" Doctrine, 198n.38
Press Clause, 16, 19–20, 22, 24, 123, 126–27, 197n.28
privacy and, 21–22
private property and, 211n.163
Protean nature of, 15–18, 181
sexually explicit speech under, 201n.65
sociolegal culture and, 2
states, as applying to, 20, 22–24
text of, 19, 280n.17
textualism and, 2–4
textual originalism and, xii
Fourteenth Amendment, 3–4, 22, 23–24, 187n.41, 202n.70, 204n.91, 285–86n.67, 286–87n.72
Fourth Amendment, 191n.74
freedom of association in, 127
gender discrimination in, 285–86n.67
gerrymandering in, 171, 279nn.9–10, 286–87n.72
Guarantee Clause, 199n.48
Israel compared, 136, 141–42, 262–63n.4

Index

United States (*cont.*)
judicial culture in
constitutional text as less important, 18, 31–32
freedom of expression, importance to, 31–32
judicial "updating," 18
role of judges in protecting freedom of expression, 15–18
judicial review in
generally, 209n.144
Constitution as supreme law and, 207n.121
de novo review, 84, 232–33n.113
First Amendment, in conjunction with, 171
racial discrimination and, 285n.66
limited relevance of constitutional text in
generally, 11–12, 13, 15, 33–34
First Amendment, 127, 169, 176
human rights and, 25–26
judicial culture compared, 31–32
sociolegal culture compared, 24–28
"Living Constitution," 194–95n.21, 199n.50
"living tree" approach in, 24–25, 27–28, 29, 33, 205n.103, 281n.28
Louisiana Purchase, 188n.51
Ninth Amendment, 191n.74
originalism in
generally, xi
common law constitutionalism as more important, 18–24
First Amendment, 31–32
infrequency of use, xii
prominence of, 26, 173, 206n.117
Protean nature of First Amendment versus, 16–17
"spirit of the law" approach, 172
"Our Federalism," 29, 210n.150
Privacy Act, 21
privacy in, 21–22, 202n.70
Privileges and Immunities Clause, 23, 106–7, 173–74
rationality review in, 254–55n.152
regulatory takings in, 210–11n.160
reverence for Constitution in, 206n.120
"reverse incorporation," 211n.161
selective-but-complete incorporation, 203–4n.90
Seventeenth Amendment, 188n.49, 189n.52
Sixth Amendment, 22, 203n.79
sociolegal culture in
generally, 10–11

abortion and, 126
constitutional text compared, 24–28
First Amendment and, 2
other legal rights and, 24–28
scope of freedom of expression, as defining, 24–28
South Africa compared, 54, 63–64, 68
sovereign immunity in, 30
spoils system in, 17–18
State Department, 66–67
students, speech rights of, 196n.23
substantive due process, 203–4n.90, 207n.125
Takings Clause, 30, 106–7, 210–11n.160
taxing power in, 7–8, 189n.58
tenure of judges in, 285n.63
textualism in
generally, 2–4
common law constitutionalism as more important, 18–24
constraint on judges, not serving as, 27–28
false premise of, 27, 28
First Amendment, 31–32
inconsistency in, 26–27, 29–31
prominence of, 173
Protean nature of First Amendment versus, 16–17
"spirit of the law" approach, 172
Third Amendment, 10, 187n.40, 191n.74, 199n.48
treaties in, 230–31n.76
2016 presidential election, 121
UK compared, 83, 84, 89, 90, 94
Vesting Clauses, 187–88n.43
Universal Declaration of Human Rights, 34

Vienna Convention on Consular Relations, 230–31n.76
Vietnam, written constitution in, 190n.67
voting rights, 218n.92

Warren, Earl, 3, 126–27
Weitzman, Avi, 175
Wells, Christina E., 263n.6, 264n.8
Westboro Baptist Church, 278–79n.8
Whitman, James Q., 237n.194

Yancey, Charles, 64

Ziv, Neta, 175
Zungu, Bhekuyise, 65